AGING, SPIRITUALITY,
AND RELIGION

AGING, SPIRITUALITY, AND RELIGION

A HANDBOOK
Volume 2

Melvin A. Kimble
Susan H. McFadden
Editors

Mee-Ock Park
Editorial Coordinator

Fortress Press
Minneapolis

AGING, SPIRITUALITY, AND RELIGION
A Handbook, Volume 2

Volume 2: ISBN 0-8006-3273-7

The Library of Congress has cataloged volume 1 as follows:

Aging, spirituality, and religion : a handbook / Melvin A. Kimble . . .
   [et al.], editors.
      p. cm.
   Includes bibliographical references and index.
   ISBN 0-8006-2667-2
   1. Aged—Religious life. 2. Aging—Religious aspects—Christianity.
   3. Church work with the aged. 4. Aging—Social aspects.
   BV4580.A446 1995
   208'.4'6—dc20   95-6351
                                               CIP

The paper used in this publication meets the minimum requirements of American National
Standard for Information Sciences — Permanence of Paper for Printed Library Materials,
ANSI Z329.48-1984.

Manufactured in the U.S.A.
07   06   05   04   03   1   2   3   4   5   6   7   8   9   10

Contents

Contributors

Richard Address
Director of Union of American Hebrew Congregations
Department of Jewish Family Concern
New York, New York

Robert H. Albers
Pastor of Central Lutheran Church
Minneapolis, Minnesota

Robert C. Atchley
Professor of Gerontology
Naropa University
Boulder, Colorado

V. DuWayne Battle
Pastor of St. Paul Baptist Church
Assistant Instructor, School of Social Work
Rutgers University
New Brunswick, New Jersey

Betty A. Birren
Director Emerita
California Council on Gerontology and Geriatrics
Pacific Palisades, California

James E. Birren
Associate Director of the Center on Aging
University of California—Los Angeles
Los Angeles, California

Helen K. Black
Senior Research Scientist
Polish Research Institute
Philadelphia Geriatric Center
Philadelphia, Pennsylvania

Paul R. Brenner
Director, Jacob Perlow Hospice
Beth Israel Medical Center
New York, New York

Thomas R. Cole
Painter Distinguished Professor
University of Texas Medical Branch
Director of Graduate Program, Institute for the Medical Humanities
Galveston, Texas

Nancy Gieseler Devor
Director of Training
The Danielsen Institute
Boston University
Adjunct Assistant Professor
Boston University School of Theology and Graduate School
Boston, Massachusetts

James W. Ellor
Professor of Human Services and Coordinator of Gerontology Programs
National-Louis University
Wheaton, Illinois
Associate Director, Center for Aging, Religion and Spirituality

Dayle A. Friedman
Director of Geriatric Chaplaincy Track
Reconstructionist Rabbinical College
Wyncote, Pennsylvania

Mark Holman
Director of Network Development, Lutheran Services of America
Minneapolis, Minnesota

Lynn W. Huber
Gerontologist, educator, retreat leader, and spiritual director
Lakewood, Colorado

Ellen L. Idler
Professor, Institute for Health, Health Care Policy and Aging Research
Rutgers University
New Brunswick, New Jersey

Melvin A. Kimble
Director of the Center for Aging, Religion and Spirituality
Professor Emeritus of Pastoral Care and Counseling
Luther Seminary
St. Paul, Minnesota

Lois D. Knutson
Pastor of Our Savior's Lutheran Church
Chaplain of Luther Haven Nursing Home
Montevideo, Minnesota

Jeff Levin
Epidemiologist and author
Valley Falls, Kansas

Elizabeth MacKinlay
Director of the Centre for Aging and Pastoral Studies
St. Mark's National Theological Centre
Senior Lecturer, School of Nursing, University of Canberra
Canberra, Australia

John T. McFadden
Senior Minister of First Congregational UCC Church
Appleton, Wisconsin

Susan H. McFadden
Professor and Chair, Department of Psychology
University of Wisconsin, Oshkosh
Associate Director, Center for Aging, Religion and Spirituality

Harry R. Moody
Director of the Institute for Human Values in Aging
Brookdale Center on Aging of Hunter College
Palisades, New York

Richard L. Morgan
Author, Consultant on Older Adult Ministry
Morganton, North Carolina

Christie Cozad Neuger
Professor of Pastoral Care and Pastoral Theology
United Theological Seminary of the Twin Cities
New Brighton, Minnesota

Douglas Olson
Assistant Professor, Allied Health Professions
University of Wisconsin–Eau Claire
Eau Claire, Wisconsin

Kenneth I. Pargament
Professor of Psychology
Bowling Green State University
Bowling Green, Ohio

Marty Richards
Affiliate Assistant Professor
University of Washington School of Social Work
Port Townsend, Washington

Robert A. Rost
Parish Pastor, Nativity of Mary Parish
Independence, Missouri
Associate Director, Center for Aging, Religion and Spirituality

Stephen Sapp
Professor of Religious Studies
University of Miami
Miami, Florida

James J. Seeber
Associate Professor of Sociology
Northern State University
Aberdeen, South Dakota
Associate Director, Center for Aging, Religion and Spirituality

Henry S. Simmons
Professor of Religion and Aging
Director of Center on Aging
Union-PSCE
Richmond, Virginia

Paul R. Sponheim
Professor Emeritus of Systematic Theology
Luther Seminary
St. Paul, Minnesota

Carole Bailey Stoneking
Associate Professor of Religion
Chair of Department of Religion
High Point University
High Point, North Carolina

Jon C. Stuckey
Director of the Office of Foundation Relations and Sponsored Programs
Messiah College
Grantham, Pennsylvania

Jane M. Thibault
Associate Professor, Division of Geriatrics
Department of Family and Community Medicine
University of Louisville School of Medicine
Louisville, Kentucky

Ladislav Volicer
Professor of Pharmacology and Psychiatry
Boston University School of Medicine
Clinical Director, Geriatrics Research Education Clinical Center
E. N. Rogers Memorial Hospital
Bedford, Massachusetts

Richard M. Wallace
Associate Professor of Pastoral Care and Counseling
Luther Seminary
St. Paul, Minnesota

Anne E. Streaty Wimberly
Professor of Christian Education and Church Music
Interdenominational Theological Center
Atlanta, Georgia

Preface

Aging, Spirituality, and Religion: A Handbook, Volume 2 is an outgrowth of the continuing mission of the Center for Aging, Religion and Spirituality (CARS), which
was established in 1993. CARS, a nonprofit organization housed at Luther Seminary, St. Paul, Minnesota, encourages education, research, and publication on the
religious and spiritual components of late-life experiences. It offers an interfaith
and multidisciplinary approach to issues related to aging, spirituality, and religion.
The present volume builds on and extends volume 1, which was published in 1995,
and continues the development of scholarship and practice in older adult ministry.

We hope that the essays in this volume will stimulate further reflection, research,
and scholarly writing about spirituality and religion. Concomitantly, may it prove
helpful to gerontologists as well as clergy and leaders in faith communities to continue the expanding interdisciplinary dialogue on religious and spiritual themes
that emerge in later life.

It would be remiss of the editors not to express appreciation for the creative and
scholarly contributions of our distinguished group of chapter authors. A number of
these individuals are treasured friends of the editors as well as respected colleagues.
Many of us have journeyed together the last two decades in creating a space within
gerontology for the discussion of religion and spirituality. Other authors are less
well known to the editors, but their contributions are no less valued.

We also want to express appreciation to Henry French, formerly vice president
of Fortress Press, for his encouragement to publish volume 2 and to Michael West,
editor-in-chief, Harold Rast, consulting editor, and Beth Wright, assistant managing editor, for their helpfulness in bringing this volume to print. Finally, but in no
way least, we especially want to express appreciation to Mee-Ock Park for her
patient and competent work as the Editorial Coordinator.

Introduction: Continuing the Conversation

James Birren once declared that "aging is too important to leave to the scientists."[1] It was an acknowledgment that the natural science model in many respects has served gerontology well, but not well enough. It has failed to recognize that a wider frame of reference in the study of aging is needed to allow for the full exploration of the question of the meaning of growing older.

Twenty-five years ago national gerontological societies seemed to be the exclusive domain of persons from the medical, behavioral, and social sciences. There were relatively few gerontologists who were interested in the relevance and importance of spirituality and religion in the aging processes. That climate has changed. There has been a heightened interest in the role of religion and spirituality in aging and a general recognition that aging touches all the basic questions of life and dimensions of being. Aging is a multidimensional reality that demands a truly interdisciplinary approach that includes the arts and humanities.

Consequently, there is a growing recognition that a wider frame of reference is required to more fully explore the multifaceted and complex questions about older adulthood and its meaning. The natural sciences with their positivistic empirical approach are too narrow and unidimensional in their study of aging and its meaning. Insights of the medical and psychosocial sciences need to be brought into dynamic dialogue with religion and theology in order to address the phenomenological and hermeneutical structure of later life and the profound multidimensional issues of aging.

In the 1980s prescient gerontologists like James Birren and Barbara Payne encouraged several of us to undertake the challenging task of including the spiritual dimension in the study of aging and its meaning. The result was the exploration of some of the uncharted terrain of spirituality and religion and their impact on aging and older adulthood. Volume 1 of *Aging, Spirituality, and Religion: A Handbook*, was published in 1995 at a time when there was still very little literature on spirituality and aging. This volume represented a unique collection of essays by a variety of eminent scholars and practitioners from assorted disciplines of gerontology, theology, and pastoral practice. Although there was no apparent market for such a handbook, Fortress Press took the risk of publishing this volume. There was considerable surprise when the Academy of Parish Clergy in 1996 named this book one of the ten best books for parish ministry—and perhaps even more surprise when the handbook continued to record steady sales to both gerontologists and clergy.

1

The culture and climate for introducing spirituality and religion into gerontology have significantly changed since volume 1 was published. The inclusion of the spiritual dimension of aging has been widely recognized as evidenced by professional gerontological societies such as Gerontological Society of America and American Society of Aging creating study sections on religion and spirituality in gerontology. The spiritual dimension is increasingly cited as an important dimension in health today and as a critical component in "successful aging." The red carpet has been unrolled. Persons from the religious sector are now encouraged more fully to participate in presentations and symposia at national gerontological conferences.

Persons from the religious sector, however, cannot come empty-handed to this conversation. They must participate having done their own conceptual reflection and research in the areas such as theology, liturgics, psychology of religion, and pastoral care. Likewise, researchers and practitioners in the biomedical and social sciences need to critically examine their disciplines for their unspoken assumptions about the meaning of human longevity.

Some of the questions that need to be addressed include the following. How can a theological hermeneutics reshape the pervasive biomedical model of aging? What are the unique roles of the faith community in promoting wholeness and health as well as spiritual growth and maturation for persons in the last stage of the life cycle? How do religious communities and pastoral caregivers respond to the implications of an expanding older adult population nearing the fourscore years envisioned by the psalmist? What are more creative ways to implement older adult ministries with both mobile and frail elderly? What metaphors and symbols are needed in order to emphasize the transcendent meaning for life at all stages, including older adulthood? What forms do religious and spiritual development take in later life? How do faith and spiritual focus affect older adults' thinking, feeling, and acting? How are social behaviors affected by late-life religious and spiritual commitments, and what are the implications of these commitments for compassionate service to others? The findings from such research and scholarship must be disseminated in scholarly papers and publications that advance the understanding of the relevance of religion and spirituality in the field of gerontology.

Fresh breezes continue to blow in current gerontological theory, research, and practice that value and include spirituality and religion and their impact on aging. Because of the significant outpouring of interest, the editors proposed to the publisher a revised version of volume 1. It was suggested, however, that we keep volume 1 in print and publish a fresh collection of essays as volume 2 that would continue and expand the interdisciplinary conversation begun in the first volume. A core of scholars and practitioners was therefore enlisted to contribute essays to this new volume. This volume, although not without substantive theoretical essays, has more emphasis on praxis. It contains many examples of how religion and spirituality are encountered in the growth experiences and life crises of older adults and their families.

Several new themes arise in this volume that were absent in the previous work. For example, little mention was made of Alzheimer's and other dementias in the first volume. Volume 2 contains four chapters entirely devoted to issues related to dementia, and others engage the topic by addressing concerns of caregivers. Similarly, the noisy baby boomers were relatively silent in volume 1, but now several chapters focus on the ways they are reshaping expectations about religion and spirituality in aging persons. Reflecting an emerging vision for inquiry in gerontology, the need for narrative explorations of late life emerges as a strong theme in this volume. Authors in this volume are also more ready to take on the challenging discussion of dying and death, topics that did not receive much attention previously. Finally, this volume places much stronger emphasis on older adults' opportunities for service to others and the ways their love for their neighbors and for God may heal the brokenness in this world.

Although James Birren suggested that "aging is too important to leave to the scientists," he also wisely added, "but it is also too important to leave to the theologians and scholars in the humanities." He underscores the necessity for interdisciplinary and multidimensional approaches. Spirituality at first viewing is an ambiguous, vacuous term open to a range of interpretations and meanings. It is a part of the human experience that displays manifold facets that cut across many academic disciplines. The role of religion and spirituality in gerontology requires meaningful dialogue built upon mutual understanding and respect for disciplines that are usually not in dialogue with each other.

The area we have entered by introducing an examination of religion and spirituality and its impact on aging is a borderland between two often conflicting paradigms, namely, that of the natural sciences and the humanities. Those of us who work in this realm must realize that we are under surveillance from two sides. Suspicious and cynical glances are to be expected, but the result of this continuing dialogue appears to be worthwhile and important to pursue in order that spirituality and religion not remain marginalized or excluded from the study of aging and older adulthood. It is sincerely hoped that this volume advances such a dialogue and moves beyond unexamined assumptions and uninformed discourse.

MELVIN A. KIMBLE AND SUSAN H. MCFADDEN

NOTE

1. James Birren, "Methodological Problems in Religion and Aging," address given at the Conference on Religion, Spirituality and Aging in the Twenty-First Century, Luther Northwestern Theological Seminary, St. Paul, Minnesota, October 10, 1992.

Part One

LATE-LIFE SPIRITUAL POTENTIALS

The metaphor of pilgrimage weaves in and out of many chapters in this handbook, and thus it is most appropriate that for the first chapter *Lynn W. Huber* has chosen it as her guiding theme. Unlike the popular metaphor of development in childhood and youth as an energetic hike up a hill to the "prime of life," with aging as a gradual and then precipitous slide into dissolution, Huber's understanding of spiritual pilgrimage embraces the notion that losses and gains occur throughout life as one casts off the false self and journeys toward the true self of authentic wisdom.

But what if that journey carries one into the land of dementia, where the spiritual potential to become what Huber calls a "wisdom person" is clouded by confusion and disorientation? *Jane M. Thibault* addresses this life crisis with deep sensitivity born of her many years of counseling with families coming to terms with the dreaded diagnosis. By creating an imaginary journal written by a woman wrestling with her God and her doctors' verdict, Thibault affirms that God remains a source of comfort and grace.

The shadow of suffering lengthens with aging, for nearly all older people know at least a few friends and loved ones who slip into frailty. Despite these nearly inevitable experiences, and perhaps *because* of them, late life holds rich opportunities for spiritual development, as *Robert C. Atchley* so compellingly reveals. In his chapter, he describes three levels of "spiritual elderhood," from elders in training, to actualized elders, and finally to transcendent spiritual elders. Spiritual elders populate our ordinary lives, if we have eyes to see their goodness and ears to hear their wisdom. Atchley shows how to recognize spiritual elders in our midst and suggests that our lives together might be transformed by encouraging aging people to enter training to increase the numbers of spiritual elders among us.

Susan H. McFadden begins her chapter by lifting up images of ordinary older people undertaking many mundane tasks in their religious congregations. These common activities offer opportunities for expressing and sharing emotions ranging from sorrow to joy. McFadden urges both researchers and parish clergy to pay close attention to the richly patterned emotional lives of older people revealed in the worship, prayer, study, and intergenerational social interaction that occur within religious communities. In particular, she stresses the significance of older people's love for other persons and for God.

In these chapters, little is made of gender, for both men and women can undertake a spiritual pilgrimage, suffer from dementia, become spiritual elders, and experience emotions in faith communities. Nevertheless, we know that in Western cultures, social scientists have generally found that older women are more likely to acknowledge their spiritual lives and become involved with public expressions of religious faith. *Christie Cozad Neuger* explores the reasons for this and reveals the way gender training in our culture produces different ways of being spiritual for men and women in later life. This has important implications for ministry with older persons, especially in times of bereavement and the process of dying.

With *Jon C. Stuckey's* chapter, we turn again to spiritual challenges of Alzheimer's disease. This volume of the handbook gives much more attention to dementing illnesses of old age than did the preceding volume. Dementia is "out of the closet," so to speak, and those who study and encourage late-life spiritual potentials must not marginalize the many older people who suffer from it. Stuckey affirms both the cruelty of Alzheimer's disease and also the fact that the presence of the Divine within all of life—even on the dementia unit—offers meaning and hope.

The final chapter in Part One functions as a transition to Part Two, as *Henry C. Simmons* examines the ebb and flow of stable periods and transitions in many older people's lives and the implications of this for ministry. He creates a matrix of these expected life events laid out against the backdrop of what social scientists would call demographic variables of gender and sexual orientation, socioeconomic status, cohort, ethnicity, and geographic location. Simmons notes how various pathways to spiritual growth may take different forms depending upon the combination of factors that form the individuals who converge in religious communities where they worship, serve others, teach, proclaim their faith, and witness to the possibilities of late-life spiritual growth.

1

Aging as Pilgrimage: Spiritual Potentials of Late Life

LYNN W. HUBER

I choose the word "pilgrimage" instead of "journey" in the title of this chapter, although the latter is much more in use in today's literature. I do so to indicate that the life path is not only spiritual but at least to some degree an intentional path to a destination variously conceived of as a holy place, a promised land, a liberation, enlightenment, a state of being in union or wholeness, or eternal life.

As I began working on this chapter I attended a conference for spiritual directors, where Richard Rohr presented a provocative model for the life pilgrimage, serendipitously suitable to frame what I shall say. He says that the first half of life is devoted to building up the ego—learning to think, work, achieve, and (especially in modern Western culture) learning to look good.

We spend many years building a "self." There is often a desperate quality to this process; we are trying to *become* "someone," and deep down inside we may wonder if we are really anything at all. The fear of exposure as "nothing" pushes us to greater and greater efforts to create what Jung calls a persona—a face that we present to the world. It is not a false face exactly, but it certainly does not include the things of which we are ashamed, those things that are "unfinished" in us, those things of which we are not even conscious (Jung calls them shadow), nor those things of which we do not think others will approve. The persona is the part of us that we assume will be successful in getting us what we want in life.

Based in part in the work of Thomas Merton (see Finley 1978), Rohr calls this the "false self" and sees it as an obstacle to authenticity, love, and spiritual wholeness. It contrasts with the "true self," which is genuinely humble, loving, and in right relationship with the Divine, with others, and with the world in which one lives.[1]

The journey from the false self to the true self is one way to describe the goal of the spiritual pilgrimage of late life, and becoming the true self is one way to describe the fulfillment of late-life potential. This journey is not easy. It requires a strange and paradoxical balance of effort and letting go. It involves the abandonment of early life-goals in favor of those that offer more. Bertman (1999, 12) describes this as follows:

> Pursuing grand designs can be an exercise in futility; they lead us on, only to vanish before our eyes. To abandon grandiose goals, however, does not mean to live a goal-less

life. Being fully present in each moment of time and being spiritually responsive to the presence of others and to the world around us, its need and its beauty can also be a goal and, if [those who have described it to me] are to be believed, a most worthy one.

Finally, a caveat to the reader. Although some study this topic exclusively from a scholarly perspective, unless one has wrestled with these issues for oneself, it is somewhat like learning about the sexual potential of life solely from reading Masters and Johnson. I therefore make this presentation to some degree in a personal way and encourage the reader to respond likewise.

THE JOURNEY BEGINS AT CONCEPTION

We begin the process of aging at conception, and from the beginning the entire spiritual pilgrimage is an experience not only of gain but also of loss. In order to be born we must leave the comfort and security of the womb. In order to go to school, we must lose the comfort and security of our all-day, safe haven with our mother at home. In order to marry, we must lose the comfort and security of our status as a self-determining single being. No matter what we look at as growth, as achievement, as accomplishment, as new life, it always has a shadow side of loss. Every new birth is also a death. This is made patently visible in many cultures in that rites of passage include such symbols of death and rebirth as baptism (dying under the water and being reborn), receiving a new name, and gaining new status and rights.

We see both loss and gain most vividly and powerfully from midlife on, and especially in late life, which for many comes with a multitude of losses so far-reaching that they can be utterly overwhelming. We may lose health, friends, spouses, employment, status, residence, and many other things that we have come to think of as making up the basic core of who we are. An extensive and exquisite discussion of this "two-sidedness" of aging can be found in Kathleen Fischer's (1985) classic work on the spirituality of aging, *Winter Grace*.

If we are open to the lesson, we may discover that the basic core of who we are is *not* dependent on any of these things: material possessions, status, relationships, even our own bodies and our minds.[2] Our core identity is dependent not on these "accidentals" but on something deeper, which might in various cultures and religious/spiritual traditions be known as being children of the kin-dom (a gender-free term used in *The Inclusive New Testament* [Priests for Equality, 1996]), upon our living into our "Buddha nature," upon our becoming true wisdom persons. We discover this more and more if we allow ourselves to move through those losses, through the grieving of them, to be open to transformation into that true self, toward which a Higher Power is calling us.

Much has been written about the midlife crisis (e.g., Levinson 1978; Viorst 1986). One way of conceiving this crisis is as the transition point between the development of the false self and the birth of the true self. It is a time of confrontation with the likelihood that the dreams of greatness that we may have had as young persons will probably not be fulfilled, at least in the form we had anticipated. We have insufficient time, not enough resources, not enough of anything. In fact we, ourselves, are "not enough." We must confront and accept our finitude and ulti- mately our mortality. If we refuse to do this we may find ourselves going down many dead-end roads, all of which end with our becoming diminished beings full of bitterness and despair.

Erikson's (1963) classic description of ego integrity and despair is well docu- mented in the literature and confirms Rohr's framing of the options (see also Erik- son et al. 1986). Erikson has informed the thinking of many about psychosocial development and bridges the perspectives of psychologists and those who view the journey primarily as spiritual. Erikson sees the outcome of a successful negotiation of the passage to late life as resulting in wisdom, which he defines (1986) as "a detached and yet active concern with life in the face of death."

The Chinese word for crisis is formed of two symbols, one of which means "opportunity," the other "danger." This is certainly true of the midlife crisis. The danger is attempting to go on with business as usual, knowing on some level of consciousness that it is impossible to do so, and living therefore always in terror of the shadow of what is in denial. The opportunity is to allow this transformation.

EVOLUTION OF THE TRUE SELF IS NOT INEVITABLE

Rohr (2001) observes that the life trajectory of those who choose not to acknowl- edge and embrace the losses of aging results in a journey to bitterness. Others have noted this as well. Margot Hover (2000, 26) finds that some people hold on to dev- astating life experiences and may become damaged "beyond the point where a comforting spirituality appears possible."

When I gave my first lecture on the topic of aging and spirituality some fifteen years ago I spoke among other things of the importance of forgiveness. Afterwards I was confronted by a very angry woman who shrieked at me, "If you had gone through what I have gone through you could *never* ask me to forgive!" I found myself without a helpful response and answered as gently as I could manage, "You may be right." Her choice was to hold on to her rage, and she had a right to do so, regardless of the cost. But the cost she was willing to pay, consciously or not, stunned me. Years later, another woman, stuck in fresh grief over the death of a daughter some twelve years before, responded to my question, "Would you like me to help you get past your grief over Anne?" with a cryptic and final, "Not on your life!"

The evolutionary process varies, perhaps infinitely, from person to person. Sometimes people move through midlife without evidence of a real crisis. In West- ern culture many persons live protected lives of such affluence and health that they do not have to consciously face the sort of letting go that really tests us and leads us to make a radical commitment to the pilgrimage. If it has not come earlier, however, late life gives such a test for all of us. For even if we are blessed to have money, power, and health, we *will* have major losses: people we love will die, get sick, change, move away, and in other ways abandon us. Opportunities will diminish. We will have to face major letting go.

Furthermore, we will be living in a world which undervalues us simply by virtue of our age. In our society, prejudice against old age is deeper, more unconscious, and more virulent than that toward any other human diversity: race, gender, nationality, religion, even sexual preference. This virulent ageism certainly adds to the stresses of late life, and to the pressures to distort normal aging by resorting to age-denying practices (such as plastic surgery), all of which work against the successful negotiation of the transition to the true self.

I do not know what makes it possible for some to move on and to accept what life does offer while others seem committed to just grieving what is not. But before detailing the beauty that is possible to the former, it seems necessary to note that the latter also occurs.

THE GIFTS OF AGING

Even in Western culture there are some seditious pockets of folks who, at least to some degree, appreciate the gifts of aging. Among them are Jungians. One of my friends is an Episcopal priest, psychotherapist, and spiritual director who is in her sixties. When she was thirty-five her nest emptied. She felt spent, used up, useless, because her children did not need her anymore.

Just at this time she was given an opportunity to go to the Jung Institute to study psychology. As she began her studies, she met what was to become one of her primary mentors, a woman well into her eighth decade. This woman told her, "I'm not sure you are old enough to be here. It isn't until you're past forty-five that most people are ready to become whole and to explore the spiritual part of themselves. You're still a baby!" My friend was at first astonished. But this encounter led to a powerful sense of renewal; she went on to take a whole new perspective on life.

There are others who are also able somehow to resist the culture—people who have come to see the gifts of the spiritual journey that come with long travel. For if in life we are indeed on a spiritual pilgrimage, and if that pilgrimage is designed to take us to a holy destination (however it is framed), then the older we get the closer we ought to be to that place. And we come to see that primarily by looking back.

A metaphor that describes this is hiking in the mountains. When you are on your way up, you do not know what to expect. As you follow the trail, you may find yourself climbing a long hard way up, only to be forced to turn and walk almost as far (or farther) back down again. You may wonder why the trail maker did not just go straight on up. You may walk around almost in a circle and find that the waterfall you walked away from turns up again a little below you on the trail. You may think you are almost there only to find that what you thought was the top is actually a false peak, and there is more climbing yet ahead.

But when you get to the top, you can stop and look around you, and see where you have come. You know then that the trail had to skirt a deep gorge, go over or around a ridge, and take all the twists and turns it did, if you were to arrive safely where you are. The view from the peak of years can be like that—we can find the meaning in the twists and turns, ups and downs, by looking back, and come to rejoice in the trail we have taken rather than seeing it as a curse. As we see others behind us, we can encourage them: "Keep going; you're on the right trail."

Erikson (1963, 268) says it in other words:

> Ego integrity . . . is the acceptance of one's one and only life cycle as something that had to be and that, by necessity, permitted of no substitutions. . . . Although aware of the relativity of all the various life styles which have given meaning to human striving, the possessor of integrity is ready to defend the dignity of his own life style against all physical and economic threats. For he knows that an individual life is the accidental coincidence of but one life cycle with but one segment of history: and that for him all human integrity stands or falls with the one style of integrity of which he partakes.

LIFE REVIEW AND THE MUTUALITY OF THE WISDOM GIFT

One method for looking back is life review. The lovely thing about life review is that it is useful not only for the one seeking perspective but for those coming along behind. Erikson et al. (1986) point out that the successful negotiation of the adult journey results in generativity and caring—a capacity for passing along the accumulated gifts. Two of the seminal works on life review are Butler (1963) and Kaminsky (1984).[3]

My own gifts from older adults, both those in my own family and those I have worked with professionally, have largely been from their sharing wisdom gained from such a perspective of many years. The members of the Yoruba tribe in Nigeria call older adults "The Wisdom People," and this has become my favorite term for the elders who have done their work.

A metaphor for human community is that we are all members of one growing thing, the elders being roots, the descendants (literal or figurative) being fruits—neither making sense without the perspective of both. Thus intergenerational exchange provides the answer to a wonderful koan: "When one hand washes the other, who knows which one is getting clean?" Let us look at some perspectives on this two-way gift of and from older adults.

Emma Lou Benignus is an Episcopal laywoman who has worked in the area of older adult spirituality for many years. I have been blessed to work with her in some educational ventures and loved hearing her talk about a workshop she ran for affluent elders in one of the southwestern towns of retirees. One man there spoke of working in his retirement in a hospice setting, having chosen his hours to run from midnight until 8 A.M., because those were the hours when people most needed to talk and when listeners were least likely to be there. With obvious delight in his voice and demeanor, he proclaimed, "I can turn night into day, for God's sake!"

Emma Lou believes that the reason God has engineered the spectacular increase in life expectancy in the last one hundred years is because the world is so desperately in need of wisdom that God created more elders. This is a drastically different look at the explosion of older adults in the developing world than one usually sees!

Zalman Schachter-Shalomi, a Hasidic rabbi who teaches from a truly interfaith perspective, has done work on the transformation of late life, described in his book *From Age-ing to Sage-ing* (Schachter-Shalomi and Miller 1995). He proposes that elders do their spiritual work consciously in order both to find their own fulfillment and simultaneously to be a resource for the world. He calls this process "conscious aging."

Sages are needed not simply for their own sake but for the next generations. James Gambone (1999) has done work on intergenerational dialogue using all five living generations. He believes this can lead to meaningful intergenerational cooperation, and is convinced this holds the key to solving many of our nation's social problems. He sees such dialogue as having promise for bridging cultural gaps as well, for, no matter what other issues divide cultural and ethnic groups, all elders are in agreement that they want hope and a future for their grandchildren.

Although they often do not focus on the spiritual aspects of their work, there are literally hundreds of intergenerational programs springing up throughout the country, ranging from foster grandparents to university centers on intergenerational relationships to intergenerational theater projects. Generations United is a promising effort at coalition among more than one hundred national organizations working for youth and older adults. These ventures provide a variety of vehicles for understanding and engaging in intergenerational contact and cooperation that give outlet to the desire elders may have to offer their gifts and to the need juniors have for meaningful connection with their "roots." (For additional information, contact Generations Together, An Intergenerational Studies Program at the University of Pittsburgh; The Center for Intergenerational Learning at Temple University; or Generations United.)

THE IMPORTANCE OF STORY

In my professional brochure I include the following:

> I believe that the greatest gift we can offer to each other is the telling of and listening to our stories. This empowers us to appropriate and live out our own stories, unifies us in diversity, and leads to reconciliation. . . . This theme of story unifies all I do: including

work with older adults and young adults (both of whom have developmental as well as spiritual needs to recover and share their stories); . . . spiritual direction (an intimate vehicle for exploring and living into one's story); and lay pastoral care training. . . .

As this indicates, I see story as being of tremendous importance. There are many others interested in the spiritual journey who share this perspective. Jean Shinoda Bolen (1994, 272–73) says:

> *To bring about a paradigm shift in the culture that will change assumptions and attitudes, a critical number of us have to tell the stories of our personal revelations and transformations.* . . . The stories people tell have a way of taking care of them. If stories come to you, care for them. And learn to give them away where they are needed. Sometimes a person needs a story more than food to stay alive.

The absence of models for aging with grace and wisdom is both cause and effect of the ageism in our society. The effect of this on those approaching late life can be devastating. Katie Funk Wiebe, attempting to remedy this lack, wrote her lovely spiritual autobiography *Border Crossing: A Spiritual Journey* (1995). She describes her motive as follows:

> What makes the journey into old age terrifying to me is that I hear no one beyond the middle years inviting me urgently and loudly to cross the border quickly because of its splendid advantages. A little child learning to walk has admiring fans in parents, siblings, and friends, cheering every faltering step. That cheering section was missing as I began to cross into the land of the aging. And this is the reason for this book. . . . (21)

Wiebe explicitly describes how she sees the importance of story. After a visit to the Soviet Union, the place of her family of origin, she reports: "I returned with countless stories people told me about their lives. I came back with a renewed sense of the importance of story, especially for the older adult. Stories bind the generations together. Stories bring light to dense abstractions. Stories show the pattern of living. Stories assert boldly 'I am a human being'" (132). Her message can be summarized in the following way: "I wrote these things because I am convinced many older Christians . . . have lived through numerous changes, successes, and defeats in their religious life. But they hung on. . . . True faith does not become mired in obstacles. It moves through the darkness of perplexity to that stage when life becomes daily grace" (91).

WHAT DOES THE TRUE SELF LOOK LIKE?

Rohr's (2001) description of the wisdom person (which he calls the Holy Fool) is identical for men and women, even if their journeys to that place are via different routes.[4] The Holy Fool "can live with paradox and mystery, with compassion and forgiveness ... does not need to punish or shame others ... can lead, partner or follow when necessary ... has it all ... [has gone] beyond judgments, reason and control to wisdom." What does this mean?

1.   "Can live with paradox and mystery": The wisdom person realizes not only that there are grays but that there are blacks and whites that must be allowed to remain in (often painful) coexistence until truth (enlightenment) emerges. They are, like Rilke, living more in the questions than in the answers. This allows them patience with those who are caught in one side or the other of paradox, and permits a loving shrug in the face of accusation.

2.   "Can live with compassion and forgiveness, does not need to punish or shame others": The wisdom person has learned (usually from painful experience) the truth that refusing to forgive is like taking poison and expecting it to kill the other person! Having lived through one's own sin, repentance and forgiveness allows one to let others into the forgiveness process as well.

3.   "Can lead, partner, or follow when necessary": Some of us suffer from the need to be in charge, others from fearing a leadership role, while others prefer to colead. The wisdom person is able to assess the need that the situation and other participants have, and is inwardly free to take whatever role is needed. Ego demands are much less strident and irresistible than in earlier life.

     A friend once defined humility as follows. Most of the time the camera is up close and personal; we are very much aware of the impact of everything upon us. In fact it is *all* about us! Humility on the other hand is like zooming the camera lens back, back, back to see the universe and our place in it from God's perspective. This does not mean that we ignore ourselves, our gifts, our needs—only that we hold them in proper perspective with the needs, gifts, and selves of all others. Sometimes we best "fit" by leading, sometimes by following, sometimes by partnering. From the perspective of humility, we are able to tell which is which. From the freedom from personal agendas of the wisdom position, we are liberated to do what is best.

4.   "Has it all ... [has gone] beyond judgments, reason and control to wisdom": It is no longer necessary to follow the rules; the wisdom person has internalized the spirit of the law and acts in accord with it. It is no longer necessary to try to control; the wisdom person trusts the control of the Higher Power and is content to pay attention and follow in the Way, in the dance of life.

Those of us in the Abrahamic faiths (Jewish, Christian, and Muslim) hear all our lives that our purpose is to live to the glory of God. In like manner, Buddhists are called to show forth the "Buddha nature" and Hindus to reach the stage of wisdom where they can be models to others.[5]

However it is framed, the spiritual journey is geared to lead not only to our own growth but also to the benefit of those in community with us, especially the generations that come behind us. Sometimes this sounds simply like pretty words designed to paper over the losses and pain of aging. At other times it evokes a longing in us, to which we may or may not attend. And sometimes it becomes a ravenous desire that overwhelms everything and impels us to make a deeper commitment to the pilgrimage. This is true no matter our age. Yet the very old ones, who have done their work, show it forth in a special way. Tornstam (1994) calls this "gerotranscendence," a concept developed in another chapter of this handbook.

Turning away from the multitude of negative images of aging that assault us in the media and throughout our culture, one can aspire to become a wisdom person. So let us examine what leads to the development of someone with fulfilled spiritual potential—in other words, to the development of a true wisdom person.

In the Christian gospel there are many expressions of truth and many stories that illustrate them. Each of them bears within it seeds that might be called in today's vernacular "good news and bad news." Sometimes we hear of a kin-dom or realm (or dwelling, if you will) to which followers of the truth are invited. Whatever you call it, this is good news (the literal meaning of the word "gospel"). But this kin-dom is not of this world—it is not going to get us our fifteen minutes of fame—and so perhaps this is not such good news after all. Or think of it in terms of a pearl of great price, another of the images used in Christian Scripture (Matt. 13:45-46). A pearl, valuable beyond anything else—good news! But with a great price. Is *that* good news? We must admit that a pearl of great price is also bad news, for to grasp it we must let go of everything else within our purview. Eastern religions speak of *maya*, illusion, referring to the things that seem important in the first half of life, the things we must let go of. Paul of Tarsus had spent many years building up a persona, and in his time of enlightenment lists all his former achievements and said that he now considered them rubbish (Phil. 3:8).

A young seeker came to a Buddhist teacher asking for enlightenment. The teacher took him outside to a horse trough and plunged his face into the water, holding on to the hair on the back of his head with a powerful grip. After a moment or two of practicing "acceptance," the young seeker began to struggle, finally breaking away just before losing consciousness, and with a loud gasp took in a huge lungful of air. The teacher gently commented, "When you want enlightenment as much as you just wanted air, you will find it."

The destination of the wisdom person is often quite countercultural. The moment of recognition when previously sought goals no longer have value is called enlightenment in the East, conversion in the West, and is described in Twelve-Step programs as discovering that what one has been engaging in is "stinking thinking." This change in perspective is the demarcation of the beginning of the conscious spiritual pilgrimage.

Once this change in perspective is made, one enters the chosen path and learns to use life experience to ever more deeply surrender the superficial for the truly valuable. While it is framed in many languages and has many different tools for the journey, when one sticks to the end one becomes both blessed and blessing.[6]

SOME EXAMPLES OF WISDOM PEOPLE

One might look to the Bible as one source of wisdom models. It does not much address issues of aging explicitly, but many of its stories are about older adults and are worth additional reflection. Abraham was elderly before he began his journey to the promised land, and had his child-heir in very late life; Sarah, the child's mother, was also elderly, and named the child Isaac ("laughter") because of her reaction to being told she would give birth. Moses was elderly before beginning his liberation of the Hebrew people. Perhaps these and other biblical stories of those who are full of years were offered to illustrate the need for having some years under one's belt before beginning the true pilgrimage of meaning in life.[7]

There are four examples of people I know personally who have made that pilgrimage and have given me models for aging with grace and wisdom. First is a ninety-year-old black woman whom I interviewed for my dissertation. She lived on the second floor of an unappealing, foul-smelling, dilapidated shack. Furthermore, I knew in advance that she was in very poor physical condition. I reluctantly walked up the steps, not wanting to be there. I left three hours later, feeling sure that I had visited in the kin-dom of God. This woman, with failing hearing and eyesight, bad arthritis (so bad that she rarely got out), with little money and lots of pain, who had outlived both of her husbands and *all nine of her children,* was a woman living in the center of hope.

She said something that I will carry with me as long as I have my mind: "God keeps takin' stuff away from me, and every time he does I mourns a while, and then he fills me with more of himself!" The only way I could describe her was to say that she was marinated in God! Is there anything worth more for which to hope? She is perhaps my best example of how, in spite of loss (and, I am forced to admit, at least sometimes because of it), one can live in the kin-dom.

Another example was a ninety-nine-year-old woman, weighing perhaps eighty-five pounds, sitting in a wheelchair on a stage at the Kanuga Conference Center in western North Carolina during a conference on older adult ministry. She seemed to be in her own little world, and because her hearing was very poor, in a real way she was. (After hearing her speak, I later wondered if *that* world was not really the kin-dom.)

She came alive when someone handed her the microphone. She whipped out a small stack of three-by-five cards, and began to share with us her carefully chosen description of the spiritual pilgrimage of late life. Her basic message was "seize the day." She lived fully, enjoyed her life, still did volunteer work, and went to church. She said that the secret of her joy (and she *was* joyful beyond my powers of description) was to "find the yeses in God's noes."

Another very old woman from Tennessee granted me the favor of an interview. She too radiated that inner joy that I have come to see as a hallmark of residence in the kin-dom. I asked her to tell me what wisdom she had learned in her own aging. She said something I will never forget: "When I was young, I spent a lot of time kicking against the goad. I have learned to accept almost anything almost instantly." I felt cold fear, and admitted, "Oh, dear, I can't even pray for that yet!" "Don't worry, Lynn," she lightly replied, "you're not yet ninety-six years old!"

Finally, let me tell you what happened when I was talking about all of this with a very wise and very old former New York City social worker, also a black woman. I told her about these people, and as she listened she nodded wisely, instantly comprehending. Her words seemed to be saying, "Oh, you are talking about the kin-dom!" She not only *knew* about it, but she had arrived there, and *lived* there.

I am discovering that there are many more people like these than I had ever dreamed might exist. If we do not see them it is because we do not look for them. Even if we should see them, we do not often listen long enough to hear them talk about the kin-dom. Ram Dass said once at a speaking engagement that the reason the world does not have more bodhisattvas, people who exist only to be of service, and who are free of their own "stuff," is that no one wants them!

Miller (1999) interviewed a number of older adults to discover what were the common elements of spiritual maturity. Some of their responses illustrate well the mind-set of the wisdom person. Here is just one example (Miller 1999, 44): "I am not afraid any more . . . because I have been loved enough by God; he has really given me a lot of gifts. There is hope for us all, if we can just quit worrying about ourselves and just let the Lord love us and try to give love back as well. . . . The day that I found out I was lovable was the day that my life was changed."

There are distinctive characteristics that may be found in the wisdom people we meet. One is a shift not only in self-image, but in the image of God as well. A view of God as angry, judgmental, and rigid is incompatible with a view of one's self loved as is. We will discover wisdom people living in the here and now, not much in the future (and only in the past for the purposes of meaning-making and story-sharing). There is also evidence of their ability to live in the tension between self-authentication and community. On one hand, we do not need outside approval to know we are acceptable, for we find our acceptability elsewhere. On the other hand, we rejoice in sharing our vision of the pilgrimage with others on the same journey.

Thomas Kelley (1941) speaks of the community of those who seek to live in awareness of the holy. Upon meeting, they recognize each other, and find each other's company precious. Simone Weil (1973) says that there is nothing among human things with more power to concentrate the gaze ever more steadily upon God than friendship for the friends of God.

Wisdom people recognize that truth is often so large that it embraces apparent opposites. Rohr (2001) sees this capacity for living in the tension between two apparently contradictory truths embodied in the gesture of one's arms being wide open, holding opposites in tension, in a sort of spiritual and intellectual crucifixion. The Eastern mind views it as the balance of yin and yang, and there is a parallel wisdom in somewhat different language in the Jewish cabala. The Zen seeker looks for it in the paradox of the koan, the comprehension of which comes only with enlightenment.

Another characteristic of wisdom people is their ability to rest—to be—rather than always having to fit the American vision of "doing." Jane Thibault (1993) compares very late life to monastic life that offers the opportunity to learn to just be. The motto might be, "Don't just do something; sit there!" Basil Pennington (1998, 30), a Cistercian monk, speaks of this as follows:

> For me the quiet hours in my recliner have indeed become more and more precious. I look forward to them and look forward to the time when I will have more of them. Why is this? Well, for one thing, they are filled with friends and friendship. Sometimes they do afford me the time to really just enjoy a friend, waste time with the friend, with no sense of something waiting to be done, of a certain restrictive limit to the time we can enjoy together. I sense this is a bit of a beginning of the joy of eternal life, just being with friends with nothing else to do.

It is not possible to *make* this process happen. But one cooperates with it. Thus, speaking of it, one uses the language of paradox: losing one's life to find it (Matt. 10:39) or returning to the place from which we started, but seeing it as if for the first time (Eliot 1962, 145). One friend whose path includes twice-daily centering prayer (see Keating 1995) said to me that he believes the true self to be liberated by this prayer. It does not result from struggle to gain insight, but rather from letting go and trusting the Holy One to enter the deepest part of one, find and heal the wounds, and depart, leaving as evidence only the "peace that passes understanding" (Phil. 4:7). Another way to speak of it is as the dance of will and grace. Will is required simply to "show up"; grace is the part that comes to us as gift when we do.

William Butler Yeats describes the strange countercultural truth of the wisdom person economically in four short lines in his poem "Sailing to Byzantium":

> An aged man is but a paltry thing
> A tattered coat upon a stick
> Unless soul clap its hands and sing
> And louder sing for every tatter in its mortal dress. (1962, 95)

At the age of fifty-eight, I teeter on the brink of what I hope will lead to my becoming a wisdom person. Recently, when confronted with the illness of an aged mentor, I took to my journal to work out what I saw as "a good death." This led me further to tease out a description of "a good life." My spiritual director, listening to my ruminations, asked, "Isn't that what the chapter you are writing is supposed to be about?" The energy of synchronicity is an element in discerning that one is on the pilgrim path. So with a tad of uncharacteristic self-consciousness, I share this with the reader:

A good death: what is it?

1. being at peace with life, others, and God
2. having enough warning so as not to leave unfinished business

3. having freedom from the kind of pain that prevents letting go with dignity and grace
4. living each moment with a sense of rightness, and coming to peaceful closure
5. having faith, hope, and trust in the Ancient of Days and in what is to come (Ancient of Days is one of the terms used for God in the Jewish tradition, and if humanity is indeed created in the image of God, is it not a delicious way to validate the elder-journey by using this name and remembering that it refers also to us?)
6. having given permission to those left behind to do "good grief" and then to let go and move on with life
7. having been a teacher for others, and a blessing to all who have crossed my path

And a good life?

1. loving the Ancient of Days, self, and others—in relentless benevolence
2. having discovered a right balance (or rhythm) between doing and being
3. walking humbly with the Holy One
4. loving people and using things, and doing both with gratitude
5. living sustainably with the earth and her creatures
6. praying without ceasing (Other traditions might call this "living contemplatively" or "conscious living.")
7. using the gifts I have received wisely and with creativity and joy
8. full of the "fruit of the Spirit" (St. Paul enumerates this fruit in Gal. 5:22 as "love, joy, peace, patience, kindness, goodness, faithfulness, humility and self-control." I choose to add hope, generosity, and thanksgiving.)
9. self-aware but not self-absorbed (This phraseology is found in the Episcopal Diocese of Colorado handbook for spiritual directors as a characteristic of a mature spiritual director. It seems to fit a wisdom person too.)

There is no guarantee that one will have either a good life or a good death, but it is my firm conviction that setting out on pilgrimage to the kin-dom is an invitation to the universe to direct us to both of them. I give thanks for the models I have known and to my teachers. I aspire to be both to those who know me. It seems to me that the adventure and gift of this handbook is to provide a variety of perspectives to those who would understand, experience, and teach about pilgrimage so that the good news about the spiritual potentials of late life can be passed on. In the words of Robert Frost (1962), "You come too!"

NOTES

1. In 1975, the National Interfaith Coalition on Aging (now a constituent body of the National Council on Aging) affirmed a definition of spiritual well-being that expresses the same notion: "Spiritual Well-Being is the affirmation of life in a relationship with God, self, community and environment that nurtures and celebrates wholeness." I'll not attempt to pin it down further. For some efforts at so doing, see Thomas and Eisenhandler (1994), Seeber (1990), and Bianchi (1982).

2. See Viktor Frankl's (1963) work on logotherapy, a major tool for meaning-making. Frankl was a speaker at the 1989 Annual Program Meeting of the American Society on Aging, where he explicitly applied his theory to the vicissitudes of late life, including the losses associated with Alzheimer's disease.

3. For some interesting exercises to facilitate life review, see Morgan (1996) and Wakefield (1990). Kaufman (1986) gives some superb and detailed examples of people going through this process with her and emphasizes the importance of the integration of the parts of one's life in the process of coming to wholeness.

4. Rohr differentiates the journeys of men and women, but today's First World woman's journey much resembles that of the man, so this distinction will not be made here in detail. In some traditional cultures, women are subject to many social and physical forms of oppression and so have a more "down-up-down" journey.

5. For a beautifully written description of the stages of pilgrimage, see Moody and Carroll (1997).

6. For some spiritual yet practical tools that can help us cooperate in this process, see Schachter-Shalomi and Miller (1995).

7. For just a few of the multitude of additional nonbiblical examples of late life stories in the literature see Section 2 ("Case Studies") in Thomas and Eisenhandler (1994), Myerhoff (1978), Ramsey and Blieszner (1999) and Learn (1996).

BIBLIOGRAPHY

Bertman, S. (1994). "A Handful of Quietness: Measuring the Meaning of Our Years." In Thomas and Eisenhandler, 3–12.

Bianchi, E. C. (1982). *Aging as a Spiritual Journey*. New York: Crossroad.

Bolen, J. S. (1994). *Crossing to Avalon: A Woman's Midlife Pilgrimage*. San Francisco: Harper San-Francisco.

Butler, R. (1963). "The Life Review: An Interpretation of the Reminiscence of the Aged." *Psychiatry* 26: 65–76.

Eliot, T. S. (1962). *The Complete Poems and Plays: 1909–1950*. New York: Harcourt, Brace and World.

Erikson, E. (1963). *Childhood and Society*. 2d ed. New York: Norton.

Erikson, E., et al. (1986). *Vital Involvement in Old Age*. New York: Norton.

Finley, J. (1978). *Merton's Palace to Nowhere*. Notre Dame, Ind.: Ave Maria.

Fischer, K. (1985). *Winter Grace*. Mahweh, N.J.: Paulist.

Frankl, V. (1963). *Man's Search for Meaning: An Introduction to Logotherapy.* New York: Washington Square.

Frost, R. (1962). "The Pasture." In L. Untermeyer, ed., *Modern American and Modern British Poetry,* 168. New York: Harcourt, Brace and World.

Gambone, J. (1999). *All Are Welcome: A Primer on Intentional Intergenerational Ministry and Dialogue.* Spring Park, Minn.: Elder Eye.

Hover, M. (2000). "The Sacred Spiral: Spirituality and Aging." In Thorson, 16–27.

Kaminsky, M., ed. (1984). *The Uses of Reminiscence.* New York: Haworth.

Kaufman, S. (1986). *The Ageless Self: Sources of Meaning in Late Life.* Madison: University of Wisconsin Press.

Keating, T. (1995). *Open Mind, Open Heart: The Contemplative Dimension of the Gospel.* New York: Continuum.

Kelley, T. (1941). *A Testament of Devotion.* New York: Harper & Row.

Learn, C. D. (1996). *Older Women's Experience of Spirituality: Crafting the Quilt.* New York: Garland.

Levinson, D. J., et al. (1978). *The Seasons of a Man's Life.* New York: Knopf.

Miller, M. E. (1994). "Religious and Ethical Strivings in the Later Years: Three Paths to Spiritual Maturity and Integrity." In Thomas and Eisenhandler, 35–58.

Moody, H., and D. Carroll (1997). *The Five Stages of the Soul: Charting the Spiritual Passages That Shape Our Lives.* New York: Doubleday.

Morgan, R. (1996). *Remembering Your Story: A Guide to Spiritual Autobiography.* Nashville: Upper Room.

Myerhoff, B. (1978). *Number Our Days.* New York: Simon and Schuster.

Pennington, M. B. (1998). "Long on the Journey." In Weaver, Koenig, and Roe, 29–34.

Priests for Equality (1996). *Inclusive New Testament.* Brentwood, Md.: Priests for Equality.

Ramsey, J. L., and R. Blieszner (1999). *Spiritual Resiliency in Older Women: Models of Strength for Challenges through the Life Span.* Thousand Oaks, Calif.: Sage.

Rohr, R. (2001). Keynote presentations at "Men + Women: The Journey of Spiritual Transformation," a conference sponsored by the Episcopal Diocese of Colorado, January 19–20, Denver, Colorado.

Schachter-Shalomi, Z., and R. S. Miller (1995). *From Age-ing to Sage-ing: A Profound New Vision of Growing Older.* New York: Warner.

Seeber, J. J., ed. (1990). *Spiritual Maturity in the Later Years.* New York: Haworth.

Thomas, L. E., and S. A. Eisenhandler, eds. (1994). *Aging and the Religious Dimension.* Westport, Conn.: Auburn House.

Thibault, J. (1993). *A Deepening Love Affair: The Gift of God in Later Life.* Nashville: Upper Room.

Thorson, J., ed. (2000). *Perspectives on Spiritual Well-Being and Aging.* Springfield, Ill: Charles C. Thomas.

Tornstam, L. (1994). "Gero-Transcendence: A Theoretical and Empirical Exploration." In Thomas, and Eisenhandler, 202–25.

Viorst, J. (1986). *Necessary Losses.* New York: Simon and Schuster.

Wakefield, D. (1990). *The Story of Your Life: Writing a Spiritual Autobiography.* Boston: Beacon.

Weaver, A. J., H. G. Koenig, and P. C. Roe, eds. (1998). *Reflections on Aging and Spiritual Growth.* Nashville: Abingdon.

Weil, S. (1973). *Waiting for God.* New York: Perennial Library.

Wiebe, K. F. (1995). *Border Crossing: A Spiritual Journey.* Scottdale, Pa.: Herald.

Yeats, W. B. (1962). *Selected Poems of William Butler Yeats.* Ed. M. L. Rosenthal. New York: Macmillan.

2
Spiritual Counseling of Persons with Dementia

JANE M. THIBAULT

"Of what use will I be to anyone—even to God?" (a person newly diagnosed with Alzheimer's disease).

"Where is my mother's soul, now that she no longer knows who she is?" (a daughter).

"How could God abandon someone who has been so faithful for so many years?" (a husband).

"I no longer visit my father—it is a waste of time. He doesn't remember who I am, and it hurts me to see the physical shell he has become. I'd rather keep the memory of who he was" (a son).

"Why should I give communion to demented elders? They don't understand what they are doing!" (a pastor).

Their caregivers and persons suffering from dementia have asked variations of the above questions repeatedly in my twenty-five years of clinical work with them. These questions, which sound more like mournful pleas than requests for information, represent an attempt to make some "spiritual sense" of the experience of dementia. Unfortunately, answers are hard to find. Very few theologians and philosophers have reflected on the existential meaning that the loss of memory has for individuals and for society, even though Judaism, Christianity, and Islam are grounded in acts of remembrance. There are few readily available guides for the practitioner who attempts to give useful and sensitive responses to these questions, nor is there much help for the clinician who is tempted to despair when faced with yet another person diagnosed with dementia.

During the course of my work I have often asked myself the same questions. How would I create meaning if I were diagnosed with a dementing disorder? A few years ago, my own anguish became so intense that I set out to find and/or create some meaning for myself that, if appropriate, I might share with my patients and their loved ones. The work that I do involves assessments of the cognitive, emotional, social, functional, and environmental domains, as well as counseling related to the practical and existential meaning of "loss of self." In my encounters with patients and caregivers I have witnessed both great tragedy and high comedy. On rare occasions I have been the awed observer of intense spiritual experience. Sometimes I have been given the gift of participating in this experience, as though God were working through the person with dementia to reach me. My "breakthrough case" occurred a few months after I began the search for "meaning" in dementia. Here is what happened.

At the beginning of the new year I was in a state of overload, highly stressed from a hectic holiday season and burdened with a number of assignment deadlines. I felt angry and resentful that I had not made time for myself and knew that I was rapidly "burning out" both personally and professionally. I had begun to feel that the type of work I had chosen so eagerly had become too much of a burden for my body, mind, and soul and was trying to discern whether to leave human services completely (not an uncommon experience for most of us who work in any of the helping professions).

During that time a despairing daughter brought her eighty-six-year-old mother to our Geriatric Evaluation and Treatment Clinic to be assessed for the cause of her confusion, short-term memory loss, and rapidly deteriorating ability to speak. Because the patient could not utter a comprehensible phrase, it was difficult to test her cognition. Although she seemed aware of her verbal disability, she did not become frustrated but remained gracious and calm throughout my attempt to test her. As part of the Mini-Mental Status Examination I asked her to write a sentence, fully expecting that she would not be able to do so.

Instead, she took the pen and paper, looked at me intently for a few seconds, then, in lovely handwriting, wrote, "Enjoy your life *and* help other people, too!" She returned the paper to me, patted my hand gently, and smiled broadly. I was stunned by the message and exclaimed to her, "This is exactly what I needed to hear today!" The patient's daughter, who had been present for the duration of the testing, read what her mother had written, reached for a pen and paper and copied the message, saying, "I needed this, too." I have taken this woman's wisdom to heart and keep her words in the front of my appointment book.

At some deep level of human awareness, a stranger, a woman with dementia so advanced that she could no longer converse with her family nor remember how to dress herself, was able to discern my spiritual need and respond to it in a healing way. She was the blessing that I desperately needed, the blessing for which I had prayed intensely. Reflecting on this experience I wondered what had happened in this encounter. Was this an instance of pure coincidence or was God working in some way to let me know that persons suffering from dementia are God's own beloved children who can serve their Creator just as well as those of us who have no cognitive disability—perhaps even *more* effectively? The quest for meaning expanded as I began to investigate the ways in which persons suffering from dementia can actually be a blessing to those who come in contact with them.

One outcome of this quest is the following reflection, written as my own dialogue with God. It is an attempt to make meaning of the experience of the loss of self. I use the text as bibliotherapy when I am engaged in spiritual counseling with persons whose religious formation is within the domain of Christianity. When counseling a person with newly diagnosed dementia, I offer the "journal" entries as my own attempt to make spiritual meaning of the loss of personal memory and encourage the person to discuss the ideas and feelings with me if he or she chooses. In a number of cases the person has chosen to write her own reflections and share those both with me and with significant others. When a person cannot read or write, I read aloud passages that seem to relate to what the person is feeling. This usually engenders some discussion. With the use of the journal as a catalyst, a person's deepest fears can emerge for sharing and self-expression, resulting in a decline of fear, a sense of peacefulness, and renewed hope.

The following are the primary concepts I am trying to convey to persons suffering from dementing disorders and those who love and care for them:

1. Even if I can no longer remember who I am, even if others forget me, God remembers.
2. By remaining a member of the religious community, the members of the congregation will continue to remember for me.
3. Even if I do not realize how I serve God's wish for humanity, I will still be well employed by God to proclaim God's blessings in some mysterious way. I will still be able to carry out the Hebrew mandate to do *tikkun olam*—to help repair the world.
4. After death, in the next phase of life, I am promised that I will—for the first time—know myself fully. In my knowing God, I will finally know myself *as I am known.*

MOURNING PAGES

These journal entries reflect a period of six weeks after "Catherine" had been diagnosed with an early stage of Alzheimer's disease. Although fictional, the content is based on the questions I have heard asked over and over in my twenty-five years of work with persons suffering from dementia. These musings represent a possible response to the spiritual significance of the total loss of the self from this disease.

Day 1: For more than half of my life I've begun each day with morning pages—journal entries that speak of my relationship with God. They are written in that just-awakened state after sleep, before the world intrudes, while the mind still partially resides in a misty elsewhere—"dreamtime," I believe the Aboriginal people call it. I have always thought of it as "our" time, mine and God's. Not prayer, not diary keeping, not reflection. Just time to be with one another, to savor the joy and pain of being in each other's lives. This is the sanctuary from which the guidance for my outer life has always come, where the meaning of my life is made. But now, my morning pages have turned to "mourning" pages, for I have been told that who I am is slowly going away. Rather, I am being taken away without my consent from all I know and love. Yet I will continue to live for a while in a void like Sheol. So I will write to the one I love until the time comes when I can no longer emerge from the elsewhere of night to meet with the morning sun.

Day 4: Dear God, How long can I keep this a secret? I want to shout, yell, scream. I can't keep the terror of this to myself. But I must. It's not safe to speak to anyone but you now—and I know you won't be telling anyone! (Sorry, that was a cheap shot.) My soul is full of cheap shots at the moment. All I want to do is to strike out at someone, anyone, and you're the only safe one—the only one on whom I may vent my rage. I want to batter you with my words, with my fists, with my whole being. Why did you do this to me? I thought you loved me, that we were friends. I thought you needed me to do your work. Don't talk to me any longer about there being too few laborers in the vineyards. There would be if you weren't so busy getting rid of us!

Day 5: Dear God, Please bear with me. I'm angry with you and I need you—both at the same time. I hate feeling like this. There's one thing I would really like to know—no, I really need to know—why this particular disease? I'm not asking why I have to die, but why do I have to die this way? I'm willing to have cancer, a heart attack, any one of the wasting diseases. I'm willing to suffer pain. I'm a realist, have always accepted the fact that someday I would die. But please, dear God, don't let my mind die before the rest of my body. Don't let who I am die before what I am. Don't let me be a vacant house. What good can I be to you that way? I say to you what Hezekiah said, "For Sheol cannot praise you, nor Death celebrate you; those who go down to the pit can hope no longer in your constancy. The living, the living are the ones who praise you. . ." (Isa. 38:10-20, New Jerusalem Bible). I rewrite Hezekiah's prayer to make it my own and plead with you to reconsider, for surely only those in their right minds can serve you:

> In the noon of my life
> I am to depart.
> At the gates of Sheol I shall be held
> for the rest of my days.
> . . . I shall never see Yahweh again
> in the land of the living.
> My home has been pulled up, and thrown away
> like a shepherd's tent;
> like a weaver, I have rolled up my life.
> You have cut me from the loom.
> From dawn to dark, you have been making an end of me;
> till daybreak, I cried for help;
> like a lion you have crushed all my bones.
> From dawn to dark, you have been making an end of me.
> God, I am overwhelmed, come to my help.
> How can I speak and what can I say to you?
> You are the one to act.
> I must eke out the rest of my years
> in bitterness of soul.

God, you could do for me what you did for Hezekiah. I don't even ask for fifteen years—just let what is left be my own. "O Lord . . . let my prayer come before you; / incline your ear to my cry" (Ps. 88:1-2). Please?

Day 8: Dear God, the loneliness is overwhelming. I hate that no one but my physician knows what is happening to my brain, to my life. I can't settle down. I want to tell everyone I know, want them to hold me, to tell me that the tests were wrong, that all will be fine. I want them to tell me that my mind is too strong to succumb to such a disease. I wish my mother were alive, to kiss my head and make it better. But I can't let anyone know. If they found out they would dismiss all I have to say, to give, to do as the product of dementia.

I feel so ashamed—and so guilty. What did I do wrong? What could I have done to take care of myself better? Could I have prevented this in any way? If I had eaten more nutritious foods, meditated regularly, been more disciplined in exercising, taking vitamin E—would it have made any difference? I'll never know, but just the realization that these were available to me and I didn't use them washes me in feelings of guilt.

Day 10: Dear God, talk to me. Tell me what to do. Give me some sign that you hear my panic. Do you care? I can't do this alone. Help me to think—I can't think; I can't figure out what to do. O God, help me! I am caught in a whirlwind of feelings and thoughts and I can't figure out how to get out.

Day 12: Dear God, I feel calmer now, a little clearer, as though a violent storm had blown itself out. Thank you for your peace. What is it you want from me? What is it that I have to learn? I do have enough confidence in your love that I know you did not make this happen to me (even though initially I did accuse you of inflicting this on me). But how can I continue to do your work if the essence of who I am is disintegrating? If the other parts of my body were failing, I could somehow witness to my faith in your existence by loving whoever comes to see me or care for me. But if I don't have any memory of you, how can I be for you? How can I even continue to love you? Please answer me. I do not think these are trivial questions. Surely thousands of others with this disease ask you the same questions.

Day 13: Dear God, I am waiting. Please let me know you hear me. Once, during that difficult time when I was a teenager (this memory seems far more vivid to me than my meeting with the doctor), I thought I heard you talking to me. You said, "Don't be such a brat, Catherine. Let these people help you. Everything's going to be all right." I did what you said, and things really were better. What words do you have for me now? Do you think you could say something to me again? What can I do to help you help me?

Day 16: Dear God, I am so tired of trying to figure out how I am going to handle this. I would like to die right now. If I can't be of service to you or anyone else, why let me be a burden? Why not let me take care of this quickly, while I still have the ability to do it. No one would have to know. I could be in a single-car accident, drown while swimming. My children are grown; they all have full lives. My spouse is gone; it would not be a disaster for anyone. In fact, my family would be spared the pain of having to see who I am disappear, bit by bit.

It would be a service to society, wouldn't it, not to use resources someone else could use? I once heard a pastor talking about a man in his congregation who had taken his own life when he learned he had the same disease. He did it so that his frail wife would not be burdened with his care and be left bereft of all their savings. The minister said he admired this man because he had "laid down his life for his friend." Is this what I should do too? When is the deliberate and premature taking of one's life not suicide but "laying down one's life for one's friend"? Is this to be my final way of serving you and others?

Day 18: Dear God, I listen, but hear nothing, not even my own voice speaking to me. If you won't talk to me, is there something in Scripture that can guide me in this? Did they have Alzheimer's in Jesus' time? Mental illness is mentioned, but I don't recall any references to anything like dementia and there's nothing specific to it in the concordance. I looked it up. There are sixty-four references to some variation of "forget"—most of them telling us *not* forget!

The poet of Psalm 71 pleaded with you not to leave him alone in old age: "Do not reject me now I am old, nor desert me now my strength is failing." But he couldn't have had dementia because he asks that his life be prolonged in old age so that he could continue serving you: "Let me live to tell the rising generation about your strength and power, about your heavenly righteousness." This psalm does not reach me, for how will I be able to speak of you to the next generation when I do not even remember who I am? Oh, my God, will I forget you, too?

Day 21: Dear God, when you tell us to "become like little children," do you mean as little as the infant, or as psychologically small as the fetus in the womb, neither of whom has consciousness of you? But even the unborn child at least has the promise of the consciousness of you! I have the promise of the loss of my knowledge of you. Do not reject me now that I am forgetful, even if I forget you.

Day 23: Dear God, is who I know myself to be now the sum total of who I am? When the mystics talk about the loss of self as a goal of the spiritual life, are they talking about this kind of loss of self? I bet not. Bernadette Roberts has written about the experience she calls "no-self." Is this the same thing? Temporary loss of the sense of self as an intense spiritual experience is fine, but permanent forgetting of who I am? I don't think so.

Day 26: Dear God, I've witnessed how demented people are treated by their congregations and have decided not to go to church anymore. Remember when Mrs. Kay started singing with the soloist during the offertory hymn? Everybody looked at her with a frown and let her husband know in no uncertain terms that he should take her home. They've never come back. I bumped into Mr. Kay at the grocery a while back and he said he's never even been contacted by the pastor (who is probably relieved that she doesn't have to deal with any more surprise outbursts). And a number of years ago I had a conversation with a priest-professor whose father had dementia. We were talking about communion at the time and he said that he no longer gave his father the Eucharist because the man no longer understood the meaning of what he was doing. Dear God, am I going to lose your physical presence as well? Have I ever fully understood what I was doing when I received at your table? I doubt it. Does anyone?

Day 28: Dear God, I do not want to be an embarrassment to anyone. I want to retain my dignity. What is dignity, anyway? My old dictionary says that it is the quality of being worthy of esteem or honor. Who really is worthy? Who isn't? Seems to me Jesus didn't exit this life in a very dignified manner. So why am I so concerned with dignity and "death with dignity"? My doctor started to talk to me about "advance directives," saying that these decisions would assure me of dignity when I can no longer make my own decisions, but I can't bear dealing with that now. Why is dignity such a value? Is any kind of death ever really dignified? Yet, perhaps it's the most dignified thing we ever do. My head is tired. I want to go home.

Day 31: Dear God, on my birthday a few years ago someone gave me Eugene Bianchi's book, *Aging as a Spiritual Journey.* I loved it when I first read it, as it gave me a new vision of what my aging process could be. I looked at it again today, searching for the spiritual meaning of dementia. There is no reference at all to dementia. So only those in their right minds can be on a spiritual journey?

Day 34: Dear God, I constantly search your word. There are more references to aging in the Hebrew scriptures than in the Gospels. In fact, the only direct mention of old people is Luke's story of Anna and Simeon—and neither was demented!

It occurs to me that Christianity really is a religion for people whose memories are intact. Not only that, we Christians are *told* to remember, as if being a Christian depends on having a good memory. The words of Communion, "Do this in remembrance of me," are central to the entire Christian faith. Judaism requires remembrance of the Passover. So much emphasis is placed on remembrance. What place is there for those of us who no longer have the gift of remembrance? I feel so left out.

Do you have any words at all for me—and for the others in my situation? Do not abandon us to a night of the soul.

Day 37: Dear God, since the last time I wrote to you I have been thinking about the last phrase I used—"night of the soul." I used it as an expression of my fear, but as I pondered those words, I remembered that the sixteenth-century Spanish mystic St. John of the Cross used the term "dark night of the soul" to describe the most intense stage of purification of the soul in final preparation for union with God in this life.

Many years ago I had read the works of John of the Cross avidly, greatly desirous of this union about which John spoke so passionately. However, at some point I remember getting "cold feet" about my spiritual journey and what it might require of me. I'd read in John of the Cross that the most characteristic quality of this last stage was the sense of the absence of God, the feeling of being abandoned by God and, for some, a struggle to believe in the existence of God. John taught that this final "night" is necessary for those who are seeking God because the experience strips them of all their humanly comforting illusions about who God is. The person undergoing this "dark night of the soul" has all of her thoughts about God taken away so that only the pure, unknowable, transcendent God is left.

John's "night" is an experience of God-who-cannot-be-pinned-down. God in the void. I remember the terror I felt when I read about this night. I also remember intentionally putting away John's writings, realizing that I was too much of a coward to willingly go through that kind of experience. Yet, I will experience it—or something very much like it—and not willingly.

Could it be that my dementia is a kind of physiological "dark night of the soul"—could it still accomplish in me the same kind of preparation for God that St. John's dark night does? The people who intentionally allow themselves to go through this purification at least have the satisfaction of knowing that they are seeking you. Does it still "count" spiritually if I lose all memory of you and can no long seek you?

And—when I no longer recognize that you are the desire of my life, where is my soul?

Day 41: Dear God, the only possibly relevant scripture I have found is in the last part of John, where Jesus says to Peter, after telling him to feed his sheep:

> Very truly, I tell you, when you were younger,
> you used to fasten your own belt and to go wherever you wished. But when you grow old, you will stretch out your hands, and someone else will
> fasten a belt around you and take you where you do not wish to go. (John 21:18)

I was taught a long time ago that this passage referred to the way Peter was going to die—being led to his death on the cross. But the more I read it the more I think it is a better description of a person with Alzheimer's disease. Some day, sooner or later, depending on my own physiology, I will not remember how to dress myself. Perhaps I'll even take to wandering around stark naked in the neighborhood, as my grandmother once did when I was a child, to the total embarrassment of my mother. So when that day comes, some stranger will bathe me and dress me and take me where she thinks I should go—to the nursing home dining room, or to the activities room, or back into my own bed. All against my will.

Was Jesus foretelling that this is what would happen to Peter? Knowing what I know of Peter, this would be a fate worse than death on the cross upside down! He was a person who liked to be in control of the situation (as I do).

The most promising and hopeful thing about this prediction is in the next passage: "He said this to indicate the kind of death by which he would *glorify God*" (John 21:19, my emphasis). Do you really mean this? Is it possible for me to glorify God even when I no longer can dress myself and need total care? How can this be?

Day 42: Dear God, I can hardly believe what has happened. You really do answer me in my distress! Why am I so amazed? Let me write the story, so that when I have totally forgotten it, someone else can read it to me.

As you know, I have recently been trying to determine what others think about dementia. This morning I happened (?) to be sitting in my doctor's office next to a fairly young woman who works as a nurse's aide in the dementia unit of a local nursing home. I made the general comment, "Alzheimer's is the last disease I'd ever want to have. It must be hard to work with them." In truth, I was leading her on.

She responded by agreeing that it was difficult but rewarding to be able to help those who were in such need, and she had been satisfied with her job. However, she had recently learned that her mother had the disease. This completely overwhelmed her with grief. She decided that she could no longer work with dementia patients and be reminded daily of what her mother was going to experience. So she decided to find work in a hospital. On the day she was going to give her resignation, she went into the room of one of her patients, to help her dress. The woman, glad to see her, said to the aide, "Honey, what's my name?" The aide gently told her, and felt her heart break for the patient and for her mother. She couldn't wait for the day to be over. Then the woman went on with her conversation. She pointed to the cross on the wall of her room and said distinctly and with seeming total comprehension—and with a laugh, "Honey, most of the time I don't even know who I am, but he does, and that's all that counts."

The aide told me that in that moment all of her fears for her mother and for herself went away. She was flooded with peace and a sense of being protected. She told me she knew without a doubt that whatever happened, everything would be all right. She also knew that her mother would still be serving well the God she had so dearly served all of her life.

Oh, my beloved God, once again you have come to my rescue. Through the mouth of a stranger in a not-so-chance encounter I heard the words you spoke to me in my teenage distress: "Everything is going to be all right." What joy! Do the other words apply here, too: "Let these people help you"? Are you saying that I need to tell my friends, to stay in my congregation, to share my pain openly with others? I believe this is what you are telling me. So, as I did years ago, I will trust you. Even in this, the loss of who I am, I will trust you. Even when I can no longer trust, I will know that, in the elsewhere, you are there. But allow me, dear love, one more request: in my dimmest moments please let me witness to your loving care. Let me point to your cross and say to all who need to hear, "I don't know who I am, but he does—and that's all that counts!" And let me say it lightly, with a laugh!

BIBLIOGRAPHY

Bianchi, E. C. (1982). *Aging as a Spiritual Journey*. New York: Crossroad.

Kavanaugh, K., and O. Rodriguez, trans. (1964). *The Collected Works of Saint John of the Cross.* Garden City, N.Y.: Doubleday.

Roberts, B. (1989). *What Is Self? A Study of the Spiritual Journey in Terms of Consciousness.* Austin, Tex.: Mary Goens.

3 Becoming a Spiritual Elder

ROBERT C. ATCHLEY

This chapter is about experiences people have in the process of becoming a spiritual elder. It is based on the ideas of Rabbi Zalman Schachter-Shalomi (Schachter-Shalomi and Miller 1995), my experiences as a participant in the spiritual eldering work, and my research on later life spiritual development since 1990. I use the word "becoming" to suggest that being a spiritual elder is not a destination where we arrive but rather a capacity that we can become in any moment. Becoming a spiritual elder is the culmination of what has come before in terms of spiritual growth and capacity to understand and discern the demands of a specific situation. It is a moving mosaic that requires the capacity to be intensely present and at the same time to transcend our purely personal perspectives. Becoming a spiritual elder is also an evolution that couples a mature inner connection to the sacred with action in social roles.

The chapter begins with an examination of the nature of spiritual development and the role of spiritual elder. Next is a consideration of some of the personal, cultural, and social obstacles that prospective spiritual elders must often overcome and the skills they will require. The chapter then presents three types of spiritual elders associated with later stages of life: spiritual elder in training, actualized spiritual elder, and transcendent spiritual elder.

SPIRITUAL DEVELOPMENT

The study of adult development is concerned with how personality, intellect, and self-awareness evolve together over time. This evolution takes place in and is influenced by cultural and social environments. Adult development also considers the parallel development of body, mind, consciousness, and spirit and the interrelationships of these. Spiritual development is obviously the subset of adult development that concerns the evolution of the spiritual aspects of existence—our capacity to be aware of our spiritual nature and to experience spiritual growth and change.

It is important to be as clear as possible about the language used to discuss spiritual development. The word "spirit" has many meanings, but the one most useful for our purposes is "incorporeal consciousness" (American Heritage College Dictionary, 1993), that part of consciousness that does not depend on input from the body. Spirituality—experience of spirit—is neither tangible nor material. In this sense, spiritual development is about how we come to know the sacred region within consciousness and how this knowledge affects development of body, personality, intellect, and self (Wilber 1999). Spirituality is not about beliefs. Beliefs may influence experience of spirituality and experience of spirituality may influence beliefs, but they are not one and the same.

Wilber (1996) pointed out the importance of using appropriate methods of knowing for different levels of consciousness. To know the phenomenal world we use the body's senses. To know what is logical or rational we use our calculating minds. To know our spirit, which exists beyond our bodies or minds, we use our contemplative capacities. Each of these ways of knowing has its own methods for connecting with reality, achieving illumination, and confirming our insights. Because the essence of spirituality is neither body nor mind, we can know spirit fully only through methods of contemplation such as meditation and contemplative prayer. One paradox is that spirit can manifest itself in the body or mind, but the source of these manifestations is neither body nor mind. Spiritual development focuses on the source, not the manifestations.

There appears to be a relationship between spiritual development and life stage (Atchley 1997). The freedom of later maturity that occurs as a result of child launching and retirement can be used to focus attention on spiritual development with an intensity that is difficult to manage when still enmeshed in child rearing and careers. Many of those who embark on a conscious journey toward becoming a spiritual elder are just entering the later maturity life stage. Most of those who are actualized spiritual elders are in a middle stage of later life. And most transcendent spiritual elders are in old age, the last life stage.

THE SPIRITUAL ELDER

What does it mean to be a spiritual elder and how is it different from just being old? A spiritual elder is one who has done the inner work necessary to come to elderhood from the source of spirit. Spiritual elders first must come into deep and enduring contact with their spiritual nature; then they can bring that nature to whatever roles they play in society. In this sense, being a spiritual elder modifies how we play many types of social roles. This concept of the role of spiritual elder is flexible enough to accommodate the realities of our postmodern world, because it does not center the role within a religious context. However, the spiritual elder can also be a role in itself in contexts that are explicitly spiritual or religious. Spiritual elders are mentors and wisdom keepers, but spiritual elders do not see wisdom as a commodity to possess; they see it is a process that depends on connection to spirit.

The process of becoming a spiritual elder can "transform the downward arc of aging into the upward arc of expanded consciousness" by focusing on the possibility that later life can be a time of unparalleled inner growth (Schachter-Shalomi and Miller 1995, 5-7). The process of becoming a spiritual elder is an interplay between contemplation and action. Without contemplation, the capacity for action as a spiritual elder is not there. But without action, there is no spiritual elder in the community. When people are recognized as sages—venerated for their experience, judgment, and wisdom—they have become actualized as spiritual elders.

OBSTACLES

The cultural concepts of life stages and postmodernism constitute important obstacles to becoming spiritual elders. The cultural concept of life stages essentially ignores the potential for spiritual growth in later life, focusing instead on the physical aspects of aging, their effects on psychobiological functioning, and changing social roles. Later maturity and old age are seen as life stages permeated by loss, and many people react to this image by denial and avoidance. They avoid aging and older people and deny their own aging. Herein lies another paradox: To become spiritual elders, we must embrace later life; but to embrace later life we need positive visions of what later life can bring. To have positive visions of what later life can bring, however, we need images of spiritual elders. A key to overcoming this obstacle is to recognize that spiritual elders are not rare but abundant, if we only know how to look for them.

Postmodernism gives rise to a subjective worldview in which everyone's individual reality is treated as having validity. "My truth" is taken to be each person's ultimate truth. This viewpoint is often used to justify self-indulgence, but it also recognizes a fundamental aspect of human existence: we all have our own personal constructs of goodness, truth, and beauty that we use to make sense out of life and make decisions about it. This is an important starting point. But instead of taking these personal constructs as ultimate truth, we might consider them as working hypotheses that we are skeptical about and willing to subject to the test of dialogue and experience. This latter perspective creates experiences of humility in the face of a search for truth. Seeking happens more often than finding. A key is to retain the openness of postmodernism without succumbing to its potential for nihilism.

Fear is probably the major personal obstacle to becoming a spiritual elder. We spend many years of our lives learning to function as social beings, and it takes courage to distance ourselves for a time from this type of functioning to learn to function as spiritual beings. Many spiritual seekers find that nourishing a strong connection to spirit requires a period of intense focus on the spiritual region of consciousness. A key to letting go of our fear about what may happen to our social functioning as we focus on spiritual development is to recognize that spiritual development does not require that we abandon our capacity to function as social beings. In fact, retaining our capacity as social beings is essential to becoming actualized as a spiritual elder. What spiritual development offers is a capacity to see the social world and its demands with more clarity.

We also tend to fear letting go of our social roles. But if we have done our inner work, then we can shift our perspective to the spiritual level of consciousness while we continue to function in many of the same social roles. However, we need to have the capacity to remain centered spiritually in order not to be drawn into the materialistic mind-set of others we encounter in various everyday venues in which we play our social roles. Many spiritual traditions teach that this learning to be "in the world but not of it" is best begun quietly.

Fear of silence and inactivity is another major obstacle to knowing our spiritual self. In New York, London, or Tokyo, it seems as though most people walking down the street are talking on cell phones. We fill every potentially silent moment with sights and sounds. To those unaccustomed to it, five minutes of silence can seem like an eternity. Those unfamiliar with stillness find it very difficult to just sit quietly. Their bodies want to fidget and move. They feel a need to be doing something all the time.

Ram Dass wrote:

> In the process of learning to become mindful, and to age in a conscious way, fearlessness is an essential ingredient. This fearlessness involves the willingness to tell the truth, to ourselves and others, and to confront the contents of our minds. We must be willing to look at everything—our own suffering as well as the suffering around us—without averting our gaze, and allow it to be in the present moment. (2000, 54)

SKILLFUL MEANS

Contemplative practice, spiritual teachings and teachers, and spiritual community are important supports for becoming a spiritual elder. Contemplative practices teach us patience. The paradox of contemplative practices is that they are intended to lead us to spiritual experience, yet the harder we try, the less likely it is that we will have an experience of spirit. Contemplative practice requires faith because the results of practice are not predictable. By engaging in contemplative practice, we can reduce the clutter in our consciousness and create space within which spiritual experience may occur.

Contemplative practices come in enormous variety, ranging from meditation and contemplative prayer to devotional prayer to rumination on sacred texts to contemplative movement disciplines such as walking meditation and t'ai chi. All these practices hold the potential to connect us with what Aldous Huxley (1941) termed "the divine ground of all being." The ground of being can be experienced as both immanent and transcendent. It is immanent in that it permeates everything. It is transcendent in that it is experienced as an infinite sea of being. Countless people have reported that the inner experience of the divine ground of all being is one of deep silence, stillness, well-being, and peace. Once this connection has been experienced, the experiencer is motivated to experience it again. Although contemplative practices cannot guarantee a re-creation of the immediate experience of the ground of being, they represent a good strategy. Not only that, but once we get used to the silence and stillness of contemplation, it becomes a pleasant experience in itself.

Spiritual teachings and teachers can accelerate our spiritual development, but they can also get in the way—yet another paradox. Authentic spiritual teachings about the nature of the divine and the spiritually centered life are often attempts to put into words the processes and circumstances associated with an experience of the divine ground of all being. Such teachings come through human vehicles, located in a cultural and historical time and place. Another paradox is that to understand teachings fully, we need to have had our own direct experience of the ground of being. Otherwise the teachings are just thinking. Whether teachings ring true to a person depends on how the teachings resonate with that person's experience of spirit and the language that seems to be an authentic way to talk about those experiences. Some people are fortunate to grow up in a spiritual tradition whose concepts and language continue to resonate well with their experiences as they evolve spiritually. Others find that the concepts and language of their religion of origin gradually lose the capacity to describe their spiritual experiences. Often, spiritual seekers remain on the lookout for teachings that express well what they have experienced. It is not that they are necessarily looking for a different truth. They may simply be looking for more ways or better ways to express what they have already experienced.

Teachers can be invaluable bridges between teachings and experience. Some teachers are good at leading people to a direct experience of the ground of being. Others are good at leading people to ways of expressing those experiences. Some teachers model bringing wisdom into everyday life. Still others are good at many of these things. Not all teachers are gurus. As Ram Dass (1988) said, "The teacher points the way; the guru *is* the way." Gurus are the embodiment of the teaching in all its aspects. In this respect the fully realized spiritual elder is a guru, although there is no such societal position in Western societies.

Spiritual communities are a valuable support for the spiritual journey. Some spiritual communities function within the context of traditional religions; others are nondenominational collaborations. Spiritual communities provide guidance, structure, and encouragement. Many people find that being part of a spiritual community makes it easier to sustain their commitment to the spiritual journey. Spiritual communities come in many varieties. Some are loosely organized and very democratic in process, others hierarchical and doctrinaire. Most are probably somewhere in between these two extremes. Little systematic study has been made of how these variations in spiritual communities influence the nature of spiritual development in later adulthood.

Spiritual communities also serve as a check on the ego's tendency to transform spiritual insights into ego agendas. For example, the Quakers have a process called the "clearness committee" that calls a small group within the community together to help a seeker explore the extent to which a motive is spiritually rooted. Clearness committees are especially likely to be called for those who are considering membership or marriage, but other types of actions can also benefit from this process. Clearness committees create a supportive space in which people can, in the company of spiritual peers, explore fully their motives and intentions. Clearness committees are not intended to put a stamp of approval on any particular way of thinking and acting but instead to open an opportunity for the seeker to arrive at greater clarity about the matter.

Being part of a spiritual community also allows the seeker to explore the language and concepts of spirituality in the company of people who are also confronting issues of connecting with spirit, expressing that connection, and contemplating the implications of that connection for everyday life.

Becoming a spiritual elder thus occurs in the context of spiritual development. But it also occurs in a context of cultural and personal obstacles to believing that spiritual growth is the purpose of later life and to recovering a role for elders as exemplars of spiritually awakened living. Contemplative practice, spiritual teachings and teachers, and spiritual communities are important supports on the journey to spiritual elderhood. Becoming a spiritual elder is a capacity that usually takes years to develop.

I have encountered three distinct categories of people who are involved in becoming spiritual elders: spiritual elders in training, actualized spiritual elders, and transcendent spiritual elders.

SPIRITUAL ELDERS IN TRAINING

At the point when people realize that becoming a spiritual elder is a real possibility, they can become elders in training. They take on spiritual elders as their reference group, people who represent their aspirations. But how do people come to this realization? A fortunate few experience a rite of passage that recognizes their entry into elderhood, but most of us must rely on more subtle messages that we are about to enter a new stage of life.

In 1999, I attended an acknowledgment ceremony for elders at Naropa University. The Naropa elders serve as interview subjects for students, attend classes such as contemplative caregiving or the psychology of aging, and often become mentors for students and faculty. The ceremony was conducted by Subonfu Some, a West African tribal spiritual teacher. She began by gathering the elders into a seated circle facing outward. I was surprised when Subonfu took me by the hand and seated me in the circle. Although I was sixty, I did not see myself as yet being an elder, and I was easily ten years younger than the others included as elders. There were about fifteen elders in the circle. About seventy-five other attendees (students and faculty) walked around the circle for ten minutes or so, singing a lilting song of appreciation to the elders. Then Subonfu instructed the attendees to go to the elders for blessings. I had never in my life given anyone a blessing and had no idea of how to do so. A psychology faculty member whom I knew only casually approached me, knelt on the floor in front of my chair, and asked for my blessing. After a brief feeling of being at a loss, I went in my consciousness to that place that is beyond my personal concerns and found its stillness. I then lightly placed my hand behind her head and drew her forehead to mine and said, "Be peace." Tears welled in her eyes and she smiled. She then bowed two or three times to me, rose and stood quietly a moment before moving on. I looked around the room, and the other elders were involved in the same unpretentious ritual. I gave different blessings to ten or twelve people that day. It seemed that the process of blessing and being blessed was much more important than the specific words. This was my initiation into becoming a spiritual elder in the present moment.

Unfortunately, such initiations into elderhood seldom occur in our society. We do not have formal rites of passage that clearly mark entry into elderhood. Instead, if we are lucky we experience subtle messages that people are interested in what we have to offer, especially in situations that involve articulating a big picture. These experiences are openings to practice becoming a spiritual elder. Of course, the demands of speaking for the long view, what Manheimer (1999) called "the work of generations," can also spark an interest in learning more about the role of spiritual elder.

There are a few "schools" where people can learn about being a spiritual elder. For example, the Spiritual Eldering Institute is a national organization with headquarters in Boulder, Colorado. The institute offers an introductory workshop and several advanced workshops on spiritual eldering at locations throughout the country. It also has several local community organizations called Sage-ing Centers that function much like a spiritually focused senior center. The Spiritual Eldering workshops and the Sage-ing Centers facilitate both the inner work that is required to become a spiritual elder and the skills and knowledge required to bring that perspective into various roles in the community.

Mentors and role models are also helpful in learning what it means to be a spiritual elder. As mentioned earlier, spiritual elders are common, but we may need to hone our perception to be able to see them. In my experience, spiritual elders often have notable characteristics in addition to many years of life experience: clarity, patience, an air of quietude, good listening skills, a nurturing attitude toward others, and a lack of anxiety even in the face of distressing circumstances. They may or may not be verbally articulate or interested in social action. By spending time with spiritual elders and noticing how they combine their inner work with their capacity to benefit the world, elders in training can develop a better sense of what it takes to become a spiritual elder. Spiritual elders are often willing to serve as mentors to elders in training.

Inspirational discourse, mentors, and role models are helpful, but the elder in training must eventually face alone the inner tasks of spiritual development. These tasks involve cultivating spiritual disciplines, doing philosophical homework, reflecting and integrating, letting go of earlier concerns, practicing forgiveness and gratitude, and making peace with death (Schachter-Shalomi and Miller 1995). These tasks engender a rich inner mosaic that nurtures the capacity to stay spiritually centered amid the complexities of daily life. They lay the foundation for being able to become a spiritual elder in the present moment.

As mentioned, spiritual practices come in many varieties and, to facilitate a steady awareness of connection with the divine ground of being, practices are best done regularly. At first, contemplative practices such as prayer or meditation can be difficult. They require being still and quiet as much as possible. The practitioner must learn to push through the urge to abandon practice when the body aches or the mind is filled with cascading thoughts. But the more times the practitioner is able to just sit in awareness of the body and mind, whatever their current state, practice becomes easier. And developing the habit of practice creates a commitment that can carry the practitioner through times when the mind does not want to practice. Developing a mature spiritual practice takes time—years rather than weeks or months. Practitioners often report feeling that they have gained the ultimate insight only to find that there is more to learn. And much of this learning occurs at an intuitive level rather than a verbal or intellectual level. When this happens over and over again, it instills an attitude of humility, especially since it is so difficult to communicate what one has learned.

What Schachter-Shalomi and Miller (1995) call philosophical homework involves contemplating deep questions about where we come from and where we go. They quote Robert de Ropp (1979):

> "The contemplation of an individual life against the background of time brings inevitably deeper insights into the nature of being and becoming. . . . How vast a time passed by before I existed and how vast a time will be after I cease to exist! But what is I? What is this self whose days and adventures are drawing to a close? An isolated spark briefly lit, destined to fade forever into darkness? A fragment of a greater consciousness that will return again to the place from which it came? A spirit temporarily imprisoned in flesh? A traveler far from his true home and now about to return?" (Schachter-Shalomi and Miller 1995, 124)
>
> Who am I? Why am I here? What is my place in the universe? What is God? Can I know God? What is my relation to God? Rumination on these types of questions makes later life a philosophical life stage. (Manheimer 1999)

Erik Erikson initially thought that the major psychological task of old age was to develop ego integrity and thus avoid despair in the face of aging and death (Erikson 1955). But in his eighties Erikson changed his mind. Wisdom was the culminating development of old age, and wisdom was reached by understanding that integrity and despair coexist (Erikson, Erikson, and Kivnick 1986). The wise individual understands that integrity balances despair and that despair tempers integrity. Wisdom thus transcends both integrity and despair. This type of transcendent perspective grows out of years of contemplating deep questions.

In order to move forward into these deep questions, the elder in training must also overcome inertia and let go of earlier concerns. Feeling that one has been wronged or deprived in the past is a major attachment to the past. To move forward we must be able to forgive ourselves and those others we hold responsible for past circumstances that distress us. The Buddhist practice of Tonglen is an example of how we can change our perceptions of the past and develop the compassion that enables forgiveness. In Tonglen, the practitioner begins with an attitude of openness, awareness, and compassion. Then he or she focuses for a few moments on the breath, breathing in dark feelings of confusion or pain and breathing out light, bright feelings of relief. Then he or she focuses for a few minutes on a particular situation that causes pain and breathes in those feelings and breathes them back out into the entire universe. Then he or she focuses for a time on all people who experience similar pain, breathing in their pain and then breathing it out into the universe. (For more detail on Tonglen practice, see Wegela 1996.) This last phase leads the practitioner to experience that she or he is not alone in experiencing pain and to experience the relief that accompanies releasing the pain into the vastness of the universe. The result is a feeling of connection and relaxation. From this state, forgiveness and gratitude are much more possible.

Buddhists believe that the reality of death, if unexamined, is like a millstone hanging around the neck. Denying death does not really work. To be free we must face death and accept it. To die with awareness we must be willing to contemplate and ruminate on death until we reach an understanding of it. This is another part of the philosophical homework, dealing with questions such as: How will I deal with the process of dying? What happens to me at the moment of death and after I have died?

Spiritual elders in training are just getting started on a set of tasks that are seldom fully completed. Just when we think our work is done, life sends us another invitation for further learning.

ACTUALIZED SPIRITUAL ELDERS

Elders who have done the inner work that allows them to experience their ongoing connection with the ground of being are able to move about in the world as actualized spiritual elders. Generativity and wisdom are the hallmarks of this type of spiritual elder.

Generativity involves nurturing and guiding those who will succeed us in the flow of generations (Erikson, Erikson, and Kivnick 1986). It is most often manifested in mentoring relationships. Mentoring is a type of caring relationship; it focuses on accompanying a developing person and providing loving support. Support may involve giving information about a sphere of life, especially an overview, but its ultimate aim is to foster the capacity of the mentee to function on his or her own. Schachter-Shalomi and Miller (1995, 189) assert that "mentors do not impose doctrines and values on their mentees in an attempt to clone themselves. Rather, they evoke the individuality of their apprentices, applauding them as they struggle to clarify their values and discover their authentic life paths." Mentoring is a skill that takes practice and therefore time to develop.

Schachter-Shalomi and Miller (1995, 200–202) suggest several guidelines for recognizing the mentoring skills of an actualized spiritual elder. First, the elder listens with great spaciousness to the mentee's concerns before attempting to share his or her wisdom. The elder does not expect to transfer great insights unsolicited but instead offers wisdom in small increments in response to questions. Second, the elder uses Socratic questioning methods to evoke the mentee's innate knowing rather than imposing knowledge in an authoritative fashion. Third, the elder does not try to impress the mentee by claiming to be perfect, but instead is an authentic human self—seeking, tentative, and vulnerable. Fourth, the elder works with the mentee's unique human potential, not with some idealization of what everyone should be like. As Hillman (1999) pointed out, character development is what later life is all about, and character is highly individuated. Fifth, elders recognize that the mentoring relationship has phases. In the beginning, there is a gradual development of spiritual intimacy that allows for a genuine relationship. Then there may develop a frequency of interaction that allows the relationship to meet the mentor's need to be of real service and the mentee's need to have someone really understand what they are experiencing. The deep trust that this process occasions allows the transmission of wisdom to occur. Finally, the mentee becomes a peer and no longer needs to be under the wing of the mentor. The mentoring relationship comes to a conclusion. Both mentor and mentee then need to be willing to move forward into a new peer-to-peer relationship.

Mentoring relationships can occur in many different contexts. Parents often mentor their children. Grandparents often mentor their grandchildren. In the workplace, elders can be mentors for those who are at earlier stages in their careers. In community organizations, elders can mentor those who are at an earlier stage of their experience in public service. In almost any intergenerational context, elders can mentor the young. But in our society, too many contexts are age segregated and the natural tendency of the young to seek mentors among the old is stifled.

In my course Psychology of Aging, I assign the students to visit a spiritual elder. They meet with the elder weekly throughout the semester and write a life history of the elder. In the process, more than a quarter of the students become mentees of their elder and their interactions continue long after the course ends. Many of these students indicate that had they not been required to meet, they would not have sought out these spiritual elders. In our society intergenerational contact does not occur naturally, except perhaps in families. Accordingly, for actualized spiritual elders to serve as mentors requires that we develop mechanisms to facilitate intergenerational connections. The good news is that intergenerational programming is one of the latest growth areas within gerontology.

Wisdom is a quality that spiritual elders bring to their own lives and to the social worlds in which they participate. Wisdom is not a commodity that a person can possess. Instead, it is a process that requires skill. In my opinion, the essence of wisdom begins with the capacity to see the world from outside one's own personal agenda. This allows the observer to see various sides of an issue and "think outside the box." A person at a transcendent level of consciousness also experiences time in a more expansive way, which creates a more relaxed and less frenzied stance toward decision making. "Being while doing" is a learned capacity that opens opportunities for the quality we call wisdom to enter into our world.

To practice bringing wisdom into the world requires developing the habit of being still and patiently awaiting a moment that demands the special gift of nonpersonal perspective that we call wisdom. But, as one member of an elder circle put it, "In order to bring your special gifts as an elder, you have to be there. You have to resist the temptation to withdraw to the comfort of your own solitude or your small circle of friends. You have to continue to show up in those groups you care about."

Actualized spiritual elders, those who are recognized as having the capacity to be a sage in the present moment, generally recognize one another as such and enjoy each other's company. When they get together, there are often periods of comfortable silence. They share their experiences of joy as well as doubt and uncertainty. And there is almost always a sense of the humor that accompanies the human predicament. We have a tendency in our culture to treat spiritual matters very seriously, but sages know that there is also great humor in our fumbling attempts to understand the ground of being, connect with that ground, and live from that connection. As Manheimer (1999) pointed out, humor can be an expression of wisdom, the result of a heightened state of consciousness and a philosophical outlook.

Part of the wisdom of elderhood is understanding that we cannot act on every impulse we have to care for others. We have to have as much compassion for ourselves as for those we serve. Actualized spiritual elders know that to be able to serve over the long haul requires attention to pacing, establishing a humane life routine. These elders do not try to do everything. They have learned that they must choose wisely how to spend their precious energies.

Actualized spiritual elders are "fully operational" but still developing. Moody and Carroll (1997) described a circular process of spiritual growth that begins with a leading, a sense that there is more to be discovered. This creates an opening during which the seeker looks around for new opportunities for growth. There is often a struggle as the seeker attempts to understand to integrate new understanding with previous understanding. Then the seeker often breaks through to a new level of integrated understanding. Finally, the seeker focuses on how to bring that new insight back into the world. Actualized elders know that they may go through many more cycles of spiritual development. It is a territory that is very incompletely mapped, yet actualized spiritual elders have faith in the process.

TRANSCENDENT SPIRITUAL ELDERS

Transcendent spiritual elders have developed the capacity to abide in the highest levels of spiritual consciousness. They tend to be very quiet and speak only when they have something they feel compelled to say. They are holders of the spiritual field within which others struggle to become and act as spiritual elders. They are deeply in touch with a panoramic experience of time.

Wilber (1996) describes the higher levels of consciousness as a "sagely region" that includes a "subtle level," which is transindividual and intuitive; a "causal level," which is experienced as formless radiance and transcendence; and an "ultimate level," in which there is only undifferentiated, infinite consciousness, and no separate experiencer. The subtle level of consciousness is the source of the capacities of generativity and wisdom that are the cornerstone of being an actualized spiritual elder.

The causal level of consciousness, which manifests itself as radiance and deep stillness, is the source of the capacity to be a transcendent spiritual elder. At this level there is very little that one feels compelled to say, so there is much quietude. Yet there can be great joy in continuing to participate in the routine activities that constitute life, including routine religious and spiritual activities.

By abiding at a level of consciousness very close to the source of spirit, transcendent spiritual elders "hold the field." That is, their presence and quality of being consistently remind more active participants why they are interested in the process of becoming spiritual elders. Transcendent spiritual elders attract our attention through their manifest connection with the divine ground of all being. It is not what they do, but how they are that is their contribution to the group. Consider two cases.

In his mid-eighties, William projects an air of robust good health. He attends a worship group regularly but only rarely speaks. Yet he constantly serves as a living example of what it means to be radiantly at peace. He is very comfortable with his spiritual nature and it shows in his clear, soft voice, bright gray eyes, and ready smile. There is a serenity about William that many people in the group have remarked about. There is also a sense that the group is missing an important presence when William is not there.

James attends the same worship group. He is in his early nineties and suffers from numerous chronic conditions that cause him to move about very slowly. He is nearly blind and in a great deal of chronic pain. When asked, he acknowledges that his physical existence is not very enjoyable at his stage of frailty. Yet in the worship group, James will occasionally stand and ecstatically recite a psalm from memory. At these times he is completely transported by the source of the psalms, and the renderings invariably leave the group uplifted and in awe of this very gentle man's connection with God.

Neither William nor James takes a lead in the operation of the group. They are focused more on just being present and leave the logistics to the "youngsters," many of whom are in their seventies.

Schachter-Shalomi and Miller (1995) assert that spiritual elders have a panoramic view of time, and this is certainly true of transcendent spiritual elders. Transcendent spiritual elders have a type of consciousness that abides "under the aspect of eternity," that sees time not as a commodity or an instrumental need but as a vast panorama, of which our human lifetime is but a very small part. Ram Dass (2000, 141) wrote that elders are learning to live by "soul time" and that souls live by a different calendar, one in which "our egos are like mayflies that are born in the morning and die in the evening." This panoramic view of time redirects values away from the materialistic concerns of our current culture and toward more holistic values that respect the needs of the entire planet. From a panoramic view of time, we can be patient and persistent, less likely to become frustrated if we do not immediately achieve our objectives. This perspective on time supports the quietude that characterizes transcendent spiritual elders.

Transcendent spiritual elders do not stand out. They have little interest in standing out. Yet they are there to see if we only look. Another paradox is that some of the role models we desperately need are right there in front of us, but we don't see them.

CONCLUSION

The idea that elders can possess a high capacity to bring spirituality into their lives and into the world has been around for thousands of years. But what is it about later life that brings this about? The concept of spiritual development presumes that humans have the capacity to evolve spiritually, to identify their spiritual nature and over time strengthen their conscious connection to this sacred aspect of self. The concept of the spiritual elder presumes that spiritual development and later life stages can combine to affect how we play various social roles and also to prepare us to play a specific role of spiritual elder.

Becoming a spiritual elder is an evolutionary process through which spiritual development is nurtured and an individual learns what is needed to prepare for and take up the role of spiritual elder and to be a sage. The openness that aging can create through child launching and retirement can also be an opening to become a sage in training. No one knows why some elders are drawn to this possibility as a conscious journey, others unconsciously develop spiritually, and still others show no signs of spirituality.

Although spiritual development involves continuous cycles of development, being a spiritual elder is manifested in ways that are loosely related to stages of later life. At the beginning of later life (the sixties), many people are involved in being elders in training, engaging the inner tasks of spiritual growth and learning from their elders how to behave as a spiritual elder. They are becoming "rooted in their being." In the middle of later life (the seventies and early eighties) many who have been on the journey have become actualized spiritual elders, fully in touch with their spiritual nature and able to keep that nature at the center as they function in the world. They are adept at "being while doing." In old age (the mid-eighties and older), transcendent spiritual elders are common. These people are radiantly at peace and are "being more than doing."

A recurring theme in this chapter has been that spiritual elders are not rare and that by raising consciousness about the characteristics of spiritual elders and the process of becoming a spiritual elder we can better recognize them. And as we recognize the extraordinary depth that spiritual elders bring to our collective quality of life, we may come to see value in creating more opportunities for spiritual elders to be a more visible part of our world.

BIBLIOGRAPHY

Atchley, R. C. (1997). "Everyday Mysticism: Spiritual Development in Later Life." *Journal of Adult Development* 4: 123–34.

de Ropp, R. (1979). *Man against Aging.* New York, Arno.

Erikson, E. H. (1955). *Childhood and Society.* New York: W. W. Norton.

Erikson, E. H., J. M. Erikson, and H. Q. Kivnick (1986). *Vital Involvement in Old Age.* New York: W. W. Norton.

Hillman, J. (1999). *The Force of Character and the Lasting Life.* New York: Random House.

Houghton Mifflin (1993). *American Heritage College Dictionary.* 3d ed. Boston: Houghton Mifflin.

Huxley, A. (1941). *The Perennial Philosophy.* New York: Harper & Row.

Manheimer, R. J. (1999). *A Map to the End of Time: Wayfarings with Friends and Philosophers.* New York: W. W. Norton.

Moody, H. R., and D. Carroll (1997). *The Five Stages of the Soul.* New York: Anchor Books.

Ram D. (2000). *Still Here: Embracing Aging, Changing, and Dying.* New York: Riverhead Books.

————— (1988). *Finding and Exploring Your Spiritual Path.* Los Angeles: Audio Renaissance Tapes.

Schachter-Shalomi, Z., and R. S. Miller (1995). *From Age-ing to Sage-ing: A Profound New Vision of Growing Older.* New York: Warner Books.

Wegela, K. K. (1996). *How to Be a Help Instead of a Nuisance.* Boston: Shambhala.

Wilber, K. (1999) *Integral Psychology.* Boston: Shambhala.

————— (1996). *Eye to Eye: The Quest for a New Paradigm.* 3d ed. Boston: Shambhala.

4

Older Adults' Emotions in Religious Contexts

SUSAN H. McFADDEN

This is a good time to be thinking about the emotions older people experience in worship, private times of meditation and prayer, and in various activities occurring in congregational settings. In the last quarter century, there have been many exciting advances in our understanding of emotion across the life span. In addition, knowledge has been steadily accumulating about older adults' religiosity and the effects of religious beliefs, experiences, and practices on health and well-being. In general, these two lines of research have developed independently, although the search for the underlying factors connecting religious experience and practice with physical and mental health increasingly points toward emotion.

In the past psychologists tended to focus primarily on negative emotions and their adverse effects upon health (Mayne 2001). Most people are aware, for example, of studies of anger/hostility and heart disease. Now, however, researchers investigating happiness, hope, and optimism—so-called positive psychology—are increasingly open to including measures of religiosity and spirituality in their studies and they are finding intriguing connections to various indications of physical health. For example, a recent study showed that a "sense of coherence" moderates the relationship between immune system activity and life stresses in older people (Lutgendorf et al. 1999). Although this study did not specifically address religious faith, it is not unreasonable to assume that faith offers considerable support for feeling that the world can be understood and managed, and that life is meaningful. These characteristics of a "sense of coherence" would be likely to produce positive emotions and also to offer perspective to older people coping with negative emotions.

We now know that when researchers control for functional health, positive affect increases with age while negative affect decreases (Lawton 2001). We also know that as people age, they get better at regulating their emotions by choosing to participate in situations they know will bring positive emotions. For example, some older people avoid large, noisy gatherings that elicit anxiety because of hearing problems. But if these gatherings involve close family, then the older adult may decide that the joy of being with family outweighs the anxiety of not being able to hear well (Carstensen 1995). With age, people learn about the patterns of their own "ups and downs"; also, as many older people say, they learn not to "sweat the small stuff." When they deal with others, many elders demonstrate an integration of thinking and feeling, so that they are more tolerant of others' foibles, more willing to forgive, and more likely to recognize that they, too, have flaws and weaknesses, as well as hard-won perspective on themselves and others (Labouvie-Vief, DeVoe, and Bulka 1989; see also Magai 2001).

A major challenge for research on religion, spirituality, and aging is to know how to connect what we have learned about older adults' emotional lives to what we know about their experiences of religious faith and fellowship through the years. We should pursue this knowledge not only because religion appears to be so strongly tied to physical and mental health but also because the sense of life's ultimate meaning and purpose conveyed by religion influences how we feel about our own lives and our connections with other persons, with the world in general, and with God.

Research on older people's emotions in religious contexts and their effects on health and well-being has many applications to ministry. In addition to suggesting new pathways for researchers to follow, this chapter also offers ideas about how a better understanding of late-life emotion can be applied to pastoral care, adult religious education, worship, and congregational life in general. First, however, we will consider some "stories" presented in the form of dedications to the older people whose lives are often reduced to numbers reported in research. In thinking about research and practice shaped by a better understanding of older adults' emotions in religious contexts, we do well to turn to the older people themselves, for they have much to teach us.

DEDICATIONS

They untie their aprons at the end of a long day of cooking in the church basement, happy knowing that they have successfully fed yet another group of people. These elderly women can be found in all types of congregations. Many have grown old together and have prepared countless meals for their congregation. Peeling potatoes and stirring soups, they have laughed and cried together, promised to pray for one another, gossiped about the minister, and given one another ample "social support," as researchers like to say. To their devotion, tireless work, green bean casseroles, and Jell-O salads, this chapter is dedicated.

These men wear ties and jackets to usher more casually dressed congregants into worship. Sometimes they even have silk carnations pinned to their lapels. Smiling yet serious about their duties, they greet worshipers with printed programs, show them to empty seats, dutifully "count the house," and, standing straight, collect the morning's offering. In recent years, most have welcomed women and young people to their ranks. To the elderly men who faithfully report for ushering duty year after year, this chapter is dedicated.

A group of older women and a sprinkling of older men meet every Tuesday morning for prayer and devotions. They, too, have grown old together, sharing "joys and concerns," praying for one another, the congregation, the community, and the world. They have known many dark and sorrowful times of loss but they have also celebrated the births of grandchildren and great-grandchildren, offered thanks for a beautiful day, and asked God's forgiveness for themselves and others. This chapter honors their constancy and openness to shared times of prayer.

This chapter is also dedicated to the older men and women who take apart the floral arrangements after the service and deliver them to sick and homebound people. They sing in the choir, teach religious education classes, and serve on committees and boards of the congregation. Some gather on weekday mornings to laugh and talk and make crafts to sell for mission projects. Older people visit nursing homes, run food pantries, teach children to read in after-school programs sponsored by congregations, and perform countless other caring acts that enrich their communities. They have learned that a dividend of these caring acts is joy, and they often say they receive more than they give. They have the personal characteristic of "positivity," as some researchers have noted (Colby and Damon 1992), though they would probably find such language amusing rather than edifying.

Look around most congregations at worship and witness the courage and persistence of the aged men and women who arrive with walkers and oxygen tanks, often transported by other older people less encumbered by health problems. Sharing pews with noisy babies, children with crayons, bored teens, and distracted parents, they sing and pray, sit in silence, listen to scripture and sermons, rise and sit as they are able, share the Eucharist if Christian, and exit in friendly conversation with fellow travelers. In the hymns, prayers, scripture readings, and sermons, they hear of love and forgiveness, gratitude and hope, despair and lamentation, anger, fear, and awe. In no other community do persons of so many different backgrounds and ages meet regularly to consider the human condition and turn to the sacred for an enduring sense of meaning and purpose in life. For all the older people whose weeks are anchored in worship, this chapter is dedicated.

When one of their number dies, they gather for a funeral. Well-practiced in funeral-going, they say goodbye to a member of their community. Sadness combines with celebration of the life lived. Despair over losing yet another friend combines with hope of eternity. Thus, their feelings reveal a complexity shaped by years of experience and grounding in religious faith. To these elders who attend more funerals than a young person can possibly imagine, this chapter is dedicated.

This chapter also recalls the older people whose daily lives are shaped and regulated by prayer and devotion. They greet the day with prayers of gratitude, though their bodies may cause them to groan as they rise from bed. They sit down to eat and render thanks. They pray about their sorrows and griefs, worries about family members and the state of the world, fears of disability and dying, and happiness about a friend's visit or the flash of red as a cardinal lands on a bird feeder. Their prayer lives are one way they regulate their emotions, though they would be unlikely to find that to be a satisfying explanation of why they pray.

Finally, this chapter is dedicated to those elders who no longer worship, study, or volunteer with their congregations. Some still manage to attend services in long-term care settings; others are bedridden and approaching the end of life. The tedium and suffering of their days can be relieved by prayer or meditation, although dementia and other illnesses may have removed that source of solace. Some are faithfully attended by their congregations by being named in public prayers and visited often, while others, sadly, are forgotten. Some cry out to God for release, feeling angry, bitter, or just plain tired from life's trials. Others hold on to gratitude until their last breath.

The story fragments that form these dedications are undoubtedly familiar to most readers of this handbook. They are offered with the invitation to read this chapter by recalling similar images of older people and considering the vast array of emotions felt and examined in congregational communities. These include both positive and negative emotions, although, as Paul Ekman, a prominent emotions researcher, commented recently after meeting with the Dalai Lama to discuss how Western brain science might complement Buddhist meditation, "the Buddhists make it clear to us how primitive that distinction is" (Durhams 2001, B2).

RELIGIOUS PERSPECTIVES ON EMOTIONS

In Western thought there has been considerable ambivalence, even conflict, over the role of emotions in religious life. On the one hand, some religious traditions embrace asceticism and suppress nearly all feeling. This position asserts that passions distract the believer from God. Even intense love of God may be too pleasurable and thus should be carefully monitored. Likewise, this position holds that piety can stimulate pride—another emotion to be controlled. Alternatively, some in the mystical tradition have encouraged the embrace of ecstasy when believers awaken to the call to give themselves over to God in joyful union. Many variations can be found on these themes of extreme emotional control versus the conscious journey from despair and spiritual agony to the utter bliss of unification. (See Watts 1996 for an extended discussion of these views.) In some places, like the small Ohio town where I used to visit my grandmother, one can find charismatic congregations that employ music, dance, and oratory to stimulate frenzied emotion as a vehicle for religious inspiration (if not mystical union) just across the street from congregations that find inspiration only in the strict denial of the emotions. From one side of the street, the faithful criticize the other side for being coldly intellectual, while those so criticized look upon their neighbors as having submitted to mindless religious passion.

The challenge for many religious persons today is to find a balancing point—a third way perhaps—between the formalistic rejection of emotion in religious contexts and the denial of the critical faculties found in religions that view emotion as the only valid criterion of faith. Persons in our time who reject institutionalized religion in favor of individual pursuits of spirituality often do so because they believe that religious institutions are interested only in perpetuating dogma and not in providing opportunities for people to experience emotional connection with the sacred.

In between the rise of the human potential movement in the late 1960s and the proliferation of popular works on spirituality in the 1990s, Lucy Bregman, Professor of Religion at Temple University, published a work on "inner experience" that was sympathetic to contemporary persons' desire for what she called "firsthand religion" (1983, 1). What many today loosely term "spirituality" she called "psychological religiousness" (145), seen by some as an attractive alternative to traditional Christianity and Judaism. She praised its focus on direct experience of the sacred, vision of harmony with nature, and transcultural emphasis. However, in the last three pages of the book, she succinctly laid out her criticism that "psychological religiousness," like popular spirituality today, does not witness to the deep wells of melancholy, suffering, and brokenness in the human spirit, nor does it recognize the "enormous and well-attested capacity for self-deception" (167) that is "intrinsic to our existence as human beings" (168). Her work raises two issues that have deep roots in Western religious thought: the tension between reason and emotion (or, as viewed through the lens of contemporary debates over religion and spirituality, between institutionalized dogma and personal experience) and the tension between human desire for pleasure and the reality of contingency, suffering, and loss.

Throughout Western religious thought, one finds many examples of persons wrestling with these tensions. One who devoted considerable attention to this was Jonathan Edwards (1703–58). Claimed by some to be America's greatest theologian, Edwards in 1746 wrote a remarkable, psychologically astute book called *A Treatise concerning Religious Affections*. In it he sought to defend the importance of religious affections as contrasted with the frenzied religious passions that appeared to be outside of the control of the mind. At the same time he wanted to rescue Protestantism from "static intellectual propositions" (Rice 1991, 16; see also McClymond 1998). His work led to the first Great Awakening in American religious history, a revivalism that "preached a religion of the heart, but wished to avoid religion of the guts" (Pruyser 1968, 141). His keen analysis restored religious affections to legitimacy as the God-given source of human action. His writing about the integration of cognition, emotion, and motivation (or, to use his terminology, understanding, the affections, and the will) sounds very contemporary:

> I am bold to assert, that there never was any considerable change wrought in the mind or conversation of any one person, by anything of a religious nature, that ever he read, heard or saw, that had not his affections moved. Never was a natural man engaged earnestly to seek his salvation; never were any such brought to cry after wisdom, and lift up their voice for understanding, and to wrestle with God in prayer for mercy; and never was one humbled and brought to the foot of God, from anything that ever he heard or imagined of his own unworthiness and deserving of God's displeasure; nor was ever one induced to fly for refuge unto Christ, while his heart remained unaffected. . . . And in a word, there never was anything considerable brought to pass in the heart or life of any man living, by the things of religion, that had not his heart deeply affected by those things. (1746/1959, 102)

For Edwards, these "gracious affections" are grounded in *spiritual understanding*, which he identified with a "new spiritual sense"—the "knowledge of the loveliness of divine things" (271). This spiritual sense does not exist apart from the kind of everyday experience depicted in the dedications of this chapter. Rather, it *infuses* it. Spiritual understanding consists "in a sense of the heart, of the supreme beauty and sweetness of the holiness or moral perfection of divine things" (272).

Although many might doubt the applicability of Edwards's work to our post-modern times, revisiting his writings about the "spiritual sense" might prove fruitful, especially for those struggling with the split between religion in the "head" and in the "heart." Moreover, his insistence on contrasting religious "affections" that move a person toward the "fruits of the Spirit" and religious "passions" whose effects are "more violent" (Edwards 1746/1959, 98) would be enlightening for persons struggling with the terrible evidence of religious passions that burst upon the world on September 11, 2001. His writing about religious passions reflected Edwards's rejection of the overpowering emotions he observed in the extremes of religious revivalism of his day, but his careful construction of a phenomenology of emotion in religious contexts provides considerable insight into its effects upon people's actions and thoughts.

Today, as in Edwards's time, interpretations of the meaning and appropriateness of emotions in religious contexts vary widely, often as a function of a particular theological orientation and tradition. For example, one finds among many African Americans a deep, abiding, and passionate love of Jesus that has sustained them through years of hardship when worship has provided a joyous center to their lives. Older Roman Catholics have similarly experienced the transforming emotions of the Eucharist and have been stirred by visual, auditory, and olfactory stimulation in worship. But what about the Protestants, especially those of the Reformed tradition whose heritage in John Calvin's theology and in Puritanism has often been interpreted in our time to mean a dour, highly intellectual, emotionless approach to religion that denies, devalues, or simply ignores inner experience? These older people reached adulthood at a time when American Protestantism was swept into modernity's embrace of science and reason. Talk about "spirituality" reminds some of them of nothing more than "spiritualism," mediums, and Tarot cards. Nevertheless, as in previous centuries, many people in our time hunger for a recovery of religious feeling that is integrated with critical thought to produce what Edwards called "a new spiritual sense."

Older persons who have been associated for many years with Reformed denominations may find their congregations increasingly engaged in exploring various ways of integrating emotion with intellectual understandings of faith. Interestingly, the same response is occurring within Reformed Judaism (Dayle Friedman, personal communication). These congregations are showing renewed openness to various forms of religious experience, even as they continue their traditions of study and social activism (Rice 1991). This can produce conflict in congregations where efforts to invigorate worship with "religious affections" appeal to younger people but may be off-putting to some elders who feel uncomfortable when real ashes are introduced into the Ash Wednesday service, the sign of the cross is encouraged during Communion, or classes in yoga and meditation are offered in the fellowship hall of the church.

Because Western thought for so long valorized reason, emotions were often seen as disorganizers of behavior. In other words, the reasonable person set aside or controlled emotions in order not to be distracted or, worse, disabled by them. Today, however, emotions are seen as organizing systems, with effects on physiological, cognitive, behavioral, and social functioning (Mayne and Bonanno 2001).

What does this new way of thinking about emotion tell us about the elderly cooks in the church basement, the ushering crew, the prayer group, and the weekly worshipers? Week after week they bring an organization of emotions to congregational activities that has accumulated over time and that influences the way they meditate silently during services, greet one another over coffee after the service, plan to pick up a friend for choir practice, and so on. In these groups, gathered together because in some way they have a felt-relationship with the sacred, individuals experience a range of emotions. In all likelihood, most of these feelings about gathering with fellow congregants are positive, because otherwise they might not continue to participate. However, the emotions they share with one another may include fear, anxiety, despair, and sorrow. Thus, it is possible that they feel positive emotions about the connections they make to "bear one another's burdens" (Gal. 6:2). This ability to grasp the interweaving of positive and negative emotions is a sign of emotional maturity that many older adults display.

Jonathan Edwards spoke of love as the "chief of the affections, and the fountain of all other affections" (1746/1959, 106) for we are to love God and one another. We would do well to follow Edwards's lead by viewing love as the primary emotion in religious contexts. It binds the faithful to God and to community. They might not all admit to loving one another or God as they think they ought to, yet often their acts of hospitality, empathy, and simple patience with others amply reveal that love. That love undoubtedly has been repeatedly tested but, in late life, spiritual graciousness and generosity can often be observed in religious elders, including those who no longer can participate in the community life of a congregation.

In her book *A Deepening Love Affair* (1993) Jane Thibault describes a very elderly woman who clearly understood what Edwards meant when he named love as the central religious affection. This woman would probably not score well on standard measures of physical health, nor would she probably care. Rather, her focus was on loving God and all the gifts she had received from God. She said she no longer had the energy to pray or even think about her faith. Instead she said she looked out at her "little world" and just spent time loving it. She believed that her "looking and loving is enough for God" (93).

FUTURE DIRECTIONS FOR RESEARCH
ON EMOTION AND RELIGION

Most research studies count "bouts" of religious participation and private religious practices and levels of subjective religiosity, but the range of emotions connected to these measured variables is seldom noted. Yet, in the church basement, choir practice room, classrooms, and the sanctuary, one can observe older people laughing and weeping with one another, sharing anger over injustice (or perhaps the way the hymns were selected), expressing their hopes and fears about the future, and joining together in prayers of gratitude for what they have shared and received. Considerable research has suggested that activities like these may be connected with improved health and longer life (see Koenig, McCullough, and Larson 2001 for a review), though surely these elders have experienced their share of hardship and suffering and they all know that someday they will die.

Although the "mechanisms" of the relation of religion to health and longevity still need to be described and explained and will undoubtedly involve the regulation of emotion, still there are many other fascinating questions for researchers to address that go beyond what sometimes seems to be a rather materialistic, reductionistic approach to studying religion and aging. Three areas of research that relate to emotion in religious contexts are beginning to attract attention: personality, forgiveness, and gratitude. Although we do have an emerging body of literature on personality, religiosity, and health (for example, Danner, Snowdon, and Friesen 2001; Tucker and Friedman 1996) and some preliminary evidence about forgiveness and health (Thoresen, Harris, and Luskin 2000), it is not necessary always to make that connection. The unique ways we present ourselves to the world, as expressed in personality, and our willingness to forgive and be grateful testify to the power of the human spirit and enrich our lives in community.

We still have much to learn about how being religious can affect personality and the sense of self and how the latter shape our religious lives. Although many of the building blocks of personality (sometimes called the "big five" personality traits) appear to have a basis in heredity, the ways they are expressed and integrated with life goals may nevertheless both influence and be influenced by religious faith and activity. For example, a person with a high level of "openness to experience" may choose in late life to sign up for Elderhostel learning opportunities but may also volunteer for congregationally sponsored mission trips to build homes in poor neighborhoods. How do personality traits interact with religious commitments to serve others? These complex questions only now are receiving attention from the scientific community.

Another emerging focus of research concerns forgiveness. Despite the fact that much of the work on forgiveness is being conducted without reference to religion, it is nevertheless hard to avoid the testimony of ages and cultures that forgiveness is "is consistent with the worldviews of . . . Judaism, Christianity, Islam, and Hinduism. In Buddhism, forgiveness is subsumed by the concepts of forbearance and compassion" (Rye et al. 2000, 37). Assurance of God's forgiveness, along with the forgiveness of others and the self, can release people from the grip of negative emotions. Whether older persons are more likely to forgive and whether they more frequently cite explicitly religious reasons for doing so remains to be studied. We do know that small groups that gather for prayer and Bible study also promote forgiveness. These groups provide the opportunity to talk about personal problems, offer emotional support, and pray, and, compared to small groups that merely socialize, participants are far more likely to forgive others and experience the healing of relationships as a result (Wuthnow 2000).

A new area of research concerns gratitude, which, like forgiveness, is "a highly prized human disposition" in the world's major religions (McCullough et al. 2001, 249). Some preliminary data indicate that older people are more likely to be grateful (Robert Emmons, personal communication) but the connections to religiosity have not been clearly articulated. The old woman interviewed by Jane Thibault who spent her days looking and loving tells us something about gratitude. She said, "It is all so very beautiful, even the bad things somehow get washed in the beauty of everything. I am so grateful for it all, grateful for *all* of my life, for all of life" (93). This sense of gratitude was named by Edwards as one of the religious affections. Thankfulness to God, said Edwards, naturally flows from love of God. Having "seen the glory of God" and been "overcome by it," a person's heart "hereby becomes tender, and easily affected with kindnesses received" (Edwards 1746/1959, 257), just like the woman Jane Thibault described who had found a way to cope with extreme frailty. Thanks to the work of Ken Pargament and his students, we have learned much about religious coping in recent years (see Pargament 1997). Now we need to examine the gratitude people feel in response to the outcomes of that coping as well as more general gratitude for life's gifts.

MINISTRY AND OLDER ADULTS' EMOTIONAL LIVES

As shown by the many topics covered in this handbook, ministry with older people is multifaceted. In worship, for example, people have the opportunity to express gratitude, ask for and receive forgiveness, and reflect upon their worries, fears, and sorrows, as well as their joys. Worship leaders should be sensitive to the many ways emotions are woven into a service and should examine whether the service in any way *prevents* people—especially older people—from feeling love for God and one another.

Small groups have become a popular approach to adult religious programming in recent years and they offer many important opportunities for sharing, expressing, and understanding emotion. Congregations need to examine whether small group experiences are as available to older people as they are to young and middle-aged adults. Within these small groups, considerable "emotion education" can take place as people come together to pray, study Scripture, and reflect upon how their faith guides their lives. In Edwards's terminology, small groups can promote "spiritual understanding" wherein what people comprehend intellectually about their faith becomes connected to their feelings about God.

When engaging in pastoral care, clergy walk with elders through dark valleys and help them recover hope from grief and joy from sorrow. Pastoral caregivers have the privilege of hearing about the entire range of human emotions and they have the challenge of caring for their own emotional lives. As Robert Rost so aptly demonstrates in this volume, pastoral caregivers' mission is not to be psychologists in collars but rather to help elders appreciate the grace of God in their lives and the ways that grace can convey new meanings to all emotions.

Opportunities for service need to be examined in light of the needs and life situations of older persons. Are elders in the congregation seen only as the recipients of care? Or are creative approaches offered so they can experience the joy of helping other people? Referring to frail elders who may think they have no way to serve others, Wendy Lustbader has written, "Being of use makes being in need easier" (1991, 30). I observed a poignant example of this on September 13, 2001, when I visited with a group of frail people in a long-term care facility planning a prayer service for the following day to last from 9 A.M. to 5 P.M. The entire nation was struck with tremendous sorrow and fear as a result of terrorist attacks on New York and Washington, and these very old people, all of whom suffered at least one chronic, debilitating ailment, were determined that they would spend the day in prayer. As they planned how they would do this, I sensed their feelings of connection to one another and a nation in grief. They would not be standing in public vigils holding candles and flags, but they would be together, supporting one another, praying for themselves and the world, and feeling God's abiding love.

Many older people show a kind of psychological resilience that could be an important model to younger persons of how to bounce back from terrible life experiences. A wonderful study of elderly Lutheran women in Germany and America found that their spiritual resiliency was supported by their sense of community, the emotions—both positive and negative—they shared, and their personal relationships both inside and outside of the church (Ramsey and Blieszner 1999). Research on positive emotions like joy, interest, contentment, and love is showing that resilient people become expert at employing them to cope with negative emotions. As suggested by the work of Fredrickson (2001), positive emotions may broaden people's repertoires of thoughts and actions to enable them to forgive and express gratitude. This may in turn contribute to the formation of the kind of individual and communal spiritual resilience I witnessed.

Worship leaders, pastoral caregivers, and designers of congregational programs need to understand and acknowledge elders' emotions—especially their love. They also need to find ways to encourage and support older people's application of religious beliefs and activities to healthy emotion regulation. Finally, they need to provide opportunities for younger persons to appreciate and learn from the ways that older people experience emotions.

BIBLIOGRAPHY

Birren, J. E., and K. W. Schaie, eds. (2001). *Handbook of the Psychology of Aging*. San Diego: Academic Press.

Bregman, L. (1983). *The Rediscovery of Inner Experience*. Chicago: Nelson-Hall.

Carstensen, L. L. (1995). "Evidence for a Life-Span Theory of Socioemotional Selectivity." *Current Directions in Psychological Science* 4: 151–56.

Colby, A., and W. Damon (1992). *Some Do Care*. New York: Free Press.

Danner, D. D., D. A. Snowden, and W. V. Friesen (2001). "Positive Emotions in Early Life and Longevity: Findings from the Nun Study." *Journal of Personality and Social Psychology* 80: 804–13.

Durhams, S. (2001, May 23). "Dalai Lama Links Science, Spiritual Life." *Milwaukee Journal/Sentinel*, B2.

Edwards, J. (1746/1959). *A Treatise concerning Religious Affections*. Ed. J. E. Smith. New Haven, Conn.: Yale University Press.

Fredrickson, B. L. (2001). "The Role of Positive Emotions in Positive Psychology: The Broaden-and-Build Theory of Positive Emotions." *American Psychologist* 56: 218–26.

Koenig, H. G., M. E. McCullough, and D. B. Larson (2001). *Handbook of Religion and Health*. New York: Oxford University Press.

Labouvie-Vief, G., M. DeVoe, and D. Bulka (1989). "Speaking about Feelings: Conceptions of Emotion across the Life Span." *Psychology and Aging* 4: 425–37.

Lawton, M. P. (2001). "Emotion in Later Life." *Current Directions in Psychological Science* 10: 120–23.

Lustbader, W. (1991). *Counting on Kindness*. New York: Free Press.

Lutgendorf, S. K., P. P. Vitaliano, T. Tripp-Reimer, J. H. Harvey, and D. M. Lubaroff (1999). "Sense of Coherence Moderates the Relationship between Life Stress and Natural Killer Cell Activity in Healthy Older Adults." *Psychology and Aging* 14: 552–63.

Magai, C. (2001). "Emotions over the Life Span." In Birren and Schaie, 399–426.

Magai, C., and S. H. McFadden, eds. (1996). *Handbook of Emotion, Adult Development, and Aging*. San Diego: Academic Press.

Mayne, T. J. (2001). "Emotions and Health." In Mayne and Bonanno, 361–97.

Mayne, T. J., and G. A. Bonanno, eds. (2001). *Emotions: Current Issues and Future Directions*. New York: Guilford.

McClymond, M. J. (1998). *Encounters with God: An Approach to the Theology of Jonathan Edwards*. New York: Oxford University Press.

McCullough, M. E., K. I. Pargament, and C. E. Thoresen, eds. (2000). *Forgiveness: Theory, Research, and Practice*. New York: Guilford.

McCullough, M. E., S. D. Kilpatrick, R. A. Emmons, and D. B. Larson (2001). "Is Gratitude a Moral Affect?" *Psychological Bulletin* 127: 249–66.

Pargament, K. I. (1997). *The Psychology of Religion and Coping*. New York: Guilford.

Pruyser, P. W. (1968). *A Dynamic Psychology of Religion*. New York: Harper & Row.

Ramsey, J. L., and R. Blieszner (1999). *Spiritual Resiliency in Older Women: Models of Strength for Challenges through the Life Span*. Thousand Oaks, Calif.: Sage.

Rice, H. L. (1991). *Reformed Spirituality: An Introduction for Believers*. Louisville: Westminster John Knox.

Rye, M. S., K. I. Pargament, M. A. Ali, G. L. Beck, E. N. Dorff, C. Hallisey, V. Narayanan, and J. G. Williams (2000). "Religious Perspectives on Forgiveness." In McCullough, Pargament, and Thoresen, 17–40.

Thibault, J. M. (1993). *A Deepening Love Affair*. Nashville: Upper Room Books.

Thoresen, C. E., A. H. S. Harris, and F. Luskin (2000). "Forgiveness and Health: An Unanswered Question." In McCullough, Pargament, and Thoresen, 254–80.

Tucker, J. S., and H. S. Friedman (1996). "Emotion, Personality, and Health." In Magai and McFadden, 307–26.

Watts, F. N. (1996). "Psychological and Religious Perspectives on Emotion." *International Journal for the Psychology of Religion* 6: 71–87.

Wuthnow, R. (2000). "How Religious Groups Promote Forgiving: A National Study." *Journal for the Scientific Study of Religion* 39: 125–39.

5 Does Gender Influence Late-Life Spiritual Potentials?

CHRISTIE COZAD NEUGER

The question that shapes this chapter is whether gender influences late-life spiritual potential and aging. It is probably clear to most readers that the answer to this question is a straightforward yes. If there is one thing we have discovered in the past thirty or so years it is that individual and corporate lives are deeply impacted by the cultural particularities by which they have been constructed and in which they live. Who we are racially, ethnically, sexually, economically, and so on, forms the very warp and woof of our deepest selves.

Therefore, the question for this chapter is probably more appropriately understood to be: What impact does gender have on spiritual potential, spiritual practices, and the meaning-making projects related to aging in late life? Or the question may even be as simple as: Do women and men experience and practice their spirituality differently as they move through late-life aging, and can any conclusions, however tentative, be drawn about these different, gendered experiences and the ministries best suited to address them? These two questions implicitly undergird the material in this chapter.

WHY A GENDER LENS?

There is very little written material about aging and spirituality viewed through a gender lens. In fact, there is little written about gendered dimensions of aging at all. We live in a world in which gender is a central organizing category. Not only is it an organizing category but gender, from babyhood through late adulthood, carries with it a set of rules, structures through which those rules are enforced, and consequences for following the rules and/or breaking them. There are "dominant gender narratives" within the culture that shape the way we form our personal, familial, and social core narratives and that have major influence on how we make meaning in our lives. Of course, these dominant cultural gender narratives have different kinds of power and influence depending on other cultural particularities. The dominant American cultural narrative about gender looks very different in middle-class African American communities than it does in middle-class European American communities, for example.

Nevertheless, in our particular culture there is a powerful narrative strand that suggests certain people are more valuable than others. People are subtly and blatantly ordered in a hierarchy of value based on various essential (defined more or less by birth) qualities like skin color, ethnicity, sex, able-bodiedness, intelligence, sexual orientation, and physical appearance. The combination of these factors guides our placement in the value hierarchy to a large degree. The cultural narrative is the story that implicitly and explicitly defines and prescribes this hierarchy and shapes individual, familial, and societal compliance to it. Obviously, this is not as much of a mechanical or deterministic process as I have made it sound. Many factors influence how individuals and institutions internalize and live out the dominant cultural narrative. Nonetheless, the narrative about who we are as individuals and relationships is a powerful shaper of attitudes and behaviors. Gender is one such narrative.

CULTURAL GENDER NARRATIVES

Since gender training is an ongoing process in our culture and gender narratives are cumulative in people's lives, it is useful to take a very brief look at some aspects of gender training in girls and boys, women and men, as it sets the stage for spirituality in older adulthood.

It is the assumption of this chapter that cultural gender narratives are powerful and formative. They are binary and polarized. Women and men, girls and boys are defined over against each other. They are seen as opposites. This is one of the first harmful dimensions of gender stereotyping. Gender stereotypes teach girls and boys to relate to one another in ways so as not to challenge the power organization mandated by the dominant culture. Girls and boys begin their education to fit into the dominant narrative from the moment of birth in this culture. Along with their pink or blue hospital caps, they are talked to more or less, played with more or less, and given more or less freedom of movement as determined by their sex.

Sandra Bem's perspective on gender-schema theory is helpful for us as we look at the cultural contexts of gender narratives. Bem states, "Gender schema theory contains two fundamental presuppositions about the process of individual gender formation: first, that there are gender issues embedded in cultural discourse and social practice that are internalized by the developing child, and, second, that once these gender lenses have been internalized, they predispose the child, and later the adult, to construct an identity that is consistent with them" (Bem 1993, 138). She goes on to state that not only must girls and boys contend with gender polarization but also with cultural androcentrism and with a mandate to pass this schema on through the culture from generation to generation. The kinds of cultural phenomena that reinforce androcentrism and gender polarization include things like "generic" male language (including male names becoming the "family" name), child-rearing practices, advertising strategies, entertainment themes and images, and so on. Bem argues that gender polarization and its enculturation is so ubiquitous that even feminist theory building (such as the persistent emphasis on women being more relational than men) can perpetuate its legacy.

It is important to note that Bem begins here with very different assumptions than do many developmental theorists. Her assumption is that children are formed in the cultural "soup" of gender norms and power arrangements. There is no emphasis here on an epigenetic principle of positive unfolding but rather an affirmation that children use the narrative material of their families, institutions, media, schools, and so on, as the raw material for the way they shape their places and identities in those systems. The theory also assumes that girl children are immediately exposed in this culture to narrative messages that deny them, at least to some degree, the ability to develop a comprehensive sense of trust, industry, or even identity, no matter how stable or affirming their family life or their personality.

GIRLS' GENDER TRAINING

Lyn Brown and Carol Gilligan have documented that loss of voice seems to happen to many girls in late childhood and early adolescence. They summarized their findings, from a longitudinal study of girls moving from age eight into their early teen years, in this way:

> At the crossroads of adolescence, the girls in our study describe a relational impasse that is familiar to many women: a paradoxical or dizzying sense of having to give up relationship for the sake of "relationships." This taking of oneself out of relationship in order to protect oneself and have relationships forces an inner division or chasm, it makes a profound psychological shift. . . . Women's psychological development within patriarchal societies and male-voiced cultures is inherently traumatic. (Brown and Gilligan 1992, 216)

Women and other members of nondominant groups have thus learned to interpret their own stories and experiences, needs, and goals through the lenses of the other—those they have been taught to please and appease. Often they have lost access to their truths and their honest strengths.

Brown and Gilligan suggest that, during early adolescence, girls learn what it means to be a "good" woman, fearing that if they do not follow the rules of "femininity" they will experience abandonment, exclusion, or ridicule. And those rules about being feminine—quiet, nurturing, relational, supportive, full of caring feelings and empathy but rarely anger, etc.—teach girls and women how to be part of the "supporting cast" rather than actors or authors with voice and authority.

Many young women learn in adolescence what it means to be a "good" woman and to "forget what they know." They give up the ability to be in authentic relationship for the sake of being related in ways that minimize the risks of exclusion and abandonment. This seems to be a subtle process for many, although abuse and other oppressive situations may take away young women's voices in much more blatant ways.

Pastors need to understand these dynamics as well as the more tangible consequences of sexism:

- Approximately one out of two women is beaten in her intimate relationships.
- The average black woman college graduate in a full-time position receives less than 90 percent of her white counterpart's salary, which is equal to the earnings of a white male high school dropout.
- Hispanic women who work full time earn about 82 percent of what comparably employed white women earn.
- One-third of all women homicide victims are killed by their husbands.
- The group of women most at risk for depression is married women who do not work outside the home and have three or more children under the age of twelve (Neuger 1992, 39–43).
- Approximately 40 percent of all girls are sexually molested or abused by the age of eighteen—either inside or outside of their families (MacKinnon 1987).

BOYS' GENDER TRAINING

There has been a lot of important, gender-conscious research in the past ten or fifteen years about masculinity and men's psychological and spiritual health. This research has focused on the kinds of problems that men experience that may well be a direct result of their attempt to conform to male gender roles. Levant and Pollack write that these new approaches to understanding masculinity "have provided a framework for a psychological approach to men and masculinity that questions traditional norms for the male role, such as the emphases on competition, status, toughness, and emotional stoicism and that views certain male problems (such as aggression and violence, homophobia, misogyny, detached fathering, and neglect of health) as unfortunate but predictable results of the male role socialization process" (Levant and Pollack 1995, 1).

O'Neil, Good, and Holmes say that there are six problematic dynamics that result from gender socialization in men. Those are:

- restrictive emotionality
- socialized control, power, and competition
- homophobia
- restrictive sexual and affective behavior
- obsession with achievement and success
- health-care problems

They go on to say that "how men are socialized produces sexist attitudes and behavior that explains much of the personal and institutional sexism in society"

(O'Neil, Good, and Holmes 1995, 171). They also suggest that normative masculinity sets up persistent worries about personal achievement, competence, failure, status, upward mobility, wealth, and career success in men's lives as well as a drive to obtain authority, dominance, and influence over others. There is an emphasis on striving against others in competitive ways. Restrictive emotionality suggests that men have difficulty and fears about expressing feelings and difficulty finding words to express basic emotions. Levant (1995, 239) say that emotionality is socialized out of boys very intentionally and that this has four major consequences. First, boys develop a form of empathy that he calls "action empathy," which is the ability to see things from another's point of view in order to predict what they will "do" (not what they feel) and is usually employed in the service of the self (different from emotional empathy). Second, boys become strangers to their own emotional life and most develop at least a mild form of alexithymia (not having words for emotions). Men who are in the presence of an unrecognized emotion often experience only the bodily sensation of its physiological component. Third, boys pour their vulnerable emotions out through the channel of anger, one of the few emotions boys are encouraged to express. And, fourth, boys learn to channel their caring emotions through sexual activity.

We need to recognize some of the important negative consequences of gender-role strain for men. For example, probably all six of the gender-role conflict factors correlate positively with depression in men and restrictive emotionality correlates positively with depression at all life stages of men. Higher levels of gender-role conflict are associated with low self-esteem. In race studies, men from Euro-American, African American, and Hispanic races all reported problems with success, power, and competition, restrictive emotionality, and conflicts between work and family relations. Results of several studies indicate strong correlations between gender-role conflict and negative attitudes toward help-seeking (O'Neil, Good, and Holmes 1995, 188–91). Finally, older men have the highest rate of suicide of any age or gender group in the United States.

IMPLICATIONS OF GENDER TRAINING
ON SPIRITUALITY IN LATER LIFE

Men and women, especially of the cohort group that is postretirement age at this time, have rarely been given the tools to deconstruct, at an adequate depth, their gender training and its consequences for their lives. Especially for heterosexual women and men, gender has been seen as essential and determinative to a certain extent and gender roles have often been developed under the rubric of complementarity. This means that women and men have been encouraged to develop different kinds of attitudes and abilities from each other and to find their self-definition and self-esteem largely in the competent performance of those differences. In the past thirty years, much of that training and those roles have been challenged, but for the current postretirement population, these new models of gender have not adequately offset traditional gender training.

Spirituality and spiritual practices are often in line with the rest of gender training. As women and men reach young adulthood, spirituality is often defined as "feminine" and thus less accessible to men. Women have been taught emotional and relational language throughout their development with the expectation that they are the ones responsible for relational, family, and religious life. Women are often seen as the "keepers of morality" for the culture. Women are asked to consistently behave in ways that are most often associated with "religious" or "Christian" life. Men are often asked to fragment themselves, leaving religious commitments and feelings for Sundays and away from their day-to-day world of business or leisure.

These divisions leave women and men with quite different abilities with which to approach their spiritual lives and very different consequences from religious participation and spiritual practices. For women, often the submissive, relational, and dependent expectations of the culture are reinforced by religious participation. As Mary Daly once said, "The qualities that Christianity idealizes, especially for women, are also those of a victim: sacrificial love, passive acceptance of suffering, humility, meekness, etc. Since these are the qualities idealized in Jesus 'who died for our sins,' his functioning as a model reinforces the scapegoat system for women" (Daly, cited in Brown 1989, 3). Spiritual participation that is in line with a sexist understanding of gender is not usually liberating or empowering for women, despite their ability to participate freely in it. Depth spirituality is often denied to men, as it stands in contrast to the rules about being male. Language, relationality, access to emotions, and so on, have all been restricted for boys and men—resources that would offer them a deeper spiritual access. In addition, women's and men's lives in a sexist culture may well have deep implication for their spiritualities in later life. Whether it is the cultural epidemic of intimate violence against women, the implacable rules about strength and autonomy for men, the persistent silencing of women's authentic voices, or the denial of men's nurturance—all of these have an impact on spirituality in later life. Women and men bring their cultural and personal narratives about gender to their spirituality in later life, with the unique strengths and limitations that those provide.

INTERVIEW RESULTS

In order to further explore issues of aging, gender, and spirituality, I conducted in-depth interviews with ten older adults, ranging in age from mid-seventies to early eighties, four men and six women. These interviews were done in two same-sex groups. All interviewees were white, in good health, middle-class, and church attendees. I also did in-depth interviews with three ministers (two male and one female). Two of the ministers are primary chaplains in different senior apartments/assisted living/health-care complexes for older adults, and one is senior pastor of a large Presbyterian church in the Sun City, Arizona, area. I also had a number of more informal conversations with pastors of churches with significant numbers of older members. The in-depth interviews with older adults included questions on how they understood spirituality, how they had experienced their own spirituality over their life span (life span divided into quarters for the purpose of the questions), spiritual issues and questions they faced, spiritual resources and practices they used day-to-day and in crises, the role of community/church in their spirituality, questions they would like to ask God, and things they wish their pastors understood about aging and spirituality. In each of these interviews, I did not reveal that gender was an investigative variable. The questions for the chaplains and pastors were similar although directed at investigating the people they served rather than at their own spiritualities. Obviously these results are limited by both the small number of interviews and by the particularities of the interviewees. Nonetheless, the limited data generated through these interviews contribute to the rather minimal literature in gender, aging, and spirituality available at this time.

CONTINUITY OF SPIRITUAL IDENTITY AND PRACTICE

One of the most striking differences between men's and women's conversations about aging and spirituality came in response to the question about life cycle and spirituality. I asked participants to imagine their lives, so far, divided into four stages and to identify how they understood their spirituality in each of those phases through the use of a phrase, a metaphor, or an image. Each of the men talked about being "formed in the church" as children and their appreciation for that experience even though they did not understand or reflect much on it at the time. In addition, each of the men had some late adolescent or early adulthood experience, often of a miraculous nature, that cemented for them a personal relationship with God. For two of the men, there were wartime experiences—stories of survival against the odds where God's intervention provided the only meaningful explanation. Although their survival caused many questions to surface, each of the men found peace in a narrative of God's providence and their grateful response. One of the other men experienced a situation, also as a young adult, of being lost in a wilderness in adverse weather (he was serving as a forester) and, upon praying, being guided to safety. He, less ambiguously, attributed this to God's miraculous intervention. All three of these men built these stories into their spiritual narratives. However, the significance of the stories faded through much of their mid-adulthood (especially for two of the men) and surfaced again as a source of meaning in their later years. For the fourth interviewee, there was no miraculous experience but he did experience God as powerfully present in his experience as an athlete (a dominant young-adult identity for him). He described an embodied spirituality that was guiding for him in his late youth but which again faded as a narrative strand in his mid-adulthood. Three of the men described a long stretch of adulthood (thirty to forty years) of more or less spiritual dormancy, speaking with some regret that they did not pursue the practice of religion during those years of career development and family responsibilities. One of the men described a mid-adulthood of questioning and searching which brought him in later mid-adulthood to an ability to articulate his own faith commitments. This was more of an intellectual exercise for him than an experiential one.

The men describe this older-age phase of life as one of much greater spiritual interest and commitment. They have both the time and the context to devote more of their energy to their church and this is the primary outlet for their spiritual expression. When asked, each of the men understood his spirituality through his participation, especially service participation, in the church rather than through a personal devotional life or reflection time. For the men, their emphasis on finding their spirituality through doing good works for the church and by attending worship services is explained through a sense of "owing something back" to God at this point in their lives. In some ways, it is a return to a position of gratitude that was more available to them in their early adulthood than in their long span of middle-adult years.

This description of discontinuity in spiritual identity and practice fits the perception of ministers to this age group. As one pastor said, "Men's spirituality is more discontinuous. After retirement there is a shift from being 'things' oriented to a more holistic reflection." For these men who were interviewed, preparation in the church as children and their experience of divine intervention as young adults gave them something to return to as older adults: the church and its ministry.

The women interviewees consistently reported a sense of continuity about their spirituality. There was no significant shift in the way they understood themselves spiritually nor in their spiritual practices from early adulthood through later adulthood. They did tend to report that their spirituality felt both more intense and more reliable at their current age. They experienced trust in God and in God's reliability but they felt that, as the end of their life approached, their spirituality took a more intensely central place in their lives. Pastors who were interviewed concurred with this experience. There was general agreement that women are much more familiar with their spirituality and spiritual practices and have ready access to them at late adulthood than do men. As women's lives often have a greater sense of continuity and multidimensionality than men's, this spiritual continuity may not be surprising.

There has been considerable debate in the literature about whether or not older people are more religious or differently religious as they enter later life. This interview material does not answer that question but it does seem to suggest that there may be gender differences in the experience of spiritual or religious continuity. It will be interesting to continue to look at this question through a gender lens.

WOMEN'S AND MEN'S SPIRITUALITY
IN THE PROCESS OF (END OF) LIFE REVIEW

Interviews with older men and with those who minister to older men indicated that the kinds of spiritual issues that they tend to explore are nuanced differently than the spiritual issues of women. Older men report that one of the major questions they have about their spiritual lives has to do with an evaluation of how well they have done "in God's eyes" and whether God is pleased or satisfied with their lives. Several men reported that a large part of their service orientation (to the church, especially) has to do with a sense of "giving something back" or "evening up the balance sheets" of their lives. One pastor said, "Men are much more engaged in religious community after retirement and it is, in part, motivated by God's measuring stick." One of the chaplains, when responding to the question of what brings older men to you for spiritual care, said, "Men come with very specific spiritual questions like, 'Am I on the right track?'" There is a sense that, in their life review, men are seeking to look at their overall lives and use later life to balance a less active spirituality of earlier years, at least in the experiences of the groups that I studied.

The older women, both those interviewed and those in the care of the pastors I interviewed, do not seem to carry these kinds of questions into their spiritual care. When asked about women's spiritual care, the pastor quoted above said, "Women seem to experience more of a spiritual continuum. They don't seem to need having their past lives affirmed by their pastor. They seem to have more confidence in those past lives or they let it go. Men seem to agonize more about their past lives from a spiritual perspective." This sentiment was echoed by other pastors and by the women themselves. When the older women were asked about their key spiritual questions, there was general agreement with the one woman who said, "I have fewer questions than I used to. God has taken me this far and will take me the rest of the way."

SPIRITUAL RESOURCES

Another difference between the men and women in their reported reflection on who they are spiritually at this point in their lives had to do with their spiritual resources. Men had many fewer spiritual resources and practices in their lives than did the women. Men reported church attendance and service to the church as their primary or sole spiritual resources. One of the men reported that he enjoyed hearing his wife pray aloud and another man said that his wife led them in spiritual devotions each day. The women reported a plethora of spiritual practices, including listening to Christian-based radio stations, Bible readings, daily devotions, ongoing prayer, Bible study, and so on. The women and men both relied on the spiritual community of the congregation.

This difference in accessibility to spiritual resources was also reported by the institutional chaplains. One chaplain said that although both sexes attended Bible study, worship, and so on, only the women made comments that indicated they were integrating those resources into their spiritual lives. She stated, "The men [in the spirituality group] are absolutely silent. They don't speak up in the spirituality groups but they do speak up in the meetings and community organizing work— there they do most of the speaking. Men don't seem to have the language for feelings and spiritual issues. They can't get very close to spirituality issues either in the group or in one on one situations." She went on to say, "After a sermon, the women will talk about how the sermon affected them, who they want to tell, how the words impacted them. The men, even 'spiritual' men, offer critique rather than responding—they stand away from the response." Despite these differences, however, it is important to say that the men I interviewed (and the men discussed by the clergy caregivers) seem relatively content with their spirituality in later life. The spiritual resources of congregation, worship, and service seem, for the most part, to be adequate for day-to-day living, with the possible exception of when they experience serious crisis such as the final illness of a spouse. We will return to this point below.

SECRETS IN OLDER WOMEN'S LIVES

One other primary issue surfaced in regard to older women's spiritual care. It has to do with the nature of unfinished business in the lives of women, especially in terms of secrets that may have been carried through life. This surfaced tangentially in the group interview with older women where they said that they wished that pastors would pay better attention to the family issues and histories that older women brought with them to later life. They were not explicit about this, but one of the chaplains named it well when he talked about issues getting triggered for women when they engage in Bible study or spiritual-growth groups. He gave the example of a woman calling for an appointment with him after a spirituality group because she remembered abuse from earlier in her life and wanted to talk about it. This was not an infrequent occurrence.

Emma Justes, in her article "Pastoral Care and Older Women's Secrets," states, "Many older women have lived their lives with the burdens of kept secrets that have deeply affected their lives. These secret experiences have played important roles in shaping the lives of women and their children in the areas of spiritual and emotional wholeness and in self-fulfillment" (Justes 1996, 241). When we look at the statistics about how many girls and women experience abuse in their lives (child sexual abuse, rape, battering, emotional abuse, etc.) and we remember that it has only been in the past twenty or so years that it has become more acceptable to name those experiences out loud, it makes sense that many older women have wounds from intimate abuse that have never been revealed to another person. Justes ends her chapter by discussing a seventy-five-year-old woman who said, "'Tell everybody it's never too late.' She had recovered the memory of abuse when she was seventy-one years old, having endured four failed marriages. When she spoke these words she was in a new and fulfilling relationship, the first in her lifetime. When there is a possibility of redeeming women from the burdens of damage caused by pain-filled secrets, it is never too late" (Justes 1996, 251).

It is important that pastors never force or demand these kinds of revelations from older women. Instead, pastors need to (1) communicate a willingness to hear about secrets; (2) hear the secret carefully and with respect when it is shared; and (3) continue to be willing to hear the secret as it evolves from secrecy to a status of openness and integration with the rest of her life over time (Justes 1996). These secrets are more likely to be shared in productive ways if women experience a safe space with their spiritual caregivers, but there must never be an expectation that women must open up their lives to their pastors.

MEN'S AND WOMEN'S SPIRITUALITY IN THE CONTEXT OF BEREAVEMENT

Both men and women may face significant spiritual crisis in the face of a partner's final illness. That this is one of the most significant life crises of older age was apparent throughout these interviews. Both women and men deeply fear the diagnosis of terminal illness in their partners, maybe even more than they fear it for themselves. This seemed especially true for those couples who were living in assisted-living or health-care institutions. But the men interviewed or discussed by chaplains seemed to find the terminal illness of their spouse to be a particularly difficult experience. One chaplain described it by saying, "Men whose wives need (terminal) care are literally 'broken-hearted.' They have a great deal of trouble being companions in suffering. They seem to have no tools to just 'be' with the sufferer. They would far rather be the sufferer themselves." The spiritual issues in this experience are profound. As one interviewee said, "You can't help but ask God 'Why?' at a time like this. It's hard to understand." Men often seem very alone in the process of accompanying a spouse through a final illness. They seem to have trouble knowing what to do to seek comfort for themselves or for their partners. As one of the pastors said, "Men don't know how to go about spiritual meaning-making because their spirituality has often been anchored in their wife." According to one of the clergy caregivers, men do tend to turn toward God in hope that God is bigger than this horrible experience. Pastors need to understand this fearful and radical aloneness that men often experience in the final illness of their wives so that they can be present appropriately. It is easy for pastors to feel that a man will be made uncomfortable by their care when, in reality, their separateness has more to do with not knowing how to be connected than a desire to be left alone.

Women who experience the terminal illness of a spouse or partner also seem to have deep fears, mostly about future loneliness. But women seem to have at least two spiritual resources that men often do not have. Many women are used to being in caregiving roles, and so this caring for a partner does not seem to generate the same feelings of disconnection and helplessness that it does for most men. As one chaplain said, "Women suffer with their partners but they're not broken by it. They become advocates and caregivers; they know this role. Women stay connected with their partners in illness." Because of this continuity, women do not seem to lose access to their spiritual resources in this kind of crisis.

The other resource that many women have is a broader network of social relationships that offer support during this time of spousal illness. They are more open to sharing feelings and experiences with friends because they are more used to doing so. This kind of support is a valuable resource during the crisis of spousal final illness, especially because women's greatest fears seem to be about how she will live without her spouse after he is dead. From a spirituality perspective, most women find that they are also open to God's presence and resources during this time as well as to pastoral care resources, if that has been a part of their experience prior to this crisis.

When a spouse dies, both men and women generally experience radical loneliness and grief. Both women and men report feeling that they have lost a part of themselves and have trouble imagining a future. Both experience "pining" behavior, longing for the lost one to return. Men often use words like feeling that part of themselves has been "amputated." Women use words that indicate more a loss of identity—"I don't know who I am without him." Women seem to worry more about how they will manage their lives. This is in keeping with cultural messages of gender.

In their time of bereavement, men often have difficulty knowing how to grieve. Most studies indicate that in at least the first six months after spousal bereavement, men have a very high risk of their own deaths. After approximately six months, their death rate appears to return to normal for their cohort group. Men, on the whole, seem more unable or unwilling to express or display grief, stop displaying grief sooner, are initially higher in guilt feelings that decline fairly quickly, are more realistic in accepting the reality of the death more quickly, and initially require more assistance in coping with the day-to-day practicalities of life (Rando 1984, 145).

Women as a group seem to experience more fear and a sense of helplessness than do men but have more resources with which to process those feelings and fears. Women may also experience some ambivalence about the death, both the profound grief and loneliness of it and some opportunity to experience a new life of greater independence. This ambivalence may be difficult, and women may feel guilty or disloyal because of it. As one pastor said, "I would like women who have lost their spouses to know that it's OK to feel good about the liberating side of that loss." Pastors have to be able to support this ambivalence that may surface in women's grieving. In addition, women may require more assistance in coping with their emotional and social responses to the loss. They may need support in dealing with the numerous social changes that occur in their lives after partner loss, especially the change in their social desirability. Due to the increasing shortage of available men during later aging, widowed women are often not as socially desirable as are widowed men. They may find that they have no place in a coupled world. On the other hand, there is much more general support for widows than for widowers, primarily because there are so many more of them. Finally, women tend to experience more change in their lives after bereavement, especially financially and vocationally, than do men (Rando 1984, 146).

All of these realities have an impact on spirituality, especially as women and men try to make meaning out of lives that have experienced radical disruption through the loss of a spouse. One of the interviewed pastors suggested that both bereaved men and women often turn to the church as both comfort and compensation. He suggested that men tend to develop a strong resurrection theology in light of their bereavement, one that emphasizes the reunion between themselves and their spouses. He continued by saying, "Men tend to elevate the meaning of the church to compensate for their loss of spirituality they had found in their wives." This pastor also suggested that bereaved men seem to really appreciate both prayer and support offered by their pastors. However, they less often use the other resources of the church, such as grief or support groups. Women may well use these institutional resources. In one large church in Sun City, the "Solos Group" has seventy-five women and three men in it. Women may also develop different theological resources. One pastor suggested that women tend to develop a more intimate theology, drawn to a male Jesus and relationally intimate prayers and hymns, as a way to cope with the loss of a spouse and a future without a male spouse in it. This is a fascinating observation for further study.

MEN'S AND WOMEN'S SPIRITUALITY IN THE CONTEXT OF DYING

There is some evidence that life review needs become more focused and evident in the last year or two of a person's life. It is during this time that many women and men intentionally seek to make sense out of their lives and to evaluate the quality of that life. It is also during these last years that many women and men may long to reconnect with lost ones, and spirituality is often resurrection-focused. Many men and women also express a greater focus on their spirituality and on questions about afterlife.

As women and men approach their end of life, some form of life review seems to be present. Because each life is profoundly particular, there are few gender generalizations that can be made with any kind of confidence. However, the chaplains and pastors who work frequently with older dying folks were able to make some gender distinctions in their observations. They suggested that women tend to hang on to life, not necessarily out of fear but out of a clinging to relationships and connections. One chaplain said that, when there are family and friends around, there is a sense of family reunion with the dying woman at the center. God is part of this family reunion, she indicated, and women often want singing, ritual, and conversation. She said, "Women are often intimately related to God at the time of their deaths. They may have a harder time dying, though, because they hang on to life." Another chaplain said that women do not seem so alone at the time of dying as men and that they tend to reveal their needs and feelings about dying more freely than do men. Although they may hold on to life, there is a sense of peace about many women who are dying. Women who are dying in institutions often take the initiative to have their spiritual needs met.

Men who are facing death in institutions tend to be more passive about their spiritual needs. They may have questions about their lives and whether they have performed their life tasks and responsibilities adequately, and they may have saved these questions until death is imminent. One chaplain suggests that men seem to die more easily than do women. They let go more easily because they do not seem to have a lot of relational issues to process. Most religious men seem to have a trust in afterlife, even though they do ask evaluative life questions, and they seem to trust in the presence of God. Their life review seems more often to be internal, with the only external questions being about whether they have lived a good life. Men seem to be able to sense when there is nothing more that they can do to continue living whereas many women seem to wonder if they should just hold on a little longer. This makes their dying more difficult in many cases.

These are, of course, huge generalizations from minimal data, but the reports of interview subjects and pastoral caregivers of the elderly describe observations that one might expect would arise in a world that organizes, to a large degree, roles and tasks and meaning around gender.

IMPLICATIONS

This chapter has emphasized the conviction that all ministry must be approached with an attentiveness to the effects of gender, individually and culturally, on the lives of people in our care. Much more research needs to be done on the strengths and limitations women and men bring to their spirituality in later aging as observed through a cultural gender lens. Issues like women's secrets of abuse histories or issues of self-esteem and authentic voice need to be explored in order to provide appropriate pastoral care in later aging. Issues like men's limited access to emotional and spiritual language and feelings, the emphasis on doing rather than being in men's lives, and men's lack of substantive peer relationships apart from that with their partners need to be kept in mind as spiritual care is provided in later aging. Much more important than this, however, is the reality that we must all be working to dismantle gender systems that limit the full potential of women or men to have voice, experience relationships, know how to both "do" and "be," and have deep and ongoing access to their own spiritualities. This is the task for pastoral caregivers to all ages.

BIBLIOGRAPHY

Bem, S. L. (1993). *The Lenses of Gender*. New Haven, Conn.:Yale University Press.

Brown, J. C., and C. R. Bohn, eds. (1989). *Christianity, Patriarchy, and Abuse*. NewYork: Pilgrim.

Brown, J. C., and R. Parker (1989). "For God So Loved the World?" In Brown and Bohn, 1–30.

Brown, L. M., and C. Gilligan (1992). *Meeting at the Crossroads: Women's Psychology and Girls' Development*. Cambridge, Mass.: Harvard University Press.

Glaz, M. (2000). "On Becoming an Ancestor: Continuity and Change at the End of Life." In Stevenson-Moessner, 227–43.

Harris, M. (1993). "Women Teaching Girls: The Power and the Danger." *Religious Education* 88/1: 52–66.

Justes, E. (1996). "Pastoral Care and Older Women's Secrets." In Stevenson-Moessner, 240–53.

Levant, R. (1995). "Toward the Reconstruction of Masculinity." In Levant and Pollack, 229–51.

Levant, R., and W. Pollack, eds. (1995). *A New Psychology of Men*. NewYork: Basic.

MacKinnon, C. (1987). *Feminism Unmodified: Discourses on Life and Law*. Cambridge, Mass.: Harvard University Press.

Neuger, C. C. (1992). "Feminist Pastoral Counseling and Pastoral Theology: A Work in Progress." *Journal of Pastoral Theology* 2: 39–43.

O'Neil, J., G. Good, and S. Holmes (1995). "Fifteen Years of Theory and Research on Men's Gender Role Conflict: New Paradigms for Empirical Research." In Levant and Pollack, 164–206.

Rando, T. (1984). *Grief, Dying, and Death: Clinical Interventions for Caregivers*. Champaign, Ill.: Research.

Stevenson-Moessner, J., ed. (2000). *Through the Eyes of Women: Insights for Pastoral Care*. Minneapolis: Fortress Press.

6

The Divine Is Not Absent in Alzheimer's Disease

JON C. STUCKEY

ALZHEIMER'S AS THIEF OF SPIRIT

In 1906, when Alois Alzheimer began caring for Auguste D., the woman who would eventually be diagnosed with the disease that bears his name, it is difficult to believe that he had any indication of the profound impact that Alzheimer's disease would have on the late twentieth- and early twenty-first-century public health agendas. Indeed, for the nearly four generations between 1906 and the late 1970s and early 1980s, the disease was a rarely accurately diagnosed disorder; symptoms were categorized instead as "senility," "hardening of the arteries," or "organic brain syndrome."

During the past twenty years, however, Alzheimer's has become a major public health issue, both in this country and abroad. The rise of Alzheimer's as a global health epidemic has led to unprecedented gains in public funding for dementia research. "Losing a Million Minds: Confronting the Tragedy of Alzheimer's Disease and Other Dementias," which was published by the United States Congress in 1987, was a call to arms for policy makers to respond to the then four million Americans who had Alzheimer's, and the projected fourteen million Americans who would have the disease by 2050. Through impressive efforts by organizations such as the Alzheimer's Association and the disclosures of diagnoses of prominent Americans, including Ronald Reagan and Rita Hayworth, Alzheimer's emerged as a horrific disease that could strike anyone, regardless of socioeconomic status or personal fame or fortune.

The early language used to describe Alzheimer's included words like "victims," "suffering," and "loss." Certainly, Alzheimer's is a devastating diagnosis. As noted by Sapp (1997), our memories link us to the past, present, and future by connecting us to meaningful relationships with others. Without these connecting memories, persons with Alzheimer's are adrift in their life journeys.

However, the result of well-intentioned public advocacy has been to nearly eclipse the presence of the human spirit. Alzheimer's disease has become more than a "thief of the mind." It has emerged as a "thief of the spirit." For the past fifteen years of my research in this area, I have been inspired by diagnosed persons and their families who have drawn a line in the sand with respect to Alzheimer's disease. Alzheimer's can steal memories; it can steal personalities; it can steal bodily functioning. But it must not be permitted to steal the human spirit. That for me is the hope amidst the challenges of the dementias, including Alzheimer's disease.

I now base my work on the premise that the spirit—the essence, the very soul of a person with Alzheimer's—remains undiminished by the disease. Persons with a diagnosis are entitled to being treated with respect, with dignity, and to being offered spiritual nurturance, simply because they *are,* not because of what they can remember or because of a subjective assessment of what they can contribute to society at large. They are worth celebrating by their mere existence. To believe otherwise is to imply that anyone with a disease is somehow less human than those who are absent from disease. Yet who among us is absent from disease? Even those without a particular diagnosis have the disease of "aging." The process of senescence that begins at birth leads all humans to an inevitable end of life.

I have spoken with many diagnosed persons and caregivers over the years regarding the role of religion and spirituality in the Alzheimer's disease experience. There are four themes that consistently emerge in all of my discussions among persons from Christian, Jewish, Muslim, Buddhist, and nonreligious perspectives. These themes are:

1. spiritual support for those with Alzheimer's disease
2. relationships as spiritual connections
3. hope and meaning
4. cultural and ethnic considerations

SPIRITUAL SUPPORT FOR THOSE WITH ALZHEIMER'S DISEASE

Whether or not a person chooses to recognize and nurture his or her spirituality, a spiritual element is present in everyone. Similar to the fact that all people need food, air, and water to survive, I argue that all people require spiritual sustenance in order to flourish to the fullest extent of the human experience. A diagnosis of Alzheimer's disease does not negate the need for attention to spiritual matters. Indeed, my experience has shown the absolute opposite. A diagnosis of Alzheimer's disease calls for even greater attention to be paid to spiritual well-being.

Spiritually and religiously based symbols and rituals are profound ways to maintain connection with the spirit well into the progression of Alzheimer's disease. Everett (1996) has noted that traditional religious services employ an abundance of cognitive-based expressions of faith (e.g., reciting scripture, listening to homilies or sermons, responsive reading). She suggests that worship can and should be a multisensory experience, using touch, music, and even nature as pathways of connection to someone with Alzheimer's. Similarly, Clayton (1991) argues for a "right brain" approach to worship that focuses less on intellectual skills and more on music, aroma, and touch. And Richards (1990) emphasizes that early memories are often preserved in persons with dementia and can be triggered using religious symbols that may have had important meaning in past years. The common theme among all these works is that the spiritual care and support of persons with dementia are as vital as physical or emotional care and support. Loss of cognitive capacity need not be interpreted as carrying a concomitant loss of spiritual capacity.

The senses are wonderful tools for worship for those with dementia. There are many ways to incorporate the senses into very spiritual experiences that rely little, if at all, on cognitive functioning.

Hearing. Whether it is passages of sacred texts or old hymns, listening is one way to make connections with those with Alzheimer's disease. Even a person who may not recognize a close relative can often recite all verses of an old hymn.

Vision. A person with the disease once remarked to me that each time she saw a snowflake it was like seeing it for the first time. There is a profound peace that can come from simply taking in the beauty of nature and creation. Moreover, religious symbols may elicit a calming response, for example, a cross, a menorah, or a particular style of dress. Simply seeing these symbols can be meaningful expressions of worship, even among those with profound dementia.

Aroma. While the sense of smell diminishes over time, the use of aromatherapy among persons with dementia suggests that odors can trigger a calming response (Brooker et al. 1997). Familiar scents can bring a spiritual calming response, such as the smell of a holy-day meal or the aroma of incense from a worship service. Even seemingly mundane scents, for example, the odor of a church sanctuary or a sacred Bible, may serve as reminders of significant spiritual memories.

Taste. The taste and texture of the elements of the communion ritual are meaningful ways to make spiritual connections for those with Alzheimer's disease. While theological arguments may arise regarding whether or not a person with a diagnosis should participate in the sacrament of communion (Stuckey 1997), these issues can and must be resolved so that all possible tools for maintaining connections to those with Alzheimer's can be utilized.

Touch. Depending on how comfortable the person is with being touched, the close presence of another human being—a hand on the back, holding hands in a prayer circle, hugging—can bring a sense of spiritual connection with others. The process of touching is a valuable expression of our human connection with others, which leads to the second theme identified in my discussions with those affected by dementia.

RELATIONSHIPS AS SPIRITUAL CONNECTIONS

The journey of Alzheimer's underscores the need for human connection amid the disease. As "fellow travelers" (Ellor 1997), there is a sense of the need to share in the journey of Alzheimer's. Rabbi Richard Address (1991) speaks of a "caring congregation." He writes that a caring congregation reaches out to others in times of need as an expression of love for their Creator. There are ways of being "kindred spirits" that cover a holistic spectrum of needs, including emotional, physical, and spiritual.

Reaching Both the Diagnosed and the Caregiver

Interacting with and nurturing the diagnosed family member can be an important source of support to both the person with the disease and the caregiver. A woman I spoke with several years ago lamented the fact that the minister who visited with her husband and her never prayed with or ministered to her husband. Whether it is through prayer, visiting, or other expressions of support, it is critical to remember that both the diagnosed and the caregiver require human connection during the progression of the disease.

Being Proactive and Concrete

In one study where I examined the church's response to Alzheimer's (Stuckey 1997), some caregivers did not ask for help because they did not want help. Others did not ask for help because they were too proud or embarrassed to do so. It is better to ask caregivers if they need assistance rather than to help without asking or to refrain from becoming involved at all. Sometimes, "Call me if you need me" is OK. Other times, it is appropriate and necessary to simply show up on the doorstep with mop or paintbrush in hand. Serving the spiritual needs of those affected by Alzheimer's need not only focus on spirituality. Being a spiritual connection can, at times, have a very physical or emotional quality.

Being Prepared

Many well-intentioned congregants have tried to reach out to people affected by this disease only to feel that their efforts were unappreciated or ineffective. It is important to remember that interacting with a person with Alzheimer's disease or another form of dementia takes training and education. Therefore, churches, synagogues, mosques, and other places of worship are wise to offer workshops for both clergy and members on the basics of dementia.

But beyond education, there is a spiritual preparation that is required. When I speak to lay caregivers, I remind them to pray and reflect before they leave their homes. I ask them to pray for strength, pray that the family will be receptive, pray for humility, pray for wisdom, and pray for peace for both the diagnosed and the family.

HOPE AND MEANING

In speaking with families living with Alzheimer's, religion and spirituality are often described as resources that provide hope and meaning. Farran, Herth, and Popovich (1995) write about hope as a multidimensional construct, including spiritual, relational, and even rational elements. The hope of Alzheimer's is linked to both spiritual and relational elements. It is spiritual in that both the diagnosed and caregivers speak about a hope for the future that is often based on an afterlife. This concept of hope is consistent with the work of others who note that religion and spirituality can provide hope for a time of being whole again. Family members hope for a time when they will be reunited with others who have already died (Koenig 1994).

Underscoring the importance of "human connectedness," however, there is also a striking relational aspect to hope that characterizes many experiences with Alzheimer's disease. A caregiver once explained to me that he was praying every day about his wife. He no longer prayed for her to become well. He had resigned himself to the fact that she would die from Alzheimer's disease. He simply prayed that he would outlive her because he wanted to be the one to care for her until she died.

Spirituality and Alzheimer's disease also deal with meaning. Caregivers report on the meaning they derive from the experience (Farran et al. 1997). However, there is a deeper meaning—a meaning of what it is to be a person. We are no more the summary of our memories than we are the summary of our cells. As has been told time and time again by those with a diagnosis of dementia and by ethicists (Post 1995), the diagnosis does not wholly define persons with Alzheimer's disease. Who they are has much more to do with how they have found meaning in this world, whether it is through family, friendships, work, or someone or something else. Even in Alzheimer's disease it is possible to find hope and meaning.

CULTURAL AND ETHNIC CONSIDERATIONS

Finally, it bears mentioning that Alzheimer's disease is not a Christian disease, a Jewish disease, a Muslim disease, or a Buddhist disease. Alzheimer's disease is a disease that affects all of humanity. The religious thoughts and ideas a person adheres to—how someone has made sense of this world, including losses and positive experiences—are some of the most personal beliefs and practices inherent in the human experience. Often these beliefs and practices stem from one's cultural or ethnic heritage. Consequently, it is paramount to be sensitive to the personal religious or spiritual traditions of those with Alzheimer's when trying to offer religious or spiritual support.

NO POLLYANNA CONCLUSION

I want to be clear on one thing: religion and spirituality do not take away the sting of Alzheimer's disease. This disease is devastating. As a graduate student, I encountered for the first time the cruel effects of Alzheimer's. I was meeting with a woman whose husband had been diagnosed, and she and I were talking about the impact on her. She said, "He's asked me what we should do for our fiftieth wedding anniversary next year. And I know in my heart that by the time of our anniversary, he won't even know who I am." He didn't.

That is the cruelty of Alzheimer's. Simply "finding" religion or expressing one's spirituality is not a panacea that takes away all the pain. I once gave a talk on the "gifts" of Alzheimer's disease. A woman with a diagnosis came up to me and said, "Gifts? Are you nuts? This disease is terrible!" And indeed it is. Moreover, religion, in particular, may foster feelings of guilt that actually make the Alzheimer's experience more difficult to bear.

Nevertheless, the disease does not diminish the personhood of the diagnosed. As noted by Kitwood (1997), personhood implies "recognition, respect, and trust." And religion and spirituality offer ways to maintain the recognition, respect, and trust of the diagnosed throughout the disease progression—up to and including the dying process.

My own faith journey has led me to a place where I am reminded daily of the presence of the Divine. Whether it is a walk in the woods after a fragrant spring rain, the delightful eyes of my daughters, or singing a familiar hymn with someone diagnosed with Alzheimer's, my spiritual self is nourished by these glimpses of a supernatural divine presence in this at times overwhelming very real world. No, there is no Pollyanna conclusion. In the words of one caregiver: "Alzheimer's stinks."

Yet there is hope. The hope of Alzheimer's is seen most clearly in the spiritual well-being of the diagnosed and their families. There is still no cure for this disease. But there is hope and there is healing. As is often the case when dealing with this disease, perhaps a song expresses this hope best:

> Sometimes I feel discouraged and think my work's in vain,
> But then the Holy Spirit revives my soul again.
> There is a balm in Gilead to heal the wounded soul.
> There is a balm in Gilead to heal the sin sick soul.
> (Anonymous)

Those affected by Alzheimer's are not absent from the Divine, and the Divine is not absent in Alzheimer's disease.

BIBLIOGRAPHY

Address, R. (1991). "The Caring Congregation." *Journal of Psychology and Judaism* 15: 195–200.

Brooker, D. J., M. Snape, E. Johnson, D. Ward, and M. Payne (1997). "Single Case Evaluation of the Effects of Aromatherapy and Massage on Disturbed Behaviour in Severe Dementia." *British Journal of Clinical Psychology* 36: 287–96.

Clayton, J. (1991). "Let There Be Life: An Approach to Worship with Alzheimer's Patients and Their Families." *Journal of Pastoral Care* 45: 177–79.

Ellor, J. W. (1997). "Celebrating the Human Spirit." In D. K. McKim, 1–20.

Everett, D. (1996). *Forget Me Not: The Spiritual Care of Persons with Alzheimer's.* Edmonton, Alberta: Inkwell.

Farran, C. J., B. H. Miller, J. E. Kaufman, and L. Davis (1997). "Race, Finding Meaning, and Caregiver Distress." *Journal of Aging and Health* 9: 316–33.

Farran, C. J., K. A. Herth, and J. M. Popovich (1995). *Hope and Hopelessness: Critical Clinical Constructs.* Thousand Oaks, Calif.: Sage.

Kitwood, T. (1997). *Dementia Reconsidered: The Person Comes First.* Buckingham, Eng.: Open University Press.

Koenig, H. G. (1994). *Aging and God: Spiritual Pathways to Mental Health in Midlife and Later Years.* New York: Haworth.

McKim, D. K., ed. (1997). *God Never Forgets: Faith, Hope and Alzheimer's Disease.* Louisville: Westminster John Knox.

Post, S. G. (1995). *The Moral Challenge of Alzheimer Disease.* Baltimore: Johns Hopkins University Press.

Richards, M. (1990). "Meeting the Spiritual Needs of the Cognitively Impaired." *Generations* 14: 63–64.

Sapp, S. (1997). "Memory: The Community Looks Backward." In McKim, 38–54.

Stuckey, J. C. (1997). "The Church's Response to Alzheimer's Disease." *Journal of Applied Gerontology* 17: 25–37.

U.S. Congress, Office of Technology Assessment (1987). "Losing a Million Minds: Confronting the Tragedy of Alzheimer's Disease and Other Dementias." OTA-BA-323. Washington, D.C.: U.S. Government Printing Office.

7

A Framework for Ministry for the Last Third of Life

HENRY C. SIMMONS

This chapter provides a framework that allows us to (1) speak of the last third of the life-course in ways that account for stable periods and transitions, (2) attend to variables that distinguish individual lives, and (3) assess ministry with older adults using core New Testament terms. The readership of this handbook is wider than Christian. The application of language that names religious realities from other traditions is invited.

This chapter describes four transitions, three stable periods, and five variables. It then presents six tasks of the Christian life (community, prayer/worship, service, teaching, proclamation, and witness). Taken together, the first two parts of this three-part framework create a 7 x 5 matrix that allows us to describe with considerable precision the people in the last third of life with whom we engage in ministry, their life situation, and the circumstances of their lives. The six tasks allow us to be systematic in structuring our ministry responses. With the application of this threefold framework, ministry with aging persons is deliberate, focused, intentional, and dialogical.

A MORE PRECISE UNDERSTANDING OF "AGING"

A careful reading of the first volume of *Aging, Spirituality, and Religion* (1995) shows little consensus about what is meant by "aging." Some authors refer principally to those in the frail part of life; others refer to a larger span, including both the able old and the frail old (Vogel 1995, 75). Nowhere is there a clear and precise definition of who is included in the category of "aging persons" or what "aging" means. Granted, few authors fall into the trap of trying to use chronology as an adequate indicator of a person's reality in later life. They are aware that a description of a "normal seventy-three-year-old" might point us to a frail elder with a degenerative disease in a nursing home or to her identical twin sister who finishes well in the Boston marathon. At earlier ages chronology works (although still imperfectly). For a "normal seven-year-old" we have a pretty good sense of physical maturity, social skills, school tasks, peer relationships, future growth profiles, and so on. Such is not the case for people in the last third of life. We might well expect that a person at age seventy is in better physical, mental, and spiritual health than a person at age ninety-five, but case-to-case we simply do not know.

A review of the more than 1,700 books, articles, and dissertations annotated in
Religion, Spirituality, and Aging: An Online Annotated Bibliography (http://www.
gracefulaging.org) shows that *collectively* persons who write for people in congregations are in varying degrees attentive to a description of "aging" that includes the
whole of the last third of life, from retirement to death. There are books, articles, and
other materials that speak about the last third of life in quite discriminate terms, for
example, rituals for retiring, creative and responsible reordering and living out of
one's time when formal work responsibilities end, ill health and the death of a
spouse, widow- or widowerhood and the refashioning of one's life, the passage into
frailty, dependence on others, dying. These take into account informally that there
are recurring life situations that go past chronology or even functionality to shared
themes and patterns of change in the last third of life. In this chapter I assume that
"aging" should include the whole of the life-course from retiring to dying.

STABLE PERIODS AND TRANSITIONS

As Daniel Levinson (1978) noted, adult life appears to be made up of stable periods
and of transitions. The stable periods stretch out over a number of years unless
interrupted by some cataclysmic event; the transitions are short in duration and
intense in character.

This is a change theory, not a developmental schema. Developmental schemas
see the individual moving toward a goal of personal integration that is more complex, more adequate, more in keeping with preformulated and agreed-on norms.
This may be in the form of a stage theory (e.g., Fowler 1981) or not (e.g.,
Loevinger 1976). A change theory like that of Levinson, however, is not developmental. The theory simply notes predictable changes, without ascribing any attributes of better/worse, lower/higher. Unlike Fowler's stage 5 that is by its nature
more adequate than his stage 3, for Levinson the fifties are only different from, not
better than, the thirties. A change theory seems to fit better than a developmental
theory with what we know of the last third of life. Nevertheless, as noted toward
the end of this chapter, there are dimensions of spiritual growth in the last third of
life that are clearly developmental in character.

There are reasons to be cautious in what we take from Levinson's schema.
First, when *The Seasons of a Man's Life* was published, the research was done on
males only, the sample was limited in its scope, and the research did not include
persons in their sixties and beyond. Second, the research was done in the mid-
1970s, and our world has changed dramatically since then. Like all research projects with human subjects, the people, their context, and the time they lived are
important factors in the way the theory will be formulated. Think, for example,
of the effect on Kohlberg's formulation of a theory of moral development of his
initial choice of twelve- to sixteen-year-old boys in Chicago in the mid-1950s as
his subjects; or of the effect on Roger Gould's theory (1978) of his initial choice

of subjects—psychiatric residents and their friends in California in the late 1960s. Nevertheless, without subscribing to the details of Levinson's theory, we may use his stable periods/transitions model of change in the adult years at least heuristically. That is to say, we may take this schema as a starting point for inquiring whether or not the changes of the last third of life become clearer when seen from this perspective.

STABLE PERIODS AND TRANSITIONS IN THE LAST THIRD OF LIFE

At the beginning of this chapter, I noted that there are individual resources for congregational ministry that speak about the last third of life in quite discriminate terms: rituals for retiring, creative and responsible reordering and living out of one's time when formal work responsibilities end, the death of a spouse and the subsequent refashioning of one's life, the passage into frailty, a time of being dependent, and dying. If we begin with this list, we see that four of these seem to be transitions: retiring, the death of a spouse, the passage into frailty, and dying. Three of these seem to be more stable periods: creative and responsible reordering and living out of one's time when formal work responsibilities end, widow- or widowerhood and the refashioning of one's life, and a time of dependence.

In 1993, James C. Fisher published an article in *Adult Education Quarterly* entitled, "A Framework for Describing Developmental Change among Older Adults." Fisher conducted interviews with seventy-four persons over age sixty to gather information describing their experiences across the older adult life span. Using a grounded theory approach, he generated a theoretical framework of categories consisting of sequential clusters of experience. His study indicated that developmental change might be described in five age-independent periods in older adulthood: continuity with middle age, an early transition, a revised lifestyle, a later transition, and a final period (Fisher 1993, 76). As I have introduced people to this model, their reaction is predictable: "Why, of course that's how growing older goes." Somehow this model provides a framework and impetus for storytelling that shows how different kinds of folks have solved problems in recurring life situations within a common popular culture. I used this model in two books, with the addition of a final transition, "dying" (Simmons and MacBean 2000; Simmons and Wilson 2001). More recently I have added another transition, retiring, so that there are now four transitions and three stable periods. Conversations with James Fisher, my fellow authors and students, and people in ministry have informed and sharpened my understanding and descriptions of these life passages. I am indebted to them.

This four-transition, three-stable-period model helps plan and evaluate congregational ministry with the aging, particularly when joined with a set of variables that helps identify and name the particularities of the life-course. Five variables are noted: gender (including sexual orientation), socioeconomic status, cohort, ethnicity and family context, and place on the rural/urban continuum. These variables introduce critical differences in the experience of aging, although they do not get at all the variability in older adults' lives.

These variables reveal rather than hide the socially constructed nature of the life-course (Tennant and Pogson 1995). Thus they should make clear that various real-life configurations lead to an understanding of the life-course that can be other than what we (or the media) take for granted. Real life is individual life. Real-life situations are where we engage in ministry; but the particularity of real life does not preclude some general and describable phases and tasks in the last third of life. In fact, the schema modified by the variables may function to reveal more clearly the unique paths that some people's life passages take. Note, however, that the model assumes that one lives long enough to go through the whole of the life-course. Factually, this will happen more often with women than with men.

A SEVEN-STEP DESCRIPTION OF THE LAST THIRD OF LIFE

Retiring

For our purposes, retiring is a transition, not a permanent state, just as graduating or graduation are transitions, not permanent states. When we wish a graduate well by saying, "Enjoy your graduation, you've earned it," we are thinking of a time-bound series of exercises and events, not a life project. When we think of graduation, we assume a before, a during, and an after. *Before* there were the years of study, work, fellow students, learning, growth; *during* there is a passage, a threshold one steps over symbolically with ritual, costume, celebration; then, in a few days or weeks, there is an *after*, a life of work, new goals, and new commitments. The parallel works also for retiring (or "retirement," although that word seems to imply a more permanent state). There is a *before*, the years of work commitments, job, colleagues; there is a *during*, a time of passage, a threshold over which one passes. This is symbolized, usually imperfectly, by Medicare eligibility, Social Security decisions, visits with the employee benefits coordinator, the proverbial gold watch, the lunch, the promises to keep in touch. Then, in a few days or weeks, there is an *after*. The shape of this *after* is left in large measure to the individual.

Everyone who makes a transition through retiring needs to discover and embrace new goals and commitments. There need to be ways to use one's time, and new or renewed nonwork relationships. The same questions that one had to answer at the end of adolescence and the end of formal schooling need to be asked again: Who am I? What will I do? With whom will I do it? These parallel, in altered sequence, Erikson's stages of identity, intimacy, and generativity. The *after* of the act of retiring ought to be based on decisions made in an intense, soul-searching transition. For many the *after* lasts for a period of time almost as long as the work years.

Sometimes people get frozen in the *during* and the *after* gets delayed. A church educator told this story.

When the wealthy men in our congregation retire, typically they spend their days golf-ing, traveling in luxury, and buying boats—three or four, each one larger, over the course of a few years. At some point, usually four or five years out, they get a look about them of desperation, dejection, despair. That's when I get a group of them together for lunch, just to enjoy each other's company . . . no apparent agenda. In the course of lunch—if not the first time, then the second or third—one of them will break the silence and pour out how empty life feels. Once one breaks the silence, they all talk. Then, and only then, can they seriously engage themselves and each other in deliberate life planning.

When he finished this story, I asked him if he meant "break the silence," like some-one breaking the *omerta* of the Mafia. "Exactly," he said. This is a dramatic witness to the need for making the critical distinction between retiring as a passage, a *dur-ing* or transition, and the life-course that follows—the *after* that needs goals, plans, commitments just as does any long period of life. It also demonstrates that entry into the conversation may be difficult.

Extended Middle Age (Also Called "Continuity with Middle Age")

The *after* of retirement is not a single period of life. Emphatically, it is not the "good years" of a common two-stage model of aging ("good years, bad years"). It is the whole of the last third of life, made up of stable periods and transitions. The first of these stable periods we call extended middle age.[1]

Extended middle age refers to the stable period that spans the time between retiring and a transition that definitively marks the end of what we describe as extended middle age. How long this stable period lasts is unpredictable. It can be as short as a year, or as long as twenty or more years. Its basic shape is this: after retir-ing, a person replaces work with another set of activities. Life goes on with a strong sense of continuity with the life one lived and the person one was in the middle years.

Some people change jobs at this time of life. Are they now in extended middle age? If in retiring one has left what was one's highest paying, highest status job, then the person has made the transition. If a person simply changes careers, a person may have retired from a job and gone to another without having made the transition to extended middle age.

As noted above, the creative and responsible reordering and living out of one's time when formal work responsibilities end requires answering three questions: Who am I? What will I do? With whom will I do it? The answer to Who am I? needs to account for a sense of personal identity that does not depend exclusively on one's previous, dominant work identity, and is more than role identity (spouse, adult son or daughter, grandparent, etc.). The answer to What will I do? needs to account for goals and commitments that fill one's days in satisfying and responsible ways. "Responsible" is not predetermined; it is certainly not someone else's agenda. But having said that, one's life-plan ought to take others and the larger community into account. Generativity is an ongoing human need and task. The answer to With whom will I do it? needs to account for a circle of friends, colleagues, acquaintances that is larger than can be had by holding on to work relationships that inevitably attenuate as time passes. All three of these questions work together and their answers interact. There is no guarantee that one will "get it right" the first time. There may be trial and error as one discovers and uncovers a satisfying way of being in the world and being in one's world. If one is given many years in extended middle age, there may be a series of answers to these questions as life unfolds, opportunities present themselves, and needs arise.

Early Transition (Also Called "Ready or Not" and "Uncertain Journey")

The stable period of extended middle age ends in a turbulent, intense transition. Some life-events that might mark this transition are the illness and death of a spouse, a dramatic change in the physical abilities of oneself or one's spouse, a one-sided divorce, relocating to a safer place in light of expected life changes, or the culmination of a long process of repositioning oneself to better deal with changing circumstances. These are difficult transitions, bearable perhaps only because the actual transitions are brief—a year or less, typically.

This may be the story. Dad grows sick; there are a half-dozen trips to the hospital by ambulance. For mom and dad there is home hospice, pain, loneliness, hard physical tasks, helping hands. For mom there are medical procedures and unimaginably intimate caretaking; there are sleep-deprived nights and days; there is the final trip to the hospital and the diagnosis of a cerebral-vascular accident; there is the shadowland of lingering hope against hope; there are goodbyes to someone already no longer there; there is death, a funeral, and the slow, shocking, numbing, lonely days that follow.

The story may have a different ending. The stroke leaves dad quite incapacitated. This once energetic man—hiker, gardener, Little League coach, church volunteer for everything, tender lover—now must use a wheelchair.

Or perhaps it is an altogether different story, a story of hurts stored up for a lifetime, love unattended, betrayal, the shocking announcement of a new, younger woman, and nothing the kids or friends can do or say makes any difference.

People cope, get by somehow, and one way or another this transition comes to an end. But the person who emerges at the end of this year is not the same person who entered. Although there may well be an experience of continuity of self, this only accentuates the dramatic change in life circumstances.

Revised Lifestyle (Also Called "The New Me" or "The New You")

As daunting as it may seem, there is nothing to do but to pick up one's losses and begin to build a new stable life structure that has its own sense, its own integrity, and ultimately its own joys and sorrows.

A few get frozen in the transition: the sorrow never seems to abate enough to let them start over; the affront of the wheelchair dominates every possible horizon, and so on. Once in an automobile supply store, I saw a couple—he in a wheelchair, she pushing him. He was practically livid with frustration and anger, and she was near tears, as he told her what oil and filters to buy so that he could then tell her, but now never show her, how to change the oil on his truck.

Mercifully and quite amazingly, though, these seem to be the exceptions. Once again, now with diminished resources, three questions have again to be answered: Who am I? What will I do? With whom will I do it? Once again one has to accomplish the creative and responsible reordering and living out of one's life by addressing issues of identity, intimacy, and generativity. However, the shape of the answers to the three questions is quite likely to yield a different life-structure than that of extended middle age. Even where there is consistency and continuity of goals and commitments, these play out very differently. What is remarkable is the adaptability of so many people who successfully build new life-structures. I am reminded of a group of adventuresome widows who call themselves, good-spiritedly, the *A Capellas* (because they go unaccompanied).

Depending on a variety of factors (e.g., the length of time one was in extended middle age, the nature of the transition out of it, personal resources, genetic disposition) this stable period may be as short as a year or as long as twenty or more years. Truly, chronological age is not helpful for determining when or how long a person is in this period. Case by case, individual by individual, lives unfold in their own rhythms.

Later Transition (Also Called "Like It or Not" or "Reluctant Journey")

It is possible that a person will go from a revised lifestyle following the death of a spouse to dying. However, if a person lives long enough, it is likely that at some point in time, the stable period of revised lifestyle comes to a dreaded point: coping with the ins and outs of daily life is no longer possible without help. For whatever reason—emotional, physical, mental—what had always been the most ordinary tasks of life can no longer be accomplished. Home becomes a strange place, a once-familiar neighborhood a maze. Memory dims to the point of confusion. The control of bowels and bladder so hard won in childhood becomes unpredictable; no longer are cane or walker enough help to get from bed to chair and back again; preparing meals and even the act of eating becomes arduous; a bath or shower dangerous. Whatever the cause, however it plays out, you cannot get by on your own. You are becoming dependent. You are going through a transition we can hardly bear to imagine for ourselves. Craig MacBean points out that the acronym of a phrase that describes this transition, "Like It or Not," is "LION." The feelings of this transition cannot be too far from "being thrown to the lions."

This transition may be previewed bit by bit over quite a long period of time as resources diminish or health issues arise. The actual transition from *just* able to get by to *not* able to get by is more compressed—a year or less. Sometimes there is a critical incident (a fire caused by a pot left on a burner, for example) that brings about an intervention. Sometimes a series of health episodes leaves the person ever weaker. However it happens, a point of no return is passed. The transition has happened and one's life veers in an unwanted direction.

Final Period (Also Called "The Rest of Living" and "While the Light Lasts")

Once again, now with dramatically diminished resources, three questions have to be answered: Who am I? What will I do? and With whom will I do it? Once again one has to accomplish the creative and responsible reordering and living out of one's life by addressing issues of identity, intimacy, and generativity. Who am I now that I cannot manage on my own? How can I be myself when I can't even get to the toilet on my own? What will I do? How will I pass my days at home or in a nursing home? What will I do that makes a difference? How will I matter? Who will I befriend and who will be my friends? For some, there is another complicating issue because the spiritual, human, and financial costs of this period of life for caregivers, particularly involuntary caregivers, can be enormous. This fact can so overwhelm relationships that it becomes a sole focus of worry and use of energy. In this circumstance, it can dim the possibility that this time has its own goals, commitments, and satisfactions.

The poster slogan "Growing old is not for sissies" takes on particular poignancy in this stable period of life. From our vantage point and seen globally, the problems seem overwhelming, and losses seem to be almost the sole measure of this period of life. Individual by individual, the truth may be quite different. Some people make a life of this stable period. Some are confident that this is the best that can be now, given the bad spells they have been through. Some find causes they are passionate about—resident advocacy, for example. Some discover prayer and the deep satisfaction of what Jane Thibault (1993) calls "a deepening love affair: the gift of God in later life." And some people can even answer, "Right now," to the question, "Looking back, what was the most satisfying time of your life?" For others, though, the days reach a point where they seem simply too long; God seems to have forgotten to take them; pain is poorly managed; the physical surroundings of their adult home, for example, border on the inhuman.

This stable period, like the previous two, can last a long or short time—from a year to many, many years.

Dying (Also Called "Living into Dying")

The final transition of the life-course is dying—not death, the act or fact, but the transition itself. It is a human act and can even be a sacred act. Nevertheless, there are too many people who die lonely, in great pain, without the human touch and care that all desperately need at this time of passage, without the comfort of, "It's OK to go now," without the chance to say, "I love you; I thank you; I forgive you; I'm sorry; goodbye" (Byock 2001). At times it is the failure to seek or accept care—

not cure—that gets an individual trapped into extensive, intrusive, and finally failed medical procedures. Fifty-one days in an intensive care unit and only three days in one's own room with comfort care is not a good dying.

What may go unnoticed in the intensely personal act of dying is the role of the community (familial, religious, medical, political, social) in providing safe and human community standards for how the whole community will respond to its own as they die. Ira R. Byock, M.D., has done extensive work in articulating and getting in place such standards in Missoula, Montana. His work has made Missoula the gold standard for community-wide quality-of-life dying.

In a humane context for dying, the transition from this life takes place step by step. The cares of the world are let go, there is a sense of completion in relationships with community, there is a sense of meaning about one's life, there is an experienced love of self and others, goodbyes are said, and one sets one's heart on what is ahead rather than on what was (Byock 2001). It can even be a time of grace:

> [Nature] is rich enough to provide reminders of the miracle of light
> in the wordless Magnificat of the late October leaves,
> simultaneously requiem and rainbow.
> Their very passage is praise.
> Death is ultimately too deep for tragedy.
> (Nugent 1994, in Simmons and Wilson 2001, 171)

THE PARTICULARITIES OF THE LIFE-COURSE

A review of books and articles in *Religion, Spirituality, and Aging: An Online Annotated Bibliography* (http://www.gracefulaging.org) shows little systematic attention to issues that identify the particular shapes of the last third of the life-course, for example, gender, the role of families, or economic issues. By contrast, research-based doctoral dissertations and Doctor of Ministry projects are quite precise in their analysis of audience or those with whom the author engages in ministry. This reaffirms an important insight: ministry that is deliberate and studied is always with real, gendered people in real and therefore particular circumstances at some specific and describable point in their life journeys.

Most—but not all—books and articles assume that the people written about are more or less "like us," with little attempt to spell out the precise characteristics of "like us." This is uncritical. Everyone is not like us. It is only when we make explicit our assumptions about gender and sexual orientation, socioeconomic status, cohort, ethnicity and family context, and place on the rural/urban continuum that our approach then becomes critical. "Uncritical" indicates that the discourse about aging, while it purports to refer to everyone, in fact begins with the gender, color, ethnic group, and class views of the speaker. In leaving these unspoken, their weight and interests remain hidden but not without effect. For example, denominationally published books about grandparenting might leave the life-situation of the writer unspoken and thus assume that all grandparents are leisure or companion grand-parents with the financial resources and personal freedom to relate in specific ways to their grandchildren (Simmons 1997). This would leave the life-situation of the grandfather or grandmother who is raising her incarcerated child's children unat-tended and even invisible.

A critical approach locates the writer's life-situation and in so doing acknowl-edges other voices and other interests. For example, it might lay bare ways the church fosters ageism or supports a status quo in which older adults are demeaned; or it might show the connection between poverty in older adulthood and the unequal pay of women in the working years, and so on. The schema proposed here attends to variables that help make our analysis both individual/personal and criti-cal/justice-seeking. These variables are gender and sexual orientation, socioeco-nomic status, cohort, ethnicity and family context, and the rural/urban continuum.

Gender is male or female. It is also important to take into account sexual orien-tation, because people with other than heterosexual orientation have specific life-courses, needs, and gifts. Socioeconomic status is an imprecise amalgam of money, education, access to power, etc. Cohort refers to persons born around the same time who acquired attitudes from shared life experience that have bearing on the way they live. For example, children of the Depression are expected to approach the task of saving for the last third of life differently from the boomers. Date of birth is often an easy starting point for getting at cohort.

Ethnicity points to race as well as to cultural particularities associated with country of origin. When ethnicity refers specifically to race it may be less of an issue in mapping a single congregation than in mapping the congregation's wider geo-graphic context. When ethnicity points to cultural particularities associated with country of origin it can be a powerful tool in understanding and responding to aging. Family context refers to the number and type of family members (real or fic-tive) who can help or who need help. For example, one couple might have two adult children with families nearby; another person might be a widow with an adult child with handicapping conditions who will always need care; yet another might be a person with an exceptionally supportive church "family."

The rural/urban continuum is an important reality because of the general avail-ability of services in urban areas that are not available in rural areas. Such services may be increasingly unavailable in older suburbs or leapfrog planned developments (planned communities that have gone far enough out into the rural area that there is green land between them and the next development, with all that this implies for public services, transportation, etc.). This is of particular importance for congrega-tions whose members are not clustered in one geographic area.

APPLYING THIS MATRIX

The first step in applying this matrix is gathering information and data. Initially this can be done anecdotally; later it should be done with more rigorous research. The task is to describe a population of persons in the last third of life. One can begin with the members of a congregation, identifying them in categories that allow for grouping and focused response. Eventually a whole geographic area can be included. A relatively easy way to begin is get as complete a list of names as possible of congregants in the last third of life, and enter those names on a grid that has predetermined fields.

Although this task seems daunting, my students and other professionals have done it with excellent results. Some began with congregants in the last third of life known personally; then they expanded the grid by asking other staff members for help; and finally they asked people from each of the stable periods to help locate others who had, fallen out of sight. Other students and colleagues began with the database used by the congregation for management and record keeping. Many of these are quite sophisticated and some can be customized. In some cases, the database was not available because of concerns about confidentiality.

	Gender and sexual orientation	Socio-economic status	Cohort or date of birth	Ethnicity and family context	Rural/urban
Retiring					
Ext. Middle Age					
1st Transition					
The New You					
2d Transition					
Rest of Living					
Dying					

Mapping on this grid usually shows considerable clustering, with some persons quite far outside congregational norms. For example, a congregation in a new retirement area may have a preponderance of people in extended middle age, and only a few at later stages. At times, analysis of congregational rolls shows people who might be known and seem "sort of old," but little is known of their life circumstances. At times, it is discovered that some of congregants who attended regularly just a year ago have now stopped coming to church—perhaps because of a transition that was not noticed. Precise data on socioeconomic status are sometimes difficult to get. Contributions might give some indication (although these are often kept confidential) or there may be other clues—such as a person declining to go on the annual symphony outing for the first time ever. Some judicious inquiry is not out of place, especially given evidence of greater poverty among older women than older men.

This grid is an excellent beginning to a precise, critical description of the congregation, and perhaps the neighborhood. The next step is to identify appropriate ministry options. These are of two types: ministry options where the agent is the individual in the last third of life, and ministry options where that person is the object of some ministry initiative. For example, the first type includes service done by someone in the last third of life; the second type looks to services done for a person in the last third of life. The tasks of the spiritual life suggested below are of the first type; that is, the persons who engage in these tasks are themselves in the last third of life.

TASKS OF THE SPIRITUAL LIFE

In *Soulful Aging: Ministry through the Stages of Adulthood* (Simmons and Wilson 2001), we suggested six pathways to spiritual growth in a Christian context. (Again, persons of other traditions are encouraged to identify pathways to spiritual growth consistent with their own beliefs.) At every stage of life, we must attend to community, prayer/worship, service, teaching, witness, and proclamation. Briefly, these tasks may be described as follows:

- Community (*koinonia* in Greek; in some churches, *Koinonia fellowship*). Deep in the human spirit is the need to be in a place of caring, love, service, and compassion, with others of like mind and heart. At its best, a community of faith responds to this need.
- Prayer/worship (*leitourgia* in Greek, from which we get the word *liturgy*). Prayer is our personal response to our awareness of God's presence; worship is our communal response. Prayer and worship arise from our need to praise, to communicate, to entreat.
- Service (*diakonia* in Greek, from which we get the word *deacon*). Service to others, or caring for others, takes many forms. Within the congregation, it might include, for example, initiatives by older adults to make the place of worship accessible, to promote health, to visit the sick. In outreach, it includes all the ways older adults engage with those now less privileged than ourselves outside the congregation.
- Teaching (*didache* in Greek, from which we get the word *didactic*). Within the Christian tradition, this refers first of all to the teaching of the apostles. More generally it is a response to our thirst to know, to make sense of, to understand our lives, our world, and our place in it. It is the attempt of a community of faith—and here specifically older congregants—to put into words God's gracious presence.
- Proclamation (*kerygma* in Greek). This refers to the word of God that brings glad tidings to the poor, proclaims freedom to captives, and announces a year of favor from the Lord (Luke 4:18-19, paraphrased). In face of the predictable losses—and possible gains—of age, proclamation needs first to listen to those further along on the journey of age.

- Witness (*martyria* in Greek, from which we get the word *martyr*). Witness to the love of God is a lifelong task; we learn by seeing as well as by hearing. It takes on a specific focus and urgency in the last third of life when negative popular perceptions of aging weigh heavily, even though personal experience of aging may be quite rich, diverse, and passionate.

These core religious tasks and realities, these pathways to spiritual growth, take on specific characteristics at each stage. Thus, community for someone in extended middle age is not the same as community for someone enduring the transition into frailty. Or prayer/worship for one who is dying is not the same as for one who is just beginning to build a new life-structure after the death of a spouse.

We can be much more specific about this, of course, using the variables identified above. Thus, for example, community for a man in extended middle age who has retired early with a very satisfactory financial package is not the same as community for a poor woman in a rural area who is without family, and who finds herself becoming daily less capable of taking care of herself. Or prayer/worship for a man just entering a nursing home is not the same as prayer/worship for a just-retired school administrator who is now deeply engaged in using her skills to advocate for change in public school funding. And so on.

APPLICATION TO MINISTRY WITH OLDER ADULTS

Direct applications of this model of analysis in the previous examples point to its worth. Other values of this model include the following five points.

First, it helps us pay attention to people we may have missed. When we have mapped our population using the 7 x 5 matrix, we begin to ask if our map is complete. A first step in checking on this might be a comparison of Census 2000 data for a congregation's geographical context with the same data for the congregants themselves. For example, one colleague reported that she found little symmetry between the census data for her congregation's census tract about households headed by single women and the data she had gathered anecdotally about her congregation. A more thorough analysis revealed that there were nine widows raising grandchildren who had been church members but were no longer attending worship. Older congregants were able to reach out to them in service and support them in community.

Second, it helps us pay attention to pathways to spiritual growth to which we might otherwise not attend. For example, if we look at each cell we have located people in, we may then ask what we are doing to respond to our and their need to teach—that is, to discover how to make sense of and understand their lives, their world, and their place in it. Similarly we may ask what we can do to help them foster community with those in the same place on the journey. The proverbial bus trip to Atlantic City for the seniors is not an adequate response to the need for community, for example, for poor women living alone. The same can be said of prayer and worship: personal and communal reaching out to God take on specific shapes depending on where and who we are. We have some responsibility to help all congregants with each of these tasks in the place where they are and where God meets them. This task becomes less arduous as we engage all the people of God—and in particular those in the last third of life—in ministry.

Third, this framework allows for precision in describing a population (a congregation or neighborhood, for example). It therefore promotes focused and by definition limited ministry initiatives. When it comes to our service to an older adult population, we need to match our gifts with their needs, and be modest and focused in what we do. For example, a congregation might realize, after mapping a neighborhood, that the most vulnerable and underserved population is men and women in Medicaid-funded adult homes in an area where more services are available than are used. This, then, might become a service project of a group of women and men in extended middle age. Or, another example, mapping may show a number of men in the congregation, fairly recently widowed and of high socio-economic status, who need a form of community with each other that has both teaching and prayer components.

Fourth, this framework allows us to compare and contrast the effectiveness of various ministry initiatives from one context to another. It has been most helpful to use this framework with a wide range of people engaged in ministry with older adults and to have participants compare results. Sometimes the results are surprising, as when we discovered that forty-two people working in seventeen states in a wide variety of churches put by far most of their resources into working with women newly widowed. At other times, the results are particularly satisfying when we discover new ways of ministry by comparing and contrasting the effectiveness of a variety of programs with which people have hands-on experience.

In the same line of thought, this framework might encourage us to look for ministry resources we might otherwise not notice. Users of *Religion, Spirituality, and Aging: An Online Annotated Bibliography* report that this framework is helpful in sorting through doctoral dissertations and Doctor of Ministry projects. Sometimes searches come up empty, and people discover that they have to create resources where none exist for their specific situation.

Lastly, this framework discourages a false we–they dichotomy between the able (we) and the frail (they) and encourages attentiveness to and preparation for every phase of our lives. As true as it is that people in each transition and stable period of the last third of life need to be looking ahead and preparing for the rest of their life-course, it is also true that we—the not-yet old—need to attend to God's call to the fullness of life for all our days.

NOTE

1. Each stable period and transition has been identified by several names: those used in Fisher's 1993 article, in Simmons and MacBean 2000, in Simmons and Wilson 2001, and in Fisher and Simmons, forthcoming.

BIBLIOGRAPHY

Byock, I. (2001). "Working Set of Landmarks and Developmental Taskwork." Online: http://www.dyingwell.com/landmarks.htm. Accessed February 13, 2001.

Fisher, J. (1993). "A Framework for Describing Developmental Change among Older Adults." *Adult Education Quarterly* 43/2: 76-89.

Fisher, J., and H. Simmons (forthcoming). *The Age Road.* San Francisco: Jossey-Bass.

Fowler, J. W. (1981). *Stages of Faith: The Psychology of Human Development and the Quest for Meaning.* New York: Harper & Row.

Gould, R. (1978). *Transformations: Growth and Change in Adult Life.* New York: Simon and Schuster.

Kimble, M. A., S. H. McFadden, J. W. Ellor, and J. J. Seeber, eds. (1995). *Aging, Spirituality, and Religion: A Handbook.* Vol. 1. Minneapolis: Fortress Press.

Levinson, D. (1978). *The Seasons of a Man's Life.* New York: Knopf.

Loevinger, J. (1976). *Ego Development: Conceptions and Theories.* With the assistance of A. Blasi. San Francisco: Jossey-Bass.

Nugent, C. (1994). *Mysticism, Death, and Dying.* Albany: State University of New York Press.

Simmons, H. C. (1997). "Grandparenting: A Bibliographic Review." *Journal of Religious Gerontology* 10/3: 73–79.

Simmons, H. C., and E. C. MacBean (2000). *Thriving after 55: Your Guide to Fully Living the Rest of Your Life.* Richmond, Va.: Prime.

Simmons, H. C., and J. Wilson (2001). *Soulful Aging: Ministry through the Stages of Adulthood.* Macon, Ga.: Smyth & Helwys.

Tennant, M., and P. Pogson (1995). *Learning and Change in the Adult Years: A Developmental Perspective.* San Francisco: Jossey-Bass.

Thibault, J. (1993). *A Deepening Love Affair: The Gift of God in Later Life.* Nashville: Upper Room.

Vogel, L. (1995). "Religious Development in Later Life." In Kimble et al., 74–86.

Part	AGING IN
Two	FAITH COMMUNITIES

Part One documents many possibilities for spiritual pilgrimage in later life. Faith communities traditionally have offered the necessary resources and support for such a pilgrimage. Today, however, many people are challenging this tradition and are seeking alternative outfitters for the journey toward meaning and purpose in later life. Indeed, some argue that faith communities have become impediments to spiritual growth by providing outdated "equipment" and indecipherable maps. The chapters in Part Two refute the notion that late-life spirituality can be self-invented in solitary pursuit. Rather, these chapters argue for the essential role of the faith community in nurturing spiritual growth through worship, study, and service. This is not to say, however, that these chapters approach the role of faith communities in older adults' lives uncritically. These communities cannot be complacent about the challenges and opportunities that lie ahead in a rapidly aging society.

Anne E. Streaty Wimberly's chapter focuses on the particularities of the black church and its traditional support for older persons and, at the same time, offers a generalizable model of congregational care. Grounded in a clearly articulated theology, this chapter claims that black congregations engage in "soul care" as an intentional way of sharing the spirit of Christ so that both individuals and communities are strengthened. Wimberly's functional approach to congregational care as involving "attending," "mediating," and "advocating" can be seen as a foundation for the chapters that follow in this section. Together, these chapters address issues related to worship and ritual, assistance to elders (often in the form of connecting them with other social services), and advocacy and consciousness-raising to address the well-being of older persons.

As documented by several chapters in volume 1 of this handbook and in a rapidly proliferating body of literature appearing since its publication, engaging in public and private religious activities appears to be related to the physical and mental health of older people. *V. DuWayne Battle* and *Ellen L. Idler* review recent findings about older adults' attendance at religious services and reflect upon some of the reasons behind the connection between worship and well-being. They discuss the rest and celebration experienced in Sabbath observances, the importance of various sensory, emotional, and intellectual components in worship, and the ways worship opens up possibilities for other important social connections for older people.

Dayle A. Friedman continues the discussion of communal opportunities for spiritual deepening by examining the meaning of ritual, especially for older persons. Rituals connect people to the past and, simultaneously, to the future but, unfortunately, few rituals specifically address the losses and gains of later life. Friedman suggests how several Jewish rituals can provide great blessing to aging persons as together in community they celebrate their transitions, grieve their losses, and look to the future with hope. She ends her chapter with specific suggestions about constructing rituals of transition that could be adapted for use in many types of faith communities.

Strengthened and supported by their experiences in worship and other communal celebrations of life's important transitions, members of faith communities may be challenged to search for ways they can articulate the values of their faith through service to others. One approach to this is to enter into "cooperative alliances" with various social ministry programs in the community. *Douglas Olson* and *Mark Holman* explain the opportunities and constraints such alliances offer to congregations that have made a commitment to improving the lives of older persons. The formation of these partnerships offers a rich array of possibilities for both congregations and agencies and in coming years will surely take on greater urgency as more people live longer.

Just as congregations and social ministry organizations may have to conduct an inventory of their values, resources, and the needs that must be met in their communities, so too do individuals benefit from a sustained examination of their efforts to live faithfully through the years. For some, the process of writing and discussing spiritual autobiographies in group settings can provide important insights about sources of meaning, release the burden of old conflicts, and create a closely knit, supportive community of people aging together. *Richard L. Morgan* offers concrete examples of the formation and function of spiritual autobiography groups in faith communities where people discover how their individual narratives connect to the central narratives of their faiths.

One of the potential outcomes of the spiritual autobiography process is a deeper commitment to service to others. In his chapter, *James J. Seeber* details the many opportunities for ministry by and for older persons in faith communities. Seeber notes that older adults currently represent a large percentage of persons who volunteer in the United States. With a large, healthy, and active cohort of elders anticipated in the near future, older people will have numerous outlets for service. Faith communities can provide the necessary structure and training for these volunteers. Seeber describes several established programs that specifically address the needs of older persons, and he also provides information about programs like Stephen Ministries that serve all ages.

Support for caregivers is a much-needed service that faith communities are in an excellent position to provide. *Marty Richards* offers a sensitive account of the needs of people who give and receive care. She notes the importance of proper training lest good-hearted persons fail to understand issues of dependence and independence, ways "helping" can harm, and complicated conflicts that almost inevitably arise within caregiving families. In addition to providing training and support for volunteer service with caregiving families, Richards argues that faith communities must educate persons of all ages about "bearing one another's burdens."

8

Congregational Care in the Lives of Black Older Adults

ANNE E. STREATY WIMBERLY

When the world has so often been willing to say only "no" to [black] people, the church has said "yes." For black people the church has been the one place where they have been able to experience unconditional positive regard. (W. C. Smith 1993, 14)

From the era of slavery forward, the black church has continued to be a dominant force in black family life. In a society where help and guidance were not forthcoming from other contexts, black Christian congregations have functioned as extended families and as environments of nurture and support for their members, including black older adults. Moreover, through their outreach these congregations have served as a standard of hope for the larger black community. Indeed, black people have held to the belief that, as hope bearers, the black church should extend its mission beyond spiritual matters to include liberating black people from economic, political, and physical suffering (Staples and Johnson 1993, 217).

Particularly with respect to older adults, black congregations and their pastors have been consistent providers of a range of supports from spiritual uplift, social and emotional help to economic assistance (Billingsley 1999; Frazier 1966; Lincoln and Mamiya 1990; Mays and Nicholson 1969; Taylor and Chatters 1986; Walls and Zarit 1991). It is true as well that black older adults themselves have been contributors to the supportive, nurturing spirit of the black church through their leadership, wisdom-sharing, and caregiving roles (Wimberly 1979, 1997).

Congregational care in the lives of black older adults is the black church's efforts to honor these persons' need to receive a broad spectrum of care and to respond to their desires to contribute to congregational life to the extent they are able. The importance of congregational care that takes into account this dual emphasis lies in the fact that the black church remains the primary, if not the only, voluntary association to which many black older adults belong. Black older adults are more likely than other age groups to be members and supporters of congregations. Statistics show that an estimated 78 percent of older black people belong to a church (Billingsley 1999, 93). For this reason, the black church remains an important resource and mediating structure between older black adults and resources in the public sphere.

The importance of intentional congregational care efforts also stems from the reality that, compared to the rest of the population, older black adults continue to experience higher rates of multiple chronic illnesses and are overall at greater risk for negative health outcomes than are their white counterparts (Smith and King-ton 1997). Black older adults are also poorer than white cohorts, which places them at greater risk for inadequate diets, increased exposure to crime, and lessened prospects for educational, work, and leisure pursuits (Jackson and Sellers 2001, 89). Community leaders are also sounding the alarm that death by suicide is rising at an alarming rate not simply among black youths aged fifteen to twenty-four but in the seventy-five-plus group. It is true that the incidence of suicide among black older adults remains lower than the rate for older white adults. However, data indicate that suicide among black Americans over age seventy-five increased more than 50 percent from 1980 to 1992 (Neighbors and Williams 2001, 107).

Disparities exist in the distribution of transportation benefits. And people of color, including older adults, are more likely than their white counterparts to be exposed to environmental health risks due to their close proximity to hazardous waste sites, deteriorating infrastructure, and dilapidated housing (Bullard and John-son 1997; Bullard 1993). Moreover, there are apparent "psychological and social psychological costs of life among black Americans—lack of perceived control, dis-couragement and discrimination that sap energy, and thwarted aspirations and expectations of a successful life" (Jackson and Sellers 2001, 89–90).

Compared to white older adults and younger age groups, black older adults are more apt to be unaware of agencies and available services, to be faced with barriers to accessing health and other services, and therefore, to be underutilizers of helping networks (Calsyn and Winter 1999, 10; Logan 1996, 195; Wimberly 2001, 133).

There is no mistaking, of course, that black older adults currently comprise a diverse population. Black older adults vary widely in characteristics and resources (Jackson and Sellers 2001, 82). Moreover, the situation for future cohorts of black older adults has the potential for greater promise than for the present one. But there is also a caution, as indicated in the following:

> Health care has improved significantly for middle-aged and older black adults, and con-secutive cohorts are better educated and better able to take advantage of available oppor-tunities. Yet, without extensive environmental intervention, it is likely that a significant proportion of older black adults of the mid-twenty-first century, born in the mid-to-late twentieth century, are at severe risk for impoverished conditions, and poor social, physi-cal, and psychological health in older age...correlated with racial and ethnic group mem-bership in the United States. (Jackson and Sellers 2001, 90)

All of the aforementioned realities contribute to the black church's deliberate con-tinuation of congregational care and willing participation in what has become a recognizable national faith and health movement. The potential impact of the efforts of the black church is also recognized. Currently, the black church is a major and multiple institutional presence, with approximately 190 distinctly black-oriented and black-controlled church bodies and networks, with more than seventy-five thousand black congregations (Dilulio 1998). These congregations are an important resource for addressing the well-being of present and future generations of older adults.

This chapter explores more fully the nature of black congregational care which contributes to the well-being of black older adults as well as the role of these persons as care receivers and contributors to their own and others' well-being. Specifically, the chapter (1) provides a sociotheological view of congregational care, (2) describes the nature of black congregational care along with best practices that illustrate this care, and (3) presents twenty-first-century challenges faced by black congregations in maintaining vital congregational care in the lives of black older adults.

A SOCIOTHEOLOGICAL VIEW OF CONGREGATIONAL CARE

Congregational care in the lives of black older adults is the black church's activity with and on behalf of older adults because of the honor these persons are due by virtue of their longevity and because of the commitment to uphold the biblical injunction to honor them. Congregational care is the black congregations' way of being people of God in solidarity with older adults and of providing a communal and spiritual sanctuary wherein older adults experience a sense of belonging, welcomed participation, and concern for their overall well-being.

As the locus of care, contemporary black congregations also build on the traditional community of black Christians whose orientation was toward a "we-consciousness" carried out under the power of God in partnership with Jesus Christ. This we-consciousness focuses attention on both the necessity and the ability of an entire congregation to function as an extended family network in the face of black people's oppression, everyday trials and tribulations, and spiritual woundedness. Congregational care encompasses compassionate regard that contributes to black older adults' ability to cope in the midst of life's challenges and to address their very real struggles for health and well-being. At its best, black congregational care in the lives of black older adults reflects black congregations' existence as honor-giving "soul communities" (Wimberly 1997) and black congregational care as "soul care."

Soul Communities and Soul Care

As "soul communities," black congregations express the soul or spirit of Christ by the communal spirit or life within which black older adults are a part. "Soul care" exemplifies the spirit of Christ in the manner in which it demonstrates Jesus' ministry of responding to the actual experiences of people and the conditions of their lives in ways that could lead to personal and communal well-being. Intrinsic to this depiction of black congregations and black congregational care is "a paramount sense of the sacredness of persons, of their being gifts from God that make them worthy of honor" (Wimberly 1997, 12, 38). Indeed, the ministry of care derives from black congregations' sensitivity to the reality that people who feel that no one cares are people who feel unimportant and of little value (Anderson 1997, 219). Thus, congregational care in the lives of black older adults involves not only a sense of the sacredness of these persons and their worthiness of honor but also the congregations' intentional commitment to an extended family-based theology wherein mutual respect and responsibility are practiced in relationship with them.

The kind of "soul care" taking place in black Christian faith communities happens because these communities intend for it to happen. Congregational care is the congregations' entry into committed activity. Commitment is the congregations' self-propelled responsibility which, in their focus on the lives of older adults, contributes to the life of the whole community (Wimberly 1997, 45).

Congregational Identity and Congregational Care

From a sociotheological perspective, commitment is the consequence of the congregations' adherence to a self-identity that informs their ministry direction. This self-identity is an ethnic-cultural one and a Christian one.

The black ethnic-cultural identity embraces images of community and the care of older adults originating in Africa. Temba Mafico, an African and an Old Testament scholar, highlights this heritage in his insightful article "Tapping Our Roots" (1997, 28–30). In the black African heritage, older adults in community are accorded high status. Older people are revered, cared for, and regarded as indispensable resources. The young are responsible for the care of older adults. Older adults are regarded as the "living library," or the keepers and tellers of the community's history. Moreover, the role of the older adults is to guide the young through the transitions from youth to adulthood. In short, in this caring tradition, older adults are honored and accorded respect in recognition of their longevity and contribution to community.

The African caring tradition was not lost in the forced movement of black people to the American continent during the era of slavery. The tradition of respect for the elders among the slaves was a matter of social code inherited from Africa. On this basis, the black church has a tradition which emphasizes the importance of older adults in the life of the church; and the black pastor has a rich tradition on which to lead congregational care in the lives of black older adults (Wimberly 1979).

Admittedly, there is concern in black church and community life today that the images and the value system undergirding them from the black ethnic cultural heritage are being lost (Billingsley 1992, 17, 377; Martin and Martin 1978, 95–96). However, Billingsley asserts that the black family continues to reflect "the most basic values, hope, and aspirations of the descendants of African people in America" (1992, 17). And, the heritage of care and support offered black older adults through black congregations is encapsulated in Billingsley's reminder that, in this regard, "the black church has a track record" (1992, 377).

The black church's commitment to congregational care in the lives of older adults is guided by the claim of Christian identity. Care that is guided by this identity not only continues the long cultural history of honoring older adults but also embraces the biblical norm of honoring the older generation and of ensuring Jesus' love ethic of mutual care and shared resources among elders within an extended family framework. The biblical norm means acting with integrity on Jesus' words, "Just as you did it to one of the least of these who are members of my family, you did it to me" (Matt. 25:40).

THE NATURE OF CONGREGATIONAL CARE

Congregational care in the lives of black older adults functions on the premise of the black church "that God desires health and wholeness for all people, that all human life is made in God's image and is a precious and valuable gift, and that all God's people yearn for love, honor, respect, and care" (Wimberly 2001). Black congregations recognize that, like others, black older adults seek an ongoing sense of well-being. The character of the well-being they want and need is multidimensional, interrelated, and connects with understandings of well-being typically described in gerontological and pastoral care literature (Clinebell 1997; Moberg 1990, 13–16). Framed from the perspective of older adults, a summary of well-being is as follows:

Spiritual well-being is identified by older adults' affirmation of life through connectedness with an affirming, life-giving, meaning-generating force beyond the self. Moreover, it embraces beliefs, values, meanings, and commitments which make possible older adults' sojourn in life with purpose in the midst of hardship and loss. Spiritual well-being guides persons' choices, quality of relationships, and actions they take in every other aspect of well-being.

Relational well-being arises from older adults' positive linkages with their past, with other people, and with the environment; their mutual participation in social environments such as family, friends, religious, and community networks that affirm their value and belonging as human beings; and, their connectedness with life-sustaining resources in community.

Physical well-being derives from older adults' actual wellness of body, effectiveness of functioning, and attention to healthy living that contributes to the wellness of self and others.

Mental well-being is older adults' self-affirmation and capacity to deal with changes and losses occurring on life's journey. It is their uses of creative, problem-solving ability and access to opportunities that assist them in confronting life issues for the good of the self and others.

Economic and vocational well-being comes from older adults' access to sufficient economic resources and support as well as their ability to care for themselves and others for whom they are responsible, materially; and their sense of life accomplishment and fulfillment of God's purposes that encompasses more than economic and material sufficiency.

Leisure well-being happens as a consequence of older adults' experiences of revitalizing recreation that is supported by readily available, accessible, and safe leisure facilities and options.

Environmental well-being occurs through older adults' existence in environmentally safe conditions. It also happens through older adults' ongoing intentional care for all of God's creation including the natural environment and the overall health of our society.

The importance of congregational care in the lives of black older adults that focuses on these dimensions of well-being derives from the earlier mentioned realities that black older adults experience critical deficits in health and well-being. And it is clear that black congregations are addressing these dimensions. Data from the Interdenominational Theological Center/Faith Factor Project 2000 show that nearly 60 percent of black churches across the denominations (Baptist, Church of God in Christ, African Methodist Episcopal, Christian Methodist Episcopal, African Methodist Episcopal Zion, United Methodist, and Black Presbyterian) had senior citizen programs of some kind other than emergency or affordable housing for seniors. Moreover, 36 percent of black churches across these denominations provide emergency or affordable housing (Rasor and Dash 2000, 46).

FUNCTIONS OF CONGREGATIONAL CARE

Congregational care in the lives of black older adults embraces at least three primary dimensions: attending, mediating, and advocating functions.

Attending

Attending is a form of black congregational care that focuses on the members' intentional presence and participation with black older adults in ways that assist these persons' well-being and that honor their desire to contribute to their own and others' well-being. Through the attending function of congregational care, black congregations pay particular notice to older adults that goes beyond observing them at a distance. Attending consists of the members' being with older adults "up close" within and beyond the physical location of the church. Attending is the black congregations' activity of showing thoughtful caring of older adults for the sake of these persons' well-being and, ultimately, the well-being of the whole community. It is providing options for older adults that respond to these persons' interests and needs to be contributors to congregational life to the extent that they are able.

Through these efforts black congregations seek to model the ministry of Jesus Christ, who gave consistent and responsive attention to the experiences and conditions of people's lives in need of care and healing. By their efforts to emulate the attending ministry of Jesus Christ, black congregations express Christ's self-giving love that affirms older adults' valued identity and presence in community. Black congregations carry out the attending function of congregational care in the lives of black older adults most specifically through worship, small groups, and home visits.

Attending through Black Congregational Worship. Black adults in general (Taylor 1988) and older black adults in particular (Taylor 1986; Taylor and Chatters 1991) have tended to be frequent church attendees. Consequently, black worship exists as an important place and experience of congregational care which attends principally to older adults' spiritual and relational well-being but which may also inform older adults' consideration of other aspects of their well-being. The activities of worship are central means by which black older adults join with others to enter the presence of God with their joys and troubles, to praise God, and to obtain guidance. Black worship is an attending environment which is typically characterized by shared ritual acts, expressive style, and socially sanctioned release of deep emotion which are revered by black older adults. Prayer, music, testimony, and sermons are principal experiences through which the attending function of black worship nurtures black older adults' spiritual vitality and relational well-being (Wimberly 1997, 130).

In black congregations, prayer gives fervent and most often extemporaneous attention to the very real situations of joy, sadness, hope, and struggle of persons within and beyond congregational bounds. Offered by a pastor, but in some cases by older adults, prayer is impassioned conversation with God that attends to individual and communal joys and concerns and that often includes the naming of persons for whom special attention is required. In actuality, prayer is participatory congregational care in the pew or at the altar that attends to black older adults' desires to be either a quiet contemplative presence, or an active prayer giver, or an engaged participant who "joins in" by punctuating prayers given by others with "Yes, Lord." These ways in which older adults are free to participate in congregational prayer constitute congregational care that provides spiritual nurture and a communal context of support.

Worship in the black church also attends to black older adults' spiritual and relational well-being through making possible their participation with others in singing and listening to African American spirituals, hymns, anthems, and gospel music. Moreover, music in black worship has historically had therapeutic value because of its ability to help people confront their struggles and to move toward healing (Wimberly 1997, 130; 2001, 130). Music provides cultural congregational care that chronicles stories of delight, God's activity in life's fullness and loss, and approaches to living and responding to life's circumstances in ways with which black older adults readily identify (Wimberly 1997, 130). Moreover, music is an experience of black worship into which older adults may freely enter softly, with or without bodily movement, or ecstatically "as the spirit moves."

Testimonies also are a historic aspect of black worship, through which congregations attend to older adults' and others' desires to tell about recent experiences and to express faith in God's presence and activity along life's journey. Testimonies are attending opportunities for therapeutic and salvific storytelling and story-listening through which affirmation, encouragement, catharsis, and healing occur (Williams 1984, 163; Wimberly 2001).

Worship experiences include sermons as part of the ministry of attending in black congregational care. At its best, the sermonic event, along with every aspect of worship, attends to older adults' spiritual well-being by providing spiritual uplift, direction in confronting issues faced in everyday life, and sustenance and strength for the unique everyday circumstances they face. Preaching serves an attending function by giving focused attention to the care and concern for persons in crisis. Historically, through the sermon, "the black pastor has often brought preaching resources to bear upon the lives of persons in difficulty so that they might choose healthy crisis-coping skills" (Wimberly 1979, 56–57). As an attending function, then, the sermon "speaks" in ways that concretize the significance and applicability of God's word in the situations of people's lives, including in the lives of older adults.

Throughout the black worship experience, older adults are contributors not simply by virtue of the prayers they offer, but in their roles as choir members, ushers, stewards during the rites of Holy Communion and baptism, storytellers in children's sermons, caregivers in the nursery, and congregational helpers through participation on "mothers' boards." In these ways, congregational care attends to older adults' gifts to the life of the worshiping congregation.

In short, congregational care that happens in worship through prayer, music, testimony, sermons, and other means affirms the black church as an important attending environment which nurtures black older adults' well-being. The attending function of congregational care in worship reveals the importance of worship as a cultural gathering place, a context of unity, and an environment where black older adults affirm with others commonly held beliefs and attitudes and contribute to communal vitality.

Attending through Congregational Care in Group Contexts. The attending function of congregational care in the lives of black older adults happens through black congregations' provision of a variety of groups beyond the context of worship in which older adults both lead and participate. In this regard, the attending function of congregational care continues to address the mutuality of attending that takes into consideration the importance of black older adults as contributors to congregational life as well as receivers of care, guidance, and support from congregations. Consequently, activities in group environments add to the form of attending that is best described as mutual attending. This aspect of congregational care takes place principally in church-school classes, Bible and other types of study groups, prayer meetings, men's and women's auxiliaries, and social clubs. But this kind of congregational care also occurs in other group settings, such as intergenerational family-night suppers and older-adult recognition events. Black adults who are aged sixty and older routinely serve as leaders in church-school classes for younger age groups, peers, and intergenerational groups. In addition, congregational care that attends to these gifts of older adults incorporates these persons in mentoring relationships with children and youth. Older adults share their own stories with children and youth, listen and respond to the experiences of the young, as well as provide guidance and impart to the young unique skills acquired over a lifetime. An example of this form of attending is the Beulah Grove Baptist Church Senior Ministry in Augusta, Georgia. Opportunities for this and other kinds of service attend not only to the interests, abilities, and availability of older adults to serve but also to black congregations' welcoming these gifts of older persons.

In addition to attending to black older adults' contributive gifts, church-school classes—prayer and Bible study groups in particular—allow for participative attending. Through this sort of attending, older adults engage in experiences that respond to their quest to deepen their scriptural knowledge and to find scriptural guides to perplexing situations. In these groups, black older adults ponder meanings of Bible texts and potential applications of scripture to their past and present experiences in family, church, and community as well as to their unique sojourn as black people in this society. As part of participative attending, black older adults also engage in storytelling and story-listening that opens the way for them to share the state of their lives and, for example, to

- affirm, as an elder said, that "God didn't bring me this far to leave me"; and
- disclose anxiety about strength sufficient from God to carry on after the death of a spouse, to raise grandchildren amidst dire resources, to worry over the children's parents, or to face waning health.

Participative attending also occurs in special group activities that offer black older adult participants spiritual nurture and relational support. For example, this attending function of congregational care in Greater Christ Baptist Church in Detroit, Michigan, is carried out through the "Fifty and Counting Club." This club recognizes on special occasions and during church worship couples who have been married for fifty or more years. The church affirms these couples' longevity in life and commitment in marriage as well as identifies them a model of the virtue of commitment (Perkins 1999, 65–66). Moreover, special kinds of group activities are occasions for black older adults to consider ways of confronting life issues, to give attention to healthy living, to engage in enriching leisure activity, and to reflect on the meaning of life. The Jewels Club of Ben Hill United Methodist Church in Atlanta, Georgia, is an example of this multidimensional kind of participative attending. The club attends to every aspect of the members' well-being at its monthly meetings in the church location and at retreats and special forums in differing local and distant locales.

Attending through Congregational Care in Older Adults' Living Environments. The inability of frail older adults to participate in church activities requires congregations to provide attentive care for these adults' living environments. Intentionality in providing this care is particularly needed because of the potential for older adults to be "forgotten" as their church attendance wanes. However, there is evidence that congregational care does occur in the lives of black frail older adults. Black congregations carry out the attending function through the presence of pastors and members in older adults' everyday living environments, particularly in situations of illness, home-boundedness, institutionalization, crisis, grief, and loss (Gibson and Jackson 1987; Krause and Van Tran 1989; McGadney 1995; J. M. Smith 1993; Taylor and Chatters 1986; Walls and Zarit 1991). Attending happens

- when church members visit and call ill, frail, and homebound older adults and their caregivers, and are intentional in visits to institutionalized older adults,
- when prayers and Holy Communion are offered,
- when compassionate listening occurs and spiritual advice and encouragement are given, and
- when other forms of support are given, such as provision of meals and financial assistance.

It is important to note that these forms of attending in congregational care in the lives of older adults actually developed, in part, because of the unavailability of services in the public sphere for black people. As a result, there arose both the expectation and the willingness of black congregations to be present with older adults. Moreover, it is possible that attending to homebound older adults has taken place not only to maintain them for longer periods of time in their own homes but also to strengthen the older adults' and the caregivers' self-esteem and ability to continue on (Krause and Van Tran 1989).

Mediating

Mediating activities comprise a second key function of congregational care in the lives of black older adults. Mediating activities constitute a form of guidance that is designed to provide concrete means of helping a person or persons move through unfamiliar, confusing, or difficult circumstances, "often in which some kind of decision making or action is involved, as in solving family problems or making life decisions" (Mitchell 1990, 486). This aspect of congregational care in the lives of black older adults builds on the unique role of the black church as a resource for members and nonmembers and as a pastoral facilitator of God's intention for persons' well-being. Moreover, black congregations are mediating structures that respond to the reticence of black older adults to access services in the public sphere.

This mediating function is the black church's outreach to members and nonmembers and is characterized by the pastor of Agape Christian Church in Denver, Colorado, "as essential to the Christian faith as [the] worship services, maybe even more important" (Billingsley 1999, 121). Furthermore, black churches identify the mediating function in mission statements such as the one adopted by Olivet Institutional Baptist Church in Cleveland, Ohio, which establishes the church's role as a spiritual and social resource for the community (Billingsley 1999, 157–58). In another instance, Beulah Grove Baptist Church in Augusta, Georgia, refers to itself as "a church without walls" whose mission is to "seek, save, shape, support, and serve [people] from the cradle to the grave."

Congregational care that incorporates mediating actions includes black church sponsorship or co-sponsorship of resources or forums needed by black older adults to assist them in addressing important issues. Mediating actions also entail black congregations' intentionally linking black older adults with resources in the larger social sphere, including mental health and medical services and economic support services. These actions connect black older adults "to agencies that can assist them in the areas of family crises; family and community violence; crime; and hazardous environment clean-ups, fix-ups, and removals" (Wimberly 2001, 144).

The use of the term "guiding" is regarded as a useful corollary to the mediating function of congregational care in the lives of black older adults, even though guiding has received criticism because of the directive and "one up" connotation it carries (Mitchell 1990, 486). However, the mediating function of congregational care in the lives of black older adults is not assumed to be too directive. Rather, because of the historical situation of deficiencies in housing, medical, and social-service provision for black older adults and existing barriers to receiving help, these older adults have tended to rely on the black church, black pastors and members, to give forthright assistance, information, advice, and encouragement.

Evidence of the black church's attention to emergency and affordable housing for black older adults was cited earlier in this chapter (Rasor and Dash 2000, 46). Specific models of mediating actions focused on housing appear in two volumes by Billingsley (1992, 1999). Billingsley identifies model housing initiatives for black older adults offered by four Baptist churches and one African Methodist Episcopal Church, all of which are churches with memberships between 1,100 and 10,000. These churches included Allen African Methodist Episcopal Church, Queens, New York (1992); Concord Baptist Church, Brooklyn, New York; Abyssinian Baptist Church, Harlem, New York; Second Baptist Church, Los Angeles, California; and Allen Temple Baptist Church, Oakland, California (1999). It is helpful to note again, however, that the study conducted by Rasor and Dash actually showed that housing programs mediated by black churches are found across the denominational spectrum (2000, 46).

Health care is another mediating activity of congregational care in the lives of black older adults. A model program focused on health care is provided by Beulah Grove Baptist Church, Augusta, Georgia. Through its Senior Ministry, Beulah Grove partners with University Hospital in providing affordable health screening, medical checkups, and a variety of health-related classes to a black clientele, 85 percent of whom are persons aged sixty and older. In this instance as well as in other cases identified by Billingsley (1992, 1999), black congregations function as on-site mediators not simply of health services, but of a wide range of benefits including hot meals and food distribution; educational, counseling, employment, transportation, arts and crafts, and recreational services. Through transportation services, congregations link black older adults to these services in the wider community. Moreover, the congregations extend a variety of supports to homebound older adults and nursing-home residents such as those given by Valley Queen Baptist Church in Marks, Mississippi, and Allen African Methodist Episcopal Church in Jamaica, Queens, New York (Billingsley 1992, 362, 371).

Research documents the black church's provision of financial resources to needy individuals and families, including older adults. And, in recognition of the increasing numbers of grandparents raising grandchildren, the predominantly black Interdenominational Theological Center in Atlanta, Georgia, formed the Ecumenical Families Alive Project that mediates the preparation of volunteers in local congregations and the seminary community to provide telephone reassurance, friendly visits, and information forums for this increasing population.

It must be added that black older adults themselves have contributed to the mediating function on their own behalf and on behalf of others. Black older adults are volunteers in the aforementioned settings and in a variety of other service capacities. For example, older adults of Dodd-Sterling United Methodist Church in Atlanta, Georgia, run the church's "Food Pantry and Clothes Closet" as a service to indigent persons. Older adults in Beulah Grove Baptist Church in Augusta, Georgia, carry out a card and craft ministry which is utilized by members and non-members. In this ministry older adults create original greeting cards that they send to sick and shut-in members and handmade crafts that are given as gifts to homebound persons and members who celebrate special occasions. As indicated earlier, black older adults also serve as mentors and foster grandparents because they want to be useful, to contribute to the next generation, and to feel valued because of their contributions. Consequently, the mediating function of congregational care in the lives of older black adults entails the creation of opportunities for these persons to be caring agents.

Advocating

Advocacy is part of black congregational care that is designed to make positive changes in existing situations affecting the well-being of black older adults. The need for advocacy stems from the fact that older black adults constitute a marginalized group whose well-being has not received full attention in the public sphere and whose circumstances require greater attention in congregations. Far too many older black adults are unfamiliar with their entitlements, have limited know-how in ways of dealing with bureaucracies, and are unaware of the aging network and the range of services provided by it. Even though black older adults are typically considered to be survivors and effective life copers, they require support and enabling practices that contribute to their well-being (Wimberly and Wimberly 1995, 161).

Through the advocating function of congregational care, black congregations speak out on behalf of the formation of needed responses to the situations of black older adults. The advocating function includes mobilizing actions by black congregations on behalf of black older adults that result in addressing deficits in resources, creating needed resources where they do not exist, and increasing access to existing and new resources. This function of congregational care seeks to arouse black older adults' and black congregations' awareness of the various programs and benefits for elderly members and nonmembers and of how to access information and referral systems. Through this function, congregations make known legislation involving the elderly population and seek ways of participating in legislative action. Congregations also engage in consciousness-raising that supplants wellness-negating stereotypical images of aging and older adults with wellness-producing realities (Wimberly and Wimberly 1995, 172). In addition, congregational care that includes the advocating function recognizes the importance of teaching black older adults advocacy skills and "appropriately assertive behaviors" so that they can advocate for themselves (Goodman and Waters n.d., 1). Goodman and Waters propose that advocacy preparation in general may include coaching or role playing to enable older adults and caregivers to ask for what they need from health-care providers, public and private bureaucracies, or other organizations. Assertiveness training may assist older adults in developing needed skills. And adequate advocacy preparation reminds and enables groups of older adults to use community organizing skills and to seek political responses to critical needs affecting them (Goodman and Waters n.d., 3). It is possible that future generations of black older adults may be more aware of helping networks and how to navigate bureaucratic structures and develop strategies to effect changes that benefit their well-being. But congregations will need to remain alert to the circumstances and need of black older adults as means of gauging how and to what extent the advocacy function of congregational care must be activated.

There are scant data on advocacy preparation activities in black congregations. One publicized program has occurred at the Gethsemane African Methodist Episcopal Church in Charlotte, North Carolina, under the sponsorship of the Charlotte Mecklenburg Council on Aging. This program was also an intergenerational service-learning project of the University of North Carolina Charlotte (UNC Charlotte 1999, 3). Informal advocacy preparation and activity also take place through the participation of black older adults in advisory boards of organizations that are providing services to older adults, such as the Ecumenical Families Alive Project of Interdenominational Theological Center and the Beulah Grove Baptist Church Health Center in Augusta, Georgia. Moreover, black older adults participate on United Methodist and Presbyterian denominational older adult ministry boards, which accord them opportunity to advocate for church programs which may be beneficial to black older adults.

TWENTY-FIRST CENTURY CHALLENGES TO CONGREGATIONAL CARE IN THE LIVES OF BLACK OLDER ADULTS

Black congregations will continue to be challenged to incorporate attending, mediating, and advocating functions of congregational care that affects positively the well-being of black older adults. This challenge is essentially one of assuring a sustaining function in congregational care. There need to be intentional means by which congregations ensure the ongoing and maximum conduct of attending, mediating, and advocating functions of congregational care in the lives of black older adults (Wimberly 2001, 145). In addition to this, however, three specific challenges must be mentioned: (1) giving attention to generational conflict that exists with regard to black worship, (2) responding to increasing numbers of grandparents raising grandchildren/great-grandchildren as well as older adults caring for other kin of varying ages, and (3) acting with and on behalf of older adults in indigenous black African congregations and communities.

Generational Conflict

Much conflict in black congregations centers around musical preferences and styles of worship that older adults value in contrast to younger generations. Particularly in mainline black Baptist, Methodist, and Presbyterian congregations, there are black older adults who have grown accustomed to African American spirituals, hymns, and anthems. These persons tend to be alienated by the substitution of praise songs, contemporary gospel music, and ecstatic worship styles which are revered by younger church attendees. To attract and keep younger members, black church leaders often feel compelled to incorporate contemporary forms of worship. Attention will need to be given to this dilemma to assure that worship in the black church is a satisfying experience and makes a positive contribution to the spiritual well-being of all, including older adults. Helpful directions include the congregations' formation of cross-generational worship committees who discuss and have input in the design of worship as well as the congregations' willingness to incorporate a broad spectrum of musical genres and worship styles.

Grandparents Raising Grandchildren

Increasing numbers of older adults in or near retirement are caring for and raising their grandchildren as the result of family issues such as the parents' illness, divorce, death, or desertion; child abuse or neglect; incarceration; unemployment; poverty; substance abuse; teen pregnancy; or family violence (Greenberg 2000; Peterson 2001). From 1980 to 1990 there was a 44 percent increase in the number of children being reared by grandparents (Saluter 1991). Census Bureau data indicate that from 1994 to 1999 the number of children under age eighteen living in grandparent-headed households rose from 3.3 million to 5.5 million. According to 1998 statistics, 1.4 million or 35.5 percent of the 4 million children living in grandparent-headed households were black (Bryson and Casper 1999, 5; Peterson 2001).

Grandparent caregivers are prone to psychological and emotional strain and to neglect both their physical and emotional health (Greenberg 2000). These caregivers are 60 percent more likely to live in poverty compared to grandparents who are not raising grandchildren; and black grandchildren in their grandparents' care are more likely than their white counterparts to be uninsured and receiving public assistance (Casper and Bryson 1998, 13). Grandparent caregivers also experience a host of other issues related to custody, education, emotional trauma, and health care of their grandchildren, and these caregivers tend to be unaware of resources available to them (Casper and Bryson 1998). At the same time, the grandparents typically proceed with committed action that epitomizes an intercessory hope or their will to stand with and for their grandchildren "in the parents' stead in order to make possible for their grandchildren a worthwhile present and future life" (Wimberly 2000, 26). The circumstance of grandparent-maintained households demands a congregation's mutual intercession with them in the form of attending, mediating, and advocating actions.

Older Adults in Indigenous Black African Congregations and Communities

The United States has become the home of numbers of African-origin immigrant groups. The proportion of the black population that was foreign-born increased from 3 percent to 5 percent between 1980 and 1998 (Fix and Passel 1998), with most immigrants coming from Caribbean countries. However, the immigrant groups also include an appreciable number from countries across the African continent, and it is projected that the flow of immigrants from Africa may expand in the future as refugees and others find their way to the United States (Fix and Passel 1998; Hunter 2001). In addition to "reluctant immigrants" or refugees who have fled brutality and political tension and who typically become legal permanent residents, African-origin immigrant groups include legal permanent residents and other immigrants, including students, businesspeople on temporary visas, and small numbers of undocumented immigrants. These immigrants also tend to have large extended families that depend on them for assistance and sustenance (Fix and Passel 1998).

While African immigration to the United States tends to be ignored in immigration studies literature (Okome 1999), there is increasing recognition in local communities of the presence of both recent immigrants and foreign-born black people whose home in the United States is long-standing. It is also known that foreign-born black people who are Christian either become part of established black churches or form indigenous churches or fellowships. The presence of Ghanaian, Sudanese, Kenyan, and Ethiopian Christian churches in Atlanta, Georgia, and the African Christian Fellowship in Knoxville, Tennessee, are evidence of the increasing formation of indigenous churches.

Whether in established black churches or in indigenous churches, African-origin residents have concerns for the aging persons who are with them and ones who remain in their countries of origin. For families with older persons who are present in the United States, there is the need for congregations to become aware of the family's and elders' specific circumstances, to apprise them of appropriate resources, and to help them negotiate systems of care, including in instances where language difference is a factor. Moreover, there is the need for congregational care that stresses the necessity of listening to the desires and concerns of older adults, the development of visitation skills, and the maintenance of contact with elders who continue to reside outside U.S. bounds (Kufarimai 2001). In light of the multicultural nature of African-origin residents in the United States, it is imperative that black churches develop pan-African perspectives to congregational care in the lives of older adults and that their advocacy efforts direct attention to culturally sensitive responses by service providers in the public sphere.

CONCLUSION

The role of the black church in the lives of black older adults continues to be important because it is the principal voluntary association to which so many of these persons belong. Moreover, the black church is a strategic mediating structure between older adults and public resources. The efforts of the black church are directed toward assuring the well-being of black older adults and these persons' contribution to their own and others' well-being. Specifically, congregational care is the intentional and committed activity of black congregations that recognizes the sacredness of the lives of older adults and their worthiness of honor. And congregational care is activity based on the premise that all God's people yearn for love, honor, respect, and care and seek an ongoing sense of spiritual, relational, physical, mental, economic, recreational, and environmental well-being.

The black church carries out congregational care through attending, mediating, and advocating functions. Through the attending function of congregational care, the black church assures up-close attentive care of black older adults. This kind of care includes experiences in church worship and group contexts in the church and everyday living environment whereby black older adults receive relational support, nurture, care, and opportunities to share their gifts and expertise.

Black congregations help black older adults confront life changes and challenging circumstances through the mediating function of congregational care that includes linking older adults with needed services in the public sphere, offering needed resources, and providing forthright assistance, information, advice, and encouragement.

The advocating function of black congregational care responds to the imperative need to redress deficits in and limited access to the provision of services to black older adults. Black congregations thereby serve as mobilizing forces by raising the consciousness of black older adults and their families about entitlements and available programs and how to access them, by pushing for the development of needed resources, and by teaching older adults advocacy skills.

These functions of congregational care must continue. But their vitality will depend on the black church's recognition of and response to emerging challenges. Congregational care will need to address such issues as generational conflict within congregations, care for rising numbers of grandparent-headed households, and responsiveness to concerns for older adults in indigenous black African congregations and communities.

BIBLIOGRAPHY

Anderson, R. S. (1997). *The Soul of Ministry: Forming Leaders for God's People*. Louisville: Westminster John Knox.

Beulah Grove Baptist Church (May 20, 2001). "A Church without Walls." Augusta, Ga.: Beulah Grove Baptist Church.

Billingsley, A. (1999). *Mighty like a River: The Black Church and Social Reform*. New York: Oxford University Press.

——— (1992). *Climbing Jacob's Ladder: The Enduring Legacy of African-American Families*. New York: Simon and Schuster.

Braithwaite, R. L., and S. E. Taylor, eds. (2001). *Health Issues in the Black Community*. San Francisco: Jossey-Bass.

Bryson, K., and L. Casper (1999). " Nearly 5.5 Million Children Live with Grandparents, Census Bureau Reports." U.S. Department of Commerce News, Economics, and Statistics Administration. http://www.census.gov/Press-Release/www/1999/cb99-115.html.

Bullard, R. D., ed. (1993). *Confronting Environmental Racism: Voices from the Grassroots*. Boston: South End.

Bullard, R. D., and G. S. Johnson, eds. (1997). *Just Transportation: Dismantling Race and Class Barriers to Mobility*. Stony Creek, Conn.: New Society.

Calsyn, R. J., and J. P. Winter (1999). "Predicting Older Adults' Knowledge of Services." *Journal of Social Services Research* 25/4: 1–14.

Casper, L. M., and K. R. Bryson (1998). "Co-Resident Grandparents and Their Grandchildren: Grandparent Maintained Families." Population Division Working Paper #26. Washington, D.C.: Population Division, U.S. Bureau of the Census.

Clinebell, H. (1997). *Anchoring Your Well-being: A Guide for Congregational Leaders*. Nashville: Upper Room.

Dilulio, J. J., Jr. (1998). "Living Faith: The Black Church Outreach Tradition." In *The Jeremiah Project: An Initiative of the Center for Civic Innovation*, Report N#98-3:1-10. Online: http://www.manhattan-institute.org/html/jpr-98-3.htm.

Fix, M., and J. S. Passel (1998). "Immigration and Immigrants: Setting the Record Straight." The Urban Institute. http://www.urban.org/pubs/immig/immig.htm.

Frazier, E. F. (1966). *The Negro Church in America*. New York: Schocken.

Gibson, R. C., and J. S. Jackson (1987). "The Health, Physical Functioning and Informal Supports of the Black Elderly." *The Milbank Quarterly* 65 (Supplement 2): 421–53.

Goodman, J., and E. Waters (n.d.). "Advocating on Behalf of Older Adults." Advocacy Paper #1: Presidential Theme Paper. American Counseling Association. Online: http://www.counseling.org/conference/advocacy11.htm.

Greenberg, S. (May 19, 2000). "Grandparents Raising Grandchildren." Washington, D.C.: Administration on Aging. Online: http://www.aoa.gov/factsheets/grandparents.html.

Hunter, J. F. (2001). "Africans Bring Unique Appreciation of Freedom." *Knoxville News*. Online: http://www.knoxnews.com/news/diversity/14848.shtml.

Hunter, R. J. (1990). *Dictionary of Pastoral Care and Counseling*. Nashville: Abingdon.

Jackson, J. S., and S. L. Sellers (2001). "Health and the Elderly." In Braithwaite and Taylor, 81–96.

Jones, R. L., ed. (1989). *Black American Adult Development*. Berkeley, Calif.: Cobb and Henry.

Kimble, M. A., S. H. McFadden, J. W. Ellor, and J. J. Seeber, eds. (1995). *Aging, Spirituality, and Religion: A Handbook*. Vol. 1. Minneapolis: Fortress Press.

Kovar, M. G. (1983). "Health Assessment." In Moddox, 434–43.

Krause, N., and T. Van Tran (1989). "Stress and Religious Involvement among Older Blacks." *Journal of Gerontology* 44/1: S4–S13.

Kufarimai, T. (May 28, 2001) "Congregational Care of Older Adult Family Members of Immigrant African Families." An interview conducted in Atlanta, Georgia.

Lincoln, C. E., and L. H. Mamiya (1990). *The Black Church in the African American Experience*. Durham, N.C.: Duke University Press.

Logan, S. L. (1996). "Epilogue: Understanding Help-Seeking Behavior and Empowerment Issues for Black Families." In Logan, 193–206.

———, ed. (1996). *The Black Family: Strengths, Self-Help, and Positive Change*. Boulder, Colo.: Westview.

Mafico, T. L. J. (1997). "Tapping Our Roots: African and Biblical Teachings about Elders." In Wimberly, 19–33.

Martin, E. P., and J. M. Martin (1978). *The Black Extended Family*. Chicago: University of Chicago Press.

Martin, L. G., and B. J. Soldo, eds. (1997). *Racial and Ethnic Differences in the Health of Older Americans*. Washington, D.C.: National Academy Press.

Mays, B., and J. Nicholson (1969). *The Negro's Church*. New York: Russell and Russell.

McGadney, B. F. (spring 1995). "Family and Church Support among African American Family Caregivers and Frail Elders." *African American Research Perspectives*. Ann Arbor: University of Michigan. Online: http://rcgd.isr.umich.edu/prba/perspectives/spring1995/bmcgadney.pdf.

Mitchell, K. R. (1990). "Pastoral Guidance." In Hunter, 486–87.

Moberg, D. O. (1990). "Spiritual Maturity and Wholeness in the Later Years." In Seeber, 5–24.

Moddox, G. L, ed. (1983). *The Encyclopedia of Aging*. New York: Springer.

Neighbors, H. W., and D. R. Williams (2001). "The Epidemiology of Mental Disorder." In Braithwaite and Taylor, 99–128.

Okome, M. O. (June 1, 1999). "African Immigration to the United States: Dimensions of Migration, Immigration, and Exile." Africa Resource Center, Fordham University. Online: http://www.africaresource.com/scholar/globa.html.

Perkins, J. C. (1999). *Building up Zion's Walls: Ministry for Empowering the African American Family.* Valley Forge, Pa.: Judson.

Peterson, J. (January 2001). "Grandparents and Other Relatives Raising Children: Challenges of Caring for the Second Family." Generations United Fact Sheet. Washington, D.C.: Generations United.

Rasor, S. C., and M. I. N. Dash (2000). "Interdenominational Theological Center/Faith Factor Project 2000: A Report." Atlanta: ITC/Faith Factor.31.

Saluter, A. F. (March 1991). "Marital Status and Living Arrangements." In *Current Population Reports, Population Characteristics.* Washington, D.C.: U.S. Government Printing Office.

Seeber, J. J. (1990). *Spiritual Maturity in the Later Years.* New York: Haworth.

Smith, J. M. (1993). "Functions and Supportive Roles of Church and Religion." In Taylor, Jackson, and Chatters, 124–47.

Smith, J. P., and R. Kington (1997). "Race, Socioeconomic Status, and Health in Late Life." In Martin and Soldo, 105–62.

Smith, W. C. (1993). *The Church in the Life of the Black Family.* 2d ed. Judson Family Life Series. Valley Forge, Pa.: Judson.

Stapes, R., and L. B. Johnson (1993). *Black Families at the Crossroads: Challenges and Prospects.* San Francisco: Jossey-Bass.

Taylor, R. J. (1993). "Religion and Religious Observances." In Taylor, Jackson, and Chatters, 101–23.

——— (1988). "Religious Determinants of Religious Participation among Black Americans." *Review of Religious Research* 30: 114–25.

——— (1986). "Religious Participation among Elderly Blacks." *The Gerontologist* 26/6: 630–36.

Taylor, R. J., and L. M. Chatters (1991). "Non-organizational Religious Participation among Elderly Blacks." *Journal of Gerontology: Social Sciences* 46: S103–S111.

———. (1989). "Family, Friend, and Church Support Networks of Black Americans." In Jones, 245–71.

——— (1986) "Church-Based Informal Support among Elderly Blacks." *The Gerontologist,* 26/6: 637–42.

Taylor, R. J., J. S. Jackson, and L. M. Chatters, eds. (1997). *Family Life in Black America.* Thousand Oaks, Calif.: Sage.

UNC Charlotte Intergenerational Service Learning Project Sites of 1999. Online: http://www.uncc.edu/geront/islp2/sites2.htm.

Walls, C. T. (summer 1999). "The Role of Church and Family Support in the Lives of Older African Americans." *Generations* 23/2: 33–36.

Walls, C. T., and S. H. Zarit (1991). "Informal Support from Black Churches and the Well-being of Elderly Blacks." *The Gerontologist* 31/4: 490–95.

Williams, M. D. (1984). *Community in a Black Pentecostal Church: An Anthropological Study.* Prospect Heights, Ill.: Waveland.

Wimberly, A. S. (2001). "The Role of Black Faith Communities in Fostering Health." In Braithwaite and Taylor, 129–50.

——— (fall 2000). "From Intercessory Hope to Mutual Intercession: Grandparents Raising Grandchildren and the Church's Response." *Family Ministry: Empowering through Faith* 14/3: 19–37.

——— (spring 1994). "Christian Education for Health and Wholeness: Responses to Older Adults in Ethnic/Racial Contexts." *Religious Education* 89/2: 248–64.

——— (spring 1979). "Configurational Patterns in the Function of the Church for Aging Persons: A Black Perspective." *Journal of the Interdenominational Theological Center* 6/2: 94–105.

———, ed. (1997). *Honoring African American Elders: A Ministry in the Soul Community.* San Francisco: Jossey-Bass.

Wimberly, A. S., and Wimberly, E. P. (1995). "Pastoral Care of African Americans." In Kimble et. al., 161–73.

Wimberly, E. P. (1979). *Pastoral Care in the Black Church.* Nashville: Abingdon.

9

Meaning and Effects of Congregational Religious Participation

V. DUWAYNE BATTLE
ELLEN L. IDLER

Eighty years ago Presbyterian minister Henry Sloane Coffin told the story of a group of young people in a certain town on the banks of the Hudson River. They made as the theme of their conversation a discussion about the state of the universe and what it would take to improve the conditions of the world. When one of the young people made mention of the contributions that religion might make, an abrupt challenge came forth: "What is there in religion anyhow?" (Coffin 1922, 1). What is there in religion? Here is a question that cascades over the centuries and rolls down through the years. It is a question of tremendous relevance today. Using the analogy of the Hudson River, Coffin identified no less than ten benefits of religion: refreshment, cleansing, power, illumination, fertility, buoyancy, serenity and adventure, beauty, division and unity, and change and permanence. Similarly, the intent of this chapter is to identify the meaning and effects (benefits) of congregational religious participation.

WHY STUDY CONGREGATIONAL RELIGIOUS PARTICIPATION?

We think of congregational religious participation as meaningful involvement in the life and fellowship of a local congregation. It is often measured by surveys asking about the frequency of attending religious services. We distinguish congregational religious participation from personal feelings or perceptions of religiousness and spirituality that do not involve regular attendance at worship services. It is true that some people have the subjective sense that they are religious, even though they might rarely or never attend religious services. Personal worship, private Bible study, solitary prayer and meditation—all of these may be vitally important to an individual's spiritual well-being. As indicators of religious involvement, however, subjective measures of religion and spirituality often have little or no association with physical health; by comparison, attendance at services often shows strong positive health effects (Ellison 1995; Idler and Kasl 1997a). The relationships of life satisfaction to church attendance, self-rated religiosity, and private prayer have also been examined; of the three measures of religiosity, only church attendance demonstrated a significant effect on life satisfaction (Markides 1983). Apparently there is something about congregational participation that distinguishes it from private religious practices and makes it especially relevant to health. What is it about the things a congregation does together that make religious participation so meaningful?

To speak of congregational religious participation in this way does not suggest that the worship service is the only way to maintain meaningful involvement within the life of a church or synagogue. To be sure, there are other ways of being connected with a congregation. One has only to think of the wide range of programs and services offered through the local congregation that might provide room for self-help, socialization, or community involvement. There is a difference, however, between playing bingo and attending mass. There is a difference between remembering the Sabbath to keep it holy and just showing up for one or two annual "high holy days." There is a difference between dropping your child off for the preschool or after-school program during the week and attending worship services together as a family. The concern with things that take place in community rather than in solitude is important, especially since the possibility of isolation and extreme individualism is such a present danger in society.

ATTENDANCE AT RELIGIOUS SERVICES

There are many reasons why regular attendance at worship services might produce better health for individuals. The relationship between religious involvement and health behaviors, for example, is an important and ongoing area of study. Ninety-six percent of the 1,517 Los Angeles County women who were respondents to a telephone interview reported attending religious services at least monthly. These data suggested that better mammography screening was related to more frequent church attendance (Fox et al. 1998). Included in a thirty-three-item survey were three church attendance questions in a study administered in African American congregations (Lewis and Green 2000). The purpose of the study was to gather information on health beliefs and behaviors and to identify ways that culturally sensitive information and programs can be disseminated to the community to improve the health status of populations of color. In another study of an urban community sample, frequency of church attendance was among the three variables used to measure the relationship between religious involvement (also included were denominational affiliation and overall religiosity) and health status among African American males (Brown and Gary 1994). The researchers found that infrequent or no church attendance was associated with regular smoking and drinking.

The relationship between religious attendance, religious affiliation, and the use of acute hospital services by older medical patients admitted to Duke University Medical Hospital was examined by Koenig and Larson (1998). They found that frequent religious attendance was associated with fewer hospital admissions and shorter hospital stays, even when age, sex, race, education, social support, depressive symptoms, physical functioning, and medical illness were controlled. In another study of symptoms of depression in 4,000 older persons, frequent churchgoers were more likely to experience better physical health and were less likely to be depressed (Koenig et al. 1997). In this study private religious activities, such as prayer and Bible reading, were not related to depression but were correlated with poorer physical health and with better social support. Watching or listening to religious programs on television or the radio was not related to social support but was related to poorer physical health and higher levels of depression. In another study of religious affiliation and psychiatric disorder among Protestant baby boomers, it was found that infrequent Pentecostal churchgoers were at greater risk of psychiatric disorder than mainline and conservative Protestants (Koenig et al. 1994). In a study of race, religious involvement, and depressive symptomatology in a large (N = 2,956) sample from the southeastern region, frequency of church attendance was associated with lower levels of depression among whites but not among African Americans (Ellison 1995). Frequency of private religious activities such as prayer was associated with more, not fewer, depressive symptoms among both African Americans and whites.

An assortment of other health outcomes shows the pervasive relationship of religion with human health. Social research dealing with the impact of religious involvement on suicide rates dates back over one hundred years (Durkheim 1951). In the United States today, there are significant inverse correlations between church attendance and suicide rates; the association is consistent for white males, black males, black females, and white females (Martin 1984). Frequent church attendance has also been associated with lower systolic and diastolic blood pressures among white men, even when age, obesity, smoking, and socioeconomic status are controlled (Graham et al. 1978). Recent studies have also examined the biological and environmental factors relating religious attendance to individual differences in religious traits (D'Onofrio et al. 1999) and frequency of alcohol use; it appears that genetic factors determine the relationship between use of alcohol and church attendance in males, while environmental factors are better indicators of this relationship in women (Maes et al. 1999). Another study looking at the association between maternal religious attendance and the healthy behavioral and social functioning of young adolescents found that frequent maternal participation in religious services was associated with healthy functioning in adolescents (Varon and Riley 1999).

In a recent study (Battle 2001) an effort was made to determine the mitigating effects of religion and spirituality on depression in seriously ill or bereaved people. Two subsamples were created from the American's Changing Lives Data, 1986 and 1989. The illness subsample was concerned with individuals who were faced with heart disease, cancer, lung disease, and stroke within the previous year, and the bereavement subsample was made up of individuals who experienced the death of a spouse, child, parent, or relative or close friend within the previous three years. Several variables were used as measures of religion and spirituality: the importance of religious beliefs in day-to-day life, frequency of attending religious services, seeking spiritual comfort, and the belief that loved ones will be reunited in the afterlife. Sequential regression analyses were performed on both study samples, where frequency of attending religious services proved to be a reliable measure of religious participation and was associated with less depression across the models. Both seriously ill and bereaved people who attend religious services experience less depression than those who do not attend. It was also found that there was a significant race difference in the interaction between religious participation and depression, where African Americans with higher levels of religious participation experienced lower levels of depression.

The number of studies examining the relationship of religion to health is growing rapidly. This abbreviated review was not intended to be comprehensive; for a complete review see Koenig, McCullough, and Larson (2000). Our purpose for reviewing the studies was to point out that there are many aspects of "religiousness" that can be measured, such as attendance at worship services, private prayer, feelings of religiousness, specific beliefs, and many others. As a characteristic of individuals, religiousness is a complex set of behaviors, beliefs, and motivations that can be assessed in many ways. They may not, however, all be related to health in the same way. One relatively consistent finding of the studies we reviewed was that attendance at public worship services is more frequently associated with better health outcomes than solitary practices such as private prayer or watching religious programming on television. In a number of studies, in fact, frequency of prayer and intensity of religious feelings were associated with poorer, not better, health outcomes. We conclude, first, that, to detect and preserve these differences, the measurement of religiousness for health studies ought to be multidimensional; and, second, that there is something special about attendance at religious services that we should investigate.

REMEMBER THE SABBATH

"Remember the sabbath day, and keep it holy." (Exod. 20:8)

As the aforementioned studies seem to indicate, researchers have pointed out the importance of attendance at worship services as a significant indicator of religiosity. This will become more important as we continue to seek ways more effectively to define and measure the phenomena of religion and spirituality. Efforts to distinguish between religion and spirituality, however, may cause some researchers to distance themselves from organized approaches to religion. It would be most unfortunate, though, for researchers to diminish the extreme importance of congregational religious participation associated with organized religion. But what is it about this kind of religious involvement that has such salutary effects for its participants? Added to this is the question of whether and how congregational participation is different for those who are aging. We now turn our attention to congregational religious participation as Sabbath and celebration. There is also some benefit in examining the importance of worship, while paying special attention to the notion that it is a gateway to other opportunities and resources.

The earliest references to the biblical Sabbath come to us in the Hebrew Scriptures. Here at the dawn of creation is the origin of the Sabbath. Genesis 2:2-3 reads, "And on the seventh day God finished the work that he had done, and he rested on the seventh day from all the work that he had done. So God blessed the seventh day and hallowed it, because on it God rested from all the work that he had done in creation." The noun "Sabbath" is derived from the Hebrew verb *shabbat*, which means "to cease, to abstain, to desist from, to terminate, to be at an end" and, in a secondary sense, "to be inactive, to rest" (Morgenstern 1962, 135). The Hebrews were enjoined to adhere to the example set before them. God ceased from the work of creation on the seventh day, blessed this day, and declared it to be holy. Likewise, there was to be a weekly day of rest in the community of faith, when normal routines of work and business were to be set aside. A recent observer/participant of an orthodox Jewish service on the Sabbath describes the experience as extremely holy (Leo 1999).

As the nation of Israel began to emerge, Sabbath observance was recognized as an important religious practice. In the Torah, guidelines are provided to help govern appropriate conduct and behavior relative to the Sabbath. When the Ten Commandments were given, the Israelites were told, "Remember the Sabbath day, and keep it holy. Six days you shall labor and do all your work. But the seventh day is a Sabbath to the Lord your God; you shall not do any work—you, your son or your daughter, your male or female slave, your livestock, or the alien resident in your towns" (Exod. 20:8-10). In the immediately following verse, the basis for this Sabbath commandment is God's rest from the work of creation in Genesis. Other early references to the Sabbath are found in the Torah (Exod. 16:29-30; 23:12; 31:12-17; 34:21; 35:3; Lev. 23:3; Num. 15: 32-36; Deut. 5:12-17). Later additions and details about Sabbath prohibitions would be added to the Mishnah and the Talmud. Clearly, the observance of the Sabbath was vitally important to the early Israelite community.

Moreover, the Sabbath was not just a day of prohibitions. There are many positive and practical implications related to its observance. Dorothy Bass (2000) describes it as a day of rest from commerce, worry, and work, and a day of rest for creation. It is God's gift to us. Consider life from the perspective of the worker who is finally able to rest from a hard week's work, or the traveler who is not to be mistreated. Physical labor such as plowing, reaping, and chopping wood was limited. Even the animals, also a part of God's wonderful creation, were able to rest on the Sabbath. There were limitations related to business, commerce, and traveling long distances, but what was really intended was for this to be a day of rest. Additionally, the Sabbath was set aside to be an occasion for joy, and as such it was linked at least in some ways to the festivals (Hos. 2:13; Lam. 2:6). Particularly important is the notion that the Sabbath was marked by visits to a prophet or the Temple (2 Kings 4:23; Isa. 1:13). This underscores the community or congregational aspects of religious participation.

From a theological perspective, the Sabbath is a reminder of God's work in creation. It is a way of rekindling faith and hope in the belief that God has a purpose and plan for creation, of which we are all a part. It stands to reason, then, at least from a faith perspective, that God has a purpose and plan for our individual lives, our families, our nation, and our world. As a memorial, Sabbath observance is a way of calling us to remember things worth remembering. Sabbath observance, still from the vantage point of faith, encourages the pursuit of hope-filled lives. There is so much in life that is difficult and dismal. Problems abound on every level—personal, familial, regional, national, global, historical, and so forth. The elderly face issues related to physical, mental, and financial security and self-sufficiency. Sabbath calls us to remember the story of Genesis: there was chaos, then there was creation, and then God rested. We are called to take a break from our expenditure of so much creative energy to correct all that is chaotic and stressful in our lives. This can be referred to as "soul rest," where Sabbath is seen as much more than just the cessation of physical labor. It is rest at the core of one's being. It is rest for one's very own soul.

The Sabbath is also a call to celebration. John Donahue reminds us that "the Sabbath is a day of rest from all work in order to celebrate and remember God as creator and liberator" (2000, 39). Barbara Brown Taylor adds, "Sabbath was the day when Israel celebrated its freedom from compulsion. . . . On that one day every week, they remembered their worth lay not in their own productivity but in God's primordial love for them" (1999, 510). It is significant that the Sabbath was a gift to those who enjoyed a special relationship with Yahweh (Exod. 20:2ff.). In this sense we are called to value the importance of establishing and maintaining healthy relationships. In the absence of these relationships with close kindred, the religious community becomes all the more important. For some, the worshiping community becomes the extended family. Perhaps this is why the priest may be referred to as father and members of some congregations may be identified as brothers and sisters. The Sabbath is an affirmation that relationships are important, and it is a call for us to celebrate the important relationships in our lives.

THE IMPORTANCE OF WORSHIP

> Let the word of Christ dwell in you richly; teach and admonish one another in all wisdom; and with gratitude in your hearts sing psalms, hymns, and spiritual songs to God. (Col. 3:16)

When speaking of congregational religious participation, researchers are usually speaking of attendance at weekly worship services. With few exceptions, most of the Christian community has established Sunday as the primary liturgical day for worship services (Acts 20:7; 1 Cor. 16:2). This transition from the Jewish observance of Saturday as the Sabbath to Sunday as the Christian day of worship dates back to the resurrection of Jesus (Matt. 28:1). References to the gatherings of the early church provide insights into the practices of the early Christian community (Acts 2:43-47; 15:30; 1 Cor. 11:23-26; 14:26; Col. 3:16; 4:16; 1 Thess. 5:16-18). It was a close-knit, growing, and active community. There was an intentional effort to look out for the welfare and needs of those who were participating members. Their meeting times were regular, at least weekly, and at times it seems that they met daily. They were glad and generous, praising God and enjoying fellowship meals together. Their services consisted of prayer, praise, worship, singing, music, teaching, preaching, communion, prophesying, and the reading of letters.

It is not surprising to note some of the similarities that exist between synagogue and church religious services. These traditions, though rich and varied, have shared histories. What is amazing, though, is just how much of this has been retained over the last three to four thousand years for Temple and synagogue gatherings and the last two thousand years for Christian religious services. In keeping with the idea of Sabbath rest, the weekly gathering for religious services provides a rhythm for living, and it helps to restore the sacred rhythm of rest (Kriz 1999; Muller 1999). Sabbath has also been referred to in musical terms as "six beats and a pause" (Wheeler 2000). Actually, since we consider Sunday to be the first day of the week, it would seem that the pause comes first. Thinking in this way, one may assert that since God's existence precedes God's work as creator, which is represented by the stories of creation in Genesis, prior to God's work of creation God rested in God's self. The Sabbath rest that follows God's work as creator is a return to God's prior state, and the weekly Sabbath becomes a call for us to rest in the plans and intentions that God has for our lives. In any event, this rhythm for living may well be most meaningful for those who are aging. For those who may have found so much meaning in raising families, keeping a regular work schedule, and following a routine that may have existed for decades, these weekly gatherings carry with them the potential to continue much-needed patterns for life.

In thinking about worship, one cannot avoid the appeal of worship spaces to our sensory perceptions. Visual stimuli abound. Religious architecture by its very design has the ability to lift the human spirit. Even the most humble of religious meeting places may have fixed symbols, stained glass, banners, liturgical colors, and so forth, that help to indicate that worship is special and important. The odor of burning incense, fresh flowers, or the Communion wine makes an appeal to our sense of smell. In the celebration of the Eucharist, the worshiper can taste the bread and wine. There are many things that make their appeal to our auditory sense. Much of it may remind those who are aging of earlier days, when their homes were filled with activity. The sounds of people talking, laughing, singing, and even children playing or crying are joined by the sound of music, anthems raised, voices joined in song. In some houses of worship, you may hear the therapeutic sound of running water or feel the healing touch of another's hand or hug. This physical dimension of worship is also seen in some of the liturgical movements that occur during worship: the standing, kneeling, and sitting. Whether our hands are held high in praise and worship or folded with our heads bowed in humble reverence, worship involves full-body liturgical movements. This is especially true in more participatory religious services, where worship is viewed less as a spectator event and more as a place where people are encouraged to get involved.

Researchers have recently considered the benefits of prayer. Often this has much to do with how an individual benefits by having others pray for him or her. What often goes ignored, though, is the relationship that exists with those who are most likely to pray with and for you. Once again, this carries with it the idea of community but, more, it affirms that there are certain people who especially care for us as individuals. These may be members of a small prayer group, special affinity cell group, or support group of another kind. Stories of answered prayer abound in congregations where congregational prayer ministries have been established. John Maxwell (1996) identifies ways to start prayer-partner programs in local congregations, and Griend and Bajema (1990) provide a listing of some thirty-three strategies for the praying church. Included among these strategies are prayer chains, prayer triplets, prayer cells, church prayer support groups, and the traditional church prayer meetings. Of particular interest to this study are the support fellowship groups that are made up of several people who meet on a regular basis to support each other through fellowship and prayer. The prayer support that is being offered is provided in a broader context of a social and emotional support.

Additionally, it is particularly helpful to think of the benefits of prayer for those who are aging in terms of how they can pray for others. This certainly has the potential to strengthen one's sense of personal worth and give attention to the contributions that are offered by those who are aging. Involving seniors in congregational prayer programs "combats the low self-esteem that many older people suffer when they sense that society (and in some cases their own families) has put them on the shelf" (Griend and Bajema 1990, 118). Griend and Bajema identify congregational prayer-ministry programs that involve seniors in this way as senior intercessors.

The present landscape of worship, speaking most especially from the perspective of the Christian church, is varied and diverse. In Robert Putnam's (1995) book, *Bowling Alone,* he identifies a decline in U.S. civic involvement, in social organizations such as politics, labor unions, parent-teacher organizations, and also congregational participation through houses of worship. Even in his account, however, the absolute level of church and synagogue attendance in the United States remains high and continues to be the primary form of community involvement for most Americans. Mark Chaves (2000) rightly warns against the mistake of equating change with decline. A decline in church attendance, for instance, may be compensated by increased involvement in small support groups that are a part of the life and fabric of many congregations. Furthermore, it should be noted that changes in patterns for church attendance are similar to trends in other areas of civic involvement. Generally speaking, it seems that young people may be looking for different ways to express their religious involvement. Gary McIntosh (1995) helps identify some of the challenges and opportunities facing congregations interested in effectively reaching the builder, boomer, and buster generations. In any effort it is vitally important to see the relationship between past and present trends. An appreciation for what has worked in the past will help congregations more effectively plan for the future.

Richard Wolf (1999) makes a comparison of in-church worship services with worship by way of television and concludes that people find in-church worship more fulfilling. This is due to the transformative nature of congregational religious participation. People who attend church are more likely to be focused, feel secure, and experience community, which allows participants to benefit from the interaction with other worshipers. Mark Edwards (2000), alerting us to the influence of technological advancements on our approaches to worship, treats the subject of virtual worship. Virtual worship, presently in its primitive stages, is "interactive worship" through the use of the Internet. Edwards contends that theological issues related to baptism, the Eucharist, and other aspects of worship will need to be reconsidered in light of the predictions of futurologists. Paying particular attention to worship practices, John Baldovin and Michael Aune (2000) examine elements of change and continuity in today's Christian liturgy. Speaking largely from Roman Catholic and Anglican perspectives, they contend that liturgy is a combination of core principles in Christian worship, ecclesiastical codes that are significant to particular religious traditions, and cultural relevance that is determined in a specific time and place. Louis Weil (2000), also speaking from a liturgical perspective, identifies needed changes in catechetical formation and liturgy. He argues that theological education should be aimed at preparing priests for the practice of liturgical ministry and that local congregations need to improve the quality of the catechetical formation of the people. Anderson (2000) looks at the relevance of Christian liturgy and makes the case that rituals such as baptism, confession, thanksgiving, prayer, and the Eucharist are indeed pertinent to the rest of life. It is not surprising, then, that in an attempt to keep people in the pew, even when they must be on the road for business or pleasure, information on Mass times across the United States is provided on the Internet (Wojcicki 2001).

Music, which has always been significant in Jewish and Christian traditions, is another aspect of the contemporary religious scene that is in flux. Arthur Paul Boers (2001) looks at the current interest of evangelicals, Catholics, and charismatics, among others, in the Taize form of prayer and worship that is common in France, England, and Scotland. This is interesting, not only because it involves the ancient tradition of common prayer, but also because it emphasizes religious participation in the context of community. What we know from other traditional and contemporary forms of worship is that congregational singing and participatory worship keeps people coming back. Ancient, traditional, and contemporary approaches to worship that involve a strong sense of community and involvement may be particularly appealing to those who are aging.

WORSHIP AS A GATEWAY

One of the things that we find particularly useful when seeking to understand the mitigating effects that religious participation may have on negative outcomes, such as depression, poor health, and bereavement, is the "gateway" effect of the worship service. Attendance at religious services is a gateway to many other opportunities in the life of a congregation that may not actually take place when the community gathers for Saturday's Sabbath or Sunday's worship. In some traditions, one has only to read the bulletin or announcements that are made available to those in attendance. Those who say that they have strong subjective feelings of religiousness but who do not attend services will not know about many of these opportunities. For instance, information on a couples' retreat, women's health-care issues, parenting classes, Bible study and fellowship group for older adults, bowling league, dance classes, music lessons, computer classes, counseling, support groups of various kinds, and other special interests activities is likely to be shared in some way with those who attend worship services. Researchers are interested in this kind of information sharing, capacity building, networking, and resourcing. Fox et al. (1998) found that frequent church attendance is associated with better health screening.

Worship is a gateway to many things, including information, social integration, social support, and an affirmation of self-worth. This is important for older adults whose spouses may have preceded them in death. They may spend much of their time alone throughout the week and may be at greater risk of experiencing depression related to loneliness and isolation. With respect to the Sabbath, one might ponder how the Sabbath looks for those who are in retirement or who are thought to live lives of leisure. The Sabbath is a reminder of God's work in creation. Inherent in work is meaning, purpose, and a sense of productivity. It seems hard to overstate the potential benefit of available resources for those who attend religious services. Closely related to this, however, is the opportunity provided by local congregations for older people to find meaning and purpose in providing service to others. Many of those who make up the core of volunteers in local congregations are older persons. These are people who have a lot of life experience, a lot of practical insight to offer in service to others, and may also have a lot of discretionary use of their own time. Many of them have specialized training, gifts, skills, and talent, and they may be encouraged to render service to others through inspiration gained from the Scriptures, sermons, or at the invitation or advice of friends. Seniors may serve as volunteers in the church office, Sunday school, choir, community service programs, and help with a hands-on building project, or some other aspect of the congregation's mission. In all of this, the volunteer's sense of self-worth, meaning, and purpose in life is being affirmed.

So what is there in religion? What are the meaning and effects of congregational religious participation? Much of what has been offered here may be speculative, but it affirms the original presupposition that involvement in a congregation has inherent benefits for the participant and, not surprisingly, advantages for the congregation as well. Religious involvement is important because, among other things, it helps provide better health outcomes, offers a balance between work and rest, provides a setting where healthy relationships and sources of support can be established, affirms the purposefulness of life, serves as a gateway to many other resources, and allows opportunities for service to others. Although the authors of this chapter are themselves participants in local congregations, the focus of this work has been mostly from the perspective of the observer. Still, there are other benefits that members of local congregations may identify that encourage participation in religious services. Therefore, future studies in this area, especially those that are qualitative in nature, might do well to explore more thoroughly what participants themselves have to say about what keeps them coming back week after week to take up their places in the life and fellowship of local congregations.

BIBLIOGRAPHY

Anderson, E. B. (2000). "Liturgy and Life: Becoming Relevant." *Encourager* 61/4: 425–38.

Baldovin, J. F., and M. B. Aune (2000). "The Changing World of Religion." *Anglican Theological Review* 82/1: 65–93.

Bass, D. (2000). "Receiving the Day the Lord Has Made." *Christianity Today* 44/3: 62–67.

Battle, V. D. (2001). "The Effects of Religion and Spirituality on Depressed Mood in Individuals Faced with Serious Illness or Bereavement." Ph.D. diss., Rutgers.

Boers, A. P. (2001). "Learning the Ancient Rhythms of Prayer." *Christianity Today* 45/1: 38–45.

Brown, D. R., and L. E. Gary (1994). "Religious Involvement and Health Status among African-American Males." *Journal of the National Medical Association* 86/11: 825–31.

Chaves, M. (2000). "Are We 'Bowling Alone'—And Does It Matter?" *Christian Century* 117/21: 754–56.

Coffin, H. S. (1922). *What Is There in Religion?* New York: Macmillan.

Donahue, J. (2000). "Rest and Repent!" *America* 182/6: 39.

D'Onofrio, B. M., L. J. Eaves, L. Murrelle, H. H. Maes, and B. Spilka (1999). "Understanding Biological and Social Influences on Religious Affiliation, Attitudes, and Behaviors: A Behavior Genetic Perspective." *Journal of Personality* 67/6: 953–84.

Durkheim, E. (1951). *Suicide.* New York: Free Press.

Edwards, M. U., Jr. (2000). "Virtual Worship." *Christian Century* 117/34: 1262.

Ellison, C. G. (1995). "Race, Religious Involvement and Depressive Symptomatology in a Southeastern U.S. Community" *Social Science and Medicine* 40/11: 1561–72.

Fox, S. A., K. Pitkin, C. Paul, and N. Duan (1998). "Breast Cancer Screening Adherence: Does Church Attendance Matter?" *Health Education and Behavior* 25/6: 742–58.

Graham, T. W., B. H. Kaplan, J. C. Cornoni-Huntley, S. A. James, C. Becker, C. G. Hames, and S. Heyden (1978). "Frequency of Church Attendance and Blood Pressure Elevation." *Journal of Behavioral Medicine* 1/1: 37–43.

Griend, A. J. V., and E. Bajema (1990). *The Praying Church Sourcebook.* 2d ed. Grand Rapids: Church Development Resources.

Guy, R. F. (1982). "Religion, Physical Disabilities, and Life Satisfaction in Older Age Cohorts." *International Journal of Aging and Human Development* 15/3: 225–32.

Idler, E. L. (1987). "Religious Involvement and the Health of the Elderly: Some Hypotheses and an Initial Test." *Social Forces* 66/1: 226–38.

Idler, E. L., and S. V. Kasl. (1997a). "Religion among Disabled and Nondisabled Persons I: Cross-Sectional Patterns in Health Practices, Social Activities, and Well-Being." *Journals of Gerontology Series B-Psychological Sciences and Social Sciences* 52B/6: 294–305.

———— (1997b). "Religion among Disabled and Nondisabled Persons II: Attendance at Religious Services as a Predictor of the Course of Disability." *Journals of Gerontology Series B-Psychological Sciences and Social Sciences* 52B/6: 306–16.

———— (1992). "Religion, Disability, Depression, and the Timing of Death." *American Journal of Sociology* 97/4: 1052–79.

Koenig, H. G., and D. B. Larson (1998). "Use of Hospital Services, Religious Attendance, and Religious Affiliation." *Southern Medical Journal* 91/10: 925–32.

Koenig, H. G., J. C. Hays, L. K. George, D. G. Blazer, D. B. Larson, and L. R. Landerman (1997). "Modeling the Cross-Sectional Relationships between Religion, Physical Health, Social Support, and Depressive Symptoms." *American Journal of Geriatric Psychiatry* 5/2: 131–44.

Koenig, H. G., L. K. George, and B. L. Peterson (1998). "Religiosity and Remission of Depression in Medically Ill Older Patients." *American Journal of Psychiatry* 155/4: 536–42.

Koenig, H. G., L. K. George, K. G. Meador, D. G. Blazer, and P. B. Dyck (1994). "Religious Affiliation and Psychiatric Disorder among Protestant Baby Boomers." *Hospital and Community Psychiatry* 45/6: 586–96.

Koenig, H. G., M. McCullough, and D. B. Larson (2000). *Handbook of Religion and Health.* New York: Oxford University Press.

Kriz, L. (1999). "Review of *Sabbath: Restoring the Sacred Rhythm of Rest*, by Wayne Muller." *Library Journal* 124/5: 84.

Leo, J. (1999). "A Sabbath Observed." *America* 180/1: 13.

Lewis, R. K., and B. L. Green (2000). "Assessing the Health Attitudes, Beliefs, and Behaviors of African Americans Attending Church: A Comparison from Two Communities." *Journal of Community Health* 25/3: 211–24.

Maes, H. H., M. C. Neale, N. G. Martin, A. C. Heath, and L. J. Eaves (1999). "Religious Attendance and Frequency of Alcohol Use: Same Genes or Same Environments: A Bivariate Extended Twin Kinship Model." *Twin Research* 2/2: 169–79.

Markides, K. S. (1983). "Aging, Religiosity, and Adjustment: A Longitudinal Analysis." *Journal of Gerontology* 3/5:621–25.

Martin, W. T. (1984). "Religiosity and United States Suicide Rates, 1972–1978." *Journal of Clinical Psychology* 40/5: 1166–69.

Maxwell, J. (1996). *Partners in Prayer.* Nashville: Thomas Nelson.

McIntosh, G. L. (1995). *Three Generations: Riding the Waves of Change in Your Church.* Grand Rapids: Fleming H. Revell.

Morgenstern, J. (1962). "Sabbath." In *The Interpreter's Dictionary of the Bible: An Illustrated Encyclopedia*, 4:135–41. Nashville: Abingdon.

Muller, W. (1999). *Sabbath: Restoring the Sacred Rhythm of Rest.* New York: Bantam.

Putnam, R. D. (1995). *Bowling Alone: The Collapse and Revival of American Community.* New York: Simon and Schuster.

Taylor, B. B. (1999). "Remember the Sabbath." *Christian Century* 116/14: 510.

Varon, S. R., and A. W. Riley (1999). "Relationship between Maternal Church Attendance and Adolescent Mental Health and Social Functioning." *Psychiatric Services* 50/6: 799–805.

Weil, L. (2000). "Community: The Heart of Worship." *Anglican Theological Review* 82/1: 129–47.

Wheeler, D. (2000). "God's Servants Together: Keeping Sabbath," A Regional and National Staff Gathering of the American Baptist Churches USA held at Green Lake, Wisconsin, March 23–27.

Wojcicki, B. (2001). "Mass on the Go." *U.S. Catholic* 66/1: 49.

Wolff, R. F. (1999). "A Phenomenological Study of in-Church and Televised Worship." *Journal for the Scientific Study of Religion* 38/2: 219–35.

10

An Anchor amidst Anomie: Ritual and Aging

DAYLE A. FRIEDMAN

INTRODUCTION

She was seated in the place of honor. It might well have been a throne, but it was actually the sofa of her daughter's home. One by one, her nine grandchildren came before her, each bearing one of the precious trinkets accumulated over her eighty-five years. It was the "Great Grammy Giveaway," necessitated by my Grammy Anne's impending move to an assisted-living complex, where her quarters would be dramatically smaller than those in the apartment she had inhabited for years. As each grandchild took a turn choosing an object from the stunning array arranged on the Ping-Pong table in the basement, Grammy Anne told the story of that tchotchke, describing the trip on which it was acquired, or the adventure she'd had bargaining for it. I got the "Grammy swans," swan-shaped crystal bowls, bought when a local hotel went under in the Depression. Floating on circular mirrors, their necks adorned with ribbons matching the color scheme of the affair, these swans had graced countless luncheon tables. They were a perfect embodiment of Grammy Anne's elegance and graciousness.

Grammy Anne is long gone, sadly, but the swans, and the memories of that sweet moment, are with me forever. That impromptu ritual passed along a treasured legacy to each of Grammy's dear ones. It also eased a difficult and sad transition for her and her family. Instead of merely discarding those belongings which would not fit in the new home, treating her treasures as flotsam and jetsam, Grammy was given an opportunity to savor them and to bestow a priceless gift on her family members. This ritual transformed Grammy's experience and created meaning in a moment of great loss.

Aging presents enormous challenges to one's sense of significant being.[1] As this narrative suggests, ritual has the potential to infuse painful passages and periods with meaning and sustenance. This is true of traditional religious ritual as well as of idiosyncratic rituals specific to the individual or family, such as this one. This chapter examines the formidable threats to meaning faced in late life. It then turns to the promise of meaning offered in ritual and specifically examines religious ritual and rites of passage, which might be nonreligious. Although human beings are inexorably drawn to ritual, we moderns may feel intimidated by the prospect of doing so. In order to facilitate the creation of new rituals to reflect the contemporary experience of aging, the chapter closes by offering guidance for shaping and conducting a ritual.

THE CHALLENGE OF MEANINGLESSNESS IN AGING

Our twenty-first-century Western society has an instrumental view of persons. We are valued for what we do, produce, or create. The role changes in old age can therefore present a difficulty for elders: Who are we when we are no longer workers, childrearers, spouses, professionals? What now is our "job"? In the absence of clearly defined roles, elders who seek meaning may well find that the social expectations of our culture stymie them. The message of many advertising and media images to those who are retired from remunerative work is that they should spend their time in play, taking up games, travel, or other "self-indulgent mindlessness" (Blythe 1979, 22). The lack of a substantial social role can make elders feel, in the words of the late Maggie Kuhn, founder of the Gray Panthers, "like wrinkled babies" rather than esteemed and sagacious senior members of society.

Elders, especially the "old old," may be quite isolated. Geographical mobility can leave them marooned far from caring friends and family, either because they have retired far from the communities in which they spent their younger years or because family members have migrated to distant locales. As longtime friends die and move away, loneliness and alienation may intensify, especially since intergenerational ties are so scarce in our age-segregated society. This disconnection further contributes to elders' anomie.

We have a responsibility to address these threats to meaning, for, as Ronald Blythe teaches, we must not allow the old to fall into purposelessness: "To appreciate the transience of all things is one matter, to narrow the last years—and they can be numerous—down to a dreary thread is another" (1979, 23).

RITUAL AS AN ORIENTING ANCHOR

Ritual can serve as an orienting anchor in the midst of confusing, alienating losses, changes, and stresses. Ritual has been defined as an act or actions intentionally conducted by an individual or group employing one or more symbols in a repetitive, formal, precise, and highly stylized fashion (Myerhoff 1977). As anthropologist Barbara Myerhoff taught, ritual suggests predictability and continuity: "Even when dealing with change, new events are connected to preceding ones, incorporated into a stream of precedents so that they are recognized as growing out of tradition and experience" (1992a, 163). Ritual connects the individual to ancestors and those not yet born. Myerhoff noted that this sense of connection is heightened in religious rituals, in which the participant is linked also to "the forces of nature and purposes of the deities, reading the forms of macrocosm in the microcosm" (1992a,

163). With the use of sacred symbols, the present moment is no longer a strange wilderness but connected to the whole of one's life, so that one experiences one's history as "a single phenomenological reality" (1992a, 163).

Ritual also serves to reaffirm meaning. According to pastoral theoretician Elaine Ramshaw, rituals "carry core meanings of the social group performing them" (1987, 25). In moments when the sense of the coherence of one's life or the universe is threatened, ritual can reinforce the symbolic worldview, thus reaffirming order. Funerals provide a powerful example of this kind of bolstering, as they bring order amidst chaos, and affirm theological and social meanings and beliefs. The widow facing a bleak and terrifying world without her husband of sixty years is symbolically reminded at the funeral of God's care and of the goodness of life that exists alongside loss and finitude.

Ritual pierces isolation and creates community. While individuals can construct private rituals, rituals are most often shared in a social context. Ritual has the capacity to heighten a sense of shared 'values or history while also creating common memories. Even an ordinary birthday party for a man who has reached the ripe age of seventy-five may bond participants together in profound ways: informal reminiscence reminds them of precious shared experiences in the past, and those who have already passed that milestone reflect on their lives before and since, and those not yet there are given an indelible model of how a person can age (gracefully or grumpily!). Ritual can intensify our bonds and deepen our awareness that we are all in the same human boat, sailing amid fragility and mortality, seeking dignity and joy, courage and love.

Ritual can provide a safe container for ambivalence. In the context of ritual, we can have a "contained expression of unwanted, conflicting emotion" (Ramshaw 1987, 31). For example, a worker retiring from a job of many years might jokingly express both his criticisms of his employers and his ambivalence about leaving in formal or informal remarks ("You nearly pushed me out with your confusing new computer system. Now I'm *really* leaving . . . but watch out, I might decide to come back and haunt you!"). Rituals also bolster social norms, as they ultimately reinforce the "preferred emotion," so the worker is made to feel that this parting is a cause for celebration and that something better awaits him in retirement (Ramshaw 1987, 31).

Sadly, elders in our society have little ritual to mark or frame their experiences. The great transitions of older adulthood go largely unmarked. Between retirement, which might be acknowledged in a social way, and death, there is no normative or even common ceremony. "That 'old age' may last for three decades, lacking even demarcations provided by clearly named phases, goals, or features, is astonishing" (Myerhoff 1992a, 221). The result of this lack of clearly defined rituals and expectations is "cultural vagueness, anomie and isolation." Infusing old age with ritual can teach old and young "the meaning of their existence and the justifications for their continued being" (221).

Ritual can provide meaning in aging in the context of ongoing religious life, as well as in marking the transitions, losses, and gains of late life. We turn first to the role of religious ritual in bringing meaning to time.

RELIGIOUS RITUAL AND SIGNIFICANCE IN TIME

Religious ritual transforms mundane time into sacred time. For older adults, this is particularly important, for one of the great losses in aging can be the absence of a sense of significant time (Heschel 1966). Older people who no longer work or participate in busy household life can easily find themselves in what Florida Scott Maxwell called a "wilderness of time" (1979), where one day looks perilously like another, and the only thing that marks time is the rhythm of TV programs ("time for my soap opera"), or the schedule for taking medications. For those in institutions or who have moved far away from longtime residences, there may be little connection to the past. Many older adults also feel cut off from the future, either because they do not have plans to look forward to or because what is ahead is death, and they may not feel entitled or able to talk or think about that.

A Location in Time

Religious ritual can infuse time with significance. Religious life is often based on cycles of significant moments, so there are many opportunities to shape time with meaning. In Jewish life, for example, we live in the cycle of the week, from Shabbat to Shabbat; of the month, from New Moon to New Moon; and of the year, through the progression from festival to festival.[2] By marking these moments with ritual, time takes on shape and texture. The day on which I'm writing this is not just Friday, it is the eve of Shabbat, the sixteenth day of the month of Heshvan, and just five weeks before Chanukah.

In my work as a long-term care chaplain, I find that rituals that mark these cycles subvert the tyranny of institutional time in a nursing home.[3] On Friday evening, every resident can participate in celebrating Shabbat, whether through attending a service to welcome Shabbat on their nursing units, coming to the synagogue, or hearing over the public address system the blessings over candles, wine, and challah bread with which a Shabbat evening meal is begun. They know this day is special the moment they see the tablecloths in their dining room. This day cannot be mistaken for Monday or Thursday. And it has nothing to do with being sick, or frail, or a recipient of care. Even residents long removed from religious life heartily offer the greeting, *gut shabbes* (a good Sabbath) and sing along with the blessings. Throughout the week, I might be asked, "Is it Shabbes?" as older adults eagerly await that sacred day. Shabbat literally becomes, in the words of Abraham Joshua Heschel, "a sanctuary in time" (1995).

Shabbat is but one example of the way in which religious ritual can give the moment a *location* in time. The present moment can take on substance through its relationship with significant moments before and after it. Even on an ordinary day, living in the cycles of religious life allows us to savor sacred moments past and anticipate those ahead.

Rosh Chodesh, the New Moon, provides an illustration of this. In Jewish life, it is traditional to mark the beginning of the new month, which falls on the new moon. Psalms of thanksgiving (*Hallel*) are recited, and there are special additions to daily liturgy. There are also traditions that link the New Moon, a semi-holiday, with women.[4] In some communities in Europe, women did not do housework on Rosh Chodesh. Contemporary Jewish feminists have reclaimed Rosh Chodesh and have developed rituals that mark it as women's time and a context for building women's community. (See Adelman 1990; Berrin 1996.)

In the nursing home we celebrate Rosh Chodesh. Initially, I thought it would be a meaningful ritual because the institution is overwhelmingly a community of women. Rosh Chodesh turned out to be powerful for both men and women because it offers another sacred marker in time. Each month the residents perform a ritual that includes lighting a moon-shaped candle, singing psalms of thanksgiv-ing, studying something connected to the upcoming month, and creating a blessing expressing their hopes for the month ahead. When a blizzard kept us from holding our celebration, a resident chastised me: "We missed Rosh Chodesh. It's not the same without it!" Although we invented this ritual based on traditional themes and material, and although none of the participants was familiar with it, the Rosh Chodesh celebration has become a treasured part of the fabric of life in the home.

Connection across Time and Space

In addition to situating older adults amid cycles of significant moments, religious ritual provides connection. Nursing-home residents participating in a Passover Seder are not just strangers thrown together by the fact of their frailty and the whim of the home's administration but fellow members of the people of Israel, telling the story of their people's birth and liberation. As they sing "*avadim hayinu* (We were slaves to Pharaoh in Egypt)" and "Next year in Jerusalem," they are part of a common whole, both the community which has been created in this place and the wider community of Jews all over the world who are participating in this same ritual at this same moment.

The connection forged by religious ritual is not just *horizontal,* in the sense of building community across space. Religious ritual also provides *vertical* connection, linking us to past and future. When an older woman in the nursing home recites the blessing over the Shabbat candles, she says, "I remember my mother doing this." An elderly man shakes the *lulav* on Sukkot and says, "I haven't done this since I was a boy." His hands are shaking and he needs to be reminded of the words of the bless-ing, but when he performs this ritual, his face lights up with a proud smile. Sud-

denly the present is not simply a place of alienation, for there is a thread of continuity connecting this moment to meaningful moments in the past.

Religious ritual binds older adults to the future as well as the past. I was touched
and surprised one Friday night after Shabbat services when a woman suffering from
advanced Parkinson's disease and profound loneliness said, "We should live and be
well and do the same thing next year." This same woman had told me earlier in the
week, "You know, I know I shouldn't say this, but every night I pray that God
should take me, that I shouldn't wake up in the morning." It is as if the experience
of celebrating awakens a desire to be part of the cycle as it comes around once
more. Even knowing that their days ahead in this life are few, older adults can feel
connected to the future through the knowledge that this great cycle of celebration
will continue beyond them—in the words of the liturgy, *l'dor va-dor*, from generation to generation.

Rites of Passage: Continuity and Change

Even in the absence of religious or communal ritual, older people often sponta-
neously create their own ways to mark the unique experiences of aging. As Myerhoff notes:

> Just as children fastidiously work to bring some cosmos into the chaos of their emerging
> world of boundless complexity, so older people are often noted to fuss obsessively with
> trivial items, ordering a life that is ending, using the predictability and certainty that rit-
> ual provides during times of anxiety and helplessness. (1992b, 225)

For example, Myerhoff compares the sorting through of mementos and personal
belongings to nesting in late pregnancy, an effort toward "a final imposition of one's
human purpose on the last random, untidy event of all" (1992b, 225). Aside from
these individual rituals and a few paltry social markings, the passages of old age have
largely been bereft of ritual acknowledgment. As Myerhoff notes, "retirements and
funerals are crude markers for the stark beginning and end of old age; in between
there is a universe of differentiation that remains a cultural wasteland for each to
calculate and navigate alone, without the aid of ritual, ceremony, or symbol"
(1992b, 225).

Rites of passage are enormously helpful to all of us in getting through life passages, so their absence in aging is costly. Rites of passage are rituals which mark a
change in place, state, social position, or age (van Gennep 1960). These rituals serve
as a frame and call us to awareness of what we are experiencing (Myerhoff 1977).
In other words, they force us to pay attention. In the words of Ronald Grimes, rites
of passage "ensure that we attend to such events fully, which is to say, spiritually, psychologically, and socially" (2000, 5).

Rites of passage help us to place the current moment in context, both in terms
of our own life span and in terms of cultural values which orient us. Grimes writes,

"Even a single rite of passage can divide a person's life into 'before' and 'after.' An entire system of such rites organizes a life into stages. . . . These ceremonial occasions inscribe images into the memories of participants, and they etch values into the cornerstones of social institutions" (2000, 5).

The rites of passage that our society offers older people are largely moments of celebration for gains or attainments. Myerhoff suggests that we need a corresponding set of rituals to mark losses (1992b, 225). There is no end to the transitions that call out for ritual acknowledgment. Here is a list of a few examples:

Positive Experiences / Gains

- becoming a great-grandparent
- taking on a new volunteer role
- undertaking a new religious study or practice[5]
- entering a new community
- making a new friend
- recovering from acute illness or surgery
- entering a new romantic relationship
- the anniversary of belonging to a congregation or organization
- going on a journey

Negative Experiences / Losses

- adapting to a disability (hearing loss, sight loss, mobility, incontinence) and/or accepting an assistive device (hearing aid, walker, wheelchair)
- hearing bad news about one's health or prognosis
- losing a friend
- leaving a home
- leaving a congregation or community
- giving up driving
- becoming a caregiver to an incapacitated spouse or partner
- the end of menopause
- becoming a "last twig" when the last surviving member of one's generation in the family dies
- entering a nursing home[6]

The very experience of entering old age can be transformed by ritual acknowledgment. For example, the scholar Savina Teubal decided she would not approach old age with dread. Instead, Teubal created a ritual to *celebrate* becoming an older woman on the occasion of her sixtieth birthday. This ritual, *Simchat Hochmah* (the celebration of wisdom), drew upon biblical narratives and included a blessing, a change of name, a covenant, a reconciliation with death, and an affirmation of life (Teubal 1992). *Simchat Hochmah* has been emulated and adapted by many other women and is depicted in a documentary film (see www.timbrelsandtorahs.com).[7]

Some of the transitions of aging could be meaningfully marked through ritual acknowledgment in the context of a religious community. The *mi-sheberakh* blessing in Jewish liturgy provides an example of a means of doing this. These blessings are traditionally offered to members of the congregation who are called up to say a blessing over the Torah when it is read in the synagogue. The individual receives a blessing in honor of his or her performing this treasured ritual, and in acknowledgment of any significant event in his or her life, such as a birthday, anniversary, departure on a trip for Israel, or a *yahrzeit,* the anniversary of the death of a close relative. This ritual makes the community aware of the important experiences of the individual. It also enables the person to share joys and sorrows and invokes God's blessing at powerful moments.

The *mi-sheberakh* blessing could easily be a context for marking the passages of late life. Elder members of a community could receive a *mi-sheberakh* in honor of moving out of their family home, or of surrendering a driver's license, or of becoming a great-grandparent. If utilized in this way, private, isolated experiences would become visible and honored. Both painful and joyous transitions would be intimately connected to community and to the Divine. Even in a more private context, the *mi-sheberakh* ritual points to the power of giving blessings. Family members, friends, and professionals can also help older adults in our midst in their high and low moments by offering them our personal blessings, whether stated in religious language or framed in a secular context as an articulation of our own hopes for them.

Personal, family, and communal rituals can thus enrich aging and provide a container to hold our hopes, fears, dreams, and dreads in moving through the passages of later life. Many people would like to create or participate in rituals but may wonder how to do it. The next section explores some simple guidelines for designing and conducting rituals for transitions of aging.

CONSTRUCTING A RITUAL OF TRANSITION[8]

In order to have an impact, a ritual needs to reflect the transition it is marking. To begin, you need to carefully examine the transition you are addressing. What are its significant features? Is there a "before" (status quo) "during" (liminality), "after" (new state)? What are the salient characteristics of each? What are the emotional components and meanings of this transition for the person experiencing it, for family members/friends, and for members of the community, if they will be included?

Second, the ritual needs to have credibility. Essential in this regard is focusing on a guiding metaphor that has emotional resonance for those involved. The metaphor will help to anchor and orient all involved, reaching from the unfamiliar in this situation toward a known and familiar realm (Myerhoff 1977). In addition, a ritual is a kind of drama, so it is helpful to focus on physical action and behavior. *Doing something* will make the experience visceral; excessive explanation and didactic content are best avoided. Finally, the ritual should tie in to personal and communal continuity through symbols, words, or actions.

Brainstorming is a helpful tool for the next stage of creating a ritual. Once you have analyzed the transition to be addressed, let your mind free-associate. Search your tradition, literature, or whatever body of knowledge is most meaningful to you. Look for material associated with this transition, including heroes, texts, stories, symbols, blessings, prayers, and songs. Hone in on the image or metaphor that seems most apt and let that guide you as you create a ritual. Use this metaphor to frame and define the moment for the person undergoing the transition and those present.

Now you are ready to construct a structure that includes ritual action or affect-based components for each stage of the rite. Here are some things to consider:

- *Timing/rhythm.* Make sure the ritual is not too long. A relatively short ritual is often more powerful than a long, drawn-out ceremony. In addition, make sure your ritual has a beginning, middle, and end, and that there are good transitions between them.
- *Involve key people.* Be aware of people in the individual's life who need to be honored or acknowledged or who can contribute to the meaning of the event.
- *Be sensitive to the community's role.* Even though the ritual is primarily focused on the individual who is making a change, those who are in attendance will both affect and be affected by this experience.
- *Drama.* Be alert to opportunities to make the moment magic. Think about aesthetic aspects, including setting, lighting, clothing/costume, food, and adornments, such as flowers and decorations.
- *Music.* Music is an essential part of the power of many rituals. Music opens participants to the experience, touches their emotions, and provides a sense of continuity. You can include music through recorded music, performed music, and/or community singing.
- *Facilitator/leader.* Think carefully about who will be conducting this ritual. Individuals who are the focus of rituals of transition want to be present to the magnitude of the moment. For this reason, it may be best if someone else takes responsibility for facilitating the ritual. The extent of this role ranges from creating the ritual to carrying out what the subject and/or others have designed.
- *Safety.* Make sure that this ritual will be safe for the person on whom it is focused and all present. Do not make unexpected demands on anyone or violate boundaries by putting anyone on the spot. Make sure the person experiencing the transition knows about and is comfortable with what will happen in the ritual.
- *Evaluate.* Once the ritual is completed, think about what went well and what did not go as you or others had hoped. Look at what contributed to a sense of connection and what fell flat. This reflection will prove invaluable to you for the next time you set out to shape a ritual of transition.

CONCLUSION

Ritual is a powerful tool for finding and creating meaning in late life. We are all blessed with an innate human proclivity toward ritual, and we can draw upon this to enrich our own and others' experiences through the highs, lows, and in-betweens of aging. Ritual can be accessible to all older adults, religious and nonreligious, frail and well. Ritual is available to all of us, like the commandment described in Deut. 30:11-14 (*Tanakh* 1985):

> Surely, this *mitzvah* (commandment) which I enjoin upon you this day is not too baffling for you, nor is it beyond reach. It is not in the heavens, that you should say, "Who among us can go up to the heavens and get it for us and impart it to us, that we may observe it?" Neither is it beyond the sea, that you should say, "Who among us can cross to the other side of the sea and get it for us and impart it to us, that we may observe it?" No, the thing is very close to you, in your mouth and in your heart, that you may do it.

NOTES

1. For an eloquent statement of this truth, see Heschel 1966.

2. The examples in this essay are drawn from Jewish life, since that is what I know intimately. I hope that readers will be inspired by these specific examples to recognize the power of rituals within their own traditions.

3. The anecdotes that are shared are based on the twelve years I served as Director of Chaplaincy Services at Philadelphia Geriatric Center. Although these are experiences related to frail elders, I have found that religious ritual is, a fortiori, also deeply meaningful to well elders. I am profoundly grateful to the elders with whom I've worked and who have been my teachers in this work.

4. Women are linked to the cycle of the moon in the monthly cycle of their bodies. In the midrash, rabbinic exegesis, Rosh Chodesh is given to women as a reward for the merit of the women who refused to give their jewels over to be turned into the Golden Calf.

5. For example, a senior adult-confirmation program at Philadelphia Geriatric Center provided an opportunity for both study and affirmation of participants' ongoing commitment to Jewish life. See my "Older Adult Confirmation," in Berrin 1997, 298–300.

6. See, for example, Cary Kozberg, "Let Your Heart Take Courage: A Ceremony for Entering a Nursing Home," in Berrin 1997, 289–97.

7. Other examples of rituals for entering old age are Marcia Cohn Spiegel, "Havdalah: A Time to Acknowledge Growing Old," in Berrin 1997, 275–78; and Anne Tolbert, "A Personal 'Seder' to Celebrate Aging," in Berrin 1997, 279–88.

8. The following draws heavily on Debra Orenstein, "Afterword: How to Create a Ritual," in *Lifecycles: Jewish Women on Life Passages and Personal Milestones* (Woodstock, Vt.: Jewish Lights, 1994), 1: 359–76.

BIBLIOGRAPHY

Adelman, P.V. (1990). *Miriam's Well: Rituals for Jewish Women around the Year.* New York: Biblio.

Berrin, S., ed. (1997). *A Heart of Wisdom: Making the Jewish Journey from Midlife through the Elder Years.* Woodstock, Vt.: Jewish Lights.

———— (1996). *Celebrating the New Moon.* Northvale, N.J.: Aronson.

Blythe, R. (1979). *The View in Winter: Reflections on Old Age.* New York: Harcourt Brace Jovanovich.

Grimes, R. L. (2000). *Deeply into the Bone: Re-inventing Rites of Passage.* Berkeley: University of California Press.

Heschel, A. J. (1995). *The Sabbath: Its Meaning for Modern Man.* Reprint. New York: Farrar, Straus & Giroux.

———— (1966). "To Grow in Wisdom." In idem, *The Insecurity of Freedom.* Philadelphia: Jewish Publication Society.

Maxwell, F. S. (1979). *The Measure of My Days,* New York: Penguin.

Moore, S. F., and B. Myerhoff, eds. (1977). *Secular Ritual.* Assen, The Netherlands: Van Gorcum.

Myerhoff, B. (1992a). "A Death in Due Time: Conviction, Order, and Continuity in Ritual Drama." In Myerhoff et al., 159–90.

———— (1992b). "Experience at the Threshold: The Interplay of Aging and Ritual." In Myerhoff et al., 219–27.

———— (1977). "We Don't Wrap Herring in a Printed Page." In Moore and Myerhoff, 199–224.

Myerhoff, B., D. Metzger, J. Ruby, and V. Tufte (1992). *Remembered Lives: The Work of Ritual, Storytelling, and Growing Older.* Ed. Marc Kaminsky. Ann Arbor: University of Michigan Press.

Ramshaw, E. (1987). *Ritual and Pastoral Care.* Theology and Pastoral Care. Philadelphia: Fortress Press.

Tanakh: A New Translation of the Holy Scriptures according to the Traditional Hebrew Text (1985). Philadelphia: Jewish Publication Society.

Teubal, S. J. (1992). "Simchat Hochmah." In Umansky and Ashton, 259–64.

Umansky, E., and D. Ashton, eds. (1992). *Four Centuries of Jewish Women's Spirituality.* Boston: Beacon.

van Gennep, A. (1960). *The Rites of Passage.* Chicago: University of Chicago Press.

11

Cooperative Alliances between Congregations and Community Agencies

DOUGLAS OLSON
MARK HOLMAN

The history of creative and cooperative relationships between congregationally based ministries (congregations) and community agencies, especially social ministry organizations (SMOs), is long and accomplished. Some trace this history back to the first century, when the leaders of the early Christian church distinguished between the roles and responsibilities of the preachers and the administrators (Acts 6). Others trace the history farther back, through the Hebrew tradition that distinguished between the worshiping community at the Temple or the synagogues and those who do acts of charity within their communities. Today it is apparent that hundreds of hospitals and thousands of our nation's aging services programs are faith-based and linked (at least historically) to communities of faith. These organizations have been the result of creative and cooperative alliances between congregations and SMOs.

An alliance is an association to further the common interests of the members. The scarcity of resources to serve the increasing needs of today's society should be enough of a driving force to encourage cooperative relationships between organizations with common interests. More than that, however, there is the intersection of core beliefs and values. Congregations and community agencies both have an interest in serving the poor, disenfranchised, and less fortunate. Often these foci are clearly stated in the mission and strategic goals of these respective entities. One population fitting this portfolio of services and receiving the attention of both are frail elders, a population that is growing at a dramatic rate (Administration on Aging 2001). Mainstream churches are aging at a pace even faster than the rest of society (Faith Communities Today 2000a). It should make great sense for congregations and community agencies to collaborate to optimize their combined resources to serve the frail elderly population. But it is not a simple equation. It requires honest, thoughtful, and engaged commitment for congregations and community agencies to connect and maintain fruitful relationships.

A common element shared by the congregation and SMOs is expressed through the Greek term for service, *diakonia*. Social ministry is one of the hardiest stems that grow from the root of "service." Within the congregation we use language such as "faith active in love" and the "ministry of the baptized." Within SMOs we are more apt to hear language of "continuous quality improvement" and "leadership development." Both agencies, however, clearly affirm a mission that begins and ends far beyond itself. Foster McCurley affirms and articulates this theme in *Go in Peace* (McCurley 1989a). He lifts up the theological understanding of "vocation" as the daily work of the baptized. The work of the faithful is inextricably linked to God's work.

One of the largest Protestant faith-based systems of social services agencies describes the vital link between congregations and SMOs in this way:

> In response to God's love, Lutheran individuals, congregations, judicatories, and social ministry organizations seek to meet human needs, advocate for dignity and justice, and work for peace and reconciliation among all people. This ministry of service—which is part of God's mission to the broken world—is essential to the meaning of the church. (Evangelical Lutheran Church in America and The Lutheran Church–Missouri Synod 2001)

This chapter does not focus on the origin or heritage of agencies. An inherent assumption is that most agencies will welcome a greater "spiritual fullness" brought to their services. Nearly two decades ago, Martin Marty asserted that "holistic health care is an idea whose time has already come" (1986, liner notes). We focus our discussion instead on current and potential relationships of churches with existing church-affiliated SMOs, which is where much of the activity is today, especially when serving the elders of our churches and aging persons of our communities.

When it comes to older adults, integrating the mission commitment of congregations and SMOs makes a great deal of sense, based on evidence about older adults' level of religiosity. According to a Gallup poll, 76 percent of persons over age sixty-five state that religion is very important to them (Princeton Religion Research Center 1994). Older adults are also more likely than younger adults to be members of congregations and to participate in groups associated with prayer (Levin and Taylor 1997). Whether this general trend will be noted among baby boomers and subsequent generations remains an open question.

INTEGRATING THEOLOGY

Faith groups express their values and commitments to health care and services in a variety of ways. For the purpose of this chapter, we offer examples from the Lutheran tradition and draw upon the collected works of Foster McCurley and Robert Kysar, both Lutheran theologians. McCurley (1986) is particularly helpful in tracing the biblical and theological foundations of the church's commitment to social ministry. The author makes it clear: social ministry is hardly a new emphasis. From the earliest times of the Christian church, congregationally based ministries have understood one of their chief roles to be to serve the disadvantaged. Increasingly, especially in an age of incredibly complex systems of health care and incomprehensible systems of funding and reimbursements, he argues for a wise, active, and thoughtful interdependence among congregations, judicatories, SMOs, and national church bodies.

Kysar (1991) uses images in the Bible to communicate the compelling motivational message of the stories in supporting both an individual and a church role in the delivery of social ministry. He examines the images of God in the Old and New Testaments in a manner that lays out a worldview founded in love and justice. The work of compassionate people is to fulfill the exemplary caring role portrayed in these multiple images. Congregations are viewed as entities for providing effective social ministry and serving as a voice for those in need. Both McCurley and Kysar go to great lengths to make the case of biblical connection and responsibility for both individuals and the church.

The integration of theological foundations is also lived out in agencies in a variety of ways. Catholic Charities is an example of an organization that incorporates multiple views to help frame their SMO agency perspective. When stating their beliefs, they elaborate on ten ways Catholic Charities are Catholic (Kammer 2000). Catholic Charities

1   has a support ministry that is rooted in the scriptures
2. has been an integral part of the Catholic Church for 2,000 years
3. promotes the sanctity of human life and the dignity of the human person
4. is authorized to exercise its ministry by the diocesan bishop
5. respects the religious beliefs of those it serves
6. recognizes that some services require attention to the physical, mental, and spiritual needs of those it serves
7. has a special relationship to the diocese and to Catholic parishes
8. works in active partnership with other religiously sponsored charities and with the civic community
9. supports an active public–private partnership with government at all levels
10. blends advocacy for those in need and public education about social justice with service to individuals, families, and communities in need.

This belief statement focuses much attention on the connection to the church, although it also touches on other areas important in how they approach their work. This includes respect for an individual's own beliefs and an awareness of interdependence. Many affiliated church agencies maintain this same ecumenical focus for the delivery of their services. It is also true that many church-affiliated agencies are recognizing the challenges inherent in providing a quality service grounded in faith while employing an ethnically and religiously diverse workforce. This same spirit of connectedness and ecumenical openness is also the accepted norm for the mainstream church agencies and the public statements of church-wide bodies.

The history of social ministry organizations is a rich story of service at both the congregational and national church levels. Congregations have long responded to the needs of "their" people and the surrounding community. Most formal national groups or associations of church agencies have been relatively recent phenomena, in comparison to local congregational and social ministry efforts. Catholic Charities is one of the oldest and has been in existence for approximately ninety years. Yet these associations have been instrumental in providing a collective voice and making it possible for church-affiliated agencies to respond to needs on a broader scale (Catholic Charities 2001). One crucial role they assume is advocacy for the church on social issues. This role is dually served within the internal church units themselves and on a broader scale for society as a whole.

One characteristic congregations of mainstream denominations and the broader societal community have in common is that both are aging. Congregational members are aging even faster than the society as a whole. Unfortunately, this fact is too often not reflected at the congregational and denominational level in the development of strategic plans or ministry initiatives. More often plans and programs are shaped for younger cohorts. While this may be viewed as more closely aligned with the needs of a vibrant growing church, sheer demographics encourage a change in orientation. An increasingly important connection to this end is the need for advocacy related to the needs of older adults. Until a clear focus is articulated and resourced, it will be imperative for voices to be heard related to services and support for older adult programs and services. It is noteworthy that on a national level, the American Association of Services and Homes for the Aged is actively collaborating with church-affiliated health-care systems to advocate on behalf of agencies serving seniors.

CONNECTIONS

At this point we examine the underlying driving and sustaining forces that churches and SMOs are looking for as part of any relationship or alliance. We think it is naïve to assume that sheer goodwill alone can make a potential cooperative alliance work for the long term. It is clear that strong and effective collaborative efforts are sustained as the legitimate self-interests of each participating body are met.

Congregations have at their center a ministry of word and sacrament. When participants are spiritually challenged and nurtured, individuals grow in their faith. As a response to God's grace, faith becomes active in acts of love. In this sense, faithful service is an expected result. The resulting service is dependent on the congregation's age, the leadership spirit of the church, geographic location, and the resources available to the church and community. These factors play into the mission priorities of the church. There are many secondary gains for the congregation. Some are:

- an increased connection to the fabric of their community
- new avenues for members' service (ministry) opportunities
- the ability to access expertise and resources otherwise not available

- a potential new source of revenue for the congregation

Choosing the right alliances and ministry opportunities is critical for the congregation, and a thoughtful plan to proceed through this process is imperative (Voss and Hark 1997). The national Jewish association has also produced a thoughtful guide to help local Jewish communities plan service delivery to the elderly (United Jewish Communities 2001). This guide contains best practices, program planning and implementation strategies for small and large communities, resource contact information, and advocacy and public policy recommendations.

Community agencies are also looking at partnerships through their own lenses of self-interest. Yet, like any organization, they must have a delineated rationale to support the energy put into any relationship. What benefits are the agencies seeking from any proposed relationship? We suggest the consideration below as a starting point, beyond the fact that the mission of any respective church may be aligned with the agency's own core values and purposes. A congregation or church body may offer

- access to a new population to serve (expanded market)
- a location that serves as a new point of service
- a greater ability to leverage and share their core competencies
- an expanded volunteer resource base
- potential funding support from the congregational resource base, including older adults.

As mentioned earlier, the type of relationship will be dependent on a multitude of congregational factors. We propose that this variability is even greater at the congregation level than at a national level, and that congregations are where most of the activity is today (Faith Communities Today 2000b). The phrase "think globally, act locally" is a good description of this arena of activity.

One of the most important elements of effective collaboration is to find mutually compatible goals and joint benefits of any alliance. A one-sided (or out of balance) relationship will not work for the long run; neither partner will be satisfied. These relationships work best when the intersections are clearly evident to both the participating organization and the benefactors. The congregation's role in a partnership may raise attention to the spiritual needs of clients served predominately by a government-funded community agency. For example, a jointly sponsored hospice program allows congregations and agencies to collaborate with their strengths. In this case, a senior visitation pastor for the congregation and the supportive professional nursing agency staff can serve as dual assets for the client. This type of alliance can foster a conduit for service that benefits everyone involved as we walk with the person through the later stages of his/her life. This hospice example is a service-oriented alliance, which we believe is the predominate driver of alliances between churches and agencies.

PROGRAMS AND SERVICES

Building on the proposition that the primary outcome of a collaboration is service, we next outline the types of programs and services that currently compose alliances. We also elaborate on examples to illustrate, in a very pragmatic way, the nature of these relationships at work today.

Adult Day Services provide the elderly and other adults with services when their caregivers are at work or need relief and generally operate programs five days a week during normal business hours (National Council on Aging 2001). This type of program has been set up between congregations and social ministry agencies in a variety of ways. One common approach is to use space within the church Monday through Friday (which are the typical days an Adult Day Service Center is open), and allow the partnering SMO to operate and staff the program. One consideration when developing this type of service is transportation availability for clients.

Group homes serve a variety of constituencies and are places where three to four adults (generally not related to the operator) reside and receive care. Treatments or services are generally above the level of room and board and usually include some nursing care. One model is a partnership between an SMO and various sponsoring congregations. The cooperating agencies may use former parsonages or have purchased appropriate residential homes, emphasizing service to older frail adults in the early to middle stages of Alzheimer's disease.

A recent program gaining popularity is the parish nurse concept. Parish nurse partnerships continue to blossom for a variety of reasons, not least of which is resources. This type of partnership is a low-risk venture with little capital investment and long-term commitment required but with many elements that the public and older frail consumer view as positive. Parish nurses have defined roles that are flexible (depending on needs) and include being a health educator and counselor, referral source, coordinator of health-related programs, and interpreter of the relationship between faith and healing (Westberg 1990).

A more traditional venue is a cooperatively sponsored nursing home. Across the nation, approximately 1.5 million people live in nursing homes. About 4.5 percent of people over the age of sixty-five in the United States live in a nursing home, which is slightly less than ten years ago (Federal Interagency Forum on Aging-Related Statistics 2000). The resident population is changing dramatically in these settings and has more medically complex needs (Sahyoun et al. 2001). Approximately 28 percent of the facilities are operated by nonprofit organizations. The major denominations represented were estimated by using a recent (2001) survey of long-term care parent organizations by the American Association of Services and Homes for the Aged. The three major church bodies represented were Catholic (15 percent), Lutheran (13 percent) and Methodist (10 percent). Other denominations that sponsored long-term care entities included Presbyterian (7 percent), Jewish (6 percent), and Baptist, Episcopal, and United Church of Christ (5 percent each), along with a collection of other faith-based sponsors. Government-affiliated facilities comprise about 6.5 percent of the nursing-home field (American Health Care Association 2001). These statistics reflect a significant church presence in this traditional (but evolving) service venue.

Senior apartments have evolved in a variety of ways, including sponsorship and funding. The continuum ranges from lower-income government-sponsored housing to privately funded Continuing Care Retirement Communities (CCRC). The congregational and church role in these types of living settings is arranged in multiple ways and serves multiple clients or populations groups (Netting 1995). The real challenge that still confronts the church is the pressure for low-income housing, although in reality these types of programs are often costly to operate. Regulations and governmental reimbursement systems are such that congregations best not venture into this without the expertise of an agency familiar with this government-sponsored program. Congregations concerned about affordable housing can address this issue via a HUD program in collaboration with an SMO or other nonprofit agency. Many SMOs engage in these programs and find the reimbursement barely adequate to cover their costs. They need to strive to find a balance between resource-dependent and resource-generating housing services to maintain long-term financial viability.

A hybrid (or bridge) for nursing-home and independent senior housing that has continued to rise in popularity is assisted living. Assisted-living services are becoming more popular, in part due to the disdain for traditional nursing-home institutional services, compounded by the increasing frail elderly population. Assisted living offers many nursing and support services of a nursing home, with less medical emphasis and in a more residential setting. Private rooms and greater client financial resources are often the distinctive features that set these environments apart. A recent Assisted Living Federation of America (ALFA) survey reported the ownership status of properties as approximately 88 percent for-profit and 12 percent nonprofit from their responding members (ALFA, 2001). This service area's recent growth and the privatization phenomenon make formal congregational relationships less plentiful, although SMO sponsorships and informal congregational connections (e.g., arrangements for the provision of pastoral care) are part of the current developing landscape.

Many other types of programs and services exemplify collaborative efforts, and are included in the following list developed from various reports on congregational and social ministry organization activities (ELCA 2001; Olson 2001; Faith Communities Today 2000b):

- Food banks, clothing and cash assistance, and meals on wheels programs are high involvement areas of many congregations.
- Mentoring programs, such as the intergenerational program that Catholic Charities promotes, called "Across Ages," use older people as mentors to youth at risk of substance abuse (Taylor 2001).

- Counseling services are available through partnerships between a wide range of SMOs and congregationally based programs.
- Transportation is a significant challenge for seniors forced to give up driving because of frailty. SMOs can partner with congregations to most effectively utilize their existing van transportation services.
- Intergenerational day cares are unique programs that combine child care and care for adults in the same center located in a church building.

This is by no means an exhaustive list of potential service collaborations, but it does suggest the vast array of services that exist as alliances today.

KEY STAKEHOLDERS

How do these alliances happen and where does the energy come from to move these types of relationships forward? Crucial elements of any alliance are the stakeholders and their motivations. There are a number of facets to consider (Fahey 1996) when examining these individuals and groups; our goal is to identify them and lift up their driving forces and tensions.

Individuals or groups feeling a "call to service" often provide the initial impetus to explore a new service venue. Initial development is often motivated by the personal experiences of the developer, friends, or fellow parishioners during a time of need. Once the idea is born, taking it to fruition requires exposure and access to the right resources.

Associations often promote or encourage these relationships by elevating the exposure of various programs that serve as positive examples of relationships that have worked. Catholic Charities, Lutheran Services in America (LSA), Methodist Association, United Methodist Association of Health and Welfare Ministries, United Jewish Communities, and other collective groups can leverage the aggregated strengths of many agencies with their national exposure and take advantage of a broader network audience to serve this role. A good example is the recent LSA program called Joined at the Heart. Part of this program includes a published list and short description of "best practices" of social ministry agency service efforts with strong church connections (LSA 2001). One challenge is that these national groups have a wide range of social-action causes and population groups to serve, and older adults are not their only focus.

SMOs are a major driving force in the formation of alliances, especially at the leadership staff level. An openness to exploring partnerships with congregations requires a commitment of energy and time. A program example is found with Advocate Health Care (Illinois), which has a dedicated office for Community Ministry. Advocate Community Ministry provides a wide array of opportunities for social ministry and health connection and also has available a variety of resources. An organization bringing together the right players for a specific service, while often productive and creative, can experience decision delays due to lack of expertise, governance control issues, or inadequate access to necessary funds. These delays may be accentuated when working with congregations and churches. In short, collaboration shows great promise, but does not promise an easy journey.

National church-wide units and regional judicatories help foster these relationships, but not as a major initiative or focus of their activities. Their agencies' predominant mission is focused on serving the broader congregational and pastoral needs of their church members and global mission activities. Regional efforts have been traditionally underfunded and understaffed.

Proprietary, or for-profit, organizations usually bring more of an entrepreneurial spirit to the table when it comes to exploring service opportunities. These alliances are often focused on services depending on private resources and revenues that can provide a reasonable investment return. Proprietary groups have become involved predominantly in faith-based alliances focused on development of senior housing or assisted-living settings. Congregations are sometimes suspicious of these types of alliances, and generally SMOs have been more involved with these types of relationships.

CHALLENGES AND OPPORTUNITIES

The opportunities for successful alliances abound, but these efforts produce challenges. What are the challenges and opportunities faced by organizations attempting to engage in these types of relationships?

- Most agencies and churches have competing interests with multiple demands.
- A time investment is necessary to cement working and trusting relationships. Time is a commodity that does not seem as available today as it was in the past.
- Appreciating the varied interests and expertise of those involved in the development of any alliance is often overlooked. People and agencies must speak a language understandable by all.
- Third parties or consultants often provide helpful assistance to groups attempting to work fairly through the deliberations and steps involved in a collaborative effort.
- Privatization of services remains an increasing trend. U.S. national health care was again defeated this past decade, and the growth of the "senior services industry" has proliferated among private enterprises. Bringing products and services to market is quicker with private resources.
- Numerous proprietary groups are beginning to partner with nonprofit agencies to offer services. The nonprofit sector frequently does not have the

resources or risk tolerance for development and growth. However, the non-profit community does offer a credible history of service and reputation.

- Executives urge caution concerning the promise of collaborations, especially if it is only a mere reshuffling of the deck (resources). These statements are based on a system that is already stressed and not able to meet current needs.

As of early 2002, President Bush's Faith-Based Initiative has demonstrated the potential and pitfalls of fostering collaboration between faith-based care systems, worshiping communities, and the government, and clearly has brought organizational development opportunities to the forefront of the U.S. political agenda. This initiative, which may have flaws and is criticized by those concerned with the separation of church and state, has opened new ways of considering service provision in this country. The core of the initiative proposes establishing centers to report on barriers between government and community groups and also allows religious organizations to compete with secular organizations for grants to deliver human services (Office of the President 2001). Regardless of what happens with legislation in this area, it is clear that new alliances between governmental and faith-based institutions will remain a very important issue for the future.

Most research has focused on data gathering and reporting trends and statistics concerning the current delivery system. A recent initiative, "The Faith-Based Profile," primarily sponsored by Lutheran Brotherhood (now Thrivent Financial for Lutherans), is an attempt to describe the distinctive nature of SMOs in the long-term care arena (Olson 2001). Differences between the religious nonprofit and for-profit delivery systems require further exploration. Changing national and church demographics serve as a catalyst needing continued descriptive evaluation and other research-informing policy-makers about the ramifications of their decisions. This research will help guide future policy directions. One potential promise is that newly developed centers (e.g., Center for Aging, Religion and Spirituality) focused on these issues can form effective bridges with other partners in the provider (e.g., AASHA) and research-oriented worlds to produce the credible and practical work necessary. One critical need for this decade's research agenda is studying the value of effective alliances and their contributions.

CONCLUSION

The graying of the United States, running parallel with the current and projected shortage of paraprofessional service staff, provides the ingredients for a looming service crisis. Congregations and social ministry organizations providing services to older, frail adults have a long history of meeting needs. These groups have staying power, which predicts survival in the decades ahead. Alliances created by and with these organizations provide hope and promise for efforts that confront this crisis by efficiently harnessing and marshaling resources. As the best of these efforts survive and flourish, they will serve as models for enlightened executives, policy makers, and other leaders in the aging services field. Working collaboratively, these groups and organizations can be stronger, and our society stands a much better chance of bridging the approaching abyss of services needed and available for the aging population. We must nurture the creativity and growth of alliances as we continue to provide services to older, frail adults.

BIBLIOGRAPHY

Administration on Aging (2001). *A Profile of Older Americans*. U.S. Department of Health and Human Services.

Allegheny Lutheran Social Ministries (2001). "Intergenerational Day Service." Hollidaysburg, Pa.: Allegheny Lutheran Social Ministries.

American Health Care Association (2001). *The 2001 Nursing Facility Sourcebook*. Washington, D.C.: AHCA.

Assisted Living Federation of America (ALFA) and Pricewaterhouse Coopers LLP (2001). "ALFA's 2001 Overview of the Assisted Living Industry." Fairfax, Va.: ALFA Public Relations.

Catholic Charities (2001). "Catholic Charities USA's 2001 Legislative Priorities." Alexandria, Va.: Catholic Charities USA..

Evangelical Lutheran Church in America (2001). "Local Congregational Social Ministry Activities." Chicago: Division for Research and Evaluation, ELCA.

Evangelical Lutheran Church in America and the Lutheran Church–Missouri Synod (2001). "A Social Ministry Partnership." Chicago: Division for Church and Society, ELCA.

Faith Communities Today (2000a). "The Basic Demographic Profile of Respondents." Hartford, Conn.: Hartford Institute for Religion Research, Hartford Seminary.

———. (2000b). "Community Outreach." Hartford, Conn.: Hartford Institute for Religion Research, Hartford Seminary.

Fahey, C. (1996). "New Wine In Old Wineskins." In *The Catholic Identity Project*. New York: Third Age Center, Fordham University.

Federal Interagency Forum on Aging-Related Statistics (2000). "Older Americans 2000: Key Indicators of Well-Being." Federal Interagency Forum on Aging-Related Statistics, Washington, D.C.: U.S. Government Printing Office.

Kammer, F. (2000). "Ten Ways Catholic Charities Are Catholic." Alexandria, Va.: Catholic Charities USA.

Kimble, M. A., S. H. McFadden, J. W. Ellor, and J. J. Seeber, eds. (1995). *Aging, Spirituality, and Religion: A Handbook*. Vol. 1. Minneapolis: Fortress Press.

Kysar, R. D. (1991). *Called to Care: Biblical Images for Social Ministry*. Minneapolis: Fortress Press.

Levin, J. S., and R. J. Taylor (1997). "Age Differences in Patterns and Correlates of the Frequency of Prayer." *The Gerontologist* 37: 75–88.

Lutheran Services in America (2001). "2001 Award for Excellence: Joined at the Heart in Ministry, Congregations and Social Ministry Organizations." St. Paul: Lutheran Services in America.

Marty, M. (1986). *Health and Medicine in the Lutheran Tradition*. New York: Crossroad.

McCurley, F. R. (1989). *Go in Peace, Serve the Lord: The Social Ministry of the Church*. Chicago: Division for Congregational Ministries, ELCA.

——— (1986). *Witness of the Word: A Biblical Theology of the Gospel*. Philadelphia: Fortress Press.

National Council on Aging (2001). "Facts about Adult Day Services." Washington, D.C.: National Council on Aging.

Netting, F. (1995). "Congregation-Sponsored Housing." In Kimble et al., 335–49.

Office of the President (2001). "Rallying the Armies of Compassion: A Faith-Based Initiative." Washington, D.C.: The Executive Office of the President.

Olson, D. (2001). *Faith Based Profile Project*. Baltimore, Md.: Lutheran Services in America.

Princeton Religion Research Center (1994). *Religion in America*. Princeton, N.J.: Princeton Religion Research Center.

Sahyoun, N. R. et al. (2001). "The Changing Profile of Nursing Home Residents: 1985–1997." *Aging Trends* 4. Hyattsville, Md.: National Center for Health Statistics.

Taylor, A. (2001). *Across Ages Program Development and Training Manual*. Philadelphia: Temple University Center for Intergenerational Learning.

United Jewish Communities (UJC) (2001). *The Continuum of Care in the Twenty-First Century, An Action Guide: Helping Federations Meet the Needs of Our Jewish Elderly*. Washington, D.C.: United Jewish Communities.

Voss, B., and G. Hark (February 1997). "Choosing Resources for Social Ministry." *Christian Social Action* 10/2: 37–38.

Westberg, G. E. (1990). *The Parish Nurse*. Minneapolis: Augsburg.

12

Small Group Approaches to Group Spiritual Autobiography Writing

RICHARD L. MORGAN

Since the original work of Robert N. Butler in 1963, doing life review with older persons has become a major task for social workers and clinicians. No longer viewed as the meaningless repetition of "old folks living in the past," life review has found its place as a natural and necessary task of old age. James Hillman has said "Life review yields long-term gains that enrich character by bringing understanding to events. The patterns in your life become more discernible among the wreckage and the romance, more like a well-plotted novel" (Hillman 1999, 91). We are finally realizing that *every life* is worthy of a novel, and no life is insignificant or unimportant. Writing one's life review is no longer just for the rich and famous, for people with distinguished lives. It is for everyone. Written memories have become more valuable because families tend to be more geographically distant and children are less likely to hear stories at their grandparents' knees. Elders know if they do not preserve these stories, they are lost.

Members of the reticent generation, termed "the greatest generation" by Tom Brokaw, are disclosing their stories by looking at their past to make the most of the years left to them. They are wrestling with such questions as, Did my life really matter? Was my time on earth well spent? What can I look back on with pride? and What did I mean to others? A special form of life review—spiritual autobiography—helps older people to clarify these questions, discern some answers, find their voices to leave as a legacy for younger generations.

Although more people are doing spiritual autobiography, there remain two major problems. All too often it takes place in one-on-one relationships, with a social worker or family member recording the stories. A weakness of this approach is it elicits selective memories, possibly shaped by defense mechanisms serving self-regard. In a group setting, where stories are told with candor and honesty, the whole story is more apt to be told. James Magee stresses the need for group spiritual autobiography, "The shared purpose of the group facilitates self-disclosure. Members are often attentive, expect to receive the same respect in their own turn. Similarities in scenes may prompt recollection from the participants" (Magee 1988, 12).

My own experience in leading spiritual autobiography groups for the past twenty years, confirms this belief. Having companions on one's spiritual journey helps when we run into rough spots on the road, get stuck in the ditch, or lose heart. Sharing faith stories in a group becomes holy ground. Sharing what is our deepest, most personal faith connects us to what is universally bonding. Also, there is a vital connection between the storyteller and the listener, as stories trigger stories and we discover that we are both telling and listening to our own and others' stories simultaneously.

A second problem with the traditional life review process is that the faith dimension is often given scant attention concerning where God fits into one's story. Harry R. Moody addresses this deficiency:

> Today there is growing interest in reminiscence and life review; some writers even speak of spiritual life-review. . . . Yet few writers on reminiscence have understood or recognized the religious origins of life review, which was put forward originally by Robert Butler (1963) in purely psychodynamic terms and has largely remained bounded by psychology. (Moody 1994, 94)

Group spiritual autobiography becomes a preferred way to preserve the faith stories.

THE NEED

Guided spiritual autobiography is an urgent need for older persons at any stage of the aging process. For those in extended middle years, it becomes a valuable tool for discerning God's will for the years that remain. It is in the seventies or later years, however, that people feel desire for larger meaning in the story of their lives and to bestow on others the wisdom they have accrued as their legacy. Every person is an unfinished story and, by discerning God's presence in the journey, one becomes more attentive to where God is leading in the present. The longevity factor presses many people to find a deeper vocation for their later years than leisure-time activities or what Joseph Sittler called "geriatric shuffleboard." Jewish writers have described the "ethical will": handing on to future generations "the voice of our heart"—the spiritual and personal values by which we have lived. Group spiritual autobiography helps older persons craft that ethical will.

Significant events of a person's life may be kept hidden and serve to further isolate older persons. Henri J. M. Nouwen has spoken of this in moving terms as "desolation."

> Desolation is the crippling experience that the few years left to live will not allow you to widen the circle again. Desolation is the gnawing feeling of being left behind by those who have been close and dear to you during the many years of life. . . . When they leave you, you know you will have to travel on alone. Even to the friendly people you will meet on your way, you will never be able to say, 'Do you remember?' because they were

not there when you lived it. Then life becomes like a series of reflections in a broken window. (Nouwen and Gaffney 1990, 36–37)

This truth came home in one of the spiritual autobiography groups I led at a retirement community. Nonagenarian Dr. Jean Ervin, sister of former Senator Sam J. Ervin, told the group how difficult it was to share her story when so many of her contemporaries had died. "The people who had shared these memories are mostly gone," she said, "and when my nephew Sam III suddenly died, it was devastating. I thought I would die before he did, and now I am still here. I am the youngest of ten children." Despite suffering from macular degeneration, Jean Ervin used a Kurzeill 1000 computer, and painstakingly wrote her life book, *The Youngest of Ten* (Ervin 1997).

One of the most glaring needs for group spiritual autobiography is in nursing homes, where frail elderly often experience isolation and desolation. Here God's oldest friends not only suffer the devastating effects of aging but also the crippling experience of the shrinking circle of friends. It is here that our mothers and fathers have to live out their days in what Ronald Blythe calls "slow motion departure" (Blythe 1979, 73).

As Henry Simmons writes, "The spiritual struggle of the later years is a struggle to keep the human spirit from being overwhelmed by frailty" (Simmons 1998, 73). Social isolation means older people are relegated to live out their lives with the old, or very old. Often there is little communication among residents. Instead of being a community, residents stay by themselves, and instead of finding common ground, they maintain their differences. At first some residents in nursing homes feel helpless, abandoned, and angry and may not work well in a group. As they seek to reorganize their lives, they need to build relationships and establish friendships. I have found that spiritual autobiography groups become a focal place for building community and forming friendships.

THE NATURE OF THE GROUP

Three important facts need to be stated: (1) Although spiritual autobiography groups are not group therapy, they do have therapeutic value; (2) spiritual autobiography includes reminiscence but adds the faith dimension; and (3) spiritual autobiography has crucial significance for the terminally ill but is mainly intended for the elderly well.

Therapeutic, Not Therapy

Many activities are therapeutic—have healing power—without being therapy per se. Birren and Cochran write, "Like regular exercise, enjoying a cup of tea in the garden, conversing with a trusted confidant, playing a musical instrument, gardening, or spending leisure time in nature, autobiography has healing powers" (Birren and Cochran 2001, 9).

The therapeutic value of spiritual autobiography groups is especially evident in the healing of memories. Rather than being stuck in the past, harboring old resentments and regrets, healing occurs when these memories resurface, and are recontexualized in a positive way. However, some older persons resist disclosure, fearing the pain of getting back in touch with their past. "I've lived through it once," one woman commented, "and somehow survived. I don't want to reopen those old wounds."

Zalman Schachter-Shalomi counters that resistance by stating, "What frees us from the tyranny of the past is the understanding that time is *stretchable,* not linear, so we can reframe and reshape it, using contemplative techniques....We can reach back into the past and repair events and relationships that we perceive as failures or disappointments" (Schachter-Shalomi and Miller 1995, 93). Experience in leading groups over the past twenty years bears witness to the healing that does take place, so that past traumas are brought to light, reexperienced, and then healed. Even when reconciliation does not take place, healing can occur.

Beyond Reminiscence

Spiritual autobiography goes beyond reminiscence or "remembered experiences." St. Augustine provides an early model of spiritual autobiography in his *Confessions.* He tells five unusually self-disclosive events: (a) the pear-stealing episode; (b) the death of an unnamed friend; (c) his escape from his mother through an act of deception; (d) his famous garden experience; (e) the mystical vision he and his mother had shortly before her death. What marked this faith review was the way Augustine discerned the presence and providence of God in these events. By composing his faith story, Augustine was able to construct a unified view of himself and his place in God's world. With this new vision of himself, he was able to return to his life with meaning and purpose. Earlier he had said of himself, "And I became to myself a wasteland" (Book II, X, 18, Outler 1955). Later, he could write, "When I came to be united to thee with all my being, then there will be no more pain and toil for me, and my life shall be a real life, being wholly filled by thee" (Book X, XXVIII, 39, Outler 1955).

Donald Capps rightly perceives that autobiography is a metaphor of the self in the process of becoming and finding wholeness. Through his *Confessions* Augustine gives self-disclosure a central importance for spiritual autobiography groups in any age or time (Capps 1983, 270).

Spiritual autobiography seeks to connect our stories with God's story in the Bible. Its purpose is to enable group members to hear the biblical story and say, "That's my story, too." It is the Spirit of God who makes that connection. The Scriptures become a role model for us to remember, share, and interpret our stories. Participants begin to realize that each life story is a part of a Big Story. The more we are in touch with our own stories and their meaning, the more alive and powerful the stories of the Scriptures become. If the biblical stories are absent from spiritual autobiography, a gap exists and, conversely, a study of the Bible without relating them to our stories leaves a vacuum. Both need the other to celebrate the meaning of our own lives and God's story to be celebrated.

Group members can discern the master story of their lives. The master story touches core convictions and embraces recurring religious themes around which we build our lives. As our stories are grounded in biblical stories, we begin to discern their meaning. Moody and Carroll's pivotal book, *Five Stages of the Soul* (Moody and Carroll 1997), points to how our stories revolve around the themes: the call, the search, the struggle, the breakthrough, and the return.

The call is known by many names—change of heart, conversion, and so forth—but is basically a movement from the circumference of life to the center. *The search* begins with a quest for guidance. *The struggle* involves disillusionment, despair, regret, and impatience. *The breakthrough* occurs with a burst of vision, a new beginning and experience of joy. *The return* means that life goes on as before with a difference that makes the ordinary unique.

In my own experience working with spiritual autobiography groups, stories within these themes abound. Stephen expressed regret over missed opportunities in life and that he had preferred security to risk. He said he had a "Jonah complex," likening his running from responsibility to the ancient prophet. But, like Jonah, he was given a second chance after retirement, when God called him to a life of service, working with the poor and outcast in a community mission. Philip also identified with Jonah, but in a different way, Surviving cancer in his fifties, he identified with being spit back into life after being in the depths of illness.

Martha expressed how she always had to live up to her name in being a model of service and sacrifice. She was always preparing meals for the family at funerals, delivering meals to shut-ins, and waiting on tables. "Now I am working on my Mary side," she said, "and devoting more of my time to prayer and meditation."

Howard lamented the fact that his life had been spent in a far country of self-interest and the accumulation of wealth but, like the prodigal son, he "had come to himself" and was volunteering for nonprofit organizations.

Sharon talked about the conversion of Paul, a conversion from religion to faith. A diligent church worker all her life, she began to experience God in a personal way after the retirement, and told the group, "My older god was a god who demanded perfection and now I am resting in the God of love who lets me be myself."

The "Well Elderly"

Spiritual autobiography is meaningful to terminally ill persons, but it is mainly intended for the elderly who are healthy. Ebersole claims that there is an urgency for terminally ill persons to share their life review. She writes, "In preparing to relinquish their own life they seem to feel compelled to carry out some anticipatory grief work. This would add credence to the belief that a life review is essentially a part of letting go" (Ebersole 1976, 305).

There remains little doubt that doing individual life review with dying persons in hospice, hospitals, or at home is a powerful experience. Research has shown that the ethical will is especially meaningful to those who stare death in the face. Hospice workers, bereavement counselors, and psychologists frequently use writing exercises to help people come to terms with their end. The wisdom that Mitch Albom heard as he listened to Morrie, which he chronicled in *Tuesdays with Morrie*, is a classic example.

Buechner writes, "There is something more than a little disconcerting about writing your own autobiography. There is something geriatric about it too, an old codger putting his affairs in order as the end approaches" (Buechner 1983, 3). However true that may be, spiritual autobiography is not to be seen as a person's last gasp—the final words before death. Our stories continue as long as we live. Writing our stories does not mean we are putting a period at the end of our stories. Rather, we are always adding more paragraphs, or even chapters.

FOR WHOM ARE THE GROUPS INTENDED?

Spiritual autobiography groups are meant for most older people, but leaders should be aware that cases of resistance will occur. Many of the "greatest generation" were programmed to believe that to talk of themselves was neither good manners nor good taste. Earlier scripting has bred a resistance to self-disclosure. I recall an older man in his late eighties who told me he could not participate in the group because, "As a child I was taught by my parents never to talk about myself. That is the way I have lived my life, and I don't intend to change now." Others shy away from groups because of fear of disclosure, shame about their past, or the misguided view that it is better to bury the past than relive it.

Birren and Deutchman described four problem members who can appear at spiritual autobiography groups: (1) monopolizers (persons who need inordinate attention and cannot relate to others); (2) career group members (persons who have attended countless groups and consider themselves experts); (3) amateur therapists (persons who play psychologist and want to analyze everyone instead of looking at themselves); (4) nonparticipants (persons who do not share in the group experience and refuse to participate) (Birren and Deutchman 1991, 94–98). Later, Birren and Cochran added to that list: (1) participants who go off on tangents; (2) shy or reticent group members who slow the energy of discussion; (3) group members who make negative or judgmental comments; (4) all group members speaking at once; (5) participants who withdraw from the group, looking displeased; and (6) participants who persistently disturb the work of the group (Birren and Cochran 2001, 45–52). Whenever an autobiography group comes together, it faces power struggles and a need for commitment. Some will want to control or dominate the group; others may drop out.

It is significant that these nonappropriate group members appear readily in middle-age groups, but rarely in groups of older people. Older people want to tell their stories and are more often attentive to others' stories. Spiritual autobiography groups for older adults can take place in a variety of settings: parish halls in local congregations, activity centers in retirement communities, senior centers, retreat centers, storefront centers, and in hospital or hospice conference rooms with volunteers and staff.

LEADERSHIP

The ideal is that each group member functions as a full partner and takes full responsibility for the group process. In most cases, however, experience has shown that a facilitator is needed to direct the group. She or he needs to free participants to more easily enter into the spirit of the group process. The goal is that members tell their stories in their own ways. Birren and Deutchman suggest that when the group size is too large to be manageable by one leader (more than six to eight members), coleadership may be preferable (Birren and Deutchman 1992, 28).

Viktor Frankl described practitioners of his school of Logotherapy more as ophthalmologists than as painters. They seek not to convey to the person a picture of the world as they see it, but rather widening and broadening the spiritual insight of group members so that they become conscious of the meaning of their stories (Frankl 1984).

In order to be an effective group leader, Birren and Cochran claim that "participation in a guided autobiography group is an essential preparation for leading a workshop. The experience of having sought meaning in one's own life and, even more important, having risked sharing one's personal history with others fosters a sensitivity and respect for the process" (Birren and Cochran 2001, 22).

WHAT IS THE GROUP PROCESS?

An effective group consists of as few as five or six adults who have come together to share and write their life stories. The best group size for a ten-week workshop is ten to twelve persons, although the group may be larger, if time is allotted for dyads or small groups of three or four persons. The meeting place needs to be large and airy, room with space for both total group meetings and one-on-one interactions. *It is essential that chairs be arranged in a circle, and that confidentiality be required.* Participants may feel freer to share in a small group than in other situations because they know that they will not be judged and what they say will not be repeated.

Native American "wisdom circles" provide a good model. Wisdom circles are places to practice heart-to-heart communication skills, to heal wounds, and to find courage to act upon that "still, small voice within" (Garfield, Cahill, and Spring 1998). Wisdom circles attempt to create a safe place for deep truth telling, with compassionate listeners who hear other person's stories without interrupting.

The group covenants to meet once a week for ten sessions (at least ninety minutes per session), to attend regularly, and to do the written assignments (Morgan 2002). Participation is always optional, with the understanding that what is shared is entirely a matter of personal decision.

THE IMPORTANCE OF WRITING ONE'S STORY

Even more empowering than telling is the act of writing one's story, which offers more potential for the longer term. Kirk Polking says that writing, rather than telling stories around the fireplace, allows for more depth and honesty, especially in terms of feelings (Polking 1995).

One does not have to be a professional writer to participate. All that is required is the willingness to write and share one's story with a group of caring persons. No one is pressured to share what has been written, although reading aloud to one other group member, a soul friend, has meaning. Each participant is given a writing assignment that covers the major scope of the class. Writing assignments are done either in the group, or at home, and are brought to the group for sharing.

If writing is done within the group, there are several steps in the writing process. First is the invitation, the calling. This is sacred time. Participants are asked to quiet their minds and listen. When they begin to write, they are putting on paper the results of their listening. Questions are asked, and time given for freewrite. Group members write for twenty minutes without stopping. The structured freewrite allows participants to get started. Some of the simplest prompts are the following:

- The day I was born. . . .
- My mother always said. . . .
- My father told me. . . .
- The first spiritual experience I remember was. . . .
- I get angry when. . . .
- My worst moment was. . . .

Before each session, participants reflect on the life theme to be presented. Individuals are asked to write two or three typed pages of their own story as related to the theme. They will read these pages in the next group.

In one group I led, participants were introduced to the theme of transitions or turning points and asked to choose one major turning point in their life and write two pages about it. Linda told about her divorce. "I found myself relinquishing the past, and it was hard because I often wondered if I made the right decision. It was a scary time where I had to learn to live in trust. The future was not yet in sight, and all that I had left behind was gone. But I grew, and started over. It was the turning point of my life story."

Strategies devised by Birren and Feldman, which organize memories around such major themes as family, work, money, health and body, sexual identity, and life models (Birren and Feldman 1997, 154–68), have also proved helpful in the writing process. Sensitizing questions guide the writers in composing their responses.

CONCLUSION

Spiritual autobiography groups provide a means for older persons to discern the meaning of their lives, resolve old conflicts, and find community in a fragmented world. They also help to clarify and write ethical wills as legacies for coming generations. Spiritual autobiography groups also help older persons maintain continuity with their former selves, what Sharon R. Kaufman calls "the ageless self" (Kaufman 1986). She tells of interviews with older people who "express a sense of self that is ageless—an identity that maintains continuity despite the physical and social changes that come with old age" (Kaufman 1986, 7).

Margaret came into one of my groups for the first time, and when I asked her to tell us her name, she replied, "My name? Same as it's always been!" She said more than she realized. The frailties and diminishments that aging inevitably brings need not sever persons from their "ageless selves."

Birren and Deutchman provided a vision for those who work with older people when they wrote, "Older people are ripe for autobiography, and it is especially beneficial for them since contemporary society does not provide the opportunity for the old to review their lives and tell their stories" (Birren and Deutchman 1991, 6).

Although writing one's story is important and an integral part of the process, the real value of these groups is in the bonding and community experience. So many of the institutions that once contributed to the stability of our daily lives have gone. Distance from extended family, mobility, frequent moves, and divorce often leaves little sense of community. Spiritual autobiography groups create a sense of community in our broken world.

I had just concluded a two-day workshop with older adults, urging them to write their life stories. For two days we had experienced listening to stories that needed to be preserved. When I asked the group how many were going to write their stories, only two hands were raised. I looked around at those faces, with a terrible sense of failure. But colleague Stephen Sapp remarked, "Don't think this was a failure. For the past two days people have shared intimate stories, experienced the New Testament *koinonia,* and seeds have been sown that will bear fruit."

Spiritual autobiography groups offer the possibility that older persons can turn the narratives of their lives into a once-told tale. Differing from the traditional life review, focus is placed on the faith dimension, where God fits into the life journey. This faith dimension allows us to see God's presence (*kairos*), the sacred moment, in the clock time of our existence (*chronos*). Connecting our stories with the Master Story becomes a powerful experience of spirituality. The group process includes not only telling one's story, but writing it. There is no greater gift that we can give older persons than to be present in those moments when they open their hearts and share their stories. Spiritual autobiography groups make such moments a reality.

BIBLIOGRAPHY

Albert, S. W. (1996). *Writing from Life: Telling Your Life Story.* New York: Tarcher/Putnam.

Birren, J. E., and D. E. Deutchman (1991). *Guiding Autobiography Groups for Older Adults: Exploring the Fabric of Life.* The Johns Hopkins Series in Contemporary Medicine and Public Health. Baltimore: Johns Hopkins University Press.

Birren, J. E., and K. Cochran (2001). *Telling the Stories of Life through Guided Autobiography Groups.* Baltimore: Johns Hopkins University Press.

Birren, J. E., and L. Feldman (1997). *Where Do We Go from Here? Discovering Your Own Wisdom in the Second Half of Your Life.* New York: Simon and Schuster.

Blythe, R. (1979). *The View in Winter: Reflections on Old Age.* New York: Harcourt Brace Jovanovich.

Botella, L., and G. Feixas (1995). "The Autobiographical Group: A Tool for the Reconstruction of Past Experiences with the Aged." In Hendricks, 141–58.

Buechner, F. (1992). *Listening to Your Life. Daily Meditations with Frederick Buechner.* San Francisco: HarperSanFrancisco.

——— (1983). *Now and Then.* New York: Harper & Row.

Butler, R. N. (1974). "Successful Aging and the Role of the Life Review." *The American Geriatric Society* 22: 529–35.

——— (1963). "The Life Review: An Interpretation of the Reminiscence of the Aged." *Psychiatry* 26: 65–76.

Capps, D. (1983). "Parabolic Events in Augustine's Autobiography." *Theology Today* 15: 260–74.

Clements, W. M. (1981). "Reminiscence as Cure of Souls in Early Old Age." *Journal of Religion and Health* 20/1: 41–47.

Doughtery, R. M. (1995). *Group Spiritual Direction: Community for Discernment.* Mahwah, N.J.: Paulist.

Ebersole, P. (1976). "Reminiscing." *American Journal of Nursing* 76/8: 1305.

Ervin, J. (1997). *The Youngest of Ten: An Autobiography.* Chapel Hill, N.C.: Professional.

Frankl, V. E. (1984). *Man's Search for Meaning: An Introduction to Logotherapy.* Trans. I. Lasch. 3d ed. Reprint. New York : Simon & Schuster.

Garfield, C., S. Cahill, and C. Spring (1998). *Wisdom Circles: A Guide to Self Discovery and Community Building in Small Groups.* New York: Hyperion.

Hatley, B. J. (1985). "Spiritual Well-Being through Life Histories." *Journal of Religion and Aging* 1/2: 63–71.

Hendricks, J., ed. (1995). *The Meaning of Reminiscence and Life Review.* New York: Baywood.

Hillman, J. (1999). *The Force of Character and the Lasting Life.* New York: Random House.

Kaufman, Sharon R. (1986). *The Ageless Self: Sources of Meaning in Late Life.* Madison: University of Wisconsin Press.

Kimble, M. A. (1990). "Aging and the Search for Meaning." In Seeber, 111–29.

Kirkland, K. and H. McIlveen (1998). *Full Circle: Spiritual Therapy for the Elderly.* Binghamton, N.Y.: Haworth.

Leder, D. (1997). *Spiritual Passages: Embracing Life's Spiritual Journey.* New York: Tarcher.

Lewis, M. I., and R. N. Butler (November 1974). "Life Review Therapy: Putting Memories to Work in Individual and Group Psychotherapy." *Geriatrics* 29: 165–69.

Magee, J. J. (1988). *A Professional's Guide to Older Adults' Life Review: Releasing the Peace Within.* Lexington, Mass.: Lexington Books.

Moody, H. R. (1994). *Aging: Concepts and Controversies.* Sociology for a New Century. Thousand Oaks, Calif.: Pine Forge.

Moody, H. R., and D. Carroll (1997). *The Five Stages of the Soul: Charting the Spiritual Passages that Shape Our Lives.* New York: Doubleday Anchor.

Morgan, R. L. (2002). *Remembering Your Faith Story: Creating Your Own Spiritual Autobiography.* Nashville: Upper Room.

———— (1995). "Spiritual Autobiography Groups for Third and Fourth Agers." *Journal of Religious Gerontology* 9/2: 1–14.

Nouwen, H. J. M., and Gaffney, W. J. (1990). *Aging: The Fulfillment of Life.* New York: Doubleday.

Outler, A., ed. and trans. (1955). *Augustine: Confessions and Enchiridion.* Philadelphia: Westminster.

Polking, K. (1995). *Writing Family Histories and Memoirs.* Cincinnati: Betterway.

Randall, R. (1986). "Reminiscing in the Elderly: Pastoral Care of Self Narratives." *The Journal of Pastoral Care* 40: 207–15.

Ray, R. E. (2000). *Beyond Nostalgia: Aging and Life-Story Writing.* Charlottesville: University Press of Virginia.

Schachter-Shalomi, Z., and R. S. Miller (1995). *From Age-ing to Sage-ing: A Profound New Vision of Growing Older.* New York: Warner.

Shea, D. B. (1968). *Spiritual Autobiography in Early America.* Princeton, N.J.: Princeton University Press.

Seeber, J. J. (1990). *Spiritual Maturity in the Later Years.* New York: Haworth.

Simmons, H. C. (1998). "Spirituality and Community in the Last Stage of Life." *Journal of Religious Gerontology* 11: 73–92.

———— (1990). "Countering Cultural Metaphors of Aging," *Journal of Religious Gerontology* 7/1–2: 153–66.

Ware, C. (1997). *Connecting to God: Nurturing Spirituality through Small Groups.* Washington, D.C.: Alban.

Wood, S., and L. M. Seymour (1994). "Psychodynamic Group Therapy for Older Adults." *Journal of Psychodynamic Nursing and Mental Health Services* 32/7: 19–24.

13　Volunteer Ministries with Older Adults

JAMES J. SEEBER

Churches in various patterns of collaboration have helped to provide human services for centuries. As the age-wave expands across America in the twenty-first century, there is little doubt that nonpublic resources will continue to be required to serve the growing needs of elders for human support and services. One important aspect of public service by congregations and other faith-based groups is that of providing a variety of volunteer services directed toward the homebound, the frail, and those in special need. Most successful older adult ministries serve several levels of need and usually include the frail and disabled as part of such a ministry. This chapter examines the basis for volunteer service to others, offers several special examples of such organized volunteer service that are active nationwide, and suggests the direction that church/synagogue life appears to be going.

RELIGIOUS GROUPS AND VOLUNTEERS

Religious groups collectively constitute the largest users of volunteers in American society. Nearly half of all volunteer activity in society is by persons who are active in and recruited through church or synagogue (Bradley 1999, 46). Much of the service volunteered is for direct religious activity, but the range and amount of social services provided by religious groups is truly astounding. The newsletter of the Interfaith Volunteer Caregivers project affirms the importance of the religious base for their projects: "The driving force of the IVCP is the spiritual ministry of caregiving—assuming a deep personal commitment in the context of one's faith" (*Interfaith Volunteer Caregivers* 1989, 10). Furthermore, the religious motivation appears to lend perseverance to such volunteer activity. IVCP projects experienced only a 3 percent attrition rate annually during the 1980s, a truly remarkable rate when we recall that a large number of IVCP volunteers are themselves older adults.

In a national survey conducted through the Forum on Religion, Spirituality and Aging of the American Society on Aging some time ago, dozens of congregations were nominated for outstanding older adult work. The services they provided mostly through supervised volunteers included hosting information and referral hotlines about community services, visitation, telecare, and personal assistance for managing funds, planning moves, and making funeral arrangements. One church in

Florida works with the local courts to provide volunteer guardians for persons who cannot keep their bills paid and living arrangements in order. Some churches have parish nurses and social workers on staff who offer clinical health care and personal case management.

Three major ministries that have attracted thousands of persons to do friendly visitation and personal services are the Interfaith Caregivers Alliance (ICA), Stephen Ministries, and Shepherd's Centers. These programs are highlighted in the pages that follow. Many support groups of other kinds either sponsored by or meeting in church and synagogue facilities also serve thousands of people across America (Seeber 1995, 256–66). In addition, religious groups alone or in combinations support nursing and retirement homes, counseling agencies, and social service organizations such as Catholic Charities and Lutheran Social Services in most parts of the country.

OLDER ADULT VOLUNTEERS IN CHURCH AND COMMUNITY

Although churches are the source of activity reported by between one-third and one-half of older American volunteers, many other organizations and programs also involve older adults as volunteers. Studies over the past half century indicate that the proportion of older Americans who do volunteer activity has risen from 11 to 14 percent (1960s to 1970s) to 37 to 40 percent (1987) (Chambre 1991, 34). That proportion remained about the same from 1987 to 1997, according to a recent American Association of Retired Persons (AARP) study (Bradley 1999, 46). An additional 22 percent are available to volunteer but were not so engaged at the time of the survey. Volunteers providing service average 6.5 hours per week, and their donated time is the equivalent of 1.1 million full-time employees. The net worth in pay equivalence for work rendered is about $17 billion dollars annually. The volunteer work they do is not "blue ribbon" committee work, but 29 percent serve people directly and 22 percent work with their hands (National Council on the Aging 1994, 42–43). An excellent example of this is a retired businessman in Shell Beach, California, who rises each Wednesday at 5 A.M. to help distribute food to the needy until noon or later as part of the community Food Basket program. In addition to formal volunteer activities, about 30 million older Americans provide direct care to family members or friends on a regular basis.

A 1997 study by the AARP of civic involvement found that nearly 86 percent of all older Americans had spent at least some amount of time in the past year helping neighbors, friends, or disabled family members. About 33 percent in 1997 identified their volunteer work with religious groups, a decline from the 51 percent who reported church-based volunteer activity in 1991 (Helein 1991, 40). Of all volunteers, about 40 percent give more than 10 hours per month. The overall proportion who volunteer varies by age group. More than 50 percent of those age 30 to 49 volunteer, while about 40 percent of persons age 50 to 70 volunteer (Bradley 1999, 46). About 30 percent of those over 75 reported volunteering (noted as 23 percent of those over age 75 in the National Council on the Aging [NCOA] report).Volunteer activity may vary by age, but it does not end as people grow older.

A variety of government programs provide opportunities for older volunteers. Successful programs such as the Retired Senior Volunteer Program (RSVP) offer formal orientations and placements as well as insurance coverage and transportation for those who need it. Foster Grandparents (FGP) is a program that has worked within many school classrooms to give one-on-one help to youngsters.The Service Corps of Retired Executives (SCORE) matches experienced businesspeople with young businesses that need guidance and helps to reduce the rate of new business failures. In addition to such national programs, many local schools incorporate older volunteers as tutors, storytellers, and classroom assistants in varied roles, while countless service clubs in America would cease to exist were it not for the many older men and women who attend meetings and lead their community programs.

In recent years corporate America has offered encouragement to senior volunteers. Harlan Cleveland, a retired professor at the University of Minnesota, reports that the Corporate Retiree Volunteer Programs (CRVP), led by Honeywell and twenty-two other businesses in Minnesota, has grown rapidly. In the mid-1990s more than six thousand retirees in Minnesota were actively involved in doing volunteer service with corporate encouragement (Cleveland n.d., 10). Examples of corporate volunteer encouragement include human relations or other personnel who facilitate, coordinate, and recognize volunteer activity by employees; corporations that develop their own community outreach programs as well as supporting volunteer activity that is in place; "executive loans" by corporations of personnel to assist nonprofit programs; "on-site" volunteerism in which corporate facilities are made available to nonprofit groups; and a readiness to value volunteer experience that is identified on résumés (Smith 1991, 70).A tangible example of such encouragement among working employees is Wal-Mart. America's largest retailer offers employees cash bonuses if they volunteer a certain amount of time in the community during a working year.

A false assumption is that retired persons have lots of time and therefore will increase their volunteer activities. Both the AARP study and the Harris Poll (Commonwealth Fund Report) found that working people gave more volunteer time than did retirees (Caro and Bass 1997, 427–41). Those who had been formal volunteers when they worked often continued the activity after retirement. Nonetheless, the AARP study found that many nonvolunteers were open to doing volunteer activities.They just had not been approached.

Barriers to volunteering that have been reported include time constraints, physical limitations, and family concerns. Only 8 percent in one survey reported being uninterested in volunteer activity (Helein 1991, 40).

What factors appear to motivate people to volunteer? Bradley notes that the AARP study found that persons more strongly identified with their communities and more involved in religious activities volunteer most often.Twenty-nine percent of those who never attend religious services do volunteer work, while 60 percent of those who attend weekly do so (Bradley 1999, 46). Also, the tendency to volunteer is related to participation in organizations and to education and income levels among people.

What specifically motivates people to give time without pay to various activities? In broad terms, the AARP study found three sources of motivation among people. First, many volunteers report an enhanced sense of purpose in life and the desire to give something back. People most often volunteer if they are committed to the cause for which they consider volunteering. Second was a specific interest in some area (arts, music, health care, etc.) and a desire for personal growth and knowledge. Third was the structuring of daily life and the feeling of continuing productivity which volunteering gives, especially for people who were used to years of routinized work life (Bradley 1999, 47–48).

The late church educator Paul Maves suggested a more personal set of motivations, which he identified as (a) feeling empathy for those who are to be helped, (b) a sense of reciprocity (people help because someone may help them someday), (c) a feeling of religious duty to help others, and (d) a spirit of altruism among those who are healthy enough or lucky enough to be able to help others (Maves 1981, 29). In another study of motivation, Rumsey found that education level and retirement status were each positively related to greater likelihood of volunteering but that financial status and living arrangements made little difference. The extent of sociability of the individual also influenced the rate of volunteering. Younger volunteers placed a greater value on gaining knowledge in their volunteer experience than older persons, but altruism influenced younger and older volunteers alike (Rumsey 1997).

If past patterns continue, those who volunteered when they were working will tend to continue doing so after retirement. Bradley notes that, with multiple career changes becoming common, volunteer roles may serve as an introduction to new fields of work and perhaps even as unpaid apprenticeships or points of entry into positions for full- or part-time employment. Baby boomers currently have the highest rate of volunteerism across the age span and may set a trend for more professional types of volunteer activities in the future.

SPECIAL CASES OF OLDER ADULT VOLUNTEER MINISTRIES

The 1970s saw the establishing of community senior programs nationwide through the Older Americans Act and the creation of Shepherd's Centers and Interfaith Volunteer Caregivers—two international programs that develop volunteer services through local churches, synagogues, and mosques. In this era the startling discovery was made that 80 percent of all persons sixty-five and over were not frail, sick nursing-home residents. In fact, the well elderly were far more numerous than the frail elderly. Bernard Nash, President of the AARP in the early 1970s, divided older people into three functional categories—active, transitional, and frail. Thirty years later we know that these categories still describe the variety of elders and their differing needs. The active elderly can largely take care of themselves. The frail elderly are in institutions or live very sheltered lives, cared for by spouses, family, or professional caregivers. The transitional elderly are those on whom much volunteer time and energy is focused helping them to maintain a life that has meaning and to receive support services they need to avoid premature institutionalization. Both Shepherd's Centers and Interfaith Caregiver groups serve large numbers of transitional elderly.

Shepherd's Centers

In the heartland, a pragmatic American program arose to enrich the lives of older people. Shepherd's Centers began in a central-city neighborhood in Kansas City, Missouri, in 1972 when a number of congregations banded together to create programs of interest and meaning for older residents in the area. What exactly is a Shepherd's Center? "A Shepherd's Center is the interfaith expression and extension of congregations in a defined area, working together, assisting and serving older adults while at the same time establishing and developing intentional ministries with older adults within congregations" (Shepherd's Centers of America n.d., "Ten Characteristics").

Elbert Cole, the United Methodist pastor who founded Shepherd's Centers, described the three fundamental principles underlying each center. First, all centers are ecumenical and (ideally) interfaith. Second, all centers are geographically based, taking a model from the Roman Catholic concept of "parish," but on an intercongregational level. Third, all centers are focused on the empowerment of seniors; they are programs by seniors for seniors.

From a modest but successful beginning in 1972, the steady growth of Shepherd's Centers led to eighty-five such interfaith projects nationwide in 1998, with thirty-five more in planning stages. Encouraged by a national office that provides guidance and some services, all centers are locally funded and governed. One might walk through a typical Shepherd's Center and see

> people learning foreign languages, studying local history, practicing Tai Chi or discovering how to use a computer. Outside the center, in the neighborhood, you'll find Shepherd's Center volunteers delivering meals, repairing houses and giving caregivers much-needed relief. And you'll find that the people doing all these things—teaching, learning, helping, giving, and receiving—are older adults themselves. (Shepherd's Centers of America n.d., "A Vision for Life")

A Shepherd's Center mission statement notes that "the primary purpose of a Shepherd's Center is to enrich the later years with opportunities for service to others, self expression, meaningful work, and close friendships" (Shepherd's Centers of America n.d., "Vision and Mission"). A second purpose is to help older people remain independent in their home environment as long as possible. This is accomplished through four main program areas: life maintenance, life enrichment, life reorganization, and celebration. The frequent outcome of these programs is a new vision of aging, both by elders themselves and by the communities that centers serve. Life maintenance programs are practical services that enable older persons to safely remain in their homes while growing more frail. Typical services include arranging for transportation, meals-on-wheels, companion aides, telephone reassurance, or hospice. Older volunteers either provide the service or are conduits by which services in the community are secured. Life enrichment activities include intellectual and social stimulation as elders share life wisdom in classes and programs. Adventures in learning is one part of the life enrichment dimension and follows the concept of elders teaching each other from the lifetime of experiences they have gained. Life reorganization offers specific kinds of sessions or classes that help older persons grapple with life changes, personal growth, and developing skills to handle the changes that occur. These often include a variety of health-education classes and preventive health-care programs. Questions are raised about life's meaning. Persons are encouraged to find meaning by helping others in various ways, from volunteer roles to new career paths. Life celebration is a general program helping persons to recognize the deeper meaning in later life events.

Elbert Cole has observed that we have added twenty-five to thirty years of relatively healthy living after the career years. Shepherd's Centers help people imagine how to use those years fruitfully and to ask implicit theological questions about the meaning and purpose of later life. Cole believes that Shepherd's Centers are helping people to develop a new social model of healthy older age. While many Shepherd's Centers are in middle-class neighborhoods, there are also successful centers in working-class and minority communities. The number of participants in centers ranges from 100 to more than 6,000 in one program in Greensboro, North Carolina.

Interfaith Caregivers Alliance

In 1983 the Robert Wood Johnson (RWJ) Foundation offered three-year start-up grants in communities across the United States to clusters of congregations who would work together to provide voluntary caring and support services to frail and disabled persons in their communities. Approximately $150,000 per project was available to help establish these new programs. Three hundred and fifty groups of congregations filed applications from which twenty-five were funded. Given limited technical assistance and encouragement by a small staff of the national program office, all projects continued in operation under local funding after the grant period. In addition, about one hundred other local programs went forward without funds from the RWJ Foundation. By 1987 when a national organization was formed (National Federation of Interfaith Volunteer Caregivers), more than forty-four additional organizations joined the original twenty-five RWJ project groups. By 1988 more than 250 organizations and individuals were members of the national organization.

At the first national meeting of the federation in 1988, Arthur Flemming, Chair of the Board of Trustees, commented on a Gallup poll that reported that while 75 percent of people help out when asked, fewer than 45 percent volunteer on their own. Flemming recognized the need to recruit and train volunteers.

To attract and keep volunteers, we must invite their participation with a clear-cut statement of need, provide staff support and training, and include them in the organization with the same status and privileges as paid staff. We must assess volunteers' skills and needs just as we would in the hiring process, and give them work to do that allows them to both contribute and grow (Interfaith Volunteer Caregivers brochure n.d., 18). What Dr. Flemming described is a vital set of processes to ensure long-term continuation and satisfaction among volunteers in congregational ministry.

Who did the twenty-five initially funded projects serve? They reached out to a needy population of nearly 26,000 people, 58 percent of whom lived alone, 69 percent of whom were disabled in some significant way, yet only 36 percent of whom received help from formal health-care providers. Elderly persons and elderly women especially were more often candidates for caregiving in the 1980s, since about 28 percent of all Americans sixty-five and older were at or near poverty income levels and 80 percent of all elderly persons living alone were women. An initial evaluation of the twenty-five funded projects not only chronicled the successes they were having. It also revealed that clergy support in the member congregations was critical but also problematic as the time and the long-term commitment needed did not always occur due to other claims and to clergy mobility.

Some clergy and congregations had a much stronger commitment to community involvement than others; some were not even aware of needs within their own congregations, particularly if they were new to the community and did not know many of the congregation's older members who no longer attended services. "We clergy have to admit the need in our own congregations and be willing to take care of more of our own" (Interfaith Volunteer Caregivers brochure n.d., 9).

A wide variety of services was provided to care recipients, including transportation, shopping, advocacy and referral, friendly visiting, and telephone reassurance. Help in maintaining homes and in personal chores (laundry, meal preparation, and cleaning) as well as personal care (dressing, bathing, eating, respite for caregivers) was included. Even help with hair shampooing was given (Interfaith Volunteer Caregivers brochure n.d., 14). Perhaps most valuable to care recipients, personal friendships were developed. It was estimated that over half of all volunteers developed close personal relationships with those they served, something not remotely possible in many public agency programs. Project coordinators helped volunteers to maintain a balance. "There's a fine line between caring and over-involvement. We in interfaith have to integrate our services into a holistic care approach that also includes family, friends, church and community agency support" (Juanita Goodson, Mobile, Alabama, quoted in Interfaith Volunteer Caregivers brochure n.d., 12).

Growth in the number of such projects has been steady. In 1993, the RWJ Foundation Faith In Action program provided an additional 23 million dollars to help establish 200 new projects, and in 2000 the RWJ Foundation announced plans to offer up to 113 million dollars more to fund as many as 2,000 additional projects. Meanwhile, the national federation moved from New York to Kansas City, Missouri, changed its name to the Interfaith Caregivers Alliance, and prepared to do a more extensive job of providing training and technical assistance to the growing numbers of local projects. The focus remains the same, however, serving the vulnerable through religious communities. A recent flyer says, "Though we are non-denominational, the Interfaith Caregivers Alliance recognizes our nation's wonderful heritage of faith-based caregiving programs" (Interfaith Caregivers Alliance n.d.).

Recent goals and initiatives of the ICA include (a) developing and establishing program standards and assessment guidelines; (b) providing leadership trainers across the country who will assist local groups to apply for foundation funding and also offer technical assistance and training to local groups; (c) developing strategic alliances and partnerships in caregiving resources, products, and services; and (d) supporting and representing faith-based caregiving groups nationwide (Interfaith Caregivers Alliance 2001, 5–6).

Stephen Ministries

Stephen Ministries began in 1975 when a local pastor trained lay volunteers in his congregation to provide Christian care among congregational members and others in the community. Over several years volunteers in other congregations were trained as Stephen Ministers as well. In 1978 Rev. Ken Haugk began to train persons who would return to their local congregations as Stephen Leaders. They, in turn, would train persons to be Stephen Ministers. Today a national staff of 50 persons offers year-round training seminars for Stephen Leaders. More than 7,000 congregations from 90 denominations in the United States, Canada, and 20 other countries host 27,000 trained Stephen Leaders and more than 250,000 trained Stephen Ministers.

Named for Stephen, a man of great compassion and the first martyr in the early Christian community (Acts 6–8), Stephen Ministries "trains lay people in Christian caregiving so more people can receive one-on-one care who otherwise might not receive care" (Stephen Ministries 1996). These volunteers work with individuals, not with couples or families, and they serve as caregivers, not counselors. They are trained to recognize the need for professional help and to work with their supervisors to help facilitate referrals to such help where needed. Through training-the-trainers (Stephen Leaders) and through the work of these "trainers," a thorough grounding is given to volunteers, including fifty hours of preparation plus continued training while serving.

Stephen Ministers "provide high quality, distinctively Christian care to those who need it" (Stephen Ministries 1995b). Theologically credible and written with psychological depth, the Stephen series training is designed as twenty-five sessions of practical material. The series offers "how to" guidance on building support for lay ministry in the congregation, selecting the right people as Stephen Ministers, and preparing caregivers for the ministry that is to come. Topics include developing skills in listening, sensing feelings, assertiveness, confidentiality, and understanding human needs in areas such as divorce, terminal illness, and bereavement.

The national staff for Stephen Ministries state as their mission that of proclaiming "through word and deed the gospel of Jesus Christ by nurturing, edifying, educating, and equipping the whole people of God [to be] effective servants who care for the needs of the whole person" (Stephen Ministries 1995a). Objectives include serving individuals such as the hospitalized, homebound, terminally ill, aging, disabled, separated or divorced, new residents in the community or church, and others. Stephen Ministers may also seek through the Christ Care series to increase congregational participation in small-group spiritual growth and caregiving and to give pastors backup support. By developing congregation-wide sensitivity to human needs, pastors, staff, and laity evolve a strong team approach to community caring.

The establishing of a Stephen Ministries program can occur in almost any size congregation and is intended to be a basic ministry of the congregation. Volunteers therefore are recruited only from within the congregation. One or more members, hopefully including the pastor, are trained by Stephen Ministries in St. Louis and then return home to recruit and lead volunteers through twenty-five sessions to become trained Stephen Ministers. These volunteers are asked to serve for a minimum of two years.

A congregation might typically follow these steps in establishing a Stephen Ministries program: (1) self-evaluation that identifies need for more complete caring ministries to meet people's needs; (2) adopting the Stephen Ministries model and sending one or more persons for a seven-day leader training series; (3) recruiting laity for training as Stephen Ministers and preparation of the congregation for a Stephen Ministries program; (4) quality training over twenty-five sessions (or fifty hours) in Christian caregiving; (5) commissioning of Stephen Ministers by the church and assigning of care-receivers to each minister; (6) ongoing regular meetings for supervision and continuing education for all ministers with new care-receivers assigned to volunteers as the crisis passes or the circumstances improve for current "clients"; and (7) additional recruits are found, trained, commissioned, and assigned as volunteer caregivers as needed.

Additional Volunteer Ministries

Special mention should be made of a recent new volunteer ministry that reaches across health-care and social service-occupational lines to offer valuable daily help to elderly people. In Minnesota and in Texas, the Living at Home/Block Nurse Program sponsored by the Elderberry Institute is touching thousands of lives. Some 36 local programs helped prevent the institutionalization of 632 elderly in the year 2000 at an estimated saving of nearly 6 million dollars. Volunteers offer informal friendship and general social support; medically trained persons offer health education and general health assistance, while a program nurse provides case management, bringing in services available in the community. The goal is to find volunteers and health-care workers who live in the same neighborhood as the clients so that an informal long-term home-care system can develop. Costs are kept modest through the use of volunteers.[1] While not specifically church-based as are the other examples, a large number of congregations participate in the community-wide programs.

Many other examples of volunteer helping ministries through congregations and religious communities exist. In the Upper Midwest a number of Protestant congregations, many of them Lutheran, have followed a "Caring Community" model which seeks to match young singles or couples who lack family nearby with older persons who likewise lack a nearby family. These younger and older households mutually minister to one another like an extended family.[2] The United Methodist Church has offered a program of "Caring Ministry" for several years in which laity are recruited and trained to do calling on isolated or vulnerable persons in their congregations. Indeed, churches and synagogues have probably the greatest potential for meaningful intergenerational sharing of all the social institutions in society.

FUTURE DIRECTIONS OF VOLUNTEERING IN CONGREGATIONS

It was noted above that religious groups in America use more volunteers than all other organizational systems. The future direction of congregational programs in American life will increasingly be intercongregational, intergenerational, and multidimensional. The era of congregations acting as if they were in a world all their own and pastors of congregations acting like masters of a ship at sea is over. More and more, the credibility of a congregation's witness in a secular and religiously pluralistic society will be enhanced by a cooperative spirit and by fostering intergenerational, family-like relationships. Churches and synagogues are places where the compartmentalizing of "specialization" does not need to dominate the interactive lives of people.

A decade of research on the value of informal social support ties (friendships, "neighboring," volunteers, etc.) has established that while immediate families may provide "instrumental support" (financial and other material help), close friends, neighbors, and church networks provide "emotional support." Such ties promote psychological and emotional well-being and freedom from loneliness. These outcomes are a valued part of the ministry of the laity with older adults.

It appears that the idea of lay ministry touches fundamental needs of all religious communities. One author summarized the centrality of meaning that volunteering in Christian traditions provides. First, such ministry is basic to life as the New Testament describes it. All Christians are called to be Christ's body, to do God's work in the world (1 Cor. 1:12). Church leaders are not called to do it all but are to "equip the saints for the work of ministry" (Eph. 4:11–12). Deeds of love and service are clearly central to Christian life. Jesus urged his followers to "love one another just as I have loved you"(John 13:34). Second, congregations need programs such as this to empower the laity in their commitment and to provide a nurturing, healing, and caring environment in the church. Third, pastors need the help to provide regular quality care to members and to build healthy relationships among church people. Fourth, laypersons themselves need such forms of "hands-on" ministry where healing, forgiveness, and strengths can be shared by all and skills in sharing it can be enhanced (Stephen Ministries 1995a).

NOTES

1. For further information, contact Elderberry Institute, 475 Cleveland Avenue North, Suite 322, St. Paul, MN 55108.

2. Further information is available from Lake Edge Lutheran Church, Caring Community Ministry, 4032 Monona Dr., Madison, WI 53716.

BIBLIOGRAPHY

American Association of Retired Persons (AARP) (1991). *Resourceful Aging: Today and Tomorrow.* Volume 2. Washington, D.C.: AARP.

Bradley, D. B. (1999). "A Reason to Rise Every Morning: The Meaning of Volunteering in the Lives of Older Americans." *Generations* 23/4: 46.

Caro, F. G., and S. A. Bass. (1997). "Receptivity to Volunteering in the Immediate Postretirement Period." *Journal of Applied Gerontology* 16/4: 427–41.

Chambre, S. M. (1991). *Volunteerism in an Aging Society.* Working Paper Series. New York: Center for the Study of Philanthropy.

Cleveland, H. (n.d.). *A Simple and Compelling Idea: Linking Retiree Volunteers with People in Need.* Minneapolis: NRVC.

Helein, J. V. (1991). "Volunteers: Resourceful Opportunities." In AARP, *Resourceful Aging,* 39–42.

Interfaith Caregivers Alliance (2001). "ICA Caregiver." Kansas City, Mo.: Interfaith Caregivers Alliance.

Interfaith Caregivers Alliance (n.d.). "Caring for the Caregivers." Kansas City, Mo.: Interfaith Caregivers Alliance.

Interfaith Volunteer Caregivers: A Special Report (1989). Princeton, N.J.: Robert Wood Johnson Foundation.

Interfaith Volunteer Caregivers brochure (n.d.). Princeton, N.J.: Robert Wood Johnson Foundation.

Kimble, M. A., S. H. McFadden, J. W. Ellor, and J. J. Seeber, eds. (1995). *Aging, Spirituality, and Religion: A Handbook.* Vol. 1. Minneapolis: Fortress Press.

Maves, P. B. (1981). *Older Volunteers in Church and Community: A Manual for Ministry.* Valley Forge, Pa.: Judson.

National Council on the Aging (April–June, 1994). "Perspective on Aging." Washington, D.C.: National Council on the Aging. 42–43.

Rumsey, D. (1997). "Motivational Factors in Older Adult Volunteers." In *Dissertation Abstracts International, Section A: Humanities and Social Sciences* 58(3-a), No. 0699.

Seeber, J. J. (1995). "Congregational Models." In Kimble et al., 253–69.

Shepherd's Centers of America (n.d.). "Shepherd's Centers of America: A Vision of Life for Older Adults." Kansas City, Mo.: Shepherd's Centers of America.

——— (n.d.). "Shepherd's Center Vision and Mission Statement." Kansas City, Mo.: Shepherd's Centers of America.

——— (n.d.). "The Ten Characteristics of a Shepherd's Center." Kansas City, Mo.: Shepherd's Centers of America.

Smith, M. P. (1991). "Older Adults: Volunteer Resources." In AARP, *Resourceful Aging,* 67–92.

Stephen Ministries (1996). "Q & A: Answers to the Most Frequently Asked Questions about the Stephen Series." St. Louis, Mo.: Stephen Ministries.

——— (1995a). "Ministry Systems and Resources for the Twenty-first Century." St. Louis, Mo.: Stephen Ministries.

——— (1995b). "What Your Congregation Receives When It Enrolls in the Stephen Series." St. Louis, Mo.: Stephen Ministries.

14 Caring for the Caregiver

MARTY RICHARDS

Thanks to preventative health care, good nutrition, an emphasis on exercise, and a general trend toward wellness, more people are living longer and may need care in their later years. For the purpose of this chapter, caregivers are defined as those who provide material, financial, emotional, and spiritual assistance to elders. These persons may or may not be related by blood or marriage to the person being cared for. Some who become caregivers may be from the religious community.

Caregiving refers to personal care (toilet, dressing, bathing, or helping someone to eat), assistance with household tasks (meal preparation, yard work, shopping, or cleaning), emotional support (talking through frustrations related to chronic illness and dependency), and spiritual aid (praying or working through ethical dilemmas). Many elders do such caregiving—tasks often not done previously. For example, an older man caring for his wife who has had a stroke may learn to cook for the first time in his life, or an older woman caring for her spouse may write checks, a task that had always been done by her husband.

Older disabled persons who receive help rely on family or friends, often at great emotional and sometimes financial cost to the caregiver. Most caregivers are women, as they have assumed a nurturing role throughout their lives, and there is an expectation that they will continue to do this in the later years as well. It can be an overwhelming task, but some caregivers also report that they have grown closer to their loved one in positive ways and have developed skills they never knew they possessed.

Many who receive care have been active members of their communities of faith over the years. As they become home-centered, those in the congregation need to remember them and the challenges they face. Those who provide care to elders and disabled persons are also members of religious communities and can also benefit from support as they cope with caregiving. But this may be easier said than done.

A story illustrates an unfortunately typical situation in many congregations. As a very active member of First Church, Sylvia was known as someone who could be counted on to assist others in crisis. Yet, since her mother moved in with her two years previously, Sylvia had been struggling with her mom's ill health. Her mother's dementia was progressing, and it was becoming increasingly difficult for Sylvia to care for her. Reluctantly she had made arrangements for her mom to move to an adult family-care home near her own home. One Sunday shortly after the move,

Sylvia sadly shared her story in an adult education class that focused on older adults' needs. Mary, an active congregant herself, was stunned. She had considered herself Sylvia's friend, yet she had no idea of Sylvia's difficulties. Her exasperated pastor, who also attended the class, privately asked the class facilitator: "How am I supposed to provide spiritual support or any other help to families when I don't even know what is going on? I am *not* a mind reader!" Sylvia, her mother, and this congregation illustrate the dilemmas faced by religious communities as they try to assist caregivers. Caregivers may be reluctant to share their concerns, and the faith community may be perplexed as to how to respond.

Although congregations can be a source of support, at times they are also places where judgments abound. Despite the fact that many elders and caregivers could benefit from assistance from their worshiping community, it is often the last place from which many would think to ask for aid. Families may not want those they relate to at church to *really* know what is happening. And they have misguided ideas about independence or protecting their loved one from uncomfortable situations. They may not want to let those from their religious community into their private lives. Sometimes persons in their community of faith may not understand what caregivers are facing and they do not know how be helpful.

There are both challenges and opportunities for faith communities to learn about caregiving issues and how best to help in dealing with such concerns. One of the learning opportunities from caregiving experiences is for persons in congregations to rethink giving, receiving, and blessing. In considering ways of supporting those being cared for and their caregivers, congregational programs need to aid people in moving from "helping" to "serving." The former word puts those being cared for in a "one down" position. The latter emphasizes reciprocity in the relationship. It also raises the possibility that the person being cared for can *be* as well as *receive* blessings.

In her wonderful book *My Grandfather's Blessing: Stories of Strength, Refuge and Belonging* (2000), Rachel Naomi Remen stresses the serving role and how it can be a blessing. "A blessing is not something that one person gives another. A blessing is a moment of meeting, a certain kind of relationship in which both people remember and acknowledge their true value and worth, and strengthen that which is whole in one another" (6). Exploring the giving and receiving of blessing in support of those who receive care and those who give it is crucial. And it can be key to providing creative assistance to elders and their caregivers.

In the congregation there are many persons who can share with those who are cared for and with the caregivers. Obviously clergy play important roles as spiritual advisors. They may bring the sacraments, pray with caregivers and those receiving care, and explore ethical and spiritual dilemmas. Parish nurses provide a link between the medical and the spiritual and can be very supportive to the caregiving situation. Laypersons, in roles as Stephen Ministers or eucharistic ministers, for example, can offer the message that the congregation still cares for the caregiver and the receiver.

In this chapter, the focus will be on what caregivers and care receivers face, the feelings and dilemmas experienced day to day, and ways congregations can support caregivers and those receiving care. This chapter represents my observations as a social worker and gerontology educator who has worked with older adults and their families for thirty-five years in various long-term care settings and in the community. Through those experiences I have had the opportunity to work with individual congregations and with national denominations on aging and caregiving issues. The families in all of these settings have taught me a great deal about love and survival skills, and some of their composite stories are used as illustrations.

WHAT FAMILY CAREGIVERS FACE
IN HELPING THEIR LOVED ONES

Congregations need to understand the issues experienced by care receivers and their families in order to assist them optimally. Each family system and each individual within that group are unique, but universal concerns are shared by many. For example, all members of the caregiving family are interdependent, as illustrated by the image of a mobile. When all is balanced the mobile moves freely in the wind. When any part gets off-kilter, the whole mobile may become tipped or even immobilized. In other words, when something happens to one member, all of the family is affected and they may struggle with a balance shift.

Patterns of interaction and communication evolve over time in families. Throughout the years, as family members nurture each generation, they learn about caregiving. Some problems faced in caring for an elder have been concerns for a long time; other issues may surface for the first time in caring in the later years. Family crises may surface when an elder sustains a fractured hip or has a stroke and then has to deal with the consequences. Such events can raise long-buried issues or they can unbalance even a family that has existed with a good equilibrium. Through the very intimate tasks of caregiving, some families that may learn new ways to relate to each other and grow closer by sharing caregiving tasks. The religious community can assist caregivers so that they are better able to be loving to the person for whom they are caring.

CONCERNS OF THOSE RECEIVING CARE

Issues of independence and dependence are at the root of many experiences for those receiving care. Most who are cared for want to do as much as they can on their own; they do not want to be a burden to their family, and they wish to make choices about their life and how their care is provided. Indeed, elders have the right to make whatever decisions they can, as long as they do not harm or put others or themselves in danger. Yet, no matter how loving their caregiver, those receiving assistance may feel that others are trying to run their life. Concerns about safety reign paramount for those who care for disabled elders. There can be disagreements between those receiving and those giving care as to how it should be provided.

Independence can be expressed by knowing when to ask for assistance, but many have a misguided sense that they cannot request help from anyone. Sometimes there is a fine balance between elders making decisions that potentially put them in serious jeopardy and having others do too much for them. Doing too much takes away the sense of being a person of value. Thus there needs to be *cooperative* caregiving. Those who receive care should make whatever decisions they can, even if they cannot execute those plans themselves. Those with dementia also have a right to add their perspectives on care, and their ideas can be sought when caregivers make decisions. Unfortunately, however, the wishes of those with dementia are often ignored.

Caregivers and care receivers may need to adapt how they view the world, the environment, and their expectations of each other. The religious community can aid them in this process of negotiating changes and expectations.

CONCERNS FOR FAMILY CAREGIVERS

Families face physical challenges, material stress, emotional concerns, relational changes, and spiritual and ethical dilemmas when they are caregivers. Close relationships between the caregiver and others can be sorely strained. Each family has its own issues, so those who would offer help need to listen and try to understand what a particular caregiver or group of caregivers is facing. Working out a plan by which the religious community can aid caregivers should come out of a careful observation of the needs expressed in each situation.

The level of daily "hands-on" caregiving done by families cannot be underestimated. Doing personal tasks for the person who receives assistance takes its toll on caregivers, even those who are in good physical condition and stable emotional health. When caregivers themselves face ill health or other stresses, they may find it extremely difficult to provide assistance.

The religious community can remind caregivers to practice self-care. Just as people who travel in an airplane are advised to adjust their own oxygen mask before they assist others, family members benefit from support to assure that their own needs are attended to. They need reminding that they will not be able to continue care for their loved one if they are exhausted. One caregiver put it very well: "Even Superman is Clark Kent most of the time!" The congregation can offer respite programs or time away to assist those in the caring role to carve out time for themselves.

BALANCING THE CONCERNS OF ALL IN THE CAREGIVING FAMILY

Because both the person receiving care and the caregiver have needs, there is a tenuous balance when one attempts to support caregiving families. Outsiders may have a tendency to see only one side or another of the equation of care. One caregiver in reflecting on a visit from a congregational volunteer lamented, "Just one time I wish they would ask me how *I* am doing." On the other hand, some visitors, uncomfortable with the mental or physical condition of the person receiving care, will ignore that elder. All involved in caregiving need acknowledgment of their particular story, and supportive visitors who hear them.

Although it is tempting to take sides, those who support families must hear all sides of a story and not make judgments. A story illustrates a case in which a congregation made unfair judgments. Larry was a fixture at Faith Church. He faithfully cared for his wife at home for five years as her condition deteriorated. His children and a care manager encouraged him to get home help for his wife, who was diagnosed with Parkinson's disease and diabetes. He neglected his own health and ultimately was diagnosed with severe heart problems. Only after his wife had a fall and he could not lift her did he entrust his wife's care to a well-regarded nursing home connected to his church. Older members of his congregation started talking judgmentally among themselves about his "neglect" of his wife, and what he "should" be doing. One even called to ask, "What do you think you are doing bringing your wife to the nursing home?" He found this very hurtful on the part of those who had for years been close friends, and he felt abandoned by them. He felt that he had no church home anymore. The older parishioners, fearful of their own declining abilities, projected their concern onto him. They might have benefited from some education about their own concerns about what it means to be a caregiver.

FEELINGS EXPERIENCED BY FAMILIES

Families have myriad feelings about the care of someone dependent on them. These include anger, fear, sadness, guilt, helplessness and hopelessness, ambivalence, embarrassment, and loss of control. Anger can focus on the illness process, the costs of care, the loss of dreams for the future, and the lack of concrete assistance from other family members. Despite the fact that these are normal feelings in dealing with chronic illness, families' struggles are often exacerbated by internal prohibitions about expressing such thoughts and feelings. These families need someone to listen nonjudgmentally.

Caregivers have many fears as they endeavor to do the "right thing" for their loved one. They may fear what might happen if they are no longer able to provide the primary care for a loved one. And there might be worries about others who help in the home or who work in the long-term care facility. Caregivers may feel that such persons cannot do the quality job that they themselves would do if they could. If a loved one has a condition with strong genetic links, family members may fear that they one day will also have the illness.

Sadness underlies most of the feelings faced by the aging family, and those who would offer assistance need to be very aware of this grief. This distress is omnipresent as someone watches an elder radically change. There may be emotional pain about canceled plans. Grief stems from the many "little" losses faced by the person receiving care, such as the loss of memory, the loss of the ability to walk, or decreasing financial resources. A pastoral counselor or Stephen Minister could address such sadness in visits by listening and offering support.

Guilt is another common feeling. Caregivers may worry that they did the wrong thing or that they did not do enough or even that they need to try harder. Supporters from the congregation may remind them that they are "doing the best they can." Families often need a third party to sort out what they reasonably can and cannot do.

Helplessness and hopelessness are often experienced by caregivers. These feelings result from a perception that there is little that they can do to assist a loved one. While it is true that many conditions may not be ameliorated, ways of caring and communication with a loved one, as well as keeping them safe and loved, may be improved. Caregivers may decrease feelings of helplessness by getting involved in advocacy efforts around the condition that their loved one faces. The Alzheimer's Association or the National Parkinson's Foundation are two groups that offer assistance through support groups and mobilize families to advocate for concerns related to the illnesses at both a local and national level. Hope can return when persons have a sense of control in their lives.

Ambivalence is one of the most difficult feelings; families may love the person being cared for but be very angry at the illness that is robbing them of their loved one. Mixed signals from health-care personnel about the prognosis of their loved one's condition can aggravate this feeling. Caregivers may feel pulled in several directions and can benefit from persons who listen and stand by them through it all.

Many families also feel embarrassment as their loved ones become forgetful or develop physical deformities, and they may try to "hide" the problems from others in the congregation. Caregivers and receivers often become isolated because they quit attending church or social events due to these conditions. All in the family benefit from their community being accepting of the limits of their loved one's illness. Congregations can model such acceptance of the elder and assist the family to deal with the situation more normatively.

Loss of control is another feeling to be dealt with. There are so many issues related to the condition of a loved one, and medical care and financial burdens can be overwhelming. Just laying out what options and resources are available to the family aids them in feeling more in control. Parish nurses and Stephen Ministers can aid families in uncovering internal and external resources.

Families may also need to explore what it means to be independent. Reaching out for assistance may be difficult because of a misguided push by the person receiving care to be "independent." Also, there are issues of how much to "protect" a care receiver over against the real need for a safe environment in which to live. Caregivers have to be careful not to "smother" their loved one with more care than is actually required. In addition, people involved in congregational ministry have to let go of "remembering John before he was ill" attitudes, which can negate who the person is now.

Such feelings can be extremely difficult for those who have grown up with religious ideas about how they "should" or "shouldn't" feel. Those in the faith community who support caregivers need to remember the power of these feelings. Sometimes just being able to name these feelings as normative can be much consolation to those giving care. Providing listening without judgment can also assist caregivers.

THE SPECIAL NEEDS OF LONG-DISTANCE CAREGIVERS

Those who live at a distance have many of the concerns already raised, but their issues are compounded by the fact that they are not doing hands-on caregiving. Guilt may be exacerbated by not being involved in their loved one's daily life. Grief can be overwhelming when one encounters massive changes in a person not seen regularly. There may be disagreements between those who provide the day-to-day assistance to the elder and the family member who comes from a distance. Some of this may come out of differences in perceptions as to how a person should be cared for. Those who have not been around the person cared for may be shocked by the changes over time. On the other hand, they may feel that the elders are better off than they actually are because they are seeing them for a short time.

There also may be some caregivers at a distance from those live alone at home. It is very difficult for these families to ascertain what is happening day to day. Congregations can help by getting the numbers and addresses of distant caregivers and giving them updates on what they see when they visit their loved one. They also can be aware of special "family" days such as Thanksgiving and become surrogate family for the person who might otherwise spend the holiday alone.

SPIRITUAL AND ETHICAL DILEMMAS FOR FAMILIES

In her article about spirituality and the aging family, Fischer (1992) identifies the following spiritual challenges in the aging family: "facing mortality, defining the shape and limits of love and fidelity, struggling with the meaning of suffering and evil, seeking forgiveness and reconciliation, and giving and receiving a spiritual legacy" (2–9). These are all very relevant to the caregiving situation. As persons from the congregation deal with caregiver concerns, they must be aware of these challenges as well as the physical and emotional concerns that may be present. Dealing with life-and-death issues is omnipresent in caregiving for persons with chronic and terminal illnesses.

Many questions about suffering and good and evil arise as persons sort out what they are experiencing with the illness of their loved one. If persons have "lived a good life" from their perspective, they may wonder why all of these bad things are happening at this time. A family may feel that God is being unfair in allowing a loved one to suffer. Others around the person with the physical or mental challenges may feel guilt that they are well and their loved one is suffering. Caregivers may do much questioning of their basic belief systems. Persons from the community of faith may support them by listening and reasoning through what they face. Caregivers and care receivers alike may struggle with how a God could allow this to happen to a loved one. Or they may wonder where God is in their struggles or even whether God exists, and they may question whether they have been faithful enough in their beliefs and service. These deeply felt concerns need to be addressed by those in the family and the congregation who care about them.

There are other issues related to family secrets and past estrangements. Families may have to cope with long-buried and unresolved challenges that arise again in the crisis of caregiving. Mental illness, alcoholism, abuse, adoption, and suicide are but some of the "secrets" families have hidden over the years. Even though they have been put out of day-to-day discussion, they powerfully affect how a family operates. Persons struggling with the past may benefit from help in talking it through. Even long-held perceptions that "you were the favorite son" can create dilemmas.

In the life of an aging family there may be many occurrences of saying, "I'm sorry," or asking for forgiveness and reconciliation. In his book on forgiveness in the intergenerational family, Terry Hargrave (1994) speaks to such challenges. He describes a process for assisting families to cope with such issues. Those involved need to carefully name the concern, put it in the context of the time it happened, try to understand what occurred and the person at the time, and look for ways of providing emotional or psychological restitution for the problem. Only then can real forgiveness occur. Hargrave warns against a "forgive and forget" approach. These are powerful challenges, but working through them has proved beneficial to many families, as some older families have found.

Elders often want to leave something for future generations. Sometimes it is money that they wish to conserve. Thus they may be reluctant to pay for services that would make life easier for themselves or their caregivers, because spending the resources would take away from the estate that they want to leave. There may be other ways for elders to leave a legacy, the most prominent of which could be their story or their spiritual legacy. Persons who visit from the congregation may be able to encourage them to share these stories with their families and preserve them for future generations.

Balancing family caregiving responsibility is a big concern as persons make decisions that are fair to all family members. At times difficult choices are made when more than one generation requires assistance. The rules under which the family operates may have to be renegotiated, and each person may have to decide where his or her primary allegiance lies. And roles may have to be altered as well.

Another dilemma for families relates to what has been termed the "mutuality of moral obligation" (Pratt and Wright 1987, 633–34). This relates to respect and generational reciprocity. Several questions are raised. What is owed between generations? If my mother cared for me when I was a baby, now that she is struggling with the aftermath of a stroke what do I owe her now? How do I show my love and respect and still keep my own life together? These questions—related to the commandment to "honor your father and mother" in the Jewish and Christian traditions and to filial piety and respect for older generations in Eastern traditions—loom large in the consciousness of many families.

Families also deal with dilemmas related to quality of life and quality of care. Quality of life is different for everyone and is ultimately defined by the person receiving care. But caregivers may have different perspectives, and these may be in conflict within the family. Questions such as how far to push someone one in rehabilitation after a hip fracture or whether to demand that someone bathe or eat are examples of the concerns that arise in the perception of quality of life.

Questions about technology are always present in caregiver deliberations. These include: When do you treat what? What is the benefit versus the cost of a course of treatment? How will this action today affect the long-term situation for my loved one? When is enough, enough? These are not easy answers, and caregivers and receivers alike may struggle with myriad choices about them. Not all choices are life-and-death issues. Day-to-day concerns related to care of chronic illness are fraught with such concerns. The financial and policy implications beyond an individual family cannot be overlooked as sometimes the choices made are dictated by what regulations affect the family.

The overarching question has to do with the limits of family caregiving. Each family makes its own decisions about this. At times the bottom line is that the family makes the best of the "worst" decisions. For example, while many would not choose a nursing-home option for their loved one, after a discussion and reflection, it can be the best alternative. Again, families can benefit from interactions with a listener who does not judge their choices.

How can the congregation assist families to cope with all of these concerns? Examining the morality in the simple things in caregiving as well as the larger issues of life and death can be a place to begin. Sometimes talking about the broader issues in a community forum can assist those who are dealing with very personal concerns. These discussions can plant ideas and ways to cope that may be helpful later on. People hear what they are able to at the time they are ready to hear it. Discussing things before urgent needs arise has great value. Hearing the "cover terms" as persons describe their situation can provide cues for how others can be supportive. These words cover the blocks of meaning as persons view their world and assist those who would help to get a window on what they are experiencing. Caregivers also benefit from being mentors and teachers to others going through similar situations. Assisting the caregiver better to communicate with the person needing care can also be of help.

WHAT THE CONGREGATION CAN DO TO ASSIST CAREGIVERS

Robinson (2001) reports on models of ministry to caregivers developed by Ministry of Caregiving Work Group of the Advisory Committee on Social Witness Policy of the Presbyterian Church U.S.A. A formal resolution based on these ideas was passed at their general assembly in 2001. That a national church would raise caregiving as a church-wide concern illustrates just how crucial this issue is for communities of faith. It raises caregiver concerns to the attention of congregations all over the country.

Some of that group's ideas offer a backdrop for work in any religious community. These include: to have well-trained volunteers to assist caregivers with basic needs (such as cooking meals, or respite care), to utilize a parish nurse who could aid caregivers, to educate the congregation about caregiving concerns and end-of-life issues, to share information about resources, and to encourage caregivers to take care of themselves and maintain their social support (Robinson 2001, 79).

Clergy, pastoral counselors, parish nurses, and laypeople can assist caregivers in many ways, thus adding another dimension to care. Helen, an eighty-five-year-old member of Peace Church, shared her own experience of the love and concern of her faith community: "The walls of my apartment don't reach out and touch me. The people of this congregation do." She expresses an important sentiment.

Preparation and training of those who would visit and provide support to home-centered or institutionalized persons is essential. Volunteers and paid staff alike who assist caregivers must carefully explore their own motivations for doing so. Otherwise they may offer more "helping" than an elder and their family need. A social worker who has worked with families for many years calls this "helps strikes again."

There is a need to examine carefully the countertransference issues or the personal/volunteer/professional connection. Persons who provide respite or other support need to be cognizant of their own family issues and feelings about what families "ought to do." Programs such as Stephen Ministry offer training and support on these issues for volunteers who connect with caregiving families. Other groups that provide aid to families would do well to explore their model of training and ongoing volunteer support.

Each congregation has different strengths and therefore abilities to provide assistance to caregivers. Programs should only be developed after carefully assessing the needs of a particular community and reviewing what it is realistically able to do.

There can also be an evaluation of other local religious groups with whom a congregation can collaborate to assist caregivers. Individual religious groups to not have to do it alone. Also, individual religious groups may benefit from sharing programs with other communities of faith.

Religious groups may have to put aside their theological differences in the service of community caregivers and receivers. For example, the National Family Caregivers Association has developed an interfaith service to celebrate caregivers, along with individual Catholic and Jewish services. These could be used during a celebration of National Caregivers Month in November, when caregivers are singled out and supported by their communities of faith.

Because caregivers and receivers are home-centered, the congregation can come to them with sacraments and other visible ways to connect them to the persons in that community. One Catholic parish did a homebound retreat in the season of Advent. Six frail elders at home studied and prayed the same material, and they were visited by the priest daily with communion.

PARISH NURSES OR HEALTH MINISTERS

A nurse or other health professional on staff in the congregation provides invaluable assistance to caregivers and receivers. Being able to come as a representative of the congregation to provide basic health support can be a real blessing. Parish nurses or health ministers can also provide an educative function and do preventative work as well. They provide a liaison between the myriad health-care concerns faced and the spiritual issues that are coped with.

Education

Although it has been underutilized in the past, education is one way to introduce congregations to caregiving issues before there is a critical need. I have had the experience of parish education with adult children in their middle years coming to a class "to learn more about what they can do for their parents" and leaving saying, "This is about our aging and needs too!" These classes can also plant seeds of ideas that individuals can investigate when caregiving needs become apparent later. Adult education classes also assist those in the throes of caregiving. Two reactions often occur in the class. Caregivers find there are others in their midst with similar experiences. Also, they may find an avenue for sharing their situation and for receiving support from those who may not have known what they were facing. Caregivers may become teachers and mentors to others who may also be struggling. In one congregation, an ongoing caregiver support group was formed as a result of an educational experience about caregiving. When held on Sunday morning or other times of normally scheduled classes, classes are likely to be less threatening and therefore to draw more people. For a caregiver to attend a class or a support group, there may need to be respite provided for the person being cared for. Persons of all generations need to be aware of caregiving issues. This can expand the network of persons who share in the caregiving situation.

Education also includes print and video resources. Congregations can develop a lending library of relevant books and other resources about caregiving and aging. These might also include books to assist those of all generations. Children's books such as *Wilfrid Gordon McDonald Partridge* or *Nana Upstairs and Nana Downstairs,* both positive intergenerational stories, can aid even young children to understand what older adults face.

Information about local and national resources can be available at the congregation.[1] The national Eldercare Locator might aid families looking for services. Those who answer the congregation's phone and those who have responsibility for older adult and family ministry should have these numbers available to share with distressed members. Knowing the resources available and making good referrals is a valuable service that can be provided by religious groups. Caregivers might initially be more comfortable calling the congregation than reaching out to a government resource. And caregivers can be encouraged to use their internal resources such as their faith, a sense of humor, or good family communication.

Support Groups

These groups, concentrating on caregiving itself and on care for those undergoing many illnesses, offer the opportunity for those who provide care to find out that they are not alone in the challenges and frustrations they face. There is sharing of information about resources and assistance and problem solving. The congregation can sponsor a group itself or can offer meeting space for such a group that might be sponsored by the local stroke association, Alzheimer's Association, or other group that deals with caregiving concerns. Support groups have become advocacy groups when certain issues have arisen.

Respite Care

Mary, a fifty-five-year-old caregiver to Harold, who struggled with Alzheimer's disease, credits her St. Mary's parish with keeping her sane. On Thursday nights for several years members came and spent time with him, and Mary could do whatever she wished to "take care of herself," which sometimes meant shopping for herself and sometimes just sitting next to the river and watching the sun set. The congregation set no expectations on what she should do but faithfully came each week. Respite care consists of many kinds of assistance, from one-to-one visits to giving stressed caregivers a few hours away to bringing meals or fixing meals. Adult day programs in the church building where persons can bring their loved one while they work or otherwise take time for themselves have also been a boon to caregivers.

CONCLUSION

Congregations need to become aware of the issues faced by caregivers. They can study the concerns and enlist the aid of community agencies and professionals to help them do this. They can provide love and concern. But most of all they need to remember that all of us will grow older and may need assistance. Thus the community of faith must not forget those who struggle with caregiving issues. There are indeed challenges and blessings for all involved in getting and giving care.

NOTE

1. Elder Care Locator, 1-800-677-1116 (a national referral number for aging issues); Faith in Action (Robert Wood Johnson Foundation), 1-877-324-8411 (helps to fund interfaith caregiver groups); National Family Caregivers Association, 1-800-896-3650 (has many support materials).

BIBLIOGRAPHY

DePaola, T. (1973). *Nana Upstairs and Nana Downstairs.* New York: Putnam's.

Fischer, K. R. (1992). "Spirituality in the Aging Family: A Systems Perspective." *Journal of Religious Gerontology* 8/4: 1–15.

Fox, M. (1985). *Wilfred Gordon McDonald Partridge.* La Jolla, Calif.: Kane/Miller.

Hargrave, T. D. (1994). *Families and Forgiveness: Healing Wounds in the Intergenerational Family.* New York: Brunner Mazel.

Pratt, C., V. Schmall, and S. Wright (1987). "Ethical Concerns of Family Caregivers to Dementia Patients." *The Gerontologist* 27/5: 632–38.

Remen, R. N. (2000). *My Grandfather's Blessing: Stories of Strength, Refuge and Belonging.* New York: Riverhead.

Robinson, K. M. (2001). "Long Term Illness: Too Costly to Cure?" *Church and Society* 91/4: 76–80.

Part Three

PASTORAL CARE WITH OLDER PEOPLE

Although the title of Part Three suggests that it may be addressed only to ordained persons, in actuality the chapters in this section provide useful information and wise perspectives that should also be useful for laypersons preparing to undertake volunteer ministries with older adults. For example, *Nancy Gieseler Devor* and *Kenneth I. Pargament* present four cases that demonstrate how religious faith can be a positive source of support in challenging times and how it can also be a detriment to healthy coping. Based upon Pargament's well-known empirical research on religious coping, the chapter could serve as an important component of training for volunteer service with elders. In addition, its careful delineation of different forms and outcomes of religious coping ought to remind parish clergy about the many pathways religious people take in the search for meaning in times of crisis and transition.

Lois D. Knutson's contribution could also be an important part of any training program for volunteer ministry or for clergy education in pastoral care. She suggests numerous goals for pastoral care with elders, including affirmation of their value, honoring them as important to the faith community, comforting and helping them accept the love of God and other persons. Knutson describes the dynamics of visiting with older persons in their homes and lists a number of concerns that typically arise in such visits. She also connects this kind of individual caring response to elders' needs to a large number of congregational programs that serve older persons and their families.

Not all of the issues with which aging people and the families wrestle are public and obvious. For example, addiction to alcohol and other drugs may be a deeply held, destructive secret that prevents persons from realizing their spiritual potentials as depicted in Part One. *Robert H. Albers's* chapter offers practical, sensitive, theologically grounded advice for pastors and lay volunteers working with older persons struggling with addiction. He catalogs common attitudes about addicted elders that may prevent them from obtaining treatment, and he argues that pastoral caregivers—both ordained and lay—have some culpability in reinforcing these attitudes among parishioners. He also states that pastoral caregivers have a wonderful opportunity not only to assist addicted elders and their families in receiving treatment but also to educate the faith community about the social attitudes and religious prejudices that can undermine people's efforts to be released from addiction.

Alcoholism and other addictions are often deeply hidden in the elderly population. In fact, the public often assumes that most "bad habits" and unsavory character traits diminish or disappear by the time a person reaches later life. Paradoxically, uncritical assumptions that all old people are wise, serene, gentle, and good can reinforce their marginalization. *Robert A. Rost* understands this and argues that older people must be given permission to explore issues of sin and grace. He writes about how pastoral caregivers can journey with elders as they courageously explore dark corners of their lives. He notes the pain these elders sometimes experience when all through their lives they have felt an undue emphasis on sin without assurance of God's abiding grace. Tragically, in later life some persons come to believe that their suffering is punishment and that God has turned away from them. Thus Rost speaks of the need for elders to understand and accept a theology of grace—"beholding grace," as he puts it.

Older people who do not perceive the evidence of grace in their lives may fall into despair and sometimes into a clinical depression. This is the focus of the chapter by *Elizabeth MacKinlay*. In particular she addresses the problem of depression experienced by persons living in long-term care. Pastoral caregivers who visit in nursing homes and other facilities for older people need to be able to recognize the signs of depression that sometimes intertwine with physical conditions that produce frailty. These caregivers should know that depression is a highly treatable psychiatric illness, but that it can also be a signal of an existential crisis of meaning in later life. Thus, the pastoral caregiver can be an important member of the treatment team by helping a depressed elder come to terms with sources of meaning—especially ultimate meaning. Pastoral caregivers can also journey with long-term care residents as they respond to loss, renew a sense of intimacy with God and other persons, and experience hope even in the face of frailty and impending death.

Even with compassionate pastoral care and a secure faith, older adults will experience suffering and, as *Helen K. Black* so eloquently writes, they need to tell their stories of suffering to caring listeners. Without the opportunity to relate the narratives of suffering, suffering intensifies in loneliness. Black argues that suffering is a form of cultural and religious communication; culture and religion shape the narratives of suffering and at the same time provide the one who suffers with an interpretive scheme for grasping its meaning. This chapter instructs those who would listen to these difficult narratives in ways of being sensitive to the metaphors that convey the deeper meanings of suffering.

The final chapter of Part Three also asserts that pastoral caregivers need to learn how to listen to elders' stories. *James W. Ellor* discusses the process of "spiritual assessment" and the need to be aware of underlying explanatory theories that shape the way such assessments are conducted. This chapter offers a case of an elder whose suffering cannot be fully understood without taking its spiritual dimension into account. Drawing on the theology of Paul Tillich, the developmental psychology of Erik Erikson, and the logotherapeutic approach of Viktor Frankl, Ellor shows how a holistic approach that bridges psychology and theology offers the best hope for a counselor to give support to an older person experiencing a crisis of meaning.

15 Understanding Religious Coping with Late-Life Crises

NANCY GIESELER DEVOR
KENNETH I. PARGAMENT

Pastoral caregivers working with elders soon learn that religion is an essential partner in the conversations with those they help. At times religion can be a comforting partner, a sustaining resource that helps elders hold fast amid the changes of old age. At other times religion can form a backdrop of guilt or even fear, making the older person's work of adaptation much more difficult.

Elders bring to the losses and crises of aging a lifelong effort to establish a sense of significance and purpose in life. As they face the crucible of aging and approaching death, they may grasp tightly to preserve significance, for better or for worse. But sometimes preservation no longer works, and elders must redefine themselves and their religious worlds in order to establish a new sense of significance.

Our purpose in this chapter is to elaborate the ways in which religion can be a partner in coping, for good and for ill. Through four case studies we review the ways that religion can help or hinder coping and how pastoral caregivers might utilize religious interventions to assist in caring for persons in the later stages of life. Two cases provide positive and negative examples of how elders conserve their religion as they adapt to aging. Two additional cases show helpful and nonhelpful ways elders transform their religious understandings. For purposes of clarity, we have chosen illustrations that demonstrate solely conservation or transformation. Yet the pastoral caregiver is likely to find that individuals are not usually so unambiguous and may conserve some elements of their search for significance while transforming other aspects.

It has been said that Buddhists conceptualize human development as evolving through three distinct stages. In childhood, we grow and develop physically. As adults, we rear children and practice occupations. Old age, the final stage, is reserved for spiritual growth through disciplined practice under the guidance of a teacher, in preparation for death. The Buddhist notion of retirement's goal as spiritual deepening provides quite a contrast to the popular bumper sticker plastered to recreational vehicles across the United States: "I'm spending my children's inheritance." Although our culture seems to promote the idea that retirement is about indulging previously neglected material longings, elders would be better served by reimagining the tasks of human development to include spiritual growth as a means of dealing with late-life changes. Statistics indicate that spiritual growth better describes the inner process of aging. In all studies, the elder cohort of United States citizens reveals them to be the most religious of the entire population—the most active church attendees and the most frequent prayers (Kimble et al. 1995; Koenig, Smiley, and Gonzales 1988). In spite of the religious adherence of elders, however, religion does not always provide solace in the changes accompanying aging. Whether the religious involvement of elders is a cohort effect or a stage of life effect, those who provide pastoral care for elders need to understand how religious involvement and the inner life of faith can positively or negatively impact coping with late-life crises and how to intervene effectively.

Recently, the Danielsen Institute at Boston University has been involved in an innovative training rotation to determine ways theologically trained psychology interns might help frail elders cope emotionally and spiritually with the challenges of aging. Frail elders provide an intensive view of aging and religious coping. Compared to the average "healthy" elder, frail elders have sustained significantly more physical losses. The cohort of frail elders our interns see are of a lower social economic background, affording few material distractions that might help them cope. Frail elders bring to mind Harry Moody's comment, "One can think of old age as a kind of 'natural monastery' in which earlier roles, attachments, and pleasures are stripped away" (Moody 1995, 96). Frail elders might even be described as living in a hermitage. This group has struggled to cope with poor physical health. Many have lost their homes and much of their independence. Relational losses are staggering. Frail elders encounter challenges to their spirituality not by choice but by life's demand. What they can teach us about religious coping with late-life crises is applicable to all elders, who eventually experience many of these losses, though perhaps not quite so simultaneously.

Pargament (1997) defines religious coping as an effort to enhance significance in response to threats and losses. He notes that crises are capable of disrupting our lives precisely because they endanger or harm the things that matter most deeply to us. Of course, people differ in their values of greatest significance. An event may throw one person into turmoil while the same event is met by another person with a shrug of the shoulders. Fortunately, we are not left helpless in the face of crisis. People can anticipate and respond to major life events proactively. There are two basic ways of religious coping: conservational and transformational (Pargament 1997). Although both coping methods are designed to enhance goals or values of deepest importance to us, they are quite different in character. Faced with new or mounting challenges, we are likely first to try and protect or maintain the values that have sustained us in the past. At times, conservational coping is successful. We are able to hold on to our objects of greatest significance in the midst of stress and strain. However, there are times when conservation is no longer possible or successful. Only then, when these values are lost or no longer sustain us in our new circumstances do we, often reluctantly, let go and risk attaching to new sources of significance. Thus, transformation is typically the coping option of "last resort." However, transformation may be necessary for growth, change, and the capacity to move on in life. It is important to emphasize that neither form of religious coping is good or bad in and of itself. Religious coping, conservational or transformational, is not always associated with positive mental and physical health. The challenge for the pastoral caregiver is to understand the form religious coping is taking; its appropriateness to the elder's particular needs, situation, and context; the impact of the religious coping, positive or negative, on the physical/spiritual/emotional well-being of the elder; and various ways to intervene to enhance healing.

For purposes of clarification, Pargament (1999) makes a distinction between religion and spirituality, while reminding us that the two concepts are profoundly interconnected. Either religion or spirituality can have negative or positive valences and consequences, and each can be expressed individually and institutionally. Pargament defines religion as the broader category, including individual and institutional commitments. Spirituality is considered a subset of religion, the unique expression of religion through "a search for the sacred" (Pargament 1999, 12). In this chapter we will use the concept of religious coping to include both terms, thus encompassing deep individual commitments rooted in institutional commitments to the search for the sacred.

The following clinical vignettes illustrate Pargament's coping theory. These case illustrations are drawn from the work of theologically trained psychology interns and their supervisor (Nancy Devor) and help us see how religious coping impacts late-life losses.

RELIGIOUS COPING THROUGH CONSERVATION

The losses wrought by aging test our capacity to adapt emotionally, physically, socially, and certainly spiritually in our search for the sacred. Our default position is to hang on—to try to preserve the ways of coping that have served us throughout our lives. Only when our values cannot hold are we persuaded to release old understandings and embrace new perspectives. Hanging on—conserving—can help or hinder an elder's transitions in life. Sometimes hanging on sustains us through difficulties, seeing us through pain and grief until we can accommodate a new reality. At other times, hanging on preserves a dysfunctional religious system, intensifying inappropriate guilt or self-punishment during times of crisis and need. Two cases serve as illustrations of coping through conservation.

Case One: **Mrs. R.**

Raised in the Roman Catholic faith, Mrs. R. sustained a heart attack in her early thirties. In the emergency room, Mrs. R. experienced what we would now call a near-death experience. She was so awestruck by what happened to her that she wrote a first-person account later published in a Catholic periodical. Recalling that time in her life, she remembered hearing organ music and had the experience that she was floating above her body in the operating room. Looking up, she saw people dressed in white robes, "like monks." She spoke to these people in an urgent way: "Please let me go. I have little children who need me." After she spoke these words, everything went black, and Mrs. R. regained consciousness in the emergency room. This near-death experience provided the cornerstone of a belief that has sustained Mrs. R. through many difficult life experiences, including four strokes—one in her early fifties, another in her mid-fifties, and an extremely incapacitating stroke at age sixty. At this time she was left permanently disabled and confined to a wheelchair. She has remained unable to speak clearly or to have any independent mobility other than awkward use of her right hand. Mrs. R. was placed in a nursing home more than six years ago. A fourth stroke occurred soon after her placement, and nearly resulted in her death. The religious conviction that sustains her every day is that life does not end with death; life goes "on and on and on" and life beyond death is better than the "hell" she currently endures. Her faith in God and in life everlasting helps her deal with the frustration of decreased independence from the strokes and helps her feel more relaxed and peaceful. We may die, she asserts, but our spirits live on. Mrs. R. finds ways to maintain this belief despite severe losses. Over a period of nine years, Mrs. R. lost her mother, husband, two close friends, and her adult daughter. While others might reject their faith or express anger with God, Mrs. R. states that she "got through it by believing they are better off" with God. More than a belief, her conviction is formed by experience: she has "seen" her daughter, her mother, and her husband following their deaths, and feels they have let her know that they are in a better place.

The death of Mrs. R.'s daughter occurred at a time when conservation as a means of religious coping was especially evident. Mrs. R.'s homeless daughter was cremated, and Mrs. R. did not have adequate funds to secure her ashes from the funeral home. During this time, Mrs. R. suffered from what had been diagnosed as psychotic hallucinations as she waited to receive her daughter's ashes and release her to the life she knew would bring her peace and comfort. With the expert help of her social worker, Mrs. R. finally received the ashes and was taken to the cemetery where her husband had been buried a short time earlier. Here she scattered her daughter's ashes. Being as physically incapacitated as she was, as many ashes fell on her lap and feet as on the ground. I remember her tearful face looking up at me, with ashes scattered all over her, asking, "Is this it? Is this all we are?" I reminded her that her love for her daughter was the final word, as was our love for Mrs. R. Mrs. R. threw back her head and yelled to the sky, "I love you," to her daughter. Love literally was the final word. With the support of her community of caregivers, she was able to maintain her belief in God and in life everlasting. Today she says about that service, "I believe she heard me. She wasn't alone."

Mrs. R. notes, "If you don't think God is there for you, you'll get nowhere. You have to believe." The firmness of this conviction again preserves and protects her sense that there is a better life for her and for those she loves and that if she holds on, it will be hers, despite her suffering.

Following her last stroke, Mrs. R. felt God was not hearing her. She could not understand why God had not "taken her" when she had been so close to death. She told God that she was going to give him a hearing aid for Christmas, since she did not think he was listening to her. After that, she says, things got better; God started doing things for her. She remarked that she prays all the time, "in my mind, not verbally." God speaks directly to her, also through her mind, and by giving the help she needs. For example, she prays for a decrease in pain since most of her days are spent in physical discomfort. And she feels God answers her prayer, giving her a day free of pain. She prays for help with the most intimate and personal details of her life and has found ways to get God's attention when she feels neglected. Instead of changing her belief, she finds new ways to sustain her belief. As to how she wants to die: "I'd like to go to sleep and wake up in the hands of God. When I die, I want you to look up to the sky and say, 'Thank you God,' and know that I am in the best hands of all."

Case Two: Mr. W.

Mr. W. was referred to our service because of his declining physical health and his increasing social isolation. He has received weekly visits at home over the course of several years. Over time, our trainees learned about Mr. W.'s religious beliefs. He clings tenaciously to his beliefs, despite the fact that they result in great suffering and the very symptoms that brought him to our attention.

As a teenager, Mr. W. became a novice in a Roman Catholic religious order. He left to serve in World War II and was trained to "kill as a terrorist." He reports that he has done "unthinkable things" because he was taught to "kill or be killed." Ironically enough for Mr. W., the government honored him for his heroism. Mr. W. feels otherwise. He is sure that he is going to hell and does not believe that he can be forgiven for his actions.

Initially Mr. W. described in vivid detail the deaths he caused. He went on to describe his belief that his religion condemned killers and therefore condemned him. His therapist tried in numerous ways to help Mr. W. access a more graceful understanding of his faith, where trusting in God's mercy could help him feel forgiven and experience some measure of peace. Despite numerous confessions, both with priests and with his therapist, Mr. W. could not believe he was forgiven nor develop a sense of compassion for himself. Regardless of his years of religious training that could have reminded him of another possibility—that even on a cross, Jesus forgave killers—Mr. W. could not shake his sense of judgment.

In Mr. W.'s case, conservation condemns him to a living hell and the anticipation of eternal punishment. He recounted that he once told a priest that he had only one request of God—that God would destroy hell. The priest reportedly told Mr. W. that this was "not a good prayer." Was it this experience with religious authority that kept Mr. W. stuck in a conserving religious coping that to us seems so harmful and contradictory to the religion he professes? Or was conservation his only way of coping with a conflict he could not adjudicate: psychologically, he had to "kill or be killed" and was honored for his ability to do so; religiously, he believed he had intentionally committed an unforgivable sin. Perhaps to Mr. W., accepting religious forgiveness might cheapen the wrong he committed, cheapen the value of human life, and therefore destroy the power of his religious system and his sense of significance. Accepting forgiveness might destroy the religion that through condemnation also provides him some way of repairing his extreme guilt.

It is of no account to Mr. W. that he acts redemptively on behalf of others. He is known for caring for the poor and for strangers in extravagant and touching ways. The suggestion that Mr. W.'s acts might be a form of penance, or that he offers compassion in a Christ-like way, is rejected by Mr. W. And yet, he does appear to draw meaning from his care for others. For Mr. W., to conserve his religion may preserve and even extend his profound respect for human life, albeit at heavy cost—his own personal condemnation and sense of eternal damnation.

RELIGIOUS COPING THROUGH TRANSFORMATION

In contrast to conservation, in religious coping through transformation a shift occurs in the elder's religious worldview or operational theology. Similar to conservation, this shift may help or hinder the elder's adaptation to the losses and crises besetting his or her life. In transformation, the values, understandings, even relational valences of the past are discarded when they no longer seem to help elders make sense of the world they inhabit. Instead, elders replace old strivings toward significance with new values, understandings, and relational patterns.

Case One: Mrs. L.

Mrs. L. was first referred to our service when her adult grandson, to whom she was quite close, committed suicide. Mrs. L. is a lifelong Catholic who raised five children following her young husband's death. One of her three sons became a missionary priest, working in a dangerous setting in Latin America. She herself has received enormous benefits from her church following her husband's death, and she has contributed a great deal to her church through volunteering her time and leadership. Now unable to walk independently, her days of attending her local parish have ended, but she faithfully listens to mass on television and prays the rosary as she falls asleep each evening.

Mrs. L. and I began meeting weekly immediately after her grandson's death. In our visits, I listened to her feelings and her questions. I also offered my thoughts about the process of grieving she was experiencing. Despite Catholic teachings on suicide, she came to believe that God understood her grandson's suffering, and that her grandson was at home with God. Known throughout her residence and among her caregivers for friendliness with new residents, high level of activity (despite her physical dependence), and general good humor, she soon resumed her usually cheerful and outgoing state. After two months, she dismissed me stating, "I don't need to see you anymore; others need your time more than I do now."

A year later, I was again called in to meet with Mrs. L. This time, her countenance was significantly changed. Four months before our meeting, she began to suffer poor health for which her health-care providers had no explanation and few remedies. She became convinced that she was going to die. In her experience, bad things happened in threes. Her grandson's death was followed by the death of her next-door neighbor; she was certain her death was to be the third bad thing. She explained to me the sequence of three deaths much earlier in her life that had taken away her beloved husband.

Terrified of dying, Mrs. L. resisted sleeping, which exacerbated her physical symptoms and her emotional distress. Her priest son was home for the holidays and, as he had in the past, stayed in her home. Generally she took great comfort in his presence and slept best when he was staying on the sofa just outside her bedroom. This time, however, she kept him awake all night, calling out to him over and over to make sure he was still there. Both of them were at the ends of their ropes when I was called in.

This time there was no easy cure for Mrs. L.'s discomfort. Despite the therapeutic techniques I tried, she would yell at me in panic, "You're not helping me!" Her physical caregivers were frustrated with her as well, unable to do anything to help her symptoms. Finally, over a series of months, we began to explore her relationship with her parents, the death of her husband, and her fears about death. What was striking was that the faith that had sustained her throughout her life no longer worked for her. In our explorations, two beliefs in particular proved troublesome. First, she was used to "bargaining" with God—asking in prayer for God to keep her alive until the next time her priest son could return home. She no longer believed that God would hear or honor this prayer, since she was so certain her death was imminent. Second, Mrs. L. was afraid of dying. She experienced the thought of dying as a wrenching separation from her children. The religious belief she had espoused throughout her life—that death was reunion with God and loved ones and not to be feared—was of no use at all to her in the midst of facing her own death and separation from those she loved.

Over many agonizing months, we explored the grief she felt about leaving her children. Mrs. L. often said, "I just want to stay here and hold on tight." She rehearsed her grief every time I left her apartment, crying at my departure. Over time, her fear found expression as profound anticipatory grief.

One morning Mrs. L. greeted me with the announcement that she had decided to stop bargaining with God for more time. Mrs. L. commented on her age and said that she had lived a long time, with many more pluses than minuses. She was no longer going to ask God for "one more visit" with her son but instead "accept that whatever God gives you, he gives you." To ask any more would be "greedy." She commented, "God did his part. Now I need to do my part and graciously accept whatever God gives." How do I account for this remarkable transformation? Perhaps grief counselors, like midwives, help a transformed faith emerge. For within the grief of a lost relationship is buried the gift of the relationship itself, the very glimmer of God's presence on the horizon of our lives. Contained within all she was to lose was all she was to gain. But this eternal love could only be found when Mrs. L. was able to give up her greatest treasure—her children.

This surrender marked the beginning of a transformation in Mrs. L. as she has become more serene and once again resumed her cheerful presence and resilient sense of humor. No longer does she cry when I end our visits. Her faith has been profoundly changed. No longer does she give intellectual assent to belief in life beyond death while operating out of fear, grief, suspiciousness, and a sense that one has to bargain with a God who could be withholding and punishing. Her faith now is a simple trust in God's care. Although she is still in constant pain, Mrs. L. is able to sleep. When she is awake at night, she tells me she hums Christmas carols to herself and returns to sleep, comforted by the beautiful words of the songs. She has retained close and loving relationships with her children and caregivers, yet gained a new sense of independence through her deeper faith.

For Mrs. L., anticipatory grieving led to a confrontation with religious beliefs that no longer worked. Supported by her children and caregivers, she has now transformed her relationship with God. She no longer fights and bargains but rests (literally) in acceptance and peace. No longer does she need to stay awake and alive to avoid the loss of her children. Rather, she has let go into a trusting relationship with God, whom she experiences as a constant presence in life, in death, and in the face of immense loss.

I knew our work in this area had come full circle when one day Mrs. L. greeted me with the news that her children, in cleaning her apartment, discovered that she had set aside two complete burial outfits, not just one! She told me this in great good spirits, and I knew that she no longer feared God and death.

Case Two: Mrs. A.

Mrs. A. was admitted to hospice for care and comfort while in the terminal phase of cancer. Filled with admiration for Mrs. A., her nurse nevertheless expressed concerns about her spiritual well-being and referred her for home visits. When I first met with Mrs. A. I did indeed find an angry woman who had severed any relationship with God. She was intrigued by my being a woman and a member of the clergy, but she was too angry and hurt to hold out any wish for a reconciliation with God. Toward the end of a very painful bout with cancer, Mrs. A. nearly died. Against her expressed and written wishes, she was resuscitated. She firmly believed this was because her physician was about to go on vacation and found it easier to resuscitate her than to provide the time needed for her to die. Not one to spare others' responsibility, Mrs. A. also blamed God, telling me firmly that "God was out to lunch" when she was most in need. God, like her physician, was on vacation rather than taking the time to help her die. She wanted nothing to do with God or the clergyman from her local church, although she was willing to sit and talk with me.

Mrs. A. was raised in a "fire and brimstone" religion in the southern United States, and learned to fear God as a moral judge. Her religion was an essential part of coping with a difficult early life, including a nuclear family impaired by alcoholism and her own violent first marriage. She left this marriage and struggled to cope as a single mother of small children. Eventually she remarried a stable and loving partner. The stress of raising small children became complicated by an additional burden of caring for her alcoholic parents. Due to his work, Mrs. A.'s second husband frequently traveled for long periods. Despite their initial happiness, he was unable to offer the support she needed in her daily life. Mrs. A. and her husband were active in their local church, where they met a couple who became close friends with them. Soon thereafter, Mrs. A. had a two-year affair with the husband of this couple. The affair ended when Mrs. A. and her husband moved out of state. Mrs. A. never confessed the affair to anyone, especially her husband. After the move, Mrs. A. gradually fell away from church attendance although she maintained a nominal relationship with a liberal Protestant church. She threw herself into parenting and her marriage and felt happy with much of her life.

Now severely limited by her illness, Mrs. A. relied on her husband for most of her care and mobility. The kindness and tenderness between them was tangible. Yet Mrs. A. lived in fear that if medicated for pain, she would in an unconscious state confess the details of the affair that had remained a secret for so many years. She could not stand the thought that she might hurt the husband who had been so faithful and caring for her.

Mrs. A. feels that her religion offers her nothing in facing the end of her life. Up until the point of nearly dying, Mrs. A. maintained a distance but essentially held on to a faith that condemned her earlier faithlessness, helped her cope with the alcoholism in her family, and gave her a social community. But because she had wanted to die and could find no purpose in being alive, her sense of God has changed. Enraged with being alive, she feels God has failed her completely. Mrs. A. does not view this as a punishment for her affair; she feels her guilt is appropriate enough punishment. What she cannot understand is how God allows her to go on living when it means condemning her to excruciating physical pain on a daily basis and a grueling caregiving situation for her husband. A new source of tension now has grown between them: Mrs. A.'s anger that she is still alive and waiting to die; Mrs. A.'s husband's gladness in her life and still being able to care for her. Mrs. A. cannot bear the situation. Filled with fury, her solution is to abandon God, as she feels God has abandoned her. In her poignant, angry words, "God is out to lunch."

Mrs. A. illustrates eloquently how impossible it is for some to conserve religious faith in the face of a painful death and a meaningless life. Others might have been able to use their religion to find meaning or cope with pain, but not Mrs. A. A religion that had worked for her in the stresses of her early life, a religion that even offered a system of judgment for wrongdoing, Mrs. A. was able to preserve. But faced with ongoing suffering, Mrs. A. now transforms her religion from "turning the other cheek" to "turning away." Her religious coping is to slam the door in God's face, as she feels she has been rejected at death's door. In the same way that families disown their members and believe they have solved the problem but remain at some level deeply and disturbingly connected, Mrs. A. believes she had disowned God. Her anger and rage give me a different message, however. The religious system that "worked" earlier now is transformed into an ongoing relationship marked by feelings of anger, betrayal, and loss that are ultimately destructive for Mrs. A.

PASTORAL INTERVENTIONS

In all of these cases, one of the most central interventions is the presence of a listener. These frail elders rarely experience the presence of someone listening to them with an ear attuned to the wounds that interfere with emotional, physical, and spiritual well-being. It is integrating in and of itself to have someone listen, not just to the repeated words and phrases, but to the core feelings and needs being expressed, often in symbolic fashion.

In addition the listener helps through an ongoing process of assessment. A listener might be asking: What role does religion play in this person's struggle with loss? Is her understanding helping or hindering? Is God present or absent? How is God helpful or hurting? Is holding on the best form of religious coping? Or is holding on a way of preserving a dysfunctional religious system? Can transformation help this person adapt? Is the transformation in some way alienating this person from a helpful religious understanding? Or is the transformation shifting the person away from a life of significance to a life devoid of value and meaning?

In our work with frail elders, some interventions help to maintain or conserve religious coping. Memorial services help people remember the values of their religious history and those of their ancestors and provide a way of linking themselves to the living, the recently deceased, and the long lost relationships of earlier life. Use of religious ritual, whether praying the rosary or the stations of the cross, help elders conserve the faith that filled their lives.

Other interventions aid those in need of transformation. The act of pastoral counseling or psychotherapy can provide consolidation of one's faith when that is assessed to be helpful. It can also provide challenge through deep understanding and being a companion in the wilderness of transformation. Groups that discuss the way religious beliefs impact our daily life (for example, a focus on pain management or death and dying) can assist those struggling with beliefs that provide more harm than help. The proximity of death—experienced through the onslaught of loss of friends, family, and neighbors, or through significant physical illness—can bring about a raw awareness of one's own mortality. A short horizon of life brings into sharp focus old wounds and broken relationships with others and with the religion that has shaped the central meaning and value of life. Pastoral caregivers, alert to the signs of transformation, provide invaluable ministry as confession yields to repentance, and forgiveness to acceptance.

CONCLUSIONS

In this chapter we have reviewed case vignettes of four frail elders who utilized religious coping in adapting to the severe losses that marked their lives—coping that could either hinder or foster the elder's emotional, spiritual, and physical well-being. We also discussed ways to intervene by using religious resources or pastoral counseling to assess and develop helpful ways of religious coping. These cases and suggestions are the fruit of training psychology interns with theological backgrounds to listen to the ways religion can lead to greater fragmentation or greater wholeness through conservation or transformation. This work is very much in process. We need to continue to find ways to assess the powerful role religion can play in the emotional and physical health of those facing the losses and crises of old age. We can make a good beginning by listening carefully to elders themselves as well as to the remarkable people who accompany them in this life-changing journey.[1]

NOTE

1. The authors would like to thank the elders and students who have provided the inspiration for this work.

BIBLIOGRAPHY

Kimble, M. A., S. H. McFadden, J. W. Ellor, and J. J. Seeber, eds. (1995). *Aging, Spirituality, and Religion: A Handbook.* Vol. 1. Minneapolis: Fortress Press.

Koenig, H. G., M. Smiley, and J. A. Gonzales, eds. (1988). *Religion, Health, and Aging: A Review and Theoretical Integration.* New York: Greenwood.

Moody, H. R. (1995). "Mysticism." In Kimble et al., 87–101.

Pargament, K. I. (1999). "The Psychology of Religion and Coping? Yes and No." *International Journal for the Psychology of Religion* 9: 3–16.

——— (1997). *The Psychology of Religion and Coping: Theory, Research, Practice.* New York: Guilford.

16   Pastoral Care of Elders and Their Families

LOIS D. KNUTSON

As a pastor who specializes in senior-adult ministry, valuing and cherishing aging persons is both my vocation and my personal life. Throughout my twenty years of ordained ministry, I have served senior adults as a solo parish pastor, hospital chaplain in a major medical center, and nursing-home chaplain. I currently serve both as visitation pastor in a congregation of 1926 members (in which more than 500 members are above the age of sixty-five) and as chaplain in a 120-bed nursing home. As a result of graduating from the Gerontological Pastoral Care Institute at the Center for Aging, Religion and Spirituality, at Luther Seminary in St. Paul, Minnesota, I developed a senior-adult ministry program that is detailed in my book *Understanding the Senior Adult: A Tool for Wholistic Ministry* (Knutson 1999). As a workshop and seminar speaker, I share both my program for senior-adult ministry and my insights into the aging person with congregations, conferences, synods, and national conventions.

Personally, as an adult-child caregiver to my aging mother, I feel deeply blessed that mom and I can grow older together. Mom is a wonderful role model of faith, love, and how to survive suffering, as well as my best friend. As her long-distance caregiver who lives a 400-mile round-trip drive from her, I visit her at least monthly, during which time I help her with the holistic needs of life. I telephone her every morning and every evening. We vacation together in the summer. I developed my program for senior-adult ministry based on what I believed would be meaningful to mom as well as to my parishioners. I dedicate this chapter to my wise and loving mother. Thus, ministry with senior adults is not only the focus of my vocation but also the focus of my personal life.

BIBLICAL AND THEOLOGICAL GOAL-SETTING IN PASTORAL CARE

Just as both the Old Testament and New Testament mandate that God's people love and compassionately serve the elderly, pastoral care for elders and their families has a biblical and theological foundation. Through a combination of God's love and goal-centered, well-coordinated, high-quality, structured congregational caregiving programs, aging persons and their families will experience spiritual meaning and peace in life. Goals for pastoral care in both congregations and long-term care settings of ministry are based upon this foundation. Among such goals are the following.

Affirming the God-given Value of Aging Persons

God lovingly gifts the human person with a life that is created in God's image and proclaimed to be "very good" (Gen. 1:26, 31). This God-given value continues throughout the course of life, apart from one's ability to always be productive, as illustrated by Jesus: "Look at the birds of the air; they neither sow nor reap nor gather into barns, and yet your heavenly Father feeds them. Are you not of more value than they?" (Matt. 6:26). Senior adults continue to be the same valued persons in advanced years as they were in younger years. Pastoral care proclaims to elders, their families, and all settings of ministry that people do not become less important as they grow older, even as the holistic challenges of the aging process increase.

Honoring Aging Persons

The mandate to honor aging persons is commanded by God in the Decalogue: "Honor your father and mother" (Exod. 20:12), proclaimed in the Holiness Code: "You shall rise before the aged, and defer to the old" (Lev. 19:32), modeled by Jesus: "Then he said to the disciple, 'Here is your mother'" (John 19:27), and expounded by the Pastoral Epistles: "Do not speak harshly to an older man, but speak to him as to a father; . . . to older women as mothers" (1 Tim. 5:1-2). Both families and faith communities alike are instructed to honor their elders. In fact, as aging persons move from independence to dependence, they need more "honoring" to keep their self-esteem alive (Knierim 1981). Pastoral care helps them feel respected by their congregation, synagogue, and/or other settings of ministry.

Comforting Aging Persons and Their Families

Assure elders that as they experience the challenges of the aging process, God brings them good news when they feel oppressed, binds them up when they feel brokenhearted, liberates them from captivity, and comforts them when they mourn (Isa. 61:1-3). Remind them that the incarnate Christ, who himself knew suffering, empathetically invites them, "Come unto me all you that are weary and are carrying heavy burdens, and I will give you rest" (Matt. 11:28). Through an incarnational ministry of presence, reading of Holy Scripture, prayer, ritual/sacraments, and conversation, pastoral care assures elders and their families that God is with them and comforts them as they encounter the challenges of the aging process.

Being Vehicles of Peace for Aging Persons and Their Families

For persons who have a works-righteousness theology, God's unconditional love may be difficult to comprehend and accept. Yet unconditional love is the manifestation of God's goodness (e.g., John 3:16). When pastoral care proclaims the unconditional, forgiving love of God and regularly shares the peace of the Lord—"The

Lord bless you and keep you; the Lord make his face to shine upon you, and be gracious to you; the Lord lift up his countenance upon you and give you peace" (Num. 6:24-26)—elders and their families experience the "peace of God which surpasses all understanding" (Phil. 4:7).

Assisting Aging Persons and Their Families to Discern Spiritual Meaning in Life

Although meaning (for each day, as well as for the end of life) cannot be "given" by pastoral caregivers, spiritual guides can assist the elders and their families to find purpose in life. This is accomplished as pastoral caregivers listen and draw out insights from all family members as well as frame their reflections with the love of God. William E. Hulme wrote, "God's providential care gives us a consistent sense of meaning amid the vicissitudes of our lives. We are in God's hands" (Hulme 1986, 113). As senior adults and their families discern the spiritual meaning of their lives, pastoral care helps them to remember that God who was with them in the past continues to be with them in the present and promises to be with them in the future. While pastoral caregivers provide spiritual guidance, they also need to remember that the persons who interpret meaning for elders and families are those persons themselves.

As these goals are implemented on both the visitation level and programmatic level of senior-adult ministry, pastoral caregivers need to initiate ministry with aging persons and families rather than wait for them to ask for help. Just as structured ministry is developed and offered to congregational members in areas of worship, youth, education, and social ministry, so too ministry with aging persons and their caregivers needs to be planned and implemented. Such a caregiving ministry does not just happen! If it is not prioritized through intentional planning, it may only occur "when and if there is time." Consequently, it may "fall through the cracks" of the pastor's and congregation's schedule. Ministry for elders and their families must be given the "firstfruits" of pastoral care rather than the "left over" time. As baby boomers age (and sometimes retire early), they will demand high-quality, meaningful, structured ministry for themselves and their aging parents!

FAMILY SYSTEMS AND PASTORAL CARE

Virginia Satir's "family systems" method of counseling, which initially focused upon problem children and youth, can be applied also to pastoral care with aging persons and their families (Becker 1986, 161). Here the pastoral caregiver relates not just to the elder, who may be unfairly identified as the problem person who is in need of care, but to all family members, since that which affects the elder also affects others in the family. Family members who need care include spouses, adult children, grandchildren, siblings, nieces/nephews, and close friends of the aging person.

Roles change and become more complicated in aging family systems. Some elders gradually transition from self-sufficiency to dependency upon others in the family for the needs of daily life. Caregiving spouses may eventually grieve becoming homebound, along with their partner who is in need of care. Some caregiving spouses who previously were submissive may have to take control of domineering partners. Adult children strive to balance elder care with child care, career responsibilities, personal health care, social relationships and preretirement planning. Pastoral care offers support to each person in the family system.

Pastoral caregivers assist all members of the family system to interface the bigger picture of life with the day-to-day caregiving tasks. They remind family members that God is with them and God is in control. They offer assurance that life is still good, even though they may struggle with changes that take place related to the aging process. They point out that God has given each person a calling in life: to love one another as well as to love God, neighbor, and self (Matt. 22:36-40). Pastoral caregivers assure elders that their calling to love does not cease as they grow older. Finally they help family caregivers to reframe their elder care into a spiritual calling to love. As adult children do so, they will be reminded that their parents continue to be valued children of God who need spiritual meaning and peace in life, just as they themselves do. As pastoral caregivers assist the family system to see the bigger picture, family members will grow in faith and know that God loves them.

MEANINGFUL VISITATION

One-on-one visitation is essential in high-quality pastoral care. Persons who visit include pastors, chaplains, parish nurses, and lay visitors (both trained and untrained). The settings in which visitation is carried out includes elders' homes (private homes, senior apartments), institutions (nursing homes, assisted-living facilities, hospitals, convalescent centers, hospices), and family members' homes. Short hospital stays mean that more pastoral visitation takes place in senior-adult homes. Prior to making visits, visitors who explore their personal feelings about their own aging process as well as explore any stereotypical ideas they may have about aging persons will be more likely to avoid countertransference and transference issues. The visits will thereby be more helpful for aging persons and their families. What follows are concrete suggestions for making visitation more meaningful.

Active Listening and Creating a Sacred Space

Active listening and creating a sacred space is of vital importance in visitation. Approach the time together with prayer, attention, and sensitivity. The church visitor may be the only person with whom members of the family system have the opportunity to talk, especially if they are unable or unwilling to join support groups. Integrate the biblical and theological goals for pastoral care into the conversation as you are able. Respond compassionately to the feeling level of each person in the family.

Visits with elders who are active are often stimulating and occur at a pace that is congruent with the visitor's personal pace. Follow the agenda of the senior adult. Include relevant rituals of the faith tradition, such as the reading of Holy Scripture, sacramental practices, and prayer. Visitors also may bring the worship bulletin and sermon tape/videotape for the aging person to enjoy at a later time. When the senior adult has no agenda, a guided format for visitation, such as the Parish Spiritual Assessment Tool (Knutson 1999), can be used effectively by visitors. This holistic format for visitation assists visitors to integrate the biblical and theological goals for pastoral care with elders and guides visitors as they address issues related to spirituality, psychology, family dynamics, socioeconomic concerns, and medical conditions. The Parish Spiritual Assessment Tool also includes a format through which the visitor can identify, assess, and address aging persons' areas of strengths and weakness as well as address acute problem areas in elders' lives.

Visits with elders who experience multiple challenges in their aging process may be slow and less exhilarating, as visitors need to give these persons time to ascertain their thoughts and feelings, formulate words, and speak. In such visits, the empathic visitor also speaks slowly, distinctly, and unhurriedly. When elders are unable to communicate, even with all the visitor's imaginative attempts at using symbolic items (e.g., cross, Bible, rosary) and pictures (e.g., Moses parting the Red Sea and Jesus the Good Shepherd), visits may be shorter. During these visits, sharing unspoken presence, expressing comforting facial and body language, and offering familiar prayers aloud may be the most loving form of visitation.

Visits with Family Members

Pastoral visitors should acknowledge that elder care is a complicated and stressful responsibility for which few persons are trained. All areas of the family caregiver's life are affected (e.g., the cognitive need for information; ethical and moral end-of-life issues; social-life dynamics; family conflict; employment complications; and emotional feelings of anger, guilt, shame, or sadness). "What can be most difficult to deal with is the lack of understanding and appreciation for this role of caregiver. Family caregivers often feel isolated and alone in their roles, which adds the feeling of loneliness to feelings of stress and anxiety" (from "Family Caregiver Platform Focuses on Caregiver Needs"). Pastoral care offers the opportunity for family caregivers to ventilate feelings and to articulate theological questions that have arisen. Some of these questions might be:

- Has God abandoned us, my spouse/parent and me?
- Why does my spouse/Mom who has been faithful to God all her life have to suffer so greatly with Alzheimer's while my best friend's spouse/mother died suddenly and didn't have to struggle with dementia?

- When I die, do you think I will be as confident of the gift of salvation as my wife/father is?

Pastoral caregivers need to be willing to enter the "dark night of the soul" with family members as well as provide them with resources related to finances, legal issues, housing, medical concerns, counseling needs, and home health-care agencies (many of which are available on the Internet).

Encourage family caregivers to engage in self-care. Often family members do not feel that they are as important as their aging loved one, nor do they think it is appropriate to take time to love themselves. Empower them by helping them to focus upon their relationship with God. Remind them that God fills them with everything they need. Suggest the following forms of spiritual self-care: pray (provide them with sample printed prayers, such as the Serenity Prayer); read Holy Scripture (provide a list of recommended passages, e.g., Deut. 31:8; Matt. 11:28-30; John 14:18; 1 Peter 5:7); worship regularly; participate in the rituals of their faith tradition; and view elder care as a spiritual "calling." Advise them that no one is perfect in caregiving and that God forgives their shortcomings because God created human persons with limited emotional, physical, and spiritual strength. Family members also may need to forgive themselves. Remind them that God is their refuge and strength, and source of comfort and peace.

Encourage family members also to practice psychological self-care. These forms might include joining a support group; setting priorities and concentrating on one task at a time instead of many demands at once; asking for help from professionals, other family members, and friends; accepting the role reversal; dealing with feelings of denial, anger, shame, fear, resentment, sadness, sympathy, and grief; acknowledging that some family members cannot emotionally handle visiting their loved one in a setting such as a nursing home or hospital; and scheduling caregiving escapes, such as a lazy morning in bed, watching a movie/video, reading a novel, visiting a museum or art gallery, or listening to music while doing nothing else.

In addition to spouses and adult children, other members of the family system also need to be included for pastoral visitation. For an elder who never married or whose spouse died or who had no children (or their children died), a sibling may be the only family caregiver. This sibling may provide in-home care, serve as power of attorney for legal and health-care matters, sit at the bedside when the elder is dying, and plan the funeral (if the elder has not already done so). When caregiving siblings, who have lovingly taken their loved one into their own home, become worn out due to the caregiving task, remind them that nursing-home placement may be necessary so that both siblings do not wind up in a nursing home. When the elder who needs assistance has a spouse and/or adult child to provide care, pastoral visitors need to intentionally reach out to the elders' siblings during times of crisis, including at the time of the funeral/memorial service because when siblings have experienced close relationships their grief is great and they need to receive care.

Grandchildren also need to be offered pastoral care as their grandparents age. Listen to their feelings and concerns; encourage them to sit with grandparents during worship and hold the cumbersome worship book for their grandparents; encourage them to walk with grandparents to the altar for Holy Communion and steady them so they do not fall; suggest that they read Holy Scripture out loud to grandparents who cannot see to read; assure them that they have not caused their grandparents' change in behavior, and invite them also to participate in church/synagogue support groups and educational programs.

When an elder's only family is a niece or nephew, the church can consult with that relative and set up a spiritual care program for the elder as well as advise the niece or nephew about services for the aging in the community. Close friends of the aging person may experience great stress and grief when their aging friend is ill as well as when their friend dies. Congregations that develop a Preplanning Your Funeral Service form should include an item in which the person who completes the form indicates the names of close friends who should be notified in case of death and, accordingly, offered pastoral support.

COMMON PASTORAL-CARE ISSUES IN VISITATION

Retirement

Pastoral visitors quickly learn that retirees who have a sufficient income and good health take pleasure in their retirement years as they travel, engage in hobbies, and pursue enjoyable goals. In contrast, persons who retire with limited income and poor health may experience depression in the later years. During visitation explore the retirees' feelings about retirement and encourage them to view this time in life as a spiritual calling, regardless of their socioeconomic situation. Remind retirees that there is no retirement for persons of faith. They are called "to love"—God, neighbor, and self. As they frame their retirement with a spiritual perspective, they will experience deeper meaning in life and will have a reason to get up each morning—whether they are active or homebound.

As a way to affirm retirees' value and being, faith communities can hold periodic "Celebration of Retirement" and "Reaffirmation of Baptism" worship services. Additionally, active senior adults can be encouraged to participate (as they are able) in the following opportunities: worship assistant, lector, choir member, usher, Sunday school teacher, Senior Advisory Committee member, Bible-study participant/leader, prayer chain, women's or men's organization participant, home visitor to homebound senior adults, short-term volunteer missionary in another country, and mentor to youth. Homebound members can be encouraged to serve (as they are able) by praying for the congregation and its members, daily telephoning other homebound members to make sure they are okay, and advising the faith community of senior-adult concerns based upon discussions with other aging persons and based upon that which elders read and see in the media.

Loss and Grief

Elders. During visitation, acknowledge and address both the variety of loss experiences and the multiple occurrences of loss in aging persons' lives. In addition to loss through death, elders may also grieve many other types of loss, including the ability to attend or to participate fully in the worship service (e.g., because of inability to hear or clearly see the worship leaders, or to see the small print in the church bulletin and hymnal). Elders may also lose physical proximity to their own church if they relocate to be near an adult child who lives in another community. Loss of visual acuity precludes reading the Bible and devotional material (congregations should make these available in large-print versions), and loss of physical ability may prevent pursuit of enjoyable hobbies. Some elders can no longer handle stress well and others cannot engage in active conversation with other people. Others losses include income, identity as an employed person, their own home, driving privileges, respect from persons in authority, physical health, and ability to physically care for self. Help elders to reflect upon what these losses mean for them spiritually. Assure elders that God is their companion who understands them and gives them strength.

Family members. During visitation, pastoral caregivers acknowledge and address the following losses which family members often grieve:

- their loved one's ability to participate in previous spiritual disciplines—and wondering how the loved one views the afterlife, especially when the elder is unable to articulate thoughts
- the elder's ability to acknowledge the family member's name and identity— and wondering why God allows this to happen
- the elder's ability to express love—and learning how to handle no longer receiving their loved one's affectionate support
- the elder's ability to cognitively engage in stimulating conversations—and wondering what is going on in the elder's mind
- the elder's energy and ability to perform the activities of daily life—and wondering how to problem-solve.

Encourage family caregivers to express their grief feelings as well as to reflect upon what these losses mean for them spiritually. Assure family members that God is their companion who understands them and gives them strength.

Family members also sometimes experience "ambiguous loss," in which the aging loved one is perceived as physically present but psychologically absent (Boss 1999). This is the experience of families whose elder exhibits symptoms of Alzheimer's disease, other forms of dementia, and/or stroke. Since this form of loss is difficult to master, it can lead to depression, anxiety, and even conflictual relationships within families. Ambiguous loss is frequently unrecognized by friends of the family. Family members find it helpful when pastoral visitors not only "label" this form of loss, but also support family members in the ambiguity and confusion of their experience.

Finances

Although the pastoral visitor frequently may feel a need to develop a trust level with elders prior to raising the topic of finances, sometimes such conversations are necessary earlier for the well-being of aging persons. If the visitor observes or senses that the aging person does not have the financial means to obtain sufficient food and medicine (especially toward the end of the month when the Social Security check runs out), it becomes necessary to develop a plan for addressing the problem. Possible approaches include consulting with the elders' families for assistance, providing food through the community or congregation's food shelf, temporarily purchasing what is needed through the pastor's discretionary fund, and/or contacting community social service agencies. Elders' financial situations are frequently related to their experience of God and the church; for example, when the aging person's basic needs of life are met, her or his experience of God may be positive, but when those needs remain unmet, the opposite can be true.

Additionally, elders who live on low fixed incomes usually are relieved when the pastor gives them permission to reduce (and if necessary, eliminate) their financial contribution to their faith community so that they can better provide for their basic needs of daily life. Relatedly, family members who financially support their aging loved ones will also be relieved when the pastor not only commends them for their support but also refers to their support as family financial benevolence and gives them permission to reduce their financial commitment to the faith community, if they need to do so. Most often when family members financially support their aging loved ones, they do so without the benefit of a tax deduction (as is the case with their financial contribution to their faith community).

Medical

Elders frequently engage pastoral visitors in discussions about their medical conditions. Solid pastoral care includes not only listening and empathizing with elders' concerns but also helping them to explore the spiritual meaning of their health condition. Remind them that the God who gave them strength for life's challenges in their younger years continues to give them strength in the present—and will continue to do so in the future. Assist elders to identify the inner resources (spiritual and otherwise) that have worked for them in the past and put those resources to work in current situations.

Sometimes pastoral visitors find it necessary to intervene for elders who need medical assistance. Families may need to be contacted and informed that a medical consultation is advised. In other situations, pastoral caregivers may need to encourage both elders and family members to begin home health services or to expand the services that they already use. Keep a resource file of credible home health agencies and independent home health-care workers in the church office for easy accessibility. Encourage family systems to do background checks on home health-care workers as an attempt to ensure the safety of their loved one and of the elder's material resources.

Dementia and Alzheimer's Disease

Elders. Pastoral visitors may be one of only a few persons to whom elders with dementia will relate. Confused elders need spiritual nurture. "Being with" persons who have dementia is the focus of pastoral care, rather than "doing something." It is important when visiting aging persons with dementia to validate them rather than to correct them with factual information, even though that may be the temptation. Validation communication skills involve rephrasing elders' statements, reminiscing with them, maintaining comfortable eye contact, using a loving voice tone, using slow speech and body movements, and lovingly responding on a feeling level to their emotions. Do not quiz aging persons about whether they remember who you are. Do not argue. Do not interrupt. Address persons with dementia by name, and state your name as well as the name of your church/synagogue. Assure them that they are missed by the church/synagogue and state that you are visiting them on behalf of their faith community and God.

Family members. Pastors sometimes are the front-line people who advise families that their loved one suffers from dementia. Based upon the pastor's observations during worship and visitation as well as congregational members' reports to the pastor about a confused elder's behavior, the pastor sometimes needs to initiate contact with a family, share documented anecdotes, and advise the family to seek medical advice. Some family members will respond positively and accept the pastor's recommendation, while other family members will deny the documented evidence. When families accept the fact that their loved one suffers from dementia, the pastor may be the only person with whom they are able to share their distress. This is true because some spouses may be unable or unwilling to join an Alzheimer's support group in which they would be called upon to openly share their feelings in front of other people, adult children and teenagers are frequently too busy to attend support group meetings, and children may have no transportation to attend meetings.

When family members deny the pastor's documentation and recommendation that their aging loved one exhibits signs of dementia and needs to be medically evaluated but their loved one is not a danger to herself or himself or others, another meeting with additional anecdotal documentation can be held in an attempt to break through the denial. But when the elder is a danger to herself or himself or to others, the pastor needs to initiate consultation with community adult-protective services and request an evaluation of the aging member who is at risk.

Assure youth whose grandparents suffer from Alzheimer's that they are not to blame for their grandparents' erratic behavior and outbursts. Educate them about the disease. Seeing the changes in their grandparent as well as observing the stress in the family caregivers can be troubling for young people. Youth need to verbalize their feelings about the situation and know that their feelings are normal and are shared by other family members. Youth may also need to be assured their confused grandparent understands their feelings and loves them. Suggest that families hold scheduled conferences during which all members are given the opportunity to express their feelings, dialogue about what they have learned about Alzheimer's disease, and coordinate caregiving responsibilities. Encourage the faith community to become an extended support system to the family.

Dying and Death

Elders. Pastoral visitors need to invite dying senior adults to openly discuss what death means to them, including their view of the afterlife. This also can open up a discussion with those who doubt their salvation. David Callahan has observed that "people who are young become middle-aged and then old; people who are middle-aged can become old. But people who are old have nowhere to go. If they don't stay old, they die" (quoted in Nelson and Nelson 1998, 55). For Christian pastoral care providers, ministry with dying persons needs to include the assurance that one's relationship with God does not cease with death but becomes even more wonderful and meaningful after death. St. Paul writes, "For to me, living is Christ and dying is gain" (Phil. 1:21).

Invite aging persons to preplan their funeral services, reflect upon what they want to tell their families before they die, and share what will be meaningful for them as they die, for example, the reading of specific passages of Holy Scripture, participation in sacraments and rituals, "commendation of the dying" services, listening to specific musical selections, pastoral presence, specific family members' or friends' presence, being alone. Comfort dying persons who have no family by maintaining vigil at their bedside during this sacred time on their spiritual journey.

Family members. Some family members can face death. Some cannot. Families may never have experienced such an overwhelming event in their lives. Invite them to explore their feelings and beliefs about the pending death of their aged loved one. The feelings of a spouse may be exacerbated if the loved one who is dying is the partner in a second marriage because the surviving spouse has once previously experienced the emotional pain and grief of saying goodbye to a hoped-for life partner. Now the residual feelings from the death of the first spouse may compound the grief experience of watching a perceived life partner die. A spouse whose dying loved one was unchurched may feel like a failure for not being able to get him or her to attend worship and may question whether their loved one will be granted the gift of salvation. Adult children who have siblings may or may not get along with one another, even as their parent is dying. Conflict may ensue regarding equality of time spent with the dying parent, life support decisions, and funeral arrangements. It is often helpful for adult children to be reminded that they are learning how to die from their parent. Since grandchildren may not have previously experienced death, pastoral visitors need to talk with them (at the appropriate times) about the teachings of the church regarding the afterlife, the format of the funeral/memorial service, and the final nature of the service at the cemetery/mausoleum, as well as about what their grandparent means to them.

Encourage all family members to say goodbye in their own ways, possibly forgiving the dying his or her shortcomings as well as thanking the elder for having shared love (if appropriate), values, everyday life's lessons, and specific gifts (e.g., items, education). In some situations, family members may need to be advised to give their dying loved one permission to "let go" and die. A "rite of commendation" may help the family do this. Families are comforted when they know the pastor has proclaimed the promise of salvation to their loved one. Some families also appreciate being advised about possible behaviors and symptoms of dying persons. Throughout the dying process, help the family tell the story of their loved one—who the elder is to each of the family members, as well as the joys and struggles which their loved one experienced in life.

Following the death, assist all generations to realize that they mourn in different ways and that they need to respect each other's unique grief process. Initiate pastoral visitation prior to the funeral/memorial service, and visit or telephone at regular intervals during the first year following the death. If possible, hold one of the early postfuneral visits with the family at the cemetery or mausoleum. If any family members were unable to get to the bedside of the dying loved one prior to death (or attend the funeral/memorial service) due to inclement weather, travel complications, or career conflict, pastoral caregivers may need to address related guilt feelings. One year following the death, hold an Anniversary of Death Service with the family. Surviving spouses may need to be encouraged to reengage in life, especially if they had become temporarily homebound as they cared for their marriage partner. Adult children who experience the death of their second parent may feel like orphans and may experience the reality of their own mortality for the first time, as they reflect upon the passing of the generations. Initiate pastoral conversation with all surviving members of the family.

NURSING-HOME AND ASSISTED-LIVING FACILITY VISITATION

Because it is not unusual for senior adults whom pastoral caregivers have visited in their private homes to move into supervised living situations, the same biblical and theological goals for visitation apply to visitation in nursing homes, assisted-living facilities, and senior-adult living facilities. Pastoral caregivers need to visit these aging members and their family caregivers with the same frequency—and greater frequency when these families experience crisis experiences—that home visits were conducted prior to the relocation. Love, tenderness, and high-quality pastoral care need to characterize these visits.

Pastoral Caregivers

Regularly encourage (through sermons, church newsletters, and worship bulletins) members to notify the church office when nursing-home placement is being considered for a loved one as well as when their loved one enters a nursing home or assisted-living facility. Both pastors and lay visitors should continue to visit the elder in the new home. Do not neglect these older members. Visit them with the same regularity as they were previously visited (if they were on the homebound visitation list); otherwise, they may feel abandoned by God and by their faith community. Continue to send them congregational mailings. Do so even when they have a visual handicap, because their family or the facility staff will read them the mailings.

Prior to visiting in senior-adult facilities, telephone the staff and ask advisement regarding the best time to visit (i.e., when the elder has no appointments or required facility activities). This will save time and avoid frustration for the visitor. Visitation that takes place in the new home can follow the same format for conversation that was followed when the senior adult was homebound, keeping in mind the cognitive level of the elder. Assist the member-resident to inform the facility staff (including the chaplain) about their preferences for spiritual care within the facility. This easily can be accomplished by using the Nursing Home Spiritual Assessment Tool (Knutson 1999) or something similar. Encourage member-residents to attend chapel services. If they are not encouraged to attend, some elders will choose not to attend because they may believe that such participation means disloyalty to one's home congregation. Offer to lead a Blessing of the New Home Service (Knutson 1999) in the member-resident's room. This service is an opportunity to bless the elder's new home and to assist all members of the family to get through this time of transition and adjustment. Inform senior facilities how to contact the pastoral staff for emergencies. Make additional visits when the member-resident is dying, even if the facility has a chaplain.

Family Caregivers

When families notify the church office that they are considering moving their loved one to a senior-adult facility, pastors have a wonderful opportunity to suggest that they consider a facility that is served by a chaplain. Senior adults who were active in the congregation are accustomed to continuity of pastoral care and will appreciate the pastoral relationship that will develop with the facility chaplain. Since some families (including grandchildren) have no experience with senior-adult facilities, help them deal with their feelings of discomfort and confusion, and provide them with tips for what to expect (e.g., the structured schedule of nursing-home life) and how to visit (e.g., talk about what is going on in the family, bring family photographs).When appropriate, also support families in the following ways: acknowledge their financial stress, e-mail long-distance family members, and encourage spouses and other family members who are verbally and/or physically abused by their elder to reduce the amount of time they spend in the facility.

PASTORAL CARE AND CONGREGATIONAL PROGRAMS

As the same biblical and theological goals that were implemented on the visitation level of pastoral care are carried out on the congregational programmatic level, caregiving ministry gains greater visibility within the intergenerational faith community. This can educate members of all ages about the importance and value of aging persons and their families to God and the congregation.

1. *Planning and implementing* congregational-level pastoral care in large faith communities needs to have a full-time senior-adult pastor. Clergy in small congregations need to designate specific time blocks for ministry with older members and their families. If senior-adult ministry is not planned and scheduled, in all likelihood it will receive only leftover time, if it even receives that. Form Senior Advisory Committees (comprised primarily of older members) which will offer additional ideas and support for aging persons and their families within the faith community (Knutson 1999).

2. *Worship.* Plan corporate worship services that are user-friendly, handicapped accessible, sensitive to the challenges of the aging process, and inclusive of the gifts of aging persons. Worship bulletins can be printed in a large font, handrails can be installed leading to the altar where communion is served, good lighting and appropriate room temperatures can be monitored, and elders who are able can serve in leadership roles. Faith communities can reach out to homebound persons by broadcasting their services on radio and/or television or, if that is not financially feasible, by having visitors bring informally produced videotapes of worship services to the homebound. When videotapes are brought to senior-adult facilities which house more than one congregational member, encourage those members to sit together to view the worship service. This assists them to experience their larger faith community. Special worship services can be held throughout the year which address the biblical and theological goals for pastoral care, e.g., annual services exclusively devoted to valuing and honoring aging persons (Knutson 1999), regularly scheduled healing services in which persons receive God's promise of strength and peace for their challenges of life, services in which couples renew their marriage vows, and annual services which honor loved ones who have died and address survivors' grief. As pastors regularly share the Sacrament of Holy Communion during one-on-one visitation, homebound members experience an intimate form of worship, with the pastor and with God.

3. *Support groups* provide loving care for aging persons and their families from congregational members who experience similar life situations. In addition to the

usual types of support groups (grief groups, widows/widowers groups, etc.), faith communities may offer a grandparent-caregiver support group because more and more grandparents provide child care for their families. Senior adults will value "spirituality" support groups, in which aging persons share everyday happenings as well as their joys and sorrows. Offer some of these groups during daytime hours when many older persons feel more comfortable leaving home. If possible, offer an ongoing caregivers support group to enable new family caregivers to receive immediate support and help. This is especially important for families whose loved one has just moved into a nursing home or who has just been diagnosed with Alzheimer's disease. When the congregation has a number of adult children who are long-distance caregivers, offer a support group where they can share both feelings and ideas.

4. *Educational programs* on topics of aging of aging (e.g., end-of-life issues, spiritual wellness in aging, how to visit in a nursing home) supplement the care provided to elders and their families through support groups, and educate the intergenerational faith community. Avoid always exclusively addressing the "sandwich generation" in these programs because not all adult caregivers have children. Include educational books in the church library.

5. *Respite care* provides relief and protects the health and well-being of the family caregiver as well as allows aging persons to remain in their homes longer. Family caregivers need the opportunity to attend worship, leave the bedside of a hospitalized senior adult, attend a movie, go for a walk, read a novel, or just rest. A volunteer respite caregiver program can serve in these ways and also may include giving grandparents much-needed time off to rest as they care for active grandchildren. A related form of respite care, which will be greatly appreciated by adult children, is that of providing congregational volunteers to check on aging parents when their adult children (and their families) go on much-needed vacations. Vacations can be times of high stress for conscientious adult children caregivers who feel guilty for taking time off, and for their parents, who wonder what they will do if they have a crisis when their family caregivers are not readily available.

6. *Visitation* needs to be structured. Aging persons and lay visitors need to be matched according to personality traits and interests, and the frequency of visits needs to be monitored in order to ensure that visitation occurs with regularity. Homebound senior adults experience great disappointment when they are told that they will be visited regularly, but they are only visited once. These elders may blame themselves for "doing" or "being" something or someone that led the visitor not to want to return. Pastors who use the previously described Parish Spiritual Assessment Tool as a format for visitation can also train lay visitors to use it, so that visits focus on areas of importance in the lives of aging persons. Encourage lay visitors also to occasionally pick up homebound friends of the person they visit and bring them together, thereby enabling these friends to see and visit with one another again. Homebound senior adults miss seeing their closest friends, who frequently are also homebound. The lay visitor at times can stay and visit with them and other times just provide the transportation. Aging members often feel isolated.

Part of pastoral care is to provide them with a sense of community—with the faith community and the world at large. Visitors may also take homebound persons for a ride in the car. The driver can show elders new things happening in their community, help them reminisce about past experiences in the community, and show them familiar sights that have special meaning. Some congregations may wish to coordinate their visitation program with community senior center visitation programs or Interfaith Caregivers Programs.

As a supplement to the visitation program, develop a telephone visitation ministry. Some homebound persons' telephones do not ring for days. Some long-distance caregiving adult children who have the desire and who can afford to do so telephone their parent daily. A daily telephone contact from a member of the congregation (regardless of whether senior adults have children who call them) assures homebound senior adults that if they need help, the person who telephones will obtain help. Volunteer telephoners can also serve as liaisons between elders and their adult children, advising adult children about any changes that they observe in the parent.

7. *Long-distance family caregivers* receive pastoral support from their aging parents' congregations through e-mail, pastoral advisement to visit aging parents when they are cognitively aware and able to speak, and providing a lay visitor who is available for a telephone appointment between the long-distance caregiver and the homebound elder who no longer is able to hold the telephone receiver.

8. *Fellowship activities* specific to aging members take the form of both day and evening group events. Some groups may want to meet in a restaurant for a meal, while others prefer to have a meal catered at the church. Provide programs of interest for aging persons at these meetings. Also, provide rides so that homebound members can participate. Senior adults who have similar interests also may enjoy forming groups such as reading groups, Bible-study groups, life-review groups, golf groups, musical instrument ensembles, walking and exercise groups, concert/theater groups, movie groups, and travel groups. Some seniors find participation in the Elderhostel program to be both fun and meaningful.

9. *Intergenerational programs* bring meaning to aging persons and their families as well as to the entire congregation as they promote positive attitudes about aging persons. Parish nurses (whether full-time, part-time, or volunteer) serve as spiritual counselors, health educators, trainers of volunteers, and liaisons to community agencies for elders and their families. Adopt-a-grandparent programs promote love and support for both young and old alike. Sunday school classes can adopt homebound members as pen pals, telephone pals, or prayer partners. Older youth can help aging members write letters, read letters, or send e-mail messages. Youth groups can engage in service projects such as raking leaves, shoveling snow, or running errands. Intergenerational Sunday school fosters learning and sharing across the generations.

10. *Advocacy* becomes a form of pastoral care as it is framed in the context of Micah 6:8, "What does the Lord require of you but to do justice, and to love

kindness ...?" Pastoral care providers need to advocate for justice for aging persons, in faith communities and society. In society, aging persons need to experience equal rights and dignity under the law. It is not unusual for aging persons to be victims of crimes and fraudulent business practices (e.g., unscrupulous repair persons, telephone solicitors, insurance agents who prey upon their fears). Pastoral caregivers need to be the voice for the voiceless homebound, reticent and quiet elders, those who do not want to call attention to themselves, aging persons who are unaware of the discriminatory structures which affect them, and the poor who do not have the financial means to advocate for themselves. Advocacy needs to include involvement in local and national governmental legislative processes, as well as active participation in organizations such as the AARP. Encourage aging persons also to become involved in advocacy.

11. *Internet* ministry supplements pastoral care to both aging persons and their families. Congregations that have their own Web site will want to include a special page for senior-adult ministry. This page will provide information about the congregation's older adult ministry program and how to access it, copies of the worship bulletin and sermon, articles of spiritual interest to aging persons, articles about caregiving for families, links to Web sites on topics of aging and health, and e-mail opportunities for prayer requests. Families appreciate receiving e-mail from the pastor when a visit is made to their loved one and the sacraments are shared. Periodic mass e-mail messages can be sent to homebound senior adults, bringing them a greeting from the church/synagogue and a brief devotional. Similar mass e-mail messages can be sent to family caregivers, offering them tips for caregiving, as well as supporting and encouraging them as they care for their loved ones.

SUMMARY

High-quality pastoral care needs to be prioritized and planned so that aging persons and their families are served—and served well—by congregations and senior-adult facilities. The biblical and theological goals for pastoral care are the same for one-on-one visitation level and for the programmatic level of senior-adult ministry.

As we affirm the God-given value of aging persons, honor our elders, comfort them and their families, and offer all members of the family system God's peace, the Spirit of God will work within them so that they will discern spiritual meaning in life and know that they are loved by God, by their faith community, and by one another.

Bibliography

Becker, A. H. (1986). *Ministry with Older Persons*. Minneapolis: Augsburg.

Boss, P. (1999). *Ambiguous Loss: Learning to Live with Unresolved Grief*. Cambridge, Mass.: Harvard University Press.

Clements, W. M., ed. (1981). *Ministry with the Aging: Designs, Challenges, Foundations.* New York: Harper & Row.

"Family Caregiver Platform Focuses on Caregiver Needs." Online: http://www.caregiving.com/yourcare/html/platform.htm. Park Ridge, Ill.: Tad, 2002.

Hulme, W. E. (1986). *Vintage Years: Growing Older with Meaning and Hope.* Philadelphia: Westminster.

Knierim, R. (1981). "Age and Aging in the Old Testament." In Clements, 21–36.

Knutson, L. D. (1999). *Understanding the Senior Adult: A Tool for Wholistic Ministry.* Bethesda, Md.: Alban.

Nelson, L. H., and J. L. Nelson. (1998). "Care at Home: Virtue in Multigenerational Houses." *Generations* 22/3: 52–57.

17

Pastoral Care of the Aged Afflicted by Addiction

ROBERT H. ALBERS

Addiction to mood-altering substances is a pervasive phenomenon that crosses the age spectrum from the very young to the very old. Accurate statistical data relative to the number of older persons who suffer from addiction are virtually impossible to obtain. There is a paucity of epidemiological studies and the criteria employed to determine what constitutes addiction in the elderly are not uniform. Attitudes about older people and their problems with addiction likewise present difficulties. Although many addictive behaviors could be addressed, the focus of this chapter on addiction will be mood-altering substances, prescription drugs, and alcohol (Clinebell 1998).

The Hazelden Foundation suggests that

> alcoholism and the misuse of prescription drugs are becoming a life-threatening epidemic in older people. It is estimated that 70% of all hospitalized older persons and up to 50% of nursing home residents have alcohol-related problems. Among older people there is reason for concern about mixing alcohol and drugs. Of people over 65, 83% take some prescription. Over half of all prescriptions for older persons have some sedative. Combining prescriptions with alcohol can be deadly at any age, and especially so among the older age groups. (Hazelden Publishing n.d., 1)

Assuming that these estimates are reliable, the problem of addiction to mood-altering substances is statistically staggering. A significant place to start in understanding this problem is the social attitudes exhibited toward older persons, especially those who suffer from addiction to a mood-altering substance.

ATTITUDES TOWARD ELDERS AND THEIR ADDICTIONS

Attitudes toward older persons with addictions spawn action or inaction relative to any given issue. Some of the attitudinal dispositions can be delineated as follows.

The Elderly as a Liability

In a youth-oriented culture, older adults are seen as a liability rather than as a rich resource of experience, insight, and wisdom. If deemed a liability, fewer actions will be taken to help them deal with their addictions. In a capitalistic society where cost seemingly is more important than care, the crass result is to ignore those who are considered nonproductive. Inaction relative to dealing with and treating their addictions is a result. Devaluation of the aged is evidence of a pervasive attitude of "ageism" that permeates this culture. The injustice of this particular "ism" has received less attention than the evils of racism, sexism, and classism.

The social fear of aging has become a serious systemic attitudinal problem. Because society is youth oriented and also because there is the awareness of how older people are viewed and treated in our society, the result is a denial of the aging process itself.

Protecting Older Persons

Some family members and caregivers seek to "protect" the aged from dealing with their addictions. It would be "disrespectful" to suggest that an elderly person has a problem with alcohol or prescription drugs. The alleged concern for protecting their dignity often precludes intervening. The dynamic of denial is in part attributed to the reality of shame (Albers 1995). The concern is not only for shaming the older person by exposing the addiction, but family members or significant others will sense shame or embarrassment in having a loved one who suffers from chemical dependency. This presumed form of protection results in a sustained deterioration of the person's physical, emotional, and spiritual well-being until the ravages of the addiction result in death.

Humoring Elders

Addiction to mood-altering substances is often dismissed as inconsequential simply because the people are aged. The rationale is that since the person has so little time to live what difference will it make? Little thought is given to the value of the quality life. We can wink at their addictions because they are old. They say and do things under the influence of their drugs that provide comic relief for family and caregivers. Intervening is contraindicated because they are not hurting anyone. This attitude, however, implies that older people have lost their status as creations of God who have worth and value.

Misdiagnosing Older Adults

Professional and familial care providers sometimes make a misdiagnosis of older people. Their unusual behavior may be attributed to the "aging process" and therefore considered as eccentric, but not indicative of an addiction. The realities of dementia and physiological conditions such as arteriosclerosis make a differential diagnosis difficult. Physiological factors notwithstanding, an accurate history of the use of mood-altering substances requires assessment. James E. Royce (1981, 109) astutely suggests that *polydrug* abuse among older people should always be suspected. Ten percent of the population over age sixty-five use 20 percent of the prescription drugs sold in this country (U.S.), most of which potentiate with alcohol. Old people tend to hoard and swap drugs, and otherwise use them in nonprescribed ways. If they can use the sanction of "doctor's orders" for either alcohol or other drugs, it is easy to rationalize overuse.

Many elderly have no understanding of the half-life of prescription drugs. Others use ingenuity to secure prescriptions from multiple physicians. Royce suggests that "iatrogenic alcoholism" is a major factor in addiction because physicians may recommend using alcohol as a tranquilizer. When alcohol is coupled with the use of prescription drugs, the problems of drug interaction and cross-addiction arise.

PASTORAL CARE AS RELATED TO SOCIAL ATTITUDES

Pastoral caregivers, whether lay or clergy, are in a unique position to challenge the ageist attitude so pervasive in society. In the context of preaching, teaching, and community involvement, pastoral caregivers have multiple roles.

Consciousness-Raising

Pastoral care must be seen as more than providing care; it must also become involved in consciousness-raising. Leaders of faith communities are in a strategic position to accomplish this. Periodic inclusion of issues related to older adults in preaching and teaching can lift up the plight of the aged, who are often forgotten or simply ignored. When negative attitudes prevail, maladies such as addiction are minimized even more. Addressing the deleterious effects of ageism in newsletters, parish publications, and through educational endeavors is a starting point for the consciousness-raising effort of faith communities.

Advocacy

The biblical tradition is replete with injunctions to advocate for the oppressed, the marginalized, and the disenfranchised of the world. The prophets urge particular concern for the widow, the orphan, and the stranger in the midst of God's people. In the ancient world the elderly were treated with great esteem and respect, but that exalted position no longer prevails in contemporary Western society.

Leaders in faith communities need to function as advocates not only ecclesiastically but also economically and politically. Pastoral care must move out from the safety of the sanctuary lights to the streetlights of the community to carry out the prophetic function of advocacy for older persons. The Spirit of God functions as our advocate (John 14), so also we in turn must function as an advocate for the neighbor who is oppressed or neglected.

Ecumenical Endeavors

Faith communities can ill afford the internecine warfare that often prevails among them. Interfaith efforts as well as intrafaith endeavors are crucial in addressing the needs of older persons. The common good of the aged seems to be a value shared by all faith traditions. Divisions that exist within faith traditions over theological and ecclesiastical practices pale in the wake of the work that awaits them when it comes to ministry among older adults who are addicted.

Ageist attitudes are not confined to one religious tradition or expression. Religious communities must join hands in an effort to lift up the reality of the prevailing negative attitudes toward older adults who are addicted.

Western cultures could learn from our sisters and brothers in Asian and African cultures, where the welfare of the elderly is a priority value. Faith and cultural traditions can be powerful factors in changing attitudes and substantive shifts in attitude can result.

Empowering Older Persons to Action

God has gifted all older adults. Empowering them to use their creativity and tapping into their resiliency to have their voices heard is a critical aspect of ministry. Educational opportunities planned and designed by older adults that lift up age-specific issues in addiction is important. Providing confidential peer-group experiences where the elderly can talk about their own addictions or that of family members serves to lift the isolation of addiction. Twelve-step groups are particularly effective in providing this kind of venue. For those suffering from addiction, Alcoholics Anonymous groups comprised primarily of older adults are effective. Alanon groups aid elders in dealing with addiction in their families or circle of friends.

In my own ministry, an older member of the community who was in recovery functioned as a resource for others. Empowered by her own recovery, she was a rich deposit of wisdom, insight, and resourcefulness in aiding others to receive care.

AWARENESS OF ELDERS AND THEIR ADDICTIONS

If there is a substantive shift in attitude toward the aging and their addictions, the next move is to gain an awareness of how addictions affect the older person. Recognition of symptoms is crucial lest the pastoral caregiver miss the malady completely. A shift in attitude can also break the conspiracy of silence that often accompanies addiction. What follows is a delineation of various dimensions of addiction and their manifestation in the one afflicted. Although the addictive process is unique to each person and no "lockstep" progression is intended, the following dimensions are sequenced in such a way as to suggest a possible paradigm of the addictive process.

Spiritual Dimension

The spiritual dimension of a person's life is usually the first to suffer when addiction is an issue. The "guilt" of unacceptable behavior as a result of addiction erects a barrier between the person and God. Even more pervasive is the phenomenon of shame (noted above). Due to the power of shame, the person who is addicted feels estranged and alienated from God, resulting in a sense of worthlessness and unacceptability. For the one providing spiritual care, the symptom of spiritual "dis-ease" may take the form of the person unequivocally stating that God does not care, God finds me unlovable, or God does not even exist.

The caregiver may be tempted to respond to the content of the statement as opposed to being sensitive to the genesis of the assertion emanating out of a spiritual crisis occasioned by the addiction. Rather than engaging in a dispute about the prevenient grace and unqualified love of God, the elderly person may in fact be communicating in religiously coded language a deeper problem that manifests itself in a spiritual crisis.

Another spiritual symptom that often comes to the fore in addiction is the sense that life is devoid of purpose and meaning. When the person is addicted to a mood-altering substance, the power of despair can be overwhelming. The downward spiritual spiral of addiction is akin to powerful whirlpools in a river that threaten to suck a person into the vortex and drown the victim in despair. In his epigenetic schema of human development, Erik Erikson writes about the final stage of life as resulting in ego integrity or despair (1963). The addiction may or may not have been precipitated by debilitating experiences associated with the aging process, but the net result is a significant spiritual symptom called despair. Life has no purpose or meaning and so one seeks to anesthetize oneself by the use of a mood-altering substance. This is a coping mechanism that works, at least temporarily. When the body is under the anesthetizing influence of alcohol or a drug, the existential angst and spiritual vacuum associated with the loss of meaning and purpose are temporarily suspended.

The reality of finitude is impressed on all of us as a result of advancing age. Sigmund Freud suggested that we all harbor within ourselves the fantasy of immortality, but circumstances impress upon us that this is truly a fantasy. The spiritual issue involves facing the reality of mortality. Whether a member of a faith community or not, the fear of death plagues many people. As the years flow by, the specter of death looms and the fear of "nonbeing" can grip the very essence of a person's spiritual life. The anesthetizing properties of alcohol or certain prescription drugs can temporarily allay those anxieties and fears. Care providers are in a unique position to address these common spiritual issues within their respective faith traditions.

The spiritual symptoms vary according to culture, faith tradition, or the lack thereof. Alcoholics Anonymous asserts that these fundamental spiritual concerns form the foundation for addiction and that alcoholism is at its core a spiritual malady (*Alcoholics Anonymous* 1976). The alcohol becomes a solution to the problems of living, including fundamental concerns about guilt, shame, meaning, purpose, and mortality. The person who is addicted likely is not able to articulate, admit, or accept that these are fundamental issues. The care provider is not advised to begin at this point but rather to keep in mind that there are underlying spiritual issues that need to be addressed at an appropriate time in the recovery process.

Social Dimension

The spiritual crisis or crises, whether acknowledged or not, leads to the social dimension of addiction. As the addictive pattern progresses with concomitant behavioral permutations, the relationships of the addicted person begin to suffer. The consequences of experiencing both guilt and shame may prompt withdrawal from the community of faith as a social support. Clergy and lay caregivers should always be sensitive to the absence of individuals from participation in the activities of the faith community. This is not to suggest that the precipitating factor is always addiction, but that may be the case in a large percentage of instances. The once-faithful are suddenly conspicuous by their absence. The one addicted often uses a defense strategy of attacking the faith community, its leaders and congregants, as a reason for nonparticipation. "Members of the faith community are hypocrites" is a common indictment. Those responses more often than not say more about the one indicting than those indicted. In the case of someone who is caught in the throes of addiction, it is an understandable defense. The disease syndrome precludes taking responsibility for life, so self-hatred and anger are often projected onto others. For the older adult this becomes a particularly painful experience because many have been faithful members of a faith community for decades. The addictive process prompts them to cut themselves off from relationships that they desperately need.

The deterioration of social relationships occurs not only in the community of faith but in the circle of friends as well. When the addictive process progresses to the point of adversely affecting relationships with friends, one of two things may happen. Either the friends will deliberately avoid the addicted person or the addicted person will withdraw from the circle of friends. No one likes an old man who is drunk or an old woman who is high. It is embarrassing and offensive, and elderly persons who are addicted may be summarily ostracized from former social relationships and left to their own devices. The person who is addicted will often make the first move and became absent from usual social circles in order to avoid being ostracized. Deep down at some level, the person is aware that these relationships are problematic and cause pain.

The same deterioration occurs in the social arena of familial relationships. Family members and significant others experience a similar process of estrangement and alienation predicated upon unacceptable behavior. Family members will initially deny, then excuse, rationalize, and otherwise cover up the behavior of an aging member and then give up on them. As a consequence this person may require more care and become dependent not only on the drug of choice but also on family members. In many family systems, a hostile-dependent relationship ensues in which both the person afflicted and those affected become enmeshed in dysfunctional relationships.

Pastoral caregivers more than likely will be sought out by family members who suffer as a result of the addiction as opposed to the person who is addicted. Significant others will lament the fact that they are experiencing a phenomenon that is out of their control and they are mystified about what they should do. The person they once knew and loved has undergone a metamorphosis. Significant others experience tremendous grief and pain or may express intense anger and disappointment that "at this age" their loved one should be thus afflicted. Family members and others in the community will often view the addiction as a moral rather than a medical issue, and that attitude only exacerbates the pain for all involved.

Sensitivity and awareness of the deterioration of relationships in the faith community, among friends, and in the family may raise the suspicion and the specter of addiction as being the primary culprit. Since social denial is so prevalent both inside and outside of the faith community, identification and articulation of addiction as the issue is often precluded. The inability or unwillingness to accept a diagnosis of addiction is the equivalent of a death sentence for the one addicted.

Emotional Dimension

The older person who is addicted will also manifest substantive changes in emotional life. Some may become morose and withdrawn with their increased use of a mood-altering substance and slip into a clinical depression. Sadness, regrets, and remorse occupy the time and attention of the elderly person who is addicted. Caregivers should be aware that pervasive sadness could be a result of addiction.

The effects of mood-altering substances on other elderly people may result in their being bellicose. Their prescription drug or alcohol blocks all inhibitions and their behavior becomes defiant, argumentative, and abusive. Elderly women and men who were convivial, congenial, and caring when sober suddenly become combative or otherwise out of control emotionally. The "Dr. Jekyll and Mr. Hyde" phenomenon is pervasive. Negative emotional outbursts are common and as a consequence the elderly person who is addicted may be feared by family and friends alike.

A different emotional response can be seen in people who are often referred to as "the happy drunks." While their behavior may be socially more acceptable than that of the bellicose or morose addict, jocose addicts often have no sense of boundaries or propriety in social relationships. They may be entertaining and humorous on occasion, but their behavior becomes old. Inappropriate language and behavior result in embarrassment for the addicted person or the family.

Physical Dimension

The deleterious effects of addiction to alcohol and prescription drugs soon take their physical toll as well. Addiction adversely affects every physical aspect of human existence. Cirrhosis of the liver, heart attacks, respiratory problems, renal failure, damage to the immune system, intestinal malfunction, esophageal varices (swollen veins), peripheral neuropathy, and a myriad of other physical maladies accompany addiction. All of these malfunctions can and do lead to death, but even in death the identified culprit often is not cited as addiction. Given the fact that the aging process itself can render one more vulnerable to physical complications, addiction both exacerbates and multiplies the possibilities. Accurate statistical research data regarding the comorbidity of various physical illnesses and addiction are difficult to determine.

It is not suggested that the pastoral care provider be conversant or even knowledgeable about all of the physiological implications of addiction. It is important to be sufficiently aware that the diagnosis of addiction is not overlooked as being the primary malady from which the older person may be suffering.

The pastoral care provider must recognize that addiction affects every aspect of a person's life. It is a personal disease, a family disease, and also a social disease that both afflicts and affects older adults.

PERSONAL ASSESSMENT AND PASTORAL CARE
WITH ADDICTED ELDERS

The compelling question for lay and clergy pastoral care providers with regard to addiction among the elderly is to ask what can be done. Before delineating particular concrete actions that might be taken, it is judicious for the caregiver to conduct a personal assessment.

Assessing Our Own Attitudes

As mentioned above, attitudes spawn actions. It is imperative that caregivers become aware of their own attitudes. Many people who are involved in ministry have developed attitudes predicated on parental, familial, and personal experience. As Gary Harbaugh states so accurately, we do not have a history, we are our history (Harbaugh 1991). Those who have been raised in a family where addiction was an issue will need to deal with that reality. To ignore our own history with addiction, whether with significant others or in our own lives, is to invite disaster. People frequently replicate attitudes and thus actions that emanate from their own personal experiences. Addicted persons perceive these attitudes immediately and will know if the caregiver cares or condemns them. Caregivers are not to become a part of the problem as opposed to being part of the solution. For the sake of ourselves, those with whom we minister, and thus for God's sake as well, honesty and humility about who we are becomes the sine qua non for ministering with the elderly who are addicted.

Assessing Our Awareness

Caregivers must be aware of the pervasiveness of addiction when ministering with the aged. The pastoral care provider need not become a diagnostician but a "truth teller" when interacting with the elderly and observing their behavior and general demeanor. If care providers are unwilling to consider addiction among older people as a primary possibility, effectiveness is severely curtailed. Clinical pastoral education, training seminars, workshops, and schools of addiction studies are readily available. In my own professional pastoral life, associating with and learning from those who are in recovery was the richest source of information.

Assessing Our Theology

As servants of God caregivers ultimately need to reflect upon the nature of God's will for God's people. Creation theology affirms that every person is not only created in the image of God but is of inestimable worth and value. Ignoring or disregarding the elderly who happen to suffer from addiction is no more thinkable than ignoring or disregarding an older person who is dying from cancer.

God's acceptance of people is not predicated on human assessment or human conditions. God's love, acceptance, mercy, and grace are inclusive, not exclusive. This radical and revolutionary message of love and concern for all signals that ministry with the older folks who are afflicted by addiction is a critically important ministry.

God's promise for God's people is of faithfulness even in the wake of human unfaithfulness. God's promise for healing in a disease-ridden world is never to forget or to ignore those who have been created in God's image.

Both the Hebrew and the Christian Scriptures are replete with references to the nature of God in relationship to humankind. The apostle Paul, speaking out of the Judeo-Christian conviction, states that God's disposition toward humankind is always a "yes" (2 Cor. 1:19). In that eternal yes uttered in the context of an eternal now, God has both spoken and acted decisively on behalf of all creation.

Our various theological traditions, however they come to expression, proclaim the eternal love, grace, mercy, and concern of God for all. Faith communities therefore are unilateral in their love, concern, and acceptance for all people even as God's disposition toward humankind is unswerving and unconditional. Having established the essence of the theological tradition and its message of inclusiveness for all people irrespective of their maladies, race, color, class, gender, or age, the following functional roles are proffered as guide for pastoral care providers in ministering with the aged who are addicted.

PASTORAL CARE ROLES IN MINISTERING
WITH ELDERS WHO ARE ADDICTED

Catalyst

An outside catalytic agent is often required to precipitate change in any chemically dependent family system. If the person is an older adult, inertia is often a serious issue. "What is the point?" "What good will it do?" "Let the person just be, rather than stirring the cauldron."

Pastoral care in this kind of setting requires some risk because of the resistance often encountered on the part of the one afflicted as well as those affected. The pastoral caregiver who is incarnationally present as an embodiment of God's love for the persons involved can exemplify the grace of God if there is movement toward health and recovery. In addiction circles it is often termed "tough love." This requires the caregiver to tell the truth in love concerning what is happening to the person and significant others. This does not mean playing the role of "rescuer" and assuming total responsibility for fixing the situation. The word "catalyst" fits well. It signals the posture of one who in love comes from the outside, who is detached from the situation and can provide the impetus for change. Functioning in this capacity, the pastoral caregiver needs to be prepared not only for risk and resistance but the ever-present specter of failure. Efforts toward change may stall and nothing may change. The responsibility of the pastoral caregiver as a catalyst is to plant the seed that hopefully will develop and mature into movement toward recovery and positive change.

Correlator

Pastoral care providers are in a unique position to provide the bridge between their respective tenets of faith and the existential experience of addiction. Members of the faith community often clamor for "relevance" concerning what they believe as it relates to the ecstasies and exigencies of life. If the tradition of faith is relevant to what people experience, then interpreting the role of faith for all involved is a crucial matter.

The fundamental meaning of faith in the biblical tradition is trust. It is a trust that God can do for us what we cannot do for ourselves. Recovery from addiction requires that kind of faith or trust; it is perhaps best expressed by the word "surrender." The first three steps of the Alcoholics Anonymous way of life embody the essence of faith. The first step is to admit being "powerless" over the substance. That is true for those afflicted as well as for those affected. The second step is also a step of faith in coming to believe that there is a Power greater than self that can restore one to sanity. Step three is the "surrender" or "giving over" of one's life to the care of God as God is understood by the person and family.

Perhaps the first application of this understanding of faith rests with the pastoral caregiver. Is the caregiver ready to relinquish the situation in trust to God? Modeling this kind of faith is critical if one is to minister effectively with those afflicted and affected by addiction. Practicing surrender likewise absolves the pastoral caregiver from assuming responsibility for the recovery of the person and the family.

Living out faith as trust in God is a principal concern in relationship to significant others who are adversely affected by addiction. The pattern for family members, friends, or significant others often is an attempt either to control the person and the substance use or to enable the process. These well-intentioned but misguided efforts prevent the person as well as the whole system from recovering. Control with an elderly person may take the form of moving the person geographically, assuming responsibility for finances, attempting to manipulate the environment, or asking others to monitor their use. Enabling with the elderly often means capitulating to their threats and demands to provide them with their drug of choice. I recall one instance in which the patriarch of the family threatened that the whole estate would be wrested from his children if they did not continue to provide him with alcohol.

For significant others in the life of the one addicted, relinquishing control and giving up enabling are frightful and threatening prospects. The homeostasis or equilibrium of the relationship may be put in jeopardy. Faith as trust ultimately means that no one has power over the situation. That concerned others must "Let go and let God" is a well-known Alcoholics Anonymous slogan.

Perhaps most challenging is to suggest surrender to the addict. In many instances the drug of choice has become the person's constant companion, friend, and "god." The person will go to any lengths to ensure the availability of the drug of choice. Waking moments are consumed with strategies and plans to get the drug and use it. Even a gentle confrontation with regard to the person's use can bring either an angry tirade or sullen withdrawal. Helping the addict to see that surrender of the mood-altering substance as a leap of faith, to use Kierkegaard's term, is often beyond comprehension. It is well for the pastoral caregiver to remember that reason and logic are basically powerless to effect change. If pain and suffering begin to overwhelm the addict more than the relief or pleasure of using, the possibility of recovery becomes a reality.

Physical pain occasioned by the use of the substance can precipitate surrender, but more often it is emotional pain that bears fruit. If the person is denied access to any important person, surrender of the drug of choice may loom as a preferable option. For example, there are adult children of addicts who have stated that the parent will be denied access to grandchildren if the person will not submit to treatment. Obviously, the whole family system needs to be prepared for taking such measures. The addict does not see the action as being "loving." If by the grace of God the person does recover, that person is often extremely grateful for the measures that were taken in order to break the addictive cycle.

Surrender in faith and interpreting it through the eyes of faith is but one important way in which the pastoral care provider can serve as a correlator between the faith tradition and the experience of addiction. The pastoral care provider is in a unique position to talk about the power of grace, love, forgiveness, and reconciliation.

Coordinator

The pastoral caregiver who is informed can function as a coordinator of efforts for the persons afflicted and affected by addiction. Every pastoral care provider should network the resources that are available in any given community for ministering to the aged who are chemically dependent. If one lives in an area where such services are not readily available, it is important to know where the closest resources are located—just as one would for any potentially fatal disease.

This pastoral role may take the form of coordinating the concerns and efforts of people who are related or close to the elderly person. Securing information from other caregivers with regard to the behavior of the elderly person is in order. The purpose is to gather as much salient information as might be available so that effective action can be implemented.

Unfortunately, some pastoral care providers may see their roles as nonessential or incidental to the whole process. As Vernelle Fox so eloquently stated, a multidisciplinary approach is imperative if one is to deal with the person in a holistic fashion (Fox 1974). Pastoral care providers may be in the best strategic position to coordinate these efforts because they know the older person and often may know members of the family as well as service providers in the area.

In addition to networking service providers, a significant coordination effort is to know where twelve-step meetings are held. Whether it be Alcoholics Anonymous, Narcotics Anonymous, or some other twelve-step group for the addict, knowing where these groups meet and becoming familiar with people in the groups is important. It is imperative in working with families and significant others that the location of Alanon, AlaFam, and other twelve-step groups for family members and friends also is known. Since addiction is a family or social illness, those adversely affected likewise are in need of someone to assist them in becoming acquainted with groups that serve their needs and concerns.

Efforts within the context of the congregation or faith community likewise need to be coordinated so that consciousness can be raised through education to inform other people in the community of faith. Education concerning addiction among the elderly should be encouraged and teams of congregational members can make it their mission to be at the forefront of such educational endeavors.

Confessor

Pastoral care has historically embraced the role of listening to the confessions of God's people. Addiction is the source of a tremendous amount of alienation, estrangement, and pain. The attitudes and actions of both those afflicted and those affected by addiction need to be heard. Many times this confession is not in the context of a rite provided by the liturgy of the church, although that is not precluded. Rather it is the confession of wearied people who tire of struggling with unacceptable behavior as a result of their chemical abuse and significant others who feel guilty about their attitudes and relationships with those who are addicted. This often takes the form of "purifying the spirit" of the person who is given permission to ventilate feelings regarding the addictive situation and system. Although clergy are often sought out, any pastoral care provider can provide this important role of listening carefully to the confessions.

In the twelve-step program, steps four and five represent an opportunity to clean house spiritually, emotionally, and physically. The person is encouraged in step four to take a fearless moral inventory and in step five is asked to share that inventory with God, themselves, and another human being. This process is not called "confession" in the twelve-step program per se, but it functions in many respects in the same manner. Healing begins to occur when the depth of degradation, hurt, alienation, and pain is named.

The confessor role enables all persons involved in the addictive system to name their complicity in the disease. These confessions are heard with care, understanding, and empathy. In some instances the one making the confession may in fact ask for absolution. This can be granted as a way of affirming the fact that a confession has been made and that the person remains an accepted and loved child of God despite what has occurred as a result of the insidious work of addiction. For many elderly people who are acutely aware of their own mortality, the opportunity to make confession of their shortcomings and sin is a positive healing force in dealing with their addiction.

Conciliator

Finally, the person in the pastoral care role may be called upon to function as one who helps to effect reconciliation. Inevitably there are alienation, estrangement, and shattered relationships that result in walls and barriers being erected. Relationships are at risk and sometimes completely destroyed. It can be an arduous task to attempt to facilitate reconciliation in this kind of a situation, but it has happened many times and can result in strengthened and renewed family and friendship bonds. However, it is also important to acknowledge that in many instances the deterioration of the relationships is such that reconciliation is rejected as a viable option.

This is an excruciatingly painful process to observe, but often the determination is made on the part of the people involved that separation rather than reconciliation is the preferred choice. The pastoral caregiver should not appropriate such a situation as a failure to provide adequate care. Rather, it is evidence of the depth of suffering that can preclude all efforts at reconciling. It is only the Spirit of God that can ultimately effect reconciliation if that is to occur, because human hostility, animosity, and anger over what has happened or has not happened leave little hope for renewal of relationships.

This takes on an added weight of pain when the elderly are involved. Because of the reality of mortality, some resolution, if not reconciliation, seems necessary. Perhaps this would happen in a perfect world, but we are dealing with the world of reality. Pastoral care in the form of accepting reality is critical whether it is with the person afflicted with addiction or those affected by it.

Vernon Johnson writes most persuasively about the matter of forgiveness and reconciliation with all of the concomitant hazards that it brings:

> Moreover if he [the injured party] is to be truly forgiving, he will be forced to look at, recognize, and accept certain specific negative attitudes and postures within himself. And he must work out these problems if he is to regain spiritual and emotional balance in his own life. This is particularly difficult, since the injured party almost never feels any responsibility for the situation or for his own negative attitudes. (Johnson 1980, 107)

The pastoral caregiver once again needs to come to terms with personal limitations in providing care given the fact that not everyone involved in the addictive system will be open to reconciliation or having the pastoral care provider function in the role of conciliator.

CONCLUSION

Providing pastoral care for the elderly or the aged who suffer from addiction presents its own unique challenges. Dealing with the prevailing attitudes toward the aged and aging in this society is an initial step. Addressing attitudes toward addiction and addicts is equally challenging.

It is imperative to raise the awareness in both the faith community and society concerning addiction, but the challenge in working at the community level of consciousness-raising can be formidable. In some faith communities, the denial with respect to addiction is so intense that all efforts to raise consciousness are met with resistance. Other communities of faith may wish to relegate the addicts and their families to the ash heap of society. Still other members of religious communities might propagate the idea that dealing with a disease like addiction is the exclusive domain of medicine and social work and has no place in the faith community.

It is important to be aware of what action can be taken to deal with addiction among the aging in our communities of faith. Faith communities and their pastoral care providers need accurate information, sound training, and a passion for those diseased by addiction. This is particularly true regarding the elderly who are addicted. It is far too easy to forget about them, ignore them, or devalue them because of their age.

Reliance upon the mercy, grace, love, forgiveness, and power of God alone can sustain the pastoral care provider through the challenges of providing care to addicted elders and their families. Pastoral caregivers are enjoined to take to heart and apply the wisdom contained in the Serenity Prayer that sums up in simple form what it is that we ask from God for this challenging ministry.

> God, grant me the serenity to accept the things I cannot change,
> the courage to change the things I can,
> and the wisdom to know the difference.
> Amen.

BIBLIOGRAPHY

Albers, R. H. (1998). "Spiritual Barriers in Recovery." *Journal of Ministry in Addiction and Recovery* 5/1: 1–11.

——— (1995). *Shame: A Faith Perspective.* Binghamton, N.Y.: Haworth.

——— (1994). "Spirituality and Surrender: A Theological Analysis of Tiebout's Theory for Ministry to the Alcoholic." *Journal of Ministry in Addiction and Recovery* 1/2: 47–69.

——— (1982). *The Theological and Psychological Dynamics of Transformation in the Recovery from the Disease of Alcoholism.* Ann Arbor, Mich.: University Microfilms.

Alcoholics Anonymous (1976). 3d ed. New York: Alcoholics Anonymous World Services.

Clinebell, H. J. (1998). *Understanding and Counseling Persons with Alcohol, Drug, and Behavioral Addictions.* Nashville: Abingdon.

Doweiko, H. E. (1990). *Concepts of Chemical Dependency.* Pacific Grove, Calif.: Brooks/Cole.

Erikson, E. H. (1963). *Childhood and Society.* 2d ed. New York: W. W. Norton.

Fox, V. (1974). "The Best Prime Therapist for an Alcoholic Is an Interdisciplinary Team." Unpublished paper presented at the Second World Congress of International Rehabilitation Medicine.

Fuad, Margaret A. (1992). *Alcohol and the Church: Developing an Effective Ministry.* Pasadena, Calif.: Hope.

Harbaugh, G. (1991). *Pastor as Person.* Minneapolis: Augsburg.

Hazelden Publishing (n.d.). "How to Talk to an Older Person Who Has a Problem with Alcohol or Medications." Center City, Minn.: Hazelden.

Johnson, V. (1980). *I'll Quit Tomorrow.* San Francisco: Harper & Row.

Keller, J. (1985). *Let Go, Let God.* Minneapolis: Augsburg.

——— (1991). *Alcoholics and Their Families.* San Francisco: HarperCollins.

Kurtz, E. (1984). *Not God: A History of Alcoholics Anonymous.* Center City, Minn.: Hazelden.

May, G. (1988). *Addiction and Grace.* San Francisco: HarperCollins.

Mercadante, L. (1996). *Victims and Sinners: Spiritual Roots of Addiction.* Louisville: Westminster John Knox.

Morgan, O., and M. Jordan, eds. (1999). *Addiction and Spirituality: A Multidisciplinary Approach.* St. Louis, Mo.: Chalice.

Nuechterlein, A. M. (1993). *Families of Alcoholics.* Minneapolis: Augsburg.

Royce, J. E. (1981). *Alcohol Problems and Alcoholism.* New York: Free Press.

Schaef, A. W. (1987). *When Society Becomes an Addict.* San Francisco: Harper & Row.

Vaillant, G. E. (1995). *The Natural History of Alcoholism Revisited.* Cambridge, Mass.: Harvard University Press.

World Services (1974). *Alcoholics Anonymous.* 3d ed. New York: World Services.

18

Issues of Grace and Sin
in Pastoral Care
with Older Adults

ROBERT A. ROST

A CATALYTIC EXPLORATION

There are already many volumes of outstanding theological treatises written on the realities of sin and grace as such and how these are understood by different faith traditions down through history in their respective theologies of justification and sanctification. Moreover, it is far beyond the scope of this chapter to get involved in such theological deliberations, which have been centuries in the making. This chapter instead will be an initial exploration into the issues of sin and grace as these surface in the practice of gerontological pastoral care. Such an exploration will also be more restricted to a Christian perspective only because of the limitations of my own experience and competence.

Thus, for the purpose of this investigation I would like to use the following definitions, taken from the *Dictionary of Pastoral Care and Counseling,* which seems to be an acceptable source devoid of overt denominational bias.

Grace in Christian theology refers to the unconditional, comprehensive, empowering love of God for the world. As one of the central concepts of Christian theology, grace combines the covenantal theme of God's overflowing, undeserved forgiveness of sinful humanity with a sense of divine power to liberate, redeem, and renew human life. God's grace empowers human beings to live graciously, in faith and gratitude to God and in a spirit of forgiveness and peace with others (1 Cor. 1:3ff.), and is expressed also through particular spiritual "gifts" (or "graces") that God gives to the church for its upbuilding and edification (1 Cor. 12:4ff.; Eph. 4:11-16) (Hunter et al. 1990, 468).

Sin (or *sins*) is the most comprehensive and distinctive term in ancient Israelite religion and its modern heirs (Judaism, Christianity, Islam) that describes the human predicament as a state of corporate and individual moral corruption originating in the human being's inclination to ignore, disobey, or replace God, plus the acts and dispositions prompted by that state (Farley 1990, 1173).

Pastoral care derives from the biblical image of *shepherd* and refers to the solicitous concern expressed within the religious community for persons in trouble or distress. Historically and within the Christian community, pastoral care is in the cure-of-souls tradition. Here cure may be understood as care in the sense of carefulness or anxious concern, not necessarily as healing, for the soul, i.e., the animating center of personal life and the seat of relatedness to God (Mills 1990, 836).

Such general definitions of grace and sin in the realm of pastoral care are substantiated by current biblical scholarship (Cover 1992; Kselman 1992; Sanders 1992; Shogren 1992), although such scholarship also indicates how complex these realities are in the roots of Judaism and Christianity. Likewise, "pastoral care" has diverse understandings. "What constitutes pastoral care is rooted in the basic religious convictions of the community. But it is also rooted in the historical, political, and social fabric of a given time and place" (Mills 1990, 837). Such complexity and diversity within our three key and interrelated concepts become more significant as we continue.

Although sin and grace have been pondered by the greatest religious minds over the course of history, these issues have been conspicuously absent in the writings about pastoral care with older adults. To be more accurate, I should say that the issue of sin or the interconnected issues of sin and grace have been conspicuously absent. "Grace" by itself, on the other hand, is recently getting good press, particularly by those lifting up the possibilities of longevity and the stories of extraordinary people who have realized these to an exemplary degree (Fischer 1995; Ramsey and Blieszner 1999; Thibault 1993; Wicks 1996). Given the negative images of aging we have inherited from our youth-oriented culture, such efforts to make integral connections between grace and aging are absolutely necessary for the development of a positive spirituality for later life. Still, the spiritual and moral issues of sin and grace, in connection with each other and in the context of pastoral care with older adults, seem to be neglected. Thus I hope that this chapter will serve as a catalyst for further insights to surface and to be shared.

A DISCONNECTION FROM OUR RELIGIOUS ROOTS

With regard to the reasons for this neglect, Karl Menninger, in his landmark book *Whatever Became of Sin?* (1973), asserted that our current society and culture do not want to acknowledge the reality of sin and its consequences in human life. Rather, people are viewed by "the new psychology" as by nature somewhat flawed and either make mistakes or manifest symptoms. When their mistakes are discovered by others, they can admit and even try to correct them. When they manifest symptoms, they can seek treatment (44–45). But in this view people do not commit sins and so do not have to repent, confess, seek forgiveness, do penance, make amends, undergo conversion, and work through a process of reconciliation. Thus, even the reality of grace, while still acknowledged and even prayed for, is far less than amazing, since people are no longer wretches who need to be saved, justified, or sanctified.

Indeed, Menninger perceived it is just these *corollaries* of the sin doctrine that are rejected. "For sin traditionally implies guilt, answerability, and, by derivation, responsibility" (20). In particular, it is the ingrained association of sin and penalty that is discarded. "Thus, sin, or designating something sinful, began to disappear because it was too expensive in terms of the current standards of comfort. Instead of reducing the penalty, people merely negated the sin" (29). Although such an understandable reaction to past, punitive rituals and unenlightened explanations of human behavior does make the treatment of certain actions more humane, it also clouds some real personal and societal issues.

I have pursued the possible usefulness of reviving the use of the word "sin"—not for the word's sake but for the reintroduction of the concepts of guilt and moral responsibility. Calling something a "sin" and dealing with it as such may be a useful salvage or coping device. It does little good to repent a symptom, but it may do great harm not to repent a sin. Conversely, it does little good to merely psychoanalyze a sin and sometimes a great harm to ignore a symptom (Menninger 1973, 48).

For well over a quarter a century, issues of sin and grace have been viewed as academic, historical, and denominational, but not relevant to our society's self-understanding. Given this fact, it may be no wonder that the field of pastoral care has been more wedded to psychology than to constructive and moral theology or to spirituality. As mentioned above, pastoral care is shaped not only by religious convictions but also by the historical, political, and social milieu of a particular time and place. Thus, theologians and spiritual directors still speak in the language of sin and grace, while those trained in the CPE (Clinical Pastoral Education) model of pastoral care may be much more comfortable with the language of symptoms and treatments. Although this may make for a closer working relationship and greater respectability with other health-care professionals, there is a downside to the disconnection between pastoral care and its religious roots.

Paul Tillich wrote:

> There is a mysterious fact about the great words of our religious tradition: they cannot be replaced. . . . All attempts to make substitutions—including those I have tried myself—have failed. . . . They have led to shallow and impotent talk. There are no substitutes for words like "sin" and "grace." But there is a way of rediscovering their meaning, the same way that leads us down into the depth of our human existence. In that depth these words were conceived; and there they gained power for all ages; there they must be found again by each generation, and by each of us for himself. (Tillich, cited in Menninger 1973, 47)

In the field of pastoral care Tillich and Menninger now have company in this assertion. There are those whose fundamental paradigm is grounded in biblical theologies of deliverance and covenant (Patton 1993, 3–6), as well as those who describe the process as a spiritual transformation guided by the Spirit of God leading toward a new eschatological identity (Gerkin 1984, 70–75). John Patton, Charles Gerkin, and others like them are reconnecting the practice of pastoral care to its biblical, theological, and spiritual roots. Rather than substituting more currently comfortable concepts for "grace" and "sin," they are making room for the meaning of these realities to emerge and be rediscovered within the pastoral encounter.

Since the focus of our exploration is pastoral care with older adults, we need to see how these issues are affected by the multidisciplinary arena of gerontology. While expanding beyond the biomedical paradigm, with which it began, toward a much more holistic approach inclusive of many other dimensions inherent to quality of life, only recently have religion and spirituality become acceptable and respectable subjects for serious research in the lives of older adults. Such research has focused on how religious and spiritual practices can and do have a beneficial effect on the overall well-being of those who practice them (Koenig 1994; Levin 1994). Although such research "can support efforts to offer meaningful spiritual services to older people, researchers have rarely addressed religious experience from a phenomenological perspective" (McFadden 1999, 116). It is precisely this phenomenological perspective on the lived experience of grace and sin that pastoral care with older adults needs to develop.

Given such a limited focus on the role of religion and spirituality in the lives of older adults, it is predictable that most discussions of ethics in the gerontological literature are confined either to how older adults are being treated by the institutions of health care and government or to how end-of-life decisions should be professionally handled. Although these two areas of ethical debate are most important for the quality of life for many older adults, there is no discussion about the ethical responsibilities older adults themselves can and should have in all the time prior to their end-of-life choices. What we currently have in the field is a developing sense of the rights of older adults without any corresponding sense of their responsibilities. Although this is very typical in our current society for persons of all ages (Frankl 1988, 49, 62, 65), those who have lived beyond the expected responsibilities of parenting and career are left in what Viktor Frankl called an "existential vacuum" (1984, 111, 151–52).

Nevertheless, there are a few gerontologists of a more philosophical mind-set who have stepped beyond a focus on a more generic spiritual well-being to the realm of meaning and how older adults are finding, making, and witnessing meaning in the midst of the transitoriness and precariousness of later life (Ellor, McFadden, and Sapp 1999; Kimble 2000; Seeber 1990). Once one crosses over into the realm of meaning, by necessity one enters the arena of responsibility and faces the reality of mystery. As Viktor Frankl said, it is life itself that both holds us responsible for the meanings we create and plunges us into the darkness of mystery each time we encounter suffering (1988, 62, 145–46).

THOSE WHO ARE STILL CONNECTED

When we take this step into the realm of meaning as older adults experience and name it, we must accept their categories of language. To do otherwise would be to impose foreign constructs onto their experience and invalidate their own interpretations. This would violate a most fundamental principle of pastoral practice

(Gerkin 1984, 26–28). Ironically, given the previous discussion about our current culture, even going back three decades or more, the language categories of older adults often come from a prior age and culture, an age and culture that was more formally religious. For the current cohort of older adults, the age and culture in which their categories of meaning were formed was one where there was such a thing as sin, such a dialectic as sin and grace being constantly played out in the course of human life, and the final outcome of this dialectic determined one's immortal and eternal future. Although this framework of meaning may be considered passé by many in our current age and culture and even by many who would claim religious affiliation or spiritual beliefs, it remains quite significant for a number of our current older-adult population.

This is not to say that the validity of these categories depends on their being personally significant to a particular portion of the population. As Paul Tillich noted, they obviously have a biblical, theological, historical, and ecclesial validity independent of any current or future cohort of people. Still, valid and helpful pastoral care needs to accept the framework of meaning that the person brings to the encounter and, whenever possible, to connect this with the larger faith tradition which both share (Gerkin 1984, 58–62). The issues of sin and grace in pastoral care with older adults come not only from these traditional religious sources but from their own search for meaning in the categories of language which make sense to them.

I claim this assertion as a Roman Catholic pastor whose decades of pastoral care with older adults involves hearing their confessions as well as the rest of their life stories. I also state this as a teacher and supervisor of gerontological pastoral care with chaplains and pastors from many different traditions. Although there may be different pastoral settings and distinct categories of language according to religious and ethnic backgrounds, there is much common ground where the issues of sin and grace surface in our mutual ministry.

As these issues do surface in the course of the pastoral encounter, the minister is placed in a most privileged and humbling position of hearing older persons' personal interpretations of very private and often painful experience in their own language. Such interpretations may not be a part of current research instruments or spiritual assessment tools for use with older persons. Yet older persons are the ones who struggle with the issues of sin and grace. And because they do, they have the spiritual right for a receptive, competent, compassionate, and challenging person to walk in step with them.

FROM CONFUSION TO ENLIGHTENMENT

The most common theme that arises out of these interpretations by older adults is a moral and spiritual confusion. They have witnessed so many changes in social mores, such fundamental transitions within their own religious traditions, such differences between generations in their own families, and such a vacuum of responsibility for their own current status in life. They are genuinely and validly confused about what is right or wrong, what is virtue or vice, what is pleasing or displeasing to God, and what is appropriate for praise or for confession. Like most of us who do not have a high tolerance for ambiguity, when we are confused about something that really matters to us, we want to get it cleared up. We want answers. And, so do they. Since classic CPE training espouses a very nondirective, therapeutic approach to pastoral care, this poses a real dilemma for pastoral caregivers and frustrated older persons. Such a dilemma demands a paradigm shift on both sides.

Pastoral caregivers need to enlarge their approach to include an educative function in the mode of Viktor Frankl. He claimed the primary purpose of education is the formation of conscience, i.e., that intuitive capacity we all have to discern the meaning and responsibility we have for any given situation we encounter (1988, 18–19, 63–66). "In an age in which the Ten Commandments seem to lose their unconditional validity, man must learn more than ever to listen to the ten thousand commandments arising from the ten thousand unique situations of which his life consists. And as to *these* commandments, he is referred to, and must rely on, his conscience" (64–65).

If Frankl is correct, then simply giving older adults definitions of sin and grace updated from the 1921 edition of *Baltimore Catechism* to the 1994 edition of the *Catechism of the Catholic Church* (to use a sectarian example) is not going to clear up all their confusion around their issues of sin and grace. Nevertheless, it is very helpful to be aware that the 1921 catechism, the King James Version of the Bible, the former Book of Worship, or the Sunday school teaching are where their fundamental religious principles and language originated. In order to walk them through their confusion we must connect with that original learning experience and its proper place in their conscience today.

As an aging baby boomer I have often found it helpful that I memorized the same catechism answers as persons my parents' age. As a pastor, I have often found it equally necessary to remind myself of the extreme luxury of advanced education and spiritual direction which have made possible my own transition from that catechism to my current, operative credo.

On the older persons' side of the paradigm shift, they need to expand their own sense of self-responsibility. Each person has a responsibility and a capacity to care for his or her own soul, not outside faith community but within faith community. When persons are confused or wounded they may well need our pastoral care to assist them, but they are still responsible for and capable of their own soul care. The answers they seek are not monolithic or completely external to themselves. Even though they may well uphold the Ten Commandments, they also need ten thousand commandments to guide them in the ten thousand distinct and different decisions they still have to make in their lives. While they need sensitive listening and accurate information from persons competent in their respective faith tradition, they also need to take responsibility for how this should be applied to their own relationships and decisions.

This demands that they get and stay in touch with their own inner voice, the voice of their own souls. They need to be more in tune with this voice than the sermons of their own pastor. Indeed, it is truly an act of responsible care on the part of the pastor to affirm and assist them in that process and not only offer either nondirective receptivity or theological information. When the interpretation of one's life becomes painful or conflicted, especially in the midst of suffering, Gerkin perceives the need for the person to look "for a listener who is an expert at interpretation, one who can make sense out of what has threatened to become senseless" (1984, 26). From Frankl's point of view, such an expert does not take the role of teacher or preacher. "To put it figuratively, the role played by a logotherapist is that of an eye specialist rather than that of a painter" (1984, 114). Such an expert enables and empowers persons to "see" for themselves the meanings of their own lives rather than scripting them with meanings from another source.

Thus the way through the moral and spiritual confusion that clouds the realities of grace and sin in the lives of our elders is not "Father Knows Best." Rather, it is a soul-searching journey that is best assured by respectful, prayerful, and honest accompaniment. To employ a culinary image, the identifications of "grace" and "sin" that are sought are neither prepackaged nor microwaveable. They start with raw ingredients of human experience. They involve a whole range of recipes drawn from tradition and practiced wisdom, which both elder and pastor share. Individual dialogue and adaptation are always required out of respect for the person and his or her own sense of responsibilities (U.S. Catholic Bishops 1999, 22). Slow and prayerful cooking in the crucible of conscience is essential to give time for the Spirit to work.

Moral and spiritual confusion is always contextual and relational. There is always a story, and within the story very personal interpretations which need to become the focus of attention and examination. Often such interpretations arise out of convergent thinking and thus are taken to be the only interpretation that is valid. But upon more careful review motivated by the need for clarification, a more divergent thinking can emerge which allows for other interpretations to be considered (Birren and Deutchman 1991, 80–87). Since the soul itself is in the continual process of interpretation and reinterpretation (Gerkin 1984, 97–105), the occasion of confusion can actually become the opportunity for greater inner insight once the soul is given proper attention, assistance, and encouragement.

THE PRIMARY CATEGORY OF SELF-UNDERSTANDING: SIN OR GRACE?

This phenomenon is an indication of a deeper dimension to older adults' confusion around issues of sin and grace. I can speak here only for older Catholics. But I do so with the intuition that this possibly applies to older persons of other faith traditions. Older people who were raised Catholic even as recently as the fifties (which would thus include older baby boomers) were taught from that very Baltimore Catechism that sin more than grace is the primary category of human self-understanding. Human beings were born into sin, not grace. People, even once graced, could lose that grace through sin at any moment up to the moment of death. Sources of sin were everywhere, whereas sources of grace, especially that grace necessary for salvation, were limited to certain rituals, which, currently and especially for the more frail elderly, are in shorter and shorter supply (McGuire 1941, 23–26, 35–36).

Ironically, this teaching of spiritual self-understanding may well have contributed to the disappearance of "sin" from our language and culture by the time of Menninger's book. Once the catechism changed, the long lines outside confessionals disappeared. When the burden of chronic guilt was lifted, regular confession was seen as unnecessary. Among those who remained regular recipients of that sacrament most were older and many were those whose spiritual self-understanding had not changed.

It is the proper educative function of compassionate pastoral care to convey spiritual orthodoxy. "Right belief about God and right relationship with God are intimately connected" (Leech 1977, 154–55). Our spiritual self-understanding is at the very heart of our image of God and who we are and where we stand in God's eyes, whatever our faith tradition. If God's grace is something which can be lost and gained and lost again, then what is the very foundation of our existence, our identity, and our destiny? It cannot be grace, because grace is too tenuous, too transitory, too dependent on variables which are under human rather than divine control.

If our faith and our trust are to become unconditional, then grace, not sin, must be the primary category of our self-understanding. We are graced from the very first moment of our existence by our Creator (Ps. 139:13). As contemporary Catholic theologian Michael Himes asserts, to lose this "state of grace" would not mean condemnation but rather loss of one's very existence. As long as we exist, we are in the state of grace, that is, in relationship with our Creator, at least from our Creator's side of the relationship (Himes 1994). For our faith and our trust in our Creator to become unconditional, grace must be unconditional. The sources of grace, the very grace necessary for this relationship to survive and thrive, are everywhere at all times (Rom. 8:38–39). The pastoral care of the church community may be limited, even unjustly and artificially so. But God's grace is not limited to those rituals, that ministry, or a particular tradition.

All human beings form but one community. This is so because all stem from the one stock that God created to people the entire earth (cf. Acts 17:26) and also because all share a common destiny, namely, God. His providence, evident goodness, and saving designs extend to all men (cf. Wis. 8:1; Acts 14:17; Rom. 2:6-7; 1 Tim. 2:4) against the day when the elect are gathered together in the holy city which is illumined by the glory of God, and in whose splendor all peoples will walk (cf. Rev. 21:23ff.) (Flannery 1975, 738).

This is exactly why orthodox doctrine and good pastoral care must be intimately and permanently connected. We must have the proper doctrine of grace to appropriately respond to the issues of sin and grace as they arise in our pastoral encounters. "God wants all people to be saved and to come to know the truth"

(1 Tim. 2:4, NAB). If God wants this, then God provides the means, the "grace," for this to happen. "For the One whom God has sent speaks the words of God; he does not ration his gift of the Spirit" (John 3:34, NAB). Grace is not rationed; it is not in short supply. On the contrary, it is far greater than the supply of sin, whether claimed or denied. "There is no comparison between the free gift and the offence. If death came to many through the offence of one man, how much greater an effect the grace of God has had, coming to so many and so plentifully as a free gift through the one man Jesus Christ!" (Rom. 5:15, NJB).

LEARNING TO BE BEHOLDERS OF GRACE

"The whole of life is in grace. That grace is to be found everywhere. The grace of God is there, always there. What's missing is someone to behold it. All of us are learning to be beholders of grace" (Himes 1994). Here Michael Himes identifies the crux of the issue. We are all, from the youngest to the oldest, learning to be "beholders of grace." This is our fundamental vocation as well as our lifelong learning curve. The grace of God is everywhere, at every time, for everyone, yet every one of us has to spend our whole life learning to behold it. If there is any evidence for "sin" as spiritual blindness (Luke 27:32; John 9:39-41), this would be it. If there is any reason for the pastor to act in Frankl's role of the "eye specialist," this would be it. If there is any issue of grace and sin in pastoral care with older adults, this would be it.

Our older adults have to work at, pray for, be encouraged and assisted in beholding grace in their lives, in their own aging. Because in every person, in every situation, in every moment they do not behold grace, that person, that situation, and that moment are experienced as devoid of grace and, thus, absent from God. This, I believe, is a critical issue. Too many of our older people, especially those who are facing serious loss(es), are experiencing too many parts of their lives as devoid of grace and absent from God. Their fundamental spiritual concern is not what they are doing wrong, not the commission of sin, but rather what they are struggling to do right, overcoming the omission of beholding the grace in the very midst of their aging and their loss.

Then fixing his eyes on his disciples he said:

> How blessed are you who are poor; the kingdom of God is yours.
> Blessed are you who are hungry now; you shall have your fill.
> Blessed are you who are weeping now; you shall laugh.
> Blessed are you when people hate you, drive you out, abuse you,
> denounce your name as criminal, on account of the Son of man.
> Rejoice when that day comes and dance for joy, look!—
> your reward will be great in heaven.
> This was the way their ancestors treated the prophets.
> (Luke 6:20-23, NJB)

For many older persons the learning curve of beholding grace in their present lives is the same as that of grasping the mystery of beatitude in Luke's Sermon on the Plain. Although many of us who are younger can spend our whole lives, even as religious persons, avoiding that mystery, quite a number of our elders cannot. Maybe it is in coming to the end of avoidance when they/we discover that learning to behold grace is a grace. It is not just an act of our will. It is a fulfillment of the will of God.

I believe that there is a correlation between the spiritual learning curve of beholding grace and Frankl's search for meaning. He perceives this search for meaning as taking shape in three distinct groups of values. "The first is what he gives to the world in terms of his creations; the second is what he takes from the world in terms of encounters and experiences; and the third is the stand he takes to his predicament in case he must face a fate which he cannot change" (1988, 70). This second group of values refers to human relationships. He holds that each person establishes unity and completeness with a community, not within himself or herself (Kimble n.d.). In love, human beings have the capacity to transcend themselves to grasp another in his or her innermost core, which holds not only the person's character but also his or her potential. "Furthermore, by his love, the loving person enables the beloved person to actualize these potentialities. By making him aware of what he can be and of what he should become, he makes these potentialities come true" (Frankl 1984, 116). Ethically speaking, Frankl asserts that we are responsible for what we create, whom we love, and how we suffer (1988, 74).

I find this perspective most helpful for the issue at hand, precisely because it emphasizes personal responsibility and opportunity in a comprehensive way that is applicable to all elders in any and all circumstances. It is possible to behold grace in what we create, whom we love, and how we suffer, and we are responsible for doing so. As we are already learning with our more positive attitudes toward aging, later life can be a very creative time for many elders. It can hold many opportunities for loving relationships old and new, peer and intergenerational, to blossom and thrive. Learning how to lovingly grasp another in his or her innermost core only increases with age and experience. These are the more obvious graces for those who are engaged in them. Yet, in our pastoral care, we should not take them for granted, because both the opportunities and the motivation for these may need some encouragement and assistance. A greater beholding of grace in an older person's life does not just happen when he or she is in prayer with us. Ninety-nine percent of their beholding needs to happen beyond the pastoral encounter.

Because of our natural avoidance of suffering, the most difficult learning curve is beholding grace in *how* we suffer. Frankl holds that "attitudinal values are the highest possible values," the *how* of suffering, and that "the meaning of suffering—unavoidable and inescapable suffering alone, of course—is the deepest possible meaning" (1988, 75). For, if there is meaning in the attitude one takes toward unavoidable suffering, then "life's meaning is an unconditional one" (1984, 118). Neither suffering nor dying can detract from it. Thus, "life never ceases to hold a meaning, for even a person who is deprived of both creative and experiential values is still challenged by a meaning to fulfill, that is, by the meaning inherent in an upright way of suffering" (1988, 70). But the ultimate meaning of human suffering cannot be grasped by the human intellect because it exists in a higher dimension than thought. What people need is "unconditional faith in unconditional meaning" (156). And it is Frankl's contention "that faith in the ultimate meaning is preceded by trust in an ultimate being, by trust in God" (145).

In the realm of suffering and attitudinal values, beholding grace is indeed a grace, the grace of faith preceded by the grace of trust.

> Now that we have been justified by faith, we are at peace with God through our Lord Jesus Christ. Through him we have gained access by faith to the grace in which we now stand, and we boast of our hope for the glory of God. But not only that—we even boast of our afflictions! We know that affliction makes for endurance, and endurance for tested virtue, and tested virtue for hope. And this hope will not leave us disappointed, because the love of God has been poured out in our hearts through the Holy Spirit who has been given to us. (Rom. 5:1-5, NAB)

> From his fullness we have all received, grace upon grace. (John 1:16)

Frankl and the Scriptures are indeed correct. Maintaining a meaningful attitude in the midst of suffering is not a matter of the intellect but rather grace upon grace that is sought out, prayed for, and chosen.

Especially the Scriptures focus our attention on the revelation of what grace *we* have received. It is in this realm of grace in the face of suffering that both individuals and community are challenged to affirm their interdependency as members of the same body sharing the same Spirit (1 Cor. 12:1-31; U.S. Catholic Bishops 1999, 3).

Whatever forms the suffering takes—physical or mental, interpersonal or spiritual, or any combination thereof—the homeostasis of both the person and the body is disrupted and anxiety is created. With this disruption and concurrent anxiety come a whole host of temptations: scapegoating, victim thinking, binding anxiety through triangling, avoidance, denial, rescuing, patronizing, distancing, etc.

These temptations become the attitudinal focal point of the dialectic between sin and grace. In a negative way they highlight the choice of attitude that suffering places before each person involved. What attitude will I choose to take toward my own suffering? Toward the suffering of someone I dearly love? Toward both the suffering and the attitude of the person suffering with whom I am called to extend pastoral care?

These choices of attitude, which suffering demands, cannot just be made once for all but must be continually reviewed and renewed as long as the suffering lasts. Thus it is indeed "grace upon grace" that must be sought out, prayed for, and chosen.

There are interrelational implications of these choices. The choices of attitude determine whether the relationships are conducive or not conducive of grace specifically in the face of suffering.

These choices highlight how much suffering is *the* test of our trust. Suffering tests not only our trust in the God who will ultimately bring victory over suffering (Rev. 21:1-11) but also our trust that each and every one of us is given a manifestation of the Spirit for the common good here and now (1 Cor. 12:7). In the courageous choices of attitude that transcend the temptations generated by the suffering, the Spirit is manifest and the victory has begun.

Charles Gerkin asserts that the grace of such trust in grounded in the gospel's fundamental revelation. "Suffering thus replaces power and omnipotence as the primary characteristic of God." In the event of the cross, both Father and Son suffer in the act of abandonment. Now, for all time, Jesus "is to be sought wherever there is human suffering." He identifies with all who suffer and long for redemption. The Holy Spirit "is to be found wherever there is suffering in the not-yet-ness of the final unity of all things." The Spirit works in history as the "creator of a new future" (Gerkin 1984, 67).

To transcend the attitudinal temptations human suffering generates takes the grace of the Spirit as creator of a new future. This is where Frankl's three categories of values merge together. The development of the attitudinal value of finding meaning and beholding grace in the midst of suffering requires creative and loving work which is both ours and God's. When the attitudes will no longer work, new attitudes must be created. When the actual has reached its limits, the potential can only be grasped—love from God, love from another, and love from one's own self.

FROM PASTORAL CARE BACK TO SOUL CARE

This is at the heart of the *cura animarum* (care of souls) mode of pastoral care out of the classic tradition (Oden 1984). Beholding grace and transcending temptations requires soul care. The first major articulation of the care of souls, particularly for pastors (bishops and priests) was the *Regula Pastoralis* by Gregory the Great, who served as pope from 590 to 604. In this work he advises pastors on how they ought to counsel the many kinds of persons for whom they bear pastoral responsibility. His principle in this is *juxta uniuscuiusque qualitatem*, i.e., "in accordance with each one's character." He comments at varying length on thirty-six pairs of qualities (Leinenweber 1998, x–xi).

Long before my time Gregory Nazianzen, whose memory we hold in honor, taught that no single exhortation suits everyone because we are not all bound by the same character traits. What helps some often harms others. Teachers have to accommodate their language to the characters of those who are listening to them so as to meet their individual needs, but they must never renounce the art of building up everyone (Leinenweber 1998, 1).

Gregory's enumeration of thirty-six pairs of qualities range from circumstances of birth, characteristics of personality, qualities of motivation, and life choices to life situations beyond individual choice. Although some of these qualities may seem a bit dated by 1,500 years of history, the very thoroughness and diversity of the enumeration demonstrate quite a depth of pastoral perception. The pastor must discern the unique opportunities and dangers of a whole range of characteristics and circumstances, most of which are far beyond the personal experience of the pastor.

Gregory's thirty-six pairs are actually the pairing of polar opposites. By this method he demonstrates that no matter what character trait dominates one's life situation or personality, each person has both a unique grace and a unique temptation in relation to his or her call to holiness. No person is without the unique grace or the unique temptation.

Some persons' temptations may seem more obvious because their character traits can tend toward more obvious or more public failings. Gregory actually includes the seven capital sins among his dominant character traits. Other persons' temptations are much more subtle because their character traits can appear to be ready-made for sanctity, as those he lists which seem to come from both the Beatitudes (Matt. 5:3-11) and the "fruits of the Spirit" (Gal. 5:22). Gregory indicates that these people actually need greater care of their souls so that the more subtle temptations do not go undetected and thus become as deadly as the more obvious ones. No one is ready-made for salvation or damnation. Each soul, no matter what the dominant character trait, has the capacity for grace and sin. Each soul needs care, by the person and the pastor, for sanctification to be assured.

Thus Gregory provides us with a discernment model of pastoral care directed specifically at the issues of grace and sin as they take unique form in each and every individual as well as in his or her relationships and responsibilities. Among the many gifts and challenges this model brings to both elders and pastors is that it is really about ongoing spiritual direction. Its focus is truly soul care, not temporary symptoms and treatments. "Pastoral care in the Christian understanding is not restricted to the troubled or distressed or to crisis points in life. . . . It is a continuing ministry to life's normality. The ministry of spiritual direction indeed is more important when there are no particular crises" (Leech 1977, 100–101).

In Gregory's mode an ongoing relationship is necessary to practice discernment. The specific graces and temptations of the person's dominant character traits take time to reach mutual awareness. The focus is not crisis intervention but rather the whole journey to salvation. That shift of focus alone would demand both a new model of gerontological pastoral care as well as many more pastoral caregivers trained in this model for most communities and institutions to begin to practice this level of soul care. Yet it is at this very level that our awareness as pastors and elders is opened to a much broader and deeper realm where grace and sin reside.

Gregory concludes his work, as I would like to conclude here, by offering more personal advice to pastors themselves concerning self-awareness of their own dominant character traits as well as the opportunities and temptations inherent therein.

At this point zeal for love leads me back to what I said above: preachers must express themselves more in actions than in words. They must first be concerned to punish their own faults by their tears and then denounce what needs to be punished in others. Before they deliver words of exhortation their deeds should proclaim all that they are about to say.

> Frequently almighty God, although perfecting in large part those who guide others, leaves them in some small part imperfect. Then, even as they are resplendent with marvelous virtues, they may pine away with disgust at their own imperfection. While they toil on, struggling against little things, they do not exalt themselves because of the great. As they are not strong enough to overcome their smallest weaknesses, they do not dare take pride in their outstanding accomplishments. (Leinenweber 1998, 143)

This advice corresponds very well with the investigations of Kenneth Leech into the history of spiritual direction. In order of priority, the first and essential characteristic of the director is "holiness of life, closeness to God." "Secondly, the spiritual director is a man [*sic*] of experience, a man who has struggled with the realities of prayer and life. . . . A guide who has not encountered his own passions, his own inner conflicts, who does not truly know his darkness and his light, will be of no value in the spiritual battle" (1977, 89).

Such self-awareness, which includes an honest facing of one's own human sexuality, is a necessary prelude to both emotional maturity and the knowledge of God. Third, the director must be learned in the Scripture and the wisdom of the tradition. Fourth, the director must be a person of discernment, perception, and insight who can "read the signs of the times, the writing on the walls of the soul." Such a person must be able to give way to the Spirit of God (89, 104–6, 113–16).

St. John of the Cross says that a director can spoil the wondrous work that God was painting on the soul.

> Let such as these take heed and remember that the Holy Spirit is the principal agent and mover of souls and never loses His care for them. Let them not, therefore, merely aim at guiding a soul according to their own way and the manner suitable to themselves, but let them see if they know the way by which God is leading the soul, and if they know it not, let them leave the soul in peace and not disturb it. (Leech 1977, 166–67)

The spiritual direction/discernment mode of pastoral care is a formidable challenge to any pastor, chaplain, or pastoral caregiver. It involves a lifelong journey in facing all one's own personal and professional issues involving grace and sin. This, in itself, may make it well suited for gerontological pastoral care. On this journey our elders become our teachers as well as our flock (Kimble 1990, 115). And we are kept humble and receptive in their presence, knowing that they may well be a lot farther down the road than we are.

As ancient and traditional as Gregory and Leech sound, their voices are echoed by a contemporary, CPE-trained mentor in pastoral care. Charles Gerkin asserts that in order to pastor respectfully and wisely the minister must make his or her own "hermeneutical detour" (Gerkin 1984, 43). Each of us is "embedded in our own historical process" and can never view ourselves from outside our history. Each one must become "aware of one's own bias, so that the text may present itself in all its newness and thus be able to assert its own truth against one's own fore-meanings" (45). This is especially true since the therapeutic encounter requires "that both interpreter and the object of interpretation be changed at the fundamental level of meaning" (46).

Maybe Gerkin's concept of the "hermeneutical detour" is itself an apt metaphor for this chapter. We have taken a detour through our theology, our culture, our pastoral practice, as well as our elders' own experience and language of interpretation. We have examined and challenged the notions of "sin," "grace," and "pastoral care" in both their contemporary and traditional understandings. We have raised more questions than given answers. And in doing so we may have placed the responsibility for the search right where it belongs—in our own growing personal and mutual awareness.

As Tillich so wisely said, there are no substitutes for these great words of our religious tradition. "Grace," "sin," and "soul care" are among these great words. The way of rediscovering their meaning is the same way that leads us into the depth of our human existence. Many of our elders are well along that way. We have the distinct and humbling privilege of accompanying them. As they and we learn to listen to the voices of our own souls, we will begin to peer through our spiritual and moral confusion to discover the graces that are there to be beheld and the temptations that are there to be transcended. And we will be given grace upon grace. "Write these matters down, for the words are trustworthy and true! These words are already fulfilled! To anyone who thirsts I will give to drink without cost from the spring of life-giving water" (Rev. 21:5-6, NAB). Elder or pastor, ancient or contemporary, one religious tradition or another, we all drink from the same well. We all trust in the same promise.

BIBLIOGRAPHY

Birren, J. E., and D. E. Deutchman (1991). *Guiding Autobiography Groups for Older Adults*. Baltimore: Johns Hopkins University Press.

Cover, R. C. (1992). "Sin, Sinners: Old Testament." In Freedman et al., 6: 31–40.

Dictionary of Pastoral Care and Counseling (1990). Ed. R. J. Hunter. Nashville: Abingdon.

Ellor, J., S. McFadden, and S. Sapp (1999). *Aging and Spirituality: The First Decade*. San Francisco: American Society on Aging.

Farley, E. (1990). "Sin/Sins." In Hunter et al., 1173–76.

Fischer, K. (1995). *Autumn Gospel*. New York: Paulist.

Flannery, A. ed. (1975). "Declaration on the Relation of the Church to Non-Christian Religions." In *Vatican Council II: The Conciliar and Post Conciliar Documents*. Northport, N.Y.: Costello.

Frankl, V. (1988). *The Will to Meaning*. New York: Penguin.

——— (1984). *Man's Search for Meaning*. New York: Simon & Schuster.

Freedman, D. N., et al., eds. (1992). *The Anchor Bible Dictionary*. 6 vols. New York: Doubleday.

Gerkin, C. V. (1984). *The Living Human Document*. Nashville: Abingdon.

Himes, M. (1994). *The Mystery of Faith: An Introduction to Catholicism Video Series*. Jefferson Valley, N.Y.: Fisher Productions.

Kimble, M. A. (1990). "Aging and the Search for Meaning." In Seeber, 111–26.

———— (n.d.). "Frankl's Ten Theses on the Human Person." Unpublished manuscript.

————, ed. (2000). *Viktor Frankl's Contribution to Spirituality and Aging*. New York: Haworth.

Koenig, H. G. (1994). *Aging and God: Spiritual Pathways to Mental Health in Midlife and Later Years*. New York: Haworth.

Kselman, J. S. (1992). "Grace: Old Testament." In Freedman et al., 2: 1085–86.

Leech, K. (1977). *Soul Friend*. New York: Harper & Row.

Leinenweber, J., trans. and ed. (1998). *Pastoral Practice: Books 3 and 4 of the Regula Pastoralis by Saint Gregory the Great*. Harrisburg, Pa.: Trinity Press International.

Levin, J. S., ed. (1994). *Religion in Aging and Health*. Thousand Oaks, Calif.: Sage.

McFadden, S. (1999). "Ten Years of Research on Religion and Aging." In Ellor, McFadden, and Sapp, 114–16.

McGuire, M. A. (1941). *Father McGuire's The New Baltimore Catechism No. 1*. New York: Benziger Brothers.

Menninger, K. (1973). *Whatever Became of Sin?* New York: Hawthorn.

Mills, L. O. (1990). "Pastoral Care." In Hunter et al., 836–44.

Oden, T. C. (1984). *Care of Souls in the Classic Tradition*. Philadelphia: Fortress Press.

Patton, J. (1993). *Pastoral Care in Context: An Introduction to Pastoral Care*. Louisville: Westminster John Knox.

Ramsey, J. L., and R. Blieszner (1999). *Spiritual Resiliency in Older Women*. Thousand Oaks, Calif.: Sage.

Sanders, E. P. (1992). "Sin, Sinners: New Testament." In Freedman et al., 6: 40–46.

Seeber, J. J., ed. (1990). *Spiritual Maturity in the Later Years*. New York: Haworth.

Shogren, G. S. (1992). "Grace: New Testament." In Freedman et al., 2:1086–88.

Thibault, J. M. (1993). *A Deepening Love Affair*. Nashville: Upper Room.

U.S. Catholic Bishops (1999). *Blessings of Age*. Washington, D.C.: United States Catholic Conference.

Wicks, R. J. (1996). *After Fifty: Spiritually Embracing Your Own Wisdom Years*. New York: Paulist.

Pastoral Care for Depression in Long-Term Care Residents

ELIZABETH MACKINLAY

DEPRESSION AND LOSSES IN LATER LIFE

Depression is a devastating feeling. It is not something that one can "pull oneself out of." It is often seen to be a part of growing older, because, as some suggest, the multiple losses that so often come with aging would be enough to make many people feel depressed. Depression, however, is not part of the aging process. Depression is often seen concurrently with dementia and frequently associated with suicide in later life (Butler 1995). It is evident that the quality of life is reduced for those who are depressed. Nevertheless, depression is one of the most treatable of mental illnesses of older adults (Butler 1995).

Estimates of the prevalence of depression among older adults vary considerably. According to Koenig (1995), depressive syndromes may occur in more than 25 percent of older community-dwelling people while among older people hospitalized with medical illness this proportion rises to more than 40 percent. Some chronic illnesses may first exhibit signs of depression (Butler 1995). Medical conditions that are commonly associated with depression in later life include the cardiovascular conditions of hypertension, myocardial infarction, coronary artery bypass surgery, congestive heart failure, and stroke. A study over a six-year period by Ariyo and Haan (2000) found that participants with the highest cumulative mean depression scores had a 40 percent increased risk of coronary heart disease and 60 percent increased risk of death compared to those with the lowest mean scores. Thus depression itself may be a risk for developing at least some chronic conditions rather than being the result of the condition. Robert Butler (1995) also reported that depression rates were higher among those with Alzheimer's disease, Parkinson's disease, diabetes, thyroid disorders, cancer, chronic obstructive pulmonary disease, rheumatoid arthritis, deafness, chronic pain, renal dialysis, and chronic constipation. He also noted sexual dysfunction and side effects of therapeutic medications may be sources of depression.

No single theory explains the occurrence of depression in later life (Buckwalter 1999). A better way to understand depression in later life is through an integrative etiological perspective, in which understanding the cause is a key to the most appropriate interventions. The main theories usually considered are psychological, or neurobiological and genetic. At least in some cases, however, depression cannot fully be explained by these theories but may lie within the deeper issues of life meaning and being (Close 2000). In writing of the diagnosis of depression in later life, Close says: "Thus if the biological symptoms of Major Depressive Disorders (MDD) are a crisis of the body, and the psychogenic symptoms are a crisis of the mind, then the noogenic symptoms are a crisis of one's life purpose, a concern of the soul" (2000, 124).

RECOGNIZING DEPRESSION

Depression in older people is often mistaken for a normal aging change or chronic illness. This means that depression is frequently misdiagnosed. Snowdon (1998, 58) reported that internists recognize depression in only one-quarter to one-half of depressed outpatients, while general practitioners detect a minority of potentially treatable depression. When does a loss experienced in aging and the associated depression become classified as clinical depression? The answer, in a clear clinical sense, is when the signs and symptoms match those of the diagnostic criteria of DSM-IV (American Psychiatric Association 1994). Yet, in practice it is less clear, as the grief of loss may be similar in appearance to depression. So important is it to identify older people who have depression that Snowdon (1998) recommends using a simple screening test for depression, such as Geriatric Depression Scale (Yesavage et al. 1983), on all older people who have physical, cognitive, or psychiatric disorders, unless they are *not* obviously depressed.

Traditionally depression has been classified, diagnosed, and treated on the basis of medical assumptions of a biochemical and genetic etiology. It is worth examining depression from a wider perspective, however, so that a more accurate diagnosis and hence a more appropriate choice of treatment may be made. Close (2000) proposed an alternative to the medical model view of depression—a psychotheological view. He used Frankl's (1984) noogenic, or meaning, dimension, and Tillich's (1963) ontological dimension, which points to anxiety and the threat of nonbeing in reconsidering the basis of depression.

DEPRESSION AND SIGNS OF FRAILTY

DSM-IV symptoms of a major depression include five or more of the following (on most days over a two-week period): depressed mood; markedly diminished interest in most activities; significant weight loss or gain, insomnia or hypersomnia; psychomotor agitation or retardation; fatigue or loss of energy; feelings of worthlessness or inappropriate guilt; diminished ability to concentrate; and recurrent thoughts about death or suicide.

Taking another perspective, symptoms of frailty in later life must be examined against these DSM-IV criteria. Frailty, due to the decremental physiological changes that occur in aging, is characterized by fatigue or loss of energy, weight loss, and sleep disturbances. There may also be symptoms of psychomotor retardation, feelings of worthlessness, diminished ability to concentrate, and recurrent thoughts about death or suicide, leading to confusion in diagnosis. A serious question for all who work with older adults is the relationship between frailty, depression, and failure to thrive.

A syndrome that has emerged in the gerontological literature in recent years is that of the failure to thrive, a term borrowed from the pediatric literature. This syndrome describes a set of signs in some older people that includes loss of appetite, physical and cognitive disability, and social and environmental impairment (Jamison 1997). It is a condition seen in frail older people, who are more likely to be in long-term care and who might suffer from malnutrition, dementia, delirium, or depression. It is worth considering, however, that there does come a time when physiological changes in the process of dying make it impossible to alter that dying trajectory. Thus it may be futile to try to reverse the physical decline. But may there be some instances in which the concept of failure to thrive may be reversed? How much of failure to thrive is related to lack of nourishment for the soul? Perhaps this syndrome may be a response to a loss of meaning in life, that is, a noogenic response.

If we are to consider holistic care, then failure to thrive is a major challenge. Gerontological literature recognizes it, but do we take account of this in pastoral care and chaplaincy, and do nurses and social workers recognize it in their practice? Simply recognizing and naming the syndrome is empowering. Having done that, it is possible to examine possible strategies of pastoral intervention.

DEPRESSION AND SUICIDE IN LATER LIFE

Kimble (1990) writes of the crisis of meaning in aging that many older people experience. Modern technology has added years to life, but many older people still feel cheated. These added years may lack meaning. Kimble describes a situation where there is a lack of positive symbols of aging, at least in Western society. This crisis of meaning for older people may lead to feelings of hopelessness.

Where feelings of worthlessness and hopelessness persist, the individual may ask the existential question: Is it worth continuing to exist at all (Close 2000)? It is here that Close (2000) suggests thoughts may turn to suicide. Butler (1995) writes that of all the causes of suicide in later life, depression is the most preventable. He advocates reducing the frequency of depression and providing effective treatment as the major interventions for reducing suicide in older adults.

In 1963 Butler wrote that some older people reviewing their past life events may find these too distressing to cope with and too difficult to communicate to others: "It is often extremely difficult for the reviewer to communicate his insights because of the unacceptability to him" (Butler 1963, 491). It may also be difficult for this individual to comprehend the meaning of these events. Butler noted that in the most tragic of cases the person may feel there is no other way but suicide, and this may in some way account for the raised rates of suicide in older age.

Currently, suicide rates for males over eighty-five years of age in the United States and Australia are higher than most other groups. In Australia, rates increased from 37.0 to 50.0 per 100,000 in the ten years to 1990 (Hassan 1995). Hassan writes that preliminary evidence from South Australia suggests that for older people, particularly men, suicide is often planned and rational. Further: "Suicide for many of them means not an unwillingness to live or inability to live but a willingness to die" (1995, 67). The fact that they have survived to old age demonstrates their will to live to an old age, but Hassan suggests that the economic, psychosocial, and health problems of old age "become unbearable" (1995, 66). Perhaps these problems in turn become spiritual distress in the older person. It seems that also the spiritual dimension is important in the decisions of such older people to commit suicide (MacKinlay 2001).

TREATMENT OF LATE-LIFE DEPRESSION

Providing it is properly diagnosed, depression is a highly treatable condition (Butler 1995). There is a range of treatments available including use of antidepressive medication, psychotherapy, pastoral care, and ECT (Electroconvulsive Therapy) when the person fails to respond to other forms of therapy.

Best outcomes result from accurate identification of clinical depression followed by pharmacological treatment supported by psychotherapy. Raymond suggests (2001) that too often medications are used alone. This chapter asserts that there is also an important role for pastoral care in treating depression in older adults, again supported by medications. The focus of this chapter is on depression among long-term care facility residents.

THE IMPORTANCE OF PASTORAL CARE FOR DEPRESSION IN LONG-TERM CARE

Estimates of the prevalence of major depression among long-term care facility residents varies within a range of 6 to 25 percent (Baker 2000). Due to the complexities of diagnosis, however, these figures can be taken only as an estimate of the real picture. Baker (2000) studied the giving of pastoral care with three groups of nursing-home residents: a depressed-treatment group taking antidepressive medications; a group of people identified as at risk of depression not taking medications; and a third group of subjects without depression. He visited each treatment subject for thirty minutes weekly for six months. The control subjects received only minimum pastoral care. He found pastoral care to be equally effective in both the treatment groups. The study supported the hypothesis that intentional pastoral care, nurturing the spiritual dimension, may reduce the prevalence and degree of depression. An increase in depression levels after the study was completed highlights the need to examine ways of implementing long-term support, after a period of support from a chaplain. Awareness of residents' spiritual care needs should be everyone's business—chaplains, nurses, social workers, and other care workers, including ancillary staff. The development of a spiritually aware environment may do much to lower rates of depression among older adults, especially those who reside in care facilities.

During a study of elderly nursing-home residents in 1999, I used in-depth interviews and a spiritual reminiscence method to map the spiritual dimension of these residents. One of the informants was Katie (not her real name). Her story illustrates the degree of loneliness experienced by nursing-home residents. Such people may be at risk of depression even in the midst of a large nursing home with many daily activities. Katie spoke of feeling really down at times, of how she needed to talk to someone about her life and its meaning and to work things through: "There's nobody. . . . I've just got to think things out for myself. . . . It's a lonely life for one person to come into a big place like this." Katie said that she often wished there was someone she could talk to about her life:

> No, it makes it very hard, you know. . . . There are often times you feel like a talk even if you go back over the years, just something different, because I can't see well enough to read now and I've just got to live this . . . no one to talk to or no one that I know. I've just got to lie there and think things out and try and work out something but it's almost impossible when you can't. . . . You don't know anybody.

Katie's sense of isolation was clear. It seemed too that she was attempting to search for final meanings in her life; she was reminiscing and wanted someone to help her and perhaps journey with her in this task. As she rightly said, there was no one in the nursing home who could do that with her. Time constraints and staffing would not allow for this. Her nursing home was privately owned and had no chaplain attached. The visiting clergy conducted services on a regular basis and attended those who were dying. They also had busy parishes to run.

There was an interesting follow-up to Katie's story. Several months after I had finished my interviews with Katie, a nursing assistant from that home told me that after I had interviewed Katie, she had talked about her story to that nursing assistant. She said that Katie had seemed to come to a sense of peace and died soon after. The nurse remarked that she really hadn't expected Katie to die so soon. There is a sense in which Katie had found a way to share with someone. Perhaps Katie had come to her own final life meanings, and was then spiritually ready for death.

A MODEL FOR PASTORAL CARE WITH DEPRESSED ELDERS

Studies of the spiritual dimension of aging (MacKinlay 2001) led to the development of a model of spiritual tasks of aging. These tasks may serve as a framework for pastoral care of people who are depressed. The model (figure 1) starts with an exploration of the person's sense of ultimate meaning in life, that is, the center of his or her life or what it is that forms the core of existence for the individual. In depression this sense of ultimate meaning may be disturbed. This disturbance of meaning may be related to the way individuals perceive particular and significant losses in their lives leading to a sense of meaninglessness. It is out of this ultimate or core meaning that the individual responds to life. If life appears meaningless, then it seems that there is nothing to respond to. Hence the threat to being as described by Tillich (1963) may be experienced.

Ultimate Meaning in Life

The first and central task is to find the source of meaning for the individual. It is important not to make assumptions about a person's meaning in life. For those who have an image of God or some sense of deity, pastoral care begins with an exploration of this image. This is important because a person who holds an image of a judgmental God will respond to life from this perspective, expecting to be punished, feeling unworthy, perhaps lacking in a sense of hope, and perhaps even becoming depressed. A person may believe in a distant God who cannot be reached or believe there is no God. The person who can believe in a personal and loving God will respond to life out of a sense of hope. Central meaning for many people comes from human relationship (see below).

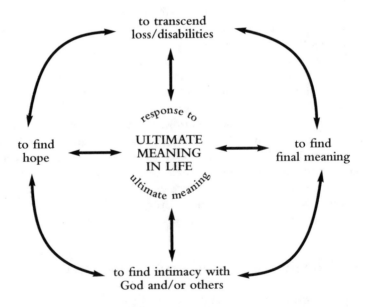

Figure 1: Spiritual Tasks of Aging

Responding to Ultimate Meaning

Humans are meaning makers and people respond to life out of their core meaning. For many, this meaning may be accessed through religious practices. Organized practices include worship, music, and liturgy. Nonorganized practices include prayer, meditation, and reading of Scripture and other religious material. Response to ultimate meaning may also be a response to the environment, mountains, gardens, the sea, art, and music. The use of symbols is an important part of human response to meaning, as symbols connect the individual to his or her sense of ultimate meaning and to others in community. For some people who are depressed, it is not possible either to respond to or find meaning in their normal religious practices, and worship itself may become meaningless (Koenig 1994). They may be able to respond more fully to worship and their other spiritual needs once the depression has been adequately treated. Thus treatments that include chaplains or other persons who offer spiritual care are essential in meeting the needs of the whole person.

The model of spiritual tasks includes four tasks: to transcend the losses experienced in aging; to move from provisional meanings in life to final meanings; to find intimacy with God and/or others; and to find hope in later life. Difficulties in achieving any of these tasks can situate the person in a vulnerable position where depression becomes more likely. Assessment of each of these tasks may provide indicators of need for growth and pastoral care. Pastoral care should be intentional, and individualized, first identifying the spiritual needs of the person, so that these may be specifically addressed. Group work using pastoral care may also be useful.

TRANSCENDING DISABILITIES AND LOSS IN LATER LIFE

Transcending disabilities and loss is an important spiritual task of later life. Many people seem to come naturally to a sense of transcendence. They appear to deal effectively with the major losses so often encountered during this life stage. This is not to minimize the seriousness of the losses, but to say that people may learn to move through and beyond the grief, and having moved through it, to find they have grown during the experience. According to Erikson and Kivnick (1986), these persons reach a stage of integrity; the alternative is to be in a state of despair.

An informant in the 1999 MacKinlay study, Violet (not her real name), seems to typify this transcendence. She has bad leg ulcers, the worst I have ever seen. She says she has had them for more than twenty years. She can't move her legs herself, but needs someone to lift each of her legs if she needs to move at all. Despite her many health problems Violet has a wonderfully positive outlook on life. She said, "You've got to accept what God gives you, haven't you?" She went on to explain, "There's nothing else you can do. You can't say to him, 'I don't want my legs to be like this or that,' but it's just that they are, you know. See, I can move myself up here but I can't move the bottom part. . . . My mother always said you take what God gives you till he stops giving, and you've got to do the best you can with it. Well, I use my hands, that's all I can do is use my hands."Violet's attitude could be described as one of transcendence. Her physical problems were real, causing both immobility and pain, yet she seemed able to move through these to rise above the awfulness of her physical disabilities. Violet still experienced joy in her life. Not only that, she was inspirational to those who cared for her.

How can people be assisted to transcend their losses and disabilities? For the Christian, a dying to self occurs at this stage, a letting go, or self-forgetting. Clements (1990) noted the same experience, a stripping of the roles of midlife in which the person may seem to have no alternative but to reevaluate life direction. This requires an acceptance of life and a willingness to enter into aging so that psychosocial and spiritual growth can continue. As physical decline becomes more marked, in the oldest people this becomes the very point from which the move to wholeness can come into its own. On the other hand, it is possible for an individual to become stuck in a midlife focus and to seek to deny the aging process. In such cases, anxiety may increase as persons become more aware of their progressive physical decline and are unable to accept the implications that may hold. Depression may arise out of this and may cause a blockage to further psychosocial and spiritual growth. It seems that transcendence is an integral part of the complex process of human aging. The freedom that is experienced and described by some older people is evidence of this process in action.

If transcendence is part of a normal process of aging, can we assist in its intentional development? Perhaps the early Christian mystics had a key to useful strategies like meditation, contemplative prayer, and spiritual exercises. These strategies, however, are not well known. In my study of the spirituality of elderly nursing-home residents, few informants knew what meditation was, although some informants practiced an Eastern-type meditation they had learned mainly through reading. Spiritual direction and guidance may be helpful on a one-to-one basis.

FINDING INTIMACY WITH GOD AND/OR OTHERS

The losses of later life, of partner, siblings, friends, and, for some, the loss of God, may be linked to depression in later life. Some independent-living older people (MacKinlay 2001) find that the most important source of meaning in their lives is their relationships—with partners, if they had them, and from children and grandchildren. For many, these relationships provided a reason for living—that is, core meaning.

Elderly residents in care facilities are even more likely to be frail and to have experienced major losses in life, such as loss of spouse or partner. They have then lost their place of residence on entering the home and, sometimes, even their identity. Often there is no one to talk to about their losses and their fears and no one to share intimacy with. Human beings need intimacy, in later life as at any time during the life span. Just as with infants and toddlers who are deprived of love, failure to thrive may be more likely in frail elderly individuals who may experience the touch of another human only in the feeding, showering, or other caring activities, but never in a non-instrumental way, as a simple act of love. (I refer not to sexual touch but touch as an expression of intimacy. This does raise the issue that many find so difficult to come to terms with, that of the need for sexual intimacy among frail older people.)

MOVING FROM PROVISIONAL TO FINAL MEANINGS IN LIFE

While the circumstances of aging may not often be able to be changed, individuals' perceptions of their circumstances based on their past *can* be changed. For some this may include blame for past actions, or guilt, justified or unjustified. In some instances negative memories may be highlighted by depression. For those who are bereaved and show a "persistent inhibited or painful reminiscence . . . [it] is a good indicator of the need for grief therapy" (Coleman 1986, 158). Coleman further notes the value of reminiscence used in mental health institutions, leading to greater socialization of those involved, including reports of higher self-esteem and fewer disruptive behaviors.

Coleman (1986) suggests that the counselor needs to hear the person out, to provide the necessary catharsis, and finally to assist the person to move from a sense of guilt to one of forgiveness. This moves into the arena of the spiritual dimension; underlying the psychosocial is the spiritual with its core values of acceptance and forgiveness. Thus guilt should be addressed not only from the psychosocial perspective but also with spiritual strategies, perhaps of a religious and ritual nature (MacKinlay 2001). Coleman (1986) notes the importance of the Christian confession in this regard.

Much has been done in recent years to develop group work in reminiscence, both within institutions and in independent living situations (Bornat 1994; Burnside and Schmidt 1994; Coleman 1986). While noting that life review has become a familiar concept in the study of aging in recent years, Coleman (1994) commented that the value of life-review therapy has yet to be determined. Still, he notes that the satisfaction gained by many who participate in reminiscence is beyond doubt. Coleman (1994) highlighted four points in reminiscence: finding positive memories; confronting painful memories; empowering memories inhibited by grief; and encouraging non-narcissistic memories. Spiritual reminiscence can effectively include these types and then explore final life meanings through focusing on these. Spiritual reminiscence differs from ordinary reminiscence by its intentional focus on ultimate meanings, on coming to final life meanings through reminiscence and reframing one's past experience, including joy, anger, guilt, forgiveness, and reconciliation. Spiritual reminiscence also focuses on the transcending of losses and disabilities, on finding intimacy with God and/or others, and on exploring hope.

Kimble (1990, 120) says, "The individual is accepted as one responsible for his or her life story and the telling of it." Allowing the person to tell the life story, being with the person, and listening are vital components of pastoral care. In the telling of the story, the person may express memories of unfulfilled self-expectations. Spiritual reminiscence offers the opportunity of reframing past memories and moving on to the present. Spiritual reminiscence focuses on the individual's core meaning; for the Christian, this includes the person's life journey and relationship with God. For many this searching for final meaning becomes more urgent as they begin to perceive their approach toward the end of life. Spiritual reminiscence may enable the person to deal with guilt, resentment, anger, and regret that may be a result of perceived failures of earlier life. Memories of guilt and regret, but also memories of positive aspects of the past, are a focus for spiritual reminiscence. These spiritual questions of life meaning help the person to answer questions such as whether life has been worth living.

FINDING HOPE IN FRAILTY

If there is hope for humanity, that hope is no hope at all if it disappears in the face of pain, suffering, or the frailty of old age. In the twentieth century many were searching for the elimination of suffering, pain, and loss but had to learn that these things are part of the human experience. People can grow through suffering, although the outcomes of suffering can ever justify unnecessary suffering, as Frankl so wisely wrote (Frankl 1984). Yet the question that Frankl posed about the human search for meaning—why some people were crushed by suffering and died in the World War II camps, while others under the same circumstance retained hope and lived—seems to lie just within that question of life meaning and hope. To survive, a person needs hope, but hope is not a commodity that can be measured out and taken as medication; it is far more elusive than that. Yet, through our journeys with others, we may become a partner in affirming and nurturing hope, helping others to find their own sense of hope in the midst of their struggles to understand their own suffering, pain, and grief. Frail elderly people who have found this elusive ingredient are an inspiration to others. One such person is a woman I call Elaine. She is not depressed, but she shows some of the struggles that nursing-home residents have to live with and that could put one at risk of becoming depressed.

Elaine has ulcers on both legs, osteoarthritis, and gout. Having had two leg fractures, she now must use a wheelchair. She says she takes twenty-five tablets each day. Elaine spoke of the pain from her arthritis and leg ulcers: "The whole leg gets very sore, even in the muscles and everything you touch." She explained how hard it was for her to learn to take something for the pain on a regular basis, not waiting for the pain to get too bad before she took her medication; she said that had made it much more manageable. And then she said, "But life's not that bad." There was more to Elaine than her physical problems. I remarked to her that she seemed quite happy in spite of all the health problems she had. She responded, "Oh yes. . . . Oh, I lost my husband fifteen years ago. It was a bit of a struggle; a lot [of people] say you forget, but you never forget. I know [it gets] a bit easier, a bit easier, but in the end you never forget." Then she started to speak of the death of her roommate at the home just a week before, and she said: "That put me back this last week, you know. I'm starting to get over that again now." She paused and reflected about the former roommate:

> Oh, she was a good roommate, you know. We got along so well together, and she was so crook [feeling really ill] the last few days. Every morning you'd wake up and you'd look over and it didn't matter whether it was five o'clock in the morning, and she'd be sitting in the corner in her chair. She couldn't sleep, you know. And it was that way after she'd gone. Every time I woke up, I could see her sitting in the chair. So I took her seat. I sit in that corner now, and I can't see her, you know, it's [a] sort of relief that. . . . [she pauses] That was hard the last night—the poor thing, she was trying to tell me something, but I couldn't catch it, and that sort of got me down, you know, what was she trying to tell me. And I couldn't hear it, you know. As I say, I'm over that now, and every day I'm getting better.

As I thought about her reflection, I kept wondering, what was it the roommate had been trying to say? Maybe she needed help in some way or maybe she needed someone to listen. We cannot tell what it might have been. And I wondered, what if there had been more nursing staff available? Or if there had been more pastoral-care staff available, would they have picked up on some issue? Perhaps some unfinished business? It seems to me that what the dying woman wanted was most likely some emotional and spiritual support, perhaps a question answered, an assurance, even an assurance that she was not alone as she died. I can only make assumptions.

And then I wondered what was happening with Elaine as she reflected on the death of her roommate. This experience may well have brought issues to the surface for her, perhaps fears of death, perhaps fears of being alone and dying, perhaps issues of the very meaning of her own life. Was there anyone in that nursing home with whom she could share her deepest concerns?

Yet, for Violet, Katie, and Elaine, as for so many others who are frail and reside in long-term care facilities, there was a deep-seated sense of hope. It was hope in the midst of frailty. This hope was born out of their struggles, and there was a depth and strength to it.

CONCLUSION

I have focused particularly on depression and pastoral care in the context of long-term care, drawing examples from residents in nursing homes. Pastoral care provides an important part of a team approach to both prevention and treatment of depression. This very treatable and common problem among older adults needs first to be more accurately identified. Older people at risk of depression should be identified for early pastoral interventions. Depression is not part of normal aging, and adequate

treatment can vastly improve quality of life for many older people. The most effective treatment of depression is most often a combined approach of antidepressive
medications and psychotherapy. Pastoral care is also effective when used with antidepressive medications. Use of the framework "spiritual tasks of aging" assists in providing a means of working pastorally with people who are either at risk of
depression or clinically depressed. Pastoral care strategies, however, are not exclusive
to the role of chaplains but are part of a holistic approach to care that needs to be
more thoroughly examined and incorporated into the roles of other health professionals, including nurses and social workers. In many aged care facilities it is often the
least qualified of all care providers who are present with residents as they voice their
deepest fears and concerns. These care providers need to have at least an understanding of their own spirituality and to be good listeners; they also need to be willing to refer to chaplains according to their residents' needs and wishes.

A spiritually aware environment may result in lowered levels of depression
among aged care-facility residents. An environment that honors the personhood of
each resident is an essential starting point. This means consciously rooting out the
last remains of ageism, evident in stereotyping and paternalistic attitudes toward
older people. Educating staff, residents, and their families about the spiritual tasks of
aging may facilitate spiritual growth for older persons, their family, and staff. It
would then be possible to work collaboratively to achieve an improved quality of
life for older people.

BIBLIOGRAPHY

American Psychiatric Association (1994). *Diagnostic and Statistical Manual of Mental Disorders.(DSM-IV)*. 4th ed. Washington, D.C.: American Psychiatric Association.

Ariyo, A. A., and M. Haan (2000). "Depressive Symptoms and Risks of Coronary Heart Disease and Mortality in Elderly Americans." *Journal of the American Heart Association* 102/15:
1773–79.

Baker, D. C. (2000). "The Investigation of Pastoral Care Interventions as a Treatment for
Depression among Continuing Care Retirement Community Residents." *Journal of Religious Gerontology* 12/1: 62–85.

Bornat, J. ed. (1994). *Reminiscence Reviewed*. Buckingham: Open University Press.

Buckwalter, K. C. (1999). "Depression and Suicide." In M. Stanley and P. Beare, eds, *Gerontological Nursing,* 2d ed. Philadelphia: Davis.

Burnside, I., and M. G. Schmidt (1994). *Working with Older People: Group Process and Techniques*. Boston: Jones and Bartlett.

Butler, R. N. (1995). Foreword. In Haight and Webster, xvii–xxi.

——— (1963). "The Life Review: An Interpretation of the Reminiscence of the Aged." *Psychiatry* 26: 65–76.

Butler, R. N., and M. I. Lewis. (1995). "Late-Life Depression: When and How to Intervene."
Geriatrics 50/8: 44–55.

Clements, W. M. (1990). "Spiritual Development in the Fourth Quarter of Life." In Seeber, 55–69.

Close, R. E. (2000). "Logotherapy and Adult Major Depression: Psychotheological Dimensions in Diagnosing the Disorder." *Journal of Religious Gerontology* 11(3/4): 119–40.

Coleman, P. G. (1994). "Reminiscence within the Study of Aging: The Social Significance of Story." In Bornat, 8–20.

——— (1986). *Aging and Reminiscence Processes: Social and Clinical Implications.* Chichester: Wiley & Sons.

Erikson, E. H., J. M. Erikson, and H. Q. Kivnick (1986). *Vital Involvement in Old Age.* New York: W. W. Norton.

Frankl, V. E. (1984*). Man's Search for Meaning.* New York: Washington Square.

Gibson, F. (1994). *Reminiscence and Recall: A Guide to Good Practice.* London: Age Concern.

Haight, B. K, and J. D. Webster, eds. (1995). *The Art and Science of Reminiscence: Theory, Research, Methods, and Application.* Washington, D.C.: Taylor & Francis.

Hassan, R. (1995). *Suicide Explained: The Australian Experience.* Melbourne: Melbourne University Press.

Jamison, M. S. T. (1997). "Failure to Thrive in Older Adults." *Journal of Gerontological Nursing* 23/2: 8–13.

Kimble, M. A. (1990). "Aging and the Search for Meaning." In Seeber, 111–29.

Kimble, M. A., S. H. McFadden, J. W. Ellor, and J. J. Seeber, eds. (1995). *Aging, Spirituality, and Religion: A Handbook.* Vol. 1. Minneapolis: Fortress Press.

Koenig, H. G. (1994). *Aging and God: Spiritual Pathways to Mental Health in Midlife and Later Years.* New York: Haworth Pastoral.

——— (1995). "Religion and Health in Later Life." In Kimble et al., 9–29.

MacKinlay, E. B. (2001). *The Spiritual Dimension of Aging.* London: Jessica Kingsley.

Raymond, J. (2001). "Psychosocial Interventions in Depression in Later Life." Paper delivered at Older People's Mental Health Network Conference, Canberra, Australia.

Seeber, J. J., ed. (1990). *Spiritual Maturity in Later Years.* New York: Haworth.

Snowdon, J. (1998). "Management of Late-Life Depression." *Australasian Journal of Aging* 17 (2): 57–62.

Tillich, P. (1963). *Systematic Theology.* Vol. 3. Chicago: University of Chicago Press.

Yesavage, J. A., T. L. Brink, et al. (1983). "Development and Validation of a Geriatric Depression Screening Scale: A Preliminary Report." *Journal of Psychiatric Research* 17: 37–49.

20 Elders' Narratives of Suffering

HELEN K. BLACK

DEFINING SUFFERING

Dictionaries give the word "suffering" a static definition: the enduring of pain or anguish, grief, injury, harm, or evil. Suffering also has been described in medical, psychological, and religious contexts as "the state of severe distress associated with events that threaten the intactness of the person" (Cassell 1982, 640); "a threat to our composure, our integrity, and the fulfillment of our intentions" (Reich 1987, 117); and "as involving crises and threats that constitute an alienation of our being" (van Hooft 1998, 14).

No definition of suffering, however broad, can show what suffering looks like or means to those who experience it. The complexity of suffering demands a wider range of categories than "suffering as illness," "suffering as grief," or even "suffering as the fear of finitude." The purpose of this chapter is to offer a place where elders not only define suffering but also attribute a cause to it, theorize about its meaning, and affirm or deny its value.

For a caring professional to ask, (1) "Would you describe an event or period in your life when you felt that you were suffering?" (2) "How would you define suffering?" and (3) "If you could draw a picture (or take a photograph) of suffering, what would it look like?" encourages elders to take an active role in relating the experience of suffering by authoring a story about it (Schweizer 1994). This request also convinces elders to make temporal and visual as well as psychological and spiritual order out of the "messiness" of suffering (Coohey 1999, 96).

These questions acknowledge the possibility that an experience as uniquely lived as suffering falls out of the lines of unidimensional portraits and asks instead for the elder's expertise in drawing her own tragedy. To elicit elders' stories of suffering recognizes that suffering in age is not only an issue of medicine, psychology, or sociology but also of existence (Kliever 1989a).

Connecting the story of suffering across the three disciplines of aging, narrative, and religious studies supplies a breadth and depth of language—a "thick description"—to the experience of suffering (Geertz 1973). Together the three disciplines explore suffering as a transformative experience rather than as an illness to be cured, an internal conflict to be resolved, or a social inadequacy to be amended

(Carpenter 2001). In other words, this interdisciplinary link expands the meaning of such an ultimate experience in human life (Bakan 1968).

This chapter is based on research on forty African American and Caucasian elders' (age seventy and older) attributions, definitions, and theories about suffering. It offers elders' discourse on suffering as a unique form of cultural and religious communication, a language that elders used to teach and from which we can learn much *if* we listen. All names have been changed to protect identities, but the words of the elders are reported verbatim.

SUFFERING AS A FORM OF CULTURAL COMMUNICATION

Suffering as a lived experience has a fluid definition. That is, it is laden with social connotations and marked by symbols that are recognized and shared throughout a particular culture (Martin 1987). Since suffering threatens the integrity of the person in many experiential domains, its fluid definition is connected to the mores of a society and to a way of communicating within that society (Scheper-Hughes and Lock 1987). It is thus defined both according to the meaning with which society imbues it and according to how individuals internalize and then objectify that meaning from the standpoint of their own experience (Berger 1967). Shared definitions and interpretations of suffering create its value as well as a rejection of its value in a particular culture (Graneheim, Lindahl, and Kihlgren 1997). In other words, suffering may be named acceptable, unacceptable, a cultural exemplar, or even an "outrage" in a given community (McGoldrick 1996; Rosen and Weltman 1996; Townes 1997; Zborowski 1969).

As a form of cultural communication, suffering lets others know not only something about the individual who suffers but also something about how various life experiences (such as illness or sorrow) and stages of life (such as old age) are perceived and valued in a culture. For example, Mrs. Sanders is a seventy-four-year-old Caucasian woman. She lives with her husband in a large home in the suburbs of Philadelphia. She half-sits, half-lies on a chaise longue in "a room of [her] own" during the interview. She explains that her lack of energy results from the medicines she takes because of a heart condition. She seldom goes out by herself, but when she does she is acutely aware not only of her physical weakness but also of her emotional frailty in the midst of a world that "seems to be created for healthy young people."

> You're invisible once you get to be a certain age. It's lonely and it's strange. I think they're not trying to be rude, but there will be young people with briefcases walking toward you, and I just stand still and they'll just crash right into me. I'm braced; I'm over as far as I can go to the wall, and I have learned to wait. "Oh, I'm sorry," they'll say. Because I used to say I'm sorry to them, because I was in the way. Do you know what I mean?

Mrs. Sanders is not only sharing her experience but also wondering whether I (the interviewer) understand the profundity of what she is telling me about her place in the world—"braced," "close to the wall"—as an older woman. She is even hoping, perhaps, that I have something to offer in return for her gift of self. For Mrs. Sanders, the meaning that is socially imputed to old age and to suffering intertwines and informs both her experience and her expression of suffering.

Mrs. Sanders allows herself to be seen (to the interviewer) as an aged female sufferer, and so communicates that life is as much about age, sickness, and tragedy as it is about youth, health, and fulfillment. In a pointed and poignant anecdote she discloses the inevitable underside of joy and agency (Connolley 1996). At the same time she informs the interviewer that she is not a passive recipient of either age, suffering, or the interviewer's questions but that she interprets the experience of suffering from the worldview of an aged woman in singular interactions with younger, healthier others. Although Mrs. Sanders expresses suffering in the manner that she perceives her culture deems acceptable for an older woman, that is, quietly and without complaint, she does so within the uniqueness of her personhood and her life as a whole (Zborowski 1969).

Sufferers in a given society usually describe their experience of suffering through commonly held definitions or shared symbols. It is thus spoken through the multiple voices of (1) bodies in pain; (2) identities and roles, however altered due to suffering; (3) religious and spiritual beliefs questioned, maintained, or rejected because of suffering, and, (4) if one is asked, through the stories one tells about suffering.

Although the voices of suffering emerge through bodies, identities, roles, beliefs, and stories told about suffering, these varied languages are not so neatly delineated. At one time of suffering the voice of the body may echo louder than one's preeminent but altered role as, say, a mother or a scientist. At another time, the voice of the story may be one's best-spoken language (Brodwin 1992). At yet another time in life, the realization that one's religion helps give meaning to bodily pain roots the interpretation of suffering in the sacred as well as the secular domain (Harrison 1985).

SUFFERING AS A FORM OF RELIGIOUS COMMUNICATION

In response to experiences that force questions about meaning in life, humans reach to aids like religion to impose order, suggest a purpose, or imbue such experiences with sacred value (Ring et al. 1997). Suffering is religiously spoken in several ways. For example, in Western culture one way to communicate suffering is to recall the biblical models that represent unmerited suffering, such as the story of Job or the passion of Jesus. Current writings on the Holocaust and various liberation theologies also communicate the meaning of suffering with contemporary slants on Jewish and Christian theologies and theodicies (Cannon 1995; Cone 1970; Gutiérrez 1973; Langer 1997; Ruether 1987).

Suffering as a form of religious communication may be thought of as "talk" about suffering and its value based on what elders think they *should* believe and express according to their religious denomination. This talk may also spring from an idiosyncratic spirituality that the elder shapes throughout the life-course, garnered from a particular religious tradition and altered or modified by personal experience. Suffering as a form of religious communication, however, may also be a silent language, spoken by the body twisted with pain, by the suffering countenance, by one's attitude of good cheer or misery while suffering, and individual perceptions that silent suffering is good or appropriate. One seventy-six-year-old Caucasian respondent explained that he never discusses an "anguish" that resulted from an act he committed in young adulthood. He believes that suffering is an appropriate penalty for this past misdeed; suffering in silence therefore adds both to his pain and to his punishment.

In other words, suffering as a form of religious communication cannot be separated from a culture's legacy of the morality of suffering, that is, whether and what kind of suffering is deserved or unjust as well as how men and women or persons of different class statuses should endure and express their suffering (Amato 1990).

Mr. Danders is an eighty-year-old African American widower who lives alone in his West Philadelphia home. He describes himself as "still grief-stricken" after the death of his wife and "kindred spirit" four years previously. When asked what a picture of suffering would show, he answered:

> Well, it would be a man with a very haggard face and obviously disheveled and perhaps if you took another photograph that included hands, for example, his hands would be clasped tightly together, indicating anxiety.
>
> Interviewer: Why disheveled?
>
> Mr. Danders: Because when a man reaches that point the last thing he thinks about is his personal appearance.
>
> Interviewer: Is there anyone else in the photograph?
>
> Mr. Danders: No, he's alone. See, that's the epitome of suffering—you're alone, empty.

Mr. Danders's suffering "man" endures a silent lack—of peace, of others, of fullness—a variation on Augustine's view of evil as privation of the good. His portrait shows an uneasy familiarity with the power of loneliness and its crippling effect on self-esteem. Although God is also absent in his portrait of suffering, Mr. Danders reveals that after his wife died and before he "refound" his faith, *he* was the man in the picture.

In order to make meaning of illness or grief, elders may enlist a religious perspective to help them remake the world that is or was disrupted by suffering (Bianchi 1984; Bregman 1996). Viewed with a religious lens, suffering may become the intersection where (1) the sacred becomes significant in the story of suffering; (2) God or the sacred is acknowledged as a player in the suffering experience; (3) individual life is seen in a dramatic aspect as both diminutive *and* cosmic; and (4) the self, despite its "littleness," is viewed as a significant and unmatched piece in the universe.

Mr. O'Hanlon is a seventy-seven-year-old Caucasian man who lives with his wife in a housing facility for retired firemen. The couple enjoys an active retirement;

they dispense food and clothing at a homeless shelter several mornings a week. Although Mr. O'Hanlon is in constant pain from a variety of chronic ailments, he contends that physical pain is *not* suffering. But he admits that he suffers from the loss of his only son ten years previously in an airplane accident. When asked what a picture of suffering would show, he answered, "Christ on the cross. That explains it all." When asked what his religion (Roman Catholic) says about suffering, he considered:

> Well, it says we all suffer. And there's suffering in various ways. I think there's more mental suffering than physical. But you can't sit there and have the rosary beads and pray and do nothing. He's not going to come down from that cross and lift your butt up. You've got to lift your own butt up because that's the only way it's [relief from tragedy, depression, physical pain] going to come.

For Mr. O'Hanlon, the passion of Jesus Christ is both the paradigm and the explanation of human suffering. To win meaning from this ultimate tragedy is to forcefully lift rather than complacently carry one's own cross. In order to fully take part in God's suffering, he believes that humans must "work hard" to alleviate their own suffering and that of others.

Like Mr. O'Hanlon, many elders testify to suffering's personal value. Its worth is gained through a nonmaterial take on suffering. Elders perceive suffering as a means to hone innate qualities such as optimism or intelligence or develop characteristics such as fortitude or patience that would remain dormant if not kindled by suffering.

Mr. Glass, a seventy-three-year-old frail African American man, lives alone in a row house in North Philadelphia since his recent divorce. He connects his "financial" suffering, which is marked by worry, stress, and harassment by creditors, to his "turning away from the Lord's word." His suffering has value because it forces him to "remember" God.

> I think biblically suffering is important. If somebody don't go through it they could lose their salvation because they would forget God. Some people can get carried away, you know.
> Interviewer: How do they get carried away?
> Mr. Glass: Well, I must say I was never a good steward. I handled the Lord's talent not in a good way. The things that he gave me, the money that I made, I didn't use it right. I suffer now because of that. I got carried away.

The value of Mr. Glass's suffering is mediated through his reading of Scripture according to his religion (African American Episcopal) and refined by his view that current suffering results from squandering his talents throughout life. Because he "lived high" in young and middle adulthood and mounted up bills that remain unpaid, he believes that his suffering is a punishment both deserved and instructional. "With what I know now," he assures himself, "I will never stray." Mr. Glass finds purpose in the suffering that is meant for his correction and to prepare him for a "changed" future.

Inherent in this need to feel individually, specially targeted by suffering is the question Why? which Simone Weil (1951) declares all humans ask with innocence. Some elders believe that to ask why is to challenge the omnipotence of God and therefore to provoke God's displeasure. Other elders' questions about suffering, whether *to* God or *about* God, suggest to them that doubt is a necessary route on their faith journey (Smith 1996). In fact, many elders, especially African American women, believe that their active, combative response to adversity invites God's concrete, immediate, and personal empathy toward them in their daily lives (Black 1998, 1999; Black and Rubinstein 2000).

Elders may address the Why? question most often to those who work with and minister to them, such as health practitioners or clergypersons. Although the question is never adequately answered, listeners can provide a welcome forum by asking an elder to "tell me the story of your life and your suffering." But it is important to remember that one gives away part of oneself in biography and listeners need to realize that *not* sharing the life story must always be an option for the elder. If the elder agrees to talk, the story must be received as a living treasure; if asked, listeners should be prepared to give back a part of their own stories.

By asking to hear the elder's life story, the listener acknowledges that the elder's suffering cannot be separated from the elder's life as a whole. The story of suffering may be embedded in a distant past that held dreams and disappointments, a recent past filled with achievement and sorrows, a present colored by "both" pasts, or an uncertain, truncated future. To elicit the story of suffering is to ask how suffering fits into a lifelong context, and to learn how elders take and make meaning of the experience as elders, as storytellers, and as religious believers or nonbelievers. Discussion of the facts as well as the mystery of suffering prompts elders to place their own anguish within the bottomless well of suffering, to view suffering within the context of both a spiritual and a social world, and to see suffering as both universal and contingent (Black and Rubinstein 2000).

As mentioned above, as a form of communication that links cultural and religious traditions, suffering lets others know something not only about a person but also about what that person treasured that is now lost, missing, or broken (Graneheim, Lindahl, and Kihlgren 1997). Sometimes when elders are unable or unwilling to reveal the loss of their own treasure they relay and interpret another's.

For example, Mr. Winchell is a self-reliant ninety-year-old African American widower. He lives alone in a luxury apartment in a Protestant home for older adults. Although he requested to participate in the study, he "could not recall" his own experiences of suffering. However, when asked what he felt when he witnessed others' suffering, he answered without hesitation.

> Well, I met a man here who since committed suicide. His wife had been dead for about four years, and he was still grieving about it. And he said, "Are you grieving about *your*

wife's death?" I said, "Absolutely not. I did all I possibly could to make her life comfortable. So I have no regrets." But there are people who just cannot get over the fact—I've lost my husband, my wife—I'm now alone. Well *I'm* enjoying my freedom. You see, suffering is those people who cannot accept what's happened and who cannot go on with their own life.

Interviewer: What did you feel for him?

Mr. Winchell: I wasn't surprised [that he committed suicide] if that's what you're asking. Because of my observation of him and his manifestations, I thought perhaps he may do something like that.

Interviewer: If you don't mind my saying, you've approached that pretty intellectually. On a feeling level, what did you feel about him?

Mr. Winchell: [Pause] Well, I felt sorry for the guy. I was sorry he hadn't been able to manage his life in a more wholesome manner. Into everyone's life some rain must fall. God usually sends sunshine shortly after.

In this anecdote, he offers at least two points about suffering: (1) although he and his neighbor had endured the same grief, Mr. Winchell "handled" his grief and therefore did not suffer, and (2) his pity for his neighbor is not based on the man's suffering and eventual suicide but rather on the "unwholesome" way the man "mismanaged" his life. His comments hold a strong indictment against dependence and self-pity. Cultural and religious notions about the propriety of expressing grief intertwine in Mr. Winchell's response toward suffering in general and in his attitude toward a particular sufferer.

STORIES OF SUFFERING: THE NARRATOR

Although elders' theories about suffering may be explained in response to specific questions asked during an interview, they validate and elaborate their theories in light of an entire life story. Through metaphors, symbols, and themes, elders explicitly spell out the implicit meaning and fit of suffering to their life (Widdershoven 1993). Their stories show that suffering does not occur in a social or even personal vacuum but interconnects the smaller and larger, private and public, and sacred and secular worlds that the sufferer has inhabited throughout life.

For example, Mrs. Brown is an eighty-two-year-old Caucasian divorcee who lives alone. Because she was the oldest of seven children and her mother worked "out of the house" as a domestic, she "just about raised" her younger siblings. In the past fifteen years, Mrs. Brown's mother and all of her siblings died from various causes; she nursed most of them through their illnesses. For her, suffering is witnessing the deaths of her mother, brothers, and sisters that occurred "out of order." "You know, being as old as I am, you think that the oldest would go first. And then down the line. But it doesn't work that way. My mother lost two before she died. She never got over it. And now, with me, they're all gone. You never know."

When asked what a photograph of suffering would show, Mrs. Brown smiled and nodded, as though familiar with the picture.

Somebody sick in bed and in pain and somebody watching. One would just try. . . . Like when my mother had pains in her legs so bad, I tried everything, you know, rubbing things [ointments] on her legs.

Interviewer: In your picture, who is suffering?

Mrs. Brown: Both, in a different way. One is suffering pain and the other is suffering because someone you love is suffering and it makes you suffer, too.

Mrs. Brown's story of suffering is integrated into her life story as well as into the role she assumed throughout life—caretaker. Her story's theme—caretaking—links the stages of her life, as well as the duties that defined them. This theme was introduced by her mother's absence during her childhood. The "climaxes" of the story are the illnesses and early deaths of her siblings. The denouement of her story occurs in the present, because now no one needs her to care for them. Just as she knits her suffering to her long-standing role as caretaker of her family, she sketches an orderly, public exhibit of familial loss based on the thickness of her private grief (Gutiérrez 1987; Wink 1986). In telling her story she redefines her personal role in light of suffering (although she still thinks of herself as a caretaker, she realizes there is no one left to care for), and allows a new role (of narrator) to emerge within an arena (the private interview) that gives that role validity. Her individual narrative gives voice to her as an expert about herself and her suffering (Coyle 1996).

Suffering stories also attempt to "stay" the narrative *and* the life forced "off course" by the experience. In the story of suffering, the narrator may use a unifying theme to heal the broken self with personal tools, such as luck or intelligence, or in the case of Mr. Bryan—caution.

Mr. Bryan is an eighty-year-old African American man who lives with his wife in a small apartment in a federally funded building. He defines suffering as being housebound due to arthritis and "bad eyes" and frustration because of his inability to "go out to work or even do for myself." When asked where he thinks God "fits into his suffering," he answered:

Well, if you're suffering too much, you just pray to God to help you to stop suffering.

Interviewer: Is prayer the key?

Mr. Bryan: If you believe, it probably is.

Interviewer: Is it for you?

Mr. Bryan: Well, for me, I just don't let things get to me. 'Cause if I don't, I'd be jumping out the window for sure. You have to be careful the way you live it. And you have to be careful the way you think.

Interviewer: What do you mean?

Mr. Bryan: [With a smile] Just to be careful.

Mr. Bryan answers questions with a quiet but firm indirectness that leaves little room for probing. He appears to have lived by his own advice—be careful—throughout his life. These words of counsel may spring from many sources—growing up in the segregated South, estrangement from his children, feeling surrounded by "mean, unfriendly" neighbors, or perhaps being interviewed by a Caucasian female stranger. Whatever his reasons, Mr. Bryan knits the theme of "carefulness" into his life story, his story of suffering, and even his relationship with God. His theme, as it explicates his worldview, helps him organize the relationships between himself, his experiences, and others. It also allows him to control whether those relationships, and the feelings that attend them, penetrate him (Gubrium and Sankar 1993; Luborsky 1993).

STORIES OF SUFFERING: THE LISTENER

The fear of one's life story not being heard, especially at the end of life, may be part of the experience of suffering (Picard 1991). Elders' desire to tell their story of suffering is tied to the moral imperative for "someone" to be an audience (Schweizer 1995). The lack of such a listener—and despairing awareness of that lack—is an important element in suffering at any age (Bregman 2000). In older age, this lone-liness is confounded by the belief that one's story is no longer interesting or impor-tant or that there are few or no persons left, especially in one's cohort group, to remember what it felt like to go hungry during the Depression or recall the jubilee at the end of the Second World War—in other words, to recognize that both living through past events and recalling them shape the present, local moral world that the elder inhabits (Kleinman 1992).

Perhaps the listener's moral imperative is first to be invited to enter the "local moral world" of the aged sufferer. If invited, the imperative is then to challenge the cultural norm of youth or health. Perhaps it is to acknowledge that every stage of life endures a suffering that is both peculiar to a time of life (such as old age) and a suffering that is unique to the individual. It is also to recognize that reminiscence is an important activity of older age (Butler 1963). Thus, listening to a narrative of suffer-ing *may be* a hermeneutical and compassionate encounter with the suffering other (Frank 1992). But another significant imperative for the listener is to concede that some elders do not wish to speak of their suffering or even admit to having suffered.

To elicit an elder's story of suffering is to hear how present suffering fits into the life story, whether past suffering influences the present quality of life, and how the experience and the story of suffering alter or reinforce an identity constructed through the life span. It is also to learn how being old relates to suffering as a cause, an effect, or relates not at all. It is to discover where suffering is "placed" temporally in the life, and in the story of that life—whether it is an elder's major theme or an odd and singular event.

Mrs. Rink is an eighty-three-year-old African American divorced woman. She has lived in her North Philadelphia apartment for over forty years. When asked to relate an incident, event, or time period of suffering, she answered without hesitation.

> When I got married at sixteen, that's it. Because you know what young men do. So I left
> him. But he was all I thought about. And I just wish I hadn't married him. And I got

down on my knees and I asked the Lord to take him off my mind. I thought that was the only man in the world; I loved him so hard. Now that is bad, miserable, suffering.

Interviewer: You wanted to forget him.

Mrs. Rink: [with animation] Oh, yeah! Just give him up! Get rid of him in my mind and just go on about my business, so I could be happy.

Mrs. Rink endured the death of her only son, was recently diagnosed with cancer, feels bereft because of the deaths of two close friends, and fears that because of her isolation she will "not be found for days maybe" after she dies. But her portrait of suffering shows herself, almost seventy years ago, as a young woman obsessed with an unfaithful man and praying to be released from that obsession. Her portrait of suffering is embellished by her belief that God would and did answer her prayer to "get rid of that man." The power of her narrative lay in its ability to graphically portray her suffering as well as her trust that God would restore sense to a mind interrupted by suffering.

USE OF METAPHOR

As mentioned above, because the understanding of suffering relies on a shared cultural context, religious value, and social symbols (Graneheim, Lindahl, and Kihlgren 1997), there is no universal definition of suffering. Finding a suitable personal definition for suffering that includes its private and extreme, yet universal and common aspects rests on elders' use of metaphor (Bakan 1968). Metaphor is defined here as a symbol that represents, stands in for, or suggests something else (Soskice 1985). In this instance a metaphor of suffering may be used to "stand in" for the experience itself.

Metaphors transfer the meaning of suffering between interpretive domains (Holstein and Gubrium 1997), such as the domains of health and religion. Metaphor helps elders formulate, dramatize, and elaborate experiences of suffering (Browning 1966), and leap beyond the essential privacy of the experience (Fernandez 1974). The elder may offer a metaphor for suffering that crystallizes, reflects, or mimics an overarching theme of the life story. Listeners can elicit metaphors by asking elders to imagine a picture or photograph of suffering.

ATONEMENT METAPHORS IN ELDERS' STORIES OF SUFFERING

Metaphors of suffering often appear in three forms: as attack (from a perceived internal or external threat), as injustice (Why me?), and as loss (of significant others, of an integrated self, or of faith).

These metaphors (suffering as attack, injustice, and loss) are used because they resonate to elders' experiences of suffering under several experiential domains. In the religious domain the three metaphorical categories of suffering relate to three theories of spiritual atonement. The metaphor of suffering as attack parallels the ancient theory of atonement as dramatic and dualistic. The metaphor of suffering as injustice corresponds to the classic theory of atonement as juridical. The metaphor of suffering as loss is analogous to the modern theory of atonement as relational (Aulen 1951).

In health idioms, suffering experienced as attack (of a virus or cancer invading the body or as a militaristic fight against illness), injustice (the unfairness of illness striking a previously healthy person; the debilitation of age), and loss (a weakening of physical and cognitive functions) is well documented in aging literature (Kaufmann 1986; Kenyon, Birren, and Schroots 1991; Sontag 1978).

Because of the all-encompassing nature of suffering, the three metaphors have the ability to translate the material reality of suffering into stories that can be read as both personal and universal and with both sacred and secular interpretations. The metaphors build an inductive bridge leading from the intimate spiritual significance of suffering in an elder's story to its universality. Metaphors also offer rubrics to organize the phenomenological or lived experience of suffering. They show that atonement speaks to the reintegration of both physical and spiritual fragmentation. Atonement metaphors depict "where" people in suffering live—in both secular and sacred places, in both rational and spiritual states of confusion, and in the tumult of both body and soul.

Suffering as Attack

The metaphor of suffering as attack, related to an ancient theory of atonement, exposes the unexpectedness of suffering. The previously intact self is laid bare to poor health or tragedy and moves suddenly from personal security, however illusive, to the liminal state of "betwixt and between." The swiftness of suffering's attack hurls both identity and self-worth into disarray.

Mr. Carson is a seventy-five-year-old unmarried Caucasian man. He has lived alone in his childhood home since the death of his parents more than twenty-five years previously. When asked what a picture or photograph of suffering would show, he replied:

> Hmmm. Well, I would say it would be like a painting coming to life or possibly the tentacles of an octopus reaching out. I would be trying to keep my distance from those tentacles grabbing me. (Pause) Or, it could be like an oil painting. I remember a movie years back, *The Picture of Dorian Gray*. That picture started to move. "Ooohhh," I heard one woman let out a yell, and I thought that was the way I felt, too. I don't know if I stayed to watch the end.

These two "pictures" portray Mr. Carson's suffering as an imminent attack from an external "demon" and an internal threat of self-disclosure. In the first picture, although he is just shy of the octopus, it is close to "grabbing" him. The second picture shows the "real" face of Dorian Gray as aged and twisted while the "living" Dorian remains young and handsome. Perhaps this "moving picture" reveals what Mr. Carson thinks he and others would find—were someone able to "look inside" of him.

Suffering as Injustice

The metaphor of suffering as injustice, similar to the classic theory of atonement, discloses the "unfairness" of life and of suffering. Suffering as injustice shows how little control the self has over major events in life, such as unexpected illness or an untimely death. It reveals our surprise when tragedy befalls us. We are not special after all?

Mrs. Lowell is a seventy-five-year-old African American widow who names the "shocking" death of her sister as the event that precipitated her suffering. Mrs. Lowell knows that her sister's doctor was "too tired" to perform a minor surgical procedure, but "too proud" to admit it. A mistake during that procedure resulted in her sister's death.

> It was late at night. He [the doctor] was supposed to do some kind of test on her but he got to the hospital late and he was tired. I said, "Why don't you wait and do this tomorrow?" "No, I can do it right in her room." Then the nurse called back and said, "Your sister wants you right away." That doctor got on the phone and said, "Oh, we have to take her to the operating room." I said, "Don't touch her 'til I'm there." She was in the operating room when we got there. Then he [the doctor] comes out and says, "We're sorry but your sister passed." That was the worst moment *because it didn't have to be* (respondent's emphasis).

Mrs. Lowell continually relives the events preceding her sister's death. *If* she had been firmer in telling the doctor not to perform the test, *if* the doctor had not been tired, *if* she had been at the hospital instead of at home, perhaps her sister would still be alive. Although her sister died more than four years previously, the intensity of her shock, grief, and anger remains. She believes that she will never feel "at peace" about her sister's death because of its eminent injustice—her sister died, in good health, because of a tired and arrogant doctor—yet no one, neither the doctor nor the hospital, will be held accountable.

Suffering as Loss

The metaphor of suffering as loss is analogous to the modern theory of atonement. This metaphor reveals the contingency of life. Elders' awareness of finitude affirms that at any moment they may lose or have lost those significant others who most sustain them or interpret the world for them, such as their children, their spouses, or their most beloved. Also, elders reveal their unbearable sense of loss when they fail to connect with themselves, others, or God. The metaphor of suffering as loss also exposes a deeper contingency. At any moment, the ground on which one is firmly rooted may give way, revealing the abyss that is, one realizes, always underfoot.

Mrs. Anderson is a seventy-six-year-old married Caucasian woman who gave birth, more than forty years ago, to a son with cystic fibrosis. She remembers the night that she accepted the fact that even if her child grew to adulthood, he would never be a "normal" person. In one vividly recalled moment of that evening Mrs. Anderson stopped believing in God.

> When we found out what was wrong with him, one doctor said, "He's just a vegetable. He won't live past three." I didn't believe them. I thought I could pray him well. I can remember one night, he was crying and I was crying. And I was standing at his crib praying like crazy. [Pause] Then I realized that nobody was listening.

Perhaps the desperation with which she prayed equaled her sudden certainty that no one heard her. Soon after that evening Mrs. Anderson placed her son in an institution, where he remains today. She returned to school and received an advanced degree. She fulfilled her need for an Absolute by excelling in mathematics. She trusts the elegance, precision, and "infiniteness" of numbers. Yet, when asked what a picture of suffering would look like, Mrs. Anderson answered, "The idea of drawing suffering would be totally beyond me. I immediately think when you said that I would try to re-create the *Pietà*. I think suffering has to do with a mother and child."

Although the perfection of numbers cannot hurt her, neither can it give comfort. To depict a portrait of suffering she turns not to math nor to God but to the Mother of God who holds her grown child's lifeless body in her arms. The grief that Mrs. Anderson feels for her son, still alive, may be deepened by her grief for the God in whom she no longer believes. She bases her picture of suffering on his own mother's loss of him.

The use of any metaphor enriches the singularity of the narrative. Atonement metaphors lend themselves well to both the physical and spiritual breakdown of suffering and the elder's desire for reintegration. But, while elders' portraits fit well into metaphors of atonement, they are not constrained by them. As will be seen when actually listening to stories, elders employ other metaphors, similes, and symbols to represent experiences of suffering. It is the work of the listener to tease out the metaphor that best captures this representation and link its meaning to the suffering experience as well as to the elder's life.

CONCLUSIONS

Talking through an experience of suffering holds the potential for entering another phase of suffering, i.e., to plot a route toward meaning (Reich 1989). In previous research conducted by the author, when elders were asked open-ended questions about a variety of subjects, such as "Whom would you name as the person closest or most important to you right now?" they often named God (Black 1999). This response emphasizes that an elder's primary and perhaps sole audience is God. Although popular culture encourages personal revelation, and current media welcome "telling all," the voyeuristic stance of a disengaged audience cannot help a sufferer reframe experiences or rechart a life plan (Bregman 1999). To listen committedly to another is to become coactor in weaving meaning and value into his or her story of suffering and, perhaps most significant for this discussion, to welcome elders' inclusion of religion and spirituality in their story of suffering.

Metaphors are significant in elders' stories. They form a bridge between the reality of suffering, which is often ineffable, and discussion about it. They help elders describe the tension between living in a society that lauds worldly security and experiencing the spiritual uncertainty of suffering. Within storytelling, metaphors may aid elders in trying out a reasonable, yet hopeful future chapter to their story, whether or not suffering actually ends.

Certainly, to invite stories of suffering also permits the "dangerous" memory of social suffering to come to light (Langer 1997; Metz 1987). It elicits stories of those who are economically or politically disenfranchised—the elderly poor. It is important to recognize that economic, political, and social injustice (Kleinman, Das, and Lock 1997; Soelle 1975) is intricately and inextricably tied to suffering in the daily lives of many elders and is revealed in their narratives.

Elders' stories of suffering are also filled with evaluative expressions, such as suffering is "good" or "wrong," as well as words of moral duty, such as how to "fight suffering" or "rise above it." In other words, elders pull sense for suffering from the gamut of attitudes, behaviors, experiences, memories, and traditions of a personal lifetime intertwined with an internalized cultural morality about both age and suffering.

When asked what a picture of suffering would show, an eighty-year-old African American man responded: "Your mind. You would be your own suffering. You make it [suffering] yourself. You're doing it with your own mind. So you got to get rid of it yourself." He proposes that both the cause and alleviation of suffering rest with the sufferer. The Western cultural notion that we are "masters of our fate" suggests that one who suffers is a victim of himself and the mind he cannot control. This elder's comment exemplifies the cultural notion that the value of suffering is measured by the sufferer's ability to "get rid of it." Suffering becomes the judging ground of who has strength and power—qualities highly touted in an individualistic society.

Conversely, suffering has inestimable value in Christianity (Amato 1990). It is measured by Christians' share in the suffering of the paradigmatic innocent sufferer, Jesus Christ. The meaning of suffering is gained through one's belief about how this share converts, transforms, and ultimately empties the self in order to turn outward toward suffering others (Smith 1996). Expressions such as "suffering servant" or "to bear witness" are positively evaluated in traditional Christianity (Townes 1997); words of moral "duty" include service and humility. For most elders, whether religious believers or nonbelievers, suffering exposes the contingency of personal attributes, such as power *or* humility. It is perhaps here, at the juncture of cultural and religious notions of suffering and the reality of elders' experience, that suffering touches the sacred milieu of the self.

It is also at this juncture that elders weigh the ambiguities, contradictions, and paradoxes of suffering in this society. All respondents in this study believe that "everyone, at some point in life, suffers." Still, they strive to find a way "out of suffering" and at the same time to find a meaning in suffering that denies its cruel absurdity in the face of finitude.

Kleinman (1992, 13) noted that in the present "language of suffering" there is a "relative weakening" of moral and religious vocabularies. Suffering is "disease," pathology replaces "crises of the soul" (Frank 1992, 480), and death is an entity to be delayed by technology (Schweizer 1994). If it is the role of cultural anthropologists to chart these changes in definitions of suffering, I suggest that religious scholars rediscover suffering's religious vocabulary within narrative. Narrative, as the intersection between the humanities and social sciences, acknowledges the cultural backdrop that frames a morality of suffering and sets the experience within a structure of meanings, traditions, and roles.

"Let us all tell our stories," said Elie Wiesel in another setting of suffering. Let there be enough of us who listen to them.[1]

NOTE

1. My heartfelt thanks go to the men and women who, with great warmth and openness, shared their life stories with me. I also thank the Fetzer Institute for funding this research.

BIBLIOGRAPHY

Amato, J. (1990). *Victims and Values.* Westport, Conn.: Greenwood.

Aulen, G. (1951). *Christus Victor: An Historical Study of the Three Main Types of the Idea of Atonement.* New York: Macmillan.

Bakan, D. (1968). *Disease, Pain, and Sacrifice: Toward a Psychology of Suffering.* Chicago: Beacon.

Berger, P. (1967). *The Sacred Canopy.* New York: Anchor.

Bianchi, E. (1984). *Aging as a Spiritual Journey.* New York: Crossroad.

Black, H. K. (1999). "Poverty and Prayer: Spiritual Narratives of Elderly African American Women." *Review of Religious Research* 40: 359–74.

———— (1998). "'Keener than Any Two-Edged Sword': Three Elderly Christian African American Women Living in Poverty Interpret the 'Living Word.'" *Journal of Religious Gerontology* 10: 45–63.

Black, H. K., and R. L. Rubinstein (2000). *Old Souls: Aged Women, Poverty, and the Experience of God.* Hawthorne, N.Y.: Aldine de Gruyter.

Bregman, L. (2000). Personal correspondence of January 17.

——— (1999). Personal correspondence of December 8.

——— (1996). "Stories Better Left Untold: Failed Autobiographies of Dying and Grief." Paper presented for "Final Gifts" Conference, November 14-16, Omaha, Nebraska.

Brodwin, P. (1992). "Symptoms and Social Performances: The Case of Diane Reden." In Good et al., 67–99.

Browning, D. (1966). *Atonement and Psychotherapy*. Philadelphia: Westminster.

Butler, R. N. (1963). "Life Review: An Interpretation of Reminiscence in the Aged." *Psychiatry* 24: 68.

Cannon, K. (1995). *Katie's Canon*. New York: Continuum.

Carpenter, E. (2001). Personal correspondence of August 7.

Cassell, E. (1982). *The Nature of Suffering and the Goals of Medicine*. New York: Oxford University Press.

Chopp, R. (1986). *The Praxis of Suffering*. Maryknoll, N.Y.: Orbis.

Cone, J. H. (1970). *A Black Theology of Liberation*. Philadelphia: Lippincott.

Connolley, W. E. (1996). "Suffering, Justice, and the Politics of Becoming." *Culture, Medicine, and Psychiatry* 20: 257–77.

Coohey, P. (spring 1999). Editorial: "The Messiness of Dying." *Journal of Feminist Studies in Religion* 15/1: 96–98.

Coyle, N. (1996). "Suffering in the First Person: Glimpses of Suffering through Patients' and Family Narratives." In Ferrell, 29–64.

Ferrell, B. R., ed. (1996). *Suffering*. Sudbury, Mass.: Jones and Bartlett.

Fernandez, J. (1974). "The Mission of Metaphor in Expressive Culture." *Current Anthropology* 15/2: 38–57.

Frank, A. (1992). "The Pedagogy of Suffering" *Theory and Psychology* 2: 467–85.

Geertz, C. (1973). *The Interpretation of Cultures*. New York: Basic.

Good, M. D., P. E. Brodwin, B. J. Good, and A. Kleinman, eds. (1992). *Pain as Human Experience: An Anthropological Perspective*. Berkeley: University of California Press.

Graneheim, U. H., E. Lindahl, and M. Kihlgren (1997). "Description of Suffering in Connection with Life Values." *Scandinavian Journal of Caring Sciences* 11: 145–50.

Gubrium, J. F. (1993). *Speaking of Life*. New York: Aldine de Gruyter.

Gubrium, J. F,. and A. Sankar, eds. (1993). *Qualitative Methods in Aging Research*. New York: Sage.

Gutiérrez, G. (1973). *A Theology of Liberation*. New York: Orbis.

——— (1987). *On Job: God-Talk and the Suffering of the Innocent*. Maryknoll, N.Y.: Orbis.

Harrison, B. W. (1985). *Making the Connections: Essays in Feminist Social Ethics*. Boston: Beacon.

Holstein, J., and J. Gubrium (1997). *The New Language of Qualitative Method*. New York: Oxford University Press.

Kaufman, S. (1986). *The Ageless Self*. Madison: University of Wisconsin Press.

Kenyon, G. M., J. E. Birren, and J. Schroots (1991). Introduction to *Metaphors of Aging in Science and the Humanities*. New York: Springer.

Kleinman, A. (1992). "Pain and Resistance: The Delegitimation and Relegitimation of Local Worlds." In Good et al., 69–197.

Kleinman, A., V. Das, and M. Lock (1997). *Social Suffering*. Berkeley: University of California Press.

Kliever, L. D. (1989a). "Dax and Job: The Refusal of Redemptive Suffering." In Kliever, 187–211.

———, ed. (1989b). *Dax's Case: Essays in Medical Ethics and Human Meaning*. Dallas: Southern Methodist University Press.

Josselson, R., and A. Lieblich, eds. (1993). *The Narrative Study of Lives*. Vol. 1. Newbury Park, Calif.: Sage.

Langer, L. (1997). "The Alarmed Vision: Social Suffering and Holocaust Atrocity." In Kleinman, Das, and Lock, 47–66.

Luborsky, M. (1993). "The Identification and Analysis of Themes and Patterns." In Gubrium and Sankar, 189–210.

Martin, E. (1987). *The Woman in the Body*. Boston: Beacon.

McGoldrick, M. (1996). "Irish Families." In McGoldrick, Giordano, and Pearce, 544–66.

McGoldrick, M., J. Giordano, and J. K. Pearce, eds. (1996). *Ethnicity and Family Therapy*. New York: Guilford.

Metz, J. (1987). *The Praxis of Suffering*. Maryknoll, N.Y.: Orbis.

Parkin, D. (1990). *The Anthropology of Evil*. Oxford: Basil Blackwell.

Picard, C. (1991). "Caring and the Story: The Compelling Nature of What Must Be Told and Understood in the Human Dimension of Suffering." *National League for Nursing Publications* 2401: 89–98.

Reich, W. T. (1989). "Speaking of Suffering: A Moral Account of Compassion." *Soundings* 72: 83–108.

——— (1987). "Models of Pain and Suffering: Foundation for an Ethic of Compassion." *Acta Neurochirurgica*, Supplement 38, 117–22.

Ring, N. C., K. S. Nash, M. N. MacDonald, F. Glennon, and J. A. Glancy (1997). *Introduction to the Study of Religion*. Maryknoll, N.Y.: Orbis.

Rosen, E. J., and S. F. Weltman (1996). "Jewish Families: An Overview." In McGoldrick, Giordano, and Pearce, 611–30.

Ruether, R. (1987). *Sexism and God-Talk*. Boston: Beacon.

Scheper-Hughes, N., and M. Lock (1987). "The Mindful Body: A Prolegomenon to Future Work in Medical Anthropology." *Medical Anthropology Quarterly* 1/1: 6–41.

Schweizer, H. (1994). "To Give Suffering a Language." *Literature and Medicine* 14/2: 10–21.

Smith, R. (1996). "Theological Perspectives." In Ferrell, 159–72.

Soelle, D. (1975). *Suffering*. Trans. E. R. Kalin. Philadelphia: Fortress Press.

Sontag, S. (1978). *Illness as Metaphor*. New York: Farrar, Straus & Giroux.

Soskice, Janet (1985). *Metaphor and Religious Language*. Oxford: Clarendon.

Townes, E. M. (1997). *A Troubling in My Soul: Womanist Perspectives on Evil and Suffering*. Maryknoll, N.Y.: Orbis.

van Hooft, S. (1998). "The Meaning of Suffering." *Hastings Center Report* 28: 5, 13–19.

Weil, S. (1951). Reprint 1973. *Waiting for God*. New York: Harper & Row.

Widdershoven, G. (1993). "The Story of Life: Hermeneutic Perspectives on the Relationship between Narrative and Life History." In Josselson and Lieblich, 1–20.

Wink, W. (1986). *Unmasking the Powers: The Invisible Forces That Determine Human Existence*. Philadelphia: Fortress Press.

Zborowski, M. (1969). *People in Pain*. San Francisco: Jossey-Bass.

21

The Role of Spiritual Assessment in Counseling Older Adults

JAMES W. ELLOR

THE CASE OF JOHN

John is an eighty-six-year-old white male. He lives in a small apartment in a large urban center with his wife, Ruth. John and Ruth never had any children. His mother and father worked long hours at a local factory. As a result John was generally alone much of the time. When John entered school he continued to be quite independent, often referred to by his teachers as a loner. John contracted an unusual number of illnesses as a child. While he somehow managed good grades, he often missed more school than most other children in his class.

John went to a two-year business college to learn accounting. Upon completion of this degree he went to work in the accounting department of the same boiler factory that his father had worked for. John worked as an accountant at this firm until he retired at age sixty-five. He seemed to be satisfied with his employment, even though he reported that he had never received any type of promotion.

When asked about the things outside his family and former employment that interest him, John quickly turns the discussion to his church and religious faith. When he had finished high school, he went to visit an uncle for a year. Uncle Bob was a missionary on an Indian reservation. John's family belonged to a Roman Catholic church. John talked a lot about becoming a priest. He was particularly attracted to a religious order that he noted was celibate and lived in a monastery. His mother was supportive of this idea, referring to it as "his vocational call" and a "blessing for the entire family." His father, however, a nonpracticing Roman Catholic, felt that a "real man" would not go into such a profession.

While John was at the mission, he had what he describes as a call to vocation. When he discusses the event, he notes that it was evening. He was in a prayer meeting. The group was praying particularly hard this evening for further guidance for John. As they prayed, John began to feel exceptionally good about the idea of becoming a priest. He talked it over with this uncle, who referred to this as his calling. John recalls sitting down immediately to write his mother the good news. About a week later, John's uncle received a scathing letter from John's father, demanding John's immediate return home.

John recalls returning home to a raging battle with his father. John talked about his confusion and inner turmoil at being denied what he felt so strongly to be a call from God. John went to business college instead.

His wife, Ruth, referred John for pastoral counseling. Ruth noted that when John was sixty-five, the company retired him with a big party and a gold watch. After that John simply stayed home. In the beginning he played cards with a few friends from church. But they had either died or moved away in recent years. Attendance at church was John's only consistent activity.

For about the last year, John has become quite "sickly." He has developed numerous back problems. This was extremely unusual. John had never missed work due to illness. He had no prior history of back problems. He was hospitalized twice, but each time all the tests came out negative. Ruth particularly became alarmed when John stopped attending Mass. He feels too ill to leave the apartment or even to get dressed, except to see his doctor. He often does not even get out of bed. He spends most of his days lying around the apartment. John has shown no signs of any cognitive disorder. During the first visit, John notes that he feels very isolated and alone. "Even God seems to have abandoned me!"

THE NEED FOR SPIRITUAL ASSESSMENT

Many elements of John's case are common among older adults. He had disappointments in his employment and vocation; his retirement was not goal-directed or even well thought through, and now he is depressed. All of this suggests an intervention for clinical depression. Also common, but less clear in our current assessment environment, is the spiritual material presented. Does this material simply justify the diagnosis of depression, and thus can it be ignored? Or does it reflect a dimension of John that can both be a part of the assessment and thus intervention? Is it possible that while the spiritual is clearly a source of some pain it might also be a strength for his recovery from the depression? If this is the case, then we are challenged to ask about the spiritual assessment and how it is integrated into other clinical assessment procedures.

Spiritual assessment challenges the practitioner to move beyond methods that are limited to observable behaviors of religious practice, such as church attendance and frequency of prayer, to new approaches that reflect a deeper understanding of the spiritual, emotional, and physical needs of older adults. Pastoral counselors and other counseling professionals concerned with holistic assessment need tools that offer a cogent assessment across disciplines. In order to develop such tools, approaches to counseling also need to benefit from holistic theories.

Holistic counseling and spiritual assessment became popular terms in the late twentieth century as the counseling disciplines returned to a modest willingness to listen to the voices of spiritual concern. Yet this new openness exposed the continued failure to develop adequate definitions for the spiritual dimension. Reflection on the work of theologian Paul Tillich (see Tillich 1967) suggests that this failure echoes the use by psychology of social-scientific definitions for a dimension that cannot be defined by the tools of these disciplines. For Tillich, while psychology is concerned with human existence, theology is concerned with ultimate or essential being (Tillich 1967, 1: 18). Only with adequate holistic tools can conceptual insight be developed to support counselors to fully understand the spiritual dimension.

Clinical assessment is the point in any counseling relationship where theory is most exposed and practice engaged. The point of any assessment is to move from theory to action. If the conclusion of the assessment is that the senior is depressed, then the clinical intervention should be for depression. Therefore the two need to be hand in glove. Indeed, one can argue that without spiritual assessment spiritual concerns will be hard to address in the actual counseling session. Spiritual assessment is important at every stage of life, but particularly critical for older adults as they struggle through the final stage of life.

Spiritual assessment should be a part of every clinical assessment, not just for those with obvious religious or spiritual concerns. Today the Joint Commission on Accreditation of Health Care Organizations (JCAHCO) mandates spiritual assessment. Thus, at least in JCAHCO facilities, it must be a part of all assessment processes. In every clinical intervention, however, "ultimate concerns" are not far from the minds and hearts of most seniors. Some articulate these concerns strictly in terms of death and an afterlife. Others reflect on their lives as a whole. Most seniors are not obsessed with this topic, but it is clearly one that most have thought about and should be a part of an honest dialogue between any therapist and the senior.

In the case of John, it is easy to understand two or three good reasons for him to be depressed. He never achieved the vocation that he clearly aspired to; his plan for retirement was unclear and a fertile basis for depression in his later years; and his friends had moved away or died—not to mention the spiritual aspect of John's life. On the other hand, is there some correlation between his wanting to join a celibate religious order and his not having children? If so, does he understand this in spiritual or religious terms? Does it represent for him a spiritual or religious failure to achieve his vocation? What does it mean for him to be abandoned by God? Does this reflect some major vacuum that has existed for much of his life? These and many more questions in concert with the traditional questions of depression constitute a fuller perspective that can aid counselors in seeing a more holistic basis for clinical intervention.

ISSUES IN THE HOLISTIC-ASSESSMENT PROCESS

In any clinical setting the first step is in assessment. For an assessment to be holistic it needs to include the spiritual. The challenge in spiritual assessment is to try to understand what is being assessed. Behind every assessment is a theoretical paradigm of some sort. This is equally true for eclectic therapists. A theory of explanation offers insight into the nature of the pathology or problem being addressed with the client. No matter what paradigm is employed, there are several common elements, as seen in figure 1. Hidden in these basic assumptions is an understanding of the spiritual nature of the person. It is reflected in both the view of human nature and the value system understood by the therapist. From the perspective of an assessment, even DSM IV reflects the paradigms of those who have developed it.

For centuries in Western Europe the accepted view of human nature was drawn from the Christian church. Only in the last 150 years have new theories arisen. Especially Sigmund Freud's theories led to alternative explanations. More recently, scientific theories have become influential. By reintroducing some understanding of the spiritual into their theory of care, counselors are not taking a step backward but are simply acknowledging the needs, concerns, and explanations of their clients. As Wallis notes, there is a new awakening on the part of the counseling professions to the spiritual needs of clients: "Twenty years ago, no self-respecting M.D. would have dared to propose a double-blind, controlled study of something as intangible as prayer. Western medicine has spent the past one hundred years trying to rid itself of the remnants of mysticism"(Wallis 1996, 68). Paul Tillich, in dialogue with Carl Rogers in 1965, notes, "If this word were not forbidden in the university today, I would call it something in our *soul* but you know it as a psychologist, as somebody who deals with the soul, that the word 'soul' is forbidden in academic contexts" (Tillich and Rogers 1984, 201).

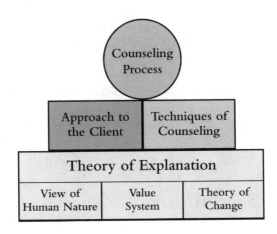

Figure 1: The Counseling Process

As noted above, prior to the nineteenth century much of psychology was developed from a philosophical base that was consistent with the Christian tradition. Today the counseling professions operate from the humanistic philosophies with little or no acknowledgment of theology. This transition in the basic theory of interpretation means that religious and spiritual issues must conform to the expectations and professional *norms* of psychology. It also offers the basis for removing any ecstasy and/or mysticism from the spiritual by placing the entire emphasis on a reality that is measured by the experiences of the here and now. Thus an ever-growing body of literature utilizing the term "holism" has emerged where the nature of the person is understood to include physical, social, emotional or psychological, and spiritual aspects (or essences). The challenge that this approach elicits reflects the integration or combination of these elements. Are they separable? Is one superior to or more powerful than the other? These questions are often unanswered.

Pastoral counseling, on the other hand, has always embraced religion and spirituality but has now embraced the behavioral sciences as well. Strunk notes, "Pastoral counseling is as old as the church and as new as the birth of psychoanalysis" (Strunk 1993, 14). The term "pastoral counseling" is defined by the Association of Pastoral Counselors, which accredits pastoral counselors, as "a process in which a pastoral counselor utilizes insights and principles derived from the disciplines of theology and the behavioral sciences in working with individuals, couples, families, groups, and social systems toward the achievement of wholeness and health" (Strunk 1993, 15). Key to this definition is the understanding of the blending of the "disciplines of theology and the behavioral sciences." The historic care of the soul did not have benefit of the modern behavioral sciences. Yet, pastoral counseling today reflects the interaction of these two powerful traditions.

For both behavioral science and pastoral counseling, the challenge is not in recognizing the potential benefit of bringing them together but in developing a coherent approach. The behavioral sciences see humanity as the focus for their theories of explanation. Relationships conceived by the social and behavioral sciences to that which is beyond human comprehension beg questions about the basis for understanding. Both behavioral science and pastoral counseling are searching for approaches that can offer bridges between the various theories to enhance understanding.

DEFINITIONS OF SPIRITUALITY AND RELIGION

Each person who develops a spiritual-assessment tool needs to struggle with how to employ it as a part of the theory of explanation for his or her theoretical paradigm. For many seniors religion and spirituality play an important role in the individual and community quest for meaning in human existence as well as in the quest for ultimate meaning. The term "religion," as defined by Koenig, McCullough, and Larson (2001), refers to "an organized system of beliefs, practices, rituals, and symbols, designed (a) to facilitate closeness to the sacred or transcendent (God, higher power, or ultimate truth/reality) and (b) to foster an understanding of one's relationship and responsibility to others in living together in a community" (18). Organized religions first emerged more than six thousand years ago. As such, religion reflects both the nature of the organization as well as the beliefs that are orchestrated by these groups.

Most spiritual-assessment tools actually reflect questions of religiosity rather than spirituality as a broader concept. The idea of "religiosity" dates back to the turn of the twentieth century, when psychologist of religion Edwin Starbuck (1911) conducted empirical studies of religious phenomena. Since then many have been developed that attempt to identify the key elements of religion or spirituality that would be acceptable to therapists and researchers. Many assessment instruments include questions like, "How often do you attend church or synagogue?" or "How often do you pray?" or even "How important is your faith to you?" These questions are important, but they address the behaviors of religion. They should not be understood as interchangeable with the fullest understanding of the spiritual needs of older adults.

Spirituality is generally understood to be distinctive to each individual. Koenig, McCullough, and Larson (2001) define spirituality as "the personal quest for understanding answers to ultimate questions about life, about meaning, and about relationship to the sacred or transcendent, which may (or may not) lead to or arise from the development of religious rituals and the formation of community" (18). Religion and spirituality are not mutually exclusive terms; each has its place with the other. It is generally thought, however, that an individual can be spiritual without being religious, but one cannot be religious without being spiritual.

THE ASSESSMENT PROCESS

As noted earlier, spiritual assessment should not be done in isolation but as a part of a holistic assessment. This means that the person developing the assessment tool will need to be able to understand his or her results in light of the physical, social-emotional, and spiritual needs of the senior. Particularly critical to this process is the insight as to how these three impact each other.

Developing a Tool

Three key questions must be asked: Who will do the assessment? What will be assessed? What will the information be used for? These questions help to guide development of the proper tool for the individual situation. Who will do the assessment will shape both the perception of the senior of the questions as well as how the questions are interpreted. It has long been understood that clergy are seen in a different light from other helping professions. For some seniors, clergy are associated with a "magic" that comes from their relationship with God. For these clients, if the person doing the assessment is a priest or other clergyperson, answering the questions is like talking to God, or at least God's representative. Other helping professions are generally not given this type of vocation by seniors. Thus to have a social worker, activity worker, or volunteer do the assessment does not evoke these images and may alter the answers given. At the same time, on spiritual matters many clergy have a broader education upon which to base an understanding of the answers than other professionals. This is not to suggest that volunteers, social workers, psychologists, and other counseling professionals should not do this type of assessment but only that the other professions may need to gain more knowledge of spiritual matters in order to interpret the information given.

The question of what will be assessed is key to the interface of the spiritual questions with the other aspects of the holistic assessment. If the activity team needs to know what types of worship services should be sought for their community, then the questions about the history of the faith traditions of the senior become relevant. If the counselor needs to understand the influence of religion on the coping patterns of the senior, then these types of questions should be asked. An important point here is that unless this tool is to be used for pure research, questions that are solely for the interest of the counselor or his or her agency would not be appropriate to ask. All questions should be based upon the client's situation.

Finally, what will the information be used for? This is like the question about what will be assessed in that it queries the context for the use of the information. It may be used in counseling, program development, or even end-of-life care. Understanding the spiritual needs of seniors can help focus a Bible study as easily as it can help a counselor interpret feelings. But in every case there is a context. As noted above, questions should not be asked out of pure curiosity but rather to meet individual needs in specific contexts.

Common Elements

It is important that two groups of questions be developed. The first are demographic. Such questions as "What is your faith tradition?" and "What rituals or activities of your religion are important?" provide important information. This group could even include the question, "How important is religion in your life?" Clearly these questions need to be guided by the needs of the common religious traditions in the community where the assessment tool will be used. If there are only Christians in the community, then the question need only be, "What church do you attend?" rather than, "What church or synagogue do you attend?" On the other hand, where other religious traditions are present, a consultant may need to be engaged to be sure that questions are appropriate for all of the traditions that may be engaged by this approach.

The second group of questions is harder to develop. These are the questions that reflect spirituality and meaning. They need to directly reflect the theory of explanation operative by the person developing the instrument. Doug Olson and Rosalie Kane (Olson and Kane 1999) did a study of the common variables used in spiritual assessment. They found that the most common demographic variables were relationship with God, religious history, questions about organizational practice, and the degree of commitment.

Olson and Kane found that the most common questions at the heart of the spiritual domain reflected themes of private daily experience, value systems, beliefs, and spiritual development. For counselors, questions about religious coping would also be helpful following the pattern of those asked by Pargament (1997) or Koenig (1994).

How Will It Be Done?

The final aspect of spiritual assessment is to understand the format for information collection. Will it be done in an interview or in another clinical assessment format? Will it be done on a computer or with paper and pencil? Will it be a kind of test given to the senior to fill out and present to the counselor? Some even do this as a part of group discussion. This is often a very pragmatic question. It depends in part on the resources of the persons collecting the information. If there is one chaplain in a facility of 1,000 residents, then a paper and pencil instrument that can be self-administered, scanned for reporting, and analyzed as needed may be more practical than the labor-intensive instruments that require the chaplain to go door-to-door assessing the entire population.

REFLECTION ON THE CASE OF JOHN

Referring to the case of John, once the assessment process is concluded, the counselor will move with him into the counseling phase. As the pastoral counselor listened, John began with lengthy discussions about health problems. In between glimpses of his story, in the first several sessions, John had a hard time understanding why a counselor had been called rather than a physician. After all, the primary referral came as a result of the physician stating to his wife that John's physical problems were not real. Hypochondriasis is generally understood to be a stopping-off place for a person who is clinically depressed. It is common among older adults, particularly those for whom it is unacceptable to think in terms of emotional or spiritual needs.

In these initial discussions, the counselor confirmed the physician's statement that John did not suffer from any form of cognitive impairment or other organic disorder that would inhibit treatment. In this example holistic assessment has been done based on an eclectic paradigm that includes the theological interpretations of Tillich (1967) and the psychologies of Frankl (1967, 1969) and Erikson (1950; Wallerstein and Goldberger 1998). This combination has the advantage of reflecting three thinkers whose vocabulary and conceptual base can bridge psychology with theology. This is clearly not the only approach that could be taken. Family therapy and process theology would make natural bridges, as would liberation theology and cognitive behavioral psychologies. However, when working with older adults the questions of meaning are often at the heart of many depressions. Therefore an existential approach is employed here.

Tillich's Ontology

Listening to John, the pastoral counselor notes a chronic lack of centering, lack of courage to be, and the existential anxiety that comes from having been overwhelmed with the finite nature of his existence. Specific assessment of John's spiritual center begins with examination of polarities. Possibly the most consistent concern throughout John's life has been in terms of his struggle with individualization and participation. As John relates his childhood, the family and cultural impact on John's decisions with regard to this polarity are enormous. His father seems to have had a narrow perspective of who John should have been and how he should have acted. His mother disagreed with these assumptions, yet did not seem to have been able to stand up for John in these areas.

From the beginning, John seems to have struggled with this self-world polarity. One sees glimpses of John's potential participation, particularly at his uncle's mission. Yet his inability to find the courage to move beyond his father's image of who John should be did not allow him to fully grasp this potential. John spent much of his life working as an accountant with his books, in a marriage in which he and his wife slept in separate bedrooms, and with some casual friends whom he could not replace when they died or moved away.

On the second polarity, dynamics and form, John seems to have been defined by his form with little ability to comprehend dynamic being. John seems to have led a patterned life, living within safe repetitions of reality. Once his vocational call had been given up, John settled into an existence that included the routine of office, home, and even church. It is as if his potential reached out to him only once. When he felt that he could not grasp it, he refused to even try to find it again. This imbalance is symptomatic of his hypochondriasis, as it became safer to blame his physical form for his anxiety than to find the courage to live life in some new fuller way.

The call to vocation that John understood that he experienced at his uncle's mission would be understood by Tillich as experiencing the *power of new being*. This is more than an experience; it is a moment when the individual is fully grasped by the ground of being and able to perceive elements of essential nature. John fully felt grasped by God and was ready at that moment to pursue potential in this new way. Unfortunately, his father stepped in and John gave up his potential. While John continued to attend church and keep the traditions of his faith, he was unable to fully accept his own spiritual potential from that time on.

Finally, John exercised his freedom to the extent that he only developed a very narrow destiny. As John described his past, it quickly became predictable where his future was headed. John was almost afraid of his own freedom to change or to grasp anything that reflected his potential, a potential that he seemed to understand as a youth. But now as an adult he could not move beyond the event that redefined his life and then molded his future. At the time of the first interviews, John had a difficult time grasping any concept of freedom. He simply felt trapped by his destiny.

John fully understood the nature of his finitude. This comes out in the way he discusses his relationship with his father as well as his sense of being unable to be reached by God. He felt even God had abandoned him in his struggle to grasp his future. Thus both life's boundaries and those created to keep John safe from the anxiety of the boundaries of his own creation are clear. John's anxiety can be understood as normal anxiety in terms of coping with the loss of his friends and his later discussions of the potential for his own death. But they are pathological when viewed in terms of his father's response and his own reactions throughout his life to his father and his own lifestyle. John met the anxiety about his work by turning in to himself and protecting his need to be angry with his father. He often said that his father destroyed him. John was unable at first to take any responsibility for his own decisions that led to the fulfillment of the destiny that he had allowed his father to establish in his life.

Finally, John was unable to find any resource in the passing of time. For John life hinged on his understanding and interpretation of the past. Starting from this one significant event, John was fully aware of his past in space and time. But he saw little hope in the future—only more of the same. With the lack of balance between past and future, John struggled to make any sense out of today.

Assessing John from Tillich's perspective suggests imbalances in individualization and form and destiny. In place of finding his center, John dug himself into an increasingly finite existence that failed to acknowledge the fullness of his freedom as an individual. His self-creativity and his self-transcendence were sacrificed to protect himself from the anxiety of accepting his finitude in terms of achieving vocation and even in finding the self that he had envisioned. Thus his experience of his spiritual center is of abandonment by other people and even by God.

Erikson's Developmental Psychology

Developmental psychology, particularly Erikson's formulation (1950), reminds us that John was not always the John we have met today. He had struggled with the many crises of life from early on. John came into young adulthood with reasonably normal responses. However, with the event in the mission field, John became *stuck* in the crisis of intimacy and isolation. Similar to Tillich's notion of individualization and participation, it is in this stage where the resolution to this developmental crisis is supposed to be love. John did not feel love, particularly from his father, and never seemed to learn to love. As noted above, his failures in self-transcendence and self-creativity make love nearly impossible for the human spirit.

As John aged, his struggle to attain ego integrity or the ability to maintain coherent sense of self became apparent. After retirement his world became even bleaker. Thus he fell into despair and failed to achieve any sort of wisdom or perspective on his life as a whole.

Frankl's Logotherapy

Existential psychology calls John's type of depression an existential vacuum. Logotherapy, the therapeutic approach developed by Viktor Frankl, understands this to be a state of the loss of meaning in life. Logotherapy's approach is to work to help him to find something positive in his past that can be used to help him grasp the concept of meaning in life. Clearly John did a consistent job as an accountant at a factory that employed more than one hundred people. When the accountant fails at his or her job, the potential is always there for loss of income and thus loss of wages to employees and profit for the factory. From this basis, even though John was feeling quite mediocre about his life, existential counseling would start by trying to show John that his work had some meaning. From this meaning in the past, the logotherapist would then press John toward the movement of responsibility to his future. Thus the logotherapist would model for John the experience of time in all three tenses as well as help him to begin the search for meaning. Frankl notes that human existence is not authentic without transcendence. By finding meaning in his work, John would also be able to see an example of the role of transcendence in his life.

An Integration

John clearly does suffer from an existential vacuum. But the picture offered by employing all three theorists moves the counselor beyond the singular theoretical framework. The counselor will need to work with John to claim his potential through understanding the nature of his finite freedom. With this he can begin to build the social skills offered by Erikson to be able to develop participation in a new being. John is not a person who would in the beginning fully grasp the goal of being a spiritually centered person. He clearly has not experienced centeredness in himself or others in a full way. As he works to address each level, however, he can begin to grasp and be grasped by new being. With this he will not only overcome the feeling of his abandonment by God and other people but will be able to reach out to others as he begins to find meaning in his own new being.

There is hope for John if he can embrace a new vision as a spiritually centered person. John's essential nature and the ground of being have not failed John. John has failed to grasp them. John's time to fully realize the possibility of becoming a centered person has not run out. But he cannot go back and undo the past to make life look like he thought it should in the first place. Thus, moving toward a centered sense of spirituality would enable John to see the potential of who he is capable of becoming in actuality.

CONCLUSION

Clients like John who raise religious and spiritual concerns are common among older adults. The various counseling professions can ignore the spiritual and might still be able to help John. But there is so much more to John and his needs. A holistic approach gathers together all of the otherwise hidden aspects of John's life, affording a clear and more complete picture. Although there are many theoretical ways to approach this, bridging psychology and theology needs to be at the heart of the approach. Psychology by its very nature cannot ask or find answers to all of the ultimate questions of life. Together, psychology and theology can seek to draw together an explanation for the nature of the person such as John. This allows a fuller walk with John and the greater potential for him to find meaning in his struggles and a fulfillment of his life.

BIBLIOGRAPHY

Erikson, E. (1950). *Childhood and Society*. New York: Norton.

Frankl, V. (1969). *The Will to Meaning: Foundations and Applications of Logotherapy*. New York: New American Library

———— .(1967). *Psychotherapy and Existentialism*. New York: Washington Square.

Kane, R. L., and R. A. Kane, eds. (1999). *Assessing Older Persons: Measures, Meaning, and Practical Applications*. New York: Oxford University Press.

Kimble, M. A. (2000). *Viktor Frankl's Contribution to Spirituality and Aging*. Binghamton, Eng.: Haworth.

Koenig, H. G. (1994). *Aging and God: Spiritual Pathways to Mental Health in Midlife and Later Years*. Binghamton, Eng.: Haworth.

Koenig, H. G., M. E. McCullough, and D. B. Larson (2001). *Handbook of Religion and Health*. New York: Oxford University Press.

LeFevre, P., ed. (1984). *The Meaning of Health: Essays in Existentialism, Psychoanalysis, and Religion*. Chicago: Exploration.

Olson, D. M., and R. A. Kane (1999). "Spiritual Assessment." In Kane and Kane, 300–319.

Pargament, K. I. (1997). *The Psychology of Religion and Coping: Theory, Research, Practice*. New York: Guilford.

Starbuck, E. D. (1911). *The Psychology of Religion: An Empirical Study of the Growth of Religious Consciousness*. New York: Walter Scott.

Strunk, O. (1993). "A Prolegomenon to a History of Pastoral Counseling." In Wicks, Parsons, and Capps, 14–25.

Tillich, P. (1967). *Systematic Theology: Three Volumes in One*. New York: Harper & Row.

Tillich, P., and C. Rogers (1984). "Paul Tillich and Carl Rogers: A Dialogue." In LeFevre, 194–202.

Wallerstein, R. S., and L. Goldberger (1998). *Ideas and Identities: The Life and Work of Erik Erikson*. Madison: International Universities Press.

Wallis, C. (1996). "Faith and Healing." *Time* 24: 58–68.

Wicks, R. J., R. D. Parsons, and D. Capps, eds. (1993). *Clinical Handbook of Pastoral Counseling.* New York: Paulist.

Part
Four

THEOLOGICAL
PERSPECTIVES
AND ETHICAL ISSUES

Theological perspectives on aging and older adults' lives, along with ethical concerns about care and support for people in later life, form a subtext in many of the chapters found in the preceding three sections of this handbook. In Part Four, theology and ethics are engaged directly. These chapters assert that a vision of old age formed wholly by the biomedical and social sciences is radically flawed and limited in its ability to tolerate the inevitable ambiguities that arise in later life.

Carol Bailey Stoneking's chapter begins this section with a critical analysis of much scientific and theological writing about aging as an abstract problem separate from the lives of real human beings. In addition, she observes that many churches embrace cultural prejudices about late life and split the problems of older people from their potentials. Continuing the theme of narrative begun in the chapters on pastoral care, Stoneking places images of aging before the mirror of the Christian story. This narrative of suffering and redemption powerfully gathers in the paradoxes of later life and places them in the context of sacred time where hope prevails despite the unquestionable facticity of death and where problems coexist with continuing potential for spiritual deepening. Older people who understand this have many gifts to offer by teaching the young about living *and* dying.

Working from another Christian theological position—that of process theology—*Paul R. Sponheim* reflects on what it means to know that life inevitably ends. He depicts three functions of this knowledge: it can define our lives, inspire us to pass love and wisdom on to others, and offer hope for resurrection into timelessness. Sponheim understands that Christians struggle to know what lies beyond death. He counsels acceptance of the notion that in death "we are indeed with God" and rejection of the desire to take God's place in judging one another's destinies. For older people drawing close to the end, Sponheim offers a comforting metaphor: we spend our lives rowing toward God, but in old age we can rest the oars and drift with the current that flows back to the Creator.

If Sponheim's chapter has us drifting with a stream's current, then *Richard M. Wallace*'s contribution has us on our feet singing. He writes about the special meanings of the African American church where for many generations, elders provided sustenance to the community. He warns that the African American community risks being tainted by the dominant, materialistic, youth-oriented culture of our times and argues that if it gives up its traditional respect for elders, then it will lose its very soul. In the experiences of older people in the African American church and community, Wallace finds a basis for theological reflection on aging. Grounded in the work of George Lindbeck on a cultural-linguistic approach to religion as well as Charles Gerkin's narrative hermeneutical model of pastoral care, Wallace finds theological inspiration in several African American narratives of aging and old age. He thus binds the particularities of biography to the generality of his call to African Americans to hold firm the connections in their communities between the living witness of elders and their theological foundations in faith and hope.

Richard Address also reflects upon the end of life by writing about how Jewish tradition and sacred texts offer guidance for decision making in the difficult circumstances that commonly arise when medicine can sustain life but at the same time threaten its "dignity and sanctity." Preservation of this dignity and sanctity represents the core of Jewish ethics, yet this core is challenged in our time of increasing longevity. Today, many people facing end-of-life decisions struggle with what Address calls the "wild cards" of personal autonomy, technological possibilities for life extension, and the search for meaning in life. What happens when the culturally reinforced desire for personal autonomy encounters life-sustaining biomedical technology, all in the context of the desire for spiritual significance? Address guides his readers through this thicket of difficult questions and concludes that life's dignity and sanctity are sometimes preserved best by removing impediments to death.

The last two chapters of this section focus on what some believe to be a "living death": dementia. In Part One, Jane Thibault and Jon Stuckey reflected on the potential for spiritual engagement that persists despite the degradations of dementia. In this section attention is shifted to those who care for persons with dementia and the often painful ethical challenges they face. *Stephen Sapp* implores leaders of faith communities to lift their voices in affirmation of the continuing personhood of elders with dementia. This witness is an important—though often overlooked—component of an ethic of dementia. Not only are clergy and chaplains in a unique position to provide ethical guidance to people with dementia and their families, but they also occupy roles in which they can proclaim to contemporary society the dignity and worth of all persons, including those whom dementia so cruelly afflicts. Sapp describes a number of ethical concerns that faith communities will increasingly confront beginning when their members receive the dreaded diagnosis on through to the end when decisions must be made about terminal care.

Writing from the perspective of biomedical ethics, *Ladislav Volicer* and *Paul R. Brenner* continue this discussion of ethical issues raised in the care of persons with Alzheimer's disease (AD). Their chapter begins with the difficult question of definitive diagnosis and whether persons should be told that in all likelihood they have AD. Volicer and Brenner review reasons why some physicians may not want to tell their patients, but conclude that "telling the truth" has more beneficial consequences than withholding the information. Next they explore the ability of patients to make decisions for themselves and urge that advance planning be done in the face of this progressive illness. This includes planning for the time when the individual can no longer make autonomous decisions and someone else may need to step in to determine when driving must cease, when institutionalization is necessary, when the use of restraints is debated, and when life draws to an end.

22

Postliberal, Postmodern Theological Views of Longevity

CAROLE BAILEY STONEKING

AGING IN THE ORDINARY[1]

Like files in a filing cabinet . . . we're organized on the vertical. Feebler we get, higher up we live. Floor below this one is the hale-and-hearty. Some people there go to work still, or clip coupons or whatever it is they do; use the golf course and the Ping-Pong tables, travel south for Christmas. This floor is for the moderately, er, challenged. Those of us who need wheelchair-height counters or perhaps a little help coping. Fourth floor is total care. Nurses, bed with railings. . . . Everybody hopes to die before they're sent to Four. . . . It's certainly preferable to burdening your children, . . . [still] something about the whole setup strikes me as uncomfortably, shall we say, symbolic. See, I've always pictured life as one of those ladders you find on playground sliding boards—a sort of ladder of years where you climb higher and higher, and then, *oops!,* you fall over the edge and others move up behind you. I keep asking myself: couldn't Thelma have found us a place with a few more levels to it? (Tyler 1995, 193–94)

It is at least in part his desire to back down the ladder of years that leads the septuagenarian widower Nat to marry a woman in her thirties and father a child. Next to the double doors of Senior City is erected a four-foot-tall wooden cutout of a stork, sporting pale-blue waistcoat and carrying a pale-blue bundle. Nat is elated, but his elation ends in tears. Three weeks later, a frail Nat is confessing to his friend, Delia, "It's a time trip . . . just a crazy, half-baked scheme to travel backwards and live everything all over again." Nat's plight is both comedic and tragic. His innocence, his very nearness exposes our failure to meet the conflict and mystery of aging, our failure even to construe the "problem of aging" within the context or grammar of the experience of aging. Unlike the text of sophisticated modern theories of aging, Nat offers us the text of his rather ordinary life, intensely personal, firsthand, peculiar, confused, fated. The failure of his "crazy, half-baked scheme" uncovers problems that modern theories of aging, for all their promises, cannot solve. Indeed, modern theories of aging view aging not as a fated aspect of our individual and social existence but as another of life's problems that will soon be solved through willpower, aided by science, technology, and expertise. Modern scholars of aging know that an accumulation of empirical facts will someday produce total understanding of the natural and social worlds, allowing us to grow old, or perhaps even stay forever young, without disease or suffering or fear of dying.[2] The mythology of the scientific management of aging construes the "problem of aging" such that it requires only one question, What are we going to do about it? Travel backwards and live everything over? Nat's story exposes the need for different questions: What does aging mean? What does it mean to live a full life? What does it mean to die well? These questions pose a deeper range of challenges—which no particular policy, strategy, or technique will overcome. These questions require that aging be examined in the context of our moral and spiritual commitments, in the context of our connectedness, our ordinariness, in the context of our years.

A DIFFERENT PERSPECTIVE?

Unfortunately, the majority of theologians who have focused their attention upon aging have not offered us much theological insight—no doubt because they have not taken their basic orientation from the text of lived lives but from the social and biomedical sciences. Theologians have too often focused on aging as simply an object of social policy, an object of unemployment, poverty, disease, health care, retirement, and pensions. Thus it is that the so-called problem of aging, even from the perspective of these theological experts, goes hand in hand with the cultural and symbolic impoverishment that has beset the last half of life since the late nineteenth century. Theories of aging, generalizations about the status of aging, attitudes toward aging or the elderly, class and gender differences, or treatment of the poor or frail old frame important questions, but the picture is stolen from us. The desperate voice of a woman turned and tuned to her ripening, suddenly feeling expendable, left behind, will never be calmed by modernity's traditional dissociation of ideas, images, and attitudes from the "facts" of aging. The epistemological stance of most theories of aging makes aging an abstraction and places us at a comfortable distance away. Modern theories of aging treat ideas, beliefs, and feelings about aging as if they were merely subjective reactions to an objective reality. This dissociation impedes a richer understanding of growing old. When internalized it feeds a kind of false consciousness, a separation of body and self, a feeling of dispossession that is common in our culture.

By focusing solely on the abstract "problem of aging" apart from the actual lives and voices of people growing older, the scientific management of aging also denies our universal participation and solidarity in this most human experience. It creates a cultural representation of human aging as wholly comprised of loneliness, dispossession, disempowerment, and fear of death. By elevating scientific meanings of aging and allowing them to dominate public discourse and much else—including, unfortunately, much "theological discourse"—we deny ourselves a critical vision, a larger story, within which one's experience makes sense. Christians have such a story. But unless there exists an essential and creative tension between the empirical facts of aging, the meaning systems of science and medicine, and the story of Christ with its ideals, images, and social practices that conceptualize and represent the end of human life, growing old will never be more than the dreary denouement of an individual's life drama. This is not to say that shaping one's vision according to the Christian story will remove all the challenges of aging. Instead, emphasizing the story of Christ as the grammatical setting for our moral commitments regarding aging holds the possibility of helping us to understand, accept, and imaginatively transform the unmanageable, ambiguous aspects of our existence. It is the movement between the sacred— the story of Christ—and the ordinary and mundane— the graying hair, a tattered favorite pair of shoes, the house we once lived in—that stretches our minds and allows us to suddenly glimpse a pattern repeated in the fabric of our personal history or to realize that some struggle or personal triumph links us to the larger movement of communal life. It is a movement that requires tolerance for ambiguity and incongruity precisely because it allows for the paradoxes of later life: aging is a source of wisdom *and* suffering, spiritual growth *and* physical decline, honor *and* vulnerability.

The elderly even within the church, however, are encouraged not to think about growing old within the story of Christ but rather about how to remain young as long as they can. The elderly even within the church are not inspired with meaning, solace, or challenge for this time but are the captives still of the story of an impoverished Protestant culture of the nineteenth century. This culture, impelled by a belief in perfectionism in physical and spiritual matters and a belief in the power of the individual will, dichotomized and rationalized experience in order to control it. These beliefs created pressures to master old age rather than accept it and generated a dangerous dualism: anyone who lived a life of hard work, faith, and self-discipline could preserve health and independence into a ripe old age, followed by a quick, painless, natural death; only the shiftless, faithless, and promiscuous were doomed to premature death or a miserable old age. Thus we are today in the twenty-first century, a culture relentlessly hostile toward decay and dependency. We quite literally imagine that the only way we can relieve the pathos of aging is by disencumbering ourselves of one another, by removing all disorder, by attempting to redefine our very selves, to solve through our own devices the enigmas of our individual histories. Ancient—and more animate—images of aging such as the tree of life have been felled, only to be replaced by the peculiarly modern, peculiarly uniform rungs of the Ladder of Years (see Cole 1992; also Troyansky 1989). Like Nat, we are left to wonder whether we can find a place with a few more levels, a ladder with a few more rungs.

Modern society has in fact evolved into a fully age-segregated society in which most of the aged do not occupy a vital role. It is a society that supports a burgeoning aging industry but one that does not otherwise value the aging of the mind, body, and spirit. It not only offers no moral endorsement or meaning to growing older but fears growing old, identifying aging with the obsolescence that it both creates and perpetuates, and ultimately merges aging with the fear of death, a fear of slipping and sliding into nothingness. In the late medieval period images of a rising and falling staircase charted a cognitive map of life's course (see Cole 1992); such images might still serve, as well as Nat's ladder and slide, as an important visual source for idiomatic language still used in English today: "going downhill" or "slipping fast."

A CHRISTOCENTRIC VIEW

How might aging be envisioned differently? What different perspectives on aging do the ages offer? A beautiful example of a different vision survives in a fourteenth-century Psalter that belonged to Robert de Lisle of Yorkshire. The Psalter depicts the ages of life arranged around the wheel of life. Christ is at the center, governing the wheel on which the fate of humans revolves. Radiating from the center are eight medallions illuminating four ages of life; two medallions, a coffin and a tomb, emphasize the natural end of life. The image conveys a sense of eternal turning as a human life progresses from season to season until death breaks the cycle, opening the passage to eternal life. Significantly, each age is equidistant from God, stressing their subordinate but equal status. The inscription around the central Christ medallion reads, *Cunta simul cerna totum racione guberno* (I perceive all ages at once, I rule all with reason) (see Cole 1992). In redeeming human life from its natural cycle, this Christ-centered vision subordinates seasonal time to sacred time. Earthly time becomes a mere shadow of eternity. And, significantly, since no individual regardless of age can attain the transcendent stature of Christ, no one can ever consider herself or himself a fully completed person. This biblical ideal of adulthood affirms that all ages of life are equal in God's eyes. A wise old person retains the capacity for growth. Such is the hope of eternal time.

We are, I think, blinded to the possibilities of growth in old age by modernity's celebrations of the goals of the first half of life: education, expansion, efficiency, child rearing, and social utility. We have been trained to see the second half of life as all "downhill," the diminution of one's capacity to achieve these goals. This image of the second half of life as literally barren of possibilities gives rise to the peculiarly modern lament delivered in Ruth Harris Jacob's *Becoming Sixty*: "Would I give birth only to my old age" (Jacobs 1991, 125).[3] So it is that we attempt to "master" old age rather than yield to it, to eliminate rather than explore the final stage of our earthly life. Trollope's (1882/1990) satirical novel *The Fixed Period* unveils the trajectory of modern thinking: chronological age is an efficient tool for regulating life and even more crucially for managing generational replacement in primary labor markets. Why not extend the logic, if old age is irrelevant and burdensome? If a certain number of years mark the limit of human productivity and rationality, why allow anyone who has passed this fixed period to hold office or control land or other forms of wealth? Why not—painlessly and efficiently, of course—dispose of all people who have outlived their usefulness? If in fact life has no significance that transcends one's capacity for productivity or, literally, for women, re-productivity, it stands to reason that we might simply eliminate the final stage of life by eliminating the aged or, at the very least, the frail aged.[4]

In this respect it is ironic that the critics of ageism, including many theologians who have sought to debunk modern "myths" of old age, sound the very values that would inform a "fixed period." While campaigns against ageism have enjoyed considerable success, particularly in expanding the range of choices for the middle-class elderly, the same drive for accumulation of individual health and wealth, the same preoccupation with control of the body that gave rise to ageism in the nineteenth century, informs the attack on ageism. Instead of offering a different perspective on aging, the critics of ageism simply replaced the old negative stereotype of the older person as conservative, unproductive, disengaged, inflexible, senile, poor, sick, or in a nursing home with a more fashionable positive stereotype. Yet this positive stereotype, captured, for example, in advertisements that feature a sky-diving older woman or a jet-skiing older man, shows no more tolerance or respect for the intractable vicissitudes of aging than the old negative stereotype; old people are (or should be) healthy, sexually active, engaged, productive, and self-reliant, else they have hit the mark, they have outlived their usefulness—and down the slide they go. From this peculiarly modern perspective, the meaning of aging still amounts to no more than the sum of its empirical parts. Whether it is the optimistic or the pessimistic stereotype that holds sway, what these images lack and what we need is not optimism but hope.

THE SPECTER OF AGING

The dark side of modernity's "optimism" regarding aging is a generational war. Critics of Social Security and Medicare blame the deteriorating condition of children and families on the "graying of the federal budget." Since 1985 this view has been widely publicized by an advocacy group known as Americans for Generational Equity. This group has argued that society is postponing current costs onto future generations and is ignoring its obligations to children and the unborn; at the same time, it contributed to an increasingly powerful image of a greedy gerontocratic lobby, ruthless in its pursuit of hard-earned tax dollars to underwrite increasingly golden retirements (Kaplan 1987).

Until the early 1980s, the elderly as a group had enjoyed a privileged status of sorts, at least among welfare-state beneficiaries, a "status" built on the image of older people as a group as poor, frail, and dependent (Moody 1988). Ironically, as the opposite, more optimistic image of aging was promoted by the "new" old, and as the generational equity campaign portrayed them as politically powerful, selfish, and potentially dangerous, the dynamics of interest-group liberalism turned against the elderly. Old age emerged once again as a lightning rod for the storms of liberal capitalism and of middle-class identity. Personal anxieties about the aging of primarily middle-aged, white baby boomers merge with fears about declining fertility and the burden of an aging population and merge also with the fiscal and ideological crises of the welfare state and create a specter of old age that completely obscures its possibilities. What the middle-aged baby boomer senses, even if she cannot articulate it, is that while the middle-class elderly have become healthier, more financially secure, and more politically potent, they nevertheless suffer from the cultural disenfranchisement imposed on older people in general. Having satisfied the social requirements of middle age and avoided or survived many previously fatal diseases, older people are often able to live ten or twenty years beyond gainful employment. But then what? Is there something special one is supposed to do—or not do? Is old age really the culmination of life? Or is it simply the anticlimax to be endured until medical science can abolish it?

GROWING OLD AS CHILDREN OF HOPE

Neither superficial optimism nor false pessimism can provide a response that does not destine us to live in fear of failure, for neither can accommodate the realities of decline and death. No matter the quality or quantity of our hygienic regimen or our medical care, our place on the biological continuum between "normal" aging and disease is only partly controllable. We are all vulnerable to chronic disease and death. This vulnerability defeats all efforts to write our own endings; our moral existence is inextricably historical and thus fragile. The wisdom of the gospel, however, is distinguished from both pessimism and optimism, because it is derived from a source finally not subject to the contingencies of history, not subject, that is, to our own ability to create meaning. From a Christian perspective, individual as well as collective history remains morally ambiguous to the end. Hope takes the form of Christian eschatology, that is, it moves beyond history. As subjects within God's time Christians are taught that they are not subject to fortune in a manner that makes them impotent. Christians are children of hope, no matter their chronological age.

Thus it is that Christians celebrate hope even as we struggle to resist the seductiveness of optimism and the barrenness of pessimism. Hope requires such resistance; it requires we face the unraveling of the knot that ties us to needing and wanting more for ourselves. It requires we assemble reminders that enable us to recognize that self-deception is a permanent possibility. It requires we attend to the disorderly text of our lives and learn to recognize moral commitments that are in fact more profound than our customary descriptions can suggest. Story is hope's midwife.

THE EYE OF THE STORY[5]

We need the text of lived lives, for we all are in a profound sense not unlike Tyler's accidental tourist, bewildered postmodern travelers, moving hesitantly toward our own fantastical dance with fate and mutability, toward an acceptance of mortality and finitude. But each of us alone is like Percy's (1975) lonely castaway, combing the beach for fragments, for messages washed ashore in bottles. We may emerge with different criteria for sorting and unfolding messages, but without an explanation "why." If we are lucky we may emerge seeing our world in its surprising variety, its surprising sameness, its complexity and mysteriousness, its flawed and imperfect beauty, but we cannot express what we see except in a language and in forms more complex than theory, more allusive, more attentive to particulars, conjoined to furies. We may emerge laden with the knowledge of our timefulness, our connectedness, with the challenge of how we ought to say goodbye to our children. We may emerge upon a threshold, a threshold that holds out the possibility of continued growth in wisdom. There is much to be shared.

We need to hear these stories. We need to know the text of lived lives, lives of people who weave a collective past into the present, a personal past into a journey of hope. Of course, the text of lived lives will not offer simple prescriptions or romantic visions of *the* proper way to grow old, no promise that we will be unscathed by life's vicissitudes. But like Bunyan's (1684) Christiana, the overlooked heroine of part two of *Pilgrim's Progress*,[6] the texts of lived lives are assembled reminders that each journey of life is lived in relation to others. If we but would, we the gifted people, are called "to give to others, so that when we leave this world we can be what we have given" (Nouwen and Gaffney 1974, 13). Death from this perspective can be made into our final gift. "We belie it daily," wrote Florida Scott Maxwell at age eighty-five, "but is it not possible that by living our lives we create something fit to add to the store from which we came? Our whole duty may be to clarify and increase what we are, to make our consciousness a finer quality. The effort of one's entire life would be needed . . . to return laden to our source" (1968, 40). How profound is our need for these voices of wisdom, for particular stories that may yet train us to understand "how the Christian story may fit over our lives" (Hauerwas 1988, 29).

We need the stories of Christianas; we need elder tales, stories of growing older, stories of transformation, self-transcendence, humility, and wisdom, stories not limited by a denial of physical decline and mortality. We need communities capable of hearing these stories, capable of viewing these time travelers not as fearfully alien old strangers but as pilgrims, children of hope like ourselves. We need to revalue aging, to embrace the aging body as also a sacred space, to emphasize the spirituality of nurturing in all the ways that nurturing is both given and received throughout our lifetimes. Perhaps herein the irony lies: an aging woman's body and her earthly relationships, those very things that appeared to Bunyan as impediments, offer the ground for a recovery of spirituality in later life, the ground of practical wisdom.

We need the stories that flow from lived lives. In particular, Christians need the elder tales of elder Christians, peculiarly hope-filled tales, tales of the gift of years. It is the text of lived lives that assembles for us, quite literally, bodies. Reinstating moral agents as concrete selves, embodied selves, reasserts the *inter*subjective nature of morality, thus redefining the second half of life as a moral category, not primarily a biological or psychological category. In other words, it is within the spiral of highly charged intimate relationships persisting over time that the possibilities for understanding are the greatest and the greatest understanding is possible. To be sure good stories require many tellings and certainly any one telling of a good story will intersect in different ways with the grammar of the hearer and the hearer's tradition. Mired as we are in the modern tradition, captive to its images of aging, chained to its charting of life's course, it is tempting to imagine the telling of a story as itself an Archimedian point—the end of ambivalence. Indeed, that is Nat's tragedy, "a crazy, half-baked scheme to travel backwards and live everything all over again," for Nat's scheme sacrifices still the text and meaning of ordinary life.

But imagine Nat's story intersecting with a tradition that does not presume that all moral ambivalence will one day end, or even that it should. Christians are gifted with such a tradition. We need not be so dependent upon luck if we attend to the Story in which we imagine all our stories are embedded. We did not learn to "know" God any other way than through the Story. Story is the way in. It is the threshold.

Endowing the relationships of elders, in particular their relationship to the Christian community, with moral significance and linking personal interpretation with an overall narrative understanding, a Christ vision, involves a shift from determinate rules regarding the first or the second half of life to models of practical wisdom and the unity of life. Such a shift, for example, may inform the moral decision not to ask physicians to do more than physicians can or should do. Being formed by hope in fact requires that we be more provocative and less abstracted from the wellsprings of our own thought and action. Being formed by hope requires that we take seriously the story of Jesus, the church's own normative (if not descriptive) tradition as well as the text of our sometimes mundane existence. Genuine theological reflection moves between the sacred and the mundane; it is distinctive because of this peculiar posture toward the world and because of its peculiar intersection with the stories of ordinary women and men. Its grammar should not be structured on the principle of detachment but on the impulse of hospitality. This is the peculiar claim that Christians imagine denotes the truth of who we are, of why we are, a people whose possibilities for caring, whose arc of action, and whose hopefulness loop around and around and around the Lord's table, spiraling back onto the human site, remaking, returning, remembering us, without distortion, without sacrificing the text of any part of our lives.

Christians can offer alternative understandings of the moral significance of growing old exactly because the cross is not a symbol of the fragility of a virtuous life. It is not "just a story" but the ground of a reality that subsumes the stories we would tell; the cross of Jesus is the grace of God. It is the ground of our hope and it is the promise of our deliverance. To grow old as a child of hope is to come to the table laden. The church must insist we do so.

MORAL OFFERINGS: THE GIFTS OF THE ELDERS

The church needs the gifts of its elders. Those who have grown in years are not relieved of moral responsibilities. "They cannot," Stanley Hauerwas and Laura Yordy write, "leave the church to survive on its own and move to Florida. For Christians, there is no 'Florida' even if they happen to live in Florida" (Hauerwas and Yordy, forthcoming). The Christian community cannot allow aging to be a lost opportunity, but the church must insist on a transformation of what the world understands to be a loss of power into service for the good of the Christian community. We cannot afford to isolate the generations one from the other any more than we should expect the elderly to live as if we never grow old. Isolation and denial leads only to barrenness. We need the memories and experiences of those who have grown old in Christ to midwife, literally to remember the skills necessary for the telling and retelling of the gospel story. The gospel is a story with myriad subplots, intricacies, colors, and textures. Stories live through memory, through being told over and over again, and, in the telling, new aspects of the story are discovered. How, for example, does an eighty-three-year-old woman tell the story of Jesus, a young man, a Savior, who died at thirty-three? We are in fact dependent upon those who help us remember the complexity of the story that constitutes who we are. The church requires the wise, particularly the elderly among us, to exist.

Thus the church needs to find a way not only to avoid the isolation of the young from the old but to encourage friendship between the young and the old. The church must find ways to have children and youth, as well as the midlife parents of youth, to sit at the feet of their elders where they learn the wisdom of the those whose very bodies are assembled reminders of being oriented toward witnessing God's work in God's time rather than achieving our goals in our own time. Perhaps the hardest thing the church must ask of the elderly is to teach us how to die. Such a teaching requires a vulnerability none find easy, particularly in a society based on autonomy. Yet, as Hauerwas and Yordy (forthcoming) note, "none of us know how to die 'by nature.' Rather, we must be taught how to die through friendship." We must learn how to die in hope.

DYING WELL: THE STORIES OF SIMEON AND ANNA

The gospel offers us moral examples in the persons of Simeon and Anna. We know little about Simeon when he appears at the beginning of the gospel story. His own story is near its end; we know he was old and thus approaching death. We know he was a devout and righteous man who, inspired by the Spirit, came into the temple when the parents brought in the child Jesus. Even as the infant settled into his arms, we are told, Simeon blessed God. He can now go to his death in hope, for he has glimpsed God's salvation for the whole world ("Master, now you are dismissing your servant in peace, according to your word; for my eyes have seen your salvation, which you have prepared in the presence of all peoples," Luke 2:29-30). Simeon is not thereby released from his own story, but his story is now transformed; he in fact dies outside the story. Again, we know little about Simeon's death except that it will shortly occur. Thus the narrative suggests that the significance of Simeon lies in his hope. Simeon's hope in Jesus carries him to his death in the knowledge that what he has lived is not futile precisely because it need not save itself.[7] Christians are in fact a people who do not have to hurry to accomplish all our goals before we die; rather we testify to the truth of Christ's kingdom in the midst of the world, without expecting that we can enact it ahead of its appointed time. The completion of our lives, just as in Simeon's case, lies ahead, in the fullness of a story that is still unfolding. Simeon's virtue is that he prays in hope for himself, which is not to say hope in himself. Significantly, there is no indication that arduousness of death is removed; indeed, Simeon, having caught just a brief glimpse of what is to come, and then "dying" to the story, sees that what is to come will also be arduous since, as Simeon must tell Mary, "a sword will pierce your own soul too" (Luke 2:35) (see Pinches, forthcoming).

Of Anna we know even less. We are told she was of "a great age, having lived with her husband seven years after her marriage, then as a widow to the age of eighty-four" (Luke 2:36-37). She also is devout: she "worshiped . . . with fasting and prayer night and day" (Luke 2:37). Otherwise, all we know of Anna is her hope and her witness to that hope: she praised God and spoke "about the child to all who were looking for the redemption of Jerusalem" (Luke 2:38). Anna is looking ahead, not toward the completeness of her own life, but to the continuation and ultimately the completion of the story into which her life is taken up. This is knowledge glimpsed only in and through hope. Formed by this hope she witnesses to the full completion of God's story, *godspell,* the gospel, to the redemption of the whole world. Again, as with Simeon, the focus of the narrative, indeed Anna herself, is directed toward new life.

This is significant, for one could image that Anna would be obsessed with death. As a woman of "great age," she differs from those of other ages in knowing that she will die soon, maybe in a few weeks, maybe in six months, maybe in six years, but nonetheless. Yet the story tells us that it is now at this great age that she engages in pointing her life beyond itself: "*at that very hour,* she spoke of him to all who were looking for the redemption of Israel." Anna dies to the story, but she fades from the story drawing the attention of all whom she encounters beyond themselves, beyond even the lives and troubles of the current ruling generation, to the truth that anchors all our lives. She points in hope beyond what is now to what is yet to be.

Anna and Simeon fade from the story, because through the eyes of the story our gaze (like theirs) is fixed not on them but on Jesus. Their gaze teaches us. We need their witness not only because we need to know where to fix our gaze but because we need to learn from them how to die well. Ned, like many modern elders, is awash in the terrifying fear that the best is behind him. He desperately wants to back down the ladder of years, to live everything over again, to find something new and more meaningful to pin his life upon. Although Anna and Simeon may have literally died alone—we simply do not know the particulars—they are carried to their deaths together, for they share a hope that stretches toward what lies ahead.

Still, teaching us to die well is hard. The physical and spiritual realities of dying and preparing for one's own death are difficult work. This remains true for those who die in hope, although it is a different sort of work than that of those who die without it. "Retirement" for Christians ought not represent just the time when what we do in life changes; it ought instead to represent the time of the final work of our lives. Anna was at work, she was worshiping; glimpsing the completion of God's work, her resolve was set to go forth witnessing.

WHAT THEOLOGIANS MUST LEARN TO RECEIVE

Unfortunately, theologians in the modern era have too often patterned themselves after the "experts" of the social and biomedical sciences. The expert is not expected to be wise but to know the best ways to achieve results through the use of technical rationality. As Hauerwas and Yordy (forthcoming) observe, "the whole point of a society constituted by the authority of the expert is to be a community that can live without stories" (see also MacIntyre 1984, 79–84). Modern society thus has no need for the elderly. But the church is called to be a community dependent on the wisdom of the elders; therefore the church, when it is church, inevitably stands in tension with the culture of modernity. Theologians, as those who are charged with the task of helping us live more faithful lives through serious intellectual engagement, must learn to receive the wisdom of the elders, the wisdom of Anna and Simeon. Theologians must learn to fix their gaze rightly if they are to offer us some help in dying-into-life.

Perhaps the first task is reflection on the significance of the absence of cruciform stories and cruciform practices. Theologians whose gaze is rightly fixed can help us see how modernity requires aging individuals—all of us—to shed the garment of our physical selves, to set aside what it would label the distorting lens of each of our particular experiences of aging, and to hold fleeting thoughts steady. Modernity would require us to relinquish the features of a weathered face, the remembered touch of a cool, small hand, or leave out the pathos of someone's tale of hardship or her laughter of having come through life's travails, all in order to "manage" aging, to conquer death. Theologians whose gaze is rightly fixed can expose how impoverished is modernity's story of self-determination, autonomous rationality, and productivity. Such a story can only name aging a burden; the language of aging in modernity's story can only be the language of crisis.

Theologians whose gaze is rightly fixed can juxtapose this language of the crisis of aging to the language and grammar of the Christian tradition and the practices of the Christian community. An account of aging, accommodated to neither the economists nor the sociologists, but shaped rather by the story of Christ, can provide that which is genuinely needed to sustain the gift of a long life, namely, meaning, solace, celebration, and challenge. So it is that we embrace the hope glimpsed by Anna and Simeon when we participate in worship, when we see worship as a site for reclaiming the storied truth that all of us—from the very youngest to the very oldest—are creatures made in the image and likeness of God, destined for communion with God and worthy of participation in the praise of God. To see worship in this manner is to embrace the notion that personhood is not circumscribed by memory, mental activity, or the *mind in isolation from* other faculties or other people! The work of God's people is not only the task of the elderly; it is also on behalf of the elderly. For example, when persons suffering dementia in old age forget all that they know and all who know them, those surrounding them do not forget. Those surrounding them, the Christian community, are called to remember for them; we are called to narrate each other's lives faithfully, grateful that, while we may forget God, God in Jesus does not forget us. This is the truth we must learn to receive.

> In old age they still produce fruit;
>> they are always green and full of sap,
> showing that the LORD is upright;
>> he is my rock, and there is no unrighteousness in him.
>> (Psalm 92:14-15)

NOTES

1. Much of the substance as well as many of the particulars of this essay were initially penned for "Modernity: The Social Construction of Aging," a chapter in a forthcoming book, *Growing Old in Christ,* edited by Stanley Hauerwas, Keith Meador, David Cloutier, and Carole Bailey Stoneking. This collection, particularly Part 3, which focuses on constructive practices of Christian aging, would serve well the audience of this handbook.

2. This traditional positivist approach has been increasingly challenged in recent years. See, for example, Manheimer (1989) and Birren and Benston (1988).

3. Our culture imposes its hostility toward physical decline with particular vengeance on women. See Susan Sontag (1979).

4. It might be said that Trollope anticipated our society's capacity to legitimize Jack Kevorkian.

5. The phrase is borrowed from the title of a short story by Eudora Welty. See *The Collected Stories of Eudora Welty* (New York: Harcourt Brace Jovanovich, 1980).

6. That Bunyan treats Christiana at all can be contrasted to classical and medieval writers who restricted their reflections upon the journey of life to men only; but Bunyan does not break with tradition in his presentation of chastity as the primary female virtue and sexual misconduct as the characteristic female sin. Since patriarchal portrayals of female frailty and subordination have been well documented by liberal feminist scholars, it is more intriguing at this point to note that Bunyan's treatment of Christiana is in at least one other significant way more traditional then his treatment of Christian. In medieval versions the male hero's journey through the stages of the spirit took him through the stages of life as well. A faithful journey also meant enduring the ravages of time and the body's vicissitudes. Yet it is Christiana whose body ages; it is Christiana whose aging body remains the symbol of earthly imperfection; it is Christiana of whose death we are told, a death which takes place in the warmth and security of a Christian community.

7. There is significant difference between dying in hope and hoping for death. Hoping for one's own death can be a sign of despair, precisely the opposite of Christian hope. Nor does Simeon's hope appear to be rooted in a Stoic resolution. Simeon's hope is grounded in redemption.

BIBLIOGRAPHY

Birren, J. E., and V. L. Benston, eds. (1988). *Emergent Theories of Aging*. New York: Springer.

Bunyan, J. (1684/1965). *Pilgrim's Progress*, Part 2. Ed. Roger Sharrock. Harmondsworth, Eng.: Penguin.

Cole, T. R. (1992). *The Journey of Life: A Cultural History of Aging in America*. Cambridge, Eng.: Cambridge University Press.

Hauerwas, S. (1988). *Christian Existence Today*. Durham, N.C.: Labyrinth.

Hauerwas, S., K. Meador, D. Cloutier, and C. B. Stoneking, eds. (forthcoming). *Growing Old in Christ*. Grand Rapids, Mich.: Eerdmans.

Hauerwas, S., and L. Yordy (forthcoming). "Friendship and Aging," In Hauerwas et al., *Growing Old*.

Jacobs, R. H. (1991). "Becoming Sixty." In Martz, 125.

Kaplan, S. (March/April 1987). "The New Generation Gap: The Politics of Generational Justice." *Common Cause* 13: 13–15.

Manheimer, R. J. (1989). "The Narrative Quest in Humanistic Gerontology." *Journal of Aging Studies* 3/3: 231–52.

Martz, S. H. ed. (1991). *When I Am an Old Woman, I Shall Wear Purple*. Watsonville, Calif.: Papier-Maché.

MacIntyre, A. (1984). *After Virtue*. South Bend, Ind.: University of Notre Dame Press.

Moody, H. R. (1988). *Abundance of Life: Human Development Policies for an Aging Society*. New York: Columbia University Press.

Nouwen, H., and W. J. Gaffney (1974). *Aging: The Fulfillment of Life*. New York: Doubleday.

Percy, W. (1975). *The Message in the Bottle: How Queer Man Is, How Queer Language Is, and What One Has to Do with the Other*. New York: Farrar, Straus, and Giroux.

Pinches, C. (forthcoming). "The Virtues of Aging." In Hauerwas et al., *Growing Old*.

Scott-Maxwell, F. (1968). *The Measure of My Days*. New York: Knopf.

Sontag, S. (1979). "The Double Standard of Aging." In Williams, 462–78.

Stoneking, C. B. (forthcoming). "Modernity: the Social Construction of Aging." In Hauerwas et al., *Growing Old*.

Trollope, A. (1882/1990). *The Fixed Period: A Novel*. Ed. R. H. Super. Ann Arbor: University of Michigan Press.

Troyansky, D. (1989). *Old Age in the Old Regime*. Ithaca, N.Y.: Cornell University Press.

Tyler, A. (1995). *Ladder of Years*. New York: Knopf.

Welty, E. (1980). *The Collected Stories of Eudora Welty*. New York: Harcourt Brace Jovanovich.

Williams, J. H. (1979). *Psychology of Women: Selected Readings*. New York: W. W. Norton.

23 Rowing toward the Creator: Eschatology and Aging

PAUL R. SPONHEIM

As Christians live toward the ending of their lives, they may repair for perspective to the claims their faith makes about "last things"—to eschatology. Christians do make claims about "the end." They are not alone in this. There are, of course, other moves that are made by human beings caught in the grip of time. Perhaps many non-Western voices may be inclined to locate themselves in a more "vertical" transcendence of time. Through myth and ritual the worshiper "escapes from historical time" and returns to whatever Eden his faith offers (Eliade 1960, 34–38). Indeed, even such a Euro-American movement as existentialism held out a time-transcending encounter with the eternal (Bultmann 1957, 155; Moltmann 1996, 13–22). For the most part, however, post-Enlightenment people, living in a period and place marked by the "discovery" (Toulmin and Goodfield 1965) or "rediscovery" (Prigogine and Stengers 1984) of time, look to the "end." Perhaps it is too much to speak of the "ultimate" significance of time (Griffin 1986), but we do live with the strong sense that we are "timeful" creatures. We live toward and look to the end.

It is not only believers who do so. In the last century atheist Ernst Bloch in *The Principle of Hope* could devote more than 1,400 pages to looking to the end. The scope of Bloch's vision was vast, as he drew together material from music (e.g., *Symphonie Fantastique* and funeral marches), religion (e.g., astral myths, Nirvana, exodus, and resurrection), and philosophy (e.g., Hegel's phenomenology and Marx, "the true architect"), among other fields (Bloch 1986). On the specifically American scene Catherine Keller (1996) has noted Bloch's sense of "temporal depth" by which hope "cannot be reduced to a subjective emotion" but "has a kind of ontological status" (122). There is power here, and ambiguity as Keller notes how popular culture "offers a cornucopia of apocalypses," citing sources ranging from Hollywood to Washington, D.C., to Waco (3–5). We live with a "sense of ending" (Kermode 1968). Ernest Becker's (1973) classic work *The Denial of Death* noted that "the irony of man's condition is that the deepest need is to be free of the anxiety of death and annihilation; but it is life itself which awakens it, and so we must shrink from being fully alive" (66). But if we cannot deny death, we will somehow take the end into our hands—perhaps violently.

Perhaps this looking to the end has been intensified more keenly in the last century and a half. We are not merely children of René Descartes and John Locke; we are descendants of Darwin. Charles Darwin published his monumental work *On the Origin of Species* in 1859, and the consciousness of the evolutionary character of life has steadily penetrated the popular mind. Yet putting a question to the many who acknowledge or emphasize the significance of evolution elicits disparate answers. Things are on the move, but where are they headed? We look to the end, but shall we do so with hope or with fear? Traditional religious teaching about the end combines symbols of doom and deliverance, of judgment and joy (Miller 2000). Darwin's discovery, deepened by more recent work in genetics and molecular biology, carries something of the same ambiguity. Shall we exult in evolution's ascent—say, the promise of stem-cell research to banish disease? Or shall we settle grimly back in a reductive naturalism, recognizing that nothing beyond "natural" selection guides the evolutionary process? We have such questions as we look to, even as we live toward, the end. Christian claims provide perspective in that looking. I will write briefly of seeing the end as terminus and telos and more fully of the hope that claims end as advent.

END AS TERMINUS: LIFE DEFINED

We look to the end as defining the meaning of our lives. Martin Heidegger was wont to speak of "being toward death." Human beings seek to realize some wholeness in their lives. That quest typically takes a temporal form, as Robert Jenson has noted: "Human life is possible—or, in recent jargon, meaningful—only if past and future are somehow bracketed, only if their disconnection is somehow transcended, only if our lives somehow cohere to make a story" (Jenson 1984, 87). Death holds out promise for such questers. After all, as long as we still are alive "something is always still outstanding, what it can and will be" (Heidegger 1962, 215–16). In our dying we are summed up, and the identity of our living is revealed. So do we look to the end as terminus in living toward death, for we recognize that only then will our life story be complete.

There is wisdom in this, wisdom that Christian faith can affirm. In a culture where considerable effort is devoted to suppressing the realization that we will die (Mitford 1963; Moltmann 1996, 49–51), it is to be hoped that in "numbering our days" we may get a heart of wisdom (Ps. 90:12, RSV). God's creation provides us with ample opportunity for such timely attentiveness. Alfred North Whitehead (1929) offers a cosmological sketch shot through with "perpetual perishing": "The past fades . . . the present fact has not the past fact with it in any full immediacy" (340). More specifically, even (especially) the very best moments in human life are fleetingly momentary. In the honest recognition of such daily dying there can be preparation for the defining last death. "In the midst of life we are in death" (The Protestant Episcopal Church 1976, 332), marking us as finite and anticipating the final closure that completes our living. Older folks may sense this most keenly as they increasingly experience the loss of friends and associates.

The end as terminus does not call the individual to passivity. Before we die, the story of our lives is not complete but is being written. And part of the writing may well be the anticipatory gathering up of the chapters of the past into a vision of the future whole. Mel Kimble (1995) has written of the task of "life review" as a process of scanning and reclaiming the past. As Christians engage in such a process their faith comes into play as the felt need for a forgiving and healing God. In that faith it becomes possible to say with creational wisdom, "It is enough," and, "For all that has been, thanks" (Hammarskjøld 1965, 89). And yet such acceptance, while wise, seems insufficient. What of the infants who died tragically without "enough"? What of those whose lives offer mainly the plot line of undeserved suffering? And can the older person close his eyes in peace when he ponders the perils and predicaments sure to confront those younger ones whom he loves and now leaves?

Perhaps the ability to accept one's finitude indirectly reflects recognition that there is One who does not die. It is faith in that God that leads the believer to speak of the end with additional sentences. If the God who does not die is the Creator, may one hope for an end in which there is healing and flowering for those who did not live fully? Could the End reveal the Advent of a life that is truly new? And short of that, can the believer place anything in the hands of that God who does not die? In our passing can we pass on something of genuine value?

END AS TELOS: LIFE PASSED ON

Looking to the end as terminus gives the individual some measure of peace in anticipating the self finding the identity death brings in completing life. But our lives reach out beyond themselves. We can, of course, deny or ignore this connectedness. But then one may doubt that the self-defining death will be received as the gift it is. Indeed, Jürgen Moltmann (1996) may be right that it is "the reduction of the consciousness to individual awareness, and the concentration of individual awareness on one's own life, which makes death so frighteningly 'the end of it all'" (51). It need not be so. Perhaps in life review the older person finds herself reaching back before birth to ponder her span of years in the context of ancestral rhythms. And perhaps that backward movement is connected with a looking ahead, to passing life on. Moltmann (1996) has put the connection strongly: "Because individualized men and women know no life before birth in their ancestors, they know no life after death in their children either" (51).

But it need not be so. End may be looked on as telos, with the last years understood as passing life on to those who follow. Students of the later years have seen this. Erik Erikson emphasized the development of a sense of autonomy and initiative in the early stages of life leading to a generativity in mature adulthood. He appropriated the Hindu notion of "maintenance of the world" to speak of involvement in "what one truly cares for" (Erikson, Erikson, and Kivnick 1986, 50). But he saw generativity giving way to the wisdom of integrity in the final stage of life.

Thus he called for a "truly involved disinvolvement," lest one get stuck in an emphasis on procreativity or productivity.

Christian faith can frame this transition as a telos in which faith recognizes creatureliness and affirms finitude, while giving what one can to those who will follow. Robert Rubenstein (1994) has written of the "ambiguous" relationship between generativity and narcissism in Erikson's thought (171–73). Such a judgment may understate the difficulty if one is looking for the self in the pool of American culture and seeing the image of an autonomous and self-reliant entity. But what if faith sees the self as essentially connected with the other(s)? Faith knows the ecological wisdom of the Creator and trusts the Creator working still (John 5:17) with "a tender care that nothing be lost" (Whitehead 1929, 346). In that trust there is the courage to find genuine fulfillment, believing one's life will reach its telos through the providential care of the God who does not die. In one's living and in one's dying one gives to those who will follow. A striking illustration is the matter of intercessory prayer. The nursing-home grandmother finds herself physically "disinvolved" perhaps, but she prays fervently trusting that God will use the energy of her entreaties as "new stuff for the weaving" that lies beyond her reach both now and later (Suchocki 1996, 46).

Such creational wisdom counters the human arrogance that would build an earthly fortress against the night. Moltmann (1999) has written of the need to critique the "progressive syndrome" that looks to a secular "end of history," as in a "globalized and totalized capitalism" following the collapse of communism (194–96). Against such "brave new worlds" creational faith finds a telos more humble than heroic: in our passing we pass life on. Thus Sharon Betcher, theologian and midlife amputee, hails "the ironic divine potency of humility" as her disabled body "dissents from our culture's infatuation with the technological sublime" (2000, 97). And as we grow older most of us know something of disability, but the Spirit grants us the breath (*pneuma*) "to affirm finitude while averting finality. Finitude without end" (Keller 1996, 274). But still we ask: Is this sufficient? May there be more?

INTERLUDE

With or without, faith individuals may find it possible to accept with some equanimity their personal ending in death. Keller and Betcher plead eloquently against formulations that rage against finitude. The evident wisdom of recognizing and accepting finitude is more readily available to the individual who can look to his personal end as life-defining terminus or life-passing telos. Faith in God can support such a perspective. Why should we ask for more?

Such asking arises as we consider our social connectedness. The octogenarian who seems prepared to close his eyes a final time after a reasonably happy and healthy life may be roused to concerned wakefulness by thinking of "the others." Helmut Peukert (1984) puts the point thusly:

> This generation has inherited everything from the past generations and lives on what they have paid for. The exploited are no longer living among them, but are in the past, those who have gone before them. The happiness of the living exists in the expropriation of the dead. Is happiness at all conceivable under these presuppositions? Is it not the presupposition of happiness that the unhappiness of those who went before is simply forgotten? Is amnesia, the utter loss of historical memory, the presupposition of happy consciousness? (69)

One need not dwell on whatever sense of personal guilt may be evoked in resistance to such amnesia. The issue is the claim on life held by the many who have lived all too briefly or suffered far too much. Moreover, one may well extend the satisfaction-disturbing reflection by referencing not merely other human beings but also all the suffering experienced by other forms of life. Any anthropocentrism of the octogenarian may well be challenged by the question, Did all this happen so that I can close a comfortable life by dying quietly in my sleep? Does the "whole creation groaning" (Rom. 8:22) make no difference?

Such questions are intensified for the person of faith. If faith assigns to God some major responsibility for the creation and maintenance of life, then surely God is "in the dock" in the face of the suffering and death that surround us at every hand. Furthermore, even the believer who sees her death closing a good finite life may ask for more. She sings "Abide with me, fast falls the eventide," reaching for some hope in the faithful presence of One who does not die. Rightly so, for her faith is in God the Creator. As creator, God surely has some responsibility for the suffering embedded deeply in the world's living and dying. As creator, God holds out the promise of "doing a new thing" (Isa. 43:19) for this world beyond this world. Thus Hans Weder (2000) can write of how "finitude is a positive presupposition for an eternal life that is created afresh by the same creator who has created the finite one" (193). I mentioned above how the person of faith looks to the end as terminus and telos as he "rows toward God," who does not die. But if that God not only lives but creates life, may it be that what we look to is not so much the ending of life as it is the coming of God (Moltmann 1996, xi)?

END AS ADVENT: NEW LIFE

What Would We Do (if It Were True)?

If we start from where we are, what changes are needed? Let us try to fill out the concept of this advent of life. Clearly the life at and/or beyond the end must be truly new—different. If death is given with finitude, a life that would not know death would surely be different. But simply to be granted unending life of the same highly mixed quality we now know would not meet our need. Perhaps much of the physical suffering we now know is connected with conditions in the natural world that are part of the "package deal" (Polkinghorne 1994, 45) entailed in a universe where creatures are granted freedom by the Creator. If those physical sufferings are to be no more, freedom must also come to an end. Moreover, the human moral evil that creates genuine victims is to be traced to a misuse of that same freedom. Putting matters in the terms of the biblical creation myth, we can see that it will not do simply to return to Eden with its possibility (probability?) of continuing cycles of fall and renewal. In sum: as we ponder our condition we come to see that for moral reasons a metaphysical change is needed. This life must be new.

Another way to speak of this newness is to look to transcending the sense of limitation or separation that seems to follow from our finitude. Marjorie Suchocki (1988) has stretched to picture this: "One could envisage then a multiple transcendence of personality in God: first transcendence of seriality into the fullness of the self; second, a transcendence of selfhood through mutuality of feeling with all other selves and occasions; and third and most deeply, a transcendence of selves into the Selfhood of God" (108). Again, such a life would truly be different, not just "more of the same."

Yet clearly that new life will need to carry some continuity, some "sameness," in relation to the old. Otherwise how could it truly be "our" life? The promise of a new heaven and a new earth brings us beyond Eden, but the language of earth and sky carries needed continuity. Other elements of continuity calling for recognition would include something like space-time. Embodiment, so essential to human life, speaks of spatial reality, and personal agency suggests some kind of time. The fundamental fact that human life is life in relationship again argues for something like space-time as needed for the reconciliation with others (Volf 2000, 268–69, 275). In the claim for continuity we not only recognize the gift that the new is for us; we face the reality that our choices in this life have some bearing for that future. It is this concern for continuity and care of the present life which should chasten us from overplaying the contrast caught up in advent. Thus W. Paul Jones (1987) may skate near error in describing advent as "a process of interpolation from the future to the present" (17). If the God of the future is the creator God, then the one who comes is none other than the omniactive God before whom we presently "live and move and have our being" (Acts 17:28).

Some such delicate combination of discontinuity and continuity does indeed seem to be what Christian faith stretches to see. The Bible's last book stands on tiptoe to speak of the day when "death [the "last enemy," 1 Cor. 15:26] will be no more; mourning and crying and pain will be no more" (Rev. 21:4). That is new enough; indeed, "the first things have passed away" (Rev. 21:4). And if in their later years Christians know all too well of the limitations given with finitude, they hear a new word when they hear "God himself will be with them" (Rev. 21:3). Older folks know painfully well that their participation in the life of God is now partial, and it comes as genuine news to be told that "when the complete comes, the partial will come to an end" (1 Cor. 13:10). That life will be different . . . as surely as to see "face to face" is not to "see in a mirror dimly." And yet clearly these promises of the new are spoken to persons who yet live here as words of promise that they will live there. That is why when Christians gather for funerals, one often hears read John 14:2: "I go to prepare a place for you."

Little wonder that when in 2000 a group of scientists and theologians emerged from a three-year study process on *The End of the World and the Ends of God* (Polkinghorne and Welker 2000), they said this:

> The strongest theme to emerge from all our discussion . . . is the need to wrestle with the necessity for both continuity and discontinuity. . . . Too great an element of discontinuity would threaten the trust that it is "Abraham, Isaac, and Jacob" (and not some new persons bearing those names) who live with God. It must be that each generation will attain to fulfillment, never merely serving as a stepping stone to the future of others, and that those whose lives have been cut short by oppression and violence receive what was denied to them on earth. Yet too great an element of continuity would threaten belief in the new creation, redeemed from the old creation's bondage to death and decay. (12)

In such wrestling a new question emerges: Is this claim true? In answering yes, two tasks challenge us: first, to show that such discontinuity and continuity can be coherently integrated in principle so that we are not talking about a contradiction in terms and, second, to offer what "evidence" can be mustered for the claim that this coherent concept will correspond to something real.

Jürgen Moltmann (1996) tackles the first task. He notes how that "even in this life before death, we experience the Spirit of life as the wide space in which there is no more cramping" and "as the power of divine hope which leaves us time, because it gives us future" (118). And so he concludes: "That eternal life gives the broken and the impaired and those whose lives have been destroyed space and time and strength to live the life which they were intended for, and for which they were born" (118). The sentences strain to convey their meaning. Perhaps poetry has better range to serve us. Ford Madox Ford (1936, 15) wrote "On Heaven" to "V. H.," who asked for a working heaven." Among his lines were these:

> So it is, so it goes, in this beloved place,
> There shall be never a grief but passes; not, not any;
> There shall be such bright light and no blindness;
> There shall be so little awe and so much loving-kindness;
> There shall be a little longing and enough care,
> There shall be a little labour and enough of toil
> To bring back the lost flavour of our human coil;
> Not enough to taint it;
> And all that we desire shall prove as fair as we can paint it.
> For, though that may be the very hardest trick of all
> God set Himself, who fashioned this goodly hall.
> Thus He has made Heaven;
> Even Heaven.

We may strain with Ford to ask when it is that God will wipe away every tear (Rev. 21:4), and we may pause over proposals to employ "a suitably demythologized concept of purgatory" as a transitional category (Polkinghorne 2000, 41; Moltmann 2000, 247–48). In any case, as Christians reflect on the relationships of the blessed Trinity and recall God the Creator finding the creation to be "good," "very good," we can move toward thinking "progressive movement and contentment together" (Volf 2000, 269), as did Gregory of Nyssa (Gregory of Nyssa 1987, 128). In such ways poets, philosophers, and church fathers help us to the sense that a coherent vision of the new life is possible. It could be true. But then perhaps the second question rises in us with new force: What evidence is there that the vision may be not only coherent but true?

Is there evidence to consider that does not depend on testimonies of explicitly religious faith? Voices from the natural sciences speak of alternative catastrophes so emphatically that it would seem the only "positive" use a theologian could make of their speaking is to say we are shown that the new world will not come to be through immanental, evolutionary development. It does seem a dark saying that eventually "just as surely as the sun has given us life and continues to do so, it will eventually ensure our demise" (Stoeger 2000, 24). Lest we should hurry to colonize other solar systems, we are further told that, from "all that we know about the evolution and dynamics of the observable universe and about the laws of nature that govern it, the universe itself will eventually evanesce or possibly collapse in a fiery conflagration" (Stoeger 2000, 27).

It is not in Christian faith's interest to dispute these highly likely cosmological forecasts. Ironically, it is more promising for faith to consider suggestions that the story of the universe is indeed one of radical change, such as the grim alternatives sketched. May it be that the contingency of natural occurrences such as genetic mutations is a signal of nature's "fundamental openness to new creation" (Haught 2000, 100)? May the astrophysically unpredictable generation of a star using old matter in a new structure offer a launching pad or, better, a connection point for theological reflection about the future (Weder 2000, 188)? It is important to move with care at this point. Take the recently emerging emphasis on information as a concept needing recognition alongside such basic notions as mass and energy. What shall one make of this? It seems highly rash to offer an eschatological vision of the universe "offering an infinite amount of information in its final dying gasp" (Polkinghorne 2000, 33). In such a move the scientist (Tipler 1997, for example) seems to be wearing clerical garb. But it may be interesting for the theologian to consider how the patterning of information could provide needed continuity in a very different material embodiment (Polkinghorne 2000, 39).

Eulalio Baltazar is a theologian who has used the paleontological reflections of Teilhard de Chardin in such a way. He argues that it is mistaken to posit "time" as a single container, self-identical regardless of what happens "in" it. He notices the differences between the electronic and atomic, the organic and the human in terms of a decreasing contingency. In such steps he prepares himself to look toward a new time that could yield "activity without contingency" (Baltazar 1970, 119–25). Somewhat similarly, the great mathematician/philosopher Alfred North Whitehead (1927) tried to help us understand how time as "pure succession is an abstraction of the second order, a generic abstraction omitting the temporal character of time" (36). Time, it would seem, might differ significantly depending on the actual relationships from which it abstracts. It is well known that Whitehead was deeply concerned with the seemingly universal experience of "perpetual perishing." His quest for something more than "objective immortality" (here, end as telos) is clearest in the final part of his magnum opus, *Process and Reality* (1929), where he writes: "In the temporal world, it is the empirical fact that process entails loss: the past is present under an abstraction. But there is no reason, of any ultimate metaphysical generality, why this should be the whole story" (340).

Earlier Whitehead had written in *Religion in the Making* (1926) that his understanding of reality was "entirely neutral on the question of immortality," adding, "There is no reason why such a question should not be decided on more special evidence, religious or otherwise" (107). If we accept that invitation to enter the community of faith, what do we see? In the world of science there do seem to be intriguing connection points for the Christian theologian to consider appropriating as she fills out her faith's vision of the ultimate future. What about that vision itself? What reasons does the believer have to hold that this vision is true?

The central biblical witness at this point is surely to the resurrection—the resurrection of Jesus and the resurrection to which the believer looks in faith. The resurrection is prominently included in Paul's "short list" of matters of "first importance" (1 Cor. 15:3-8). Moreover, this teaching has such internal systematic importance that Paul argues that without a real resurrection Christian faith is "futile" and Christians "are of all people most to be pitied" (1 Cor. 15:12-19). Elsewhere Paul makes the connection explicit: "For if we have been united with him in a death like his, we will certainly be united with him in a resurrection like his" (Rom. 6:5).

This primary witness is clear. I think it is not particularly helpful for the Christian, turning outward, to try to "prove" this resurrection claim by reference to an empty tomb or resurrection appearances or the remarkable transformation of the disciples from timidity to courage. But it is interesting to note that the witnesses' description of the resurrected Jesus does nicely conform to the blend of continuity and discontinuity we arrived at in asking, "What would we do if it were true?" Michael Welker (2000) has put this well: "The pre-Easter person and the pre-Easter life here continue in a new way. . . . The pre-Easter Jesus is transcended and yet remains true to himself. The biological body is not restored. The biblical texts speak of a 'glorified' body or of a 'spiritual' body" (283).

Turning inward, it is important to note how the claim of resurrection is supported by the fabric of Christian faith more generally. This is well suggested by a key distinction. Jesus did not *rise* from the dead—he "*was raised* from the dead by the glory of the Father" (Rom. 6:4). The point here is God's commitment. On the

Christian reading of history, the plot line centers in a triune God who in love chooses to create an "other" and who will do what is needed to see that commitment through to completion. It is the creator God who is at work in the resurrection. On Easter the Christian theologian does not find himself appealing to an arbitrary interruption "from" the future. The surprise of resurrection is precisely what we might expect from a God who does new things . . . in creation, in incarnation, in resurrection.

What Two or Three Questions Press for Consideration in Filling Out This Claim?

Many Christians ask, What happens to us when we die? Perhaps it is wise not to try to say too much in responding to this question, for some of our surest knowing in this is to know that we do not know finally or fully. But we can appropriately frame a response by ruling out certain options and then orienting ourselves in a direction between these "ditches." The extreme views we do not choose to follow would say that at death, as it were, either we are simply gone, dead altogether, or we are "home free." In choosing to reject these positions I do not mean to reject the element of truth in each of them. The "dead altogether" view attaches itself to the truth that the human person is a psychosomatic unity. That truth does need to be asserted, most notably against the opposite view that we are "home free" because we possess an essentially immortal soul that cannot die. In its most extreme expressions, this second view risks suggesting three errors: (a) that life after death is a statement about human capacity and (b) one that honors the essential individual now, (c) sloughing off the dross of materiality. Even so, this view does serve faith by challenging the first position's grim word that the individual's death is simply the end of the story.

What lies between these ditches? I have titled this chapter "Rowing toward the Creator," and the most helpful response to the "when we die" question is that we are indeed with God. This can be formulated variously. The image of soul-sleep serves this concern. Christ is "the first fruits of those who have fallen asleep" (1 Cor. 15:20). More abstractly, one may say the relation with God does not die, for God does not die when we do. Michael Welker (2000) puts it so: "If God is God, his relation to his human image cannot be destroyed, either through the antagonism and recalcitrance of human beings or through their death" (245). As such that does not seem to say much about the human side of the relationship, and perhaps more does need to be said. A strong motivation for saying more is the biblical witness that believers in this life "are surrounded by so great a cloud of witnesses" (Heb. 12:1). Moltmann (2000) makes this point well: "When in the worship of the Latin American base communities the names of 'the disappeared' and the martyrs are read out, the congregation responds with the cry, 'Presente.' They are present, and we sense our fellowship with them and their fellowship with us" (254). This is a helpfully communal emphasis and protects against the individualism of the "me and my immortal soul" view. Moreover, it coheres well with the conviction that any continuing life at death is incomplete until the "general" resurrection, when God is "all in all" (1 Cor. 15:20–28).

That brings up a second question: How universal can our hope be? Will God indeed be "all in all" or, as popular piety puts the question, Will everyone be saved? The Christian cannot answer this question by citing scripture. Or perhaps he can, but the thorough reader will find himself giving more than one answer. Arland Hultgren (1987) is helpfully candid in stating the difficulty, demonstrated most dramatically by the Pauline writings and the Gospel of John: "Paul envisions the redemption accomplished in Christ as effective for all humanity. . . .In the gospel of John it must be concluded that the world is lost; salvation is given only to those who hear the word of Jesus and believe in him" (179). There are strong theological tendencies embedded in these textual differences. Johannine dualism can appeal to the capacity of human beings in their freedom (or their bondage) to resist God, and such a choice surely cannot be without consequence. Pauline universalism, on the other hand, appeals to the capacity of a God who wills all to be saved (1 Tim. 2:4). As Langdon Gilkey (1976) puts it:

> However we argue, so long as there is a dual destiny, faith is a merit that saves—unless God has inscrutably chosen us above others (or perhaps he has not!). In either case, the width, efficacy and supremacy of the divine love is abrogated in favor of an ultimate partiality that contradicts the glory of that love, and the divine agape has as its own background an arbitrariness that abrogates the essential meaning of agape. (105)

So what are we to say to this? We can say at least three things. (a) We are not given the responsibility of deciding who has accepted God's call. Perhaps the person who goes to his deathbed cursing God protests too much, remembering all too keenly the stupidity or perversity of persons claiming to be God's servants. (b) We may need to recognize the "mixed bag" of our own responses to God's call. "I believe; help my unbelief" (Mark 9:24) and "I do not do the good I want, but the evil I do not want is what I do" (Rom. 7:19) may sum things up fairly well. (c) So finally we appeal to the mercy and dexterity of a God who has demonstrated the ability to make out of chaos something that is good, very good. Perhaps the biblical differences and theological strengths can be distributed in a process in which an always-loving God through judgment exercises mercy. Earlier I alluded to contemporary theological interest in a reappropriation of the notion of purgatory. The key point is that God be understood to be the lead actor on any such stage.

BUT HOW SHALL WE LIVE NOW?

We have come some considerable distance in our time with tour guides as we look to the end. Perhaps we have come too far. These visions of the absolute future and these appeals to divine mercy and dexterity may serve to distract us from the urgent reality of our present life. Sharon Betcher (2000) wisely warns us against the temptation to "theologize our frustration with dependence on the earth as a transcendent longing for elsewhere" (98). At the very least we must respond by asking how looking to the end as terminus, telos, and advent may affect our living even now up to the end.

I want to agree with Jürgen Moltmann (1996) when he writes:

> Jewish and Christian apocalypses speak to people in the terror of historical and cosmic catastrophes, but they do not talk like Cassandra; nor do they interpret humanity's crimes and cosmic catastrophes religiously, so that people may accept them, collaborate with them, or simply resign themselves to them. They awaken the *resistance of faith* and the *patience of hope*. They spread hope in danger, because in the human and cosmic end they proclaim God's new beginning. (203, emphasis his)

I want to make this testimony to the empowering work of hope in response to the challenge raised by Betcher and countless others. Yet I need to join many other people of faith in confessing that often it is not so. Death may seem the final dark reality. Hope's efficacy may only serve to diminish actual effort in this present life. In such times guilt joins death in constituting the nadir or zero point. Walter Brueggemann (2000) speaks of this as the "*nullpunkt*" for Israel. What was Israel—what are we—to do? Two things, says Brueggemann—to *relinquish* what is gone and to *receive* "what is inexplicably and inscrutably given" (145, emphasis his).

The older person can make this double movement. There is much for that person to give up—including perhaps certain perfectionist projects for this life and projections for the next. The Christian can do this because she believes that the God who does not die did go through death for a needy creation. And that Christian can receive what is given because she knows that death did not defeat that God. In this receiving there is the present-tense experience of a quality of life that holds a promise beyond the grave. Thus the writer of John's Gospel can speak of how the one who hears and believes "has" eternal life, "has passed from death to life" (5:24). In this quality there is what A. N. Whitehead (1926) called peace. This is not a state of anesthesia (which Betcher rightly fears), for "it is a positive feeling which crowns the 'life and motion' of the soul" (285).

Christians can look to the end as terminus, telos, and advent. But actually, as they row toward the end Christians find themselves looking to the God of beginnings, the Creator. And so, when strength fails, they may find themselves placing their oars at rest. The current seems to carry them forward quite nicely. And they can imagine some day singing a new song:

> You are worthy, our Lord and God,
> To receive glory and honor and power,
> For you created all things,
> And by your will they existed and were created.
> (Rev. 4:11)

BIBLIOGRAPHY

Baltazar, E. (1970). *God within Process.* Paramus, N.J.: Newman.

Becker, E. (1973). *The Denial of Death.* New York: Free Press.

Betcher, S.V. (2000). "Wisdom to Make the World Go On: On Disability and the Cultural Delegitimation of Suffering." In Fretheim and Thompson, 87–98.

Bloch, E. (1986). *The Principle of Hope.* Cambridge: MIT Press.

Braaten, C. E., and R.W. Jenson, eds. (1984). *Christian Dogmatics.* Vol. 2. Philadelphia: Fortress Press.

Brueggemann, W. (2000). "Faith at the *Nullpunkt.*" In Polkinghorne and Welker, 143–54.

Bultmann, R. (1957). *History and Eschatology.* New York: Harper.

Eliade, M. (1960). *Myths, Dreams and Mysteries: The Encounter between Contemporary Faiths and Archaic Realities.* London: Harvill.

Erikson, E., J. Erikson, and H. Kivnick (1986). *Vital Involvement in Old Age: The Experience of Old Age in Our Time.* New York: W. W. Norton.

Farley, M. A., and S. Jones, eds. (1999). *Liberating Eschatology: Essays in Honor of Letty M. Russell.* Louisville: Westminster John Knox.

Ford, F. M. (1936). "On Heaven." In *Collected Poems.* 3–17. New York: Oxford University Press.

Fretheim, T. E., and C. L. Thompson, eds. (2000). *God, Evil and Suffering: Essays in Honor of Paul R. Sponheim.* St. Paul: Word and World.

Gilkey, L. (1976). *Reaping the Whirlwind: A Christian Interpretation of History.* New York: Seabury.

Gregory of Nyssa (1987). *Song of Songs.* Brookline, Mass.: Hellenistic College Press.

Griffin, D., ed. (1986). *Physics and the Ultimate Significance of Time.* New York: State University of New York Press.

Hammarskjøld, D. (1965). *Markings.* New York: Knopf.

Haught, J. F. (2000). *God after Darwin: A Theology of Evolution.* Boulder, Colo.: Westview.

Heidegger, M. (1962). *Being and Time.* New York: Harper.

Hultgren, A. (1987). *Christ and His Benefits: Christology and Redemption in the New Testament.* Philadelphia: Fortress Press.

Jenson, R. (1984). "The Triune God." In Braaten and Jenson, 79–191.

Jones, W. P. (1987). "Theology and Aging in the Twenty-first Century." In Oliver, 17–32.

Keller, C. (1996). *Apocalypse Now and Then: A Feminist Guide to the End of the World.* Boston: Beacon.

Kermode, F. (1968). *Continuities.* London: Routledge & K. Paul.

Kimble, M. A. (1995). "Pastoral Care." In Kimble et al., 131–47.

Kimble, M. A., S. H. McFadden, J. W. Ellor, and J. J. Seeber, eds. (1995). *Aging, Spirituality, and Religion: A Handbook.* Vol. 1. Minneapolis: Fortress Press.

Miller, P. D. (2000). "Judgment and Joy." In Polkinghorne and Welker, 155–70.

Mitford, J. (1963). *The American Way of Death.* New York: Simon & Schuster.

Moltmann, J. (2000). "Is There Life after Death?" In Polkinghorne and Welker, 238–55.

——— (1999). "Liberating and Anticipating the Future." In Farley and Jones, 189–208.

——— (1996). *The Coming of God: Christian Eschatology.* Minneapolis: Fortress Press.

Oliver, D. B., ed. (1987). *New Directions in Religion and Aging.* New York: Haworth.

Peukert, H. (1984). *Science, Action and Fundamental Theology: Toward a Theology of Communicative Action.* Cambridge: MIT Press.

Polkinghorne, J. (2000). "Eschatology: Some Questions and Some Insights from Science." In Polkinghorne and Welker, 29–41.

——— (1994). *Quarks, Chaos and Christianity.* London: Triangle.

Polkinghorne, J., and M. Welker, eds. (2000). *The End of the World and the Ends of God: Science and Theology on Eschatology.* Harrisburg, Pa.: Trinity Press International.

Prigogine, I., and I. Stengers (1984). *Order out of Chaos.* London: Heinemann.

The Protestant Episcopal Church (1976). *Book of Common Prayer.* New York: Seabury.

Rubenstein, R. R. (1994). "Generativity as Pragmatic Spirituality." In Thomas and Eisenhandler, 169–82.

Stoeger, W. R. (2000). "Scientific Accounts of Ultimate Catastrophes in Our Life-Bearing Universe." In Polkinghorne and Welker, 19–28.

Suchocki, M. (1996). *In God's Presence: Theological Reflections on Prayer.* St. Louis, Mo.: Chalice.

——— (1988). *The End of Evil.* Albany: State University of New York Press.

Thomas, L. E., and S. A. Eisenhandler, eds. (1994). *Aging and the Religious Dimension.* Westport, Conn.: Auburn.

Tipler, F. (1997). *The Physics of Immortality: Modern Cosmology, God, and the Resurrection of the Dead.* New York: Doubleday.

Toulmin, S., and J. Goodfield (1965). *The Discovery of Time.* New York: Harper.

Volf, M. (2000). "Enter into Joy! Sin, Death, and the Life of the World to Come." In Polkinghorne and Welker, 256–78.

Weder, H. (2000). "Hope and Creation." In Polkinghorne and Welker, 184–202.

Welker, M. (2000). "Resurrection and Eternal Life: The Canonic Memory of the Resurrected Christ, His Reality, and His Glory." In Polkinghorne and Welker, 279–90.

Whitehead, A. N. (1933). *Adventures of Ideas.* New York: Macmillan.

——— (1929). *Process and Reality: An Essay in Cosmology.* New York: Macmillan.

——— (1927). *Symbolism: Its Meaning and Effect.* New York: Macmillan.

——— (1926). *Religion in the Making.* New York: Macmillan.

24

The Theological View of Aging that Permeates the African American Experience

RICHARD M. WALLACE

The young lions suffer want and hunger,
 but those who seek the LORD
  lack no good thing. (Ps. 34:10)

This passage of Scripture appears to challenge some of the cultural assumptions about growing old. Implicit is the notion that what one loses as a result of the aging process is more than compensated for by the wisdom that one gains. In fact, it could be argued that of the two, youth and wisdom, wisdom is the more valuable. Maya Angelou expresses this another way in her description of the values of rural African Americans when she says, "Age has more worth than wealth" (Angelou 1993a, 65). This is perhaps what Temba Mafico (1997), a Zimbabwean, is also alluding to when he recalls the lessons he learned at the beginning of his pastoral ministry.

When I became a pastor at a very early age, I was asked to chair a meeting at which everyone was older than I. Though I had the knowledge to run the church and had received more schooling than my church members, I did not have as much experience of life as they had. One elderly man with whom I was disagreeing touched his gray hair and told me that he was "not gray as a joke." In other words, I was arguing from what I had learned, whereas the elder was arguing from tested knowledge acquired through experience (Wimberly 1997, 28).

This is especially true when knowledge is gained from the experience of relying on something other than oneself—something other than one's own strength or power.

Upon reflecting upon aging in the African American experience, it is almost impossible to distinguish the inherent theological perspective in this passage from a given datum about African American cultural identity that the elders are a communal treasure from God. They are the community's custodians of hope, for they have sought the Lord.

This is particularly evident in the song "We've Come This Far by Faith," from the genre of African American music known as gospel. Without the living witness of the elders, there is no possibility of singing "We've Come This Far by Faith." We know what God is capable of doing in the present and the unknown future, by hearing through the living witness of the elders what God has done.

In her book *The Spirit of Intimacy,* Sobonfu E. Somé, a woman from the Dagara people of Western Africa, offers a slightly different insight. In describing the various ways that the capacity for developing intimate relationships is dependent on the wisdom of the elders, she demonstrates how the wisdom of the elders belongs to the entire community. In recounting her initiation experience, she writes, "I particularly enjoyed the frankness and openness between the youth and adults—especially the elders. They did not hide anything from us. They talked to us about their own experience, the kinds of difficulties they encountered in their own intimate lives, and how they were able to overcome them" (Somé 1997, 73). Accordingly, the wisdom of the elders is the inheritance of hope for the next generation, held in community trust. Similarly, Anne Streaty Wimberly identifies the elders as "repositories of wisdom" (Wimberly 1997, 8).

VICTIMIZED BY THE ARROGANCE OF THE PRESENT

Perhaps when we consider all the internalized pathologies that plague the contemporary African American community, we may attribute them to the arrogance of the present. We are victimized by the arrogance of the present when the community, severed from the living witness of the elders, defines itself solely in terms of its present reality. This is conceivably what is at the bottom of what Cornel West is delineating in his definition of nihilism.

> Nihilism is to be understood here not as a philosophic doctrine that there are no rational grounds for legitimate standards or authority; it is, far more, the lived experience of coping with a life of horrifying meaninglessness, hopelessness, and (most importantly) lovelessness. The frightening result is a numbing detachment from others and a self-destructive disposition towards the world. Life without meaning, hope, and love breeds a coldhearted, mean-spirited outlook that destroys both the individual and others. . . . In fact, the major enemy of black survival in America has been and is neither oppression nor exploitation but rather the nihilistic threat—that is, loss of hope and absence of meaning. For as long hope remains and meaning is preserved, the possibility of overcoming oppression stays alive. The self-fulfilling prophecy of the nihilistic threat is that without hope there can be no future, that without meaning there can be no struggle. (West 1993, 22)

As a result of being severed from the living witnesses of hope—the elders—the community is ripe for the nihilistic threat. This severing is epitomized in the actions of the young African American male who broke into the home of Rosa Parks, the respected elder from the civil rights era, and assaulted and robbed her. At one level it is disturbing because he either did not know or did not care whose home he was breaking into. Yet, at another level, the fact that he assaulted and robbed an eighty-one-year-old woman is profoundly more disturbing because Ms. Parks was not afforded respect by virtue of being an elder. In effect, the custodian of the community's hope, the mother of the civil rights movement, came to symbolize nothing to this young African American male but an object, a thing. One of the ironies is that this happens in a community for which respect and valuing of elders is constituent of its identity. In a sense it is the phenomenon of a community destroying its own hope.

Although it could be argued that the lack of respect for elders is a feature of the dominant culture, the fact that it happens in the contemporary African American culture is both inevitable and insidious. It is inevitable that African American culture could not remain exempt from the hegemony of the dominant culture. And it is insidious because the detrimental consequences are exacerbated for a community whose very survival has always depended upon the contribution of its elders. When one considers all the ways that elders have functioned in the African American community as surrogate parents, particularly now in the midst of the devastation wrought by crack and HIV/AIDS, this is not an exaggerated claim. This is consistent with a theological perspective that resides in the soil/soul of the African American culture—that the God who can make a way out of no way can even use those who, according to the prevailing cultural norm as a result of the aging process, have outlived their usefulness.

This view of aging in the African American community was forged from an encounter between the African American experience and the God who was revealed in the biblical drama. This is a God who is always working through the disenfranchised, the despised, the rejected, and the discarded. In fact, Paul's words in 1 Cor. 1:26-31 are theologically definitive for the African American community's experience with aging:

> Consider your call brothers and sisters; not many of you were wise by human standards, not many were powerful, not many were of noble birth. But God chose what is foolish in the world to shame the wise; God chose what is weak in the world to shame the strong; God chose what is low and despised in the world, things that are not, to reduce to nothing things that are, so that no one might boast in the presence of God. He is the source of your life in Christ Jesus, who became for us wisdom from God, and righteousness and sanctification and redemption, in order that, as it is written, "let the one who boasts, boast in the Lord."

TRUE TO OUR GOD AND TO OUR NATIVE LAND

These closing words from the hymn "Lift Every Voice," by James Weldon Johnson, which is also known as the black national anthem, reflect the telos of the theological view of aging from the African American experience. First, the state of the elders in the African American community is a barometer of the relationship between God and the people of God, similar to the Old Testament prophets, who used the state of the widows and orphans in Israel as a barometer of the relationship.

Tangentially, an increase in the abuse and neglect of elders may be similar to the rising temperature in a thermometer that indicates the presence of an infection. The health of any community is directly correlated with the extent to which the neglect and abuse of its elders are tolerated, which in Israel's case reflected a warped relationship to the God of Israel. Somewhat similarly, for African Americans the neglect and abuse of the elders, which adversely affects the entire community, are further indicative of a distortion of a cosmology[1] where the gulf between the Creator and the created is considerably narrowed, and also where, according to Albert Raboteau, "elders are respected in part because they preserve the memory of the dead and are closer chronologically to the ancestors" (Raboteau 1980, 12). These ancestors, I might add, are closer to the Creator but are nevertheless still a vital part of the community. This clearly has the potential of ancestor worship, but the salient point is that dying does not sever one from the community, and the living still have access to the wisdom of those who have preceded them.

This in turn produces another approach to dying in that death is not feared as the end but instead is regarded as a transition to a new status. Molefe Asante alludes to this when he says, "Libations are still poured in some places in the American South as an indication of respect for 'those who are not with us,' and despite the Christian religion, much of African American religion is devoted to the idea of transition from life to death to life eternal" (Asante 1987, 100).

Interestingly enough from a medical and scientific perspective, one finds this theme being similarly articulated by Sherwin Nuland in *How We Die: Reflections on Life's Final Chapter*. In the concluding comments for the chapter "Doors to Death of the Aged," he says:

> Far from being irreplaceable, we should be replaced. Fantasies of staying the hand of mortality are incompatible with the best interest of our species and the continuity of humankind's progress. . . . Among living creatures, to die and leave the stage is the way of nature—old age is the preparation for departure, the gradual easing out of life that makes its ending more palatable not only for the elderly but for those also to whom they leave the world in trust. . . . I speak only of the useless vanity that lies in attempts to fend off the certainties that are necessary ingredients of the human condition. . . . When it is accepted that there are clearly defined limits to life then life will be seen to have a symmetry as well. (Nuland 1995, 86f.)

It could well be that this symmetry to life, which Nuland appeals to as a way we should approach the inevitability of death, is what Temba Mafico is describing in his partial appropriation of John Mbiti's work *African Religions and Philosophy* (Mbiti 1988):

> In the circular view, life events accentuate the rhythm of community life. The primary life events of birth, adolescent rites of passage, marriage and child rearing, and death are processes that connect members in the kinship circle. They also connect the living with the departed, or "living dead," who remain alive in the memories of surviving families.

Consequently, event A, the birth of a child, is the concern not simply of the immediate family but of everyone in the community including the elders and the living dead. The child owes its existence to the existence of the elders and the departed and is evidence of the circularity of life. (Mafico 1997, 24)

Characteristically speaking, what this means is that the aging process is not necessarily something that is bad or to be avoided. It is a natural process that can be embraced and may even be regarded as a victory of sorts.

In this regard, elders often pray, "Lord grant me three score and ten." To live to seventy years was itself a blessing and had its own victory. Whenever one reads the narratives of former African American slaves who were then in their eighties and nineties, particularly the ones interviewed by the "Federal Writers Project" and Fisk University,[2] it seems that their old age is itself a quiet act of defiance against all that was done against and to them. Obtaining old age is an embodiment of what Nicholas Cooper-Lewter and Henry Mitchell describe as a particular core belief of "Soul Theology"—the justice of God expressed in the proverb "What goes around comes around" (Cooper-Lewter and Mitchell 1986, 32).

Similarly, one may recall the elders in the church giving thanks that on that particular morning they awoke "clothed in their right mind," as acknowledging that the aging process that included senility was in God's hands. Even the humor that African American elders express, which is characteristic of the humor that has assisted the African American community in resisting the daily darts and arrows of racism, functions as a joyful affirmation in the face of the inevitability of the aging process with all of its aches, pains, and challenges. An example of this is the following anonymous exchange.

Pastor: How are you doing today, Mrs. Evans?
Mrs. Evans: Oh, Arthur's messing with me today.
Pastor: Who's Arthur and why is he messing with you today?
Mrs. Evans: Arthritis.

The intent is not to suggest that all African Americans approach death and the aging process this way but rather to suggest, as have Howard Thurman and Gayraud Wilmore (Thurman 1975; Wilmore 1998), that there resides within the collective psyche of African Americans a joy in spite of all that life can impose. In fact, Wilmore's words are so illustrative that they need to be cited in their entirety:

This is to say that an essential ingredient of black Christianity prior to the Civil War was the creative residuum of the African religions. The defining characteristic of that spirituality was its spontaneous fascination with, and unselfish response to, the reality of the spirit world and the intersection between that world and the world of objective reality. Such an ontology called for a release of the human spirit, the sacred vessel in which the vital forces of the universe coalesce, from every power—whether of humans or the gods—that would exercise unauthorized dominion over it. Those who profess such a religion cannot be bound by anyone or anything indefinitely. Freedom is intrinsic to its very nature. The African attitude literally created the image of the preexistent God in the free-dom of the religious imagination and opened human life to the influence of divinity that flowed out of history and the natural world. The liberation of the whole person—body, mind, and spirit—from every internal and external constraint not deliberately and pur-posely elected was the first requirement for one who would be possessed by the Spirit. God alone had the authority to command, to invoke life and death, blessing and cursing; alto-gether it is clear that God customarily exercised this power through many intermediaries. But the indispensable condition for life and human fulfillment in the religious and philo-sophical tradition of Africa was freedom—the untrammeled, unconditional freedom to *be,* to exist, and to express the power of being, fully and creatively, for sheer joy and profound meaning of *Muntu,* man in the genderless sense of basic humanity. (Wilmore 1998, 49f.)

This brings us to the second point, the latter portion of the closing words from the hymn "Lift Every Voice": "true to our native land." This is indicative of how the theological view of aging in the African American experience is rooted in Africa. Without engaging all of the arguments about the degree of African retentions among North American slaves, it is simply being asserted that respecting and valu-ing elders is a retention that did indeed survive the slave experience. About this par-ticular retention, Molefe Asante writes:

Perhaps the African American version is truncated by Christianity or Islam or some other non-African expression, but even in modified form we see how ancestral myths are a part of our communicative sense. . . . For example, the admonition frequently heard in south Georgia, "Call me like you gon' call me when I am dead," had as much imbedded conti-nuity as the passed down banjo or the hot irons used to press clothes. The elders find a connectedness with their past when they hear such a direct reference to the adoration given to the dead. However, beyond what appears to be metaphysical attachment is the continuation of practices that find their source in the traditions. (Asante, 1987, 99)

The reason the reflections of Molefe Asante, along with those of Wade Nobles and Asa Hilliard, are so interesting is that they appear to be proposing an "Afrocentric" aesthetic that attempts to redefine black culture relative to an antecedent place. Such an aesthetic counters a cultural relativism that would enslave black culture to the arrogance of the present. In lifting up respect and valuing of elders as one of the enduring values of African culture, these proponents are transmitting to the next generation the profound origins of a cultural practice that appears to have lost its etymology. This is to say that respecting and valuing the elders is indeed to remain true to the native land.

Again there is need to qualify this: I am not suggesting that respecting and valu-ing the elders is always the reality in either contemporary Africa or the African dias-pora but rather insisting that it is a specific communal orientation born out of what John Mbiti describes as "the cardinal point in the understanding of the African view of man [humanity]" (Mbiti 1988, 108), that is, "I am, because we are; and since we are, therefore I am." Similarly, as it takes a whole village to raise a child, it takes a whole village to grow old.

It is not simply that the theological view of aging emerges from the African American experience or that the African American experience is reflected in the theological view of aging, but rather that there is no causative relationship between the two.

This means that the African American community is not engaged in doing theology first and then applying the theology to the experience. Nor is the African American community engaged in the task of formulating a theology out of its experience. But rather it is engaged in the task of reflecting about the communal experience with God. Therefore, the theological view of aging would permeate the whole of the African American experience, so that if there were any lines between the theology and the experience they would become so fused as to be nonexistent. When one looks at several different sources that express the African American experience, one finds in all of them the theological view of aging that is "true to their God and native land."

EXPLORING THE THEOLOGICAL VIEW OF AGING PRESENT IN EXPRESSIONS OF THE AFRICAN AMERICAN EXPERIENCE

I begin by appealing to the cultural-linguistic approach to religion proposed by George Lindbeck. The appeal of his model for the current discussion is that he proposes a synthesis that suggests a way to overcome a perceived dichotomy between theology and experience, which he describes, respectively, as the "cognitivist" and the "experiential-expressive."

According to Lindbeck, the cultural-linguistic can accommodate and combine the distinctive and often competing emphases of the other two approaches (Lindbeck 1984, 34). The task of accommodating and combining of the cognitivist and experiential-expressive approaches is twofold. First, the cultural-linguistic approach reverses the order in the experiential-expressive, so that, instead of deriving external features of a religion from inner experiences, it is the inner experiences that are viewed as derivative (34). Lindbeck describes this task: To become religious involves becoming skilled in the language, the symbol system of a given religion. To become a Christian involves learning the story of Israel and of Jesus well enough to interpret and experience oneself and one's world in its terms (34).

Being emancipated from the potential for tyranny of subjective truth by inverting the derivative relationship, the cultural-linguistic approach resembles cognitivist approaches for which external (i.e., propositionally statable) beliefs are primary, but without the intellectualism of the latter (35). Concerning this aspect of the accommodating and combining task of the cultural-linguistic approach, Lindbeck says:

> A comprehensive scheme or story used to structure all dimensions of existence is not primarily a set of propositions to be believed, but is rather the medium in which one moves a set of skills that one employs in living one's life. Its vocabulary of symbols and its syn-

tax may be used for many purposes, only one of which is the formulation of statements about reality. Thus while a religion's truth claims are often of the utmost importance to it (as is the case of Christianity), it is, nevertheless the conceptual vocabulary and the syntax or inner logic which determine the kind of truth claims the religion can make. The cognitive aspect, while often important, is not primary. (35)

The appeal of Lindbeck's synthesis to the proposed task of exploring how the theological view of aging permeates these three expressions of the African American experience is that it provides a nondichotomous way of thinking about the theological view of aging and the African American experience. More specifically, it appeals to the derivative relationship that already exists within the African and African American experience with regard to the internal reality, that is, the inner reality of the individual that is always derivative of the external reality of the community. This is to say that the cultural linguistic reversal of the derivative relationship between external and internal realities has always been reversed in the African American experience. This is an important assertion because, given Lindbeck's critique of modernity, it would appear that the African and the African American experience is inherently resistant to modernity. "The structures of modernity press individuals to meet God first in the depths of their souls and then, perhaps, if they find something personally congenial to become part of a tradition or join a church" (22). In the African and African American experience one cannot speak of the self as a priori to the community.

Edward Wimberly and Anne Streaty Wimberly have an excellent discussion of this in *Liberation and Human Wholeness: The Conversion Experiences of Black People in Slavery and Freedom*, where they explore the conversion experience of Nat Turner in particular and suggest that he suffered from the absence of a community to interpret his conversion: "Even though God was working at the depth of the person's life in periods of transition and life crisis, how one perceived God's work depended on the social symbols permeating the culture of the slave community. Relationship to others and participation in communal religious activities were essential to bring meaning and perspective to significant feelings and experiences" (1986, 63).

Second, when Lindbeck proposes that in "linguistic and cultural approaches a comprehensive scheme or story is used to structure all dimension of existence," he is describing precisely what African American slaves did when they read themselves into the Exodus narrative. It was the Exodus narrative that gave meaning and purpose to their experience. Consequently, it is the biblical-theological view of aging that gives meaning to the African American experience of aging.

An exploration of three expressions of African American experience shows how the permeability of the theological view of aging in the African American experience demonstrates Lindbeck's critical notion:

Rather, to become religious—no less than to become culturally or linguistically competent—is to interiorize a set of skills by practice and training. One learns how to feel, act, and think in conformity with a religious tradition that is, in its inner structure, far richer and more subtle than religion can be explicitly articulated. The primary knowledge is not about the religion, nor that the religion teaches such and such, but rather how to be religious in such and such ways. . . . Thus—insofar as the experience-expressive contrast between experience and knowledge is comparable to that between "knowing how" and "knowing that"—cultural-linguistic models, no less than expressive ones, emphasize the experiential or existential side of religion, though in a different way. . . . The proclamation of the gospel, as a Christian would put it, may be first of all the telling of the story, but this gains power and meaning insofar as it is embodied in the total gestalt of community life and action. (Lindbeck 1984, 35f.)

The cultural-linguistic model is evident through the theological view of aging that permeates the African American experience, as an interiorized language and cultural mode of how to age as a child of God.

Additionally, this exploration of the three expressions will provide an opportunity to utilize Charles Gerkin's narrative hermeneutical model of pastoral care, which draws from Lindbeck's proposals. Gerkin proposes a schema in which pastoral care resides dialogically between the story of the Christian community and its traditions, on the one hand, and the particularity of life stories, on the other (Gerkin 1995, 111):

> The schema is intended to indicate that the dialogue between life stories and the Christian story involves a tension or dialectic. Even through, as Lindbeck has shown, the language, meanings, and even the feelings persons use in experiencing their life stories, including the story of their religious community, life stories have a particularity of their own. The images and meanings attached to those stories have been given a particular cast by the life experiences of the individuals, families, and other groups involved. The fit between the particularity of life stories and the Christian story is never exact. They virtually always stand in some degree of tension with each other. (112)

The expressions that will be explored are *Having Our Say,* the story of the Delaney sisters; *I Know Why the Caged Bird Sings,* by Maya Angelou; "My Sparrow," by Ronald Stodghill II; and *Colored People,* by Henry Louis Gates Jr.

Having Our Say

The phenomenal public response to the book *Having Our Say,* about the Delaney sisters, Sarah Louise and Annie Elizabeth, who were 104 and 102 years old when the book was published, indicates that it touched something deep within the collective psyche. In some way it may relate to what Erik Erikson said in discussing the eighth and final stage in his psychosocial developmental theory: "Ego Integrity vs. Despair: And it seems possible to further paraphrase the relation of adult integrity and infantile trust by saying that healthy children will not fear life if their elders have integrity enough not to fear death" (Erikson 1963, 169). This would also address the particularity of the phenomenal response of the African American community to the Delaney sisters' story. In addition, it has elements of what Mafico defines as a distinctively traditional African view.

The prayer of a traditional African was to live a long life. One major distinguishing factor between traditional Africans and contemporary people is that traditional Africans did not fear aging. Every old person desired to be the oldest person still living. In the past, as today, old age accords a person significant status in the community. An old person is understood as having experienced the vicissitudes of life. It is for this reason that young people consult old people for advice (Mafico 1997, 28).

The way they embrace their own aging teaches us something about our own living. We as the young lions attempting to overcome by our own means and strength need the wisdom of those who have sought the Lord, as have these two African American women who have survived "Jim Crow" and a host of other injustices and lived to tell about it. Knowing that their trust in God's holy Word has enabled them to survive all that confronted them as African American women gives hope to the next generation that it, too, trusting in God's holy Word, will survive what it will confront. The integrity that Erikson spoke of is evident in the words of Amy Hill Hearth, who collaborated in the writing of their story.

Among those who read my article were editors at Kodansha America, Inc., who felt that the Delaneys' story deserved to be a book. At first the sisters demurred, unsure that their life stories were sufficiently interesting or significant. But they came to see that by recording their story they were participating in a tradition as old as time: the passing of knowledge and experience from one generation to the next (Hearth 1993, xii).

On an even deeper level, however, there is within their written story an implicit and subtle language and culture that will communicate the theological view of aging to African Americans in a particular way. There is this sense in which "the Story," that is, the Christian story, permeates their story. As one reads their narrative, one hears throughout the echo of the language and cultural metaphors that have shaped the African American Christian experience. Theirs is a story about reaping what you sow, about running with perseverance the race that is set before, and proleptically coming through the great tribulation. While these are all biblical themes that have been accessible to everyone, they have permeated the African American experience in a particular way so that the very language and culture are imbued with them. In the written words of the Delaney sisters, coauthored with Amy Hill Hearth, one hears the gospel song "How I Got Over," which contains the language that the African American community has used to talk about its experience of aging as children of God.

> How I got over, How I got over,
> Oh, my soul looks back and wonders how I got over,
> Yes, soon as I can see Jesus, the man that made me free,
> The man that bled and suffered and died for you and me,

I thank Him because He taught me, I thank Him because He brought me,
Thank Him cause He never left me, Thank Him for the Holy Bible,
Thank Him for good old revival,
Thank Him for heavenly vision. Thank Him for old time religion,
I'm going to sing well, you know I'm goin' to shout,
Well, I thank Him for all He's done for me. . . . (Ward 1982, 188)

I Know Why the Caged Bird Sings

In *I Know Why The Caged Bird Sings,* Maya Angelou's autobiography, the theological view of aging that permeates the African American experience is found in the prominent role of her paternal grandmother, Annie "Momma" Henderson, to whom Maya and her brother had been sent to live when they were three and four. Although being sent to live with their grandmother satisfies what Peter Paris identifies as a practice of African American parents sending their children to live with grandparents in order for the children "to learn about their values and to experience the practical import of those values" (Paris 1995, 144), Maya and her brother being sent to live with her testifies to the ongoing contributions of the elders in spite of their age. Elders do not cease active parenting and, because of that expectation, remain active and vital participants in the community. In spite of age, God continues to work through the elders. It was not an unreasonable expectation of Maya's and Bailey's parents, Bailey Sr. and Vivian Baxter, that the grandmother, Annie Henderson, would take in Maya and her brother. An expectation of this magnitude may appear to Western minds an unjustified imposition, but in a community and culture defined by a communal worldview it is an expectation based on what it means to belong to community. In the midst of a society where 50 percent of grandparents no longer live in close proximity to their grandchildren (Adams and Kinney 1996, 335), this is more than an appeal to return to a pristine past. Instead it speaks to the literal value and contribution of elders to the overall welfare of the community. The fact that elders function in this way is not simply for the convenience of a capitalist society in which two incomes are increasingly essential but is definitive of a communal worldview where, as Sobonfu Somé and John Mbiti point out, the children belong to the community.

Although parents often sent their children to live with their grandparents out of necessity precipitated by a crisis, as was the case with Maya and her brother, it was nevertheless an assumption that grandparents were both capable and willing to take care of and, if necessary, raise their grandchildren. And these were aging grandparents who, while not necessarily possessing the material resources to take care of or raise their grandchildren (although that was not the case with Maya's grandmother, who owned a general store in Stamps, Arkansas), did so because of the responsibility of kinship and faith in a God who would make a way out of no way. At a time when more grandparents have to fill the breach as a result of drug addiction and HIV/AIDS, rather than an indication of the African American community's impoverishment, it is a witness to its wealth.

Even though this particular assumption—that grandparents were both capable and willing to take care of and, if necessary, raise their grandchildren—may be more ideal than actual practice, it is a resident ideal in the African American experience that is attested to through its ongoing presence in the various expressions. The assessment of the relative health of the African American community needs to take into consideration the existence of the reciprocity between respecting and valuing of elders and their level of functionality. In other words, the health of the community can be determined to the degree that there exists a mutuality of need that can be expressed by the realization that the children need the elders and the elders need the children. This is the circularity of which the theological view of aging is a significant component, and a consistent thread that permeates the African American experience.

"My Sparrow" and *Colored People*

In the concluding expressions of this exploration, the theological view of aging is manifest in the understanding of aging as a process of transition. This is particularly interesting, given the reports that African Americans as a whole generally do not avail themselves of hospice care or advance directives (Moyers 2000), which would appear to be in contradistinction to the theological view.

In "My Sparrow" Ron Stodghill II writes about his initial struggle in accepting the condition of his grandmother who was stricken by a series of strokes. In fact, the opening paragraph is itself significant as a description of a context in which unfortunately too many elders in the African American community find themselves. This context is the antithesis of a community where the respect and valuing of elders are a constituent of its identity.

> Three years ago a crack dealer moved into the house next door to my grandmother. He did a good amount of business there. Customers came by during the day and at all times of the night. Many stayed and partied until morning. And while there was occasional gunfire, it was never enough to draw police. But if the drug dealer prospered, my grandmother did not. He and his entourage brought great stress. In the span of a year my grandmother suffered several strokes, each one pushing her closer to her deathbed. (Stodghill 1995, 251)

He is struggling with the continued deterioration of a person who was not only vital in his life but a former college professor and community activist. He is writing about a visit to his grandmother's bed, to which she was then confined, for the purpose of introducing her to the woman he is seeking to marry.

> We had been dating several months and had come to a point in our relationship where I though it best she meet my family. I had not yet brought myself to pop the question, but I wanted to marry Robyn. Two days spent with my mother and sister had introduced her to two of the most important women in my life. Now, as we prepared to meet the third, I could feel my heart pounding in my chest. I took a long, deep breath. (251)

During the visit there comes a point when he realizes on the basis of Robyn's gift of a song to his grandmother ("His Eye Is on the Sparrow") that this new woman who has come into his life has the same qualities as the woman he is losing. He describes this realization in the following way: "Still, as I pulled away into traffic, with Robyn sitting close beside me, I felt a great sense of relief surge through me. I was not afraid anymore. For now I knew that if God was taking one great woman out of my life, he had been merciful enough to bless me with another" (255). What may be deeply implicit in this is what Mafico describes about the circularity of time as the belief in certain tribes of West Africa that a dead person is reborn as a baby (Mafico 1997, 24). In Stodghill's reflection this belief is manifested in the belief that God has sent him someone who will fill the void that will exist when his grandmother is gone, and a portion of her spirit will reside in Robyn. This is particularly evident in the way he describes what happened during Robyn's singing:

> As Robyn sang, my grandmother's eyes opened wide and alert. She began to clap her hands and sway as though in a church pew, and Daddy Grady was watching his wife with a face of astonishment. For this moment, as we sat enveloped in the rich and sonorous melody of her song, the air around seemed weightless and ablaze, time felt suspended, and it was as though my grandmother was suddenly unburdened by her illness and she was young again and full of great joy. It was magical, and I felt giddy and proud that I had brought such a gift. For in this moment I would have sworn that Robyn had healed my grandmother, that in the power of her song all my grandmother's pain, fear, and sorrow had been cast away. Robyn peered at the woman and sang gloriously:
>
> > His eye is on the sparrow
> > And I know he watches me
> > I sing because I'm happy
> > I sing because I'm free
> > His eye is on the sparrow
> > And I know he watches me. (Stodghill 1995, 255)

In a somewhat similar vein, Henry Louis Gates in his autobiography, *Colored People,* writes about the death of the matriarch of his extended family, "Big Mom":

> Them coons loved Miss Maggie, and no one wanted to let her go, least of all Miss Maggie herself, not even at the ripe old age of ninety-two. I wrote the eulogy for her funeral, and Rocky [his brother] read it at the service. Let her go, was my refrain; we've had her long enough. Let her go. Be thankful for the life she's lived, and our time together, all the things she did that made life special. (Gates 1995, 168)

Letting go is an interiorization of 1 Thess. 4:13b, "So that you may not grieve as others do who have no hope." This also relates to Erikson's notion about the relationship between the integrity of the elders who do not fear death and children not fearing life. This may in turn account for the vulnerability of the contemporary

African American community to nihilism. It is not just being severed from the living witness of the elders, but that the elders have themselves been severed from a theological view of aging that is countercultural—a theological view of aging that is "full of the faith that the dark past has taught us . . . and full of the hope that the present has brought us" ("Lift Every Voice," in Johnson and Johnson 1999).

NOTES

1. Scott Sullender, in "Saint Paul's Approach to Grief: Clarifying the Ambiguity," introduces an interesting discussion about the differences in cosmologies between Paul and the modern psychologies and their impact upon their respective approaches to grief. The point of his discussion for my thinking is that cosmology matters (Sullender 1981, 72).

2. The Federal Writers Project sent fieldworkers to interview blacks who had lived under slavery and recalled their experiences of it. Most of the ex-slaves were found in the South, although a sizable number reported from states not generally regarded as Southern. The project yielded oral histories on a scale unprecedented at the time (Hurmence 1989, x). *God Struck Me Dead* is the compilation of the interviews conducted by Andrew Polk Watson, a graduate student in anthropology at Fisk University during the 1930s (Watson 1993, ix).

BIBLIOGRAPHY

Adams, W. L., and J. Kinney (1996). "The Elderly." In Kinney, 333–48.

Angelou, M. (1993a). *Gather Together in My Name*. New York: Bantam.

———— (1993b). *I Know Why the Caged Bird Sings*. New York: Bantam.

Asante, M. K. (1987). *The Afrocentric Idea*. Philadelphia: Temple University Press.

Boyd, H., and R. Allen, eds. (1995). *Brotherman: The Odyssey of Black Men in America—An Anthology*. New York: Ballantine.

Cooper-Lewter, N., and H. Mitchell (1986). *Soul Theology: The Heart of American Black Culture*. Nashville: Abingdon.

Erikson, E. H. (1963). *Childhood and Society*. 2d ed. New York: W. W. Norton.

Gates, H. L. (1995). *Colored People*. New York: Vintage.

Gerkin, C. (1995). *An Introduction to Pastoral Care*. Nashville: Abingdon.

Hearth, A. H. (1993). *Having Our Say: The Delaney Sisters' First 100 Years*. New York: Kodansha.

Hurmence, B. (1989). *Before Freedom: When I Just Can Remember*. Winston-Salem, N.C.: Blair.

Johnson, J. W., and Johnson, J. R. (1999). "Lift Every Voice." In *This Far by Faith: An African American Resource for Worship*. Minneapolis: Augsburg Fortress.

Kinney, J., ed. (1996). *Clinical Manual of Substance Abuse*. St. Louis: Mosby-Year Book.

Koslow, P., ed. (1999). *The New York Public Library African American Desk Reference*. New York: Wiley & Sons.

Lindbeck, G. (1984). *The Nature of Doctrine: Religion and Theology in a Postliberal Age*. Philadelphia: Westminster.

Mafico, T. L. J. (1997). "Tapping Our Roots: African and Biblical Teaching about Elders." In Wimberly, 19–33.

Mbiti, J. (1988). *African Religions and Philosophy*. London: Heinemann.

McClain, W. B., et al., eds. (1982). *Songs of Zion: Supplemental Worship Resources 12*. Nashville: Abingdon.

Moyers, B. (2000). "Living with Dying." First program of the series *On Our Own Terms: Moyers on Dying*. Produced by Public Affairs Television, Inc.

Nuland, S. (1995). *How We Die: Reflections on Life's Final Chapter*. New York: Vantage.

Paris, P. (1995). *The Spirituality of African Peoples: The Search for a Common Moral Discourse*. Minneapolis: Fortress Press.

Raboteau, A. (1993). Introduction. In Watson.

—— (1980). *Slave Religion: The Invisible Institution in the Antebellum South*. Oxford, Eng.: Oxford University Press.

Somé, S. E. (1997). *The Spirit of Intimacy: Ancient Teachings in the Ways of Relationships*. Berkeley: Berkeley Hills.

Stodghill, R., II (1995). "My Sparrow." In Boyd and Allen, 251–55.

Sullender, R. S. (spring 1981). "Saint Paul's Approach to Grief: Clarifying the Ambiguity." *Journal of Religion and Health* 20: 63–74.

Thurman, H. (1975). *Deep River and The Negro Spiritual Speaks of Life and Death*. Reprint. Richmond, Ind.: Friends United, 1990.

Ward, C. (1982). "How I Got Over." In McClain et al., 188.

Watson, A. P. *God Struck Me Dead: Voices of Ex-Slaves*. Ed. C. H. Johnson. Cleveland: Pilgrim.

West, C. (1993). *Race Matters*. New York: Vantage.

Wilmore, G. (1998). *Black Religion and Black Radicalism: An Interpretation of the Religious History of African Americans*. Maryknoll, N.Y.: Orbis.

Wimberly, A. S., ed. (1997). *Honoring African American Elders: A Ministry in the Soul Community*. San Francisco: Jossey-Bass.

Wimberly, E. P., and A. S. Wimberly (1986). *Liberation and Human Wholeness: The Conversion Experiences of Black People in Slavery and Freedom*. Nashville: Abingdon.

25 Making Decisions at the End of Life: An Approach from Sacred Jewish Texts

RICHARD ADDRESS

It takes three things to attain a sense of significant Being:
God, a soul, and a moment.
And the three are always here.
Just to be is a blessing,
Just to live is holy.

—Abraham Joshua Heschel

THE EVOLUTION FROM JEWISH TEXTS

We are instructed in Jewish tradition to make choices for life. Human life remains the fundamental value within Judaism that serves as the foundation for our entire religious and ethical system. This is to be life that is in the "image and likeness of God," imbued by a sense of devotion to doing sacred acts (*mitzvot*) that affirm and support the power of our relationship to the mystery we call God.

In recent decades medical technology's progress has surpassed society's ability to absorb the impact and implications of an expanding possibility of choices. From new technologies at the beginning of life to the ability to extend the boundaries of life at its end, we are often presented with unique scenarios that challenge our relationship with God. A challenge is to establish a method of decision making that, while acknowledging the realities of medical technology, draws strength from the guidelines established by Jewish tradition. These moments, as Heschel reminds us, are sacred moments when the power of God is present. However, as science and medical technology have progressed, the contexts for creating sacred moments of decision making have evolved in new and often dramatic ways. It is the purpose of this chapter to explore a model of decision making that focuses on the moments at the end of life. It is a model that is supported by the fundamental values of Jewish tradition while embracing the twin challenges of evolving medical technology and the belief in personal autonomy.

At the beginning of the twenty-first century, we find ourselves at the beginning of a great revolution, a revolution of longevity. The Jewish community is no different in

345

this regard from the non-Jewish world. Indeed, demographic studies of the Jewish community contend that it is "graying" at a faster rate than non-Jewish communities, due in large part to longer life spans and the fact that Jewish birth rates for much of the non-Orthodox community barely reach two children per family. Theodore Roszak introduces the concept of this revolution by noting that

> longevity is far more than a human interest item; it marks not only a massive change but a permanent one. . . . The largest growing sector of our population as of the early twenty-first century comprises those over eighty-five. By the middle of the twenty-first century, those who fail to reach that age, except by reason of accident, will fall into a new medical category: premature death. (Roszak 1998, 10)

We know that this is the longest-living, most health-conscious, mobile, and affluent older adult population ever. This reality is restructuring the way our society looks at work, retirement, leisure, sexuality, and political power.

The Jewish community reflects these new realities. These became obvious during a series of population studies of the Jewish community sponsored by local as well as North American Jewish communal agencies during 1990s. The majority of the current generation of Jewish older adults was born in North America and thus may have more in common with their grandchildren than their grandparents. Their "old country" may be the "old" neighborhoods of Philadelphia, Los Angeles, Baltimore, and Brooklyn—and not Eastern Europe. Like the non-Jewish population, this generation is more affluent, mobile, and educated than any in Jewish history.

What is also striking is that this longevity revolution is providing our society with a spiritual revolution as well. The gift of long life and life experience is being unwrapped in a desire to see how one's life and experience can make sense in a transcendent fashion. Pediatric responses are quickly cast aside. A life fully lived now demands a religious community that will provide adult responses to deeply spiritual questions.

As powerful as this revolution in longer life is, it faces a unique challenge as the cohort of the "baby boom" revolution joins their parents in a virtual aging explosion. As revolutionary as the current older adult generation is, their children, the "boomers," promise to expand the horizons and challenges of what it means to grow older. We can expect the spiritual search that marked much of the last decade to continue to expand. While the parents of the boomers may be seeking meaning at the end of their life, their children, once dubbed "a generation of seekers" (Roof 1993), will push the exploration of spiritual meaning into new directions. One of the greatest challenges for contemporary synagogues is exactly how to respond to and anticipate the growing appetite for spiritual meaning that is so much a part of the baby boom generation.

Many of the moments that bring these generations together in their spiritual search are those involved with issues of decision making as life ends or is radically altered. The current longevity revolution can be seen as the foundation for this reality. Because of longer life, better health, greater mobility, and access to health care, the denial of mortality is ever-present. In distinction to past generations, few people are given the gift to say goodbye to a loved one in person, to experience the sacredness of those moments, and, in their loved one's face and struggle, to see themselves. Roszak puts this in another format when he says that "never before have so many people entered their senior years by way of a medical crisis, a contemporary rite of passage that brings them face to face with their own mortality. The cultural and political importance of that increasingly commonplace experience should not be overlooked. Death, if one survives its first call, is a great awakener of conscience and a call to serious reflection" (Roszak 1998, 11).

Making decisions at the end of life, no matter what the context, produces moments of powerful spiritual potential. Hopefully, families will be afforded the opportunity to discuss their own feelings and wishes. Often, however, these moments arise suddenly and are filled with quiet fear and desperate loneliness. Yet, no matter how these situations arise, they are instances in which people seek the strength and guidance of their tradition to provide support and caring. Our textual tradition gives us the insight to construct a method of making sacred decisions at the end of life. Passages from Exodus provide us with interpretations that teach the importance of healing in light of illness (Exod. 15:26; 21:18,19). Leviticus 19 calls on us not to shirk our responsibilities to seek healing when we witness illness, and an interpretation by Maimonides of a text in Deuteronomy underscores that it is a *mitzvah* to try to restore lost health to someone who is ill (Deut. 22:2). The mood of these and other Rabbinic texts underscores what can be called a fundamental ethic upon which decisions can be constructed. That ethic is *the dignity and sanctity of human life and the preservation of that human life in dignity and sanctity.*

CONTEMPORARY "WILD CARDS"

This fundamental ethic or basic value in Judaism serves as the foundation for a methodology of decision making. The difficulty in the application of this value to all cases is manifest by the presence in our culture of two "wild cards": autonomy and technology. These two realities flow as twin currents through the social fabric of our world. They impact the fundamental value by introducing shades of gray, reminding us that decisions at the end of life are often not between what is good or bad but variations of those themes, reflected against the wishes of the individual and a family.

Autonomy presents the contemporary Jew with a great challenge. As products of our contemporary North American culture, we have been taught since childhood that individual rights are an inherent part of our society. The post–World War II generation raised this concept of personal autonomy to almost idolatrous levels. This stands in conflict with Jewish values. The individual, as *tzelem elohim* (image of God), does not exist in a vacuum. By virtue of our being born, we exist in a fundamental relationship with God and are called to model that relationship with others in the world. The prayer book speaks to a theology that reminds the individual that the body and the soul spring from the mystery that is God. We are partners with God in this mind-body-soul dialectic. Traditional prayers acknowledge the miracles of daily life. They celebrate the ability of the body to function as a balanced network and recognize that, should something occur that would impede this network, our bodies would suffer and we would be unable to stand in life with God. Likewise, the tradition teaches that the soul that has been given to us by God will be taken at the time God chooses. This fundamental relationship between us and God is underscored in the prayer's final words, which remind us that we are to bless God, "in whose hands are the souls of all the living and the spirits of all flesh." Judaism teaches that we are not free to do what we want when we want. Autonomy has limits and, in situations requiring extraordinary medical treatment at life's end, these limits can create profound spiritual tension.

The "wild card" of personal autonomy has an ally in the continually evolving arena of medical technology. The progress being made in the diagnosis and treatment of illness has further added to the vagueness of the absolute application of the fundamental ethic by providing people with greater choices than in any time in history. In end-of-life situations this is especially true. The ability to prolong a life is measured against the same technology being able to delay the inevitability of death. Issues such as "quality of life" now occupy substantial amounts of dialogue. The lack of proper guidance, discussion, and preparation can lead to confusion, doubt, and guilt in the decision-making discussions. That is one reason why every major denomination in Judaism now affirms the need to discuss end-of-life situations in anticipation of need. The creation of a personal Advance Directive for Medical Care accompanied by a Durable Power of Attorney for Health Care has become a modern *mitzvah*. Medical technology has made these discussions a necessity.

Too often individuals find themselves in situations where their wishes for treatment have not been made known. They exist in a coma, at the end of a prolonged siege of dementia or in a vegetative state. With no discussion beforehand, physician and family members are left with few answers to difficult questions. The challenge is how to have these discussions in light of the widely held cultural belief in personal autonomy. This is where significant conflict may occur. How can we understand the wishes of an individual in light of the guidelines of Jewish tradition? How can we balance the belief that "this is my life" against the Jewish tradition's belief that life is a gift from God and that the end of that life is in God's domain? This tension may be understood by looking at the mood of Jewish tradition, which reminds us that while the amount of life this is granted to us may be out of our control, what we do with that life—its quality or meaning—rests squarely within our hands.

This introduces us to the possibility of a third wild card, one that is emerging with increasing regularity and one that needs to be part of the discussion of how we apply Judaism's fundamental ethic to a particular life situation. This third factor is the desire for spiritual significance, the search for one's own meaning and purpose. This new dynamic is a direct result of the longevity revolution. As we age we renew our sense of search for how our life can be lived so as to achieve meaning. The Jewish tradition stresses this point. Life is to be lived, even to the last moments. In each moment there is opportunity to find and provide meaning. More and more we give credence to the theme of Sherwin Nuland's book *How We Die* in that we choose how we die influenced by the ways in which we chose to live. As each life is unique, so too is each individual's death. "Every one of death's diverse appearances is as distinct as that singular face we each show the world during the days of our life. Every man will yield up the ghost in a manner that the heavens have never known before: every woman will go her final way in her own way" (Nuland 1994, 3).

GUIDELINES AND BOUNDARIES

In each person's life there is always the possibility of meaning, even as that life winds down. The works of Abraham Joshua Heschel reinforce our continuing need to search for the mystery of our own meaning within our existence. A theme of Heschel's writings is that we human beings are constantly in search of meaning, and this search is cemented in a partnership with God. "To the biblical mind man is not only a creature who is constantly in search of himself but also a creature God is constantly in search of. Man is a creature in search of meaning because there is a meaning in search of him, because there is God's beseeching question, 'Where art thou?'" (Heschel 1959, 238–39).

Judaism reminds us that even at the end of life there can be meaning and the opportunity for *mitzvot*. This gives even greater importance to the need for families to discuss the issue of how to approach, treat, and manage the decisions that arise as life ends. In spite of the belief in personal autonomy, there still exists the desire for life to have meaning, a desire made all the more urgent in light of the choices brought about by medical technology. The fundamental value of life's dignity and sanctity and the preservation of that life in dignity and sanctity still remain our foundation. Yet, given the wild cards, how can we begin to apply this ethic? Is it absolute in every situation?

No, and this the gift of Jewish thought in the area of decision making at the end of life depends on the context of the case before us for the application of the fundamental value. Each individual case is best judged on its own, based on the particular situation. Decisions regarding a person's quality of life are best left to that individual or to a duly appointed surrogate if the individual becomes unable to make his or her wishes known. Again we see the importance of creating opportunities for these discussions to take place, discussions that will lead to the creation of necessary Advance Directives for Medical Care.

The importance of examining the context of a particular situation is reinforced by the specific legal guidelines that may impact when and how decisions are made. These guidelines are based on specific categories drawn from Jewish textual tradition. It is safe to assert that, with the dignity and sanctity of human life as our fundamental value, it is not permitted to actively end a human life. It is safe to assert that everything should be done to return a person to wholeness and life. Jewish tradition emphasizes this value when it reminds us that to save a human life (*p'kuch nefesh*), we are permitted to abrogate almost every Jewish law. Yet there does exist a boundary, drawn from Jewish legal tradition, beyond which different approaches to treatment apply. Up until that boundary is reached, the mood of Judaism is to mandate that everything must be done in order to save a human life. Once, however, that boundary is crossed, a different mood exists. That boundary is called *goses*, and it refers to a patient who is moribund and whose death is imminent. Here the wild card of technology comes into play for, while tradition defined imminent as within three days, current technological prowess has rendered that definition moot. It is possible to prolong a moribund life via technology. The question then asserts itself as to whether you are prolonging a life or delaying the death.

The *goses* is a person whose flame of life is flickering out and, while we may not be permitted to actively snuff out that flame, we are enjoined to do everything in our power to make sure that the flame flickers out in dignity and sanctity. For the *goses* all aggressive medical treatment options have been exhausted. An individual may be hooked up to many machines; debilitating therapies may have been tried; and in the worst-case scenarios, the patient may even be unconscious. The arsenal of medical treatment has been exhausted. Are we still commanded to pursue aggressive treatment in such cases? Judaism says no. When the end of life is clear, when the journey has been completed, when the flame is flickering out, we are under no obligation to prolong suffering or pain, because that only reduces the value of dignity and sanctity. Ongoing communication between a family, a patient, a health-care provider, and a rabbi is fundamentally important in determining when a person crosses this boundary. There are no set rules. There is no set standard. Each individual case stands on its own.

Jewish tradition's position that there are times when it is permissible to allow the flame of life to flicker out is based on classic Jewish texts. Jewish life draws its vitality from the evolving analyses of texts, analyses that allow current issues to be viewed through a historic lens of faith and relationships. The text that informs much of this discussion centers on the death of the beloved Judah Ha-Nasi.

Rabbi Judah was in the last stages of life. His students gathered outside his house in Jerusalem and prayed that he might live. Judah's maidservant, seeing that these prayers were actually hindering the natural process of Judah's death from taking place, ran to the top of the house and threw down a large pottery jar. The crashing of the jar on the ground caused the prayers of the students to stop and at that instant, Rabbi Judah's soul departed (Babylonian Talmud, *Kettubot* 104a). Rabbi Judah, in other words, was definitely *goses*. Given those facts, it was permissible to seek relief and allow the flame of life to flicker out in dignity and sanctity. This story also opens us to a discussion of the role of prayer in the healing and caring process. Many scholars understand that in certain contexts it is permissible to pray that an individual be granted release from the pain and suffering associated with the final moments of life. Given the realities of medical care that presently exist, we need to be reminded that dignity, sanctity, and comfort are basic Jewish values that need to be a part of the decision-making process as the final moments of life unveil themselves.

Too often as life ebbs families are called upon to make a decision as to a loved one's care. The textual tradition of Judaism reminds us that while we are not permitted to actively end a life, when the category of *goses* is operative it is permissible to remove what may be impediments to the natural, dignified means of dying. Rabbi Judah's story has echoes in other texts as well. Rabbi Chananya ben Teradyon, as he was being martyred, allowed the removal of water-soaked tufts of wool that would have delayed the impact of the fires that were consuming him (Babylonian Talmud, *Avodah Zarah* 18a). The classic Jewish law code of the sixteenth century, the *Shulchan Aruch,* continues this discussion when it permits the removal of that which may impede the final process of death. Contemporary commentators interpret the imagery of loud pounding sounds such as the chopping of wood (*Yoreh Deah* 339.1) to permit the removal of extraordinary machinery or treatments when life's final stage is reached.

Keep in mind that Judaism is clear on its insistence that no one may actively end a life. The *goses* is considered a living person. Yet, many people are faced with agonizing decisions regarding end-of-life treatment that go beyond simply removing so-called impediments. Can we find guidance in situations where someone is dealing with great pain and suffering? Here as well we see possibilities of action. Pain and suffering are not values that bring dignity to a person or enhance a person's sanctity. In cases such as this, the category of *goses* is critical. In such a situation is it permissible to increase types of medication in order to relieve excruciating pain and suffering, even though this increased dosage may hasten the person's death? If it is our intent to relieve the pain and suffering of a dying person, then the answer is yes. If it is our intent to end a life, to "put this person out of his or her misery," then the answer is a resounding no. A discussion drawn from Reform Jewish sources on the issue of relieving pain in the final hours of a person's life concludes that

> we may take definite action to relieve pain, even if it is of some risk to the *chayei-sha-a,* the last hours. In fact, it is possible to reason as follows: It is true that the medicine to relieve his pain may weaken his heart, but does not the great pain itself weaken his heart? And: May it not be that relieving the pain may strengthen him more than the medicine might weaken him? At all events, it is a matter of judgement, and in general we may say that in order to relieve his pain, we may incur some risk as to his final hours. (Jacob 1983, 256–57)

A discussion from the Orthodox point of view affirms the basic mood of Judaism regarding these "quality of life" issues in the contexts of decision making at the end of life. "Judaism is concerned about the quality of life, about the mitigation of pain and the cure of illness whenever possible. If no cure or remission can be achieved, nature may be allowed to take its course. To prolong life is a *mitzvah,* to prolong dying is not" (Tendler and Rosner 1993). These situations of decision making reinforce the need for families to have the necessary conversations among themselves so that decisions can be made with knowledge of an individual's wishes. During many of the discussions, the concern for an individual's quality of life is often raised. Here again, the concept of seeking to understand the context of an individual and a situation is helpful. Quality of life is by definition a subjective issue. Decisions regarding a person's quality of life are best left to that individual or to a duly appointed surrogate if the individual is incompetent. The completion of appropriate documents in connection with honest family discussion can be seen as a modern-day *mitzvah.*

The emphasis on examining the context of an individual's medical situation in light of treatment decisions points to a way of looking at these considerations in a nonlinear manner. The wild cards that impact our current society have allowed us the opportunity to see the end of life as a gradual unfolding of stages. Elliot Dorff has been instrumental in helping to develop the point of view. Responding to the impact of medical technology, and the need for people to seek more control over their treatment options, Dorff has reintroduced a classic Jewish term into the discussions of decisions at the end of life. Building on the work of David Sinclair, Dorff writes of the concept of *terefah,* which he defines as someone who has been diagnosed with an irreversible, terminal illness. This is a person for whom it would be permissible not to treat in an aggressive manner. The person who has become *terefah* is really no longer a healthy person and evolves into the status of *goses* in the last days, hours, and moments of life. Dorff echoes other scholars when he reminds us that in these final stages of life we are mandated not to prolong death. Rather, the intent of our actions needs to be, by appropriate palliative and comfort care, to sanctify and dignify life (Dorff 1998).

This category represents a new stage in the process of dying. Many individuals now function in this category. They may be in this stage for a long time, given the reality of medical technology. In this category greater leeway is available for decision making that may in fact prolong life. Indeed, it is in this stage that often someone will opt for more aggressive treatments or say to their physician and family, "Enough." Again, the value of open and honest discussion and the evaluation of the particular context in which the individual finds himself or herself is of crucial importance. Few of these decisions are arrived at without great anxiety, fear, and doubt. These are profoundly spiritual moments in which, as Heschel reminds us, the relationship between man and God is present.

The fundamental value of Judaism, viewed against the context of a particular case, allows us to make informed Jewish choices. Choice, a basic component of Jewish thought, is the final aspect of this decision-making construct. In Deuteronomy we are reminded that we are given choices all the time in our life. They are choices between life and death, good and evil, the blessing and the curse. We are called upon to "choose life" (Deuteronomy 30), so that those who follow us will be blessed. Often it is difficult to see how the decisions that people must make regarding end-of-life situations can be seen as a blessing. The texts, as mentioned above, often remind us that there is no blessing in pain and suffering and that there actually may be times when prayers are said so that a person can be released from the final stages of life. Examining the context against the values of Jewish tradition can give us secure guidelines for making Jewish choices. The discussion with family, caregivers, and clergy of these values in light of a particular context is the pathway for coming to a sense of wholeness in what is a difficult stage in a family's life.

There is also another opportunity to see in these stages a way to sanctify and dignify the life that has been given to us. There is a Jewish tradition, based on the stories at the end of Jacob's life in the book of Genesis, of the "ethical will." This is a practice that urges one generation to leave behind a document in which is bequeathed a spiritual, moral, and ethical legacy. In essence, this is another way in which we transmit the fundamental values of life's dignity and sanctity and fulfill our responsibility to pass on those values to the people who remain after our death. A personal ethical will is a gift that a parent gives his or her child. It is a testimony about living, a prescription based upon one's own experiences in living a righteous life. It should be compiled with the same detailed thought and planning that we devote to creating documents that instruct about the distribution of our property and assets as well as our wishes regarding medical treatment.

The choices we make, individually or as a family, in preparation for life's final stages speak volumes about who we are as human beings. Jewish tradition has evolved guidelines and approaches, based on sacred texts that can inform and support our discussions in these most difficult times. The decision-making model of value, context, and choice springs from a belief that in facing the ultimate aloneness and alienation of death, we can strive to embrace these final stages of life with a sense of the sacred. It is in the contexts of these final stages that the mystery of God so often is present, as are our souls and the preciousness of the moment.

BIBLIOGRAPHY

Address, R. (2000). "Making Sacred Choices at the End of Life." In *Life Lights* (pamphlet series). Woodstock, Vt.: Jewish Lights.

Dorff, E. (1998). *Matters of Life and Death: A Jewish Approach to Modern Medical Ethics*. Philadelphia: Jewish Publication Society.

Heschel, A. J. (1959). *Between Man and God*. New York: Free Press.

Gordon, H. (1998). *When It Hurts Too Much to Live: Questions and Answers about Jewish Tradition and the Issues of Assisted Death*. New York: Union of American Hebrew Congregations, Department of Jewish Family Concerns.

Jacob, W., ed. (1983). *American Reform Responsa: Collected Responsa of the Central Conference of American Rabbis, 1889–1983*. New York: The Conference.

Jacob, W., and M. Zemer, eds. (1994), *Death and Euthanasia in Jewish Law*. Pittsburgh: Freehof Institute for Progressive Halakha/Rodef Shalom.

Kogan, B. (1991). *A Time to Be Born and a Time to Die*. Hawthorne, N.Y.: De Gruyter.

Nuland, S. (1994). *How We Die: Reflections on Life's Final Chapter*. New York: Knopf.

Ochs, C. (1994). *Song of the Self: Biblical Spirituality and Human Holiness*. Valley Forge, Pa.: Trinity Press International.

Roof, W. C. (1999). *Spiritual Marketplace: Baby Boomers and the Remaking of American Religion*. Princeton, N.J.: Princeton University Press.

——— (1993). *A Generation of Seekers*. New York: HarperCollins.

Rosner, F. (1991). *Modern Medicine and Jewish Ethics*. 2d ed. Hoboken, N.J.: K'tav, and New York: Yeshiva University Press.

Roszak, T. (1998). *America the Wise: The Longevity Revolution and the True Wealth of Nations*. New York: Houghton Mifflin.

Sinclair, D. (1989). *Tradition and the Biological Revolution*. Edinburgh: Edinburgh University Press.

Tendler, M. and Rosner, F. (1993). "Quality and Sanctity of Life in the Talmud and Midrash." *Tradition* 1/28: 22–27.

Union of American Hebrew Congregations (1996). "The Role of Pain and Suffering in Decision Making." New York: UAHC Bio-ethics Study Guide VIII.

——— (1994). *A Time to Prepare: A Practical Guide for Individuals and Families in Determining One's Wishes for Extraordinary Medical Treatment and Financial Arrangements*. New York: UAHC Press.

——— (1991). "The Living Will: Advance Medical Directives." New York: UAHC Bio-ethics Study Guide IV.

26

Ethics and Dementia: Dilemmas Encountered by Clergy and Chaplains

STEPHEN SAPP

Seventy-five years after German pathologist Alois Alzheimer first described the syndrome we now know as Alzheimer's disease (AD), the late medical essayist Lewis Thomas dubbed it "the disease of the century." Two decades later *Time* magazine still called AD "the aging brain's most heartbreaking disorder" (July 17, 2000). Nonetheless, optimism about this disease (and related dementias) is more justified now than at any time in the past century because Alzheimer's researchers are pursuing a number of hopeful leads in identifying the causes and thus possible cures (and/or preventions).[1]

Currently, however, such hope remains only that—hope—because truly effective prevention and treatment still lie at least several years—and possibly a decade or more—in the future. Clergy and chaplains—and the faith communities they represent—therefore must address AD as it manifests itself in the here and now, and it is an illness that presents a number of problems for the caring religious professional. Some of these concerns reach far beyond dementia itself while others involve matters more distinctive to this particular set of illnesses. These few pages offer some reflections on the most important of these issues, not so much in a "how-to" mode as from a perspective of underlying conceptual considerations that must be addressed as the foundation for effective pastoral care.

First, though, parish clergy especially should consider if they want to serve the needs of their parishioners with regard to dementia as fully as possible. As just indicated, despite significant progress, a great deal of research lies ahead before AD falls into the same category as, say, heart disease—that is, an illness that is potentially deadly but nonetheless one for which effective prevention and treatment strategies exist. Thus, although it is a sensitive matter for some religious traditions, becoming an advocate for increased funding of research would be a tremendous service with impact far beyond any individuals to whom one might be able to minister, especially as the 76 million baby boomers begin to approach the age of susceptibility.

Alzheimer's care is already estimated to cost $100 billion annually for the 4 million Americans currently afflicted, and predictions about the number of afflicted by the middle of this century reach as high as 14 million. Because of the demographics of life expectancy and the increased incidence of AD as one gets older, delaying the onset of the disease just five years would mean that one-half of those who would otherwise exhibit significant symptoms will die before they become disabled by the disease (McConnell and Riggs 1999). Thus clergy who see speaking out on matters of public policy as part of their religious calling can play an important role in raising awareness of the needs in this area. Indeed, their advocacy can be especially effective because most clergy will be able to speak from firsthand experience in their congregations about the problems that AD brings to families. At the very least, congregations that want to do something about AD should support research programs financially and encourage affected congregants to participate in studies for which they are eligible.

A CRITICAL ISSUE: ALZHEIMER'S DISEASE AND PERSONHOOD

Underlying any pastoral approach to dementia—and arguably the key to any appropriate religious response to the illness—is one critical question that must be faced squarely: How are we to understand the personhood of those with AD? At first blush this may seem a strange and overly theoretical question in light of the many practical concerns AD raises for those affected but, unless we address this question honestly and faithfully, we run the risk of tacitly sanctioning the increasingly dominant view of the culture around us to the detriment of those we are charged to care for.

In ethicist Stephen Post's (2000) now familiar but still felicitous phrase, we live in a "hypercognitive culture," one in which personal value resides primarily in our capacity to think rationally and produce economically. AD undeniably attacks both of these abilities,[2] leading to a tendency—likely to become only more prevalent—to devalue persons with Alzheimer's disease and to regard them as less than fully human and therefore only an expendable "drain on society's limited resources." After all, what do they contribute? And, as we have seen, they certainly do incur expense.

Why is this situation of particular concern for clergy and chaplains? Let me begin to respond with a personal experience. On a bitterly cold, gray day in February 1999, my wife and I stood on the grounds of the former Nazi concentration camp at Dachau, just northwest of Munich, Germany, as the piercing wind blew the few remaining leaves off the twin rows of trees the inmates had planted more than a half century ago to try to beautify that horrible place. After walking through the crematorium and the gas chamber disguised as a shower (inexplicably never used at Dachau) and seeing the film and still photographs in the visitor center, we made our way back toward our car. As we passed under the reconstructed guard tower and through the opening in the fence of concertina wire, my wife voiced questions that force their way unbidden into one's mind at such times: "How could people do such things? How could other people let them do such things?"

As I reflected on her questions, the answer struck me as relatively simple, on one level at least: the Holocaust happened because the people who were its victims had been systematically and thoroughly rendered *non*persons. They had been stripped of their identity as human beings, as *persons* to whom other humans instinctively grant moral standing, with attendant rights, consideration, and protection. And once they were no longer human, because they had become qualitatively different from those making such judgments, it really did not matter what happened to them.

At the risk of sounding overly dramatic, for elders in our country, especially those with dementia, the same process may be occurring, although perhaps more subtly. If our "humanhood" is assumed to rest simply in our economic productivity and even more in our rational capacity, persons with AD are relatively easy to classify as "less than fully human."

Surely no explanation is necessary, however, for why such an attitude is totally alien to the basic teaching of the historic Western faiths—enunciated clearly from Genesis through the Hebrew prophets to Jesus, Paul, and Muhammad—that *all* human beings are created in God's own image and are worthy of respect and protection, especially those who cannot care for themselves or who do not measure up to the world's standards of value. As just suggested, we have only to look back to the Holocaust and more recent examples of genocide to see what can happen when an entire group of people is deemed by society to be less than fully human and thus expendable. Clergy and chaplains have a special responsibility to wrestle seriously with what their faith says it means to be human and then to make their voices heard in the public square.

In this regard I cannot help but think of the most memorable point I learned in the first pastoral psychology course I took at Duke Divinity School three decades ago. The late Richard A. Goodling reminded us constantly throughout the semester, "The individual and not the problem must be your focus," which reminds me of the admonition Sir William Osler, the great medical educator at Johns Hopkins and Oxford, is said to have offered to his students: "It is more important to know all you can about the person who has the disease than all you can about the disease the person has." The only way we can provide truly ethical dementia care—certainly within our dominant religious traditions in this country—is to keep our focus first and foremost on the *person* for whom we are caring. If we allow our priorities and attention to drift anywhere else, we run the risk of losing sight of the inherent worth of every human being, whatever the person's cognitive capacity, productivity, or ability to "contribute" to society.

Sadly, even many people of faith exhibit the disposition to buy into our dominant cultural values. We increasingly accept the "self-evident" proposition that a person who does not think is less than fully human (if even that), that someone who is no longer "productive" is not really a person (of value, anyway), that losing one's independence and "becoming a burden" is the worst fate that can befall a human being. In short, we assume that the inherent value that we have heretofore automatically attributed to humans as beings created in God's own image is unquestionably lost or certainly diminished by the loss of rationality, economic productivity, and independent functioning.

If we buy into these currently dominant attitudes of our society, we make certain judgments about the worth of individuals and our responsibilities to them. We are then likely to categorize them as less than fully human, as not really *persons*, because they fail to meet our criteria of personhood. To coin my own word, I think we can legitimately say that such people are *dis-membered*, removed from being seen as a "real" part of the organic entity—the *body*—that constitutes any social grouping, whether secular or religious, and that can be very dangerous (obviously therefore the task before people of faith is to find ways to re-member such people and incorporate them back into the body).

Along these lines, an e-mail I received a while back from a friend in Arkansas demonstrates one of the major problems with dementia care in our society. After telling me that her father has begun to have "more than just annoying memory loss" but that his doctor isn't sure whether it is actually Alzheimer's, she wrote, "We are not pushing for a diagnosis, as I think the AD diagnosis carries such *unfortunate social consequences* that there is no reason to go further" (my emphasis). Although some people may not agree completely with her decision about not pursuing a diagnosis, anyone who has been involved in dementia care understands what she means about what can happen to someone as soon as he or she enters the class "persons with AD."

The likely social consequences that she fears if her father were to be diagnosed as having AD are probably based in part at least on the way many people feel about it with respect to themselves. For example, in my "Religious Issues in Death and Dying" class recently, the high incidence of Alzheimer's disease in those over eighty-five was mentioned (almost 50 percent), and one of my senior students (twenty-one years old) immediately responded, "I'm going to die before I get that old." When I asked her if she were just being flip or meant what she said, she said, looking me directly in the eyes with no hint of a smile on her face, "I'm completely serious." Most Americans simply cannot accept that *we* would want to go on living our lives with the loss of those characteristics that our society says give us worth, and it is not too great a step to project that feeling onto others.

SOME FACTORS UNDERLYING NEGATIVE ATTITUDES TOWARD PERSONS WITH AD

What specifically are some of the things that contribute to this negative attitude toward persons with dementia—and thus cause such people to be treated in a way that overlooks their personhood and neglects the spiritual dimensions of their lives? The first factor is a trap that we often fall into with older people—especially those with dementia—one that is indicative of a certain failure to respect each person as a unique individual: when a person is impaired in *one* way (e.g., incontinent or aphasic), there is a tendency to treat that person as if he or she were impaired in *many* or even *all* ways, to generalize from a deficit in one function to a deficient *person*. In fact, many older people (and many younger ones as well!) have deficits—cognitive or physical—that only become more or less of a handicap depending on environmental factors, one of the most important of which is the way *others* react to the deficits. And just because a person has trouble remembering people's names or even much more does not mean the person cannot still benefit from attending worship or experiencing other religious rites.

Closely related is the common tendency to assume that the person's deteriorating cognitive capacity eliminates the many characteristics that have made the person who he or she always has been. This assumption leads to a number of actions that one can almost say progressively render the person "generic," treated in ways that fail to respect preferences and patterns built up over a lifetime. Instead of giving in to this temptation, we must seek in every way possible to continue to respect the person's uniqueness as an individual. This includes remaining aware of all those everyday preferences unimpaired people are able to act upon and honoring such values as long as we can, even if the person with AD seems unaware of our doing so. Did she like to sit in the first pew? Then she should continue to do so. Was his favorite dessert at family-night suppers apple pie? Then he should be served that instead of ice cream whether or not we think he knows the difference because that's what *he* likes.

One way to express this point is to say that the community—whether the faith community or the community of the individual's family or some broader community—can honor the cognitively impaired person by *remembering for that person* even when the person can no longer remember for himself or herself, thus affirming the person's continuing humanity, individuality, and value. Such "collective consciousness" has precedents in our dominant religious traditions (e.g., the "corporate personality" of ancient Israel described by H. Wheeler Robinson and the "communion of saints" or even the "earthly body of Christ"). Perhaps the time has come to revive the notion.

Another common way in which we dehumanize people with dementia is to assume that the things they do that "don't make sense" to us are merely random, pointless actions that have no meaning whatsoever, another sign of a less than fully human person. As soon as we see people with dementia as merely "behaving" (in the sense of engaging in meaningless body movements and vocalizations), we deny an essential part of their personhood and thus their value. Consider, for example, the common practice of wandering—only one of many behaviors that are so frustrating for caregivers. The person may be tired but not remember where her bed is, or hungry but not recall where food is kept; so she looks for them, just as anyone would who could not find something she knew (or felt) she needed. The same goes for the human need to feel safe and secure. One way people accomplish this is to say, "I've taken care of this and that." The person with dementia cannot *remember* whether he has taken care of something and thus has to keep asking about it or trying to deal with it. Again, everyone wants to be in control—of one's own life if nothing else. The person with AD cannot really control anything and therefore may try to be in control of everything. And it is essential to remember that persons with AD have the same needs as everyone else but may have lost the social conditioning that builds up over the course of lifetimes and controls what is acceptable in public. Many behaviors that others find embarrassing make great sense apart from normal social conventions. Perhaps her underpants are too tight and she just wants to be comfortable, and that is why she tries to take them off, even in the mall. Or maybe his social inhibitions have deteriorated to the point where he subscribes to that philosophy everyone has wanted to follow at one time or another: "If it itches, scratch," even if one is in a public place!

The eminent social worker/researcher Elaine Brody tells about a very old woman admitted to the Philadelphia Geriatric Center with advanced AD. She had been unable to communicate for some time, but her only real behavioral problem was that she screamed without letup every time she was bathed. The staff, concerned about her obvious distress, talked to her family, who could offer no explanation. So they tried changing the water temperature, playing soft music, and talking to her in a soothing way. Nothing helped. Then, during one of her baths, a staff member came into the room to tell the nurse's aide something she did not want other residents to overhear. As soon as she closed the door, the woman stopped screaming. From then on, as long as the door was closed she accepted her daily bath with no protest; if the door were inadvertently left open, however, she screamed until the bath was over and she was dressed.

This story is important for two reasons. First, it challenges many assumptions about what persons with AD can understand but, second and more important, it illustrates quite clearly that even in conditions of severe mental and physical impairment people still hold on to their sense of dignity, and they suffer if that dignity is violated.

THE IMPORTANCE OF EMPATHY

If those charged with the spiritual care of others—even of those with severely limited ability to comprehend traditional religious formulations and forms and to respond in "appropriate" ways—made a greater effort to "live into" the world of the person with AD, they would have a deeper appreciation for what it feels like to have one's very worth as a human being called into question, not only by others but, perhaps more sadly, even by oneself. After all, our dominant religious traditions teach that we should love our neighbors as ourselves and do unto others as we would have them do unto us. Part of putting that injunction into practice must surely be to try as much as possible to imagine what it would feel like to be experiencing what that neighbor and those others are.

Most people have probably had some time in their lives—deep grief or great stress, personal failure or serious illness affecting mental functioning—that might resemble to some small degree at least what a person with dementia is experiencing constantly: feelings of intense loneliness, abandonment, betrayal, powerlessness, incompetence, and confusion. Or it may be something as simple as those "senior moments" so many people blame for momentary lapses of memory or the common "tip-of-the-tongue" phenomenon when a familiar word or place-name simply will not come into consciousness, however hard one tries to recall it.

How must it feel if the world one has known and lived in for seven, eight, nine decades is now changing every day in ways that make no sense, if things one has done every day since childhood and somehow knows are expected and important begin to be more than one can manage, such as tying one's shoes or wiping oneself? Everyone has experienced the frustration of seeing someone familiar who just cannot be placed or whose name will not surface. What if now all the people one has known and relied on for years start to be replaced by strangers, maybe familiar strangers but still *not* the people one has known, or at least one is no longer sure exactly who they are? And certainly in everyday dealings with various government agencies, businesses, and especially the health-care establishment, most people know a little about how it feels to be treated more like an object than a person.

Unfortunately, accepting the dominant medical model of dementia—that it is an inexorably advancing neuropathy that cannot be arrested, with inevitable results that strip one of personhood—may have lulled us into believing that people with dementia do not really experience suffering, at least none above the most basic *physical* level, and therefore have no needs beyond essential physical care. With this attitude it is certainly easy to neglect the spiritual dimension of such people's lives, which is to treat them in an inherently unethical way.

A "CONTRARIAN" POINT

This emphasis on remembering the humanity and thus fundamental worth of people with dementia suggests an important point that will run contrary to the received wisdom of the day with regard to Alzheimer's care. In the past two decades, a commendable movement to focus attention on the caregivers of persons with AD has arisen, stated clearly by two of the leading figures in the field, Donna Cohen and Carl Eisdorfer: "Caring for the patient by working with the family . . . is the best strategy available. The latest evidence supports the idea that the patient's family, where available, is the key to truly helping the patient" (Cohen and Eisdorfer 1986, 325–26). This emphasis is not surprising, given that for every demented person in an institution at least two similarly impaired people are cared for at home, and families provide between 70 and 80 percent of all care received by persons with dementia. In fact, studies have shown that whether or not a person suffering from dementia will be institutionalized depends as much on the kind of family the person has as it does on the characteristics of the ill person. Attention to family caregivers therefore must be a major focus of all pastoral care and of efforts of religious congregations to respond to the challenge of dementia, a focus unfortunately too frequently neglected.

Why is the question being raised here, given the clear need to care for family caregivers? This laudable effort to recognize and respond to the needs of family caregivers has both been driven by and perhaps contributed to an unintentional but nonetheless dangerous devaluation of the person with AD as one for whom "nothing can be done anyway." The focus then shifts from the one who should be of primary concern, thus further diminishing that person's worth. Indeed, if one felt cynical, one could even say that the status of those afflicted with dementia has been lowered in part because they have come to be seen as the *cause* of the many problems now so clearly recognized among AD family caregivers.

This should not suggest a reduction in efforts to provide support and assistance of every kind possible to family caregivers. A great deal more needs to be done in this regard, especially by communities of faith who all too often tend to withdraw from individuals and families where dementia makes it difficult to know how best to help. In these efforts, however, great care must be shown not to further the devaluation of the person with AD that is already too evident in the values of society. Such people remain human beings, and they need and deserve the most humane care possible.

THE DENIAL OF MORTALITY AND DEPENDENCE

Another issue that clergy and chaplains must confront more honestly contributes to the difficulty of dealing adequately with dementia but goes far beyond it. Put simply, Americans do not like to admit their mortality! But if the Abrahamic religions—indeed, virtually all religions we know—teach us one thing about ourselves, it is that "you are dust, and to dust you shall return" (Gen. 3:19). Closely linked with this inescapable fact is another reality—though equally distasteful to contemporary Americans—that lies at the very heart especially of the Christian gospel but is also an element in the beliefs of most other religions: Not only must we die but we are fundamentally *dependent,* first, on a gracious and merciful God and, second, on other human beings.

Why are our faith communities so afraid to confront these facts and to encourage recognition of them, leaving us unable to deal with them in a healthy and constructive way? The one institution in our country that should be the center of frank and open discussion about the fragility of life and the legitimacy of accepting dependence is curiously silent. Apart from the *theological* appropriateness of such discussion, in mainline Protestant denominations a *demographic* imperative also exists. For example, in my church, the Presbyterian Church (U.S.A.), 67 percent of members are over the age of forty-five, 57 percent are over fifty, and 35 percent are sixty-five or older (the median age is fifty-four, whereas the median age for the U.S. population as a whole is about thirty-six). These numbers make clear the reality of mortality and impending dependence for the individuals who increasingly constitute such congregations.

THE PROBLEM OF ASSISTED DYING

Related to this matter is an issue that will not go away, despite our discomfort and refusal to face it, namely, the question of assistance in dying, under whatever guise it appears (physician-assisted suicide or euthanasia, which may be lumped together under the heading "encouraged" or "accelerated" death). As the number of persons with AD rises, increasing pressure will be brought upon (and by) them to spare themselves and others "the funeral that never ends." Yet little thoughtful, theologically informed, and practical guidance exists from most religious institutions. Why are faith communities not in the forefront of wrestling with this perplexing issue? More specifically, what about the question of whether to provide or withhold antibiotics and artificial nutrition and hydration for people with advanced Alzheimer's, a real concern for their caregivers? What guidance can they find on this difficult issue from their congregations and spiritual leaders? However complex and conflicted the questions are, responsible clergy need to determine where they stand on such questions and guide the people under their spiritual care into serious discussion of them.

Clergy and chaplains must also face the fact that, with increasingly accurate diagnostic methods, more and more people will know their diagnosis of AD earlier in the course of the disease, raising the bar considerably for dealing with the situation. Until recently, diagnosis almost always has come too late in the progression of the illness for the person to be able to take concrete action in response. Now the diagnosis is coming early enough and with enough confidence that those told of their illness will still be able to choose to avoid its inevitable progression and outcome, especially if the movement toward "encouraged" death continues to gain momentum across the nation and the means to do so become more readily available. Again, leaders of faith communities have an obligation to address this issue and to provide much greater support to those wrestling with it than is currently being offered.

This discussion raises the classic question of whether to tell the person about the diagnosis at all, especially if it comes relatively early in the manifestation of symptoms. Another chapter in this volume explores the ethics of disclosing the diagnosis. My own view is that no justification exists for trying to keep it from the person most directly affected, except perhaps in those cultures where such truth telling is contrary to other important values. Little empirical evidence exists for either position, though it seems intuitive that many people may handle developing symptoms better if they know why they are experiencing them. The most important consideration, however, is the main point of this chapter: if we are to respect persons with AD as fully human individuals and not treat them as problems to be managed so as to minimize the impact upon others, the act of informing such people of what is happening to them in as serious a matter as the diagnosis of dementia is fundamental. Sensitive clergy who know the family well can play a critical role in helping everyone involved to get through this difficult step in the long journey they all face.

SUPPORT FOR FAMILIES AFFECTED BY ALZHEIMER'S DISEASE

This discussion suggests another area of concern, the general support and care of persons with AD and their families. With new medications people are living longer with the early symptoms of AD, a situation that raises serious questions about making that time meaningful. In its most basic form, the question might be simply whether such people are really made to feel welcome in worship, even if they may be somewhat "disruptive." Is there any instruction for members of congregations in how to interact with persons with AD in ways that make them feel they continue to be valued as members of the "covenant people," the "body," or the *ummah?* Do congregations do anything to help a caregiver attend even when the person with AD no longer can come or to provide care for the individual during worship so the caregiver can still participate?

Beyond this, most people know that Alzheimer's caregivers face years of "thirty-six-hour days," with little help available. What better source of such assistance could exist than their faith communities, made up of people who are supposed to understand their obligation to reach out and help those in need, even at some cost to themselves? As the membership of many congregations continues to age, more and more retired members will have time to put this basic belief into practice, and in doing so they may be able to regain some of the sense of self-worth that gerontologists have noted for years our youth-oriented society strips from Americans as we get older. Clergy can and should take the lead in urging their congregations to explore ways to provide support and care to Alzheimer's families, both formally and informally.

THE PROBLEM OF GENETIC TESTING

Another area of ethical concern has to do with genetic testing, which raises many questions about the use to which such information may be put (another chapter in this volume deals with this issue more thoroughly). Suffice it to say that despite great progress recently in identifying genes associated with AD that appear to increase susceptibility to the illness, the current state of knowledge does not permit clear diagnosis (except for relatively rare "early-onset AD"). Therefore none of the major national panels of Alzheimer's authorities currently supports genetic suscep-tibility testing, which in any case holds no value with regard to treatment. Clergy and congregations, however, need to begin thinking about the ethical and practical implications of further discoveries in this area, because they *will* come and clergy need to reflect on how they will counsel their increasingly older congregations on the matter.

THE SEXUALITY OF PEOPLE WITH AD

Finally, an ethical concern that has received far too little attention in faith com-munities (not surprisingly, because it ranks right beside mortality and dependence among topics studiously avoided by most clergy) is the sexuality of people with dementia—indeed, of older people in general. Most younger people—even trained professionals like clergy, physicians, social workers, and others—have a great deal of difficulty picturing elders engaging in sexual activities like inter-course, masturbation, or even fondling and kissing, despite considerable evi-dence—both data-based and anecdotal/observational—that humans remain sexual beings throughout the life cycle. National accrediting bodies for schools of medicine and psychology do not mandate sexuality training (Davies et al. 1998), and it is certainly not prominent in the curricula of any theological institution I know. Yet the issue is a real one for persons confronting dementia, with several facets, and when the topic arises in support groups, participants usually respond with relief that finally they can talk about it.

In one sense, this may not be too much of an *ethical* issue as long as the couple remains in their own home and the person with AD is still basically functional, though excessive demands for sexual activity often accompany the diminution of inhibitions characteristic of the illness, leading to questions about the right to refuse one's partner. As the illness progresses, practices normally engaged in by the couple may become difficult or impossible, and new avenues of expression and satisfaction between the couple may have to be sought, some of which may be contrary to the teachings of some religious traditions. Still, given the level of pastoral care available for sexual problems in general in our culture, what goes on in the privacy of a cou-ple's home will probably remain private.

If the person with AD becomes incapacitated, or especially institutionalized, the problems become considerably more complex, especially from the standpoint of clergy and chaplains who may be called upon to offer spiritual/ethical counsel to family members and staff. What if the community spouse—facing years of sexual inactivity and emotional loneliness—wants to become sexually active or simply pursue another relationship solely for companionship, at least initially? In our dom-inant religious traditions, licit sexual expression is strictly confined to married het-erosexual couples, and even then at least tacit limits on permitted activities often exist. Marital fidelity lies at the heart of the sexual ethics of Judaism, Christianity, and Islam (and other religions as well). Does the definition of that central concept change when one partner becomes cognitively impaired, especially if he or she can linger for years in a debilitated condition? And if the answer is that there must be some modification to allow for the needs of the healthy partner, does that support the dehumanization of the person with dementia discussed earlier?

And what of the institutionalized partner, especially if the spouse is dead? What if he or she begins to exhibit a sexual morality at odds with that expressed throughout life, becoming, for example, excessively amorous when previously almost "prudish"? Does the "then self" or the "now self" win out? We trust family members to make end-of-life decisions, supposedly based on the loved one's known preferences before incapacitation. Can they be counted on in this arena to make wise and reasoned choices for the person, or is this area actually *more* difficult to deal with than termination-of-treatment decisions?

The ethical and pastoral issues are numerous and complex, and they should be addressed openly and honestly (as of this writing the Ethics Advisory Panel of the national organization The Alzheimer's Association is wrestling seriously with them). If parent religious bodies are not going to do it, individual clergy and especially chaplains in institutions need to, not only for the sake of those they serve but also because they themselves may well confront these issues in their own families.

Dementia for the time being remains what I have called it since I first encountered Alzheimer's disease more than two decades ago—"a damnable disease." Hope glows more brightly now than ever before, but it is only *that* at the moment—hope. For those who approach the world from the perspective of religious faith, though, some directions to take and even mandates to follow appear to be clear. "God never forgets" even the least of God's children—which from contemporary society's perspective is an apt description of people with Alzheimer's disease (Sapp 1977). If we fail to take seriously the issues raised above, we who claim to be followers of that God risk forgetting that people with Alzheimer's—however impaired—are still God's children.

NOTES

1. For an accessible overview of recent research on AD see the *Time* article mentioned in this chapter and others in this volume. Although unexpected side effects in human trials dashed the hope engendered by early reports of the vaccine AN-1792, which not only prevented the onset of symptoms in vaccinated juvenile mice but actually reversed damage already done by the disease process in adult mice, the promise of such advances is enough to evoke joy in all those familiar with the toll of Alzheimer's disease. The prospect of a successful treatment or even cure, however, raises a potential problem for those charged with spiritual counsel of families with AD: A long-heard lament among people with Alzheimer's disease and their caregivers is what I will shorthand as the "theodicy" issue: Why is this horrible thing happening to us? If the vaccine ultimately proves effective, the agony of that question may be compounded by the feeling of many that "we got Alzheimer's just a little too soon"!

2. The effect of AD on rational capacity is readily apparent to all who know anything about the illness, but less well known is the impact on economic productivity: According to some estimates, American business loses more than $30 billion annually through lost productivity on the part of workers who are AD caregivers. And many people with AD would also continue to contribute to the economy if they were not disabled by the disease.

BIBLIOGRAPHY

Cohen, D., and C. Eisdorfer (1986). *The Loss of Self: A Family Resource for the Care of Alzheimer's Disease and Related Disorders.* New York: Norton.

Davies, H. D., A. M. Zeiss, E. A. Shea, and J. R. Tinklenberg (1998). "Sexuality and Intimacy in Alzheimer's Patients and Their Partners." *Sexuality and Disability* 16/3: 193–203.

McConnell, S., and J. Riggs (1999). "The Policy Challenges of Alzheimer's Disease." *Generations* 23: 69–74.

McKim, D. K., ed. (1997). *God Never Forgets: Faith, Hope, and Alzheimer's Disease.* Louisville: Westminster John Knox.

Post, S. G. (2000). *The Moral Challenge of Alzheimer Disease: Ethical Issues from Diagnosis to Dying.* Baltimore: Johns Hopkins University Press.

Sapp, S. (1997). "Memory: The Community Looks Backward." In McKim, 38–54.

27 Ethical Issues in Care of Individuals with Alzheimer's Disease

LADISLAV VOLICER
PAUL R. BRENNER

With increased life expectancy of our population, Alzheimer's disease (AD) is becoming one of the most important problems facing future health care. The prevalence of AD increases with age from about 3 percent in individuals 65 to 74 years old to 47 percent in individuals 85 years old or older (Evans et al. 1989). Currently, about 35 million people in the United States are aged 65 and older, and it is estimated that 4 million of them suffer from AD. By 2050 the number of Americans aged 65 and older will have doubled, to 70 million people, with the people over the age of 85 being the fastest-growing segment of the population. Therefore, it has been estimated that the number of individuals suffering from AD will reach 14 million in the year 2050 unless significant progress in prevention and treatment of this condition is made.

AD poses many ethical issues to caregivers and the whole society. Ethical dilemmas faced by caregivers are caused by an impaired ability of the individual with advanced AD to make rational decisions about activities of daily living, living circumstances, participation in research, and medical treatments. The whole society is challenged to allocate resources that would allow provision of appropriate care for individuals with AD and other progressive dementias. This chapter summarizes some of the ethical issues and suggests strategies for minimizing ethical dilemmas.

COMMUNICATION OF DIAGNOSIS OF AD

The principle of truth telling governs ethical deliberation regarding communication of diagnosis of AD. The factors that should be considered when making decisions regarding communication of diagnosis of AD include uncertainty of the diagnosis and rate of progression, consequences of the diagnosis label for individuals with cognitive impairment and their families, and advantages of becoming aware of nature of the problem for these individuals.

Uncertainty of the Diagnosis and the Rate of Progression

The definite diagnosis of AD requires presence of both clinically significant dementia and specific pathological changes in the brain tissue obtained by autopsy. There is no definite diagnostic test or procedure that would determine presence of AD in a living individual, and clinical diagnosis of AD is confirmed by autopsy in about 85 percent of the cases (Lim et al. 1999). A significant number of individuals diagnosed with other forms of dementia, however, have Alzheimer changes present on autopsy examination, and most of the individuals who were falsely diagnosed as having AD have a progressive degenerative dementia that causes the same impairments and practical consequences as AD. In addition, autopsy findings in many individuals include not only Alzheimer changes but also other processes that can cause progressive dementia, such as vascular lesions and Lewy bodies (Lim et al. 1999; Volicer, McKee, and Hewitt 2001). Thus we can never be sure about the patient having AD, but the exact diagnosis is not very important from a practical point of view.

The rate of development of functional deficits due to AD varies widely and, although on average the individual with AD lives eight years after occurrence of the first symptoms, the disease can last up to twenty years. It is also unclear when AD can be first detected. Diagnosis of AD requires presence of dementia that includes memory problems and additional deficits in two or more areas of cognition, and results in functional impairment. It was recently recognized, however, that isolated memory problems, called Minimal Cognitive Impairment, predispose individuals to development of AD and are considered by some an early stage of AD (Morris et al. 2001). Thus the safest course of action is to tell the patient that the current condition could be AD, leaving open the possibility that the impairment could be due to other causes and not predicting the future course.

Consequences of the Diagnosis Label for Individuals with Cognitive Impairment and Their Families

Some physicians hesitate to make diagnosis of AD because of the diagnostic uncertainty and because they fear the effect of the diagnosis on patients and their families. Such hesitation may be increased by a requirement to report patients with diagnosis of AD to government authorities, such as California's requirement to report individuals with AD to the county health department.

Many physicians do not report diagnosis of AD to their patients because they are afraid of the patient becoming depressed and even committing suicide (Smith and Beattie 2001). Similarly, family members often urge physicians not to report the diagnosis to the patient, although they themselves would want to know the diagnosis if they should develop AD (Smith and Beattie 2001). Suicides of several individuals with AD have been reported (Ferris et al. 1999), and AD changes were present in brains of elderly individuals dying from suicide more often than in brains of elderly individuals dying from other diseases, which indicates that AD may be a

risk factor for committing suicide (Rubio et al. 2001). Compared with the prevalence of AD, however, the number of individuals committing suicide is very small,
and early recognition and treatment of depression and the availability of effective
treatments for cognitive deficits should help in decreasing risk of suicide. Overall,
most professionals think that the risks of depression and suicide are outweighed by
benefits of communicating early diagnosis.

Advantages of Becoming Aware of Nature of the Problem for Individuals with Cognitive Impairment and Their Families

The importance of telling a patient the truth about possible causes of the cognitive
impairment was recognized by the Alzheimer Association, which published a guide,
"Telling the Truth in Diagnosis" (Alzheimer's Association 2001). The beneficial
consequences of communicating the diagnosis are several:

- Reassurance of the individual that she/he is not "going crazy." Many elderly
  individuals perceive their cognitive impairment and are afraid of a psychiatric
  illness. They are comforted by the assurance that their problem is not a sign of
  psychiatric illness but a memory problem that is common in aging individuals.
- Ability to plan for optimal life experiences in remaining years of relatively
  preserved capacities, and to make decisions regarding the estate and early treatment of cognitive impairment. Currently available medications for treatment
  of AD, which include donepezil (Aricept), rivastigmine (Exelon), and galanta-
  mine (Reminyl), are most effective when started early in the disease course
  (McLendon and Doraiswamy 1999). These drugs do not stop or reverse progression of the disease, however, but only postpone inevitable deterioration.
  The considerations concerning their use should include realistic expectations,
  possible side effects, including more difficult caregiving caused by a slight cognitive improvement, duration of medication use, and cost of medications.
- Ability to prepare legal documents concerning care in more advanced stages
  of the disease that include advance directives or living will and designation of
  a proxy decision-maker. Advance directives allow the person to express
  wishes regarding the use of aggressive medical interventions to sustain life,
  such as cardiopulmonary resuscitation, transfer to ICU and other acute-care
  setting, use of tube feeding, and use of antibiotics to treat life-threatening
  infections. Such advance directives may not eliminate the need for a proxy to
  make specific decisions but they greatly facilitate formulation of a proxy plan
  described below (Mahoney, Hurley, and Volicer 1998).
- Ability to do life review, plan life legacy, and maximize family relationships
  while cognition is still available. Spiritual preparation for the future could be
  also made at this point.
- Ability to consider possible enrollment in research projects. Participation in
  studies that pose more than minimal risk and do not provide any direct benefits for their participants may require advanced consent from individuals

who can no longer give informed consent at the time of the study. Procedures that would be considered as belonging in this category include lumbar puncture for development of diagnostic test or basic research in pathogenesis of AD, genetic testing, etc.

- Ability to participate in Alzheimer support groups. Support groups are an important resource for both an individual with AD and the family. Support groups for individuals with early stage AD have positive effects on participants' understanding of the disease and its consequences, their coping behavior, and general well-being (Petry 1999). Support groups for caregivers are important component of the general support that was shown to delay institutionalization of individuals with AD (Mittelman et al. 1996).

DECISION-MAKING CAPACITY

Health-care providers may err by both overestimating and underestimating the capacity to make decisions. Overestimation may occur when individuals are not tested for their cognitive functioning and is more common if the patient agrees with the health-care provider. Many people in the early stages of dementia are good at maintaining a social façade. If they are not tested, their impairment may not be apparent on simple questioning. On the other hand, underestimation may occur, especially in residents of long-term care facilities.

Five standards were proposed as necessary to assure that an individual possesses decision-making capacity (Roth, Meisel, and Lidz 1977). They are, in order of increasing stringency:

1. the capacity to evidence treatment choice
2. the capacity to make reasonable treatment choice
3. the capacity to appreciate the consequences of a treatment choice
4. the capacity to provide rational reasons for a treatment choice
5. the capacity to understand the treatment situation and choices

Although a large amount of research was done by the Marson group regarding application of these standards (Marson et al. 2000), they are not uniformly accepted. One problem is that even some cognitively intact individuals do not meet all the standards and would require a substitute decision-maker. The other problem is that the requirement of "rational decision" is open to different interpretations. Because of that, some ethicists omit this standard from their recommendation for decision-making capacity determinations (Pearlman 1997).

An alternative recommendation is that not all standards are required for all treatment decisions. Drane (1984) proposed a sliding scale of decision-making capacity that specifies three different levels of standard requirement according to the nature of decision. The first level includes treatments that are clearly beneficial and do not pose serious danger; this is the most commonly encountered situation in treatment of acute conditions. Decision-making capacity for these treatments would require only the awareness of the situation and assent from the patient. If the disease is chronic or the treatment is more dangerous or of less definite benefit, the decision-making capacity would require understanding of the risks and outcomes of different options and choice based on this understanding. The third level would apply for decisions that are dangerous and fly in the face of both professional and public rationality. In this situation, the decision-making capacity would require appreciation of the consequences of the decision, and the patient would have to provide reasons for his or her decisions.

The principle of the sliding scale was endorsed by the President's Commission for the Study of Ethical Problems in Medicine and Biomedical and Behavioral Research (1983) and by some ethicists (Pearlman 1997). Other authors, however, object to this method because it is less objective than the strict application of five standards (Kloezen, Fitten, and Steinberg 1988). They argue that less stringency is achieved because different treatment situations present different levels of complexity for the patient to understand but that the five standards should always be used.

Some authors attempted to develop an instrument for determination of decision-making capacity. Janofsky et al. (Janofsky, McCarthy, and Folstein 1992) suggested that responses to a questionnaire administered after patients hear an essay provide information about the patient's understanding of the essay and indicate that even some moderately demented individuals have the capacity to make treatment decisions. It is also possible that moderately demented individuals, who do not have ability to make decisions regarding their care, are still able to appoint a health-care proxy (Mezey et al. 2000).

Advance Proxy Plan

With the progression of dementia all individuals eventually lose their decision-making capacity. It is often at this point that difficult decisions regarding end-of-life care have to be made. These decisions may be made more easily if the patient executed a living will or advance directive statement specifying which treatments he or she would accept. Unfortunately, most living wills are very general, do not provide guidance regarding specific treatment procedures, and do not take into account the slowly progressive nature of dementing diseases that makes unclear when the living-will decisions should be applied. Therefore in most situations specific decisions have to be made by a patient's surrogate or proxy. Ideally, this proxy should be appointed by the patient and should have discussed the patient's wishes and philosophy with the patient before he or she became demented. In this situation the proxy can make decisions on the basis of substituted judgment, putting herself or himself into the "patient's shoes." Even if the proxy was not appointed by the patient, some family members or close friends may have this knowledge and make decisions in the same way. Substituted judgment is also promoted by a living will that can be interpreted by the proxy and used to make specific decisions.

Often, however, appointed proxy or family members do not have any evidence of what the patient would want in the present situation. In that case, the proxies have to decide on the basis of the best interest of the patient as perceived by them. These decisions are very difficult, and the proxies need guidance from the treatment team. Otherwise they may feel overwhelmed and guilty if they decide to forgo some treatment modalities. Recommendations for the proxy should be made not only by the physician but also should be developed as a consensus of the whole treatment team. It should be recognized that nursing staff are moral agents who have to be consulted before treatment decisions are made, because they have to work with the residents and execute these decisions (Hurley et al. 1998). Several factors are important for the process of reaching consensus: patient decline, family coping, professional development of nursing staff, and nursing-unit philosophy (Hurley et al. 1995). Timing and trust are influential catalysts to family, and staff readiness is a factor in achieving consensus.

Treatment decisions should be made ahead of the time of crisis at a meeting of proxy and other family members or friends with the treatment team. The treatment team should include the physician or physician extender, nursing staff representative, and social worker who acts as a meeting moderator. The presence of a chaplain is also useful for answering concerns regarding religious or ethical matters. This family conference is a good opportunity to answer all concerns expressed by the proxy and others close to the patient regarding patient condition and treatment (Mahoney, Hurley, and Volicer 1998). During the conference the treatment team should clarify the patient's prognosis and describe options for management of complications and intercurrent diseases. The risks and benefits of all the management strategies should be clearly explained as described below. Presence or absence of previous patient's wishes has to be determined at the beginning of the discussion. The discussion may be framed as an opportunity for deciding on priorities regarding the goals of care: survival at all costs, maintenance of function, or comfort care (Gillick, Berkman, and Cullen 1999). According to these priorities, decisions are made to accept or forgo cardiopulmonary resuscitation, transfer to acute care setting, treatment with antibiotics, and tube feeding. These decisions (advance proxy plan) are not permanent and may be changed by the proxy any time. Therefore it is necessary to maintain good communication between the treatment team and the proxy, notifying the proxy of any significant change in the patient's condition. The decisions should be reviewed periodically and if the proxy dies or becomes incapacitated a new proxy should update the advance proxy plan.

LIMITATIONS OF AUTONOMY OF A PERSON WITH AD

Respect for autonomy is an important ethical principle that should be honored whenever such action does not expose the person with AD or other individuals to danger. Unfortunately, because individuals with AD have impairment of executive function and may not be able to comprehend their functional impairments, they may lose their ability to make rational decisions and engage in activities that are dangerous. These activities include driving, wandering and getting lost outside, using appliances unsafely, attempting to walk unassisted when their gait is unsteady or they are unable to perceive obstacles in their path, and ingesting inedible objects. Persons with AD may also engage in activities that decrease their dignity and may affect the ability of caregivers to provide care, such as undressing and having inappropriate sexual behavior. Although limitation of autonomy is often required for these reasons, the caregivers should always allow the individual with AD to make as many decisions as it is possible considering their consequences.

Termination of Driving

The diagnosis of AD is not by itself a sufficient reason for loss of driving privileges. However, sooner or later AD progression impairs one's driving ability. There are no simple criteria that would determine at which stage of AD the individual is no longer able to drive safely. Driving should be terminated when there is evidence that the individual poses a serious risk to self or others. This decision should include the person with AD if she or he retains decision-making capacity.

Legislative approaches to this problem vary from state to state. California requires physicians to submit a confidential report to the county health department when individuals are diagnosed with dementia severe enough to impair driving abilities. Persons with moderate and severe dementia automatically have their licenses revoked, and persons with mild dementia have to undergo testing. Other states (e.g., Missouri, Florida, and Maryland) provide that anybody may submit a confidential report to motor vehicles licensing authority concerning an individual with questionable driving skills. This report results in investigation and requirement for testing. This approach is preferable, because mandatory reporting may cause avoidance of physician examination by persons who have memory impairment and delay effective treatment.

Institutionalization

Whether to institutionalize an individual with AD is one of the most difficult decisions the family caregiver has to make (Brown, Lyon, and Sellers 1988). It is difficult because the caregivers may consider this event a sign of their failure to cope, and they may feel guilt and despair over their inability to continue safely to manage their loved ones at home. It should be recognized, however, that institutionalization has both drawbacks and benefits that should be considered by both family and professional caregivers.

Quality of life of an individual with AD may be decreased by institutionalization, because it deprives the individual of familiar home environment, privacy, and freedom of individualized routine. With progression of AD, however, these factors become less important because persons may not be able to recognize their home and initiate meaningful activities. Institutionalization at this point may therefore improve the quality of life, if the patient is provided an opportunity to engage in meaningful activities organized by the staff. Institutionalization may also improve the patient's safety by providing a safe environment in which to wander and improve the patient's nutrition by providing regular meals with staff assistance. Institutionalization may also prevent the risk of injuries happening to either the patient or family caregiver during caregiving activities because resistance to care caused by the patient's inability to comprehend why care should be provided may escalate into combative or abusive behavior by either the patient or the caregiver.

Use of Restraints

Two types of restraints are often discussed: chemical and physical. Chemical restraints are defined as "any drug that is used for discipline or convenience and not required to treat medical symptoms" (Guidance to Surveyors: Long-Term Care Facilities 2001). Legitimate treatment of psychiatric symptoms of dementia does not constitute chemical restraint, but the resident has to have appropriate diagnosis (e.g., depression or delusions/hallucinations) to justify administration of psychoactive drugs.

Use of physical restraints varies in different countries, being reported as low as 3.8 percent in Scotland (Evans, Strumpf, and Williams 1998). Scottish facilities, however, routinely use beanbag chairs or deep chairs from which patients may not be able to rise without assistance, and they do not consider those to be restraints. Elsewhere, restraint use varies and is currently about 20 percent in the United States (Phillips et al. 2000). Clinical trials may reduce restraint use significantly below 20 percent (Evans et al. 1997), but even individualized-care alternatives may not eliminate physical restraints completely (Werner et al. 1994). There are three main reasons for use of restraints: fall risk, treatment interference, and disruptive behaviors.

Fall prevention is the most legitimate reason for use of physical restraints. As the dementia progresses, patients lose their ability to recognize obstacles and their gait becomes unsteady and narrow-based (scissors gait). At the same time patients do not recognize their limitations and attempt to get out of a bed or chair and walk unassisted. This results in falls and sometimes in a serious injury, such as hip fracture. More than half of patients with Alzheimer's disease lose their ability to walk independently 7.8 years after their first symptom of dementia (Volicer et al. 1987). The only way to avoid the use of physical restraints completely would be to allow patients to crawl on the floor. Although this practice was adopted in one Colorado facility, it has a problematic effect on patients' dignity and may not be accepted by patients' families.

Risk of falls, however, may be decreased by modifying drug therapy and by evaluating patients for treatable causes of gait disturbances. It is important to maintain independent motor activity as long as possible. Walking provides an outlet for the patient's physical energy, allows for more social contact and involvement in activities, and helps to prevent pneumonia and urinary tract infection. Bedfast patients have a 6.8 higher risk of pneumonia and a 3.4 higher risk of urinary tract infections than ambulatory individuals (Magaziner et al. 1991). Safe mobility may be enhanced by physical therapy, combination of assisted walking with conversation (Tappen et al. 2000), safe footwear, and the use of assistive devices such as the Merry Walker (Trudeau 1999). Injury from falls can be reduced by hip protectors (Kannus et al. 2000), low beds, and bed and chair alarms with adequate monitoring. Falls from a chair can be also reduced by fitting the size and type of chair to the patient and by employing reminders or delayers such as placing an overbed table in front of the chair (Evans 1991).

Treatment interference may require short-term use of restraints to prevent removal of a medical device such as an intravenous line or urinary catheter. Use of restraints may be minimized if the reason for an intervention can be explained and if appropriate pain control is provided. Distraction by personal attention, environmental modifications, or other activities may also be helpful (Evans 1991). However, the need for restraint should be always considered when an aggressive medical intervention is planned, and the burden of restraints should be weighed against the benefit of the procedure.

Disruptive behavior should not be a reason for long-term use of physical restraints, but restraints may be necessary for a short period until an appropriate management of the disruptive behavior is achieved. Behavioral and environmental strategies should be employed, such as providing sufficient meaningful activities to prevent apathy and agitation and assuring a safe and/or controlled environment for independent ambulation. If the disruptive behavior is caused by psychiatric symptoms of dementia, appropriate treatment with psychoactive agents should be instituted.

Use of restraints has many undesirable effects. Restraint use results in increased agitation (Werner et al. 1989) and was rated the third most uncomfortable medical procedure by a panel of cognitively intact individuals (Morrison et al. 1998). Restraint use leads to muscular deconditioning, development of contractures, and other detrimental effects. Use of restraints does not decrease the incidence of falls (Capezuti et al. 1996) and may actually increase their frequency (Tinetti, Liu, and Ginter 1992). Physical restraints may also lead to pressure sores, thrombosis (Hem, Steen, and Opjordsmoen 2001), and even death (Miles and Irvine 2001).

END-OF-LIFE DECISIONS

Decisions regarding end-of-life care have to take into consideration the burdens and benefits of various procedures. Patients with advanced dementia are unable to comprehend the need for therapeutic interventions, do not cooperate with treatment, and may even actively oppose it. Thus the burden of therapeutic interventions in patients with advanced dementia is larger than the burden in cognitively intact individuals. Benefits of therapeutic interventions may be also limited by the dementing process as described below.

Cardiopulmonary Resuscitation (CPR)

CPR performed in a hospital provides immediate survival for 41 percent of patients and survival to discharge for 13 percent of them (Ebell et al. 1998). However, success is three times less likely in the presence of dementia—almost as rare as in metastatic cancer. In addition, many cardiac arrests occur in long-term care institutions caring for demented individuals. The immediate survival of resuscitated nursing-home residents is 18.5 percent, with only 3.4 percent discharged from the hospital alive (Finucane and Harper 1999). If the decreased success rate observed in a hospital population is present also in the nursing-home population, only 1 percent of demented residents suffering cardiac arrest can be expected to be discharged alive from the hospital.

This potential benefit is, however, diminished by several considerations. CPR is a stressful experience for those who survive, who may experience CPR-related injuries such as broken ribs and often have to be on a respirator. Intensive-care-unit environment is not conducive to appropriate care for demented individuals, who are confused and often develop delirium. Many patients who are discharged alive from the hospital after CPR are much more impaired than they were before the arrest (Applebaum, King, and Finucane 1990). The experience of CPR is very traumatic for patients and their families as evidenced by the fact that even residents who have reported no change from prearrest status frequently execute a "Do Not Resuscitate" (DNR) directive preventing repetition of the CPR (Tresch et al. 1993). Performance of a CPR also adversely affects other residents of long-term care facilities, who may be upset by witnessing the procedure.

Transfer to an Acute-Care Setting

Transfer of demented individuals to an emergency room or hospital exposes them to serious risks. Even cognitively intact hospitalized elderly individuals develop depressed psychophysiological functioning that includes confusion, falling, not eating, and incontinence (Gillick, Serrell, Gillick 1982). These symptoms are often managed by medical interventions, such as psychotropic medications, restraints, nasogastric tubes, and foley catheters, which expose the patient to possible complications including thrombophlebitis, pulmonary embolus, aspiration pneumonia, urinary tract infection, and septic shock. It was reported that shortly after hospital admission of elderly individuals, functional deterioration occurs in mobility, transfer, toileting, feeding, and grooming—and none of these functions improves significantly by discharge (Hirsch et al. 1990).

Transfer from a long-term care facility to an acute-care setting is most often due to an infection and/or breathing difficulties (Volicer, Hurley, and Blasi 2001). Pneumonia is a leading cause of infection among patients in long-term care facilities, and its median reported incidence is 1 per 1,000 patient-days (Muder 1998). Risk of development of pneumonia is increased in residents who are confined to bed, have a debilitating neurologic disease, and who require tube feeding (McDonald et al. 1992). Other risk factors include older age, male sex, swallowing difficulty, and inability to take oral medication (Loeb et al. 1999). Many of these risk factors are not amenable to intervention in an individual with progressive dementia. Persistence of the risk factors is responsible for high rate of recurrence in individuals who experienced an episode of pneumonia. Patients discharged from a hospital after admission for pneumonia have a five times higher risk for development of another episode of pneumonia than patients admitted for other conditions (Hedlund et al. 1992), and 43 percent of nursing-home residents who survive an episode of pneumonia develop another episode within twelve months (Muder et al. 1996).

Transfer of long-term-care facility residents to an emergency room or hospital for treatment of infections and other conditions may not be optimal for management of these problems. A recent study, which reviewed hospital records of one hundred unscheduled transfers to a hospital, found that 36 percent of emergency-room transfers and 40 percent of hospital admissions were inappropriate (Saliba et al. 2000). These numbers increased further to 44 percent of emergency-room transfers and 45 percent of hospital admissions when advance directives were considered. The rate of hospitalization varied widely between different long-term care facilities (Thompson, Hall, and Szpiech 1999) and could not be predicted by any patient characteristics if all hospitalizations were considered (Barker et al. 1994).

Hospitalization is not necessary for optimal treatment of pneumonia of nursing home residents. Immediate survival is similar in residents receiving treatment in long-term care facilities and in hospitals (Fried, Gillick, and Lipsitz 1997). Similarly, mortality due to pneumonia was similar in two nursing homes despite a double rate of hospitalization in one of them (Thompson, Hall, and Szpiech 1999). Longer-term outcomes are actually better in residents treated in a nursing home. It was reported that the six-week mortality rate was 18.7 percent in nonhospitalized residents and 39.5 percent in hospitalized residents, despite no significant differences between the hospitalized and nonhospitalized groups before diagnosis (Thompson et al. 1997). Similarly, a larger proportion of hospitalized individuals had worsening of their functional status or died two months after the episode of pneumonia (Fried, Gillick, and Lipsitz 1997).

The available data indicate that transfer to an emergency room or hospital has a significant degree of risks and relatively few benefits for individuals with advanced dementia. Therefore this management strategy should be used only when it is consistent with overall goals of care and not as a default option or in response to family panic. A decline in the rate of hospitalization of severely cognitively impaired residents has been reported (Mor et al. 1997), and this change may be due to improved assessment or changing treatment philosophy.

Antibiotic Therapy

Antibiotic therapy is quite effective in treatment of an isolated episode of pneumonia or other systemic infection. In most patients it is possible to limit antibiotic therapy to oral preparations. Medina-Walpole and McCormick (1998) reported that residents receiving only oral antibiotics were more likely to be cured. However, patient characteristics might have been different in the case of patients who received oral and parenteral therapy. In other studies oral antibiotics were shown to be as effective as parenteral antibiotics (Hirata-Dulas et al. 1991). It is preferable to limit the use of intravenous therapy in cognitively impaired individuals who do not understand the need for intravenous catheters, try to remove them, and often have to be restrained or given psychotropic drugs to allow the treatment to continue. If patients have poor oral intake, it is possible to use intramuscular administration of cephalosporins for treatment of infections.

The effectiveness of antibiotic therapy, however, is limited by the recurrent nature of infections in advanced dementia. We have shown that antibiotic therapy does not prolong survival in cognitively impaired patients who are unable to ambulate even with assistance, and who are mute (Fabiszewski, Volicer, and Volicer 1990). Similarly, Luchins, Hanrahan, and Murphy (1997) found no significant difference in survival rate between very advanced dementia patients (characterized as at or past Stage 7C) who were and who were not treated with antibiotics. In addition, our results indicate that antibiotics are not necessary for maintenance of comfort in demented individuals. Using an observational scale for measurement of discomfort (Hurley et al. 1992), we have found that discomfort increases during the first three to five days of an episode of infection similarly in patients treated and not treated with antibiotics (Hurley et al. 1993). Similarly, there was no significant difference in discomfort during the resolution of infection. This indicates that use of analgesics and antipyretics, and of oxygen if necessary, assures comfort without antibiotic administration.

Antibiotic use is not without adverse effects. Patients may develop gastrointestinal upset, diarrhea, allergic reactions, hyperkalemia, and agranulocytosis. Diagnostic procedures such as blood drawing and sputum suctioning, which are necessary for rational use of antibiotics, cause discomfort and confusion in demented individuals who do not understand the need for them. In addition, diagnostic procedures fail to indicate the source of infectious episode in 30 percent of cases (Fabiszewski, Volicer, and Volicer 1990). Use of antibiotics in patients with advanced dementia should therefore take into consideration the recurrent nature of infections, which are caused by persistent swallowing difficulties with aspiration and by other factors predisposing for development of infections (Volicer, Brandeis, and Hurley 1998) that significantly reduce the benefits of antibiotic treatment.

Tube Feeding

Eating difficulties develop in all individuals as dementia progresses. They are caused by apraxia that initially prevents patients from using utensils but eventually makes them completely unable to eat independently. In addition, patients often develop intermittent food refusal that can be caused by depression, dislike of institutional food, or inability to perceive hunger. With further progression of dementia, patients often develop swallowing difficulties that provoke choking on food and liquids. Choking and food refusal are often exhibited simultaneously (Volicer et al. 1989). Eating apraxia can be managed by hand feeding, and food refusal often responds to antidepressant treatment (Volicer, Rheaume, and Cyr 1994) or to administration of appetite stimulants (Volicer et al. 1997). Swallowing difficulties and choking may be minimized by adjustment of diet texture and by replacing thin liquids with thick ones (e.g., yogurt instead of milk) (Frisoni et al. 1998). Unfortunately, some practitioners still consider introduction of tube feeding as necessary to assure appropriate nutrition and prevent aspiration (Golden et al. 1997).

Two excellent reviews recently summarized available evidence considering the risks and benefits of tube feeding in individuals with advanced dementia (Finucane, Christmas, and Travis 1999; Gillick 2000). They agreed that there is no evidence indicating that the long-term feeding tubes are beneficial in individuals with advanced dementia. Tube feeding does not prevent aspiration pneumonia and actually might increase its incidence because it does not prevent aspiration of nasopharyngeal secretions and of regurgitated gastric contents. Tube feeding also does not prevent occurrence of other infections. Nasogastric tubes may cause infections of sinuses and middle ear, and gastrostomy tubes may cause cellulitis, abscesses, and even necrotizing fasciitis and myositis. Contaminated feeding solution may cause gastrointestinal symptoms and bacturiuria. Tube feeding does not prevent malnutrition and it does not increase survival in individuals with progressive degenerative dementia. Use of a tube may actually cause death from arrhythmia during insertion of a nasogastric tube and from perioperative mortality in percutaneous endoscopic gastrostomy tube placement. Occurrence of pressure ulcer is not decreased by tube feeding and it may be actually increased because of the use of restraints and increased production of urine and stool. There is also no evidence that tube feeding promotes healing of pressure ulcers or improves functional status of individuals with advanced dementia (Finucane, Christmas, and Travis 1999).

In addition to the lack of benefits, tube feeding has many adverse effects. Tube feeding increases discomfort of the patients by both the tube presence and by the use of restraints that are often necessary to prevent tube removal. A survey of cognitively intact patients indicated that nasogastric tube is considered the most uncomfortable procedure, even more uncomfortable than mechanical ventilation, and mechanical restraints were considered the third most uncomfortable procedure (Morrison et al. 1998). Thus, imposing tube feeding on an individual with dementia results in significant impairment of comfort without commensurable benefits.

Tube feeding also deprives the patient of taste of food and of contact with the care-givers during the feeding process. In addition, feeding tubes may cause many local, pleuropulmonary, abdominal, and other complications (Finucane, Christmas, and Travis 1999). This imbalance of burdens and benefits of tube feeding justifies rec-ommendation that tube feeding should not be used in individuals with advanced dementia. This recommendation is supported by secular and most religious ethicists (Gillick 2000).

The alternative to tube feeding is modification of diet texture and fluid thick-ness that decreases episodes of choking and careful hand feeding (Frisoni et al. 1998). It is important to realize that even if a tube feeding was instituted in an indi-vidual with progressive dementia, it does not have to be continued indefinitely. Some patients have a tube inserted during hospitalization for intercurrent disease, during which their ability to eat is compromised. In these patients it is possible to convert tube feeding to hand feeding, and in some cases the patients may even be able to feed themselves again (Volicer et al. 1990).

Hospice Care

The distinct trajectory of AD reveals that the present model of care for chronic pro-gressive diseases and the structure of the hospice benefit are unable to provide ade-quate and appropriate end-of-life care for individuals with advanced AD. The existing model assumes that a person mentally, spiritually, and physically experi-ences the progression of illness as a unitary whole and arrives at a definable point at which curative care ends and palliative care begins. Hospice care is then initiated for the patient and family to achieve life review and closure and to address the bereave-ment needs of family members. In this model the beginning of the "end-of-life" phase has clear symptomatic markers that indicate that it is time to implement comfort-oriented goals of care. The conclusion of this "end-of-life" phase occurs when imminent or active dying begins, that is, when the major bodily systems begin actively to shut down in preparation for the moment of death.

This model does not work well with AD for several reasons. First, the trajectory of AD is marked by two quite widely separated events in time that measure the pro-gression of the disease. The first event is the loss of the ability of the person with AD to have rational engagement in her or his life and health care. The second event is the death of the body, which may occur anywhere from three to five years later, depending on the kinds of medical interventions utilized.

Second, hospice care cannot be implemented without a licensed physician indi-cating that, to the best of her or his predictive ability, the person has six months or less of life expectancy "if the disease continues its expected course." This means that hospice services cannot be provided to the patient with AD and his or her family while there is still an opportunity for cognitive engagement with the patient in life review, life closure, discussion of treatment choices, clarification of quality-of-life needs, issues, and values, and attention to the spiritual dimension of life's ending.

Since patients with advanced AD cannot speak or choose for themselves, the hospice referral staff must clarify who has the authority to make the election to hospice care for the patient as well as the medical choices for treatment of symptoms. The two sides to this question involve, first, the determination of who has the legal authority and, second, sensitivity to the moral and/or ethical authority of the culture and values of the family. These two levels of authority may be congruent or not, and if not, they have the potential to create conflict and disruption in care.

If the person who is referred to hospice care is also a resident of a long-term care facility, nursing home, assisted-living facility, or specialized residence for persons with AD, the referral and decision-making process may be even more complex. The process will then also involve staff members of the facility and the facility's standards of practice involving the treatment of infections, use of artificial hydration and nutrition, and the assessment and treatment of symptoms, including pain. If the facility's standards of practice do not provide appropriate strategies for end-of-life care, a conflict and disruption in care between hospice, facility, and family may occur.

Whether the source of referral is a family member, a facility, or a hospital, complications for admission into hospice care or palliative care can be due to any or a combination of the following:

- absence of a written affidavit of patient wishes or recollection of discussion that family members had with the patient about specifics of end-of-life care and treatment choices
- presence of ambivalent and conflictive emotions and/or beliefs in members of the patient's family that may affect treatment decision making
- challenges integrating best practices and accurate medical information with a family's cultural and/or religious traditions as end-of-life care decision points occur, such as treatment of infections and tube feeding
- hesitancy, reluctance, or inability of physicians to present clear, unbiased, best-practice options to families due to their own values, beliefs, or ambiguities regarding end-of-life care
- existence of dysfunctional or conflicting relationships between family members that interfere with decision making
- inability of family members to come to a consensus about treatment options and choices, especially when those choices may involve allowing some physical condition to become the direct cause of death
- financial stressors on the family due to the long trajectory of the disease and its care

These complications can make the election to hospice care a lengthy, difficult process requiring multiple meetings, repeated communications, and consensus-building time with family members, the source of referral, members of the Alzheimer's Association, religious leaders of the family, staff of a facility, facility physician, hospice medical staff, hospice admission team, and, at times, ethics committees.

Significant issues with ethical, moral, and religion/spiritual dimensions are created by the present structure of the hospice benefit for Medicare-eligible patients and the characteristics of AD itself. These include at least the following key issue areas:

- It is often a challenge to physicians responsible for prognostication to assess the patient's medical condition by the criteria that can admit the patient with AD for a six-month benefit "if the disease continues its expected course." Treatment choices, such as implementation of artificial nutrition and hydration, can influence life expectancy.
- Both the election to hospice care and choices to be made about treatment options must be made by family members or others with legal authority for the patient, since the patient is unable to articulate this for herself or himself. This can be an intense spiritual and psychological burden for the family members involved.
- The inability of patients to be cognitively involved in their lives and its care limits the "traditional" role of nurses, social workers, chaplains, and others in life review, life closure, and death preparation work with patients and restricts that activity to family members alone.
- The inability of patients to articulate their own needs and causes of distress and/or suffering especially challenges the abilities of hospice nurses to identify, assess, and treat the patient's symptoms and measure the effectiveness of treatments to achieve a satisfactory level of comfort.

CONCLUSIONS

Several ethical dilemmas are faced by everybody involved in care of individuals suffering from AD and other progressive dementias. These dilemmas include communication of diagnosis of AD, determination of decision-making capacity, proxy decision making, limitation of autonomy of persons with AD, and end-of-life decisions that include involvement in hospice care. Professional caregivers have to be especially careful to respect the sensibility of individuals suffering from dementia and their family members. Attention to their religious and spiritual background helps in minimizing stress involved in addressing these ethical dilemmas.

BIBLIOGRAPHY

Alzheimer's Association (2001). "Telling the Truth in Diagnosis." Chicago: Alzheimer's Association.

Applebaum, G. E., J. E. King, and T. E. Finucane (1990). "The Outcome of CPR Initiated in Nursing Homes." *Journal of the American Geriatrics Society* 38: 197–200.

Barker, W. H., J. G. Zimmer, W. J. Hall, B. C. Ruff, C. B. Freundlich, and G. M. Eggert (1994). "Rates, Patterns, Causes, and Costs of Hospitalization of Nursing Home Residents: A Population-Based Study." *American Journal of Public Health* 84: 1615–20.

Brown, J., P. C. Lyon, and T. D. Sellers (1988). "Caring for the Family Caregivers." In Volicer et al., 29–41.

Capezuti, E., L. Evans, N. Strumpf, and G. Maislin (1996). "Physical Restraint Use and Falls in Nursing Home Residents." *Journal of the American Geriatrics Society* 44: 627–33.

Cassel, C. K., H. J. Cohen, and E. B. Larson (1997). *Geriatric Medicine.* 3d ed. New York: Springer.

Drane, J. F. (1984). "Competency to Give an Informed Consent: A Model for Making Clinical Assessments." *Journal of the American Medical Association* 252: 925–27.

Ebell, M. H., L. A. Becker, H. C. Barry, and M. Hagen (1998). "Survival after In-Hospital Cardiopulmonary Resuscitation: A Meta-Analysis." *Journal of General Internal Medicine* 13: 805–16.

Evans, D. A., H. H. Funkenstein, M. S. Albert, P. A. Scherr, N. R. Cook, M. J. Chown, L. E. Hebert, C. H. Hennekens, and J. O. Taylor (1989). "Prevalence of Alzheimer's Disease in a Community Population of Older Persons: Higher Than Previously Reported." *Journal of the American Medical Association* 262: 2551–56.

Evans, L. K. (1991). "Nursing Care and Management of Behavioral Problems in the Elderly." In M. S. Harper, ed., *Behavioral, Social and Emotional Aspects of Nursing in Long Term Care,* 191–203. Newbury Park, Calif.: Sage.

Evans, L. K., N. E. Strumpf, and C. Williams (1998). "Redefining a Standard of Care for Frail Older People: Alternatives to Routine Physical Restraint." In Katz, Kane, and Mezey, 81–108.

Evans, L. K., N. E. Strumpf, S. L. Allen-Taylor, E. Capezuti, G. Maislin, and B. Jacobsen (1997). "A Clinical Trial to Reduce Restraints in Nursing Homes." *Journal of the American Geriatrics Society* 45: 675–81.

Fabiszewski, K. J., B. Volicer, and L. Volicer (1990). "Effect of Antibiotic Treatment on Outcome of Fevers in Institutionalized Alzheimer Patients." *Journal of the American Medical Association* 263: 3168–72.

Ferris, S. H., G. T. Hofeldt, G. Carbone, P. Masciandaro, W. M. Troetel, and B. P. Imbimbo (1999). "Suicide in Two Patients with a Diagnosis of Probable Alzheimer Disease." *Alzheimer Disease and Associated Disorders* 13: 88–90.

Finucane, T. E., C. Christmas, and K. Travis (1999). "Tube Feeding in Patients with Advanced Dementia: A Review of the Evidence." *Journal of the American Medical Association* 282: 1365–70.

Finucane, T. E., and G. M. Harper (1999). "Attempting Resuscitation in Nursing Homes: Policy Considerations." *Journal of the American Geriatrics Society* 47: 1261–64.

Fried, T. R., M. R. Gillick, and L. A. Lipsitz (1997). "Short-Term Functional Outcomes of Long-Term Care Residents with Pneumonia Treated with and without Hospital Transfer." *Journal of the American Geriatrics Society* 45: 302–6.

——— (1995). "Whether to Transfer? Factors Associated with Hospitalization and Outcome of Elderly Long-Term Care Patients with Pneumonia." *Journal of General Internal Medicine* 10: 246–50.

Frisoni, G. B., S. Franzoni, G. Bellelli, J. Morris, and V. Warden (1998). "Overcoming Eating Difficulties in the Severely Demented." In Volicer and Hurley, 48–67.

Gillick, M. R. (2000). "Sounding Board: Rethinking the Role of Tube Feeding in Patients with Advanced Dementia." *New England Journal of Medicine* 342: 206–10.

Gillick, M. R., N. A. Serrell, and L. S. Gillick (1982). "Adverse Consequences of Hospitalization in the Elderly." *Social Science and Medicine* 16: 1033–38.

Gillick, M., S. Berkman, and L. Cullen (1999). "A Patient-Centered Approach to Advance Medical Planning in the Nursing Home." *Journal of the American Geriatrics Society* 47: 227–30.

Golden, A., C. Beber, R. Weber, V. Kumar, N. Musson, and M. Silverman (1997). "Long-Term Survival of Elderly Nursing Home Residents after Percutaneous Endoscopic Gastrostomy for Nutritional Support." *Nursing Home Medicine* 5: 382–89.

"Guidance to Surveyors: Long-Term Care Facilities." (2000). Medicare State Operations Manual. HCFA-Pub. 7. Washington, D.C.: Health Care Financing Administration, Department of Health and Human Services.

Hedlund, J. U., A. B. Ortquist, M. Kalin, G. Scalia-Tomba, and J. Giesecke (1992). "Risk of Pneumonia in Patients Previously Treated in Hospital for Pneumonia." *Lancet* 340: 396–97.

Hem, E., O. Steen, and S. Opjordsmoen (2001). "Thrombosis Associated with Physical Restraints." *Acta Psychiatrica Scandinavica* 103: 73–75.

Hirata-Dulas, C. A., D. J. Stein, D. R. Guay, R. P. Gruninger, and P. K. Peterson (1991). "A Randomized Study of Ciprofloxacin versus Ceftriaxone in the Treatment of Nursing Home-Acquired Lower Respiratory Tract Infections." *Journal of the American Geriatrics Society* 39: 1040–41.

Hirsch, C. H., L. Sommers, A. Olsen, L. Mullen, and C. H. Winograd (1990). "The Natural History of Functional Morbidity in Hospitalized Older Patients." *Journal of the American Geriatrics Society* 38: 1296–1303.

Hurley, A. C., B. J. Volicer, M. A. Mahoney, and L. Volicer (1993). "Palliative Fever Management in Alzheimer Patients: Quality Plus Fiscal Responsibility." *Advances in Nursing Science* 16: 21–32.

Hurley, A. C., B. J. Volicer, P. Hanrahan, S. Houde, and L. Volicer (1992). "Assessment of Discomfort in Advanced Alzheimer Patients." *Research in Nursing and Health* 15: 369–77.

Hurley, A. C., L. Volicer, V. F. Rempusheski, and S. T. Fry (1995). "Reaching Consensus: The Process of Recommending Treatment Decisions for Alzheimer's Patients." *Advances in Nursing Science* 18/2: 33–43.

Hurley, A. C., S. A. MacDonald, S. T. Fry, and V. F. Rempusheski (1998). "Nursing Staff as Moral Agents." In Volicer and Hurley, 155–68.

Janofsky, J. S., R. J. McCarthy, and M. F. Folstein (1992). "The Hopkins Competency Assessment Test: A Brief Method for Evaluating Patients' Capacity to Give Informed Consent." *Hospital and Community Psychiatry* 43: 132–36.

Kannus, P., J. Parkkari, S. Niemi, M. Pasanen, M. Palvanen, M. Jarvinen, and I. Vuori (2000). "Prevention of Hip Fracture in Elderly People with Use of a Hip Protector." *New England Journal of Medicine* 343: 1506–13.

Katz, P. R., R. L. Kane, M. D. Mezey, eds. (1998). *Advances in Long-Term Care*. New York: Springer.

Kloezen, S., L. J. Fitten, and A. Steinberg (1988). "Assessment of Treatment Decision-Making Capacity in a Medically Ill Patient." *Journal of the American Geriatrics Society* 36: 1055–58.

Lim, A., D. Tsuang, W. Kukull, D. Nochlin, J. Leverenz, W. McCormick, J. Bowen, L. Teri, J. Thompson, E. R. Peskind, M. Raskind, and E. B. Larson (1999). "Clinico-Neuropathological Correlation of Alzheimer's Disease in a Community-Based Case Series." *Journal of the American Geriatrics Society* 47: 564–69.

Loeb, M., A. McGeer, M. McArthur, S. Walter, and A. E. Simor (1999). "Risk Factors for Pneumonia and Other Lower Respiratory Tract Infections in Elderly Residents of Long-Term Care Facilities." *Archives of Internal Medicine* 159: 2058–64.

Luchins, D. J., P. Hanrahan, and K. Murphy (1997). "Criteria for Enrolling Dementia Patients in Hospice." *Journal of the American Geriatrics Society* 45: 1054–59.

Magaziner, J., J. H. Tenney, B. DeForge, R. Hebel, H. L. Munice, and J. W. Warren (1991). "Prevalence and Characteristics of Nursing Home-Acquired Infections in the Aged." *Journal of the American Geriatrics Society* 39: 1071–78.

Mahoney, M. A., A. C. Hurley, and L. Volicer (1998). "Advance Proxy Planning." In Volicer and Hurley, 169–88.

Marson, D. C., K. S. Earnst, F. Jamil, A. Bartolucci, and L. E. Harrell (2000). "Consistency of Physicians' Legal Standard and Personal Judgments of Competency in Patients with Alzheimer's Disease." *Journal of the American Geriatrics Society* 48: 911–18.

McDonald, A. M., L. Dietsche, M. Litsche, R. Spurgas, R. Ledgerwood, C. J. Subitha, and F. M. LaForce (1992). "A Retrospective Study of Nosocomial Pneumonia at a Long-Term Care Facility." *American Journal of Infection Control* 20: 234–38.

McLendon, B. M., and P. M. Doraiswamy (1999). "Defining Meaningful Change in Alzheimer's Disease Trials: The Donepezil Experience." *Journal of Geriatric Psychiatry and Neurology* 12: 39–48.

Medina-Walpole, A. M., and W. C. McCormick (1998). "Provider Practice Patterns in Nursing Home-Acquired Pneumonia." *Journal of the American Geriatrics Society* 46: 187–92.

Mezey, M., J. Teresi, G. Ramsey, E. Mitty, and T. Bobrowitz (2000). "Decision-Making Capacity to Execute a Health Care Proxy: Development and Testing of Guidelines." *Journal of the American Geriatrics Society* 48: 179–87.

Miles, S. H., and P. Irvine (2001). "Deaths Caused by Physical Restraints." *Gerontologist* 32: 762–66.

Mittelman, M. S., S. H. Ferris, E. Shulman, G. Steinberg, and B. Levin (1996). "A Family Intervention to Delay Nursing Home Placement of Patients with Alzheimer Disease: A Randomized Controlled Trial." *Journal of the American Medical Association* 276: 1725–31.

Mor, V., O. Intrator, B. E. Fries, C. Phillips, J. Teno, J. Hiris, C. Hawes, and J. Morris (1997). "Changes in Hospitalization Associated with Introducing the Resident Assessment Instrument." *Journal of the American Geriatrics Society* 45: 1002–10.

Morris, J. C., M. Storandt, J. P. Miller, D. W. McKeel, J. L. Price, E. H. Rubin, and L. Berg (2001). "Mild Cognitive Impairment Represents Early-Stage Alzheimer Disease." *Archives of Neurology* 58: 397–405.

Morrison, R. S., J. C. Ahronheim, G. R. Morrison, E. Darling, S. A. Baskin, J. Morris, C. Choi, and D. E. Meier (1998). "Pain and Discomfort Associated with Common Hospital Procedures and Experiences." *Journal of Pain and Symptom Management* 15: 91–101.

Muder, R. R. (1998). "Pneumonia in Residents of Long-Term Care Facilities: Epidemiology, Etiology, Management, and Prevention." *American Journal of Medicine* 105: 319–30.

Muder, R. R., C. Brennen, D. L. Swenson, and M. Wagener (1996). "Pneumonia in a Long-Term Care Facility: A Prospective Study of Outcome." *Archives of Internal Medicine* 156: 2365–70.

Mylotte, J. P., B. Naughton, C. Saludades, and Z. Maszarovics (1998). "Validation and Application of the Pneumonia Prognosis Index to Nursing Home Residents with Pneumonia." *Journal of the American Geriatrics Society* 46: 1538–44.

Pearlman, R. A. (1997). "Determination of Decision-Making Capacity." In Cassel, Cohen, and Larson, 201–9.

Peterson, P. K., D. Stein, D. R. Guay, G. Logan, S. Obaid, R. Gruninger, S. Davies, and R. Breitenbucher (1988). "Prospective Study of Lower Respiratory Tract Infections in an Extended-Care Nursing Home Program: Potential Role of Oral Ciprofloxacin." *American Journal of Medicine* 85: 164–71.

Petry, H. (1999). "Support Groups for Patients in the Early Stage of Dementia—Usefulness and Experiences." *Therapeutische Umschlag* 56: 109–13.

Phillips, C. D., K. M. Spry, P. D. Sloane, and C. Hawes (2000). "Use of Physical Restraints and Psychotropic Medications in Alzheimer Special Care Units in Nursing Homes." *American Journal of Public Health* 90: 92–96.

President's Commission for the Study of Ethical Problems in Medicine and Biomedical and Behavioral Research (1983). *Making Health Care Decisions.* Washington, D.C.: U.S. Government Printing Office.

Roth, L. H., A. Meisel, and C. W. Lidz (1977). "Tests of Competency to Consent to Treatment." *American Journal of Psychiatry* 134: 279–84.

Rubio, A., A. L. Vestner, J. M. Stewart, N. T. Forbes, Y. Conwell, and C. Cox (2001). "Suicide and Alzheimer's Pathology in the Elderly: A Case-Control Study." *Biological Psychiatry* 49: 137–45.

Saliba, D., R. Kington, J. Buchanan, R. Bell, M. Wang, M. Lee, M. Herbst, D. Lee, D. Sur, and L. Rubenstein (2000). "Appropriateness of the Decision to Transfer Nursing Facility Residents to the Hospital." *Journal of the American Geriatrics Society* 48: 154–63.

Smith, A. P., and B. L. Beattie (2001). "Disclosing a Diagnosis of Alzheimer's Disease: Patient and Family Experiences." *Canadian Journal of Neurological Sciences* 28: S67–S71.

Tappen, R. M., K. E. Roach, E. B. Applegate, and P. Stowell (2000). "Effect of a Combined Walking and Conversation Intervention on Functional Mobility of Nursing Home Residents with Alzheimer Disease." *Alzheimer Disease and Associated Disorders* 14: 196–201.

Thompson, R. S., N. K. Hall, and M. Szpiech (1999). "Hospitalization and Mortality Rates for Nursing Home-Acquired Pneumonia." *Journal of Family Practice* 48: 291–93.

Thompson, R. S., N. K. Hall, M. Szpiech, and L. A. Reisenberg (1997). "Treatments and Outcomes of Nursing-Home-Acquired Pneumonia." *Journal of American Board of Family Practice* 10: 82–87.

Tinetti, M. E., W. L. Liu, and S. F. Ginter (1992). "Mechanical Restraints Use and Fall-Related Injuries among Residents of Skilled Nursing Facilities." *Annals of Internal Medicine* 116: 369–74.

Tresch, D. D., J. M. Neahring, E. H. Duthie, D. H. Mark, S. K. Kartes, and T. P. Aufderheide (1993). "Outcomes of Cardiopulmonary Resuscitation in Nursing Homes: Can We Predict Who Will Benefit?" *American Journal of Medicine* 95: 123–30.

Trudeau, S. A. (1999). "Prevention of Physical Impairment in Persons with Advanced Alzheimer's Disease." In Volicer and Bloom-Charette, 80–90.

Volicer, L., and A. Hurley, eds. (1998). *Hospice Care for Patients with Advanced Progressive Dementia*. New York: Springer.

Volicer, L., A. C. Hurley, and Z.V. Blasi (2001). "Scales for Evaluation of End-of-Life Care in Dementia." *Alzheimer Disease and Associated Disorders* 15/4: 194–200.

Volicer, L., A. McKee, and S. Hewitt (2001). "Dementia." *Neurologic Clinics of North America* 19/4: 867–85.

Volicer, L., B. Seltzer, Y. Rheaume, J. Karner, M. Glennon, M. E. Riley, and P. B. Crino (1989). "Eating Difficulties in Patients with Probable Dementia of the Alzheimer Type." *Journal of Geriatric Psychiatry and Neurology* 2: 169–76.

Volicer, L., B. Seltzer, Y. Rheaume, K. Fabiszewski, L. Herz, R. Shapiro, and P. Innis (1987). "Progression of Alzheimer-Type Dementia in Institutionalized Patients: A Cross-Sectional Study." *Journal of Applied Gerontology* 6: 83–94.

Volicer, L., G. Brandeis, and A. C. Hurley (1998). "Infections in Advanced Dementia." In Volicer and Hurley, 29–47.

Volicer, L., K. J. Fabiszewski, Y. L. Rheaume, and K. E. Lasch (1988). *Clinical Management of Alzheimer's Disease*. Rockville, Md.: Aspen.

Volicer, L., and L. Bloom-Charette, eds. (1999). *Enhancing the Quality of Life in Advanced Dementia*. New York: Brunner-Routledge.

Volicer, L., M. Stelly, J. Morris, J. McLaughlin, and B. J. Volicer (1997). "Effects of Dronabinol on Anorexia and Disturbed Behavior in Patients with Alzheimer's Disease." *International Journal of Geriatric Psychiatry* 12: 913–19.

Volicer, L., Y. Rheaume, and D. Cyr (1994). "Treatment of Depression in Advanced Alzheimer's Disease Using Sertraline." *Journal of Geriatric Psychiatry and Neurology* 7: 227–29.

Volicer, L., Y. Rheaume, M. E. Riley, J. Karner, and M. Glennon (1990). "Discontinuation of Tube Feeding in Patients with Dementia of the Alzheimer Type." *American Journal of Alzheimer's Care* 5: 22–25.

Werner, P., J. Cohen-Mansfield, J. Braun, and M. S. Marx (1989). "Physical Restraints and Agitation in Nursing Home Residents." *Journal of the American Geriatrics Society* 37: 1122–26.

Werner, P., V. Koroknay, J. Braun, and J. Cohen-Mansfield (1994). "Individualized Care Alternatives Used in the Process of Removing Physical Restraints in the Nursing Home." *Journal of the American Geriatrics Society* 42: 321–25.

Part Five

ANTICIPATING THE FUTURE: RELIGION, SPIRITUALITY, AND AN AGING SOCIETY

During the last two decades of the twentieth century, anyone who spoke about demographic projections about an aging population probably pointed to the demographers' touchstone: the year 2030. Now that the twenty-first century has arrived, that year looms more clearly out of the mists of the future as older people in the wealthy nations of the world experience longer, healthier lives. These final chapters of this handbook contain what might be called "meditations" on the future, both social and personal. Appropriately, this section begins and ends with chapters by the eldest of the group of authors whose work appears in these pages. These three wise people—James and Betty Birren and Mel Kimble—offer us intimate and courageous personal reflections on aging and dying. Between their chapters appear writings by middle-aged baby boomers considering the implications of the "longevity revolution" for research on religion and spirituality, for the church, and for a just and humane society. In many ways, this last section circles back to Part One, which spoke of "late-life spiritual potentials."

James E. Birren and *Betty A. Birren* begin their chapter by noting that models of aging have not kept up with the actual experience of aging today. These outdated models function in both the social and the personal realms of contemporary life, affecting everything from public policy about airline pilot retirement to older people's attitudes about exercise. Old models of aging, based upon expectations created by earlier cohorts of elders, provide few guides for older people today. A key point reverberating throughout this chapter is that older adults need to take control of their own aging; granted health in longevity, they can make responsible decisions about how they use their resources—decisions which have important implications for themselves, their families, and society as a whole. As a way of coming to terms with taking responsibility for one's old age, the Birrens suggest that older people begin by engaging in autobiographical reflection. By articulating the values that have shaped them, older people can make wiser decisions about how they will manage life in old age.

One of the recurring themes in James Birren's work has been the emphasis on asking good questions. The next chapter in this section poses a question Birren would appreciate: has the scientific study of religion and aging failed to ask the right questions? *Jeff Levin* believes that by ignoring inner experience, religious gerontology risks becoming superannuated in its efforts to understand late-life spirituality.

Unless researchers begin to attend to what Levin broadly describes as "mystical" experience, the split between research on religion, spirituality, and aging and the actual religious and spiritual lives of older people will become profound as baby boomers move into old age. This has implications not only for researchers but also for clergy and religious institutions as they attempt to provide opportunities for spiritual growth among aging persons—aging persons, that is, who still believe that religious institutions retain relevance for their spiritual lives. Many other aging people will pursue mystical, transcendent experiences outside of "organized religion," and Levin argues that these persons' pilgrimages need to be studied and understood. Levin urges researchers to become knowledgeable about these alternative pathways, to be open to studying consciousness, and to employ qualitative methodologies that can reveal more about numinous experience than what he calls the all-too-common "bean-counting" of today's empiricism.

From a researcher who argues that research in religious gerontology risks becoming unable to study the spiritual quests of tomorrow's elders, we turn next to a member of the clergy who claims that his colleagues and the institutions they serve are increasingly perceived as irrelevant by aging baby boomers. In what may be the most unusual chapter in this handbook in that it takes the form of a dialogue between two baby-boomer ministers sitting at a bar, *John T. McFadden* argues that mainline white Protestant churches are so busy trying to "grow" by emphasizing programs for young families that they fail to notice when people whose nests have emptied no longer remain engaged in their congregations. Moreover, some churches fail to hold older people accountable for their spiritual development and offer precious little guidance for growing in faith in late life. In fact, these two fictional clergy agree that religious institutions may be far too smug about the people who do arrive at their doors on Sunday mornings, preferring to reinforce their "extrinsic" religiosity in exchange for an occasional check in the collection plate rather than challenging them to develop a faith that can bear up under the inevitable challenges of later life.

Echoing some of the themes discussed at McFadden's fictitious tavern, *Harry R. Moody* suggests that aging baby boomers face a choice between wallowing in cynicism and narcissism or shedding their illusions and embracing the challenges of conscious aging. Moody describes a movement building in this country to promote conscious aging, not as an elixir yielding unending health and productivity but rather as a humble embrace of life's vicissitudes and the beautiful possibilities for loving God and other persons in later life. Conscious aging can be nourished within the traditional religious institutions although, increasingly, many are turning to groups outside the faith communities that have failed to address the spiritual hungers of this new aging generation. Moody argues that aging persons must learn how to hold the inevitable suffering and loss of old age in creative tension with the potential for spiritual growth and expanded consciousness in late life. Out of this may emerge new appreciation for late-life learning, creativity, holistic health, and spiritual growth. In addition, Moody believes that people who accept the challenges of conscious aging will be equipped to turn outward to help to "repair the world." Surely a vast generation of healthy, active, aging persons who have rejected self-serving spirituality in favor of spiritual disciplines rooted in the world's religious wisdom has great potential to show courage in the struggle for peace and justice in our world.

One finds in the chapters by McFadden and Moody hints of the traps and pitfalls as well as the opportunities inherent in the postmodern world of aging. In *Thomas R. Cole*'s contribution, the postmodern challenge is confronted directly. Cole carefully delineates the conflicts between postmodern thinkers and humanists that arose at the end of the twentieth century and argues that the attack on humanism as falsely preaching immutable "truths" was in error. Rather, he argues for a fresh view of humanism that can be self-critical while retaining valuable insights that are examined in light of current appreciation for diversity. The humanism of which Cole writes is not an alternative to religion or science. Indeed, Cole argues that we can celebrate the advances of Western science while not yielding it authority in the spiritual realm. Likewise, we can appreciate the humanistic impulse for human freedom and creativity without being exclusive humanists who deny the possibility of transcendence. This is why Cole states that a stance of postmodern religious humanism offers to gerontology important intellectual, emotional, and spiritual resources that embrace pluralism, encourage dialogue, appreciate the shaping influence of culture and history, and value the wisdom found in the world's religions.

McFadden, Moody, and Cole all reflect upon contemporary wishful fantasies about perpetual youth and the denial of the vicissitudes of aging. None of them, however, confront the question of death as clearly as *Melvin A. Kimble* does in this final chapter of this volume. Kimble's own encounters with the specter of death have granted him hard-won insights about what he calls its "paradoxes." Drawing upon theology as well as drama and poetry, Kimble practices the kind of gerontology Cole encourages—a reflection on aging and dying that respects the awe and fear that humans feel about these inevitabilities. In response to the paradoxes of death, Kimble urges us to be more mindful about the creation of metaphors and rituals about death. These will enable us to locate transcendent meaning in aging, dying, and death—transcendent meaning in the gracious gift of time that comes to an end for individuals but continues eternally in the loving embrace of God.

28 Our Responsibilities for Our Old Age

JAMES E. BIRREN
BETTY A. BIRREN

Old age can bring many needs for personal services, ranging from economic support, physical care, and personal attention to contacts with family, friends, and other people. These needs may take time and create work for others. We often talk about family and government responsibilities for meeting the needs of our old age but less often do we discuss our own responsibilities. The purpose of this chapter is to review the evolving picture of our personal responsibilities for our old age and to make suggestions about defining them.

Families are usually expected to provide shelter and care to aged parents and grandparents who can no longer provide for themselves. Also, the government is expected to provide basic Social Security and Medicare benefits. Now that people are living longer and more actively, questions may be raised about the overlapping of responsibilities, particularly about family care in relation to the older person. A colleague of ours took her sixty-two-year-old widowed mother-in-law into her household. The mother-in-law was still living with her at age 102. Forty years was almost a lifetime when she was born. This leads us to wonder about the personal initiative and responsibility of the mother-in-law for her own maintenance and social life as well as about her minimizing the responsibilities she was placing on others. If we were in a similar relationship, what would we consider to be our expectations from our family members and what would we consider to be our own responsibilities for managing our needs and wants in our later years? At any age there is the moral principle of minimizing demands on other persons. There is more ambiguity about older persons' responsibilities for themselves, however, as people live longer and society changes.

OUR OUT-OF-DATE MODELS OF AGING AND OLD AGE

Our contemporary society has been described as being in an age revolution. Persons over the age of sixty are now becoming the largest segment of society, in contrast to the shrinking population of young children. The services of society will increasingly need to be directed toward mature and older adults, a shift in direction that requires reexamining individual and societal priorities and responsibilities for the well-being of older adults. Sociologist Matilda White Riley and her colleagues

(1994) have pointed out that there are lag effects in institutions that need to reorient themselves to serve the increasingly mature society. Churches, universities, businesses, and entertainment are serving an increasingly older population. The models of old age that guide the activities of these institutions and organizations are carried forward from past eras when children and young people were given the highest priority. Lag effects are clearly obvious in films and videos produced for a model population of young people, whereas mature audiences are the most frequent viewers. Older people get "hand-me-up" entertainment from scenarios written for the young.

In addition to the institutions of our society that show lag effects in their outdated models of the older people they are servicing, our public policies also show lag effects. For example, airline pilots must retire at age sixty, a rule that was made in 1959. At that time commercial airline pilots occasionally died of heart attacks in cockpits during flights. Methods of detecting heart disease were not sophisticated in 1959; someone could walk out of the physician's examining room having been pronounced healthy and then collapse with a heart attack on the way home. Not only have health examining methods improved but the health of older adults has also improved. Additionally, we have ways of measuring the competence of pilots from in-flight performance observations and performance on flight simulators. But the retirement-age policy is still based on an out-of-date model of what older pilots were like a generation or more ago and what assessments of flying skills and health were like in 1959. In recent years there is some evidence that young pilots tend to have more frequent accidents than do the healthy older, experienced pilots who are forced to retire at age sixty.

There have always been generation gaps and lag effects in information dissemination but with rapid changes in contemporary society at all levels, the lag effects appear even greater. Our society and its institutions have lag effects in their models of aging and old age that provide a basis for policy, organization, services, and public decision making. In addition, our personal models of aging tend to be out-of-date as well, which requires that we update them. The ways we expect to live and structure our lives in our old age are often based on the models of life derived from our grandparents' and parents' lives. Past generations were not as healthy, nor as active in their later years, and did not live as long as we do. How should we carry forward the best of the past but add to it new features of our personal models of living longer in a changed society?

We may have observed wisdom and emotional maturity in older relatives when we were growing up. Selecting vital elements from the values and goals of the past, yet creating new models of living long lives, is a crucial task as we get older. In the past, young people expected that the job or career in which they started their work life would last their entire lives. Today, rapid contemporary changes in the business world usually seem to leave little opportunity for lifetime employment with one's original employer. The lack of stability of spousal relationships must also be noted. The divorce rate is about 50 percent, which has enormous effects on relationships within families. Thus change is a basic feature of the information age. Accompanying the external changes are the changes in individual lives, an important one being our increased length of life.

In addition to living longer and more actively, there are other reasons for attaching greater importance to examining our personal responsibilities for our own old age. In the past, caring for elderly parents was primarily the responsibility of women. Often an unmarried daughter was expected to live with and care for her dependent older parent. Families now have fewer children so there are fewer potential caregiving children for elderly family members. Also, most women are now working outside the home, often in jobs that produce great time pressures. The combination of work, caring for growing children, and taking care of a household results in tremendous time and physical demands, limiting the time and effort that can be devoted to an older family member. Overload is often the fate of the contemporary middle generation, the so-called sandwich generation. Also, younger family members often live in another part of the country in housing that probably does not include an extra room for a dependent older person.

Moving into the home of a grown child can dramatically increase the dependency of a parent, who more than likely has come from an area where he or she had many longtime friends and belonged to various groups that helped define a way of life. Loss of long-standing social contacts means that the older person needs to find new friends and new activities—not always easy to do in the busy younger household and new region. The atmosphere of unfulfilled needs and expectations caused by the new situation can be difficult for the younger generation to meet. Thus many features of our changing society and family life require forethought by the older generation about their responsibilities for their own old age.

EVOLVING RESPONSIBILITIES FOR OLD AGE

About thirty years has been added to the average life expectancy since 1900, when most workers and families lived on farms. Families were large, and older people and children were useful hands in meeting the many farm tasks. As steam, gas, and electricity replaced manpower, people moved into cities to serve the industrial age, often finding employment in making high-energy machines such as tractors and automobiles. Housing and households became smaller.

At the beginning of the information age there have been different demands on the labor force. Manual skills have been replaced as computer skills have become important for employment. Many skills that parents and grandparents knew are no longer useful in the information age, although emotional balance, love, and wisdom are still in short supply. Grandmothers have little need to tell granddaughters how to bake bread in a wood-heated oven except as a story of the past. There is little utility in having a grandfather demonstrate to his grandson how to sharpen a tool on a grindstone. But with a loss of the value of skills learned in the past, there is an increased value in knowledge about emotional relationships in this impersonal information age. Perhaps more grandparents need to learn to use e-mail so they can keep in touch with their grandchildren who do not live nearby.

A traditional role for older people is still to tell their grandchildren and their great-grandchildren about the "good old days" of their youth and, in particular, the history of their own families and traditions. But part of that responsibility is to be aware of the level of interest of their listeners to be sure that the listeners stay interested in the family lore and their own "ancient" history. This is made easier, if less interactive, by a written autobiography. While talking about the good old days it is important to realize that the good old days of our younger audiences are now.

The current oldest generation grew up during the Depression and then coped with the austerities and shortages of World War II. They spent much of the next thirty years raising the baby boomers. Luxury or even simple pleasures were not always as available as they appear to have been in movies or on TV. As older people, might it not be their responsibility to their following generations to expand their understanding and acceptance of their lives which would help define them as *people* and not just as those old parents who constantly seem to need attention and things, which can lead to their becoming regarded as "greedy geezers"?

Management of our old age requires an emphasis on emotional factors as well as on the practical matters of daily life. Perhaps the issue might be formulated thus: How should I manage my life in my old age to minimize the negative impact on others of any changing or increasing needs I may have and also to maximize the quality of my own life and to be of benefit to others?

There are many personal issues that arise from living a long life in a changing society. These range from the practical to transcendent issues of philosophy to spirituality (Kimble et al. 1995; McFadden 1996; Reker and Chamberlain 2000). These issues can be phrased as statements that direct older persons to actions that are presumably based on an accepted common set of values and common circumstances of later life. Diversity in older persons' life experiences, health, and present life circumstances is coming to be regarded as characteristic. For this reason, questions that provoke thought are more appropriate than prescribed "laws of living." The following sample questions are designed to help stimulate our maturing population to think about their responsibilities for their old age.

- How can I live my life so as to minimize the support from others to serve my needs?
- How should I conserve my resources, e.g., money, property, and access to services, so as to maximize my independence of living?
- How can I reduce the risks of poor health or disabling diseases?
- What can I do to maintain or improve personal relationships with family, friends, and organizations?
- What can I do to be of greater service to my family members?
- What can I do to better serve my community?

LOOKING BACK AND LOOKING FORWARD

Writing an autobiography is a productive way to gain a perspective on life and to help define values and responsibilities in old age (Birren et al. 1996). It is even better to share one's autobiography—one's life story—in a structured group to take advantage of the group's help in priming memories. Writing an autobiography provides insights into how life has flowed. A paraphrase of philosopher Søren Kierkegaard's statement illustrates the point: "You live your life forward but understand it backward." Understanding where we have been, what we have lived through, gives us a basis for making judgments in our later years that are not only good for us but also good for others (Birren and Deutchman 1991).

Writing an autobiography following a structured plan makes it much more likely that it will actually be written (Birren and Cochran 2001). Sharing this writing about the major themes of life with other people helps clarify the backward understanding of the "threads" that have run through the major themes and fabric of life. Is it our responsibility for our own old age to achieve such understanding? Insofar as this understanding leads us to a greater appreciation of our lives—and therefore an appreciation of others and their lives—yes, it is.

The afternoon of life can provide the time and the motive for doing autobiographies. A written autobiography is a family asset that provides family members with a map of a person's life. In the lines (or between the lines) there are lessons to be learned from the writer's survival. Another value of autobiography is that it helps provide a basis for understanding the development of one's philosophy of life and principles of living. Taking next steps in a transition stage in life is always necessary, and the later years are no exception. Doing an autobiography nudges us toward the future and shows us ways of getting there. Where to go from here—and how to go from here—are always questions of life (Birren and Feldman 1977). For our present purposes, a relevant question is what values underlie our intentions in the afternoons or evenings of our lives, and how we would like to live our remaining years.

CLEANING UP YOUR "HOUSE"

Individuals often leave behind complex and messy issues that others must manage and have to make decisions about without knowing what the departed person might have wished. These decisions extend from the disposal of possessions, the content of wills, power of attorney for health care, to last wishes for burial and memorial services. Our households and our lives can have many aspects that we expect to get around to but often never quite do. Leaving behind unfinished business can place a load on those who follow us, since they may not know our thoughts and wishes. Also, sibling rivalries may be evoked. Siblings may feel that others who inherited or received property from a formal or informal process have been favored. There may be family heirlooms or symbols of the past that have no monetary value but represent family traditions. These often cause severe family tensions and lead to estrangement of some members.

In addition to anticipating and preparing our wills and other formal documents, attention should be given to the symbols of our lives. A book might be given to an old friend, grandfather's antique watch might be given to an older grandson, or a picture that hung on the wall when the family was growing up might have a cherished place in one of the homes of the next generation. A letter can be written expressing our wishes about the disposition of personal possessions. Not only will a letter reduce confusion when we die but it will also reduce the prospect of inadvertent antagonisms derived from the uncertainty of "of who gets what."

In a broader sense we need to clean our households as we approach the end of life. Leaving a mess to be sorted our by children and others does not help them in their grief. Some of our possessions might be left to a church or preferred charity or to friends rather than being trashed. This requires that we think about them in advance and let our wishes be known. For example, the first author has a hand-forged ax that belonged to his grandfather. Would some potential great-great-grandson want this as a symbol of the past or should it go anonymously in the trash?

A feature of the expression of our late-life wishes that often creates uncertainty is the memorial service we would like to represent our lives. What music would we want? What person should conduct the service? A minister friend told us that he occasionally is called upon to conduct a funeral service without having any notes from the deceased person and without family members being aware of what might have been wanted. As a result of lack of this information, impressions given at memorial services might be inappropriate. The authors know of two persons who walked out of two different funeral services for a parent because they felt it did not represent the life of the parent. The services had been arranged by family members and others who did not know what the deceased would have wanted. The deceased would most certainly have been upset that the memorial funeral services left a legacy of family tension.

Another task of late-life planning is to prepare a list of friends and colleagues who should be informed of our death. A fifty-year friendship and collegial relationship of the authors ended when the friend died without their knowing. For years, telephone conversations on holidays had kept the relationship alive. When a letter of ours was returned with "no such party" stamped on the envelope, we felt a void. By tracing though his last address, we discovered that the friend had died. His son, who lived in another part of the country, was probably unaware of our long-standing relationship that had begun before he was born.

The best way of reducing the possibility of postmortem tensions and resentments is to discuss our plans, intentions, and wishes with family members and close friends. This can include circulating documents and statements of wishes. The process of circulating end-of-life documents and discussing them can help all members of our network to relate to each better after our death. Knowing that we did our best to express our wishes and regards for others may also contribute to our own inner peace at an important time.

STATEMENT OF INTENTIONS

The Bible, Torah, Quran, and other religious and philosophical writings provide durable lifetime values for guiding choices. The American Constitution also provides a durable guide to human values. Yet there are times when the literal interpretations of these guiding texts should be brought into a personal contemporary context. These writings were made before our age of genetic research, computers and Internet communication, knowledge of infectious diseases, men on the moon, and nuclear and germ warfare, for example. We face new choices by living longer in a profoundly changed society, and these choices touch upon our personal values and responsibilities.

The first author of this chapter once examined the values and beliefs he held that related to his responsibilities for his old age (Birren 1985). This led to an evolving list of his responsibilities for his own old age which are given in the following section. They are presented here to stimulate thought and discussion about our personal responsibilities in living long in a changing society.

My Guide to Old Age

- to honor my children and all children, to foster their growth and to remain close to them
- to keep a joyous spirit and to avoid becoming bitter if I am overlooked by the young or by the events of the times
- to continue to learn so that I may be a resource for solving or moderating the problems of life
- to continue to weed the garden of my life, remove yesterday's flowers and dead branches, so that I may foster personal growth in myself
- to refrain from seeking an unreasonable share of resources and placing a disproportionate load upon others if I become ill
- to jettison old resentments and prejudices, so that I may be emotionally free and intellectually open to others
- to use the experiences of my years to obtain fairness and justice for others, so that I may remain an active citizen in a free society
- to manage the passing on of my possessions with fairness and avoid manipulating them to gain attention or to cause loved ones to vie for material gain
- to prepare myself and others for my death, so that I may pass with poise, dignity, and peace (and to consider donating my body parts to others)
- to leave the land and its people better than I found them by my own deeds and through the efforts of others whom I have influenced

The interested reader should prepare a list of his or her responsibilities for old age. These may include such practical matters as wills for settling the transition of property to heirs and durable power of attorney for end-of-life health care. In our work with guided autobiography and listening to many life stories, we have found that many mature children have been deeply upset by the way their parents had passed on their resources. Siblings sometimes may not speak to each other for years, if ever, after disputed bequests. Most parents would undoubtedly be disappointed that their failure to be explicit about their material possessions had left such disputed legacies.

ASPIRATIONS AND GOALS

Although we may develop limitations in our ability to manage the demands of everyday life as we grow old, we should not overlook our aspirations for tomorrow. These can range from rather simple goals, such as obtaining and reading a sought-after book or writing to an old friend, to complex goals of political actions and world peace. The young may not recognize that individuals are never too old to have aspirations so they do not take the time to ask older persons what they would like for tomorrow. But it is also the responsibility of older people to think about their goals and aspirations, to discuss them with others, and to see what steps they can take to realize them.

New books are appearing that deal with the age revolution and with using our added active years to advantage. The metaphors that are used vary from an emphasis on health to useful social roles, e.g., successful aging, productive aging, and vital aging (Butler and Gleason 1985; Morrow-Howell, Hinterlong, and Sherraden 2001; Rowe and Kahn 1998). Ending personal habits that erode the body's functional capacity to use the gift of long life is not only a responsibility of our health-care institutions but also our own personal responsibility. Science is expanding our understanding of the body's capacity for self-repair and of ways to supplement it. As individuals, however, we should take the responsibility to use the gains in such information. To maximize our long lives not only in physical terms, we have to articulate and discuss our long lives in terms of the values we derive from social, philosophical, and spiritual sources in our contemporary world.

BIBLIOGRAPHY

Birren, J. E. (1985). "Age, Competence, and Wisdom." In Butler and Gleason, 29–36.

Birren, J. E., and D. E. Deutchman (1991). *Guiding Autobiography Groups for Older Adults: Exploring the Fabric of Life.* Baltimore: Johns Hopkins University Press.

Birren, J. E., G. M. Kenyon, J. E. Ruth, J. J. F. Schroots, and T. Svensson, eds. (1996). *Aging and Biography: Explorations in Adult Development.* New York: Springer.

Birren, J. E., and K. N. Cochran (2001). *Telling the Stories of Life through Guided Autobiography Groups.* Baltimore: Johns Hopkins University Press.

Birren, J. E., and K. W. Schaie, eds. (1996). *Handbook of the Psychology of Aging.* 4th ed. San Diego: Academic Press.

Birren, J. E., and L. Feldman (1997). *Where to Go from Here.* New York: Simon & Schuster.

Butler, R. N., and H. P. Gleason, eds. (1985). *Productive Aging: Enhancing Vitality in Later Life.* New York: Springer.

Kimble, M. A., S. H. McFadden, J. W. Ellor, and J. J. Seeber, eds. (1995). *Aging, Spirituality, and Religion: A Handbook.* Vol. 1. Minneapolis: Fortress Press.

McFadden, S. H. (1996). "Religion, Spirituality, and Aging." In Birren and Schaie, 162–77.

Morrow-Howell, N., J. Hinterlong, and M. Sherraden, eds. (2001). *Productive Aging: Concepts and Challenges.* Baltimore: Johns Hopkins University Press.

Reker, G. T., and K. Chamberlain, eds. (2000). *Exploring Existential Meaning.* Thousand Oaks, Calif.: Sage.

Riley, M. W., R. L. Kahn, and A. Foner, eds. (1994). *Age and Structural Lag: Society's Failure to Provide Meaningful Opportunities in Work, Family and Leisure.* New York: Wiley-Interscience.

Rowe, J. W., and R. L. Kahn (1998). *Successful Aging.* New York: Random House.

29

"Bumping the Top": Is Mysticism the Future of Religious Gerontology?

JEFF LEVIN

> One who has never been bewildered, who has never looked upon life and his own existence as phenomena which require answers and yet, paradoxically, for which the only answers are new questions, can hardly understand what religious experience is.
>
> —*Shaarei Tefillah*

WHERE RELIGIOUS GERONTOLOGY HAS GONE WRONG

"Are we a nation of mystics?" That was the question posed by National Opinion Research Center sociologists Greeley and McCready (1975) based upon results from the 1973 General Social Survey. According to their findings, the lifetime prevalence of selected experiences was unexpectedly high: 59 percent for déjà vu, 58 percent for ESP, 35 percent for a general numinous experience, 27 percent for spiritualism (contact with the dead), and 24 percent for clairvoyance.

Follow-up work I conducted based on data collected as part of the 1988 General Social Survey revealed that the lifetime prevalence of four of these experiences had increased considerably over the intervening decade and a half: 67.3 percent for déjà vu, 64.8 percent for ESP, 39.9 percent for spiritualism, and 28.3 percent for clairvoyance (Levin 1993). Further, only 13.5 percent of respondents reported never having experienced any of these phenomena. Additional analyses suggested that the lifetime prevalence of these experiences has increased with successively younger persons since the 1970s and early 1980s. The near universality of these experiences (at least one such experience in nearly nine of ten adult Americans) coupled with the apparent presence of both cohort and period effects reveal this to be an intriguing and vital construct for gerontological research now and in the years to come.

From what is funded, researched, and published by empirical scientists in the field of religious gerontology, you would never know this to be so. Research in this area continues to emphasize (a) the study of differences in psychosocial and health-related outcomes by categories of religious affiliation (see Sherrill, Larson, and Greenwold 1993) and (b) patterns, predictors, and outcomes of mostly behavioral measures of religious participation (e.g., Levin, Taylor, and Chatters 1994). Granted, there is nothing wrong with this focus in and of itself. Religious identification and involvement are crucial determinants of well-being in older adults and throughout the life-course (see Koenig 1994), and these matters warrant the careful attention that they are finally receiving after years of neglect (see Krause 1997).

Nevertheless, if the data on mystical experience are any indication, then those of us who conduct quantitatively oriented basic research in religion and aging are pretty much out to lunch. With the exception of a small area of research on prayer (see, e.g., Ellison and Taylor 1996; Levin and Taylor 1991; McCullough 1995), a behavior with definite mystical components and sequelae, empirical researchers are missing the boat when it comes to what are apparently the most widely manifested phenomena in the spiritual realm. We are systematically ignoring these phenomena—and, what is more, inner experience in general, whether "mystical" or not—in favor of discrete and measurable behaviors, public or private, consistent with the behaviorist and mechanistic biases inherent in behavioral science, behavioral epidemiology, and biomedicine. In so doing we are failing to lay the groundwork for the religious gerontology of the future, which, it seems, will have no choice but to delve into the mystical realm if it is to stay current with the most popular and salient expressions of spirituality in the older generations to come.

HOW RELIGIOUS GERONTOLOGY CAN GO RIGHT

As a corrective to the purely empirical research on discrete behaviors characteristic of much of academic religious gerontology, the late Dr. L. Eugene Thomas helped to introduce and promote more qualitative research approaches (see Thomas and Eisenhandler 1994, 1999). His greatest contribution to the field was his emphasis on identifying the variety of attitudes, beliefs, and experiences critical for the well-being of older adults, especially those living contemplative lives as renunciates or initiates of non-Western spiritual paths (e.g., Thomas and Chambers 1989; Thomas 1991, 1992, 2001).

In one well-known study, Thomas (1991) conducted in-depth interviews and participant observation with Hindu *sannyasis* (renunciates) residing in Varanasi and Pondicherry, in India. His dialogues with these *sadhus* (mystical ascetics) convinced him of their remarkable spiritual maturity and of the depth of their wisdom. He noted, for example, that these *yogis* "seem to fall clearly into Erikson's eighth stage of ego integrity" (224). His concluding remarks offer a devastating critique of mainstream gerontological research on well-being:

> In talking with these men I had a clear impression of the irrelevancy of much of the research on the correlates of life satisfaction conducted in this country. By any standard, these men were socially disengaged—the number of roles they occupied had shrunk dramatically. Their economic level would place them below the poverty level. Their health ranged from fair to quite poor. They had no support from their families, and they had no personal friends. Despite these and other negative correlates of life satisfaction (at least, as

derived from research with Western respondents), *these men would have bumped the top of any scale of life satisfaction.* (225; emphasis added)

To infer from national data on the prevalence of psi or paranormal experiences that the average American adult is as accomplished a spiritual pathworker as a self-realized yogi master would certainly be a gross overstatement. A lot of ground is covered by the labels "mystical," "psi," "paranormal," and "spiritual," and these concepts, though perhaps overlapping, are far from identical. Mystical experience, for one, is typically conceived by scholars as something of an epiphenomenon of a religious life. According to Ariel (1988):

> Mysticism is a specific theory and practice of how to intensify the religious experience. It involves the transformation of the religious experience into an intense relationship with the supreme reality. It is a more intense form of religion than is normally sanctioned within formal religions. Mysticism, in many religions, is also an esoteric phenomenon restricted to, or practiced by, select individuals rather than by the masses. (39)

Psi or paranormal experiences, such as those investigated in the General Social Surveys, are considered by respective spiritual traditions to be the fruits of mystical experience, as in the *siddhis* (supernatural powers) described by Patañjali (Woods 1914) or the "spiritual gifts" described by Paul (1 Cor. 12:1–11) or, alternatively, initiation into an occult or metaphysical path (Winner 1970). While data on the growing prevalence of psi experiences among Americans therefore do not necessarily portend a nation of classical mystics or adepts, they nonetheless signal that more direct experience of higher spiritual realities may indeed be coming to characterize the religious life of "the masses" referenced above.

If these trends continue, then the realm of mystical experience—of inner, liminal experience of the numinous or holy or divine—will be increasingly relevant to gerontologists in the coming years as the baby boomers age. This particular age cohort, born after World War II and before the advent of the Kennedy presidency, was socialized through the political upheaval of the 1960s, the human potential movement of the 1970s, and the New Age movement of the 1980s. These social-structural realities and the concomitant social changes they engendered have left their mark on the spiritual life of this cohort (Roof 1993). The increasing centrality and salience of personal experience as a defining characteristic of religious expression and a defining feature of one's spiritual life are prime examples of how this cohort differs from previous generations.

The religious gerontologists of the future thus will be surveying a much different religious landscape than is present today. Tobin (1991) recognizes this when he notes, "Religious institutions, which are particularly important for the current cohort of the very old, are likely to be of less importance for future cohorts" (132). This is not to say that religion or spirituality will not weigh as heavily in the lives of older adults or will no longer represent a source of comfort and support but rather that this salutary role will not be expressed principally through formal relationships with churches, synagogues, or mosques. Older adults will find other ways to connect with the ultimate or eternal and draw meaning from these experiences.

We may eventually reach a point where a significant proportion of elders value insights that would sound more at home in workshops at Esalen or Omega or Naropa or Elat Chayyim than in traditional liturgies. There is some evidence that mainstream religions and religious denominations have recognized this trend and are beginning to prepare for the future. During the week in which I was in Cincinnati to present the talk on which this chapter is based, I paid a visit one afternoon to Hebrew Union College–Jewish Institute of Religion, the main seminary of Reform Judaism in North America. Earlier that day, there had been a noon brown-bag presentation on the use of congregations as centers for holistic healing. Since then, the Union of American Hebrew Congregations, the synagogue arm of the Reform movement, has instituted a series of annual conferences for rabbis on this theme, and special services emphasizing spiritual renewal, inner healing, and meditation are becoming commonplace in Reform synagogues throughout the country. Similar developments have occurred in Conservative and Reconstructionist Judaism, and wherever Jewish Renewal *chavurot* have been organized.

WHAT RELIGIOUS GERONTOLOGISTS CAN DO NOW

The message for empirical religious gerontologists such as myself is clear. We ought to begin exploring the history and phenomenology of the esoteric or inner paths of exoteric traditions—the "perennial philosophy"—for fresh insights about what will be relevant to tomorrow's elders. We would do well to explore Kabbalistic Judaism, Sufism, Zen Buddhism, contemplative Christianity, charismatic renewal, the multitude of yogas, sundry metaphysical and initiatory paths, and, finally, although some may bristle at the suggestion, the New Age phenomenon in all of its manifestations. There is a lot to be learned from these esoteric paths that can nourish our research agendas and often feeble theoretical and conceptual models (and perhaps even our own spiritual lives).

One major effort to redirect empirical religious gerontology was initiated by the National Institute on Aging (NIA) through support from the Fetzer Institute of Kalamazoo, Michigan. In 1995, the NIA organized a Conference on Methodological Approaches to the Study of Religion, Health, and Aging, moderated by Dr. M. Powell Lawton. This was a special invited working meeting featuring key researchers in religious gerontology as well as prominent scholars in other related fields, such as religious studies, theology, psychology, and medicine. As a result of this conference, the NIA and Fetzer convened an ongoing Workgroup on Measures of Religiousness and Spirituality, chaired by Dr. Neal Krause, and Fetzer later released a Request for Applications (RFA) on Spirituality and Religiousness in Aging and Health: Addressing Conceptual and Methodological Issues. The expressed charge of the workgroup and the stated purpose for the RFA were to encourage the development and validation of new approaches to religious assessment that would capture more completely the breadth of spiritual expression in older adults and throughout the life-course. The workgroup's recommendations, along with some preliminary psychometric findings, were subsequently issued in a summary report (Fetzer Institute 1999).

The NIA/Fetzer workgroup identified several domains of greatest potential, including spiritual experience, operationalized as ongoing moments of transcendence or connection with the divine and a sense of oneness or harmony with God or one's surroundings. The impetus for this focus was a desire to more accurately and completely characterize the spiritual life of "those aging baby boomers who claim to be nonreligious, in an institutional or organizational sense, yet nonetheless highly 'spiritual'" (Levin 1997, 21). It will be enlightening to observe the field of religious gerontology over the next decade as research in this area begins to surface at the major meetings and in the mainstream journals.

For now, if those of us who are empirical researchers would simply pull our heads out of our statistical manuals and methodology textbooks and survey printouts for a while and spend a little time learning from folks like Rabbi Zalman Schachter-Shalomi, Pir Vilayat Inayat Khan, Father Matthew Fox, Baba Ram Dass, and Dr. Elmer Green—contemporary elders of respective inner paths—then we might gain greater insight into how spirituality can manifest itself in older adulthood. The benefits of "dialoguing" with these and other modern-day elder-mystics can be of inestimable value to us in our positing of midrange theories and hypotheses, our selection of samples to study, and our choice of constructs and variables to assess. What we currently believe to be relevant—to health, well-being, adjustment, coping, whatever—in the lives of older adults, especially when it comes to religious factors, may not be the universal or eternal social facts that they are (mis)perceived to be.

One need not rely solely on famous contemplatives or esoterica for wisdom on the place of mystical experience in spiritual maturity. We are surrounded by older folks on mystical paths. According to Robert C. Atchley (1996):

> Mystical elders can probably teach us valuable lessons, but so far most traditional religious denominations have shown very little interest in listening. Although many elders quietly ripen into mystical realization on their own, many more could probably experience mystical insights if they were encouraged or enabled to do so. And these insights might revitalize a tradition of democratic spiritual dialogue and draw more young people into the conversation. (2)

Likewise, such insights might also revitalize a tradition of seeking overlooked sources of human strength that has characterized the field of religious gerontology from the beginning. While mystically inclined older adults may currently be in the minority in their respective age cohort, this may not always be so if current trends continue. Further, as has been noted (Townsend 1996), "the influence of their ideas on the general public is growing and being absorbed by those who would never think of themselves as 'New Age' " (5). Truly, this perspective "provides a different paradigm of knowing and being . . . [through which] people can verify the reality and power of the transcendent and access it for help and comfort" (5). Religious gerontologists must begin to explore this paradigm.

This critique of empirical religious gerontology should not be overstated. While those of us working in this area do a generally lousy job of documenting the spiritual lives of adult Americans in their full breadth, what we *do* document is done with immense skill and meticulousness. Most laudable is the methodological rigor present in the best of this research. It is not my contention that religious gerontologists ought to abandon empirical research. Quite the contrary! Rather, our rigorous, psychometrically and theoretically grounded approach to researching religion and aging can benefit strongly from consideration of new spiritual domains, such as mystical experience. Likewise, the study of aging and mystical experience can just as surely benefit from a renewed emphasis on this topic on the part of the very best empirical scientists working in this field. There is no reason why our LISREL models and Cox proportional hazards models, for example, cannot accommodate variables measuring features of transcendent experience. As has been noted, "The unorthodoxy of a construct, conceptually speaking, is not a particular barrier to its psychometric validation and use in subsequent analyses" (Levin et al. 1997, 1089), provided it can be reliably assessed. Epidemiological methods, especially, are quite amenable to the investigation of "mysterious phenomena" (Levin and Steele 2001), such as expressions of spirituality.

WHY THIS MATTERS FOR RELIGIOUS GERONTOLOGY

More than thirty years ago, a report sponsored by the Russell Sage Foundation outlined the most important research needs in the field of religious gerontology. These included investigation of (a) the relationship between religious attendance and health, (b) predictors of changes in religiousness in old age, (c) the possibility of private religiousness taking the place of public worship in older adults, and (d) outcomes of religiousness over time through longitudinal studies (Riley, Foner, and Johnson 1968). Anyone who is active as a researcher in this field will immediately recognize these issues as *still* the principal topics of funding, research, and publication in religious gerontology. These certainly are important areas of research and, much work remains to be done, but perhaps it is time to begin expanding the boundaries of this field. After three decades of study on the same topics, no one can possibly accuse us of being reckless if we extend our reach a little further out. Religious gerontologists might be surprised to know that other scholarly fields long ago discovered mystical experience and have mined this realm for fresh insights for several decades.

Not surprisingly, the fields of transpersonal and humanistic psychology have shown considerable interest in mystical and transcendent experience. Notable contributions include (a) discussion of the linkages among spiritual pathwork, subtle energies, and states of consciousness (Green and Green 1971); (b) exploration of the relation of "plateau experience" to transcendence of space and time (Krippner 1972); (c) speculation on how peak experience influences a mystical intuition that enhances perceptions of the absolute (Armor 1969); and (d) identification of aspects of mystical experience with features of psychotic episodes (Lukoff 1985). Other investigations of similarities and differences between mystics and diagnosed psychotics and neurotics have been conducted by psychiatric researchers (e.g., Douglas-Smith 1971). Neuropsychological (Helminiak 1984), psychophysiological (Wickramasekera 1991), and physiological (Davidson 1976) perspectives on mystical experience also have been published.

A common theme in this work is reflection on how senescence and the approach of transition to the next world may impact one's spiritual life, especially insofar as individuals may be more amenable, susceptible, or receptive to the experience of nonordinary states of consciousness. This conclusion is consonant with centuries of observations by saints, mystics, and esotericists belonging to a variety of spiritual traditions. From medieval Catholic monastics and Jewish sages to ancient renunciates on Zen or yogi paths to ordinary seekers in contemporary North America—we know that the potential challenges and life-course transitions associated with aging may facilitate mystical interludes or more lasting experiences of transcendence. In some traditional cultures the exploration of extraordinary realms of consciousness has been an acknowledged, sanctioned, and esteemed role of community elders. The course of aging and maturing throughout adulthood and into the life stage that social demographers have sterilely labeled as "old-old" may, in enlightened seekers, also trace a process of "waking up" (Tart 1987). This concept, derived from the Western esoteric tradition of Gurdjieff and Ouspensky, refers to an awakening from the trance of everyday life into consciousness of the higher spiritual reality in which all human life is embedded. Chronic or functionally limiting illness and one's impending death can be two powerful stimuli to waking up—to becoming fully conscious.

Despite this volume of evidence in the social-historical record, social gerontologists who study religion empirically have never paid much—if any—attention to this issue. "Consciousness," whether ordinary or extraordinary, is not a concept investigated or discussed by social-science researchers in gerontology, the type of aging researchers who include among their ranks most empirical religious gerontologists. To be fair, consciousness is not a concept that seems to interest social scientists in general. Perhaps by dint of a shared worldview with prominent positivist, materialist, and secular features, many social scientists act as if they find these topics embarrassing and unworthy of study. Ironically, where empirical gerontological research has been conducted and published on the topics of consciousness and transcendence, it has been done by scientists in other fields or in branches of gerontology generally uninhabited by social or behavioral scientists. Examples include a study of the link between a state of "harmonious interconnectedness" and spiritual well-being among older adults conducted by a team of nursing researchers (Hungelmann et al. 1985), and a discussion of neurochemical factors in mysticism published in a leading journal of biological gerontology (de Nicolas 1998).

Clearly, it is high time for religious gerontologists to shed both their fetish for discrete behaviors and their fear of directly engaging personal experience. Documenting patterns, predictors, and psychosocial and health outcomes of both daily and more transcendent spiritual experiences, and developing reliable means of assessing these experiences, are tasks that empirical religious gerontologists are uniquely and amply qualified to perform. The study of aging and mystical experience fits well within the research programs of many of the field's top scientists, and will require theoretical, methodological, and analytical skills that this cohort of scholars possesses in abundant measure.

The danger in delaying this enterprise, as mentioned above, is that religious gerontology, should it neglect the experiential realm, may become increasingly irrelevant as currently younger cohorts age into older adulthood. There is a vast new world of religious phenomena that have heretofore gone uncharted by religious gerontologists but that are becoming increasingly more central, meaningful, and salient to the spiritual lives of adult Americans. These adults are tomorrow's older adults, and they will be the respondents and subjects of tomorrow's gerontological researchers. If those of us who are active in religious gerontology begin today to expand our collective vision, then we are sure to discover the rewards of a renewed focus on personal experience of the divine and numinous over and above the bean-counting of today's behavioral empiricism.

BIBLIOGRAPHY

Ariel, D. S. (1988). *The Mystic Quest: An Introduction to Jewish Mysticism*. New York: Schocken.

Armor, T. (1969). "A Note on the Peak Experience and a Transpersonal Psychology." *Journal of Transpersonal Psychology* 1: 47–50.

Atchley, R. C. (1996). "Mystical Experience and Aging: Diverse Pathways and Experiences." *Aging and Spirituality* 8/3: 1–2.

Central Conference of American Rabbis (1975). *Shaarei Tefillah (Gates of Prayer): The New Union Prayer Book*. New York: Central Conference of American Rabbis.

Davidson, J. M. (1976). "The Physiology of Meditation and Mystical States of Consciousness." *Perspectives in Biology and Medicine* 19: 345–79.

de Nicolas, A. T. (1998). "The Biocultural Paradigm: The Neural Connection between Science and Mysticism." *Experimental Gerontology* 33: 169–82.

Douglas-Smith, B. (1971). "An Empirical Study of Religious Mysticism." *British Journal of Psychiatry* 118: 549–54.

Ellison, C. G., and R. J. Taylor (1996). "Turning to Prayer: Social and Situational Antecedents of Religious Coping among African Americans." *Review of Religious Research* 38: 111–31.

Fetzer Institute (1999). "Multidimensional Measurement of Religiousness/Spirituality for Use in Health Research: A Report of the Fetzer Institute/National Institute on Aging Working Group." Kalamazoo, Mich.: Fetzer Institute.

Greeley, A. M. (1975). *The Sociology of the Paranormal: A Reconnaissance.* Beverly Hills, Calif.: Sage.

Greeley, A. M., and W. C. McCready (January 26, 1975). "Are We a Nation of Mystics?" *New York Times Magazine,* 12ff.

Green, E. E., and A. M. Green (1971). "On the Meaning of Transpersonal: Some Metaphysical Perspectives." *Journal of Transpersonal Psychology* 3: 27–46.

Helminiak, D. A. (1984). "Neurology, Psychology, and Extraordinary Religious Experiences." *Journal of Religion and Health* 23: 33–45.

Hungelmann, J., E. Kenkel-Rossi, L. Klassen, and R. M. Stollenwerk (1985). "Spiritual Well-Being in Older Adults: Harmonious Interconnectedness." *Journal of Religion and Health* 24:147–53.

Koenig, H. G. (1994). *Aging and God: Spiritual Pathways to Mental Health in Midlife and Later Years.* New York: Haworth Pastoral.

Krause, N. (1997). "Religion, Aging, and Health: Current Status and Future Prospects." *Journal of Gerontology: Social Sciences* 52B: S291–S293.

Krippner, S. ed. (1972). "The Plateau Experience: A. H. Maslow and Others." *Journal of Transpersonal Psychology* 2: 107–20.

Levin, J., and L. Steele (2001). "On the Epidemiology of 'Mysterious' Phenomena." *Alternative Therapies in Health and Medicine* 7/1: 64–66.

Levin, J. S. (1997). "Religious Research in Gerontology, 1980–1994: A Systematic Review." *Journal of Religious Gerontology* 10/3: 3–31.

——— (1993). "Age Differences in Mystical Experiences." *The Gerontologist* 33: 507–13.

Levin, J. S., and R. J. Taylor (1997). "Age Differences in Patterns and Correlates of the Frequency of Prayer." *The Gerontologist* 37: 75–88.

Levin, J. S., R. J. Taylor, and L. M. Chatters (1994). "Race and Gender Differences in Religiosity among Older Adults: Findings from Four National Surveys." *Journal of Gerontology: Social Sciences* 49: S137–S145.

Levin, J. S., T. A. Glass, L. H. Kushi, J. R. Schuck, L. Steele, and W. B. Jonas (1997). "Quantitative Methods in Research on Complementary and Alternative Medicine: A Methodological Manifesto." *Medical Care* 35: 1079–94.

Lukoff, D. (1985). "The Diagnosis of Mystical Experiences with Psychotic Features." *Journal of Transpersonal Psychology* 17: 155–82.

McCullough, M.E. (1995). "Prayer and Health: Conceptual Issues, Research Review, and Research Agenda." *Journal of Psychology and Theology* 23: 15–29.

McFadden, S. H., and R. C. Atchley, eds. (2001). *Aging and the Meaning of Life: A Multidisciplinary Exploration.* New York: Springer.

Riley, M. W., and A. Foner, eds. (1968). *Aging and Society,* vol. 1: *An Inventory of Research Findings.* New York: Russell Sage Foundation.

Riley, M. W., A. Foner, and M. E. Johnson (1968). "Religious Roles." In Riley and Foner, 483–500.

Roof, W. C. (1993). *A Generation of Seekers: The Spiritual Journeys of the Baby Boom Generation.* San Francisco: HarperSanFrancisco.

Sherrill, K. A., D. B. Larson, and M. Greenwold (1993). "Is Religion Taboo in Gerontology?: Systematic Review of Research on Religion in Three Major Gerontology Journals, 1985–1991." *American Journal of Geriatric Psychiatry* 1: 109–17.

Tart, C. T. (1987). *Waking Up: Overcoming the Obstacles to Human Potential.* Boston: New Science Library.

Thomas, L. E. (2001). "The Job Hypothesis: Gerotranscendence and Life Satisfaction among Elderly Turkish." In McFadden and Atchley, 207–27.

———— (1992). "Identity, Ideology and Medicine: Health Attitudes and Behavior among Hindu Religious Renunciates." *Social Science and Medicine* 34: 499–505.

———— (1991). "Dialogues with Three Religious Renunciates and Reflections on Wisdom and Maturity." *International Journal of Aging and Human Development* 32: 211–27.

Thomas, L. E., and K. O. Chambers (1989). "Phenomenology of Life Satisfaction among Elderly Men: Quantitative and Qualitative Views." *Psychology and Aging* 4: 284–89.

Thomas, L. E., and S. A. Eisenhandler (1999). *Religion, Belief, and Spirituality in Late Life.* New York: Springer.

———— (1994). *Aging and the Religious Dimension.* Westport, Conn.: Auburn.

Tobin, S. S. (1991). *Personhood in Advanced Old Age: Implications for Practice.* New York: Springer.

Townsend, J. B. (1996). "Aging and Personal Spiritual Quests." *Aging and Spirituality* 8/3: 4–5.

Wickramasekera, Ian (1991). "Model of the Relationship between Hypnotic Ability, Psi, and Sexuality." *Journal of Parapsychology* 55: 159–74.

Winner, A. K. (1970). *The Basic Ideas of Occult Wisdom.* Wheaton, Ill.: Quest.

Woods, J. H., trans. (1914). *The Yoga-System of Patañjali.* Harvard Oriental Series 17. Delhi: Motilal Banarsidass.

30   A Pastor Ponders the Boomers

JOHN T. MCFADDEN

It was a typical Monday afternoon at Preachers Bar and Grill, where clergy representing various denominations and theological persuasions regularly gathered to ponder deep mysteries of the Spirit or to exchange ecclesial gossip. Near the front window a mixed group of Anglicans and Lutherans amiably debated the matter of apostolic succession. Similarly lively groups were gathered at tables scattered about the room but, as usual, my old friend Pastor Langston was perched alone at the bar, a bottle of Grolsch in one hand and a folded magazine in the other, squinting to read in the dim light. I called for a draft and joined him. "You appear to be quite engrossed," I said by way of greeting. "Did the new issue of *Health and Fitness for Barthians* arrive today?"

Langston grunted an acknowledgment of my presence. "Actually, it is one of those lame weekly newsmagazines my members insist on passing to me whenever something vaguely religious is squeezed in between articles on the medical breakthrough of the month and the teen pop star of the week, like when the Jesus Seminar proves that Jesus suffered from frequent migraines."

"So what article did your member believe you could not live without reading on your day off?"

"Yet another piece on the implications of the human genome mapping project. This science writer is arguing that within three years our docs will be able to tell us what parts of our bodies are going to fall apart on us long before they actually do, and consequently the average life expectancy will hit something like 142."

"That may prove to be a tad optimistic."

"Or pessimistic, depending upon whether you regard a dramatically longer life as a blessing or a curse. My brimstone-preaching father used to insist that those who died young were the lucky ones, because they got to spend more quality time with Jesus."

"If I am privileged to spend eternity with my Savior, I can't say that I would be disappointed if I were forced to wait an extra ten or fifteen years before I joined him, providing that the quality of those extra years was reasonably good."

"Given that our baby-boom generation has not adjusted particularly well to the physical realities of middle age, I suspect that we are going to insist that the quality of those extra years be very good indeed."

I sighed. "It does sometimes appear as if our entire generation has determined that we will simply refuse to grow older. An extra three pounds when we step on the scale send us running to our personal trainers, a random wrinkle has us dialing the plastic surgeon, and any hint that our sexual vigor is no longer a match for a sixteen-year-old's . . ."

Langston waved his hand in the air. "I know the litany of symptoms of the baby-boomer denial of aging. Certainly there is no sin in paying greater attention to our physical well-being: body as temple and all that. If we are smoking less and exercising more, I doubt the Almighty has any quarrel with it."

"But there are issues of balance and proportion involved. Obsession with appearing younger than we are could fairly be labeled narcissism, and the refusal to accept the very real changes and losses that accompany aging brushes up against hubris."

"Self-preoccupation is clearly the overarching sin of our generation, so it is only natural that we tend to see aging as a problem to be solved rather than a process to be embraced. But if we are already hounding our physicians to fix every ache, pain, and inconvenience we experience in our fifties, one shudders to think what a whiny and miserable lot we are going to be twenty years from now when those aches become more severe. We like the idea of doubling our life spans, because we continue to find ourselves utterly fascinating. But we insist that the quality of those extra years approximate that of a thirty-seven-year-old conditioned athlete."

"Pretty tall order."

"That's us boomers: nothing but the best ever does for us."

I took a long sip from my glass. "And of course that includes our spiritual experiences."

A small but discernible tightening in Langston's shoulders told me that I had struck a nerve. "I heard some program about American religious pluralism on the radio last week. They were interviewing a boomer woman who had been around the spiritual buffet table a number of times: raised Roman Catholic, did a stint with the Southern Baptists, then took a sharp left and joined a Wicca coven . . ."

"Pluralism indeed."

"Not so much pluralism as narcissism: always looking for a new spiritual framework with which to frame the true object of her worship, namely, herself. When asked to summarize what she had learned from all this religious tourism she replied thoughtfully, 'I really, really like prayer beads.'"

"I would like to believe that she represents an extreme case. The boomers in my own congregation have by and large continued to center their spiritual lives within our Reformed Christian religious tradition."

Langston shot me a skeptical glance. "And how many of them have ever developed a clear sense of that tradition? Have they embraced its practices and disciplines in ways that shape and form their lives? Have they invested themselves in significant service to the community of the church? Or are they showing up for worship when it's convenient and basking in the righteous glow engendered by the modest check they mail in every month?"

"I refuse to characterize an entire generational cohort of my congregation in such narrow terms. Obviously, some have embraced the practice of their faith more deeply than others."

"Fair enough. But if I can risk one generalization, I would note that I am seeing less and less of my boomers after the last child leaves the family nest. At exactly the point in life where we ought to be ready to move more deeply into the life of faith and when we have greater gifts to share with the church community, we are bailing out in record numbers."

Now it was my turn to wince. "Yeah, I have to admit that I am seeing the same thing happen. A lot of it appears to be an extension of the affluence and mobility that had already reshaped their weekends when they still had kids at home: mini-vacations at the cottage, the ski resort, or the Mall of America. When the nest empties and they no longer have to answer to their children's complex schedules, boomer couples are spending more and more of their weekends on the road."

"That's a part of it. But my hunch is that they are also spending a lot of Sunday mornings with a second pot of coffee and the *New York Times,* or out on the golf course, basking in the glow of knowing that they did the right thing by making sure their kids were properly 'exposed' to religion when they still lived at home. 'Religious duty' is just one more item checked off of their 'to do' list."

"That's harsh, but there is truth to it. A disturbing proportion of my members with children of church-school age tend to see the church as simply one more form of enrichment for the kids, taking its place alongside team sports and music lessons."

"And as we learn again and again when soccer practice conflicts with church school, even 'alongside' may be too generous a term. Many of our parents see their church as yet another service provider for the true object of their worship, which is their own family. When the children grow up and leave home, they no longer need that service."

"Assuming you are anywhere close to the truth with these harsh assessments, could it not be argued that when the nest empties the boomers should be ready to move into a more mature experience of Christian faith? Having reduced it to the utilitarian function of 'helping our children to form values' in earlier years, might they now be ready to explore its depths and experience how it can both center and transform their lives?"

"They might. But so far they show few signs of doing so. Most of my boomers are perfectly satisfied with their lives as they are and do not feel a particular need to have them centered or transformed. Our generation has displayed a particular genius for cobbling together a complicated package of consumerism, careerism, and recreational pursuits, convincing themselves that it all adds up to a full and satisfying life. I keep waiting for the house of cards to tumble, but they seem to be constructing cards from sturdier materials these days."

"But even the weekly newsmagazines like the one you are holding endlessly insist that 'spirituality' is a necessary component of a full and satisfying life."

"And, remarkably, our generation, arguably the best educated and most intellectually astute in American history, is still buying the vague and wifty definitions of 'spirituality' floating around the culture, definitions that make spiritual life one more consumer good we can purchase and squeeze into our days: spend twenty-five minutes in the hot tub with a couple of overpriced candles burning and you've got your spiritual fix for the day. A fair number of boomers seem unable to make a clear distinction between 'religion' and 'relaxation.'"

"Perhaps that is at least in part the result of a pattern of living our lives as religious dilettantes: as a generation we have tended to hop from one tradition to another—like the Catholic Baptist Wicca woman you mentioned earlier—while never staying rooted in any one of them long enough to experience a particular tradition's transforming depths."

"Studies have now clearly demonstrated what you and I have long observed: in the overwhelming majority of predominantly white Protestant churches, nearly two-thirds of current members come from some other denomination or tradition. Most of our members are utterly clueless when it comes to the beliefs and practices that are unique to the denomination they are presently a part of. Instead they have assembled their own constructs of meaning, taking a little bit from here and a little bit from there, even to blending bits and pieces of Hinduism and Christianity, so that they are not entirely sure whether Christ was resurrected or reincarnated."

"I would like to believe that good preaching and teaching can address such confusion."

"It can, to a point, but it is an uphill struggle when many members are in worship only every fourth Sunday. And, given boomers' postmodern approach to religion, where all ideas have equal weight and value no matter how bizarre or ill-informed, they often appropriate my sermons by tossing 'my ideas' into the same hopper with those of the alien abductee they saw on Oprah last week."

"It is somewhat odd that boomers who are willing to subject themselves to considerable discipline to acquire a new skill that interests them, from computer programming to rock climbing, assume that religious understanding falls in a different category, one that requires no disciplined learning because they already intuitively grasp it."

"Odd, and disturbing. It means, among other things, that when they come to a time of personal crisis and reach down for the resources of faith to sustain them that there isn't much water in the well to draw from. Some retreat to a simplistic, third-grade level of faith, praying up a storm for direct divine intervention with all the fervor they once applied to asking God to drop a pony off in their backyard."

"Then get annoyed when the Almighty fails to deliver the goods with the promptness of FedEx."

"Right. They did their part in asking for intervention; God failed to hold up his end of the deal by zapping the cancer the next morning. The notion of a God who helps us bear the weight of suffering or grieves with us in our losses; the concept of a God who can draw wonderful gifts out of even our most painful experiences—such ideas fail to meet the boomer 'Fix it right now!' standard."

"To be honest, I seem to have fewer and fewer members who truly regard their faith as an important resource in times of crisis at all. They turn not to God but to the secular experts best equipped to address their particular need: physicians, counselors, and lawyers."

"Medical centers have become the cathedrals of our time, the places to which we look for healing and wholeness. In a time of medical crisis, religion is often viewed as an ancillary service, valued because it can help foster a 'positive spirit,' which provides benefits to the immune system. The idea that religion can place the present crisis in a broader and deeper perspective—that a life-threatening illness is one more experience within the fullness of a life lived before God, an occasion where we can discover abundant grace and the rich blessings of love and support from the community in which God has placed us—is regarded as somewhere between irrelevant and downright repugnant."

"But medical centers, counseling clinics, and courts cannot fix everything that goes awry in our lives. And this will become even more true as we continue to age. Some of us will develop chronic conditions that medicine cannot cure, and along the way cherished companions will be surrendered to death. Without the wisdom and perspective provided by a mature faith, I shudder to think how poorly equipped many of our generation will be when such losses come."

A group of Methodists in the far corner launched into a spirited, if somewhat wobbly, barbershop version of "The Old Rugged Cross." Langston idly traced a pattern in the beer that had dribbled from his bottle onto the bar. "Then it is high time that the church began to address the situation."

"Address it? How? You have all but said that baby boomers, many of them only invested in the surface of church life in the first place, are disengaging from it in growing numbers. How does the church address the needs of people who are not even there?"

"For starters, it could stop pouring all of its resources and energy into attracting and holding young families. The typical local church goes into blind panic mode if the church-school enrollment dips by 5 percent, flapping around like Chicken Little and worrying aloud about becoming a dying church. Look at the newspaper ads on the religion page! All of the churches are bragging about their youth programs and family-friendly atmosphere! Church leadership positions once reserved for folks who had been around long enough to have developed a bit of wisdom and a clear sense of the mission of the church are increasingly going to members in their thirties, because 'that is the group we need to reach.' How much of the programming of the typical congregation is directed specifically at the needs and interests of members over the age of fifty? Who can blame boomers if they get the sense that their church no longer really needs them!"

"I'm not sure that is entirely fair, Langston. Our older members are very much an active presence in our mission trips and service projects, and they probably constitute the majority in adult education classes."

"But do we challenge them to teach in the church school? Do we place them in positions where they can mentor younger adult members in the ways of faith? Do we ask them what forms of adult Christian education would really speak to where they are on the journey of faith? Do we point out the obvious to them, namely, that they are the ones with the money, the experience, and the time required to make the church a faithful and dynamic community? Where is the adult education course titled 'What does God require of you now that the kids are gone, your pension is vested, your house is paid for, and your backyard grill is bigger than your first apartment was?'"

"You may want to give some thought to shortening that title."

He waved his hand impatiently. "Not all the boomers in a given congregation are clueless; some are persons of extraordinary faith and commitment. Do we ever bring groups of such people together to discuss how we might better engage other members of their cohort? If this science guy is even on the right track"—he slapped the now-soggy magazine—"then these folks in their fifties and sixties are going to be around and in reasonably good health for years to come. As more of them phase into partial retirement at younger ages but at the same time want and need to remain active and engaged, we have a remarkable opportunity to awaken them to God's call. When is the last time you sat through a confirmation service where a pack of gangly teens was not described as 'the future of the church'? Maybe it's time we lined up the fifty-five-year-olds and told *them* they are the future of the church! It is not the churches that see a modest decline in the number of toddlers enrolled in the church school that are likely to die. I am far more concerned about the churches that fail to engage the spiritual imaginations of those in midlife and beyond!"

"You have made some convincing points, Langston."

"My best guess right now is that ours is a generation that is finally poised to arrive at the meaningful adult faith that has eluded us for thirty years because we bought into the myth that our cohort had been granted immunity from the normal challenges and indignities of the human condition, and therefore we would not need it. But if we actually are granted longer and healthier lives than those who preceded us, there just may be enough time for us, with the help of God, to make something of ourselves yet. The church should be challenging us to do so in much bolder terms than it has to date."

"Any other areas where the church ought to be challenging the aging boomers?"

"Yeah, it should really be getting in our faces about taking care of our marriages."

"Marriages? I thought that statistically speaking once we reached this point in life we could all but assume that our marriages would remain on safe ground."

"I don't know about statistics, but I know I am seeing a growing number of marriages hit unexpected walls after the kids are gone. Couples who had functioned more or less competently and happily around the shared task of active parenting are suddenly forced to look at a future—and possibly a very lengthy future—of life together with no clear sense of what they really hold in common anymore. They did fine when it came to agreeing on curfews for teens and choosing new wallpaper for the powder room, but now they are facing a much more challenging question: what is the shared sense of purpose and meaning that will unite us for the remainder of our lives on earth?"

"That could fairly be called a challenging question alright."

"And it does not help that the magazines and television talk shows keep telling them that the purpose of marriage is to enhance their personal happiness and fulfillment. As our life spans increase, argue the pundits of self-indulgence, we should expect to have both multiple careers and multiple spouses, each appropriate to our current stage of self-development."

"So here we are back at boomer self-preoccupation: marriage is about what I get out of it."

"Exactly. Serial monogamy has become the great virtue of our age. We admire people who profess to be faithful to the person to whom they are currently married, even if that is spouse number three or four."

"It is a romantic and narcissistic way to define both marriage and fidelity."

"And very far removed from the church's understanding of marriage, which has much less to do with our personal happiness and fulfillment than with a divine economy that permits each partner in a committed marriage to give more to the wider community than either could have given without the other. And one of those gifts a lifetime marriage gives to the community is the gift of stability, enabling children to experience a world in which adults can be trusted to keep the promises they make, even when keeping them comes at the cost of personal inconvenience. I am not convinced that our cohort has done a particularly commendable job of behaving like adults in this regard."

"As a pastor, you are certainly aware that divorce, while always painful, is sometimes necessary."

"Of course I am. But I grieve terribly when the subtext behind a divorce, no matter how much justification is heaped around it, is 'this person does not make me sufficiently happy anymore.' With men of my generation in particular, I am seeing the beginnings of an alarming trend toward developing elaborate rationales for divorcing their wife of many years in order to marry someone who 'shares my tastes and interests.'"

"Someone who, coincidentally or not, tends to be a good deal younger."

"More often than not. And I don't think it's the old 'trophy wife' syndrome. It has more to do with an attitude that says 'I have raised my children. I have worked hard and been a good citizen. Now it is time for me to pay attention to what *I* really want and need!'"

"Somehow ignoring the fact that by historical standards that hardworking life has been one of enormous privilege and that the spouse he is now seeking to discard was a full partner in both its accomplishments and its joys."

"We seem to be buying into the idea that we are free to reinvent our lives every decade or two, to make a new start. And of course we need a new marriage to mark that new beginning."

"Which means that we never really need to grow up."

"Explain."

"A healthy, lifelong marriage is one in which our partner, by virtue of knowing us better than anyone else one earth, can both draw forth our hidden gifts and correct our less attractive tendencies over time. Such a marriage stretches us, challenges us, shapes and forms us. Sometimes it is very hard work; sometimes it is profoundly painful. If we bolt from it as soon as it begins to feel limiting and begin again with a new partner, we never have to grow beyond our comfort zone: serial monogamy can become a means of spending our entire lives in a state of arrested spiritual development."

Langston whistled softly. "I had never thought about it in quite those terms. It reminds me of the time Stanley Hauerwas argued that the church should return to arranged marriages, because at least in an arranged marriage you understand upfront that loving your spouse is a job description, not a feeling."

"I am guessing that one is not going to fly."

"Have you noticed how few of the older couples in your congregation who are struggling with their marriages ever consult you about it, much less turn to you for counseling? More than once a divorce between couples in their fifties or sixties has caught me completely by surprise, announced to the world as a fait accompli. It's as if they believe that marriage counseling, even within their church, is entirely centered on practical skills like communicating and budgeting, skills they long ago mastered and that are not at issue in their current struggles. It never occurs to them that issues concerning how they renew a common marital sphere of meaning, purpose, and shared values is precisely what the church is in the business of addressing."

"Now that you mention it, it does seem that most of my marriage counseling is with younger couples in their first few years of marriage."

"From where I sit, we might consider doing far less premarital counseling with couples so starry-eyed they aren't paying much attention anyway, and begin encouraging married couples to sit down with us every five or ten years for an 'inventory and tune-up' session. I for one would find it refreshing to discuss marriage with couples who have been together long enough to grasp just how much is at stake and what hard work it can be to maintain the health and strength of their marriage."

"The church's understanding of marriage is much informed by its understanding of the central role of community in Christian life. Many of the problems I see in marriages these days appear to arise from the effort to take marriage out of the context of community and set it in the private realm."

"Right. Weddings are public celebrations, but marital difficulties and divorce are nobody else's business."

"It seems to me that our boomer cohort has tended to view the very ideal of community with profound ambivalence."

"You bet. Back when we were the 'now generation,' communes and other forms of intentional community were a formative part of our identity. We were going to live, work, and play together forever and ever; in our more extreme examples, we were going to hold all goods in common."

"Sounds very idealistic—even apostolic—today."

"It was a lot easier to hold all goods in common when our collective goods consisted of three bread pans and a Led Zeppelin album. But we never noticed that our communes were made up entirely of like-minded people, rather than embracing the diversity that real community always encompasses. We really were ahead of the times; as early as 1969 we had already invented the gated community."

"Gated or not, we did not remain in those communes for long."

"Nope. We embraced the individualistic life with the enormous enthusiasm and self-justifying rationalism our generation has brought to each endeavor. We moved from apartments to homes to bigger homes on larger lots. In more recent years we have taken to buying vacation homes on large, secluded lots. Purely out of concern for the environment, of course."

"But does our generation not still hold some sense of the value of community?"

"I think it still percolates somewhere beneath the surface, but we have been fearful of allowing it to perk back to the surface again. After all, real community has a way of disrupting our personal agendas. It is filled with rough edges that scrape and chafe us, it is populated by needful people who intrude upon our personal space. It is also, of course, the only route through which we may be redeemed from our self-preoccupation."

"And one might find such a diverse, transforming community . . ."

Langston raised an eyebrow in my direction. "You are not in the habit of offering me such openings. But yes, a local congregation at its best is such a community, a community we do not get to select but to which we are summoned, a community that will sometimes annoy us, that will nurture and guide us in unexpected ways, a community that will help us to define who we are and who we may yet become. A community that, if all goes exactly right, will teach us that we are accountable to something greater than our own desires and aspirations. That is a hard one for boomers to accept, because 'accountability' is a word with which we have yet to make our peace."

The crowd was thinning as the clergy headed home for dinner and an evening's respite before the start of another six-day week. I pondered my old friend's thoughts. "If I may risk an attempt at summary, you believe the church must target the needs of aging baby boomers as clearly as it has attempted to speak to the various 'letter generations'—the Xers and Yers—if it is to have a vital future in a changed and changing world."

"Yes and no."

"Yes . . ."

"Yes, it must target the baby boomers."

"And no . . ."

"It must not do so for the sake of its future. It must do so in order to give baby boomers the opportunity to repent and be saved from their abundant sinning."

I signaled to the bartender. "Check, please."

31 Conscious Aging: The Future of Religion in Later Life

HARRY R. MOODY

All the sorrows of life are bearable if only we can convert them into a story.
—Isak Dinesen

What is the story we tell ourselves about our lives, especially the culmination of life in old age? Will it be a story of "successful aging" or "productive aging"—more of the same activities that once gave purpose and direction to our lives? Or might later life be a period for moving in a different direction from what our culture celebrates and cultivates from youth through midlife? William Butler Yeats once said that life is a preparation for something that never happens. But spiritual teachings the world over remind us that "the pearl of great price" is actually right before our eyes: "The kingdom of heaven is within you." It is only that we lack consciousness to open our eyes and see what could give transcendent meaning and purpose to our lives.

"Conscious aging" finds this "pearl of great price" in expanded consciousness and personal growth as guiding principles for an aging society. To celebrate conscious aging means to see later life as a period for cultivating the virtues of lifelong learning, late-life creativity, holistic health, care for others, and spiritual development. Instead of avoiding awareness of limitations, conscious aging is anchored in awareness of time and mortality but moves toward intensity of being and clarity of vision (Waxman 1997). To aspire toward conscious aging would be to broaden our vision of the purpose and meaning of the second half of life, a broader vision that has important implications for religion, spirituality, and aging.

The term "conscious aging" was apparently first used at a national conference by that name convened by the Omega Institute in 1992. The conference attracted 1,400 people and featured speakers such as Maggie Kuhn and Ram Dass. Where other definitions of a "good old age" tend to see the older person as a worker or a citizen, conscious aging depicts elders as spiritual seekers, in short, as individuals aspiring toward a higher stage of fulfillment, what Maslow termed self-actualization. In recent years, a growing literature in gerontology has promoted conscious aging as a strategy for late-life development, a strategy very different from directions that have dominated policy and services in the field of aging for the past generation (Moody 2001). If taken seriously, the idea of conscious aging could help us imagine new and enhanced roles for congregations and religious institutions in the twenty-first century.

One of the most powerful descriptions of conscious aging is found in the journal of Florida Scott-Maxwell, *The Measure of My Days,* which she kept while a resident of a nursing home (Scott-Maxwell 2000). In this journal she describes elders as people who "carry a secret," namely, that "inside we flame with a wild life that is almost incommunicable." Her journal is a chronicle of her own inward journey toward a "place beyond resignation, a place I had no idea existed until I had arrived here."

> It is a place of fierce energy. Perhaps passion would be a better word than energy. . . . It has to be accepted as passionate life, the life I never lived, never guessed I had it in me to live. It feels other and more than that. . . . It is just life, the natural intensity of life, and when old we have it for our reward and undoing. . . . Some of it must go beyond good and bad, for at times—though this comes rarely unexpectedly—it is a swelling clarity as though all was resolved. It has no content, it seems to expand us, it does not derive from the body, and then it is gone. It may be a degree of consciousness which lies outside activity, and which when young we are too busy to experience. (32–33)

This anticipation of late life as a time for a "degree of consciousness" beyond activity is exactly what proponents of conscious aging understand to be the purpose and meaning of old age. The sentiment is eloquently expressed by Zalman Schachter-Shalomi and Ronald S. Miller (1995) in the book *From Age-ing to Sage-ing*, which serves as a primary text for the movement of "spiritual eldering," now sponsoring local chapters and activities on behalf of conscious aging around the United States. Reb Zalman comes out of the Jewish mystical tradition, but Christian writers echo his language in depicting later life as a time of "spiritual journey" (Bianchi 1982). Robert Atchley (1993) has drawn on the Vedantic or Hindu mystical perspective to offer his own description of the wisdom attainable in the last stage of life. Eastern and Western religious traditions differ, yet on the mystical side they recognize a special contemplative virtue in later life.

We speak of old age as a "stage" of life, but we also speak of "stages" of consciousness unfolding. How are we to understand conscious aging in relationship to "stages" of spiritual growth and development, as articulated, for example, in the influential work of Fowler (1995)? Does later life open up greater possibilities of moving to a higher stage of faith, or does late-life habituation make such a move less likely unless there has been previous internalization of spiritual orientation earlier in life? There are good reasons for linking higher stages with the traditional language of spirituality and mysticism (Sinnott 1996). The problem of "stage" analysis of spirituality is complex and difficult (Wilber 2000), but if conscious aging means actual qualitative growth, there is no escaping such questions.

The other fact of life there is no escaping is loss. Conscious aging may be a strategy for promoting mental wellness (Moody 2002), but it does not guarantee escape from losses. Here we can find no better example of conscious aging as both gain and loss than the recent book *Still Here* (1999) by Ram Dass (formerly Richard Alpert). The title of Ram Dass's book recalls that he was the author of *Be Here Now,* a phenomenal best-seller that expressed the aspirations of the sixties generation on behalf of higher consciousness, first stimulated by psychedelic drugs and later by Eastern religions.

But Ram Dass's book also reflects what *Star Wars* called the "dark side of the force." His book is a product of his recovery from a nearly fatal stroke that left him paralyzed and needing years of rehabilitation. *Still Here* is a particularly valuable reminder that conscious aging is possible even in situations of physical or mental frailty. This reminder is necessary because conscious aging can too easily slip into what William James called "the religion of healthy-mindedness." James was aware of late-nineteenth-century American religious movements ranging from Christian Science to New Thought, movements that linked religious revival to an American spirit of optimism.

Conscious aging as a movement is part of the familiar American optimistic impulse that seeks to make all things new, perhaps even to abolish aging as we know it. There is a tendency for proponents of conscious aging to adopt some of the unconscious, even magical thinking conveyed by the ideal of "successful aging." The idea goes something like this: "If I engage in health-promotion activities, if I work at meditation and develop my higher self, then maybe I won't get old and frail like other people." Attention to yoga or health foods may encourage these unconscious attitudes. But these attitudes are ultimately in conflict with the genuine teaching of great religions, which arise from recognition of human frailty and radical dependency.

Some popular proponents of conscious aging in the New Age style encourage denial or magical thinking. For instance, the title and even the explicit argument in Deepak Chopra's book *Ageless Body, Timeless Mind* grows out of this cosmic "self-help" stance, which promotes a style of spiritual heroism and self-determination very different from what the great traditions of spirituality and mysticism have taught. Ram Dass's book, by contrast, finds virtues in dependency. He notes that having to rely on others for his care after the stroke was an important lesson in humility. Even losing the power of speech made him more aware than ever that genuine understanding of the universe happens at a level deeper than words— another lesson the mystics have taught from time immemorial.

These examples from the popular literature of conscious aging leave open many questions. In the first place, how old do we have to be in order to try to "age consciously"? Do we begin in midlife or wait until later? Is conscious aging synonymous with spirituality and mysticism? Does an aspiration toward conscious aging tend to cut people off from concern about wider social issues? Will interest in conscious aging increase in years to come and how is it tied to the future of religion and aging more broadly?

AGE, PERIOD, AND COHORT

One way to address these questions is to think of aging in the framework of the total human life-course. In this discussion, conscious aging is analyzed in terms of social-structural features that shape the life-course, specifically, *age, period,* and *cohort.* Social gerontology reminds us that age, period, and cohort factors remain distinct in theory but are intertwined in lived experience. Thus we can consider the effect of chronological age on today's sixty-five-year-olds, but we recognize that any particular pattern of behavior among sixty-five-year-olds is also shaped by prior historical experience (that is, historical cohort factors) as well as the current social conditions (that is, period factors) that create today's environment. Age, period, and cohort remain analytically distinct (Kosloski 1986; Schaie 1992).

The power of cohort effects reminds us that what we think of as age or aging is not limited to the biology or psychology of aging but is the product of historical factors affecting people over the total life-course. For example, to understand savings behavior among elders today, we could not look at chronological age alone but would have to adopt a total life-course perspective and a historical frame of reference—for instance, to consider the impact of memories of the Great Depression. Whatever effect chronological age has on savings behavior, we would have to take full account of the impact of this very different prior experience on the two different cohorts, sixty-five-year-olds and eighty-five-year-olds.

Note too that even past experience combined with chronological age is not the whole story. The combined influence of age and cohort factors will in turn have to be balanced by contemporary changing historical factors, such as interest rates or stock-market levels in the year 2002 (a contemporary period effect). Thus, how much money a sixty-five-year-old or an eighty-five-year-old might be likely to save or spend would be shaped by three separate variables: chronological age, earlier cohort effects, and the current historical period. In practice, we can never fully separate out the influence of these three variables of age, period, and cohort. All are operating simultaneously, whether we are looking at economics or at spirituality.

The life-course analytic framework of age, period, and cohort has been applied to changes in religiosity and religious participation (Payne 1988) and the same analytic framework can be applied to the emergence of conscious aging in the early decades of the twenty-first century. I offer this analysis quite tentatively, because the phenomena of spirituality and the search for meaning are more complex and ambiguous than measuring how much money people save or spend. They are less susceptible to quantitative measurement as well. Still, it is important to consider how chronological age interacts with cohort experience and contemporary history as we try to understand prospects for conscious aging in years to come.

First let us consider chronological age effects. Some aspects of conscious aging are likely to be the result of chronological age. For example, with advancing age there often comes a tendency toward inwardness or positive disengagement—what Lars Tornstam has called "gerotranscendence" (Tornstam 1997). This phenomenon is akin to what Rosenmayr described as the "late freedom" of expanded consciousness in old age (Rosenmayr 1981), which we have seen displayed in the passage from Florida Scott-Maxwell. The shift toward greater introspection often prompts a measure of autobiographical consciousness and accounts for the long-standing importance of life review in the literature of gerontology (Sherman 2000). However, the empirical literature also shows us that reminiscence and life review are far from universal among people who grow old, and individual differences remain important. There is no reason to expect that larger numbers of old people will necessarily mean that they will also be attracted to conscious aging as a way of life. Continuity theory in gerontology would suggest that those who have an introspective orientation earlier in life will be most likely to be attracted to psychotherapy, meditation, or life review in their later years.

Other features of conscious aging reflect current period effects, displaying the emergence of a distinctive shape to the life-course in the early twenty-first century—a phenomenon Simon Biggs has termed the "mature imagination" (Biggs 1999). The life course today is less rigidly demarcated in terms of classic "stages of life." Thus, there is far more fluidity in how we think about "age appropriate" behavior, promoting a degree of flexibility that could even be termed a postmodern style of aging. On the one hand, this fluidity and flexibility make it possible for eighty-year-olds to engage in denial of their age—"You're only as old as you feel," we often hear it said. The postmodern life-course could mean an opportunity or even an obligation for later life to become simply an extended middle age (consider the popularity of plastic surgery). On the other hand, the fluidity and flexibility of age-related expectations could also promote greater individuality and respect for individual differences of all kinds. This valuing of individuality could make conscious aging, with its emphasis on personal growth and individuation, a favored coping strategy.

This trend toward a postmodern life-course seems powerful and probably irresistible. As the adult life-course becomes less predictable, opportunities for individuation, consciousness expansion, and personal autonomy are likely to multiply. This tendency is evident in the history of Elderhostel, for example, which began in the mid-seventies and continues to grow in popularity each year. The lifestyle promoted by Elderhostel, along with parallel older adult education programs such as the European "Universities of the Third Age," display many features of conscious aging.

Older-adult education programs actually create self-sustaining social structures that have conscious aging as goal. Hazan (1996) emphasizes how education can create communities for late-life learning that serve to redefine old age as a time for personal growth and consciousness expansion. Drew Leder has explicitly pointed to conscious aging as a basis for creating new residential communities for older people (Leder 1996, 1999–2000). The possibility is not merely theoretical. For example, the Jubilados community in New Mexico is engaged in planning a residential retirement complex devoted to the goal of conscious aging and enrolling on an ecumenical basis participants from different contemplative traditions. But conscious aging could also become part of the ethos of retirement communities sponsored by more traditional religious organizations. With the aging of baby boomers in the early decades of the twenty-first century we may find a growing market for residential and educational arenas promoting conscious aging.

The mention of baby boomers draws our attention to another key element of the life-course approach, the enduring power of generational or cohort influences. Conscious aging is likely to prove especially attractive to aging baby boomers, who are a group long recognized as "a generation of seekers" (Roof 1993). Boomers have been spiritual explorers since the 1960s and they have carried along this distinctive orientation that marks them off from preceding generations like the World War II generation and the Silent Generation—groups less inclined to think of religion in terms of personal spiritual seeking or exploration.

AGING AND RELIGION IN THE TWENTY-FIRST CENTURY

Conscious aging will likely remain an attractive option for a significant segment of Americans growing older in the early twenty-first century—above all, that distinctive psychographic group known as "cultural creatives" (Ray and Anderson 2000). This subgroup of the American population consists of people who subscribe neither to traditional and conservative values, on the one hand, nor to modern and rationalistic values, on the other. Instead, the cultural creatives, numbering perhaps fifty million Americans, care about ecology and human relationships and favor social policies directed toward peace and social justice. They represent a group attached to Maslow's ideal of self-actualization and are found both in mainstream religions and in New Age movements. The influence of cultural creatives is particularly strong because of their impact in higher education, the professions, mass media, and the arts.

In the coming decades of the twenty-first century, we can expect the appeal of conscious aging to grow because of the following long-term trends at work:

Enduring Power of Religion

America remains a society where religion continues to play a potent role in ordinary life, in marked contrast to Western European societies. This deep tendency, a genuine instance of "American religious exceptionalism," shows no signs of abating (Jones and Gallup 2000; Stark and Finke 2000). Population survey research, however, suggests that American religion is taking on increasingly eclectic forms (Gallup and Michael 2000). Given the broader tendencies toward postmodern culture, it is likely that religious eclecticism will persist. The exploratory ethos of conscious aging should find this mood entirely congenial.

Aging of Baby Boomers

The aging of the baby-boom cohort, along with advances in longevity, continues to be a factor in population aging. With an older population Americans will continue to look toward religion and religious institutions for ways to cope with the losses and the existential experience of old age (Bianchi 1982; Koenig 1994). This stimulus is not limited to those in advanced age but actually begins in midlife, as boomers cope with losses linked to illness and death among aged parents as well as their own midlife transition. According to conscious aging, later life should understood as an opportunity for spiritual growth (Chinen 1989; O'Conner 1978), and boomers will look toward psychotherapy, self-help, and religion as tools for finding that growth.

Lifelong Learning

Since 1975, participation in Elderhostel has grown more than a thousandfold, from 200 to over 200,000 people each year. Rising educational levels of older Americans will make lifelong learning a more attractive alternative for retirement leisure. Preferred subjects for learning are expressive rather than instrumental topics: those related to personal history, spirituality, religion, or, more broadly, the search for meaning (Lambdin 1997)—all central to conscious aging.

Religious Individualism

The continuing power of religion coexists with the strong influence of individualism and personal autonomy as cultural ideals. The result is that Americans increasingly approach religion as a matter of personal choice. There is a "marketplace" for spirituality that responds to individual choices, essentially a "mix and match" approach based on individual preference ranging from meditation and twelve-step programs to Gregorian chants, from a Native American vision quest to dialogues with angels (Cimino and Lattin 1998; Roof 1999).

The analytic framework of age, period, and cohort does not give us a magic key to predicting the future, whether for savings behavior or for religious orientation. The interplay of age, period, and cohort factors underscores how much conscious aging remains a complex and multivalent phenomenon with different meanings for different people. For some, conscious aging could entail a return to traditional values embodied in the contemplative traditions of historical religion—for example, the revival of interest in contemplative prayer by Father Thomas Keating (Keating 1992). For others, conscious aging will involve a New Age outlook favoring a blend between psychology and religion (Heelas 1996). For still others, conscious aging could represent active social engagement on behalf of making the world better, through volunteerism and advocacy—a stance recommended by both Zalman Schachter-Shalomi and Ram Dass.

For much of the past century, religion has sought to make itself relevant to the modern world through adaptations such as the social gospel or the assimilation of the language of science. Not all of religion has taken that path, of course, and the split between liberal and conservative orientations is found in all denominations in America. Moreover, we should not forget that evangelical religion and fundamentalism retain their influential role in American life and will shape the experience of religion and aging for millions, including many boomers.

There are some writers, like Theodore Roszak (*America the Wise*), who believe that boomers will bring to old age the values of consciousness expansion that came to the forefront during the sixties. An aging America, says Roszak (1998), will be a kinder, gentler society. Indeed, Roszak presents a glowing, positive picture of America transformed by a boomer generation devoted to contemplation and ecological sensitivity. Not everyone is convinced. Others, like transpersonal psychologist Ken Wilber, are more skeptical of such an outcome, and worry that aging boomers may be tempted to carry into old age familiar attitudes of narcissism (the "me" generation castigated by Christopher Lasch and other critics). Wilber, in particular, warns of "boomeritis," a kind of self-absorption that easily slides over into relativism and lack of judgment.

What will happen to aging baby boomers has yet to be written, and we should be cautious of projecting hopes or fears onto the future. But we know that cohort factors alone will not be decisive. Age and historical period also influence how individuals, generations, and even society as a whole develop over time. In sum, Roszak's optimistic forecast cannot come to pass on its own. There are many enduring obstacles to making a better world, and some are found within ourselves. Two of the most powerful are recurrent temptations—even characteristic psychological "diseases" of old age—namely, cynicism and narcissism.

THE LURE OF CYNICISM

Cynicism is rampant today in our ironic, postmodern culture. "Been there, done that," as the saying goes. Older people more than others may be vulnerable to this mood because they have reasons to be disillusioned. Aristotle observed 2,500 years ago that the young act out of hope, while the old act out of caution born from long life experience. It is true that life experience permits us to see through our illusions; indeed, "seeing through" may be a precondition for wisdom (McKee and Barber 1999). The danger comes if disillusionment slides over into cynicism: a belief that "We've seen it all before," "We tried it and it didn't work," or "There is nothing new under the sun." Cynicism shows itself in the suspicion that events must turn out badly because human beings are governed by self-interest.

Cynicism becomes a self-confirming prophecy if it stops us from acting and thus brings about the very evil it forecasts. There is an old saying that nothing is required for evil to triumph but for good people to refrain from acting. What older people need is not cynicism but some basis for hope—and conscious aging is helpful here. Conscious aging insists that, no matter what our age, it is never too late for positive growth—and equally never too late to act to make the world better. There is a parallel between the environmental challenge and aging itself. Both demand that we face up to limits and find new ways to find growth and progress within limits. Cynicism succumbs to limits by giving up any hope for growth in the future. Growth within limits could well be the watchword both for realistic environmentalism and a movement of conscious aging.

THE STRUGGLE AGAINST NARCISSISM

Another great temptation of age is narcissism, excessive preoccupation with oneself. Here the wisdom traditions of world religions have contributed a common response through the spiritual disciplines and practices that aim at narcissism in its very roots. The most important of these disciplines is meditation or contemplative prayer. The task of meditation, as Mark Epstein suggests in *Thoughts without a Thinker*, is a deep and subtle struggle against the power of narcissism, not unlike what successful psychotherapy demands.

Narcissism in old age remains a powerful and persistent adversary. The losses of age involve predictable assaults on our sense of self, from loss of career to isolation and physical decline. It is all too easy to become preoccupied with health problems and other vulnerabilities. In a culture of capitalism, self-interest is openly expressed. Some even celebrate the self-interest of elders, as in the famous bumper sticker, "I'm spending my children's inheritance." Yet we know from studies of older volunteers that this slogan is an unfair caricature. Nonetheless, it does symbolize a psychological temptation: the temptation to say, "I'm all right, Jack," or, "I paid my dues."

Conscious aging offers a crucial antidote to narcissism by emphasizing Erik Erikson's idea of generativity—what psychologist John Kotre (1996) has called "outliving the self." As we go beyond the narrow self toward wider and wider circles of concern, we overcome narcissism in favor of devotion, first, to our local community, then for other generations, and ultimately for the planet as a whole. The Hebrew word for this widening circle of concern is *tikkun olam,* or "healing the world." It remains a transcendent ideal, important both for individual psychological growth and for contributions by elders to the wider society, as Zalman Schachter-Shalomi and Ronald Miller have described in *From Age-ing to Sage-ing*.

Still, the skeptic may wonder whether it is ludicrous for elders, for those with limited life expectancy, to be concerned with social action or making the world better. Won't it take generations to solve the problems of the world? Spiritual traditions have always been aware of this problem. The world will not soon be made perfect, the planet will not be quickly healed, and the poor will be with you always—all true, but "neither art thou free to desist" from striving to make the world better. There is no age limit in which this duty of concern would expire.

We are mistaken when we think that social action and inner-directedness must be opposed to each other. Conscious aging includes a whole range of ways in which individuals become more inner-directed and reflective as they grow older—lifelong learning, the expressive arts, holistic health practices, reminiscence, and spirituality. The danger in all of these tendencies is that they make us more focused on ourselves. Perhaps this is a necessary and even healthy shift of emphasis for a society dominated by the cult of activity and productivity. But the shift is also potentially dangerous if inner-directedness becomes narcissism. Can we afford an aging society where happy Elderhostelers travel the world but others languish on SSI? Can we afford a society where some retired people polish their memoirs or oral histories but young people are not educated enough to read them?

It is worth noting that the history of spirituality of both East and West generally does not depict the highest stage of realization as a monk sitting on a mountaintop (Kornfield 2000). On the contrary, as the Zen proverb has it, "After ecstasy, the laundry." The famous "Oxherding Pictures" in the Zen tradition conclude with a picture titled "Return to the Marketplace." After finding the ox (enlightenment), we go back to ordinary life; we chop wood and carry water. St. Teresa of Avila, like Mother Teresa in our time, spent her days not in meditative retreat but laboring to create institutions that would outlast her—"outliving the self," as Kotre put it. In my own work on the stages of the soul, I describe the spiritual journey as moving from the call, to search, struggle, and breakthrough, but finally culminating in a return to the world (Moody and Carroll 1997). This sequence parallels the journey of the hero depicted by Joseph Campbell in *The Hero with a Thousand Faces*. The last stage, return, may even be a kind of "everyday mysticism" found more commonly than we realize in old age (Atchley 1997).

"Healing the world" (*tikkun olam*) means returning to the world, and therefore testing our insights, our consciousness, by means of a reality principle. In this respect, conscious aging need not be opposed at all to the ideal of productive aging, with its insistence that the old should not withdraw but continue to be productive members of society. The Sufi mystics have always urged their followers to "Be in the world but not of it." In the Christian tradition there has always been acknowledgment of the twin virtues of action and contemplation, symbolized by Martha and Mary. The greatest mystics—figures like St. Bernard and St. Teresa, as well as Meister Eckhart and Hildegard of Bingen—have combined the virtues of Martha and Mary in their own careers.

Two nineteenth-century poets, Keats and Browning, reflect the paradox of conscious aging. Browning, we know, is easily caricatured as the author of an overly optimistic image of old age—"The best is yet to be!" But Browning also added the lines, "the last of life for which the first was made," implying that old age can be—not must be, but can be—the telos in which we can find purpose for the whole of life. That transformative purpose was conveyed by Keats when he described human life as "the vale of soul-making"—an attitude that exactly incorporates what all spiritual traditions have repeatedly taught. But how is the soul actually to be made? Another great writer of the nineteenth century, Søren Kierkegaard, put it well in a line from his journal when he says that human beings are naturally subjective toward themselves and objective toward others. The task of religion, Kierkegaard said, was to reverse this tendency.

The struggle against narcissism is what this reversal of perspective is all about. The discipline of conscious aging means nothing less than to become more objective (not narcissistic) about who we really are and to become more subjective (compassionate) toward those around us. This dual consciousness, Martha and Mary together, is expressed in Jesus' summary of all the commandments: "You shall love the Lord your God with all your heart, and with all your soul, and with all your mind," and, "You shall love your neighbor as yourself" (Matt. 22:37-39).

BIBLIOGRAPHY

Atchley, R. C. (1997). "Everyday Mysticism: Spiritual Development in Later Adulthood." *Journal of Adult Development* 4: 2, 123–34.

——— (1993). "Spiritual Development and Wisdom: A Vedantic Perspective." In R. Kastenbaum, ed., *Encyclopedia of Adult Development*. Phoenix: Oryx.

Bianchi, E. C. (1982). *Aging as a Spiritual Journey.* New York: Crossroad.

Biggs, S. (1999). *The Mature Imagination: Dynamics of Identity in Midlife and Beyond.* Buckingham, Eng.: Open University Press.

Chinen, A. B. (1989). *In the Ever After: Fairy Tales and the Second Half of Life.* Wilmette, Ill.: Chiron.

Chopra, D. (1993). *Ageless Body, Timeless Mind: The Quantum Alternative to Growing Old.* New York: Harmony.

Cimino, R. P., and L. D. Lattin (1998). *Shopping for Faith: American Religion in the New Millennium.* San Francisco: Jossey-Bass.

Dass, R. (1999). *Still Here: Embracing Aging, Changing and Dying.* New York: Riverhead.

Epstein, M. (1995). *Thoughts without a Thinker: Psychotherapy from a Buddhist Perspective.* New York: Basic.

Fowler, J. (1995). *The Stages of Faith: The Psychology of Human Development and the Quest for Meaning.* San Francisco: HarperSanFrancisco.

Gallup, G., Jr., and L. D. Michael (2000). *Surveying the Religious Landscape: Trends in U.S. Beliefs.* Morehouse.

Hazan, H. (1996). *From First Principles: An Experiment in Ageing.* Westport, Conn.: Bergin & Garvey.

Heelas, P. (1996). *The New Age Movement.* Oxford: Blackwell.

John, K. (1996). *Outliving the Self: Generativity and the Interpretation of Lives.* New York: Norton.

Jones, T., and Gallup, G., Jr. (2000). *The Next American Spirituality: Finding God in the Twenty-first Century.* Colorado Springs: Chariot Victor.

Keating, T. (1992). *Invitation to Love: The Way of Christian Contemplation.* Shaftsbury, Eng.: Element.

Koenig, H. G. (1994). *Aging and God.* New York: Haworth.

Kornfield, J. (2000). *After Ecstasy, the Laundry.* New York: Bantam.

Kosloski, K. (1986). "Isolating Age, Period, and Cohort Effects in Developmental Research: A Critical Review." *Research on Aging* 8: 4, 460–79.

Kotre, J. (1996). *Outliving the Self: How to Live On in Future Generations.* New York: W. W. Norton.

Lambdin, L. (1997). *Elderlearning*. Phoenix: Onyx.

Leder, D. (winter 1999–2000). "Aging into the Spirit: From Traditional Wisdom to Innovative Programs and Communities." *Generations* 23: 4, 36–41.

——— (summer 1996). "Spiritual Community in Later Life: A Modest Proposal." *Journal of Aging Studies* 10: 2, 103–16.

McKee, P., and C. Barber (1999). "On Defining Wisdom." *International Journal of Aging and Human Development* 49/2: 149–64.

Moody, H. R. (2002). "Conscious Aging as a Strategy for Mental Wellness." In Ronch and Goldfield.

——— (2001). "Productive Aging and the Ideology of Old Age." In Sherraden, Hinterlong, and Morrow-Howell, 175–96.

Moody, H. R., and D. Carroll (1997). *The Five Stages of the Soul: Charting the Spiritual Passages That Shape Our Lives*. New York: Doubleday Anchor.

O'Conner, G. (1978). *The Second Journey: Spiritual Awareness and the Mid-Life Crisis*. Ramsey, N.J.: Paulist.

Payne, B. (1988). "Religious Patterns and Participation of Older Adults: A Sociological Perspective." *Educational Gerontology* 14/4: 255–67.

Ray, P. H., and S. R. Anderson (2000). *The Cultural Creatives*. New York: Harmony.

Ronch, J., and J. Goldfield, eds. (2002). *Mental Wellness in Aging: Strengths-Based Approaches*. Baltimore: Health Professions.

Roof, W. C. (1999). *Spiritual Marketplace*. Princeton, N.J.: Princeton University Press.

——— (1993). *A Generation of Seekers: The Spiritual Journeys of the Baby Boom Generation*. San Francisco: HarperCollins.

Rosenmayr, L. (1981). *Die Spaete Freiheit* (Late Freedom). Vienna: Severin and Siedler.

Roszak, T. (1998). *America the Wise: The Longevity Revolution and the True Wealth of Nations*. Boston: Houghton Mifflin.

Schachter-Shalomi, Z., and R. S. Miller (1995). *From Age-ing to Sage-ing: A Profound New Vision of Growing Older*. New York: Warner.

Schaie, K. W. (1992). "Impact of Methodological Changes in Gerontology." *International Journal of Aging and Human Development* 35/1: 19–29.

Scott-Maxwell, F. (2000). *The Measure of My Days*. New York: Penguin.

Sherman, E. (2000). *The Autobiographical Consciousness of Aging*. Kearney, Neb.: Morris.

Sherraden, M. W., J. Hinterlong, and N. Morrow-Howell, eds. (2001). *Productive Aging: Concepts and Challenges*. Baltimore: Johns Hopkins University Press.

Sinnott, J. (1996). "Postformal Thought and Mysticism: How Might the Mind Know the Unknowable?" *Aging and Spirituality* 8: 7–8.

Stark, R., and R. Finke (2000). *Acts of Faith: Explaining the Human Side of Religion*. Berkeley: University of California Press.

Tornstam, L. (1997). "Gerotranscendence: The Contemplative Dimension of Aging." *Journal of Aging Studies* 11/2: 143–54.

Waxman, B. F. (1997). *To Live in the Center of the Moment: Literary Autobiographies of Aging*. Charlottesville: University Press of Virginia.

Wilber, K. (2000). *Integral Psychology: Consciousness, Spirit, Psychology, Therapy*. Boston: Shambhala.

32

On the Possibilities of Spirituality and Religious Humanism in Gerontology

THOMAS R. COLE

In 1991 I published a book titled *The Journey of Life: A Cultural History of Aging in America* in which I tried to accomplish several things at once: (1) a general overview of the dominant cultural meanings of aging in Europe and the United States from antiquity to the late twentieth century, (2) a specific historical analysis and critique of the transition from religious to scientific meanings in American middle-class culture, (3) a critique of the dominance of science in gerontology, and (4) a call for renewal of the moral and spiritual possibilities of aging in postmodern culture. This book was the culmination of fifteen years of work, during which I gradually realized that although I am formally licensed to "practice history," I am fundamentally interested in what might be called the problematic of aging and meaning.

In *The Journey of Life* I argued that the vast gerontological literature that has appeared since World War II is dominated by a kind of instrumental reasoning that ignores (or presupposes answers to) the essential moral and spiritual questions that arise in the second half of life. The dominant forces in American culture have little or no interest in why we grow old, how we ought to grow old, or what it means to grow old. Like other aspects of our biological and social existence, aging has fallen under the dominion of scientific management, which is primarily interested in how we age in order to explain and control the aging process. American culture thrives on the mythology that aging is not a fated aspect of our individual and social existence but rather one of life's problems to be solved through willpower, science, medicine, and the accumulation of wealth. The most recent evidence for this claim is the dramatic rise of "anti-aging" in American medicine and consumer culture.[1]

The problem with this mythology of scientific management is not that it is altogether false but that it is only half true. The scientific management of aging fundamentally misconstrues the "problem" of aging. As T. S. Eliot once remarked, there are two kinds of problems in life. One kind requires the question, What are we going to do about it? and the other provokes other questions, What does it mean? How does one relate to it?

The first kind of problem is like a puzzle that can be solved with appropriate technical resources and pragmatic responses. The second kind of problem is really a mystery rather than a puzzle. It poses a deeper range of challenges, which no particular policy, strategy, or technique will overcome. Faced with a mystery, the human heart cries out for meaning. Born of viable cultural symbols and rituals, moral commitment, spiritual practices, and personal reflection, the experience of meaning helps individuals to understand, accept, and imaginatively transform the unmanageable, ambiguous aspects of existence.

Clearly, growing old involves both puzzles and mysteries. Yet people do not face life with the clear light of reason alone. We are always informed (for better or for worse) by beliefs, values, and symbols that are embedded in history and society. Whether we are aware of them or not, cultural beliefs and values always shape our understanding of life's big questions.

A RATIONALE FOR HUMANISTIC GERONTOLOGY

During the 1980s it became clear that the time was ripe to formulate a rationale for and to map the boundaries of the emerging interdisciplinary field that became known as humanistic gerontology, or "age studies," among feminist and cultural-studies thinkers (see Gullette 2000). I belonged to a small band of renegade humanities scholars and humanistically oriented scientists who had operated at the interstices of the Gerontological Society of America since the mid-1970s. We decided to pool our intellectual resources and—with awareness of the inherent irony—join the ranks of authoritative "handbooks" of gerontology.

Robert Kastenbaum initiated the idea of a *Handbook of Humanities and Aging*. In November 1984, at a Wendy's in New Orleans between Gerontological Society sessions, Kastenbaum, Moody, and I began sketching a table of contents. It fell to me to try to formulate a rationale for humanistic gerontology. That rationale, outlined in the introduction to the first edition, went roughly like this: Something important is missing in a purely scientific and professional gerontology. Highly technical and instrumental, avowedly objective and value-neutral gerontology lacks an appropriate language for addressing basic moral and spiritual issues in our aging society. Researchers, teachers, students, professionals, patients, clients, administrators, and policymakers have no ready way to speak to one another about fundamental questions of human existence. The predicament of gerontology mirrors a larger historical tendency.

Since the late nineteenth century, the decline of widely shared religious and philosophical frameworks, the growth of experimental science and technology, the culture of professionalism, and the emergence of the modern university have all contributed to the erosion of a common language for discussing questions of meaning and value, justice, virtue, wisdom, or the common good. In the contemporary world of postmodern culture, where exploding communications technology both saturates personal experience and undermines traditional assumptions of the self's unity, it has become increasingly important to identify and talk about moral and spiritual concerns.

The crisis of meaning in later life is not simply an academic issue; it is a historical-cultural situation (Habermas 1984) increasingly experienced by our aging selves and our aging societies. The theoretical and practical value of life review and reminiscence, the revival of narrative as a way of knowing, and the rapid growth of life-story groups among American elders all respond to the growing need for personal and sacred narratives that craft meaning and orient identity.

In American society at least, the accelerating speed of communication and social change and the continuing extension of longevity leave many people feeling like Washington Irving's character Rip Van Winkle, who fell asleep one night before the American revolution and awoke twenty years later to an alien world: "God knows . . . I'm not myself—I'm somebody else. . . . I was myself last night, but I fell asleep . . . and everything's changed, and I'm changed, and I can't tell what's my name, or who I am."

The crisis of meaning may take its most exaggerated form in the United States, but it seems to pervade all Western societies. As Chris Phillipson suggests, "modern living undercuts the construction of a viable identity for living in old age" (1998, 53–54).

HUMANISM AND THE POSTMODERN CHALLENGE

During the 1980s, as Graduate Program Director for a curriculum in the medical humanities, I became responsible for teaching graduate seminars in the history and theory of humanism and the humanities. Virtually ignorant of early modern European history, I began reading seriously in the historiography, literature, and philosophy of humanism. I found myself attracted not to any particular "doctrine of man" but to the practical modesty of Renaissance humanists who accepted the uncertainty, ambiguity, and plurality in all human knowledge but who nevertheless sought wisdom, virtue, goodness, and human fulfillment through the critical exploration of their cultural heritage.[2] As a humanities teacher and a gerontologist, I came to embrace the "humanistic educational ideal"—the ideal of self-development, of cultivating of one's full humanity—and I saw that it held great promise for guiding late-life development and encouraging the pursuit of meaning and identity in old age.

I was drawn to the work of philosopher Charles Taylor, who argues that one's full identity, or self, is a complex ontological accretion, formed in response to external value frameworks that provide the self with a place to stand in "moral space." "The full definition of someone's identity," writes Taylor, "usually involves not only his stand on moral and spiritual matters but also some reference to a defining community" (1989). Taylor does not directly address issues of aging. But his view that modern culture's crisis of meaning is caused by the loss of widely shared religious or philosophical frameworks prodded me to think not only about secularization but also about the loss of humanism as a viable tradition.

As I began learning about the contested tradition of humanism in the 1980s, I also struggled to come to terms with the postmodern deluge that had crossed the Atlantic and first upset business as usual in American academic departments of literature a decade earlier. I grappled with the antihumanism embedded in Heidegger (ironically, in his "Letter on Humanism"), Althusser, Lyotard, and the early Foucault.[3] I could see the liberating power of the idea that "man" or "humanity" or "the subject" are not universal truths but social fictions rooted in historical relations of power and knowledge.[4] But I was not prepared to surrender the idea of existential truths that can only be represented by *yet are not reducible to* specific cultural constructions. And as I learned more about humanism, I became convinced that much of the postmodern attack on humanism was based on a inaccurate reading of the humanist tradition.

In my view it is a mistake to think of humanism as a fixed philosophy of "man." Humanism is better understood as a contested educational tradition in which imagination and the arts of language (rhetoric) compete with and complement the search for rational conclusive knowledge (philosophy as a science). Renaissance humanism, which emerged in fourteenth-century Italy and spread to other parts of Europe, was primarily an educational movement opposing the then-dominant scholastic curriculum of the medieval university, with its emphasis on logic, natural philosophy, and metaphysics. Petrarch, Leonardo Bruni, and Lorenzo Valla, for example, laid special emphasis on rhetoric—the art of graceful, persuasive, and effective verbal communication, both orally and in writing. Based on the study, translation, and imitation of Roman orators, primarily Cicero and Quintillian, rhetoric aimed to help laypersons make sense of and act in the ambiguous, practical world of law, commerce, and public life. Its goal was not to discover eternal truth but to develop an "articulate, broadly effective personality adequate to any situation" (Bouwsma 1973, 15).

From the perspective of these early Italian humanists, the medieval schoolmen overvalued abstract rationality as the defining characteristic of "man." Instead, humanists addressed real flesh-and-blood individuals, understood as unpredictable bundles of passion, intellect, and spirit. The humanists wanted "to address man, every man, at the vital center of his being" (Bouwsma 1990, 76–77). They were not, as is commonly thought, liberating "man" from the superstitions of religion. Grief-stricken by the mass death brought to Europe by the plague and confused by social and cultural change in the fourteenth century, they looked to "the ancients" for models of knowledge, virtue, and behavior. They remained Christians who insisted on the value of experience in *this world* and whose awareness of the limitations of all human knowledge led them toward tolerance and dialogue, which required educating men and women in the arts of language. Renaissance humanists aimed at educating active, responsible individuals by cultivating a more reflective human consciousness.

Once we grasp the postmodern insight inherent in Renaissance humanism (i.e., that formalized systems of rational knowledge do not address "man at the vital center of his being"), the critique of humanism as metaphysical and naively anthropocentric loses its force. We can understand, for example, that Protagoras's famous dictum—"man is the measure of all things"—implies not that a unified humankind is capable of objective knowledge but rather the opposite—that individuals are limited by their experience yet entitled to measure their own experience. Postmodernism, then, has reiterated what the premodern humanist tradition already understood: all efforts to find an Archimedean point or a God's-eye view from which to observe ourselves are vain attempts—as Hannah Arendt put it, to "jump over our own shadows" (Arendt 1958, 10).

Humanism is no longer intellectually viable as an "ism" in the modern philosophical and political sense. That is, there can be no single, unified theory of human being or human nature that requires our allegiance because it is universally true. But this does not mean there can be no humanisms after postmodernism. Acknowledging that all truths are "man-made" does not require that we disdain them for being "merely" human and strive to recover the false idol of Being. The alternative to standing outside the hermeneutic circle or transcending mere human consciousness is to strive to enlarge both. We need to overcome the moral and political paralysis induced by the stance of permanent skepticism toward all ideals and by the assumption that race, gender, ethnicity, religion, or nationality creates incommensurable worlds of difference. We need to reappropriate humanism not as any particular "philosophy of man" but as an educational ideal that explores and promotes personal growth and public action regarding two key questions: What does it mean to be human? and How do we promote human flourishing?

The humanist task today is not to find our way back to a forgotten Greek origin (the way of Heidegger and Arendt) or to preserve the values of heroic Western civilization (the way of Bloom and Bennett) or to recover timeless truths from the corrosion of historical contingency (Arnold, Eliot, and Kermode). Rather, the goals are (1) to recover our bearings through a critical interrogation of the humanist past (the way of Gadamer), (2) to build on this tradition through education and scholarship aimed at expanding human consciousness through continuous dialogical engagement with plurality and alterity (Buber, Bahktin, and Habermas), and (3) to publicly address real human problems (Dewey) by personal engagement in various scholarly, educational, professional, and political practices.

Human beings who are morally equal and distinct cannot be adequately understood or properly educated through the monologic, disembodied, decontextualized rationality of modern philosophy and science. But the critique of rationalism need not lead to relativism or thoughtless pluralism. Instead, we need a rationality that is engaged, dialogic, fallible, and open-ended.[5] Summarizing Gadamer's approach to the human sciences, Bernstein (1992) has aptly captured this kind of dialogical rationality.

> The basic condition for all understanding requires one to test and risk one's basic convictions and prejudgments in and through an encounter with what is radically "other" and alien. To do this requires imagination and hermeneutical sensitivity. . . . Critical engaged dialogue requires opening of oneself to the full power of what the "other" is saying. Such an opening does not entail agreement but rather the to-and-fro play of dialogue. (4)

HUMANISM AS AN EDUCATIONAL IDEAL, HUMANISTIC GERONTOLOGY, AND RELIGION

So what does this have to do with gerontology, religion, and spirituality? I believe that the contested tradition of humanism has a great deal to offer gerontology: sensitivity to the formative power of language, an emphasis on historical and contextual thinking, a commitment to imagination as a way of knowing, a tradition of moral and spiritual reflection, and a primary insistence on dialogue. A postmodern humanism does not set religion and science against each other but recognizes religion and spirituality as constituent elements of human identity and development. This recognition is already present in the work of Giambattista Vico (1688–1744), an ambivalent believer, humanist professor of rhetoric, and author of the first major work of interpretive social science, *Scienza Nuova* (1725). Vico thought that religion originated historically in the terrorized imagination of ancient peoples. He argued that all societies everywhere invent sacred stories based on three core principles: divine providence (which requires a fable of the gods or God); marriage (which requires a fable of the passions restrained); and burial (which requires a fable of the body decaying and of the soul's fate). For Vico, as Stephen Greenblatt (2001) points out, "the fact that the whole enormous structure of belief is based on a universal poetic invention is not a source of disillusionment. Instead it underwrites the very possibility of scientific understanding" (48–49). Vico placed human poetic invention at the core of his basic axiom: "[T]he world of civil society has certainly been made by men, and . . . its principles are therefore to be found within the modifications of our own human mind" (Vico 1968 [1744], 48–49).

"Know thyself," inscribed above the entrance to the ancient oracle at Delphi, might be considered the basic mantra of humanistic thought and practice. But what makes knowledge or practice *humanistic?* By using the term humanistic, I refer to knowledge (not necessarily in the humanities) and practice that are informed by or conform to the ancient Roman ideal of *humanitas*—which originally meant "human feeling" and later came to encompass a holistic blend of feeling, knowledge, and compassionate action in the world.

Humanistic knowledge is more difficult to achieve than cognitive knowledge alone, because (in contemporary terms) it demands heightened awareness that all knowledge resides in particular individuals who are embodied, embedded in social relationships, and limited. Humanistic knowledge requires attention to the context of knowledge-making and to the practical needs and problems of any given situation. It requires a depth of self-understanding that allows both detached discernment and personal engagement, depending on the human needs of any given situation and the scholarly, practical, or pedagogical aims of the knower. The personal integration essential to humanistic knowledge is a fluid, holistic ideal that can occasionally be achieved and exemplified but cannot be taught directly or didactically. It is a spiritual ideal, an ongoing personal and interpersonal practice. Humanistic education seeks, as Erasmus put it, "nourishment for the soul instead of a mere scratching of the intellect" (cited by Tracy 1987a).

Humanism's basic commitment to cultivating personal integration, its concern with self-knowledge and the conditions of human flourishing, can bring a rich variety of perspectives and practices to bear on the basic question of humanistic gerontology: What does it mean to grow old? This question has no single or universal answer—at least not one that finite, historical beings can provide. Indeed, the question itself is abstracted from other innumerable questions that arise in historically and culturally specific forms—what is a "good" old age? Is there anything important to be done after children are raised and careers completed? Is old age the fulfillment of life? What happens after we die? What does God require of us? What are the possibilities of flourishing in old age? What kind of elders do we want to be? What are the paths to wisdom? What are the vices and virtues of the elderly? What kinds of support and care does society "owe" its old? What do the elderly owe their society?

In the last few years I have come to believe that these questions are unanswerable without culturally viable religions and/or worldviews, that is, without cosmological maps and ultimate meanings that give us reasons and guidance for living with the flow of time rather than against it. Religions and worldviews (for better and for worse) authorize ideals of old age. They provide cultural cognitive maps that chart a way into the unknown territory of later life. They illuminate the moral and spiritual work of aging. And they require not only cognitive answers but human practices that cultivate living answers in communities and in individuals.

I am evolving into a (not yet fully formed) religious humanist. Perhaps I exemplify a trend that Robert Wuthnow (1998) has identified in American spirituality since 1950 from a spirituality of "dwelling" to a spirituality of "seeking" and on to a spirituality of "practice." (As a practicing Jew influenced by contemporary Buddhist spiritual teachings, I am learning to rebalance and integrate what Matthew Arnold called "Hellenism" and "Hebraism.")[6]

As a scholar I am still recovering from an overdose of the "positive" (or "exclusive") secularism built into American university education. In *The Soul of the American University: From Protestant Establishment to Established Nonbelief* (1994), historian George Marsden argued that the American academy over the last century has essentially replaced one domineering, totalizing orthodoxy with another. In place of the old Protestant Christian Orthodoxy, Marsden claims that universities now operate under the aegis of a strictly secular understanding of human existence, which suppresses explicit religious discourse and is intolerant of religious perspectives in scholarly discourse. If Marsden's view is basically convincing, we need to think more carefully about the meaning of secularism in scholarship and society.

The last twenty years have witnessed a growing reaction to the dominance of the secular in the United States. My own thinking about these subjects has been influenced by Wilfred McClay (2001), who notes that the god of scientific rationality and the Comtean religion of humanity are now on the defensive. Renewed interest in spirituality, which may or may not take explicitly religious forms, is evident in popular culture. In religious, academic, and theological circles, fundamentalists and postmodernists alike are supported by a new wave of interest in the sacred. In gerontology there is new interest in spirituality and personal narrative in the creation and re-creation of identity, in the effects of religion on health, and in the place of religious beliefs and practices in caring for the elderly.

McClay asks a central question: Is there a way to enjoy the fruits of secularism without making it into a substitute orthodoxy, an establishment of irreligion? He suggests that we begin by distinguishing two basic concepts of secularism, analogous to Isaiah Berlin's "Two Concepts of Liberty": (1) a "negative" concept, which opposes established belief—including a *nonreligious* establishment—and protects the rights of free exercise and free association; and (2) a "positive" secular ideal that is a proponent of established *unbelief* and a protector of strictly individual expressive rights, including the right of religious expression. A "negative" secularism allows the possibility of a nonestablished secular order that is equally respectful of religionists and nonreligionists. "Such an order," writes McClay, "preserves a core insistence upon the freedom of the uncoerced individual conscience. But it has a capacious understanding of the religious needs of humanity, and therefore does not presume that the religious impulse should be understood as a merely individual matter" (60).

A "positive" secularism, on the other hand, affirms the secular ideal as an ultimate and alternative comprehensive faith, undergirded by a modernist view of science that supposedly competes with and ultimately triumphs over traditional religion. Actually, "positive" secularism relies on scient*ism*—an inflated view of science whose claims to metaphysical and cosmological certitude are unsupportable by scientific methodology alone. On the other hand, a more modest and defensible view of science sees it as an "inherently tentative and provisional form of knowledge, defined by strict adherence to certain procedural norms involving the formulation of hypotheses, and the careful conduct of observable and replicable experiments to test those hypotheses" (61).

We can, in other words, celebrate the enormous accomplishments of Western science, modestly construed, while also denying its authority to serve as a substitute metaphysics or an alternate faith. In these terms, one might say that my earlier work in the cultural history of aging demonstrated the emergence of a "positive" secularist and scientific approach to aging in American culture, emerging full-blown by the middle of the twentieth century. Only in the last thirty years have theologians, religious communities, physicians, and scholars begun to chip away at the cultural dominance of "scientific management of aging" (Cole 1991). Even now, the primary emphasis in the academic literature of religion and aging revolves around an effort to show that religion is good for your health. This is fine as far as it goes, but promoting health is the business of medicine, not the primary business of religion—except for the secular religion of health that seems to reign in contemporary America. Before what Philip Rieff calls "the triumph of the therapeutic," health was a means toward living well, living according to a vision of the good life. Today health has become an end in itself; capitalism's medicalized consumer culture responds to all qualitative questions with the quantitative answer, "More." Longevity has eclipsed eternity in the hierarchy of cultural values.

My point of view might be characterized as postmodern religious humanism. That is, my humanism belongs neither to the camp of exclusive, or "positive" secular humanists (who look to science as the demystifying power that can expose and dissolve the fears and illusions which support human irrationality), nor to the camp of traditional religionists unaware of the irreparable damage done to modern conceptions of self, the unity of knowledge, and the eternal truths of fixed sacred texts.

I write as a "negative" secularist and a strong supporter of science, modestly construed. I have no wish to return to ancient and medieval social structures or worldviews, in which aging is understood as a fixed element in the eternal order of things. But we are culturally impoverished by modernity's tendency to remove old age from its place as a way station along life's spiritual journey and to redefine it as a problem to be solved by science and medicine. We need to reconceive and resymbolize aging as a spiritual journey, as an opportunity to fulfill one's own humanity, to continue learning, developing, creating, and serving in a pluralistic world where nonfundamentalist religious views are an essential part of public dialogue as well as scientific and professional discourse.

I support modernity's affirmation of everyday life, its commitment to relief of pain and suffering, its dedication to social justice and universal human rights. I agree with liberal pluralism that human freedom is best served when no particular view is in charge, but this does not by itself accredit the view that human life is better off without transcendental vision altogether. We tend to identify modern freedom with an exclusive secular humanism, one based entirely on the notion of human flourishing, which recognizes no aim beyond itself. As Taylor puts it, "the strong sense that continually arises that there is something more, that human life aims beyond itself, is stamped as an illusion and judged to be dangerous . . . because the peaceful coexistence of people in freedom has already been identified as the fruit of waning transcendental visions" (1999, 26). Exclusive humanism, as Charles Taylor puts it, "closes the transcendent window, as though there were nothing beyond—more, as though it weren't a crying need of the human heart to open that window, gaze, and then go beyond; as though feeling this need were the result of a mistake, an erroneous worldview, bad conditioning, or, worse, some pathology" (27).

Gerontology cannot afford to rely either on an overweening scientism or an exclusive humanism. Both thought-styles tend to study religion by reducing it to a more primary variable or by trying to show that religion is good for you—or bad for you, depending on one's point of view. Gerontology will continue to be impoverished if it excludes metaphysical, spiritual, and religious perspectives as genuine contributions to knowledge. At the same time, gerontology will remain impoverished if it grants exclusive authority over religious issues to ordained clergy, professional theologians, or other religious/spiritual teachers who have a vested interest in an established religion.

I applaud gerontology's recent narrative turn, in which reminiscence, life-story writing, oral history, fiction, and the arts are understood as vehicles for individuals to craft some kind of coherence in their lives. I have been teaching life-story writing and spiritual autobiography to older people for the last five years. It is a rich and rewarding experience. I find that many people come with unexplained gaps in their stories, unresolved conflicts in their lives, and unexplored memories in search of a story line. People often arrive at these workshops with the implicit question, "What is the meaning of my life?" Answers tend to come when they ask, "What story am I part of?"

But, as essential as it is, the individual search for meaning cannot manufacture the symbols, images, and rituals that offer consolation or explanation in the face of gross inequity, intense pain, or undeserved suffering. Religious belief, as anthropologist Clifford Geertz puts it, does not emerge via a "Baconian induction from everyday experience—for then we should all be agnostics—but rather from a prior acceptance of authority" (1973, 90) that transforms those experiences. "Religion tunes human actions to an envisaged cosmic order and projects images of cosmic order onto the plane of human existence. . . . What any particular religion affirms about the fundamental nature of reality may be obscure, shallow, or all too often, perverse; but it must, if it is not to consist of the mere collection of received practices and conventional sentiments we usually refer to as moralism, affirm something" (1973, 98–99, 109).

What can gerontology—not being a religion—affirm? Certainly not the truth or untruth of any religious claim or tradition. It can, however, affirm that human beings are symbolic/spiritual animals who need love and meaning as well as food, clothing, and shelter. This affirmation carries with it a fundamental principle of interpretive social science: we do not adequately understand people of any age without viable interpretations of how they understand themselves (Taylor 1979).

Secular, scientific gerontologists need to understand that philosophical and theological perspectives do not attempt to provide rational and conclusive answers to specific questions but rather general value-orientations that guide the search for specific answers and solutions. They need to make a more serious effort to understand and respect (not agree with) religious perspectives on their own terms, which in turn will encourage them to respect religious contributions to gerontology.

From a religious perspective, for example,

the problem of suffering is paradoxically, not how to avoid suffering but how to suffer, how to make of physical pain, personal loss, worldly defeat, or the helpless contemplation of others' agony something bearable, supportable—something, as we say, sufferable. . . . For those able to embrace them, and for so long as they are able to embrace them, religious symbols provide a cosmic guarantee not only of their ability to comprehend the world, but also, comprehending it, to give a precision to their feeling, a definition to their emotions which enables them, morosely or joyfully, grimly or cavalierly, to endure it. (Geertz 1973, 104)

The world's religions came into existence when "aging" itself was not a prominent feature of human experience. There is little fully developed speculation, say, in Christianity, Judaism, Islam, Hinduism, or Buddhism. What was written in the founding sacred texts of these traditions could afford to idealize the aged, to author-ize the wisdom of elders in support of existing social and ideological regimes. There were not enough old people around to demand careful thinking about how to care for them, how to promote their well-being, how to balance the claims of youth against the prerogatives of age. In the Hebrew Bible, for example, the primary injunction to care for the vulnerable specifies "the widow, the stranger, and the orphan," not the elderly per se. I think we need a great deal more careful mining, critique, and reinterpretation of the world's classic sacred texts as we examine their resonance, guidance, and limitations in today's world of mass longevity.

Most of the work in religion and aging falls under two rubrics: the study of health-outcomes among practitioners of religion and the use of religion in care-giving, most often among clergy or hospital chaplains who use moral and spiritual resources in caring for the frail, demented, or dying elderly. But gerontology can also encourage theologies of aging. Theology was long ago dethroned as the queen of the sciences, but she should be welcomed back as an equal partner in the human search for self-knowledge. Theological traditions today must acknowledge their own plurality and ambiguity. But they need not feel or think defensively in relation to science. As science in any field gets closer to completing its task of explanation, all the questions that God was an answer to will still be waiting: What was there before the Big Bang? Why were human beings designed to live a certain maximum life span? Should we try to intervene genetically to alter the aging process or the maximum life span?

I am not a theologian or a scholar of religion per se; I have no systematic thoughts on these issues to offer. But here are some thoughts about encouraging a much-needed partnership between gerontology and theology. We need more gerontologists to become accomplished in the study of religion and we need more theologians and religious studies scholars to become accomplished gerontologists. What are some of the issues which might be tackled?

Take wisdom. I am personally skeptical of the idea that wisdom emerges natu-rally in old age. I am more impressed by the Talmudic saying that a person who is a fool in his youth will also be a fool in his old age and a person who is wise in his youth will grow in wisdom as he gets older. Robert Atchley's notion of "everyday mysticism," Theodore Roszak's idea in *America the Wise,* and Lars Tornstam's studies of gerotranscendence imply that wisdom is somehow a natural developmental feature that accompanies aging. This perspective leaves out the formative roles of culture and education in human development. I suspect (and this could be empirically investigated) that people who become wise or reach higher levels of consciousness are *either* consciously doing what we might call the "moral and spiritual work" of aging *or* they are living off their cultural inheritance (whether they are believers and churchgoers or not). I worry that a scientific, secular society is squandering that inheritance by not renewing sacred canopies to guide, motivate, inspire, and console us in what Ronald Blythe calls "the long, late afternoon of life."

Postmodern critics have done excellent work in deconstructing old age and in demonstrating the extent to which aging is a cultural construction, which gerontology itself helps shape.[7] Images of health, vigor, successful aging, and leisure activities in consumer culture tend to trivialize the moral responsibilities, existential issues, and spiritual possibilities inherent in later life. But the political and cultural deconstruction of gerontological knowledge and the popular culture of aging is only half the battle. I think that there is an equally important place for constructing theological and cultural construction of ideals of aging, as partial and limited as they will be.

Here are some questions that might aid in resymbolizing and culturally reconfiguring of old age.[8] What might it mean to reconvert aging from a solvable problem into a fated mystery that brings unique challenges and opportunities? What would happen if we viewed long life not as a reward for proper behavior or the result of good genes but as a sign of God's ongoing interest in us, who might think of ourselves not in terms of re-creation or procreation but in terms of co-creation, as God's partners in the ongoing work of creation? What would it mean if we were to imagine longevity from the perspective of eternity rather than from the perspective of mortality? What would it mean if gerontology took seriously (not as universally true) various religious symbols and beliefs of Ultimate Reality and helped us in the work of aiming toward and aligning ourselves with the "Ground of all Being"?

What would happen if we stopped using scientific methodology as an excuse for not raising questions that it cannot answer? "Is there any reason," asks Huston Smith, "for thinking that consciousness, or sentience, or awareness—all of these being names for the point where Spirit first comes to attention—is any less fundamental than matter?" (2001, 261). If we no longer assume (as science assumes) that "consciousness is not simply an emergent property of life but is instead the initial glimpse we have of Spirit, perhaps we can stop wasting our time trying to explain how it derives from matter and turn our attention to consciousness itself" (264).

In one way or another, the world's major religions all insist on the paradox of physical decline and spiritual growth, not as a testable hypothesis but as an existential possibility. It is time to think more deeply about the "ageless self"—not at the level of ego or individual identity but at the level of pure consciousness or pure awareness, with no content or images imposed on it.

Huston Smith suggests that we think about pure consciousness both as infinite potential (as opposed to God's consciousness, which is actual infinitude) and as the common property of all of us. Conscious human beings have an innate tendency to ask ultimate, unanswerable questions: What is the meaning of existence? Why are human bodies built to decline and die? Why, in the end, is life worth living? What is "real," after all?

The growth of the infinite potentiality of the human spirit requires that we wrestle with these great mysteries and how to live our lives in relation to them. When confronted with such questions, I do not follow the pragmatist Richard Rorty, who advises us to "change the subject"; nor should we allow science to rule these questions out of bounds because all answers are tentative and involve a leap of faith.[9] We need gerontological theologies today that are radically pluralistic, that speak to universal concerns from within specific traditions which involve texts, symbols, gestures, and beliefs that are not universally shared. "We have long been," writes George Steiner, "I believe that we still are, guests of creation. We owe to our host the courtesy of questioning" (2001, 338).

NOTES

1. The American Academy of Anti-Aging Medicine, founded in 1992, is dedicated to addressing "the phenomenon of aging as a treatable condition." See T. Cole and B. Thompson, eds., "Anti-Aging: Hype or Hope," *Generations* (winter 2002), for a collection of articles on this topic.

2. For a philosophical account, see Stephen Toulmin, *Cosmopolis: The Hidden Agenda of Modernity* (New York: Free Press, 1990).

3. See Tom Rockmore, *Heidegger and French Philosophy: Humanism, Anti-Humanism, and Being* (New York: Routledge, 1995); Jean-François Lyotard, *The Postmodern Condition: A Report on Knowledge*, trans. Geoff Bennington and Brian Massumi (Minneapolis: University of Minnesota Press, 1993); and Michel Foucault, *The Order of Things: An Archaeology of the Human Sciences* (New York: Vintage, 1973).

4. For an excellent Foucauldian critique of gerontology, see Katz 1996.

5. See David Tracy, *Plurality and Ambiguity: Hermeneutics, Religion, Hope* (San Francisco: Harper & Row, 1987).

6. See the classic essay of this title in Matthew Arnold, *Culture and Anarchy*, ed. J. Dover Wilson (Cambridge, Eng.: Cambridge University Press, 1996).

7. See, for example, Andrew Blaikie, *Ageing and Popular Culture* (Cambridge, Eng.: Cambridge University Press, 1999); Gullette 1997; Katz 1996; and Haim Hazan, *Old Age: Constructions and Deconstructions* (Cambridge: Cambridge University Press, 1994).

8. In the United States this reconfiguration is being initiated in popular culture by groups like Earth Elders, From Ageing to Sageing, the conscious aging movement, creative retirement, lifelong learning, and volunteerism. For related scholarship and performance art, see A. Basting, *The Stages of Age* (Ann Arbor: University of Michigan Press, 1998); R. Kastenbaum, *Defining Acts: Aging as Drama* (Amityville, N.Y.: Baywood, 1994); A. Wyatt-Brown and J. Rossen, eds., *Aging and Gender in Literature: Studies in Creativity* (Charlottesville: University Press of Virginia, 1993); Kathleen Woodward, ed., *Figuring Age: Women, Bodies, Generations*

(Bloomington: Indiana University Press, 1999); Margaret Urban Walker, ed., *Mother Time: Women, Aging, and Ethics* (Lanham, Md.: Rowman & Littlefield, 1999).

9. Rather I am influenced on these issues by the pragmatist William James, especially the essays "What Makes a Life Significant?" and "The Will to Believe," in *Pragmatism and Other Writings*, ed. Giles Gunn (New York: Penguin, 2001), 198–218, 286–304.

BIBLIOGRAPHY

Arendt, H. (1958). *The Human Condition*. Chicago: University of Chicago Press.

Armstrong, K. (2000). *The Battle for God*. New York: Knopf.

Bernstein, R. (1992). *The New Constellation*. Cambridge, Mass.: MIT Press.

Bouwsma, W. J. (1973). *The Culture of Renaissance Humanism*. Washington, D.C.: American Historical Association.

———— (1990). *A Useable Past: Essays in European Cultural History*. Berkeley: University of California Press.

Chopra, D. (1993). *Ageless Body, Timeless Mind*. New York: Harmony.

Cole, T. R. (1991). *The Journey of Life: A Cultural History of Aging in America*. New York: Cambridge University Press.

Cole, T. R., R. Ray, and R. Kastenbaum, eds. (2000). *Handbook of the Humanities and Aging*. 2d ed. New York: Springer.

Geertz, C. (1973). *The Interpretation of Cultures*. New York: Basic.

Gillman, N. (1990). *Sacred Fragments: Recovering Theology for the Modern Jew*. Philadelphia: Jewish Publication Society.

Gould, S. J. (1999). *Rocks of Ages: Science and Religion in the Fullness of Life*. New York: Ballantine.

Greenblatt, S. (2001). *Hamlet in Purgatory*. Princeton, N.J.: Princeton University Press.

Gullette, M. (2000). "Age-Studies as Cultural Studies." In Cole, Ray, and Kastenbaum, 214–33.

———— (1997). *Declining to Decline*. Charlottesville: University Press of Virginia.

Habermas, J., ed. (1984). *Observations on the Spiritual Situation of the Age*. Trans. A. Buchwalter. Cambridge, Mass.: MIT Press.

Hiltner, S. (1975). *Toward a Theology of Aging*. New York: Human Sciences.

Katz, S. (1996). *Disciplining Old Age*. Charlottesville: University Press of Virginia.

Kimble, M. A., S. H. McFadden, J. W. Ellor, and J. J. Seeber, eds. (1995). *Aging, Spirituality, and Religion: A Handbook*. Vol. 1. Minneapolis: Fortress Press.

Lawler, P. A. (1999). *Postmodernism Rightly Understood: The Return to Realism in American Thought*. New York: Rowman and Littlefield.

Levin, J. S. (1994). *Religion in Aging and Health: Theoretical Foundations and Methodological Frontiers*. Thousand Oaks, Calif.: Sage.

Marsden, G. M. (1997). *The Outrageous Idea of Christian Scholarship*. New York: Oxford University Press.

———— (1994). *The Soul of the American University: From Protestant Establishment to Established Nonbelief*. New York: Oxford University Press.

McClay, W. (2001). "Two Concepts of Secularism." *Journal of Policy History* 13/1: 47–72.

Milbank, J. (1990). *Theology and Social Theory: Beyond Secular Reason.* Oxford: Blackwell.

Milbank, J., G. Ward, and C. Pitstock, eds. (1999). *Radical Orthodoxy: A New Theology.* London: Routledge.

Moody, H. R. (1993). "What Is Critical Gerontology and Why Is It Important?" In Cole et al., xv–xli.

Moody, H. R., and D. Carroll (1997). *The Five Stages of the Soul.* New York: Anchor.

Phillipson, C. (1998). *Reconstructing Old Age: New Agendas in Social Theory and Practice.* Thousand Oaks, Calif.: Sage.

Rabinow, P., and W. M. Sullivan, eds. (1979). *Interpretive Social Science.* Berkeley: University of California Press.

Raitt, J. ed. (1987). *Christian Spirituality: High Middle Ages and Reformation.* New York: Crossroad.

Roszak, T. (1998). *America the Wise.* Boston: Houghton Mifflin.

Santner, E. L. (2001). *On the Psychotheology of Everyday Life: Reflections on Freud and Rosenzweig.* Chicago: University of Chicago Press.

Schachter-Shalomi, Z., and R. S. Miller (1995). *From Age-ing to Sage-ing: A Profound New Vision of Growing Older.* New York: Warner.

Smith, H. (2001). *Why Religion Matters: The Fate of the Human Spirit in an Age of Disbelief.* San Francisco: Harper & Row.

Smith, H., and D. Griffin (2001). *Primordial Truth and Postmodern Theology.* San Francisco: Harper & Row.

Steiner, G. (2001). *Grammars of Creation.* New Haven: Yale University Press.

Taylor, C. (1999). *A Catholic Modernity?* New York: Oxford University Press.

——— (1989). *Sources of the Self: The Making of Modern Identity.* Cambridge: Harvard University Press.

——— (1979). "Interpretation and the Sciences of Man." In Rabinow and Sullivan, 25–71.

Tracy, D. (1987a). "Ad Fontes: The Humanist Understanding of Scripture as Nourishment for the Soul." In Raitt, 254.

——— (1987b). *Plurality and Ambiguity: Hermeneutics, Religion, Hope.* San Francisco: Harper & Row.

——— (1981). *The Analogical Imagination: Christian Theology and the Culture of Pluralism.* New York: Crossroad.

Turner, J. (1985). *Without God, without Creed: The Origins of Unbelief in America.* Baltimore: Johns Hopkins University Press.

Vico, G. (1968 [1744]). *The New Science of Giambattista Vico.* 3d ed. Trans. T. G. Bergin and M. H. Fisch. Ithaca, N.Y.: Cornell University Press.

Ward, G., ed. (1997). *The Postmodern God: A Theological Reader.* London: Blackwell.

Wuthnow, R. (1998). *After Heaven.* Princeton, N.J.: Princeton University Press.

33

Final Time: Coming to the End

MELVIN A. KIMBLE

> They think it's a mistake, they think it's going to last forever. . . . My God, it's the one thing in this world you can be sure of. No matter who you are, no matter what you do, no matter anything—sooner or later—it's going to happen. You're going to die.
> —Michael Cristofer, *The Shadow Box*

The price of arrival on this amazing planet remains the same—the necessity to leave it! Human life consists in a variety of virtues and graces, of foibles and failings blended together in the paradoxical unity that constitutes our humanness. This enigmatic amalgam of shadow and light, of angelic and demonic, does ultimately decay and end. Death is the extreme point of self-creation. Every person is called upon to create a self to the fullest degree. It is at death that the process of our own self-creation ends.

But dying is part of life also—it just happens to be the last part. As Viktor Frankl (1979) reminds us, persons do not become a reality at their birth but rather at their death; we are still creating ourselves at the moment of our death. Our self is not something that "is" but "something that is becoming and therefore becomes itself fully only when life has been completed by death" (113).

The following are some musings about dying and death—the final time—as I have reached three-quarters of a century in my own aging process. The accompanying narrowing boundaries of growing older have resulted in my reflecting more frequently and deeply about coming to the end.

Ann B. Ulanov (1981) notes a truth about aging that I also am experiencing. She writes:

> Aging brings home to us what we have done or failed to do with our lives, our creativity or our waste, our openness to or zealous hiding from what really matters. Precisely at that point, age cracks us open, sometimes for the first time, makes us aware of the center, makes us look for it and for relation to it. Aging does not mark an end but rather the beginning of making sense of the end-questions, so that life can have an end in every sense of the word. (122)

Death itself, and particularly our modes of relating to it, partakes of a strangely paradoxical character. This chapter explores such paradoxes that relate not only to us personally but also to our various roles and relationships in society. I live and will die with my own personal faith-orientation and commitment. But the following reflections on paradoxes of death are presented without any primary or specific religious connotations. Death as a biological event related to the cessation of life is religiously neutral. We are all going to die, irrespective of our religious beliefs. The final section of this chapter sets forth some of my own responses to these enigmatic paradoxes.

FIRST PARADOX: DEATH IS UNIVERSAL BUT MY DEATH IS UNIQUE

The first paradox is that, although death is an inevitable and universal event about which little can be done, at the same time it is an event that we cannot demote to the status of a common everyday happening.

On the one hand, death is widespread. It is certain for each of us. It is an experience all persons undergo. From a distance it remains something largely beyond our control. In this sense death is an abstract, ordinary, commonplace event. The daily obituary notices remind us of this. Because of its generality there have been those who have sought to treat it abstractly, "nothing to get concerned about."

Yet some cracks are apparent in this solid wall of insulation concerning death. The events of September 11, 2001, and the "war on terrorism," for example, have brought death on the world's radar screen. It shockingly reminded Americans, for example, that they live not far from the valley of the shadow of death.

But, there is still something about *my* death that resists this kind of secondhand treatment. *My death* asserts itself as an *extraordinary* event. Subjectively speaking, my biological death is an ultimate time boundary of my life. Certainly it is the most important existential situation toward which I must take some kind of conscious or unconscious stance—a stance that undoubtedly affects the whole of my orientation toward the present and the future. Psychologically, I am not free simply to remain indifferent to it. Moreover, although when seen from the outside death is a generic experience, seen from the inside it is special and unique. It is an experience I will go through only *once*. My death is uniquely mine. No one can do my dying for me. Death individualizes and throws us back on ourselves. My death is intensely personal to me and it may well be that the awareness and appropriation of this is at the root of personality. For all of these reasons—as least in Western culture—one cannot regard death as just an everyday occurrence, just an ordinary event.

SECOND PARADOX:
DEATH IS TERMINUS BUT PERMEATES ALL OF LIFE

The second paradox is that, although death occurs as the terminus of life, it is not only located at the end but its reality permeates the whole of our existence. Life moves inexorably toward death. More than fifteen hundred years ago, Augustine understood this and stated:

For no sooner do we begin to live in this dying body, than we begin to move ceaselessly towards death. For in the whole course of this life (if life we must call it) its mutability tends toward death. . . . For whatever time we live is deducted from our whole term of life, and that which remains is daily becoming less and less; so that our whole life is nothing but a race towards death, in which no one is allowed to stand still for a little space, or to go somewhat more slowly, but all are driven forwards with an impartial movement, and with equal rapidity. (Cited in Oates 1948, 217)

It seems as if we derive intimations of mortality from a somewhat early age. Tom Stoppard (1967) introduced this conjecture in his play *Rosencrantz and Guildenstern Are Dead:* "Whatever became of the moment when one first knew about death? There must have been one, a moment in childhood when it first occurred to you that you don't go on forever. . . . We must be born with an intuition of mortality. . . . For all of the compasses in the world, there's only one direction and time is its only measure" (71–72).

Similarly, the English poet Gerard Manley Hopkins (1957) captured this intimation of death in a brief poem, "Spring and Fall," that describes the reactions of a very young girl to the fall of leaves in an autumnal woods. As the young girl, Margaret, contemplates the unleaving of the trees, she is disturbed by a vague disquietude. Hopkins interprets this in the poignant concluding lines:

What heart heard of, ghost guessed:
It is the blight man was born for,
It is Margaret you mourn for.

If it be true that we have these "intimations of mortality," they are not the sort of thoughts we can keep in conscious awareness—they would engender too much anxiety. As the philosopher François duc de La Rochefoucauld said, "Neither the sun nor death can be looked at with a steady eye."

We do not have much public discourse about death in our society; yet we may be more thoroughly engaged in attempting to do something about it than we realize. This accounts for our obsession these days with our bodies, with jogging, dieting, and eating healthy foods.

Not only are there these obvious efforts to ward off premature death by staying healthy and looking young but there are even more subtle and pervasive projects around which we organize our lives. Undoubtedly our inordinate desire for things and for power reflects in some measure our awareness of the end, which for the most part we do not name. Has any culture so obsessed with longer life been in such denial about aging and dying? This has resulted in a gerontophobic attitude toward aging and the chronological passing of time. It has generated a particular glorification of youthfulness and an irrational denial of the natural process of aging and dying. One might well speculate that the basis of the fear of aging is the fear of the ultimate life event, namely, death.

Even though it is at the terminus, death permeates all of life. Death is the decisive determinant of human life. Life and dying, being and nonbeing remain the ultimate existential challenge. Death marks the cessation of what we value as precious. Human life is understood as sacred because it is irreplaceable. It deserves an absolute sense of sanctity. Death is a uniquely significant event of life because it is the end of everything we have known and lived. This accounts for why most people want their death to have some continuity and integrity with their whole life cycle. The sacred nature of life finds an unparalleled focus in its conclusion. As a result of intensity we bring to a life that is precious and meaningful, dying is regarded as "holy ground" and to be in its presence fills us with respectful awe.

THIRD PARADOX: INTELLECTUALLY WE KNOW BUT EXPERIENTIALLY WE HAVE DIFFICULTY IN BELIEVING IT

The third paradox surrounding death is that while intellectually we know we are going to die, experientially we have difficulty in believing it. Humans differ from animals in that though animals die, a human person knows that he or she is going to die. At an early age we learn that death is universal. We read accounts in newspapers, watch it on TV, and witness it in video games. We are acquainted with actuary tables. Death is introduced in logic courses in college through syllogisms beginning, "All persons are mortal." Yet, notwithstanding this overwhelming knowledge of and evidence for the fact that we are going to die, experientially we still have difficulty in believing in the reality of our own death. The tendency to eliminate death from life is pointed out by Freud (1959): "Our own death is indeed unimaginable, and whenever we make an attempt to imagine it we can perceive that we really survived as spectators. Hence . . . at the bottom no one believes in his own death, or to put the same thing another way, in the unconscious every one of us is convinced of his own immortality" (304–5).

Indeed, our experience in part disconfirms the fact that we are going to die. For example, by the time we are forty years old we have gone to bed at night some 14,000 times and awakened in the morning to find ourselves still alive. By time we are seventy-five, we have done it 27,394 times! Talk about reinforcement! Consequently the idea of a new day and finding oneself still alive becomes directly associated with and strongly reinforced by one's own immediate experience. With aging and increased frailty, however, this conditioned, quasi-instinctive response to life becomes mitigated and tempered. But it is true, nevertheless, that there is a factor in conscious experience that encourages us to avoid considering that which we know is our destiny.

FOURTH PARADOX: TEMPORALITY AND MORTALITY

All cultures have to deal with the issue of time, aging and mortality. Shakespeare captured so poignantly the mystery of the passage of time in a sonnet:

> Like as the waves make towards the pebbled shore
> So do our minutes hasten to their end;
> Each changing place with that which goes before
> In sequent toil all forwards do contend.
> Nativity, once in the main of light,
> Crawls to maturity, wherewith being crowned,
> Crooked eclipses 'gainst his glory fight,
> And Time that gave doth now his gift confound. . . .
>
> (Wright and LaMar 1969, 232)

Martin Heidegger (1962) called death "an open wound." He believed that the anticipation of the experience of death propels the person to view time in a subjective sense: "But just as he who flees in the face of death is pursued by it even as he evades it, and just as in turning away from it, he must see it, nonetheless even the innocuous infinite series of 'nows' which simply runs its course, imposes itself 'on' the human person in a remarkably enigmatical way" (477–78).

Aging and death, theologian Diogenes Allen suggests, induces an "ontological humility" and allows us to value the time that we live (cited in Post 2000, 9).

Viktor Frankl, like Heidegger, speaks of the ontology of human finiteness and mortality. The ontological structure of temporality makes possible the interpretation of death, not as an enemy but as a source of meaning in the midst of boundaries of temporality and death. Human possibilities are situated between the boundaries of temporality and death. The temporal boundary of life does not constitute a wall of enclosure but is a container of accomplishments and meanings. Every person is dominated by the *horror vacui*. Everything is transitory because everything is "fleeing from the emptiness of the future into the safety of the past" (Frankl 1979, 111). Frankl reminds us that

> An hourglass can be turned over when the upper part has emptied. This, however cannot be done with time—time is irreversible. Another difference: by shaking the hourglass we can mix up the grains of sand, changing their positions in relation to each other. This we can do with time only in part: We can "shake up" and change the future—and with the future, in the future, we can change even ourselves—but the past is fixed. In terms of the hourglass, it is as if the sand becomes rigid once it has passed through the narrow opening of the present, as if it had been treated by a fixative, a preservative, a conservative. (104)

The present is the narrow passage, the opening into the safety of the past, the admission to eternity. "The present is the borderline between the unreality of the future and the eternal reality of the past" (Frankl 1979, 111). The boundaries of time define and shape the possibilities and are transformed into realities and deposited in the granaries of the past. Frankl's analysis and interpretation of the finiteness of human existence may be viewed as being quite similar to the existential hermeneutics of death in Martin Heidegger. For example, the present fleeting moment is nothing else than the opportunity to change a possibility into a reality. Frankl maintains that life in this world of time is not a manuscript written in secret code which we must decipher, but rather it is a record which are must dictate (110).

Every human being is called to face the limitations of his or her life and to respond to this call in a personal and unique manner. Temporality and mortality do not take away the meaning that is found in human living, but rather propel the person to find and create meaning in the midst of transitoriness and the finiteness of human existence. Death is a great equalizer and a powerful personalizer of human existence. Temporality is not simply an aspect of the external process of becoming but rather it is an essential element in the inner self of the person. The reality of death, the finiteness of a person in time, does not make life meaningless. The key thesis to the interpretation of the phenomenon of death is the affirmation of the meaning-generating function of death.

FINAL PARADOX: DEATH IS BOTH A BIOLOGICAL AND A SPIRITUAL PHENOMENON

The final paradox is that death is both a biological and a spiritual phenomenon. The sense in which death is biological is both obvious and indisputable but, humanly speaking, we must also always confront the question of what death means to us.

The meanings of death for many people and the attitudes they hold concerning it are complex and dynamic. The intrusion of death into life is managed, explained, and represented in a variety of approaches. Death figures in our lives as the earthly ending of our possibilities, our aspirations, and our relationships. Solomon (1998) contends, "Being human—not just being philosophical—involves having some complex set of beliefs, expectations, hopes, worries and fears about death, death as death, death as disappearance, death as absence" (171).

Ernest Becker (1972) reminds us that "primitives often celebrate death . . . because they believe that death is the ultimate promotion, the final ritual evaluation to a higher form of life, to the enjoyment of eternity in some form. Most modern Westerners have trouble believing this anymore, which is what makes the fear of death so prominent a part of our psychological makeup" (ix). Commenting on this fear, Herman Fiefel (1971) suggests:

> With the fragmentation of the family, decline in neighborhood and kinship groups, the growing impersonality of a culture dominated by technology, and the waning of providential faith, death no longer signals atonement and redemption as much as man's loneliness and a threat to his pursuit of happiness. Fear of death . . . is perhaps greater today

when we find ourselves in a period of instability, a period in which we seem to be losing command of our communal relationships. At the same time institutional frameworks and conceptual creeds no longer bolster our sense of continuity or help us to thus transcend death meaningfully. (4)

In a society devoid of transcendent symbols that facilitate confrontation and acceptance of the natural process of aging and dying, persons frantically search for deliverance in the latest medical messiah or technology. They await the discovery of an "immortality enzyme" that will delay the aging process and holds out the promise of achieving embodied human immortality. By challenging the idea of a natural life span, anti-aging biotechnology introduces the idea of "immortalization."

The abrasion of time and physiological diminution introduce nagging and annoying reminders of our finitude and that we are death-bound creatures. Indeed, to live in time is to live toward death. Facing one's own death is the final developmental stage of life. Human life has a limit. Our society conspires to disguise the fact that death occurs and to deny its reality. When it occurs, it is frequently perceived as a medical failure, not a natural event. But we are all going to die. The question is under what circumstances and at which stage of the life cycle. Medicine's proper job is to make sure people do not die prematurely or for the wrong reasons.

The algebra of suffering and the dying process is complicated. Death does not always come in the life cycle as a bright autumnal end, as "a shock of corn in its season." Death is different at age thirty than it is age at seventy-five. There are many different styles of dying and ways to choose to respond to death. One can rage, bargain, compromise, comply, acquiesce, surrender, welcome, and even embrace death. But if it comes prematurely it is an unwelcome predator. Edna St. Vincent Millay (1956) captures this unwelcome response to death in her poem,

> Down, down, down into the darkness of the grave
> Gently they go, the beautiful, the tender, the kind;
> Quietly they go, the intelligent, the witty, the brave.
> I know. But I do not approve. And I am not resigned. (240–41)

What I fear about death has very little to do with the physical. What I fear has to do with the loss of consciousness, the end of all meaningful experience (as I know it), the cessation of creative engagement with life, the dissolution of my personality. The awareness of this is often somewhat overwhelming, for example, when we view a corpse of someone we have known. In a sheer massive physical way there is not much difference between the dead body and one that is asleep. Yet we are aware that somehow there is all the difference.

Even as we can err in undervaluing life, so we can err in overvaluing it. Time leans forward and life has a limit. Dying is not an occasion but a process. Being prepares for nonbeing. This is what it means to be finite. The constitutive construction of life begins interiorly to crumble so that death can become acceptance, a *Gelassenheit* (a letting go). To live is to be utterly dependent on what Tillich calls "the ground of being." In the face of death such absolute dependency becomes clear.

For those who believe in something beyond the end of life, death is a transition and a change of state. It is not complete destruction; something endures and is transformed. Human persons are whole persons only to the extent that they understand themselves, *sub specie aeternitatis,* under the aspect of eternity. There is no way for a human being fully to understand himself or herself other than in terms of transcendence, a sense of the mystery of the holy and the sacramental dimensions of life. In many faith traditions this is called the spiritual dimension of death.

Faith communities in their rites and rituals, their symbols and liturgies introduce this transcendent dimension. Responsible and creative use of the salvific symbols of the Jewish-Christian tradition, for example, introduces rich sources of meaning that speak to suffering and dying. We are called to reverence both the Creator and the creation in our living and in our dying. The human body is God's most perfect icon, created in his image. We are challenged to respect that image in ourselves through reverence for what is human and sacred in birth, growth, and suffering and even what is sacred in dying and death.

What responses can be made to these paradoxes? Let me suggest at least two that reflect something of my own faith orientation.

THE NEED TO DECIDE HOW TO ORGANIZE OUR METAPHORS AND RITUALS ABOUT DEATH

Anthropologists remind us that no society can avoid being involved with rituals, whether they be religious or secular. Rituals of death are ubiquitous and indispensable. They are necessary in order to transit around the boundaries and crisis detours of the flow of life. They place death within a frame of reference and allow the bereaved to deal with death in a contained and purposeful way. We use rituals in order to invest meaning in that event which challenges it and by so doing seek to maintain some order in the face of chaos.

At the time of death a number of ritual forms converge to facilitate or declare the transition from life to death, to make an acknowledgment of the loss, and to convey at the very least the meaning of the life now ended. Rituals evoke emotions, explore beliefs, and enact meaning. In other words, through words and actions they honor the dead and commit them to their destiny. They express something of the significance of the relationship that has ended. Rituals allow people to deal with the ambiguities of change and give them meaning. Much of the ritualistic response to death is a creative declaration that death is more than biological cessation. Death has social, symbolic, temporal, and spiritual significance. The ritual response to death can place it in a sacred frame in which all may not be lost. Symbols and rituals emphasize the transcendent meaning of life conveyed by an Ultimate Being.

THE NEED TO FIND MEANING

The problem of how to dispose of time so that it will yield a sense of fulfillment and meaning is as old as the human race. But the problem takes on special urgency in our day. This is because we try so hard to convince ourselves that we can find all we need in a purely prolonged temporal existence.

Death forces persons to ponder this life in the knowledge of finitude and to deal meaningfully with death. Whether through religion, philosophy, or the arts, people have maintained that death matters and that it has meaning beyond the inevitable biological ending it imposes.

Death, illness, and suffering are universal experiences, but they are understood variously by different faith traditions, which in their eclectic eschatologies introduce and frame different meanings. The palliative care of the dying with its holistic approach, which includes spirituality, is resulting in a revival of *ars moriendi*. It introduces pluralistic perspectives that contribute to the care of the whole dying person, including the spiritual dimension. Such care challenges the medicalization of dying and death and focuses more on the dying person and the unique meaning of his or her life.

What language can we use to describe the "spiritual"—the often unspoken but present "other," the experience of transcendence and the *mysterium tremendum fascinans?* What language can we use to describe the syntax of the spiritual—where we cannot articulate anything more than an inadequate vocabulary of approximation? What language and metaphors can we borrow? It seems as if symbols, myths, rites, rituals, music, and art express something of the spiritual, because through their transparency we recognize transcendent meaning beyond empirical fact. From the perspective of a Christian faith orientation, Reinhold Niebuhr (1949) captures this challenge as he writes, "All structures of meaning and realms of coherence which human reason constructs, face the chasm of meaninglessness when men discover that the tangents of meaning transcend the limits of existence. Only faith has an answer for this problem. The Christian answer is faith in the God who is revealed in Christ and from whose live neither life nor death can separate us" (295).

Our respective faith traditions can be critical guides as well as supportive resources in our quest for a fuller understanding of aging and its limits, including dying and death.

CONCLUSION

We mislead ourselves when we imagine that medical science will indefinitely postpone death as a human problem. But how do we give meaning to something that our society seeks to eliminate by all means? The last stage of life loses all meaning if it is devoted to mere survival. This simply is a prolongation of biological life without a mission and without meaning.

At this stage of my own life, I am stranded in the uncharted territory of longer life expectancy with a body that daily reflects its planned obsolescence. I need to be reminded that I am more than a psychosomatic organism suffering from biological angst.

There is a transcendent destiny built into my transitory life. Dying and death is the ultimate test of my spiritual thickness. My faith tradition probes the interior as well as the exterior dynamics of my life. It speaks to the deepest substrata of my being and modifies the meaning of my death. It involves all of my nature—the senses, feelings, memory, and mind. The introduction of such salvific symbols of meaning does not deny the reality of my aging and dying, but rather transcends it.

It is such an understanding of the transcendent mystery of God's love that envelopes life and that enables one to let loose of life in the death event with the same peaceful and confident faith that Roman Catholic theologian Karl Rahner (1990) confessed shortly before his death at the age of eighty: "The real high point of my life is still to come. I mean the abyss of the mystery of God into which one lets oneself fall in complete confidence of being caught up by God's love and mercy forever" (38).

BIBLIOGRAPHY

Becker, E. (1972). *The Denial of Death*. New York: Free Press.

Cristofer, M. (1977). *The Shadow Box*. New York: Drama Book Specialists.

Clements, W., ed. (1981). *Ministry with the Aging*. New York: Harper & Row.

Erikson, E. H. (1985). *Life Cycle Completed*. New York: Norton.

Fiefel, H. (1971). "Meaning of Death in American Society." In Green and Irish, 3–12.

Frankl, V. (1979). *Unheard Cry for Meaning*. New York: Simon & Schuster.

Freud, S. (1959). "Thoughts for the Times on War and Death." In *Collected Papers* 4: 288–317. New York: Basic.

Green, B. R., and D. P. Irish (1971). *Death Education: Preparation for Living*. Cambridge, Mass.: Schenkman.

Heidegger, M. (1962). *Being and Time*. Trans. J. Macquarie and E. Robinson. New York: Harper & Row.

Hopkins, G. M. (1957). *Selected Poems of Gerard Manley Hopkins*. Ed. J. Reeves. New York: Macmillan.

Malpas, J., and R. C. Solomon, eds. (1998). *Death and Philosophy*. London: Routledge.

Millay, E. S. V. (1956). "Dirge without Music." *Collected Poems*. Ed. M. Norma. New York: Harper & Row.

Niebuhr, R. (1949). *The Nature and Destiny of Man*. New York: Charles Scribner's Sons.

Oates, W. J. (1948). *Basic Writing of St. Augustine*. New York: Random House.

Post, S. (July 2000). "Extended Life, Eternal Life: Is Longer Life Always Good?" *ITE, The Newsletter of the John Templeton Foundation* 8/3: 1, 7, 9.

Rahner, K. (1990). *Faith in a Wintry Season: Conversations and Interviews with Karl Rahner in the Last Years of His Life.* New York: Crossroad.

Solomon, R. C. (1998). "Death Fetishism, Morbid Solipsism." In Malpas and Solomon, 152–76.

Stoppard, T. (1967). *Rosencrantz and Guildenstern Are Dead.* New York: Grove.

Ulanov, B. (1981). "Aging: On the Way to One's End." In Clements, 109–23.

Wright, L. B., and V. A. LaMar, eds. (1969). *Shakespeare's Poems.* New York: Washington Square.

Index of Names

West, C., 331
Westberg, G. E., 150
Wheeler, D., 127
Whitehead, A. N., 317, 319, 324, 327
Wickramasekera, I., 408
Wicks, R. J., 240
Widdershoven, G., 274
Wiebe, K. F., 13
Wiesel, E., 282
Wilber, K., 34, 44, 423, 429
Willams, D. R., 102
Willams, M. D., 102
Williams, C., 375
Wilmore, G., 334–35
Wilson, J., 92, 95
Wimberly, A. E. S., 101, 102, 103, 104, 105, 107, 108, 111, 113, 114, 115, 330, 331, 337
Wimberly, E. P., 113, 337

Wink, W., 275
Winner, A. K., 404
Winter, J. P., 102
Wojcicki, B., 129
Wolf, R., 129
Woods, J. H., 404
Woodward, K., 446
Wright, L. B., 453
Wuthnow, R., 55, 440
Wyatt-Brown, A., 446

Yeats, W. B., 18, 422
Yesavage, J. A., 256
Yordy, L., 311, 313

Zarit, S. H., 101, 110
Zborowski, M., 269, 270
Zeiss, A. M., 365

Index of Subjects

addiction and pastoral care, 193, 224–37
  ageism and, 224–25, 227
  emotional dimension, 230
  misdiagnosing addiction, 225–26
  pastoral care roles, 233–37
  personal assessments by caregivers,
    231–32
  physical dimension, 230–31
  rates of addiction, 224, 226
  shame and, 225, 228
  social attitudes and, 224–27, 237
  social dimension, 229–30
  spiritual dimension, 228–29
  twelve-step programs, 227, 235, 236
Adult Day Services, 150
Advance Directives for Medical Care, 348,
  349
advocacy, 148, 221–22, 226, 355–56
Advocate Health Care (Illinois), 152–53
African American adults and congregational
  care, 97, 101–17
  advocating function, 112–13, 116–17
  attending function, 106–10, 116
  black congregational worship, 107–8
  church communities, 101, 102–5, 109,
    110–12, 113, 115
  and ethnic cultural traditions, 104–5
  functions of congregational care,
    105–13, 116–17
  generational conflicts and, 114
  group contexts, 108–9
  health and, 101–2, 115, 123, 124
  immigrant congregations and commu-
    nities, 115–16
  mediating function, 106, 110–12, 116
  sociotheological view of care, 103–5

soul communities and soul care, 103–4
  twenty-first century challenges, 114–16,
    117
African American view of aging, 299–300,
  330–43
  African roots, 104, 335–36, 339, 342
  blessing and victory, 334, 339
  cultural linguistic approach, 336–38
  examples of, 336–43
  God's use of elders, 332
  joy and freedom, 334–35
  as natural process, 333–34, 341
  preserving memories of dead, 333
  state of elders as societal barometer,
    332–35
  and threat of nihilism, 331–32
  wisdom of elders, 330–31
African Christian Fellowship (Knoxville,
  Tennessee), 115
Agape Christian Church (Denver), 110–11
ageism
  addiction and, 224–25, 227
  and aging as pilgrimage, 10, 13, 15
  and alternative theological views, 306–7
  consciousness raising and, 226, 266
  stereotypes and, 266, 307
Alcoholics Anonymous, 227, 228, 235
Allen African Methodist Episcopal
  Church (Queens), 111, 112
Alzheimer's Association, 74, 185, 191, 366,
  370
Alzheimer's disease
  anger toward God in, 26–27
  in Bible, 28, 29, 30–31
  caregiving concerns, 183, 215–16,
    361–62, 364

social injustice and, 281
suffering's personal value, 272
and those refusing to communicate,
273–74, 276
suicide
Alzheimer's and, 369–70
black older adults and, 101–2
depression and, 255, 257–58, 369–70
rates, 63, 123, 258
and religious involvement, 123
See also depression

theological perspectives on aging and
ethics
African American view of aging,
299–300, 330–43
Alzheimer's and, 300–301, 355–66,
368–83
eschatology and aging, 299, 316–27
Jewish texts and decisions at end of
life, 300, 345–53
postmodern views of longevity, 299,
303–14
theology of aging, 444
time
meaning and, 137–41
science and, 323–24
for transcendent spiritual elders, 45
See also eschatology and aging
Tonglen (Buddhist practice), 41

United Jewish Communities, 149, 152
United Methodist Association of Health
and Welfare Ministries, 152
United Methodist Church, 177
University of North Carolina, Charlotte,
113

volunteer ministries, 98, 168–78
corporate America and, 170
and functional categories of the elderly,
171–72
future directions of, 177–78
government and local programs, 170
New Testament traditions of, 177–78
rates of volunteer activity/civic
involvement, 169–70

religious groups and, 168–69
sources of motivation, 170–71
special cases, 169, 171–77

wisdom
and African American view of aging,
330–31
of elders, 11–12, 313–14, 330–31
and humanistic gerontology, 444–45
pilgrimage of aging and wisdom
people, 13–19
spiritual elders and, 14, 40, 43
and theologians' tasks, 313–14
women
and aging as pilgrimage, 20
aging rituals, 140–41
gender and spirituality, 64, 65–66,
67–72
suffering and African American, 273,
279
worship, 126–31
for Alzheimer's patients, 75–76
benefits of, 128–29
biblical tradition of, 126–27
black congregational, 107–8
civic involvement through, 128–29
depression and, 122–23, 124
music and, 129
prayer programs, 128, 129
services and traditions, 127
virtual, 129, 222
worship spaces and rituals, 127
See also congregational religious participation

Yoruba tribe, 11